UNIDROIT

International Institute for the Unification of Private Law

UNIDROIT PRINCIPLES

OF INTERNATIONAL COMMERCIAL CONTRACTS

2010

国际统一私法协会

国际商事合同通则
2010

张玉卿　主编／审校

中国商务出版社

图书在版编目（CIP）数据

国际统一私法协会国际商事合同通则 2010／张玉
卿主编．—北京：中国商务出版社，2012.6
　ISBN 978-7-5103-0723-2

　Ⅰ.①国…　Ⅱ.①张…　Ⅲ.①国际贸易－贸易合同－
合同法－2010　Ⅳ.①D996.1

中国版本图书馆 CIP 数据核字（2012）第 023056 号

Translation into the Chinese language of the official integral version of the Principles of International Commercial Contracts 2010 published by Unidroit—The translator gratefully acknowledges permission to translate given by Unidroit in April 2010. The Chinese not being an official language of Unidroit, Unidroit has not reviewed this translation.

本书为国际统一私法协会 UNIDROIT 国际商事合同通则 2010 官方完整版中文译本。译者衷心感谢国际统一私法协会 2010 年 4 月允予译成中文。中文并非国际统一私法协会的官方语言，协会亦未审查本译本。

国际统一私法协会国际商事合同通则 2010
UNIDROIT PRINCIPLES OF INTERNATIONAL COMMERCIAL CONTRACTS 2010
张玉卿　主编／审校

出　　版：中国商务出版社
发　　行：北京中商图出版物发行有限责任公司
社　　址：北京市东城区安定门外大街东后巷 28 号
邮　　编：100710
电　　话：010—64245686（编辑二室）
　　　　　010—64266119（发行部）
　　　　　010—64263201（零售、邮购）
网　　址：www.cctpress.com
邮　　箱：cctp@cctpress.com
照　　排：嘉年华文排版公司
印　　刷：北京市松源印刷有限公司
开　　本：787 毫米×980 毫米　1/16
印　　张：58.5　字　数：951 千字
版　　次：2012 年 7 月第 1 版　　2012 年 7 月第 1 次印刷

书　　号：ISBN 978-7-5103-0723-2
定　　价：98.00 元

国际统一一私法协会
国际商事合同通则
2010工作组成员合影
前排右一为本书主编张玉卿

 INTERNATIONAL INSTITUTE FOR THE UNIFICATION OF PRIVATE LAW
INSTITUT INTERNATIONAL POUR L'UNIFICATION DU DROIT PRIVE

The Secretary General · Le Secrétaire Général

Mr Zhang Yuqing
Beijing Zhang Yuqing Law Firm
B-1912 U-Space Building
8 Guang Qu Men Wai Street
Chao Yang District
Beijing 100022

Rome, 18 May 2011
Our refce: S57/367

Dear Mr Zhang Yuqing,

I was delighted to learn that you would be prepared to again shoulder the burden of translating or coordinating translation of the 2010 edition of the UNIDROIT Principles of International Commercial Contracts.

I much appreciate your personal interest in the matter and the support you gave in your capacity of member of the Working Group for the preparation of the new edition, and I am very pleased to grant your request.

Wishing you all the best for the work, I am,

Yours sincerely,

José Angelo Estrella Faria

VIA PANISPERNA, 28 · 00184 ROMA · ITALIA · TEL: (+39) 06 69 621 51 · FAX: (+39) 06 69 621 52
ja.estrella-faria@unidroit.org · http://www.unidroit.org

国际统一私法协会
国际商事合同通则 2010 中文版

主　编　　张玉卿

2010 通则新增条文、注释审校	张玉卿
2010 通则新增条文、注释翻译	兰　磊
2004 通则条文、注释审校	张玉卿　兰　磊
Bonell 教授 2010 通则评介翻译	张玉卿

CONTENTS

总 目 录

CONTENTS

目　　录

2010 年中文版前言

UNIDROIT 经过六年的努力，于 2010 年 5 月又完成了《国际商事合同通则》第三版（简称《通则 2010》）的编纂工作。

《通则 2010》在《通则 2004》基础上主要增加了如下内容：在第三章增加了第三节：违法(共 2 条)；第五章增加了第三节：条件(共 5 条)；第七章完善了恢复原状制度（修改了第 7.3.6 条，新增第 7.3.7 条），另外整个第十一章(共 17 个条文)——多个债务人与多个债权人，全部是新增加的内容。《通则 2010》或第三版《通则》共十一章，211 个条文，较 2004 年第二版的十章，185 条增加了一章和 26 个条文，还对一些相关条款做了修改。

下面将《通则 2010》主要增加和改动情况做一简要介绍。

1. 改进"强制性规则"的注释

首先，《通则 2010》几乎重新解释了《通则》第 1.4 条关于"强制性规则"的注释。对于源于一国的强制性规则，注释指出是那些由国家自主制定的规则，如那些对合同特殊形式的要求、罚金条款无效规定、行政许可、环境保护等规定；而源于国际的或超国家的"强制性规则"，则是指来源于国际公约或一般国际公法中的规则，如《海牙—维斯比规则》、《国际统一私法协会关于被盗或非法出口文物的公约》、《联合国反腐败公约》、《联合国世界人权宣言》中的强制性规定，或者超国家组织（如欧盟）法律（如欧盟竞争法等）中的强制性规定。强调对"强制性规则"的概念应做宽泛解释，以涵盖具体制定法的规定和公共政策的一般原则。

另外，对于规则的强制性质，注释指出既可通过法律的明确陈述判断，亦可通过对法律的解释推导而出。

在国际仲裁情况下，注释虽然提到仲裁庭没有义务适用仲裁裁决做出地国家的强制性规则，但在决定是否考虑法院地国家或与争议案件具有重要联系的其他国家的强制性规则时，仲裁庭有责任考虑到"尽一切努力确保仲裁裁决能够依法执行"。

关于强制性规则对当事人意思自治的限制，《通则 2010》对《通则

2004》第1.1条注释3第二段的文字做了改进，指出"强制性规则，无论是一国的、国际的，还是超国家的，如果根据国际私法的相关规则得以适用，则它们优先于通则的规定，并且当事人不得减损该等规则"。原注释仅囿于一国的"强制性规则"，现增加了"国际的，或超国家的强制性规则"的概念，以与第1.4条规定相一致。为此，第1.4条的注释特别提醒"对合同自由的限制也可能源于公共政策的一般原则"，例如源于"禁止从事或引诱犯罪、禁止行贿和投标舞弊、保护人类尊严、禁止性别、种族或宗教歧视、禁止不当限制贸易"的国际法的规定。注释还指出当事人在选择合同适用法的情况下，不得以合同约定规避或减损管辖该合同的国内法律的强制性规定，而该国内法律应依国际私法规则予以确定。

《通则》通过条文和注释对"强制性规则"的范围、解释方法、确定手段、与《通则》的层级关系以及与契约自由的关系等，都规定、诠释得非常清楚，无疑都有利于《通则》的适用。

2.《通则2010》的强制性规则

第三章第3.1.14条是新增条文，规定第三章有关欺诈、胁迫、重大失衡及违法的条文属于强制性条款，当事人在订立合同时排除或修改这些条文，将构成违反诚实信用。欺诈、胁迫、重大失衡在《通则2004》中已有规定，违法则是《通则2010》时增加的内容（第3.3.1－3.3.2条）。当然正如注释所述，本章并不阻止以欺诈、胁迫和重大失衡为由有权宣告合同无效的当事人，在得知事实真相或者能够自由行事之后，放弃该权利。另一方面，本章条款对协议本身的拘束力、自始不能或错误的条款不具强制力。

3. 恢复原状

《通则2010》在恢复原状方面对《通则2004》的结构重新进行了安排，条文数量也有增加。

首先，《通则2010》将恢复原状在宣告合同无效的第三章和终止合同的第七章中分别规定，即将《通则2004》中第3.17条第(2)款对宣告合同无效时恢复原状与折价补偿的规定，经适当调整后改为《通则2010》的第3.2.15条的第(1)款（恢复原状）和第(2)款（关于折价补偿），同时增加了第(3)款，因对方原因无法实物返还，无须折价补偿；以及第(4)款，可就保存或维护履行物发生之费用，请求赔偿。关于合同终止时的恢复原状，《通则2004》第7.3.6条第(1)款关于一次性履行合同终止的恢复原状与折价补偿的规定，仍维持在该条内，但分两款：第(1)款为恢复原状的规定，第(2)款为折价补偿的规定。同时增加了前面第3.2.15条的第(3)和(4)款的规定。两条内容完全相同，只是针对解除合同的不同情况。

其次，第三章第三节关于违法合同以及第五章第三节关于满足解除条件的合同，同样也涉及恢复原状问题，为了避免重复，条文只是指向适用第三章的第3.2.15条的规定。

另外，对一次性履行的合同终止与一段时间内履行的合同终止，采取平等处理，各设一条，即第7.3.6条处理一次性履行的合同终止与恢复原状问题。第7.3.7条处理一段时间内履行的合同终止及恢复原状问题，但其恢复原状问题的处理也只是指向适用第7.3.6条的规定。

最后，对于从履行中可能获取的利益是否需要返还的问题，《通则2010》只是在注释中做了处理，指出在商业实践中通常难于确定当事人是否从履行中获取了利益，因此，并未在条文中明确规定需要返还从履行中所获取的利益。

通过上述规定及注释，《通则2010》对允许恢复原状的情况、要求、折价补偿、费用赔偿以及利益返还等问题都做出了清晰的规范。但由于条文分散有关章节，需要相互索引，特别是有的条文提到适用第3.2.15条时还要"经适当调整"，这些在具体适用、解释时应加以注意。

4. 违法合同

《通则2004》第3.1条(b)项曾明确排除《通则》对因违法导致合同无效的管辖问题。但后来在征求对2010版新增主题时，各界及专家却强烈要求将违法合同纳入新版之中。故现已将排除违法问题从第3.1条删除，仅保留"本章不处理无行为能力问题"。违法问题专门作为一节放在了第三章的第三节，其中共分两条，第一条，即第3.3.1条，规定如果一个合同违反了依《通则》第1.4条所适用的强制性规则而且该强制性规则对合同效力有明确规定，应从其规定；当被违反的强制性规则未对违反行为于合同效力做出明示规定时，只要情况合理，当事人仍然可以寻求合同救济。第3.3.2条处理的是违法合同的恢复原状问题，规定违反强制性规则的合同，在返还属合理情况时，可准许当事人要求返还的请求；恢复原状，则依适当调整后的第3.2.15条的规则处理。两个条款中提到的何谓合理情况，条文给出了七点需要考虑的因素。

条文应该说很简明扼要，思路清晰。但理解时要结合注释以及通则的第1.1条和第1.4条的规定和注释。强制性规则，不管是一国的、国际的、还是超国家的，要依据国际私法规则确定；对其概念要做宽泛的解释；对合同自由的限制不仅可源于法定禁止，而且也可源于不成文的、应适用的国内法，包括国际或超国家法律中的公共政策的一般原则；对违反强制性规则后果的处理，《通则》首先指向的是合同适用的国内法，但条件是该被违反的规则必须对合同的后果做了明确规定，否则可适用 UNIDROIT 通则规定的提供解决办法。

《通则 2010》对于违反强制性规则的后果，做了两点规定：（一）只要情况合理，当事人可以寻求合同救济，但所适用的强制性规则必须是明确规定了违反行为的后果；（二）如情况合理，当事人对已履行部分可请求返还。对于准予返还，《通则 2010》的规定与不少国家的国内法规定差距颇大，因为那些国家的国内法规定此时拒绝给予当事方任何合同项下的救济，甚至当事方给予对方的利益也无权索回；而《通则》此时是依据合理原则，提供解决办法，即在合理的情况下，应允许返还。正如 Bonell 教授讲的"UNIDROIT 通则这样做是附和正在国际和国内层面出现的一种现代趋势，而且这一趋势特别适合于国际商事合同，尤其是那些涉及巨额投资的建造工厂合同、众多长期合同的特殊场合"。当我们阅读了第三章第三节的示例后，我们会认识到这一规定的合理性与公正性。

5. 条件

《通则 2010》第五章关于条件的第三节是新增的内容。在国际商业实践中，条件是指某个未来不定的事件，当事人以该事件的发生来决定其合同或合同义务的生效或失效。条件涉及一系列的法律问题。然而，在某些国内法，甚至国际统一法中对条件的立法却相当缺失。现在《通则》对条件制定出了基本统一规则，显然十分必要。

本节首先对"先决条件"和"解除条件"做出定义，前者指一个合同或某项合同义务在未来某一不确定事件发生时，才产生效力；后者指在该事件发生时才失去效力。理解通则的条文不能脱离通则对条文的注释。注释中此处提到两点要特别注意：（一）法律规定的条件，如公共许可要求等，不包括在条件概念之内，除非这些条件被当事人纳入合同之中，因为条件只能是源于当事人在合同中的约定；（二）本节讲的条件是指"不确定的条件"。类似于的条件，如一方当事人的履行取决于对方当事人的先履行，或就合同义务的发生或终止的效力规定一个具体的日期，它们均不属于条件，因为前者只是对当事人履行顺序的约定，后者是对履行时间的约定。

本节第 2 条意在表明，条件的成就只具朝前效力，但《通则》鼓励当事人在合同中做出条件成就具有溯及效力或朝前效力的明确约定。

第 3 条规定当事人对"先决条件"的义务是不阻止其成就；对"解除条件"的义务是不促成其成就，否则相关当事人不得依赖该条件的不成就，或成就。本节第 4 条规定的是条件成就前当事人应如何行为，指出从条件的成就中，特别是从生效条件的成就中获益之当事人所拥有的有条件的权利应得到保护；当事人应防止其行为可能为对方带来的不利影响。这两条都要求当事人承担起码的诚实信用、公平交易与合作的义务。

条件一节的最后一条是规范解除条件成就时的恢复原状问题，此时要求参照适用经适当调整后的关于终止合同时恢复原状的规定，即第 7.3.6 条、第 7.3.7 条的规定。如果当事方同意解除条件具有溯及效力，则应参照适用宣告合同无效时恢复原状的规定，即第 3.2.15 条的规定。

《通则 2010》在第五章里通过简明的五个条款将国际商业实践中经常使用的"先决条件"和"解除条件"概括得十分清晰，很具指导意义。

6. 多个债务人和多个债权人

《通则 2010》的第十一章，是对多个债务人与多个债权人的规定，全部是新增内容，由于内容比较复杂，分了两节 17 条来规范。第一节是规范多个债务人(第 11.1.1 条至第 11.1.13 条)，第二节是规范多个债权人(第 11.2.1 条至第 11.2.4 条)。

当多个债务人对同一债务向同一个债权人承担清偿义务时，《通则》将该多个债务人履行清偿债务的义务分为两类：(一)是"连带债务"，指每一个债务人要对全部债务承担清偿责任，换句话说，就是债权人可要求债务人中的任何一人对债务进行全部清偿；(二)是"可分债务"，指每个债务人只对其份额内之债务承担清偿义务，换句话说，债权人只有权向每个债务人请求其份额内的债务。商业实践中，除非当事人有明确的相反约定，通常都倾向推定多个债务人承担"连带债务"。这是第一节第 1 条至 3 条规定的内容。第 4 条至 6 条处理的连带债务人的抗辩权或抵销权，以及清偿、免除或和解的法律效力问题。第 7 条处理的是债权人对一个连带债务人债务的时效期间届满或中止对其他连带债务人的影响问题。第 8 条处理的是法院判决的效力。第 9

条至 11 条规定，连带债务人之间对债务承担的份额被推定为均等份额；超出自身份额清偿债务的连带债务人有权请求其他未履行清偿义务的债务人分担其超额清偿之部分（分担请求权），并可行使债权人的权利，但该权利不优于未获清偿债务的债权人的权利。第 12 条意在表明，虽然一个连带债务人对债权人全部履行了清偿义务，但如果未履行债务的共同债务人对债权人拥有自身或共有的抗辩权或抵销权，此时，该共同债务人可用此来对抗履行了清偿债务的连带债务人的分担请求权。第 13 条规定，如果超出份额履行清偿债务的连带债务人虽经努力，其超额部分仍不能得到补偿，则所有连带债务人的债务份额都要同等增加，以共同承担风险。

第二节规范的是多个债权人，依然从定义开始，将债权分为"可分债权"，即指每一债权人只能请求其自身的债权份额；"连带债权"，即指每一个债权人可以请求清偿全部债务；"共同债权"，即指所有债权人必须一同请求清偿债权。实践中，究竟属哪种债权？通则注释提醒当事人在合同中应规定清楚。

第 11.2.2 条规定的是对连带债权清偿的效力，即债务人对其中一个债权人进行了全部债务清偿，即解除了他对所有债权人的清偿义务。第 3 条处理的是债务人的抗辩权和抵销权，同时指出第一节的第 5 条至 8 条，经适当调整，可以适用多个债权人的情况。本节最后一条，规范的是债权人之间的债权分享，即如无明确相反约定，推定连带债权人之间对债权享有均等份额，同时规定，债权人如果超出其债权份额获得清偿，应在其他债权人的债权份额内将其超出部分转交给其他债权人（债权分配）。

如本节注释所讲的，在国际商业实践中的工程承包合同、贷款合同、技术转让合同，或保险合同等经常涉及或多个债务人，或多个债权人的情况。此时，多个债务人之间、或多个债权人之间，乃至多个债务人与债权人之间，或多个债权人与债务人之间的关系如何？如何处理相关的抗辩权、抵销权、债务清偿、免除与和解，以及债务分担或债权分担等一系列的法律问题，不但国际统一法缺乏这方面的规范，就是法制发达国家的规范也存在缺失。现在 UNIDROIT 率先制定出了这方面的全套规则，不能不说是对国际商事统一法的一个贡献，也必然对商业实践及纠纷处理起到重要的指导作用。

除此之外，《通则 2010》对《通则 2004》中存在的一些表述或文字问题，例如原第 8.1 条注释 4 - 5 示例的 6 - 10 就存在类似问题，这次都全面做了修正、改进。当然新增条文使得一系列索引条文的号码也必然发生变更，这些读者在阅读中会自然发现。

对新增章节的必要性、诠释与评论，请读者进一步参阅附在本书中由本人拙译的 Bonell 教授的文章：《UNIDROIT 2010 通则——国际统一私法协会新版国际商事合同通则评介》一文。

在《通则 2010》出版之前，我们对《通则 2004》的条文和注释再次进行了全面的审校、改进，大多数调整是属于语言文字性的，例如，为了保持前后用语一致。但个别地方的修改也涉及原来对条文和注释翻译的准确性问题，约有十几处，细心的读者可以在新、旧版对比研究中发现，我们就不一一列举了。

《通则 2004》附有《通则 2004》与《欧洲合同法原则（PECL）》逐条对照表（Synoptical Table），由于《通则》已有了 2010 版，而欧盟继 PECL 之后又开始编纂 DCFR（Draft Common Frame of Reference，共同参考框架草案，或欧洲私法原则、定义与示范规则）并于 2009 年公布，其内容远宽泛于 PECL，例如其中包括保护消费者的措施，因此两个范本都有很大变化，再将对照表收入书中已无甚实际意义。故本书不再收录该对照表。同样，Bonell 教授对《通则 2004》的评介文章，也由他最新的对《通则 2010》的评介文章代替。

《通则 2010》的翻译出版得到了国际统一私法协会（UNIDROIT）的鼎力支持。首先得到了协会秘书长对本人从事翻译的书面授权，并且协会还主动与本人签署了翻译出版合同，工作组主席 Bonell 教授的评介通则 2010 文章完成后即发给本人，希望与中文版的《通则》一同发表。本人对协会秘书长及 Bonell 教授的信任、支持以及与本人的良好合作关系表示衷心的感谢。

商务部条法司是中国政府主管 UNIDROIT 工作的部门，在《通则2010》翻译出版过程中，他们与协会联系，举荐本人继续承担《通则》的翻译出版工作，并提出了很多指导意见与建议，他们的支持与鼓励是本人完成本书的重要动力，我愿在此对我原来的工作单位——商务部条法司及同事们的信任与支持，表示诚挚的感谢。

我在开始《通则 2010》翻译工作之前，就计划对我主编的《国际统一私法协会 UNIDROIT 国际商事合同通则 2004》重新进行全面的审校，包括黑体字条文和逐条注释，以便修正可能存在的语句或翻译错误等问题，保持概念与称谓的前后一致性。2010 年下半年，我请兰磊博士承担对《通则 2004》的初审以及 2010 版新增部分的翻译工作，由我最后审校定稿。兰磊是我很信赖的年轻人，2004 年我们就在《通则》翻译上合作过，他国际商法非常扎实，有相当出色的法律英文水平，工作认真负责，一丝不苟。对《通则 2004》的条文和注释除遣词造句的偏爱之外，他的确发现一些翻译上的毛病与不足，此次出版我们都做了改进。兰磊对新增内容的翻译也十分专业。对兰磊认真、辛勤的工作，我在此表示诚挚的谢意。

这次对《通则 2010》新增部分的翻译以及对《通则 2004》的全面审校与改进由我和兰磊完成，但这仍与先前参加《通则 1994》、《通则 2004》条文与注释翻译与审校同志的辛勤、认真的工作分不开，在此我要对他们过去的工作表示深切的感谢。

中国商务出版社严卫京社长、李学新副社长对《通则》的出版一直十分重视和支持，赵桂茹编辑和汪沁编辑对本书的设计、编排、文字，甚至一些具体翻译都提出了中肯的意见，没有他们的无私支持，本书很难奉献给读者。我在此表示诚恳的谢意。

《通则 2010》是国际商事合同的统一法典，对其条文和注释的理解与翻译绝非易事，鉴于本人水平，肯定还会存在不准确或更好的落笔，本人诚恳希望读者能随时发现问题，提出宝贵批评和改进意见。

总之，《通则 2010》是当今国际上唯一的一部关于商事合同总则部分的统一法，正如我在《通则 2004》前言中所讲的通则是"一部极具现代性、广泛代表性与权威性的商事合同统一法"。我希望《通则》能在中国合同法现代化的进程中，在中国的商务法律实践中能起到应有的作用。

张玉卿

2012 年 2 月 16 日于北京

2004 年中文版前言

2004 年版《国际统一私法协会国际商事合同通则》（UNIDROIT Principles of International Commercial Contracts 2004）（简称 UNIDROIT《通则2004》）是当今世界上一部极具现代性、广泛代表性与权威性的国际商事合同统一法。

《通则》是"国际统一私法协会（International Institute for the Unification of Private Law UNIDROIT）"主持制定的。协会成立于 1926 年，是一个政府间国际组织，目前有成员国 59 个。我国于 1986 年加入该协会，国家商务部是协会工作的归口管理单位。协会的主要任务是协调与统一各国实体私法领域的法律，并使其现代化。协会原则上涉足私法领域的冲突规范问题，即国际私法规则，该领域的法律统一工作主要由设在海牙的国际私法会议承担。协会的具体职责是起草相关的国际公约、示范法、统一规则或法律指南。四种模式体现了国际上对统一法的不同诉求与不同的运用层面。协会制定统一法的目的是为了排除国际民商事中的法律障碍，促进国际经济贸易的发展。协会至今已起草、制定了以上述四种模式所体现的几十部国际民商事方面的统一法律，对国际私法领域的统一工作做出了杰出的奉献。《国际商事合同通则》是协会过去三十多年来取得的一项最主要，也是最成功的统一法项目。

1971 年，协会的决策机构—理事会（UNIDROIT Governing Council）决定起草制定通则（最初称《国际贸易法典》），目的是要制定一部可被各国采用的国际商事合同的统一法典。为此，协会成立了由分别代表大陆法系、英美法系和当时社会主义法系的三位法学家，法国的大卫（Rene David）、英国的施米托夫（Clive Schmitthoff）、罗马尼亚的波波斯库（Tudor Popescu）组成的指导小组，研究其可行性，就通则的宗旨、范围等提供指导意见。协会最终决定拟制定的《通则》仅涵盖适用于国际商事合同的通用条文部分，或称总则部分，对于特殊合同的相关条文留待以后或其他组织去处理。

1980 年，协会正式成立工作组，起草《通则》的各个章节。工作组成员来自世界不同法律制度的国家，以个人身份独立参加工作。他们都是合同法、国际贸易法方面的专家。1994 年，《通则》第一版的起草工作完成（UNIDROIT Principles 1994，简称"《通则 1994》"），共七章一百二十条。内容主要包括：总则、合同的订立、合同的效力、合同的解释、合同的内容、合同的履行与不履行。《通则 1994》条款在获得理事会通过后，同年在世界各地出版，被译成多种文字，受到各国法律界广泛关注与欢迎。其中文版的条文部分由本书主编最终审定。

协会在 1994 年通过《通则》时，就曾提出要关注《通则》在实践中被接受与适用的情况，并适时扩展其内容。为此，1997 年协会决定继续《通则》的编纂工作，再次成立工作组。工作组仍由来自世界不同法系或国家的 17 名专家组成，其中不少人是第一次工作组的成员。中国参加第一次工作组的成员是黄丹涵博士。《通则 1994》的成功，引起了其他国际组织的重视。在第二个工作组期间，联合国国际贸易法委员会、巴黎国际商会国际仲裁庭、米兰仲裁庭和瑞士仲裁协会作为观察员，一直积极参加工作组会议。经过近七年的努力，一部扩增的《通则 2004》，终于完成。

《通则 2004》同《通则 1994》相比，其第八章：抵销，第九章：权利转让、债务转移与合同转让，第十章：时效期间，属新增章；第二章增加了代理人的权限一节，第五章增加了第三方权利一节；序言部分增加了两个段落；在第一章和第五章的第一节分别增加了两个和一个条款。对《通则 1994》条文的修改仅属个别现象。唯一修改的条文是《通则 1994》的第 2.8 条。另外，为适应日新月异的电子商务的实践需要，《通则 2004》对原第 1.2 条等还做了一些文字调整。再者，为了便于理解与适用，工作组对条文的注释与举例做了全面的审查与改进。《通则 1994》已有"诚实信用与公平交易"的规定，新版《通则》中又增加了"不一致行为"（Inconsistent Behaviour）条款，进一步强调在国际商业中当事人诚实信用的行为准则，强调当事人不能出尔反尔，前后行为不一致，这是为了确保国际交易的可预见性与安全，是开展国际贸易的起码条件。

《通则 2004》共十章一百八十五条，比《通则 1994》有了很大篇幅的扩增，更具广泛的适用性。

《通则 2004》总结、概括了世界上大多数国家关于商事合同的基本原则以及国际上已达成的一些国际公约，如《联合国国际货物销售合同公约》（CISG）的规定，同时 还对一些现行的国内规则做了发展。《通则》在遣词用语上同联合国制定统一法一样，避免使用某一特定法系或某一国家法律的特定概念，以避免在适用与解释时各取所需，最终堕入国内法的误圈。《通则》的制定注意到了当事人之间权利义务的平衡、体现了公正与公平，同时也注重贯彻国际公共政策。同时，为了适应当前经济全球化，各国经贸交往不断加深的形势以及现代科技的发展，《通则》的条文适应了这一趋势，体现了现代化与前瞻性，能满足各种不同实践的需要。因此，《通则》得到了广泛的接受、适用。另外，《通则》附有详细具体的注释，更便于理解和掌握条文的真实含义，更好地帮助实现法律的基本属性所追求的可预见性和确定性。

2004 年在协会的第八十三届理事会上，理事们对《通则》的编纂工作给予了高度评价，要求工作组的工作不要就此停止，还应就未涉及的问题，诸如恢复原状（Restitution）、条件（Conditions）、多数数债权人与债务人（Plurality of Creditors and Debtors），保证与担保（Suretyship and Guarantees），等等，继续开展工作。所以，国际统一私法协会（UNIDROIT）合同通则工作组的工作仍在继续。

这部《通则》具有广泛的功能，从私法的基本属性角度看，它可以由当事人自主选定作为合同适用的实体法，解决当事人之间的合同纠纷；当各国立法机关在制定或修改其合同法时，他们可将《通则》作为示范法，参考、借鉴《通则》的条文，以使其合同法更加适应于现代的国际商事交易，使其法律更加现代化。《通则》是统一规则，亦可视为国际惯例。即便当合同适用某个具体国内法、或某项公约时，由于适用法或公约本身的缺略或条文的含混不清，《通则》此时尚可对合同的适用法律辅以解释和补充的作用。《通则》由于不带国籍、法系特色，内容又翔实具体，公平、衡平，不但适于为合同各方当事人选择其为合同的适用法律，法院或仲裁庭也会乐于接受、适用《通则》，解决案头的争议。特别是当合同的适用法律不足以解决合同纠纷所涉及的问题，或当事未选择适用法或选择无效时，法院或仲裁庭会主动地把《通则》作为"法律的一般原则"或"商人习惯法"，予以适用，作为解决问题的依据。当然，《通则》在教学、法律研究、商业合同谈判等实践工作中，也具有重要的价值。《通则》事实上已成为当今世界上首屈一指的一部统一合同法，是一部国际合同法编纂，或如 Bonell 教授所讲的是一部"国际合同法重述"。

合同法是调整各种契约关系的基础性法律制度，是人类经济乃至生活中最普遍、最基本、最主要的法律关系。合同关系及其法律制度的建立与发展，合同制度的贯彻与实施，代表着社会进步的程度。合同关系建立在当事人地位平等、意思自治，以及符合法律的强制要求的基础上；合同要依约定和法律的要求履行，对不守承诺的违约行为必须进行法律的必要制裁，这是确保经济秩序稳定、市场经济发展的根本保证，也是社会现代文明的标志与要求。

我国合同法律制度的建立与发展尚处在一个初级阶段，《通则》中的一些条文，如艰难情形、错误陈述、默示条款、不一致行为，等等，在我国合同法中尚属阙如。我相信《通则2004》会对我国合同法律制度的不断完善，或为解决实践中的问题起到有益的借鉴和补充作用。

本人自1983年起就陆续参与协会的工作，中国政府在1986年参加协会就是本人当时对协会研究与报告的结果。协会主持制定的《国际贸易销售代理公约》、《关于国际保付代理公约》、《国际贸易运输港站经营人赔偿责任公约草案》以及《关于被盗或者非法出口文物的公约》等，本人都曾参加过起草、论证的工作，并代表中国政府做过提案。

本人自1999年起一直为协会的理事会成员。2004年在协会的第八十三届理事会上，《通则》2004版正式获得协会理事会的批准。我在会议期间曾向协会秘书长 Herbert Kronke 教授和工作组主席、协会顾问 Michael Joachim Bonell 教授提议将《通则2004》译成中文出版发行。他们都欣然支持。秘书长还专门为此写了一封授权函。Bonell 教授还同意我将其新近发表的文章 UNIDROIT Principles 2004: The New Edition of the Principles of International Commercial Contracts adopted by the International Institute for the Unification of Private Law 作为《通则》中文版的开篇介绍。我在此谨对他们的信任与支持表示衷心的感谢。本书出版时，一并奉上 Kronke 先生的信和 Bonell 先生文章的中译文，以飨读者。

我们把 Bonell 教授的评介文章放在《通则》之前，不仅仅因为他是《通则》工作组的主席，他还是意大利知名的民商法专家，长期参与联合国贸法会的统一法制定工作。Bonell 教授作为工作组主席，自始至终主持《通则》的研讨、编纂工作，他是名副其实的《UNIDROIT 国际商事合同通则》的专家。Bonell 这篇文章如同《通则》的概论，详细介绍了《通则》的功能及其在实践中的适用情况，穿插有具体的实例，很具说服力。他评介了新增篇章的内容，同时比较了《通则》与《欧盟合同法原则》的异同。文章可以帮助我们了解和掌握《通则》，帮助我们认识《通则》在国际上的地位及其作用。我相信读者会从文章中获益匪浅。当然，也应补充一点，一部统一的国际合同条约法的制定，以及它被广泛接受、认可与采纳是个漫长的过程，各国都有自身文化和法律传统，这些都是法律统一的制约因素。

《欧盟合同法原则》也是一部颇具影响力的区域性统一法，但其地位、功能如何，尤其是与《通则 2004》有何异同？我们把 Bonell 教授和罗马大学 Roberta Peleggi 教授对《通则》与《欧盟合同法原则》两个法律文件的对照表以英汉对照的方式奉献给读者。我们可以发现两个文件有众多条款相同，同时也可很容易发现它们的立法意图、适用范围存在重大差异。我们希望这个对照表对读者具体研究、使用这两个法律文件时会有所指导、帮助。

通则的条文和注释是本书的主体。本书中《通则 2004》新增章节六十五条条文和通则全部条文的注释部分由本书的作者们独立翻译、审校，原有章节的一百二十条条文则基本沿用了《通则 1994》的中译本。《通则 1994》条文的中译本是本人和黄丹涵博士（当时她是《通则》工作组的成员，亦在外经贸部条法司工作）一起审校定稿的。在这次新版本的翻译出版过程中，我们发现原有章节的个别条文存在译法不妥之处。例如第七章第一节的 "non performance in general"，过去译为 "总则" 似过于简单，现改为 "不履行的一般规定"。第 2.1.17 条 "a contract... cannot be contradicted or supplemented by evidence of prior statements or agreements." 原译文为 "该合同不得与此前存在的任何声明或协议相冲突，或受其补充。"译文与原文含义恰好相反，原文意在表明订立合同前双方当事人的往来文件及其他表述在合同达成之后，不得再对抗合同之内容，如与合同内容不同的话，不再具有法律效力，这即是 "全部合同内容"（entire contract）的条款。现改译为 "此前存在的任何陈述或协议不能被用作证据，对抗或补充该合同。"《通则》中很多条文经常使用 "to the extend that..."，原译文充分体现这一介词短语的含义，而它又具有较强的限制性，这次均做了改进。例如第 5.1.4 条、第 6.1.4 条和第 7.1.2 条等我们都增加了 "在一定限度内"，或 "在……限度内" 或 "在一定范围内"，以确切表达原文含义。在翻译审校 1994 年版《通则》注释部分时，我们在原译文基础上进行了全面的审查、改进，其中更正了不少我们认为的不准确、甚至错误之处。比如第 2.1.22 条的注释 3，英文的 "the knock out doctrine"，其本意是讲排除两个标准合同中不一致的条款，过去译为 "意思一致"，现改为 "排除异议原则"。另外，第 7.4.2 条的注释 3 "Damages must not enrich the aggrieved party"，应译为 "受害方不应从损害赔偿中不当得利"，而原译"损害赔偿不一定满足受害方当事人",是有误的。再例如,注释中对"subject to"的理解多处不够确切,在第 6.1.3 条注释 3 中,"subject to paragraph(2),正确译法应为"需满足第(2)款的规定"或"受第(2)款制约",而不是"根据本条第(2)款"的意思,我们对此做了调整。

《通则 1994》英文版制定出来后,工作组主席 Bonell 教授与我联系,要我将《通则 1994》英文条文(即黑体字)译成中文,因为协会要出版一本含《通则》条文的英文、法文、中文、俄文、西班牙和阿拉伯文等文字的综合条文版本,在世界各地发行,以供需求。由协会向译者支付翻译稿酬。我接受了这项工作,并与黄丹涵博士合作,由她组织人员翻译,我和黄博士作审校。经过数月努力,我们终于完成任务,将译文交付协会并由协会出版。当时计划在中国再出版一本《通则》条文的中文版册子,并约好了出版社,写好了前言及介绍。但由于种种原因,小册子未能出版。1996 年,法律出版社出版了一本《国际商事合同通则》,包括《通则》条文和注释的中英文。该书使用了我和黄博士等人翻译审校的《通则》条文中译本。法律出版社于 2003 年 8 月第二次印刷此书。2004 年 11 月,法律出版社又出版了新版的《国际商事合同通则》,除 2004《通则》新增加的六十五条条文及注释,其余一百二十条条文及注释基本维持旧版本的内容,一些地方稍有改动和添加,1994年版条文部分几乎未做什么改动,原译文存在的一些不妥之处也沿袭下来。我们这本书对《通则》条文的翻译做了全面的审校,对一些旧有的不妥翻译做了逐一校正,以免给读者错误的引导。

附录中关于国际统一私法协会的介绍文章是本人于 1985 年发表于《中国国际法年刊》的。为了使读者更全面了解协会及其工作进展,此次做了修订。

另外,可能由于时间关系,原英文版注释本身也存在一些打印或排版错误,我们经认真推敲,也自行做了调整。例如第 10.2 条的注释 3 中,有一句话把 obligee 和 obligor 的位置放颠倒了。

为了使本书尽早出版,中国政法大学国际法学院的覃华平老师、周超博士等放弃了 2004 年的暑假,全身心投入本书的翻译工作。其后又由我和兰磊、周超集中时间和精力进行了一个多月一丝不苟、认真负责的审校。

另外,我还特别感谢金诚同达律师事务所的吴晶律师,她在百忙中主动承担《欧盟合同法原则》的翻译工作,使本书附录中的 2004《通则》与《欧盟合同法原则》的比较得以奉献读者。

我对他们的认真、负责与敬业精神表示深切的感谢，没有他们的奉献与努力，就没有本书及时的出版。

我们还要感谢周晓燕、李成钢等参加《通则1994》注释翻译工作的同志，没有他们的努力，这部世界上唯一的合同统一法就不能及早在中国得以传播和广泛研习。故此书的出版时，他们仍列入本书的翻译人员之中，以示对他们努力工作的感谢和肯定。

中国商务出版社的赵桂茹编辑和刘建昌编辑在本书出版过程中对书稿做了认真、细致的审阅，给我们提出了很多建议，使本书避免了不少错误，对此我们表示衷心的感谢。

王蓓菁律师在本书的资料核实、编排和出版过程中也付出了艰辛努力，在此一并表示感谢。

毕竟，本书的翻译出版是一项比较浩大的工程，法律关系复杂，条文注释繁多，有些英文语句也晦涩难懂，而客观上又要求有一定的质量水准，由于时间紧促，再加上我们水平所限，译文疏漏纰缪之处在所难免，敬请读者批评指正。

张玉卿

2004 年 12 月 25 日于北京

此前言略有修改

UNIDROIT 通则 2010——
《国际统一私法协会国际商事合同通则》
新版评介

Commentary on UNIDROIT Principles 2010
—The New Edition of the Principles of International Commercial
Contracts adopted by the International Institute for
the Unification of Private Law

Michael Joachim Bonell

张玉卿　译

UNIDROIT 通则 2010——
《国际统一私法协会国际商事合同通则》
新版评介

Michael Joachim Bonell *

张玉卿　译

导　言

《国际统一私法协会国际商事合同通则》（以下称 UNIDROIT 通则），1994 年制定出第一版，2004 年制定出第二版，目前出版的是第三版。新版的 UNIDROIT 通则 2010 在 UNIDROIT 2011 年 5 月召开的协会理事会上被正式通过。本文第一部分是对 UNIDROIT 通则做一总体介绍，第二部分集中对通则新的章节做出评价，第三部分则着重介绍通则在实践中的最主要功能，特别是它作为国际合同准据法和作为背景法来解释和补充所适用的国内法的双重作用。

一、UNIDROIT 通则：一部国际合同法重述

UNIDROIT 通则 1994 年一出现，就被美国一位著名的合同法律师（J. Perrilo）称为是"法律思想全球化的重要步骤"①，是对国际合同法总体的非官方的编纂或重述。UNIDROIT 通则是由世界所有主要法律体系和地缘政治区域的独立专家所准备。UNIDROIT 通则不同于立法文

---

* 罗马大学名誉教授，2010 Unidroit 通则"工作组"主席，"违法"一章报告员（自 2009 年 4 月）。本文表达的均属作者本人之观点，不必反映工作组其他成员之观点。

Bonell 教授是 UNIDROIT 的顾问，著述颇丰，与本文译者相识近 30 年。Bonell 对每一版（即 1994 版、2004 版及 2010 版）Unidroit 通则都撰写翔实、权威的评介文章。本篇是他为通则 2010 版撰写的评介文章，撰写完毕后即通过 E-mail 发给译者，供中文版使用。译者在此对 Bonell 教授表示深切的感谢。

① 见 J. M. Perillo, *UNIDROIT Principles of International Commercial Contracts*: *The Black Letter Text and a Review*, in 43 *Fordham Law Review* (1994), p. 281 et seq. (p. 318).

件，如《联合国国际货物销售合同公约（CISG）》，不意在由国家批准从而构成相关国家国内法不可分割的组成部分。然而，通则又与其他被广泛适用的软法律文件，例如国际商会（ICC）制定的《国际贸易术语解释通则（INCOTERMS）》或《跟单信用证统一惯例（UCP）》不同，因为通则的制定是在国际间政府组织——国际统一私法协会（UNIDROIT）的指导下完成的，并且最终由其通过。另外，也是最重要的，多数国际统一法文件，无论是立法性的，还是非立法性的，或局限于交易的具体类别（如销售、租赁、保付代理，海上、公路或航空货物运输等），或局限于特定主题（如交付条款、付款方式等），但 Unidroit 通则的适用范围却相当宽泛。它像美国合同法重述一样，是从总体方面规范国际商事合同，即规定了一套几乎涵盖了一般合同法所有重要主题的广泛规则，诸如合同成立、合同解释、合同效力、合同履行、不履行及救济、转让、抵消、多数债务人与债权人，以及代理和时效期间等内容。

另外，UNIDROIT 通则与美国合同法重述在表现形式上也相似。通则由黑体字规则（即条文）组成，第三版总计11章，211条，每条都附有注释。适当情况，每条还列举了事实示例，其目的是解释黑体字规则制定的理由以及实践中可以适用的不同方法。构成 UNIDROIT 通则整体一部分的注释，有时甚至是对黑体字规则的扩展和补充，例如当黑体字规则以宽泛语言表达时就是如此①。

UNIDROIT 通则的起草风格类似于民法典的起草风格，不属英美法系的风格，其语言简明易懂，便于非法律人员的理解，而且有意避免使用某一特定法律体系的术语。为此，通则创立了法律通用语，供世界范围来使用和统一的理解。

至于 UNIDROIT 通则的内容，它是一种传统和创新的结合。换言之，虽然作为一项规则，人们总是倾向那些在国际层面上被普遍接受的解决办法（"共同核心"方法）；然而，经常遇到的情况是，当在相互冲突的规则中必须做出选择时，决定的因素不仅仅是考虑多数国家采用了什么规则，而是考虑哪项规则更具有说服力的价值，并且/或更

① 例如，第2.1.15条第（2）款规定"……一方当事人如果恶意进行谈判或恶意终止谈判，则应对因此给另一方当事人所造成的损失承担责任"，但在注释中却具体指出"……受损害方可要求偿还谈判中发生的费用，还可要求就丧失与第三人订立合同的机会给予补偿（所谓的信赖利益或消极利益），但是一般不得要求赔偿若原合同订立可能产生的利润（所谓的预期利益或积极利益）。只有当事人明确约定诚信谈判的义务，才有可能请求各种违约救济，包括请求履行的救济权利"。

适合跨境交易（"更佳规则"方法）。

在这方面，UNIDROIT 通则毫无疑问不同于《美国合同法重述》，原因是不言自明的。"共同核心"方法对像美国这样的联邦体制具有重要意义，因为其州际间的法律差别并不大。但在国际层面，各国法律制度之间的反差却相当明显，因而采用"更佳规则"的方法就不可避免。更重要的是，由于 UNIDROIT 通则专门对国际商事交易进行规范，而国际商事交易依其性质要不断发展，其本身就非常需要那些尚未在国家层面上被普遍接受的解决办法。有鉴于 UNIDROIT 通则只是部分地反映了被普遍接受的原则与规则，而其余部分的规则有待实践的检验，人们甚至可以认为通则是对国际合同法的"重述"与"先述"。

自然，此处不是深度分析哪些 UNIDROIT 通则的条文是创新的，哪些不是的地方。毕竟，正如《美国合同法重述》（第二版）报告员艾伦·方斯沃斯（Allan Farnsworth）教授正确提到的"创新有时并不采取新的实体规则的形式，而是对问题采取新的视角，反映在运用一个替代的新术语或对传统术语的分析……即便是实体规则，评估创新的程度也不是容易的事……经常由于案件的不足或法院分析的混乱，使得严格区别创新与传统成为不可能"。①

总之，可以公平地说（让我们引用澳大利亚联邦法院 Finn 法官的话），"通则包含了世界上许多法律体系中所承认的规则，即便通则没有全面具体将一个特定国家的法律规则录入其中"。② 换言之，UNIDROIT 通则相对来说没什么公开与现行国内法相冲突的条文，而是大部分条文与所有国家的法律几乎完全一致，而且在许多情况下，还是对其现行法律的有益澄清和补充。除其他条文外，属于后者（澄清和补充）的事例有：第 2.1.1 条关于合同订立的不同形式、第 2.1.11 条关于更改承诺、第 2.1.12 条关于书面确认、第 2.1.14 关于待定的合同条款、第 4.7 条关于语言差异、第 5.1.4 条和第 5.1.5 条关于获得特定结果的义务和尽最大努力的义务、第 6.1.7 条关于支票或其他票据付款、第 6.1.8 条转账支付、第 6.1.9 条关于支付货币、第 6.1.15 条至第 6.1.17 条关于公共许可要求、提出申请责任，以及未获得批准和/或拒绝申请等条文。

---

① 见 E. A. Farnsworth，《合同法重述（第二版）修订之要素》，*Columbia Law Review* (1981)，p1 et seq.（5-6）。

② 见 P. Finn，《UNIDROIT 通则：一个澳大利亚人的视角》，*Australian International Law Journal* 2010，p193，et seq.（P. 194）。

至于 UNIDROIT 通则的创新条款，首先是那些对大陆法体系相当熟悉、而对普通法体系（英美法体系）却是陌生的条款，或情况相反。属于前一种情况的有：第 1.7 条和第 2.1.15 条关于一般依诚信原则行为的义务和恶意谈判（订约前）的责任、第 2.1.22 条关于所谓合同形式之争、第 2.2.4 条关于隐名代理、第 4.3 条关于为解释之目的，当事人订立合同前后之行为的关联性、第 7.1.7 条关于不可抗力、第 7.2.2 条关于要求对非金钱债务履行的一般规定，以及第 7.4.13 条关于对罚款条款的强制执行等。对大陆法体系来说属于新的条文的例子有：第 2.2.3 条关于显名代理、第 7.3.2 条关于对不履行仅凭通知终止合同、第 7.1.6 条关于免责条款，以及第 7.2.2 条(c)项，当受害方可合理地从另外渠道获得履行时，有关排除赋予实际履行救济的规定。不用说在这方面虽然讲到普通法和大陆法两个分支，但还尚未严格地讲到英国合同法与美国合同法之间的巨大差别，以及大陆法中罗马法与德意志法之间的巨大区别。

　　对大陆法系和普通法系来说均属新的条款只是少数，最根本的理由同样是基于国际商业交易的特殊需要。下面就是一些具体的例子：第 3.1.2 条，根据该条只要当事人之间达成协议，即足以使合同有效订立或修改，而无须诸如"对价"或"约因"的进一步要求、第 6.2.1 条至第 6.2.3 条关于艰难条款的规定，特别要关注处于不利地位的当事人可以要求重新谈判合同的权利、第 7.1.4 条关于即便在受害方终止合同后，依然可赋予不履行合同当事方补救其不履行的权利，以及第 9.1.9 条关于金钱支付权利转让的有效性，尽管让与人与债务人之间已达成限制或禁止该转让之协议。

　　最令人感兴趣的是，UNIDROIT 通则中的新创条款总的来说都受到了相当积极的评价①。在某些案件中，这些规则居然能促使法院重新审查其国内法。例如，澳大利亚法院，在一定程度上英格兰和新西兰的法院，最近在不少案件中，就在国内层面尝试确认诚实信用原则与合

---

① 从普通法视角，参见 J. Gordley, *An American Perspective on the UNIDROIT Principles*, *Cento distudi e ricerche in comparato e straniero*: *Saggi conferenze e seminarin.* 22, Roma 1996, pp. 1 −6 (with respect to the abandoning of the requirement of consideration); JM. Perillo, *UNIDROIT Principles of International Commercial Contracts*, cit, pp301 −302 and R. Goode, *Commercial Law*, 3th ed, London, p970 et seq. (with respect to the provisions on hardship).

同谈判①、合同解释②以及合同履行③的关联性上，曾引用 UNIDROIT
通则作为灵感的源泉。另一方面，法国的案例法向来在商业合同遇到
艰难情形时，对合同进行再谈判与调整的做法相当敌视，但近来起码
对合同的再谈判④采取了相当灵活的态度。

二、UNIDROIT 通则 2010：新的主题

UNIDROIT 通则 2010，如同先前各版是由来自世界各国⑤的专家所
准备，包括多个代表相关国际组织、对通则感兴趣的其他机构和仲裁

---

① 澳大利亚法方面，参见：e. g. Hughes Aircraft Systems International v. Airservices Australia in UNILEX at http：//www. unilex. info/case. cfm? id = 634；United Group Rail Services v Rail Corporation Of New South Wales in UNILEX at http：//www. unilex. info/case. cfm? id = 1517.

② 新西兰法方面，参见：e. g. Hideo Yoshimoto v Canterbury Golf International Limited in UNILEX at http：//www. unilex. info/case. cfm? id = 802；Vector Gas Ltd. v. Bay of Plenty Energy Ltd. , in UNILEX at http：//www. unilex. info/case. cfm? id = 1611；with respect to Australian law, see e. g. Australian Medic – Care Company Ltd v Hamilton Pharmaceutical Pty Limited in UNILEX at http：//www. unilex. info/case. cfm? id = 1519；with respect to English law *ProForce Recruit Ltd v. The Rugby Group Ltd*, ［2006］EWCA Civ 69.

③ 澳大利亚法方面，参见：e. g. Alcatel Australia Ltd. v. Scarcella & Ors in UNILEX at http：//www. unilex. info/case. cfm? id = 648.

④ 进一步的参考文件请见：B. Fauvarque-Cosson, *Le Changement de circonstances*, *Revue des contrats 2004*, p67 et seq.

⑤ Members of the Working Group were Behrooz Akhlaghi（Iran），Guido Alpa（Italy），M. Joachim Bonell（Unidroit, *Chairman of the Working Group*），Paul-André Crépeau（Canada），Samuel Kofi Date-Bah（Ghana），Bénédicte Fauvarque-Cosson（France），Paul Finn（Australia），Marcel Fontaine（Belgium），Michael Philip Furmston（United Kingdom），Henry D. Gabriel（United States of America），Lauro Gama, Jr.（Brazil），Arthur S. Hartkamp（The Netherlands），Alexander Komarov（Russian Federation），Ole Lando（Denmark），Takashi Uchida（Japan），Pierre Widmer（Switzerland），Zhang Yuqing（China）（张玉卿，中国）and Reinhard Zimmermann（Germany）.

中心①的观察员。新版的目的不是为了对 1994 年和 2004 年通则进行修订，而是为了添加那些国际商业和法律社会所感兴趣的新的主题，诸如合同失败时的返还原状、违法、条件、多个债务人与多个债权人。

下面就将对新的章节做一简要评价，其中对违法一节将特别着重笔墨，因为在起草时曾出现过重大分歧。

1. 失败合同的恢复原状

1994 年和 2004 年版 UNIDROIT 通则都涉及了恢复原状的题目，即对合同失败前当事人已履行的全部或部分要进行返还，这也被称为"解除失败的合同"。但是，该失败的合同仅指涉及因同意瑕疵而宣告合同无效与不履行而终止的情况。更具体讲，第 3.17 条第（2）款和第 7.3.6 条第（1）款分别规定，在上述两种情况下每一方当事人均可主张对其已提供的一切要求返还，条件是该方当事人要同时返还其根据合同所收到的一切；或者如果实物返还不可能或不适当，只要合理，应以金钱予以补偿。同时，第 7.3.6 条第（2）款还规定，如果合同的履行已持续了一段时间而且合同是可分割的，则只能对在合同终止生效后那段期间的已履行的，请求返还。

但上述的方法起码基于下面三个理由被认为不令人满意：首先，与恢复原状相关的其他一些问题尚未得到解决，例如，关于风险分担问题：当不可能返还实物的原因不归咎于履行接收方时，接收方对保存或维护收到的履行而合理发生的费用是否有权请求赔偿，以及接收方是否必须对其可能从履行中收到的任何利益进行返还。另外，有关终止时恢复原状的规则很清楚是以销售合同作为范例的，这就降低了一段期间内履行之合同的地位，而实践中一段期间内履行之合同同前

---

① Observers of the Working Group were Ibrahim Al Mulla for the Emirates International Law Center, Eckart Brödermann for the Space Law Committee of the International Bar Association, Alejandro Carballo for the Private International Law Group of the American Society of International Law, Christine Chappuis for the *Group de Travail Contrats Internationaux*, Changho Chung for the Government of the Republic of Korea, Neil B. Cohen for the American Law Institute, François Dessemontet for the Swiss Arbitration Association, Alejandro M. Garro for the New York City Bar, Attila Harmathy for the Arbitration Court of the Hungarian Chamber of Commerce and Industry, Emmanuel Jolivet for the ICC International Court of Arbitration, Timothy Lemay for the United Nations Commission on International Trade Law (UNCITRAL), Pilar Perales Viscasillas for the National Center for Inter – American Free Trade, Marta Pertegás for the Hague Conference on Private International Law, Hilmar Raeschke-Kessler for the German Arbitration Institute and Giorgio Schiavoni for the Chamber of National and International Arbitration of Milan.

者一样重要。最后，其他情况下的失败合同，诸如受违法影响的合同，或满足解除条件的合同，原版中均未规范，而在新版中都要做出规定。

当决定在 2010 版中以更宽泛的方式①处理 UNIDROIT 通则对失败合同的解除问题后，首先要回答的问题是，对该主题是要单列一个新的章节，还是在每一个处理不同失败合同情况的章节中分别就恢复原状做出规定。最终后一种方法被采纳，因为这更便于使用，但为了避免不必要的重复，决定仅在宣告合同无效和合同终止章节内对返还原状定出具体规则，而在违法和条件章节只是索引那些条文。另外，对一次性履行的合同终止与一段时间内履行合同的终止，采取平等处理，由两个分别的条款处理。

结果，1994 版和 2004 版得第 3.17 条第(2)款和第 7.3.6 条第(1)款分别成为 UNIDROIT 通则新版的第 3.2.15 条和第 7.3.6 条，文字上第(1)和第(2)款对应原来的两个条款②。最后的两款是新增加的，规定：“(3)如果不能进行实物返还之原因归咎于对方当事人，则收到履行的当事人无须折价补偿。(4)对于为保存或维护收到的履行而合理发生的费用，可请求赔偿”。对于从履行中所获取的利益问题，只是在注释中做了处理，指出在商业实践中通常很难确定一方当事人，或经常是双方当事人，从履行中所获取的利益。另外，UNIDROIT 通则第 7.3.6 条只对一次性履行合同做了规范；而对一段期间履行的合同在新的第 7.3.7 条中做了规定，实体上对应原来的第 7.3.6 条的第(2)款。最后，在“违法”一节，有一款特殊的规定（第 3.3.2 条第(3)款），即当赋予返还原状时，规定要参照第 3.2.15 条来处理；同样在“条件”一节，对返还原状也有一条特殊规定（第 5.3.5 条），即当解除条件成就时，规定要分别参照第 3.2.15 条，或第 7.3.6 条和第 7.3.7 条③处理，取决于解除条件是否具有追溯效力。

2. 条件

在商业实践中，当事人将其合同，或将源于合同的具体义务置于未来不定事件（条件）的发生，是很常见的事情。尽管在案件中会经常遇到很多问题，但在国际统一法中却往往忽略条件问题：《联合国国际

---

① 本主题的报告员——德国 Reinhard Zimmermann 教授，曾提出此问题。

② 对这些新条款的全面分析，参见 R. Zimmermann《UNIDROIT 通则 2010 失败合同的解除》，载于 *Uniform Law Review* 2011，p563 et seq.

③ 原文为第 7.6.7 条，属笔误，实为第 7.3.7 条。

货物销售合同公约（CISG）》从未触及这个问题，即便最近的法律文件，如《欧洲合同法原则》和《欧盟民法典草案》对此也只有几个条款①。

另外，新的"条件"一节（UNIDROIT 通则 2010 版的第五章的第三节）的最后文本包含五个简明条文，处理了几个基本问题，而其他一些问题因分歧过大未在黑体字条文中予以规范。但起码为了提醒当事人这些问题的存在以及在合同中需要处理这些问题②，最后决定将它们放到注释之中提及。

本节从两个类型的条件的定义开始，即一个合同或某项合同义务可以未来某一不确定事件的发生作为条件，从而该合同或该合同义务只有在该事件发生时才生效（即所谓的先决条件），或者在该事件发生时失效（即所谓的解除条件）（第 5.3.1 条）。首先，注释讲的很清楚，本节只适用于源于当事方所达成之协议中的条件，而法律规定的条件（如公共许可要求），不包括在内，除非这些条件被当事方纳入合同之中（见注释 1）。注释还提醒注意这样的事实：其他一些似乎类似于条件的情况不能与本节所规范的条件相混淆，如合同规定一方当事人的履行取决于对方当事人的先履行，或就合同或产生合同的义务发生效力或终止效力规定一个具体日期。这都不属于条件，因为前者只是就当事人对合同的履行规定了一个顺序，而后者当事人只是就该情况规定了一个时间限期（见注释 2）。另外，注释还简要地提到条件必须发生之时间的问题以及条件完全依赖债务人之意愿的问题：对于前一个问题，注释提到如果合同未就条件必须发生规定具体时间，该时间可以通过对当事人意图的解释而得出（见注释 2）；对于后一个问题，同样要依据案件的具体情况，以确定债务人是否意在愿意受到约束（见注释 4）。最后，给予特别关注的是"交割"问题，即指经常发生的那些涉及较长谈判的复杂商业交易，当事方在其合同中规定在某一特定时间点（"交割日"）正式确认所有约定之条件（"先决条件"）已于该日或之前得到满足。像在注释中所指出的，尽管当事方使用这样的术语，但并不是提到的所有作为"先决条件"的事件都是第 5.3.1 条所规定的"条件"，例如可能涉及某些具体的事项，仍需当事人之间的同意；或

① 见《欧洲合同法原则》第 16：101-16：103 条；《欧洲民法典草案》（或《共同参考框架草案》）第 III.-1：106 条。

② 对这些新条款的评价请参见 B. Fauvarque-Cosson：《UNIDROIT 通则 2010 条件新规则》，*Uniform Law Review 2011*，p537 et seq.

者涉及某些真实的义务，当事人必须在谈判过程中履行，其效果、效力都是不同的(见注释5)。

第5.3.2条在于陈明，不同于许多国家的国内法律规定，根据UNIDROIT通则的规定，条件的成就只具朝前效力，当然若当事人做出了相反的约定，则除外。

第5.3.3条则规定，一方当事人如有意使先决条件不成就，或有意使解除条件成就，此时其义务分别是不阻止该条件的成就，或不促成该条件的成就；而第5.3.4条规定，期待条件成就的一方当事人的义务是，不得损害对方当事人于条件成就时可享有的权利，这两条不过是在实体上具体适用诚实信用、公平交易以及当事人之间合作的一般原则。但是，注释还恰当地指出当事方应在他们的合同中对这些事项做出具体规定，诸如一方当事人应做哪种努力以促成先决条件的成就，或应做哪种努力以阻止解除条件的成就(参见第5.3.3(a)-(d)注释)，或会从条件成就中会获得利益的当事人，在期待条件成就时应采取哪种措施，以保护其权利(参考第5.3.4条注释)。

最后，第5.3.5条处理的是解除条件成就时的恢复原状问题，此时要参照适用经适当调整后的终止合同时的恢复原状(见第(1)款)，或如果当事方同意解除条件追溯适用(见第(2)款)，参照适用宣告合同无效时的恢复原状。

3. 多个债务人与多个债权人

多个债务人与多个债权人的主题不但涉及很高的专门技术，而且也具有重要的实践意义。就涉及多个债务人而言，几个人一起从某单一金融机构借款，或数家承包商联合参加一项建筑工程，或一组共同保险人对重要风险进行投保，上述足以说明它在实践中是常见的；就多个债权人来说，几家银行共同向同一客户签署一项辛迪加贷款协议，或多个卖方与一个买方达成股票购买协议，几个合伙人在建筑领域或石油行业作为当事方参加国际财团协定。

关于多个债务人与债权人①的第11章总共有两节，17条：第一节是规范多个债务人(第11.1.1条至第11.1.13条)，第二节是规范多个

---

① 本章报告员为比利时的 Marcel Fontaine 教授。

债权人(第11.2.1条至第11.2.4条)①。

第11.1.1条规定了：当多个债务人对同一债务向一个债权人承担清偿义务时，实践中存在的两项主要义务。第一项义务，被称为"连带"债务，指每一个债务人要对全部债务承担清偿责任，换句话说就是债权人可要求债务人中的任何一人进行债务清偿(见第11.1.3条)，但后期要受到债务人之间的分担请求的制约(见第11.1.10条)。第二项义务，被称为"可分"债务，指每个债务人只承担清偿其份额内的债务，换句话说债权人只有权向每个债务人请求其份额内的债务。第11.1.2条为反映了现实商业实践，建立了倾向连带债务的推定，但这一推定可由合同条款的明确相反约定来否决，或由能推断出共同债务人只承担其相应债务份额的其他情况来否决。

第11.1.4条至第11.1.8条规定了连带债务人对债权人具有的抗辩权。第11.1.4条特别规定了，一个连带债务人只能对债权人主张那些属于其自身的抗辩权和抵销权，或那些对所有共同债务人共有的抗辩权和抵销权，而不能主张那些属于其他共同债务人中的一个或数个人自身的抗辩权和抵销权。第11.1.5条至第11.1.8条规范的是当一个债务人对债权人之债务被解除之后或另外受到影响之后，对其他连带债务人的后果问题。

第一节结束的几个条款是关于连带债务人之间的债务比例以及相关的债务分担请求权问题。

第二节是关于多个债权人问题，以对实践中存在的三种类型多个请求权做出定义开始。"可分"债权指每一个债权人只能请求其自身的债权份额；"连带"债权指每一个债权人可以对全部债权请求清偿；"共同"债权指所有债权人必须一同请求清偿债权(见第11.2.1条)。在准备条文过程中，曾花费很多时间讨论是否应对这些请求权中的某一种做出倾向性推定，但实际调查显示实践中默认规则从一个贸易领域到另一个贸易领域，大相径庭，最终决定不要默认规则，而且在注释中敦促当事方在每一个交易中做出自己的安排(见第11.2.1条注释4)。在当事方（包括他们的律师）经验充分丰富时，这种方法或许是适当的；但起码对法律欠发达的国家来说，存在一种风险，即他们会因不存在任何默认规则而感到意外，倾向连带债权的推定会对债权人和债务人都有好处：前者，因为多数情况他们的期待是其请求权是连带的；后者，因

---

① 对这些新条款的全面评介，参阅 M. Fontaine 教授的《UNIDROIT 通则多个债务人与多个债权人之新规则》，见 *Uniform Law Review 2011*，p549 et seq.

为他们通常期待通过一次性付款，并不是对每一个共同债权人分别付款，而对共同债权人解除其债务，最终遭到所有人的起诉。

第二节的其余条款处理的是连带请求权，基本上是模仿第一节的相关条文。因此，第11.2.2条规定："对其中一个连带债权人进行全部债务清偿，即解除了该债务人对所有其他债权人的清偿义务"。第11.2.3条规定的是可对连带债权人(第(1)款)运用的抗辩权，以及当一个债权人的债权被清偿或受到另外的影响后，对其他共同债权人的效力(第(2)款)。该条的规则实质上指向了连带债务第11.1.5至第11.1.8条的相关条文。最后，第11.2.4条规范的是连带债权人之间的债权分配以及相关的分担请求权问题，同样采取了第11.1.9条和第11.1.10条的方法。

4. 违法

违法的主题明示地被 UNIDROIT 通则 1994 和 2004 版给排除了，理由是"固有的公共政策……问题的复杂性，以及国内法对其处理方式的重大不同"①。

的确，国内法之间规定这种类型合同无效，起码在内容上，甚至在术语和概念结构上，差别都相当大。大多数普通法系国家存在"违法"和"违法合同"的一般分类，进而又区分为"法定违法"和"普通法违法"，前者指合同的订立被成文法明示或默示地禁止；后者指因违反公共政策，合同依普通法违法。在美国还有一个"依公共政策不可执行合同"的概念，是"违法合同"中的一个具体类型，其特点是合同起码涉及对当事人一方施加罚款的事实。就大陆法系而言，例如德国法、奥地利法和瑞士法，有"违法合同"和"不道德"合同之分，即指合同违反法定禁止，或合同违反良好道德。相反，法国和意大利的法律是基于合同"约因违法（*cause illicite or causa illicita*）"而使合同无效。加拿大魁北克省新的民法典也采取了同一模式。荷兰、葡萄牙和巴西的民法典现已放弃了任何由约因导致违法合同或不道德合同的规定，他们基本效仿了德国的模式。②

尽管本主题极为复杂，也可能恰恰因此，当国际统一私法协会（UNIDROIT）就通则 2010 版拟增加的新议题进行咨询时，违法是最受

---

① 见 UNIDROIT 通则 1994 和 2004 版的第 3.1 条。

② 进一步信息请参考 M. J. Bonell 教授的《UNIDROIT 通则 2010 违法新条文》，见 *Uniform Law Review* 2011，pp517 – 518.

欢迎的主题，因此决定将该题目纳入新版。在准备过程中，自然也就不奇怪，工作组成员对这个议题分歧特别大①，但最终还是达成了共识，通过了两条精心设计的关于"违反强制性规则合同"和关于"恢复原状"的条文，并将它们作为新的第三节，名称为"违法"②，加在第三章关于"合同的效力"之中。

对于像 UNIDROIT 通则这样的不具拘束力的法律文件，处理如此复杂而且政治上很敏感的违法这样的主题，可能会被认为太雄心勃勃了。但这个结论是没根据的。

首先，通过将本节违法的适用范围限制在违反根据国际私法规则导致适用的强制性规则的合同（见第 3.3.1 条第（1）款，第 1.4 条）。UNIDROIT 通则考虑到了根据传统的同时也是现在盛行的观点，即主要由适用的国内法律来决定合同有效的边际，不管是国内法还是国际法；而且考虑到了只有在国际仲裁领域，仲裁庭可以参考所谓的国际公共政策或国际公共秩序（见第 1.4 条注释 4）。与此同时，UNIDROIT 通则对"强制性规则"采取了较为宽泛的定义，通则表达得很清楚，对合同自由的限制不仅可源于法定禁止，而且也可源于不成文的、应适用的国内法，包括那些国际或超国家法律中的（见第 1.4 条注释 2）公共政策的一般原则。

另外，有关违反强制性规则的后果问题，UNIDROIT 通则首先指向的是适用的国内法律，但条件是该被违反的规则明示地规定了那些后果（见第 3.3.1 条第（1）款和第 3.3.2 条注释 1）。只有在被违反的规则对此问题未做规定时，UNIDROIT 通则才能适用，提供解决办法，并借此向法官和仲裁员提供国际统一指导，决定违反相关强制性规则的后果。

规定当事方可"在情况合理时"行使合同救济（见第 3.3.1 条第（2）款）以及当"情况合理时"可赋予恢复原状，可见 UNIDROIT 通则对此采取了灵活的方式。这与多数国内法的钢性规定和"缺乏救济

---

① 主要问题是在违法的范围内，基于违法行为的严重性，是否在违反"世界范围的法律制度内被广泛接受的重大原则"合同，与违反"法定禁止"合同之间，做一区分。起初，工作组倾向这种两个层次的方法，但后来放弃了这种意见，而同意采取一个更加有限制的模式，原因是"世界范围的法律制度内被广泛接受的重大原则"概念过于含混，会在世界不同国家造成不可避免的不同解释，从而会减损在国际合同实践中促进法律确定性的 UNIDROIT 通则的目标。

② 本主题的报告员为英国的 Michael Furston 教授（2006 – 2009）以及本文作者 Bonell 教授（2009 –2010）。更多见 M. J. Bonell 教授的《UNIDROIT 通则 2010 违法新条文》，见 *Uniform Law Review 2011*，pp517 – 518.

灵活性"①，形成对比。

然而，起码就有关实践中的合同救济，其结果差距并不大。事实上，根据大多数国家的国内法律规定②，也是 UNIDROIT 通则采取的原则，任何时候如果一个合同违反了公共政策的重大原则，都不会对任何一方给予合同救济，即便是属于违反法定禁止的情况，给予这种救济也纯属例外③。

UNIDROIT 通则关于恢复原状的规定确有创新性。传统的、目前依然盛行的国内法对违反强制性规则的后果的规定是，拒绝给当事方提供任何合同项下的救济，甚至当事方给予对方的利益也无权索回④。通则的确与这种观点差距很大，其在这方面所提供的解决办法是依据合理情况来解决，这就提供了最大限度的灵活性。UNIDROIT 通则这样做是附和正在国际和国内层面出现的一种现代趋势⑤，而且这一趋势特别适合于国际商事合同，尤其是那些涉及巨额投资的建造工厂合同、众多长期合同的特殊场合。

注释中提供的两个示例对这方面具有重要的意义⑥。在这两个示例中，都涉及一个外国公司和一个本地政府签订的建造大型工厂的合同，结果前者向后者实施了贿赂。当工厂已经或几乎竣工时，一个新的政府开始掌权，它以外国公司向前政府行贿为由，拒绝支付所欠合同价款。虽然当事人不正当行为的严重性足以导致得出任何一方当事人都无权获得任何合同项下的救济，但是，准予该外国公司取得与其为该国政府已建成的或几乎建成的工厂所具有的价值相当的货币补偿，应是合理的。反过来，该国政府或前政府所支付的超过该金额的款项也应予以返还。对这样的腐败案件允许恢复原状救济，乍看上去可能让人有些吃惊，但仔细审查这种情况，会发现起码基于以下两点理由还是有道理的：首先，让该政府拥有这个已完成（或几乎完成）的工厂，其价值巨大，但却仅支付远远低于约定的价款，是不公平的；其次，

---

① 见 E. McKendrick, Contract Law, 9th ed (2011), p285.

② 进一步参考信息，见 M. J. Bonell, *The New Provisions on Illegality*, cit., p11.

③ 见 第 3.3.1 条注释 6.

④ 参见 M. J. Bonell, *The New Provisions on Illegality*, cit., p15 et seq.

⑤ 见荷兰《民法典》第 6.211（1）条，根据该条规定，只要准予恢复原状违反"合理性与衡平性"情况，就应被拒绝。另见，新西兰《1970 年违反合同法》第 7（1）条，该条规定法院可准予违法合同恢复原状，"但法院在其自由裁量权内应认为这样做是公正的"。另见，英国法律委员会 1999 年的《咨询文件 154》之建议，第 VII，第 7.2 段，重点 7.17 -- 7.22 段。

⑥ 见第 3.3.2 条注释 2 的 1 和 2 示例。

如果政府知道今后其可以贿赂为由，将非法交易的全部损失推给外国公司，这不仅不能劝阻该政府在授予重要合同时不要接受贿赂，还可能鼓励该政府继续受贿。

三、UNIDROIT 通则及在实践中的运用

即便 UNIDROIT 通则在实践中的适用只具有说服力的价值，它们可以，实际也是如此，在许多方面起到重要的作用。实践中可以运用 UNIDROIT 通则的最主要的方式都已写在了序言里。下面第 1 点重点关注的是它们在国家和国际立法机构中，作为示范法的功能；第 2 点介绍其作为国际合同适用法律的功能；第 3 点介绍其可作为解释和补充国际统一法律文件的手段；第 4 点介绍其可作为解释和补充国内法律的手段。

1. UNIDROIT 通则在国家和国际立法机构中的示范法功能

鉴于 UNIDROIT 通则自身的特点，它可以作为，实际上也是经常作为，国家和国际立法机构的示范法①。对那些在一般合同法法律规则上有待充分发展而又打算提升其法律制度的国家来说，或起码是在国际商业交易方面打算提升其法律制度，以便跟上现代国际标准的国家来说，通则就特别具有使用价值。另外，UNIDROIT 通则对不同的国家正在进行的法律改革方面还起着影响，而且还不局限于特定的地缘政治区域，事实上已扩展到了世界所有的地方，包括法律制度高度发达的国家。

在某些情况下，例如，在俄罗斯联邦准备其新民法典过程中，UNIDROIT 通则居然在其 1994 年版出版之前就被定为他们的灵感渊源之一。随后一年，爱沙尼亚和立陶宛又选择通则作为他们新的民法典的示范法，这两部民法典已于 2001 年正式生效。其他重要的事例有，苏格兰法律委员会于 1996 年发表的关于法律行为之解释规则的改革建议，2004 年由西班牙统一法典编纂委员会（*Comisión General de Codifición*）发表的关于西班牙商法典中商事合同一般规则的改革建议。还有德国的立法机构在准备修改其《民法典（BGB）》时，曾参考了

① 全面了解见 R. Michaels, in S. Vogenauer - J. Kleinheisterkamp（eds），*Commentary on the UNIDROIT Principles of International Commercial Contracts*（*PICC*）（*2009*），p68 et seq.

UNIDROIT 通则，尽管采用的比较有限。该民法典已于 2002 年生效。最近，法国对属于私法关系方面的时效期间进行改革，也受到了 UNIDROIT 通则关于时效期间规定的启发。

在欧洲之外，首先要提到的是中国 1999 年的合同法，它不但受到了《联合国国际货物销售合同公约（CISG）》，也受到了 UNIDROIT 通则的很大启发。还有蒙古、越南与格鲁吉亚关于合同法的现代化与协调化项目也是如此。另外，美国《统一商法典》第 2 条修改草案也索引了 UNIDROIT 通则的具体条文。非洲统一商业法律组织（OHADA）邀请国际统一私法协会就 OHADA 依据 UNIDROIT 通则准备其统一合同法提供支持。2004 年由 UNIDROIT 工作组一位成员准备的《统一合同法建议草案》（an Avant‒projet d'Acte uniforme sur le droit des contrats）已递交 OHADA 主管机构考虑。还有，日本民法典（债权篇）修改委员会目前正在制定其新的合同法，他们已将 UNIDROIT 通则用作其立法参考文件。

可以肯定，像立陶宛民法典和西班牙商法典，更不要说 OHADA 的非洲统一合同法大块照搬 UNIDROIT 通则的条文是很少见的。UNIDROIT 通则的影响力既不是排他性的，也没必要占支配地位。另外，UNIDROIT 通则提供的具体解决办法很可能在一个国家被当成示范法，而在另一个国家却被完全拒绝。典型的例子就是有关对艰难条款（见第 6.2.1 条至第 6.2.3 条）的态度：《俄罗斯联邦民法典》对该条只做了细微的修改便将其纳入，以适应前苏联政权解体后在社会经济和法律环境方面的剧烈变化；而中国的立法机构在经过紧张的辩论之后，却拒绝了这些条款，他们担心的是法院不会恰当地适用这些条款。

另外，UNIDROIT 通则还被用来作准备国际法律文件的示范法。"国际商会（ICC）2003 年不可抗力条款"和"国际商会（ICC）2003 年艰难条款"，都起码分别部分地参照了 UNIDROIT 通则第 7.1.7 条、第 6.2.1 条、第 6.2.2 条和第 6.2.3 条。同样，联合国贸易发展委员会（UNCTAD）与世界贸易组织（WTO）的国际贸易中心（ITC）2004 年公布的"ITC 契约式合资示范协议"文本，公开说明协议第 18 条、第 19 条有关艰难条款和不可抗力条款分别参照了 UNIDROIT 通则的对应条款。

2. UNIDROIT 通则作为管辖合同的法律规则

UNIDROIT 通则序言规定，"当事人约定其合同受通则管辖时，应适用通则"（第（2）款），以及"当事人约定其合同受法律的一般原则、商人习惯法或类似规范管辖时，可适用通则"(第(3)款)，或"当事人未选择任何法律管辖其合同时，可适用通则"(第(4)款)。

人们可以想象很多不同的情况，在这些情况下，当事人不管是颇具实力的"跨国公司"，还是中小企业，他们希望其合同不适用任何国内法，让合同"去国家化"，而使其适用真正的中立国家或超国家的法律制度①。过去，当事方为了这个目标，没有其他的选择办法而只能原则地引用"一般被接受的国际商法原则"、"商人习惯法"或类似的概念，而留给审判机构在每一个案件中去决定这些含混概念的真实含义。这种方法遇到了许多的批评，原因是如果不是专断的话，它不具可预见性。现在有了一个有效的方案，就是可依赖于能容易运用、宽泛的像 UNIDROIT 通则这样的法律文件。的确如此，近来的实践显示当事人在实践中越来越经常同意将 UNIDROIT 通则作为管辖他们合同的法律。同样，许多由国际组织，诸如国际商会(ICC)、UNCTAD/WTO 的国际贸易中心(ITC)所准备的标准合同，例如有关商业代理、分销、合资企业等方面的标准合同，都参照了 UNIDROIT 通则。通则或作为唯一的合同法被参考，或与其他法律渊源(即指某一个特定的国内法，或在某一特定贸易领域通行的一般法律原则与惯例)一同被参考。最近，联合国粮农组织(F. A. O.)通过的"食品与农业通用资源植物的标准材料转让协议"，提到"法律的一般原则，包括 UNIDROIT 商事合同通则2004"作为协议的适用法律。

需要继续观察的是：依据相关的国际私法规则，是否允许合同当事方选择像 UNIDROIT 通则这样的软法律文件作为其合同的管辖法律，从而取代某个具体的国内法；如果允许，应在何种范围之内②。

在国际商事仲裁领域，当今的回答是相当肯定的。联合国国际贸易法委员会（UNCITRAL）在 1985 年《国际商事仲裁示范法》的第 28(1)条中明确规定"仲裁庭应根据当事人选择的法律规则作为实体争议的适用法律，决定该争议"。世界上 40 左右个的国家以 UNCITRAL 示范法为基础制定的仲裁法，也具有类似的规定。

与此相反的是法院的程序，传统的而且依然流行的观点是，当事方自由选择的适用法仍局限于某个具体的国内法，结果当事方索引 UNIDROIT 通则仅被视为是将通则的条文纳入其合同的协议，只有在这些条文不影响合同法强制性规定的限度内，UNIDROIT 通则本身才对当

---

① 进一步参考，见 M. J. Bonell, *An International Restatement*, cit., p174 et seq.

② 见 M. J. Bonell, *An International Restatement*, cit., p180 et seq.

事人具有拘束力①。

这种观点显然是受到了国家法概念的影响，一些近期的重大发展显示，这种观点在不断受到质疑。

例如，1994 年《美洲国家国际合同适用法律公约》在两个地方提到（具体是第 9 条第(2)款和第 10 条）：为确定合同法律，可以是一个国家或一个超国家性质的法律渊源。由此，有理由得出结论，依据该公约 UNIDROIT 通则起码如果被当事人明示选择为适用法，完全可以作为管辖其合同的法律②。

另外，提及当事方同意 UNIDROIT 通则适用性的可能，还可以在《美国统一商法典》的官方注释中找到。具体可见 2001 年修订后的第 1－302 条的注释 2，其中写道："……当事方在合同中可定明，其关系将由被认可的适用于商业交易……的规则或原则，如 UNIDROIT 国际商事合同通则，来调整……"，从而改变（《统一商法典》）条文的效力"。的确，前面提到的注释是在规范契约自由原则的第 1－302 条之中，而未在当事人有权选择适用法律的第 1－301 条之中规定，其后果是当事方约定其合同受 UNIDROIT 通则管辖时，只有在法典允许当事方有权减损法典条文的情况下，该约定才会被考虑。但是，尽管这种明确提及 UNIDROIT 通则作为受该法典管辖交易的另外一组可适用的规则仅仅具有象征性的价值，但如果当事方真的实际选择 UNIDROIT 通则作为管辖其合同的法律规则，通则的具体条款因其与法典不符而被弃之不用的可能性，是微乎其微的③，更重要的是美国统一商法典的大多数强制性条款多限于是对消费者的交易④。

---

① 进一步请参考 R. Michaels, in S. Vogenauer - J. Kleinheisterkamp（eds），*Commentary on the UNIDROIT Principles*, cit., p36 et seq.

② 见 F. K. Juenger, *The Inter-American Convention on the Law Applicable to International Contracts：Some Highlights and Comparisons*, 42 *The American Journal of Comparative Law*（1994），p601 et seq.

③ 几个有冲突条款之一是 UNIDROIT 通则的第 1.2 条，该条规定合同的成立与事后的对其修改，或协议终止不受任何形式上的要求，与 UCC 的第 2－201 条：形式要求；法定欺诈。对 UNIDROIT 通则（包括《联合国国际货物销售合同公约》（CISG））与 UCC 相关条文的逐条比较分析见 H. D. Gabriel 教授的 *Contracts for the Sale of Goods：A Comparison of Domestic and International Law*。

④ 当然 UNIDROIT 通则其他一些条款可能会被美国法院弃之不顾，但不是因为这些条款与 UCC 具体条文有什么冲突，而是由于这些条文与美国已确立的一般合同法原则有冲突，具体情况如第 4.1 条和 4.3 条（与"显明含义规则"的合同解释相冲突），第 6.2.3 条（与美国法院急于改进其合同法相冲突）。

最后，《海牙国际商事合同法律选择原则》最近正由海牙国际私法会议准备①。该草案第 2 条在规定了"合同由当事方选择的法律管辖"的基本原则之后，明确"这些原则包括法律规则"，并在此清楚地指出在所建议的原则中，当事方尚可自由选择诸如 UNIDROIT 通则这样的软法律文件作为管辖其合同的法律规则。

再看实际运用，UNILEX 数据库（http：//www. unilex. info）② 收集的 271 个裁决中，反映了对 UNIDROIT 通则的不同方式的适用。其中在 55 个仲裁裁决中，UNIDROIT 通则作为调整争议的实体法律规则被适用，4 个法院的判决还确认了仲裁裁决对该规则的适用。另外，在两个法院的判决中法官的附带意见表示，当事方有权选择 UNIDROIT 通则作为其合同的管辖法律③。

在一些案件中，UNIDROIT 通则或被当事方单独明示选其作为仲裁庭裁决案件的法律基础，或一同与其他法律，如《联合国国际货物销售合同公约（CISG）》，或某一国内法律作为仲裁庭裁决案件的法律基础④。更有意思的是，当事方经常是在仲裁程序开始后，同意适用 UNIDROIT 通则，有时甚至是在仲裁庭的建议下，同意适用通则。

其他情况下，UNIDROIT 通则也得到了适用，一种情况是当事方同意其合同受未具体细化的、超国家或跨国家性质的原则与规则管辖；另一种情况是仲裁庭决定争议的是非曲直要根据未具体细化的、超国家或跨国家性质的原则与规则来决定。这些原则与规则可以是"商人习惯法的一般原则"、"国际合同法的一般原则"、"衡平法的一般原

---

① 见工作组最后于 2011 年 6 月通过的草案，工作组由世界各国独立专家组成。

② 见 2011 年 11 月 15 日之数据。

③ 见 E. Finazzi-Agrò, *The Impact of the Unidroit Principles in International Dispute Resolution*：*The Figures*，*Uniform Law Review2011*，p719 et seq. ）. For links to the relevant cases see UNILEX at http：//www. unilex. info/dynasite. cfm? dssid = 2377&dsmid = 13621&x = 1.

④ 参见. Arbitral Award of the Centro de Arbitraje de Mexico of 30 November 2006, in UNILEX at http：//www. unilex. info/case. cfm? id = 1149（Contract between Mexican grower and U. S. distributor for production and distribution on an exclusive basis of specific quantities vegetables；contract contained arbitration clause referring to UNIDROIT Principles as the rules of law governing the contract）；more recently, Arbitral Award of the Permanent Court of Arbitration of 2009, abstract in UNILEX at http：//www. unilex. info/case. cfm? pid = 2&id = 1473&do = case（licensing agreement between European company and international governmental Organisation；parties' express choice of UNIDROIT Principles as the law governing their contract）；ICC Award of 2004, No. 11880, in UNILEX at http：//www. unilex. info/case. cfm? pid = 2&id = 1427&do = case（international "guaranty" contract containing reference to the UNIDROIT Principles as the law governing the contract in conjunction with Italian law）.

则"以及"自然公平的法律和规则"。仲裁庭此时求助 UNIDROIT 通则是有道理的，因为通则是这些原则与规则的非常权威和可靠的陈述①。

最后，如果当事人在合同中未约定法律选择条款，或者其法律选择条款属明显无效，比如当事方提到的管辖其合同的法律根本不存在。在这种情况下，仲裁庭也可以适用 UNIDROIT 通则作为调整其争议实体问题的法律规则。仲裁庭这样做时，通常依靠的是法定条文或仲裁规则。例如，国际商会（ICC）仲裁规则第 17 条规定"仲裁庭（对争议）应适用它认为适当的法律规则"（第（1）款第 2 句），并且"在所有情况下仲裁庭应考虑……相关的贸易惯例"（第（2）款）②。

3. UNIDROIT 通则是对国际统一法律文件解释和补充的手段

像在序言中讲到的，UNIDROIT 通则可以用来解释和补充国际统一法律文件③。由于 UNIDROIT 通则并不是以国际条约形式制定通过的，也未以通则本身之形式被纳入任何国内法。因此在当事方未引用通则时，如何证明这一使用功能是有根据的，还有待进一步的观察。

《联合国国际货物销售货物合同公约（CISG）》第 7 条第（1）款规定"在解释本公约时，应考虑到本公约的国际性质和促进其适用的统一……"，第（2）款规定"凡本公约未明确解决的属于本公约范围的问

---

① 参考 ICC Award of 28 July 2000, in UNILEX at http：//www. unilex. info/case. cfm？id = 668（Member Firm Interfirm Agreements between the 140 Arthur Andersen member firms operating in 75 different countries contained arbitration clause stating "the［sole］arbitrator shall decide in accordance with the terms of this Agreement［...］［i］n interpreting［it］the arbitrator shall not be bound to apply the substantive law of any jurisdiction but shall be guided by the policies and considerations set forth in［its］Preamble［...］taking into account general principles of equity"；the Arbitral Tribunal, after finding that the Agreement failed to provide guidelines for a decision, declared that it would apply "general principles of law［...］commonly accepted by the legal systems of most countries" and to this effect have resort to the UNIDROIT Principles［...］"）；Partial Award of ad hoc Arbitration of 25 September 2000 at http：//www. fao. org/DOCREP/MEETING/004/Y6612E. HTM（contract for ordinary maintenance of premises between F. A. O. and an Italian company providing that contract be governed by "general principles of law to the exclusion of any single national system of law"；Arbitral Tribunal decided to apply the UNIDROIT Principles）.

② Cf. e. g. Arbitral Award of the Arbitration Institute of the Stockholm Chamber of Commerce of 2001, abstract in UNILEX at http：//www. unilex. info/case. cfm？pid = 2&id = 793&do = case；ICC Award of 2003, No. 11265, in UNILEX at http：//www. unilex. info/case. cfm？pid = 2&id = 1416&do = case；ICC Award of 15 September 2008, No. 15089, abstract in UNILEX at http：//www. unilex. info/case. cfm？pid = 2&id = 1440&do = case.

③ 见序言第 5 款。

题，应按照本公约所依据的一般原则来解决……"，类似的立法模式还可以在最近其他的国际公约中发现①。然而，即便在这方面没有如此具体的语言文字，国际统一法文件应根据其自治的国际统一原则来进行解释和补充，这是近年来已被广泛认可的做法，而诉诸国内法律进行解释和补充仅仅应是最后的手段。

过去这种自治原则与规则只是由法官和仲裁员在临时基础上去发现。现在有了 UNIDROIT 通则，这就提出了通则是否可以为此目的而被使用，或者如被使用，在何种程度上被使用的问题。

法学者对此意见是不同的。一方面，一些人断然否定这种可能性，理由是，（一）UNIDROIT 通则性质只是对私而且是不具约束力的；（二）基于形式主义的辩论观点认为，起码对于哪些先于 UNIDROIT 通则制定的文件，后制定出来的通则无论如何与前者不具任何关联性②。另一方面，一些人明确主张 UNIDROIT 通则作为解释与补充国际统一法律文件之手段的可能性，理由是通则代表了"国际商事合同的一般原则"，其本身无条件地满足了《联合国国际货物销售合同公约》第7条的要求③。

正确的解决办法应存在于这两个极端的观点之间。换句话说，原则上 UNIDROIT 通则完全可以用来解释或补充国际法律文件，对此不应存在什么怀疑，即便这些国际法律文件，像《联合国国际货物销售合同公约》，先于通则制定出来。此时需要满足的条件只是要确定所争议的问题是否属于有关公约的管辖范围，以及 UNIDROIT 通则的条文能够被认为是属于"本公约所依据的一般原则（CISG 第7条第（2）款的文字）"④。

转到实践情况，值得注意的是，尽管有学者对运用 UNIDROIT 通则来解释或补充《联合国国际货物销售合同公约》持怀疑和保留的态度，但法官和仲裁员们在为此求助 UNIDROIT 通则时，却未被所谓理

---

① 见 Art. 7 of the 2001 U. N. Convention on the Assignment of Receivables in International Trade; Art. 5 of the 2001 Cape Town Convention on international Interests in Mobile Equipment; Art. 2 of the 2008 U. N. Convention on Contracts for the International Carriage of Goods Wholly or Partly by Sea.

② 参见，R. Herber, "*Lex mercatoria*" und "*Principles*" – *Gefährliche Irrlichter im internationalen Kaufrecht*, *Internationales Handelsrecht* 2003, p1 *et seq.* (pp. 7 and 9).

③ 见 A. M. Garro, *The Gap-Filling Role of the Unidroit Principles in International Sales Law: Some Comments on the Interplay between the Principles and CISG*, 69 *Tulane Law Review* (1995), p1149 *et seq.*, at p1152 *et seq.*

④ 见 M. J. Bonell, *An International Restatement*, cit., p233。

论上的依据所困惑①。

一些案件求助于 UNIDROIT 通则就足以说明它的重要性。求助的理由是作为填补空缺而被引用的通则条文，被视为 UNIDROIT 通则与《联合国国际货物销售合同公约》所基于的一般原则的陈述。在两个仲裁裁决中，UNIDROIT 通则第7.4.9条第（2）款曾被引用——该款规定"利率应为付款地银行对主要借款人借贷支付货币的短期平均贷款通行利率"，以填补《联合国国际货物销售合同公约》第78条的空缺。适用的理由是该款可以被认为是 UNIDROIT 通则与《联合国国际货物销售合同公约》所基于的全额赔偿一般原则的陈述②。同样，一个法国法院认为它有理由引用 UNIDROIT 通则的第6.1.6条（履行地）的规定来确定《联合国国际货物销售合同公约》卖方退还买方不适当支付之价款的义务履行地，理由是该条是公约第57条第（1）款所基于之原则——金钱债务应于债权人之营业地履行，的一般陈述③。

在其他情况下，UNIDROIT 通则第7.4.9条第（2）款关于适用利息率的规定，或未讲任何理由就得到了适用④，或因其本身被视为"《联合国国际货物销售合同公约》第7条第（2）款的一般原则之一而被适用"⑤。其他的一些裁决也是未讲理由，把整个 UNIDROIT 通则等同于"《联合国国际货物销售合同公约》所基于的一般原则，并证明适用通则的具体条文来解释和补充该公约是有道理的"⑥。

其他的裁决还进了一步，它们不仅仅是因为 UNIDROIT 通则是"《联合国国际货物销售合同公约》所基于的一般原则来适用，而是基

① UNILEX 收集的索引 Unidroit Principles 解释国际统一法律文件的裁决总数为35起，24起为仲裁裁决，11起为法院判决，其中30起涉及《联合国国际货物销售合同公约》。参见 E. Finazzi-Agrò, *The Impact of the Unidroit Principles in International Dispute Resolution*: *The Figures*, cit., p723。

② 参阅 Cf. Awards of the Vienna International Court of Arbitration of 15 June 1994, SCH - 4318 and SCH - 4366, in UNILEX at http://www.unilex.info/case.cfm? pid = 2&id = 635&do = case and http://www.unilex.info/case.cfm? pid = 2&id = 636&do = case.

③ 参见 Cour d'Appel de Grenoble, 23 October 1996, in UNILEX at http://www.unilex.info/ case.cfm? pid = 2&id = 638&do = case.

④ 参见 ICC Award of December 1996, No. 8769, in ICC International Court of Arbitration Bulletin, 10/2 (1999), p. 82; ICC Award of 2004, No. 13152, abstract in UNILEX at http://www.unilex.info/case.cfm? pid = 2&id = 1419&do = case.

⑤ 参见 ICC Award of 1995, No. 8128, in Journal de droit international 1996, p. 1024。

⑥ 参见 ICC Award of December 1997, No. 8817, in ICC International Court of Arbitration Bulletin, 10/2 (1999), p. 75; ICC Award of 2004, No. 12460, abstract in UNILEX at http://www.unilex.info/case.cfm? pid = 2&id = 1411&do = case.

于通则是销售合同公约第 9 条第(2)款规定的'国际贸易中被广泛知道……的贸易惯例'予以适用"①，或者如所强调的，是因为通则被视为"国际商事合同法重述，它规范并扩展了包含在联合国公约中的原则"②。

最近这种观点的范例就是比利时 2009 年最高法院的一个判决③。该案涉及荷兰与法国公司之间签署的几个买卖钢管的合同，合同受《联合国国际货物销售合同公约》管辖。合同达成后，卖方通知买方因不可预测的钢铁价格上涨了 70%，它不得不重新计算双方已同意的价格，于是发生了纠纷。比利时最高法院发现公约并未明示提到艰难条款问题，便决定根据公约第 7 条的规定，考虑以"管辖国际商业法律的一般原则"予以填补空缺，而且未做进一步解释就确定了这种原则（除其他方面外）可以在 UNIDROIT 通则发现。法院并未直接引用通则第 6.2.3 条关于艰难情形后果的规定，得出结论认为本案卖方有权要求就合同的价金进行重新谈判。

4. UNIDROIT 通则作为背景法解释和补充国内法

根据 UNIDROIT 通则序言第 6 款的规定，"通则可用于解释或补充国内法"。

UNIDROIT 通则对依据当事方选择的，或依据法院地相关法律冲突规则确定的管辖合同的国内法的解释方面，的确起着作用，而且这种作用实际还在不断扩大。当相关的国内法是属于一个由计划经济向市场经济过渡国家的法律时，或国内法对现代商业交易的技术缺乏规范时，情况就更是如此。即便那些非常发达的法律制度国家，也不总是对产生于商事合同，特别是具有国际性质的商事合同的具体问题都能提供明确的解决办法，原因或是由于意见分歧巨大，或是由于对争议

---

① 参见 e. g. Award of the International Arbitration Court of the Chamber of Commerce and Industry of the Russian Federation of 5 June 1997, No. 229/1996, abstract in UNILEX at http：//www. unilex. info/ case. cfm? pid = 2&id = 669&do = case; more recently, Award of the International Arbitration Court of the Chamber of Commerce and Industry of the Russian Federation of 19 December 2008, No. 14/2008, abstract in UNILEX at http：//www. unilex. info/case. cfm? pid = 2&id = 1476&do = case.

② 参见 Court of Appeal of New Zealand of 27 November 2000 (per *Thomas J*), *Hideo Yoshimoto v Canterbury Golf International Limited*, 1 *New Zealand Law Report* (2001), p523.

③ 参见 Cour de cassation of 19 June 2009, in UNILEX at http：//www. unilex. info/ case. cfm? pid = 2&id = 1456&do = case.

的问题从未做过任何规定。在上述两种情况下，UNIDROIT 通则均可以用作解释和补充相关国内法的标准，以确保符合国际接受的标准和/或跨境贸易关系的特殊要求。

需要继续观察的是，首先，UNIDROIT 通则用来解释和补充某个特定国内法的手段，是否仅能局限于国际纠纷，还是也应允许对纯国内范畴的争议起同样的作用。其次，当 UNIDROIT 通则符合现代的国际标准，但却与相关国内法的法定条文或通行案例法相冲突时，是否还可以适用 UNIDROIT 通则，以证明其解决办法是合理的。

虽然对第一个问题的回答是相当肯定的，起码是对涉及商业的交易如此，但对第二个问题的回答就相当困难。一方面，毫无疑问在原则上，如果适用的国内法对争议问题已经提供了明确的解决办法，则就不应再允许背离此办法而倾向 UNIDROIT 通则所提供的不同的解决办法，除非合同当事方就此做出了明示的要求。另一方面，在一些特殊情况下采用这种不同的方法也可能是有道理的。这些情况是：适用相关国内法律的具体条文"……根据合理性与衡平法的标准，是不可接受的"（荷兰民法典第 6.2 条第（2）款使用的文字）。例如，可能会援引适用一个对拖欠款项的法定利率远比其他国家高的国内法。所涉利息如以当地货币支付可能是合理的，也可能不合理，但如以外币支付款项很可能会很高，而在国际金融市场上能谈出一个低很多的利率。在这种情况下，适当的办法是：有限地解释规定利率的法律，以便限制其适用于以当地货币支付的款项，并且由 UNIDROIT 通则第 7.4.9 条第（2）款关于以外币支付款项的规定而取代①。

回到具体实践，报道显示，超过半数的裁决（包括法院判决）把 UNIDROIT 通则用来作为解释和补充适用的国内法的手段②。案件大多数涉及的是国际争议，但也有的裁决涉及的是纯国内性质的争议，而且裁决的做出参照了 UNIDROIT 通则。更重要的是，所涉案件中管辖合同的国内法不仅仅是那些欠发达国家或向市场经济过渡国家的国内法，还包括像澳大利亚、英格兰、芬兰、法国、希腊、意大利、荷兰、

---

① 参见：For a notice of two unpublished arbitral awards in this sense see M. J. Bonell, *An International Restatement of Contract Law*, 3rd ed., Transnational Publications, Inc., Ardsley, New York (2005), fn. 195 at p244.

② According to the above-mentioned study (E. Finazzi-Agrò, *The Impact of the Unidroit Principles in International Dispute Resolution: The Figures*, cit, p725) the number of decisions falling in this category is 76, 27 of which are arbitral awards and 49 are court decisions rendered in 14 countries.

新西兰、瑞士等国的国内法，以及纽约州的州法。这说明即便那些高度发达的法律制度国家，也不总是能对现代国际商事交易的特殊需要，提供明确的、令人满意的解决办法。但 UNIDROIT 通则事实上证明，可以提供这样的解决办法。还有，就是引用 UNIDROIT 通则的目的往往并不对手头上争议的是非曲直的决定产生什么直接影响，而引用通则具体条文的目的最终是为了证明：依据适用的国内法律所采取的解决办法与现代国际接受的标准与规则是相符的①。另外，法院和仲裁庭在一些案件中求助 UNIDROIT 通则的目的，是为了支持适用国内法可提供的数个解决办法中的某一个，或是为了填补国内法中的各类缺略规定②。

2004 年版的序言明示提到，UNIDROIT 通则可用作解释和补充国内法的手段，这是令人印象极为深刻的。鉴于这些数字，人们仍一直坚持认为与 UNIDROIT 通则作为管辖国际商事合同的法律规则的功能相比，其实称 UNIDROIT 通则为所谓的"重述功能"，更显重要。的确，像美国的法律重述一样，UNIDROIT 通则依其自身特性最适合在国际争议适用国内法时，作为背景法律发挥作用，而且这样做通则最终可成为共同法律的一种或跨国合同法的全部③。

四、结束语

当联合国国际贸易法委员会（UNCITRAL）批准 UNIDROIT 通则 2004 年版时，UNCITRAL 祝贺国际统一私法协会（UNIDROIT）"通过国际商事合同的一般规则，对促进国际贸易做出了进一步的贡献"，并且 UNIDROIT 通则为其恰当的预定之目的，开始运用。

在过去的几年里，UNIDROIT 通则令人鼓舞地被学界和实务界所接受，以各种不同的方式不断扩大在全世界的适用。

特别是，UNIDROIT 通则对许多发达国家和欠发达国家立法机构的

---

① 属这类最重要决定的概述请参阅：E. Finazzi – Agrò, *The Impact of the Unidroit Principles in International Dispute Resolution：An Empirical Analysis*, *Uniform Commercial Code Law Journal*, 2011（under print）.

② 属这类最重要决定的概述请参阅：E. Finazzi – Agrò, *The Impact of the Unidroit Principles in International Dispute Resolution：An Empirical Analysis*, cit.

③ 参阅 R. Michaels, *Umdenken für die UNIDROIT-Prinzipien. Vom Rechtswahlstatus zum Allgemeinen Teil des transnationale Vertragsrechts*, *Rabels Zeitschrift vol 73*（2009）, p866 et seq.

法律改革项目中，起到了鼓舞作用。

另外，当事方对其国际商事合同选择 UNIDROIT 通则为管辖其合同的法律规则时，通则还被仲裁庭作为争议实体问题的适用法律规则予以适用，即便当事方没有如此要求时也是如此。

总之，UNIDROIT 通则不断被仲裁庭和国内法院用来作为背景法律，解释和补充所适用的国内法，包括被纳入其中的国际统一法律文件。

可以期待，包括了失败合同恢复原状、违法合同、条件，以及多个债务人与多个债权人的新增加条文，UNIDROIT 通则 2010 将会获得国际法律界和商业界的更高的重视。

国际统一私法协会
国际商事合同通则 2010

UNIDROIT PRINCIPLES
OF INTERNATIONAL COMMERCIAL CONTRACTS
2010

罗马 2010

FOREWORD TO THE 2010 EDITION

In presenting this third edition of the UNIDROIT Principles of International Commercial Contracts, we would like to begin by expressing our deepest appreciation to the Members of the Working Group, and in particular to the Rapporteurs on the new chapters. We also wish to express our gratitutde to the numerous Observers who have attended the sessions of the Working Group in representation of important international organisations and other interested institutions and arbitration associations. It was only on account of the outstanding competence and extraordinary efforts of all those experts, again so ably coordinated by Michael Joachim Bonell, that this new edition of the UNIDROIT Principles was made possible.

We would again also like to thank those who, through scholarly writings or by applying the UNIDROIT Principles in practice, have contributed to their great success of the Principles. The comments they made and their practical experience have been an inestimable source of inspiration to the Working Group, and we hope they will continue to share with us in the future their experience with the Principles.

A special word of thanks goes to Henry Gabriel who, together with Michael Joachim Bonell and Ms Lena Peters of the UNIDROIT Secretariat, undertook the important task of editing the new chapters and harmonising style and language throughout the entire volume.

Our gratitude also goes to the other members of the Secretariat, in particular Ms Paula Howarth, Secretary to the Working Group, and Ms Frédérique Mestre and Ms Marina Schneider for preparing the French language version of the Principles in co-operation with the francophone Members of the Working Group.

Last but by no means least, we would like to express our deepest appreciation to the Max-Planck-Institut für ausländisches und internationales Privatrecht (Hamburg) and its Director Reinhard Zimmermann for the generous financial and logistic support provided.

José Angelo Estrella Faria   Alberto Mazzoni
Secretary-General   President

2010 年版序

在将《国际统一私法协会国际商事合同通则》第三版呈献给大家之际，首先，我们要对为《通则》做出贡献的工作组成员，特别是新增各章的报告人表达我们最深切的感激。我们还希望借此机会表达我们对许多观察员的感激之情，他们代表了重要的国际组织和其他对通则感兴趣的机构和仲裁协会。唯有所有这些专家非凡的能力和超乎寻常的努力，加之工作组主席 Michael Joachim Bonell 教授出色的协调工作，才使得《通则》新版成为可能。

我们也希望感谢所有那些通过学术论著或在实践中通过适用《通则》，对通则的巨大成功做出贡献的人们。他们的评论和实践经验是工作组讨论《通则》的不可估量的激励源泉。我们希望他们将来能继续与我们分享使用《通则》的经验。

我们要特别感谢 Henry Gabriel 教授，他与 Michael Joachim Bonell 教授及国际统一私法协会秘书处的 Lena Peters 女士一起承担了编辑新增章节以及协调整部著作格式及语言的重要任务。

最后，但决不是最不重要的，我们还应感谢国际统一私法协会秘书处的其他成员，特别是应该感谢工作组秘书 Paula Howarth 女士以及 Frédérique Mestre 女士和 Marina Schneider 女士通过与法语工作组成员的合作，在筹备《通则》法语版本方面所做的努力。

国际统一私法协会秘书长　　　　　　国际统一私法协会主席

José Angelo Estrella Faria　　　　　　Alberto Mazzoni

INTRODUCTION TO THE 2010 EDITION

When it approved the 2004 edition of the UNIDROIT Principles of International Commercial Contracts the Governing Council recalled that the Principles were one of the Institute's most successful projects and recommended that they figure in the Work Programme as an ongoing project. To this effect it instructed the Secretariat not only to continue to monitor the use of the Principles in actual practice but also to undertake at an appropriate time an inquiry among the international legal and business communities to determine new topics for inclusion in a future third edition of the Principles.

The new 2010 edition of the UNIDROIT Principles, like the 2004 edition, is not intended as a revision of the previous editions. As amply demonstrated by the extensive body of case law and bibliography reported in the UNILEX database <www.unilex.info>, the UNIDROIT Principles continue to be well received generally and have not given rise in practice to any significant difficulties of application. Consequently, the content of the 2004 edition has been altered only marginally: only five provisions have been amended, i.e. Articles 3.1 (now 3.1.1), 3.19 (now 3.1.4), paragraph 2 of Article 3.17 (now 3.2.15), paragraph 1 of Article 7.3.6 (now 7.3.6) and paragraph 2 of Article 7.3.6 (now 7.3.7), and of these only the last three have been amended in substance so as to justify their transformation into separate articles; as to the Comments, significant changes have been made only with respect to Comments 2, 3 and 4 to Article 1.4.

The main objective of the third edition of the UNIDROIT Principles was to address additional topics of interest to the international business and legal communities. Thus 26 new articles have been added dealing with restitution in case of failed contracts, illegality, conditions, plurality of obligors and of obligees.

As a result, the 2010 edition of the UNIDROIT Principles consists of 211 Articles (as opposed to the 120 Articles of the 1994 edition and the 185 Articles of the 2004 edition) structured as follows: Preamble (*unchanged*); Chapter 1: General provisions (*unchanged*); Chapter 2, Section 1: Formation (*unchanged*), Section 2: Authority of agents (*unchanged*); Chapter 3, Section 1:

2010 年版导言

在批准《国际统一私法协会国际商事合同通则》2004 年版时，国际统一私法协会理事会回忆起《通则》是协会最成功的项目之一，并建议将其作为一个持续的项目列入工作计划。为此，它指示秘书处不但要持续密切注意《通则》在实践中的使用情况，而且要在适当的时间在国际法律和商务界展开调研，确定在未来的《通则》第三版中要增加什么新的主题。

正如 2004 年版一样，新的 2010 年版《通则》的目的也不是对前先前版本进行修订。正如广泛的案例以及在 UNILEX 数据库〈www. unilex. info〉所公布的书目所显示，《通则》持续得到良好的普遍接受，在实践中也未发生任何适用上的重大困难。因此，这次对 2004 年版本仅作了少许修改：仅修改了五个条款，即第 3.1 条（现在是第 3.1.1 条）、第 3.19 条（现在是第 3.1.4 条）、第 3.17 条第 2 款（现在是第 3.2.15 条）、第 7.3.6 条第 1 款（现在是第 7.3.6 条）和第 7.3.6 条第 2 款（现在是第 7.3.7 条），其中只对后三个条款进行了实质性修改，以适应其转变成独立条款的事实；至于注释，只对第 1.4 条的注释 2、注释 3 和注释 4 作了重大修改。

《通则》第三版的主要目的是规范国际商务界和法律界感兴趣的一些新的主题。因此，新增了 26 个条文，以调整合同失败后的恢复原状、违法、条件、多个债务人和多个债权人。

结果，2010 年版《通则》共 211 条（1994 年版为 120 条，2004 年版为 185 条）。结构如下：

序言（未改动）；第一章：总则（未改动）；第二章第一节：合同的订立（未改动），第二节：代理人的权限（未改动）；第三章第一节：一般规定（包含之前的第 3.1 条（修改））、第 3.2 条、第 3.3 条

General provisions (*containing former Articles 3.1 (amended), 3.2, 3.3 and 3.19 (amended)*), Section 2: Ground for avoidance (*containing former Articles 3.4 to 3.16, 3.17 (amended), 3.18 and 3.20, and a new Article 3.2.15*), Section 3: Illegality (*new*); Chapter 4: Interpretation (*unchanged*); Chapter 5, Section 1: Content (*unchanged*), Section 2: Third Party Rights (*unchanged*), Section 3: Conditions (*new*); Chapter 6, Section 1: Performance in general (*unchanged*), Section 2: Hardship (*unchanged*); Chapter 7, Section 1: Non-performance in general (*unchanged*), Section 2: Right to performance (*unchanged*), Section 3: Termination (*containing former Articles 7.3.1 to 7.3.5, 7.3.6 (amended) and a new Article 7.3.7*), Section 4: Damages (*unchanged*); Chapter 8: Set-off (*unchanged*); Chapter 9, Section 1: Assignment of rights (*unchanged*), Section 2: Transfer of obligations (*unchanged*), Section 3: Assignment of contracts (*unchanged*); Chapter 10: Limitation periods (*unchanged*); Chapter 11, Section 1: Plurality of obligors (*new*), Section 2: Plurality of obligees (*new*). For ease of comparison a table of correspondence of the articles of the three editions of the UNIDROIT Principles has been included in this volume.

In presenting the first edition of the UNIDROIT Principles the Governing Council expressed its confidence that the international legal and business communities to which the Principles were addressed would appreciate their merits and benefit from their use. The success of the second edition did not fall short of the Governing Council's expectations. It is hoped that the 2010 edition of the UNIDROIT Principles will be as favourably received as the previous editions and become even better known and more widely used throughout the world.

THE GOVERNING COUNCIL OF UNIDROIT

Rome, May 2011

和第 3.19 条（修改）），第二节：宣告合同无效的事由（包含之前的第 3.4 条至第 3.16 条、第 3.17 条（修改）、第 3.18 条和第 3.20 条，以及一个新增条款第 3.2.15 条），第三节：违法（新）；第四章：合同的解释（未改动）；第五章第一节：合同的内容（未改动），第二节：第三方权利（未改动），第三节：条件（新）；第六章第一节：履行的一般规定（未改动），第二节：艰难情形（未改动）；第七章第一节：不履行的一般规定（未改动），第二节：要求履行的权利（未改动），第三节：合同的终止（包含之前的第 7.3.1 条至第 7.3.5 条、第 7.3.6 条（修改），以及一个新增条款第 7.3.7 条），第四节：损害赔偿（未改动）；第八章：抵销（未改动）；第九章第一节：权利的转让（未改动），第二节：债务的转移（未改动），第三节：合同的转让（未改动）；第十章：时效期间（未改动）；第十一章第一节：多个债务人（新），第二节：多个债权人（新）。为方便比对，本书提供了《通则》三个版本的条文对照表。

在呈献《通则》第一版时，理事会就确信《通则》所面向的国际法律界和商务界将会欣赏它的价值以及通过使用它所获得的益处。第二版的成功没有辜负理事会的期望。希望 2010 年版《通则》像前两个版本一样得到欣然接受，并在世界范围内为更多人所知晓，并得到更为广泛的运用。

国际统一私法协会理事会
2010 年 5 月于罗马

FOREWORD TO THE 2004 EDITION

It is with the utmost pleasure that we present this new edition of the UNIDROIT Principles of International Commercial Contracts which comes exactly ten years after the appearance of the first edition.

We would like first of all to express the Institute's deepest appreciation and gratitude to the Members of the Working Group and observers for their achievement and, among them, especially to the Rapporteurs on the various chapters. It was only on account of their outstanding competence and extraordinary efforts, again so proficiently coordinated by Michael Joachim Bonell, that this new edition was made possible.

We would also like to thank all those who have, over the last years, through their scholarly writings on the UNIDROIT Principles or by applying them in practice contributed to their great success. Their comments and practical experience have been an inestimable source of inspiration to the Working Group in its deliberations. It is our hope that they will continue their support and will also share with us in the future their experience with the UNIDROIT Principles.

Last but by no means least, our gratitude also goes to the UNIDROIT Secretariat, in particular to Ms Paula Howarth and Ms Lena Peters for their invaluable editorial assistance and to Ms Marina Schneider for her efficiency in looking after the French version in co-operation with the francophone Members of the Working Group.

Herbert Kronke
Secretary-General

Berardino Libonati
President

2004 年版序

我们怀着无限喜悦的心情将《国际统一私法协会国际商事合同通则》的新版本呈献给大家，这恰好是第一版发行的第十个年头。

首先，我们愿为《通则》做出贡献的工作组成员、观察员，特别是各章的报告员表达协会最深切的感激和谢意。唯有他们非凡的能力和超乎寻常的努力，加之 Michael Joachim Bonell 极为精当的协调，这个新版本的出版才成为可能。

我们也愿感谢所有那些在过去的年月里通过对《通则》的学术论著或实践适用而取得巨大成功的人们。他们的评论和实践经验已成为工作组讨论《通则》的不可估量的激励源泉。希望他们能继续给予我们支持，并在将来与我们一起分享对《通则》的经验。

最后，也是相当重要的，我们还应感谢国际统一私法协会的秘书处，特别是应该感谢 Paula Howarth 女士和 Lena Peters 女士所给予的无可估价的编辑支持，感谢 Marina Schneider 女士通过与法语工作组成员的合作，在审校法语版本方面所体现的高效率。

国际统一私法协会秘书长　　　　　　国际统一私法协会主席
Herbert Kronke 教授　　　　　　　　Berardino Libonati

INTRODUCTION TO THE 2004 EDITION

When the Governing Council decided in 1994 to publish the UNIDROIT Principles of International Commercial Contracts, it stressed the need to monitor their use with a view to their possible reconsideration at some time in the future. Three years later work was resumed with a view to preparing a second edition of the UNIDROIT Principles. To this end, a Working Group was set up composed of eminent jurists representing the major legal systems and/or regions of the world. Some of its members had already participated in the preparation of the 1994 edition of the UNIDROIT Principles, while for the first time representatives of interested international organisations and arbitration centres or associations were invited to attend the Working Group's sessions as observers.

The new edition of the UNIDROIT Principles, appearing ten years after the first edition, is not intended as a revision of the 1994 edition. As is amply demonstrated by the extensive body of case law and bibliography reported in the UNILEX database <www.unilex.info>, the UNIDROIT Principles have generally met with approval and have not given rise in practice to any significant difficulties of application. Consequently, only very few amendments of substance were made to the 1994 text and these were moreover limited, with one exception, to the comments. Indeed, the only black letter rule amended was Article 2.8(2) which has now become Article 1.12. As to the comments, Comment 3 to Article 1.3, Comments 1 and 2 to Article 1.7, Comment 2 to Article 2.15 (now 2.1.15) and Comment 2 to Article 6.2.2 were substantially revised or expanded.

However, it was decided to consider whether and, if so, to what extent the 1994 edition of the UNIDROIT Principles required additions or amendments to adapt it to the increasingly important practice of electronic contracting. Eventually, only a few changes were made to this effect to the black letter rules (see Article 1.2, Article 2.8(1) (now 2.1.8), Article 2.18 (now 2.1.18)), while more changes were made to the comments and illustrations (see Comment 1 to Article 1.2, Comments 1 and 4 to Article 1.9 (now 1.10) and Illustrations, Comment 3 to Article 2.1 (now 2.1.1) and Illustration, Comment to Article 2.7 (now 2.1.7) and Illustration, Comment to Article 2.8 (now 2.1.8)).

2004 年版导言

　　1994 年，当国际统一私法协会理事会决定出版《国际统一私法协会国际商事合同通则》时，强调需要对它的使用进行监督，以便在将来某个时间可对它进行新的审议。三年后为了准备《通则》的第二版，工作重新开始。为此，建立了一个工作组，由代表世界主要法律体系和（或）地区的杰出法学家组成。其中的部分成员曾经参加过 1994 年版《通则》的准备工作，一些对此感兴趣的国际组织、仲裁中心或团体的代表作为观察员也应邀第一次参加了工作组的各次会议。

　　在第一版十年后出版新《通则》，目的不是对 1994 年文本进行修订。正如在 UNILEX 数据库〈www. unilex. info〉所公布的广泛的案例与书目所显示的，《通则》已经获得了普遍的肯定，在实践中也没有发生任何适用上的重大困难。因此，这次对 1994 年文本只作了少许实体上的修改，对注释的修改也是有限的，只有一处例外。实际上，所修改的唯一黑体字条文是第 2.8 条第（2）款，现在已经成为新版本第 1.12 条。就注释而言，第 1.3 条的注释 3，第 1.7 条的注释 1 和注释 2，第 2.15 条（现在是第 2.1.15 条）的注释 2，第 6.2.2 条的注释 2，进行了实质的修改或扩充。

　　为适应日益增长的电子合同的重要实践，我们也决定考虑是否需要以及在多大程度上需要对 1994 年版《通则》文本进行添加或修改。最终，为这一目的对黑体字条文只做了少许的修改：（（见第 1.2 条，第 2.8 条第（1）款（现在是第 2.1.8 条），第 2.18 条（现在是 2.1.18 条）），而更多的修改是在注释和举例上：（见第 1.2 条的注释 1，第 1.9 条（现在是第 1.10 条）的注释 1 和注释 4 及举例，第 2.1 条（现在是第 2.1.1 条）的注释 3 及举例，第 2.7 条（现在是第 2.1.7 条）的注释及举例和第 2.8 条（现在是第 2.1.8 条）的注释）。

The main purpose of the new edition of the UNIDROIT Principles is to cover additional topics of interest to the international legal and business communities. Thus, five new chapters were prepared dealing with authority of agents, third party rights, set-off, assignment of rights, transfer of obligations and assignment of contracts, and limitation periods. Furthermore, two new articles were included in Chapter 1 and Chapter 5, respectively dealing with inconsistent behaviour (Article 1.8) and release by agreement (Article 5.1.9).

As a result, the 2004 edition of the UNIDROIT Principles consists of 185 articles (as opposed to the 120 Articles of the 1994 edition) structured as follows: Preamble (*1994 version, with the addition of paragraphs 4 and 6 as well as the footnote*); Chapter 1: General Provisions (*1994 version, with the addition of Articles 1.8 and 1.12*); Chapter 2, Section 1: Formation (*1994 version*) and Section 2: Authority of Agents (*new*); Chapter 3: Validity (*1994 version*); Chapter 4: Interpretation: (*1994 version*), Chapter 5, Section 1: Content (*1994 version, with the addition of Article 5.1.9*) and Section 2: Third Party Rights (*new*); Chapter 6, Section 1: Performance in General (*1994 version*) and Section 2: Hardship (*1994 version*); Chapter 7, Section 1: Non-performance in General (*1994 version*), Section 2: Right to Performance (*1994 version*), Section 3: Termination (*1994 version*) and Section 4: Damages (*1994 version*); Chapter 8: Set-off (*new*); Chapter 9, Section 1: Assignment of Rights (*new*), Section 2: Transfer of Obligations (*new*) and Section 3: Assignment of Contracts (*new*); Chapter 10: Limitation Periods (*new*).

In presenting the first edition of the UNIDROIT Principles the Governing Council expressed its confidence that the international legal and business communities to which the UNIDROIT Principles were addressed would appreciate their merits and benefit from their use. The success in practice of the UNIDROIT Principles over the last ten years has surpassed the most optimistic expectations. It is hoped that the 2004 edition of the UNIDROIT Principles will be just as favourably received by legislators, business persons, lawyers, arbitrators and judges and become even better known and more widely used throughout the world.

THE GOVERNING COUNCIL OF UNIDROIT

Rome, April 2004

《通则》新版本的主要目的是为了满足国际法律界和商务界感兴趣的另外一些主题。因此，五个新增章节处理的是代理人的权限，第三方权利，抵销，权利的转让、债务的转移和合同的转让，以及时效期间。此外，在第一章和第五章纳入了两个新的条款，分别处理的是不一致行为（第 1.8 条）和协议免除（第 5.1.9 条）。

2004《通则》共 185 个条文（1994 年版《通则》只有 120 个条文）。结构如下：

序言（1994 年版，新增第四段、第六段与脚注）；第一章：总则（1994 年版，新增第 1.8 条和第 1.12 条）；第二章第一节：合同的订立（1994 年版），第二节：代理人的权限（新）；第三章：合同的效力（1994 年版）；第四章：合同的解释（1994 年版）；第五章第一节：合同的内容（1994 年版，新增第 5.1.9 条），第二节：第三方权利（新）；第六章第一节：履行的一般规定（1994 年版），第二节：艰难情形（1994 年版）；第七章第一节：不履行的一般规定（1994 年版），第二节：要求履行的权利（1994 年版），第三节：合同的终止（1994 年版），第四节：损害赔偿（1994 年版）；第八章：抵消（新）；第九章第一节：权利的转让（新），第二节：债务的转移（新），第三节：合同的转让（新）；第十章：时效期间（新）。

在向大家呈献《通则》第一版时，理事会就确信国际法律界和商务界将会理解它的价值并在使用中获得益处。《通则》在过去十年实践中的成功已经超出了最乐观的期望。希望 2004《通则》能得到立法者、商务人员、律师、仲裁员和法官的欣然接受，在世界范围内为更多人所知晓，并得到更为广泛的运用。

国际统一私法协会理事会

2004 年 4 月于罗马

FOREWORD TO THE 1994 EDITION

It is with the utmost pleasure that the International Institute for the Unification of Private Law (UNIDROIT) announces the completion of the drawing up of the UNIDROIT Principles of International Commercial Contracts. This achievement represents the outcome of many years of intensive research and deliberations involving the participation of a large number of eminent lawyers from all five continents of the world.

Tribute must first be paid to the members of the Working Group primarily entrusted with the preparation of the UNIDROIT Principles and, among them, especially to the Rapporteurs for the different chapters. Without their personal commitment and unstinting efforts, so ably coordinated throughout by Michael Joachim Bonell, this ambitious project could not have been brought to its successful conclusion.

We must also express gratitude for the most valuable input given by the numerous practising lawyers, judges, civil servants and academics from widely differing legal cultures and professional backgrounds, who became involved in the project at various stages of the drafting process and whose constructive criticism was of the greatest assistance.

In this moment of great satisfaction for the Institute we cannot but evoke the memory of Mario Matteucci, who for so many years served UNIDROIT as Secretary-General and then as President and whose belief in the Principles as a vital contribution to the process of international unification of law was a source of constant inspiration to us all.

Malcolm Evans
Secretary-General

Riccardo Monaco
President

1994 年版序

我们怀着无限喜悦的心情宣布《国际统一私法协会国际商事合同通则》的制定工作已经完成。这一成果与来自于世界五大洲的大批知名律师的共同参与分不开，这是他们多年来大量研究和深思熟虑的结果，是集体智慧的结晶。

这一成果首先归功于最初受委托准备《国际统一私法协会国际商事合同通则》的工作组成员，尤其是各章的报告员。没有他们所承担的工作和不懈的努力，没有 Michael Joachim Bonell 先生自始至终出色协调，这一宏大的工程就无法取得今日成功的结果。

我们也感谢来自于不同法律文化和职业背景、具有实践经验的众多律师、法官、公务员和大学教师最具价值的奉献。他们在起草过程的各个阶段参与了本项目，提出的富有建设性的意见具有极大帮助。

在此令人欣慰的时刻，不能不唤起我们对 Mario Matteucci 先生的怀念，他曾多年担任国际统一私法协会的秘书长，而后又出任协会主席。他坚信《通则》能成为国际法律统一进程中的一个至关重要的贡献，这种信念是不断激励我们努力从事这一工作的力量源泉。

国际统一私法协会秘书长   国际统一私法协会主席

Malcolm Evans   Riccardo Monaco

INTRODUCTION TO THE 1994 EDITION

Efforts towards the international unification of law have hitherto essentially taken the form of binding instruments, such as supranational legislation or international conventions, or of model laws. Since these instruments often risk remaining little more than a dead letter and tend to be rather fragmentary in character, calls are increasingly being made for recourse to non-legislative means of unification or harmonisation of law.

Some of those calls are for the further development of what is termed "international commercial custom", for example through model clauses and contracts formulated by the interested business circles on the basis of current trade practices and relating to specific types of transactions or particular aspects thereof.

Others go even further and advocate the elaboration of an international restatement of general principles of contract law.

UNIDROIT's initiative for the elaboration of "Principles of International Commercial Contracts" goes in that direction.

It was as long ago as 1971 that the Governing Council decided to include this subject in the Work Programme of the Institute. A small Steering Committee, composed of Professors René David, Clive M. Schmitthoff and Tudor Popescu, representing the civil law, the common law and the socialist systems, was set up with the task of conducting preliminary inquiries into the feasibility of such a project.

It was not until 1980, however, that a special Working Group was constituted for the purpose of preparing the various draft chapters of the Principles. The Group, which included representatives of all the major legal systems of the world, was composed of leading experts in the field of contract law and international trade law. Most of them were academics, some high ranking judges or civil servants, who all sat in a personal capacity.

The Group appointed from among its members Rapporteurs for the different chapters of the UNIDROIT Principles, who were entrusted with the task of submitting successive drafts together with Comments. These were then discussed by the Group and circulated to a wide range of experts, including UNIDROIT's extensive network of correspondents. In addition, the Governing Council offered its advice on the policy to be followed, especially in those cases where the Group had found it difficult to reach a consensus. The necessary editorial work was entrusted to an Editorial Committee, assisted by the Secretariat.

1994 年版导言

迄今为止，向国际统一法方面的努力基本上是采取有拘束力的法律文件形式，例如超国家立法、国际公约，或是采用示范法的形式。鉴于这些法律文件经常面临着成为一纸空文或在性质上支离破碎的风险，越来越多的人们呼吁求助于非立法的方式统一或协调法律。

其中一些人呼吁进一步发展被称为"国际商事惯例"的这种统一形式，例如，由有兴趣的商业界人士根据现有的贸易惯例和特定的交易类型或者由此而涉及的特殊问题，制定出相应的示范条款和示范合同。

其他人进而倡议以国际重述的形式详尽阐述合同法普遍通行的原则。

国际统一私法协会对于《通则》进行详尽阐述的动议源于此。

追溯到 1971 年，当时国际统一私法协会理事会决定将此项目列入协会的工作计划。由 René David、Clive M. Schmitthoff 和 Tudor Popescu 三位教授分别作为英美法系、大陆法系和社会主义法系的代表组成了一个指导小组，其设立旨在初步研究该项目的可行性。

直到 1980 年一个准备《通则》各章的草案特别工作组才成立。该工作组由合同法和国际贸易法律领域的专家组成，吸收了世界各主要法律体系的代表。其中大多数人是研究人员，还有一些是高级法官或公务员，他们均以个人的身份参加工作组的起草工作。

工作组在其成员中指定了《通则》各章节的报告员，并委托他们向工作组提交相互衔接的各章节草案及注释。然后，这些草案和注释由工作组讨论，并被发送到众多专家手中，包括国际统一私法协会广泛的联络网内的通讯员。另外，理事会还对所需遵循的方针政策提供意见和建议，尤其是在工作组觉得难以达成一致的情况下。必要的编辑工作则交给由秘书处组成的一个编辑委员会。

For the most part the UNIDROIT Principles reflect concepts to be found in many, if not all, legal systems. Since however the UNIDROIT Principles are intended to provide a system of rules especially tailored to the needs of international commercial transactions, they also embody what are perceived to be the best solutions, even if still not yet generally adopted.

The objective of the UNIDROIT Principles is to establish a balanced set of rules designed for use throughout the world irrespective of the legal traditions and the economic and political conditions of the countries in which they are to be applied. This goal is reflected both in their formal presentation and in the general policy underlying them.

As to their formal presentation, the UNIDROIT Principles deliberately seek to avoid the use of terminology peculiar to any given legal system. The international character of the UNIDROIT Principles is also stressed by the fact that the comments accompanying each single provision systematically refrain from referring to national laws in order to explain the origin and rationale of the solution retained. Only where the rule has been taken over more or less literally from the world wide accepted United Nations Convention on Contracts for the International Sale of Goods (CISG) is explicit reference made to its source.

With regard to substance, the UNIDROIT Principles are sufficiently flexible to take account of the constantly changing circumstances brought about by the technological and economic developments affecting cross-border trade practice. At the same time they attempt to ensure fairness in international commercial relations by expressly stating the general duty of the parties to act in accordance with good faith and fair dealing and, in a number of specific instances, imposing standards of reasonable behaviour.

Naturally, to the extent that the UNIDROIT Principles address issues also covered by CISG, they follow the solutions found in that Convention, with such adaptations as were considered appropriate to reflect the particular nature and scope of the Principles [*].

In offering the UNIDROIT Principles to the international legal and business communities, the Governing Council is fully conscious of the fact that the UNIDROIT Principles, which do not involve the endorsement of Governments, are not a binding instrument and that in consequence their acceptance will depend upon their persuasive authority. There are a number of significant ways in which the UNIDROIT Principles may

---

[*] See especially Arts. 1.8, 1.9, 2.2, in conjunction with Arts. 5.7 and 7.2.2.

《通则》大部分内容所反映的概念即便不是在所有的法律体系中，至少也是在许多法律体系中可以见到。因为《通则》试图专门提供一套规则以适应国际商事交易的需要，这些规则使那些被认为是最佳的解决办法具体化，即使它们还未被普遍接受。

《通则》的目标是要制定一套可以在世界范围内使用的均衡的规则体系，而不论其被适用的国家的法律传统和政治经济条件如何。这一目标在《通则》正式文本中和这些规则所反映出的总的指导方针中都能得到体现。

在正式的文本中，《通则》有意避免使用任何现存法律体系的特定术语。《通则》的国际性还体现在对每一条款所作的系统注释也避免参照各个国家法律来解释所采纳的解决办法的缘由和原理。只有当《通则》中的规则在文字上或多或少地采用了在世界范围内普遍接受的《联合国国际货物销售合同公约》的规定时，才直接以该公约作为其渊源。

《通则》在本质上充分灵活地考虑到由于国际技术和经济的发展所带来的不断变化的情势对国际贸易实践产生的影响。同时，《通则》特别阐明合同当事人应按照诚实信用和公平交易原则行事的一般义务，并在许多实例中加入了合理的行为标准，试图以此来保证国际商事合同关系的公正性。

自然，当《通则》中提到的某些问题也包含在《联合国国际货物销售合同公约》中时，则遵循《公约》规定的解决办法，这种适应性恰如其分地反映了《通则》的性质和范围。[①]

在将《通则》提供给国际法律界和国际商业界之时，理事会清楚地意识到《通则》并不是一项立即产生拘束力的法律文件，因此，对《通则》的接受和认可将在很大程度上依赖于《通则》本身具有说服力的权威。

实际适用《通则》可以有许多重要的方式，其中最重要的方式已

[①] 见第 1. 8 条，第 1. 9 条，第 2. 2 条，并结合第 5 条至第 7 条和第 7. 2. 2 条。

find practical application, the most important of which are amply explained in the Preamble.

The Governing Council is confident that those to whom the UNIDROIT Principles are addressed will appreciate their intrinsic merits and derive full advantage from their use.

THE GOVERNING COUNCIL OF UNIDROIT

Rome, May 1994

在序言部分予以充分解释。

理事会确信收到《通则》的人们将感谢其所具有的重要价值，并在使用中受益匪浅。

国际统一私法协会理事会

1994 年 5 月于罗马

PREAMBLE

(Purpose of the Principles)

These Principles set forth general rules for international commercial contracts.

They shall be applied when the parties have agreed that their contract be governed by them.[*]

They may be applied when the parties have agreed that their contract be governed by general principles of law, the *lex mercatoria* or the like.

They may be applied when the parties have not chosen any law to govern their contract.

They may be used to interpret or supplement international uniform law instruments.

They may be used to interpret or supplement domestic law.

They may serve as a model for national and international legislators.

COMMENT

The Principles set forth general rules which are basically conceived for "international commercial contracts".

1. "International" contracts

The international character of a contract may be defined in a great variety of ways. The solutions adopted in both national and international legislation range from a reference to the place of business or habitual residence of the parties in different countries to the adoption of more general criteria such as the contract having "significant connections with

---

[*] Parties wishing to provide that their agreement be governed by the Principles might use the following words, adding any desired exceptions or modifications:

"This contract shall be governed by the UNIDROIT Principles (2010) [except as to Articles ...]".

Parties wishing to provide in addition for the application of the law of a particular jurisdiction might use the following words:

"This contract shall be governed by the UNIDROIT Principles (2010) [except as to Articles...], supplemented when necessary by the law of [jurisdiction X]".

序　言

(通则的目的)

通则旨在为国际商事合同制定一般规则。

当事人约定其合同受通则管辖时，应适用通则。*

当事人约定其合同受法律的一般原则、商人习惯法或类似规范管辖时，可适用通则。

当事人未选择任何法律管辖其合同时，可适用通则。

通则可用于解释或补充国际统一法文件。

通则可用于解释或补充国内法。

通则也可用作国内和国际立法的范本。

注释：

《通则》旨在为"国际商事合同"制定一般规则。

1. "国际"合同

合同的国际性可以以多种不同的方式确定。在国内和国际立法实践中，有的以当事人的营业地或惯常住所地位于不同国家为标准，有的使用更为一般性的标准，如合同"与一个以上国家有重要联系"、

---

* 希望在合同中约定其协议受《通则》管辖的当事人可以使用如下表述，并加上任何希望的例外或调整：

"本合同应受《国际统一私法协会国际商事合同通则》(2010) 管辖，[除了某条款]"。

希望在合同中约定适用某一特定的辖区法律的当事人，可以使用如下表述：

"本合同应受《国际统一私法协会国际商事合同通则》(2010) 管辖 [除了某条款]，必要时由 [X管辖区] 的法律补充"。

more than one State", "involving a choice between the laws of different States", or "affecting the interests of international trade".

The Principles do not expressly lay down any of these criteria. The assumption, however, is that the concept of "international" contracts should be given the broadest possible interpretation, so as ultimately to exclude only those situations where no international element at all is involved, i.e. where all the relevant elements of the contract in question are connected with one country only.

2. "Commercial" contracts

The restriction to "commercial" contracts is in no way intended to take over the distinction traditionally made in some legal systems between "civil" and "commercial" parties and/or transactions, i.e. to make the application of the Principles dependent on whether the parties have the formal status of "merchants" (*commerçants*, *Kaufleute*) and/or the transaction is commercial in nature. The idea is rather that of excluding from the scope of the Principles so-called "consumer transactions" which are within the various legal systems being increasingly subjected to special rules, mostly of a mandatory character, aimed at protecting the consumer, i.e. a party who enters into the contract otherwise than in the course of its trade or profession.

The criteria adopted at both national and international level also vary with respect to the distinction between consumer and non-consumer contracts. The Principles do not provide any express definition, but the assumption is that the concept of "commercial" contracts should be understood in the broadest possible sense, so as to include not only trade transactions for the supply or exchange of goods or services, but also other types of economic transactions, such as investment and/or concession agreements, contracts for professional services, etc.

3. The Principles and domestic contracts between private persons

Notwithstanding the fact that the Principles are conceived for international commercial contracts, there is nothing to prevent private persons from agreeing to apply the Principles to a purely domestic contract. Any such agreement would however be subject to the mandatory rules of the domestic law governing the contract.

"涉及不同国家之间法律的选择"，或是"影响国际贸易的利益"。

《通则》并未明确规定这些标准，但它假定对"国际"合同这一概念应作尽可能广义的解释，以便最终仅排除根本不涉及国际因素的情形，即合同所有相关因素仅与一国有关。

2. "商事"合同

《通则》对"商事"合同的限定，其目的绝非照搬某些法律体系有关"民事"和"商事"当事人和/或交易的传统区分，即把《通则》的适用与否取决于当事人是否有正式的"商人"身份，和/或交易是否具有商业性质。《通则》的真正目的是把"消费者交易"排除在《通则》的适用范围之外，因为此类合同在很多法律体系正逐渐受到特殊规则的调整，且这些规则绝大部分都是强制性的。这些规则的目的在于保护消费者，而消费者是指不在惯常交易过程中或非基于自身职业订立合同的当事人。

在区别消费者与非消费者合同方面，国内与国际所采用的标准也不尽相同。《通则》对此未作任何明确的界定，仅假定应对"商事"合同这一概念作尽可能宽泛的理解，使之不仅包括提供或交换商品或服务的贸易交易，而且还包括其他类型的经济交易，如投资和/或特许协议、专业服务合同，等等。

3.《通则》与私人间的国内合同

尽管事实上，《通则》是为国际商事合同而制定，但这并不妨碍私人约定将《通则》适用于纯国内合同。然而，任何该等协议均须遵守管辖该合同的国内法的强制性规则。

4. The Principles as rules of law governing the contract

a. *Express choice by the parties*

As the Principles represent a system of principles and rules of contract law which are common to existing national legal systems or best adapted to the special requirements of international commercial transactions, there might be good reasons for the parties to choose them expressly as the rules of law governing their contract. In so doing the parties may refer to the Principles exclusively or in conjunction with a particular domestic law which should apply to issues not covered by the Principles (see the Model Clause in the footnote to the second paragraph of the Preamble).

Parties who wish to choose the Principles as the rules of law governing their contract are well advised to combine such a choice of law clause with an arbitration agreement.

The reason for this is that the freedom of choice of the parties in designating the law governing their contract is traditionally limited to national laws. Therefore, a reference by the parties to the Principles will normally be considered to be a mere agreement to incorporate them in the contract, while the law governing the contract will still have to be determined on the basis of the private international law rules of the forum. As a result, the Principles will bind the parties only to the extent that they do not affect the rules of the applicable law from which the parties may not derogate (see Comment 3 on Article 1.4).

The situation is different if the parties agree to submit disputes arising from their contract to arbitration. Arbitrators are not necessarily bound by a particular domestic law. This is self-evident if they are authorised by the parties to act as *amiable compositeurs* or *ex aequo et bono*. But even in the absence of such an authorisation parties are generally permitted to choose "rules of law" other than national laws on which the arbitrators are to base their decisions (see in particular Article 28(1) of the *1985 UNCITRAL Model Law on International Commercial Arbitration*; see also Article 42(1) of the *1965 Convention on the Settlement of Investment Disputes between States and Nationals of other States (ICSID Convention))*.

In line with this approach, the parties would be free to choose the Principles as the "rules of law" according to which the arbitrators would decide the dispute, with the result that the Principles would apply to the exclusion of any particular national law, subject only to the application of those rules of domestic law which are mandatory

4.《通则》作为管辖合同的法律规则

a. 当事人明示选择

因为《通则》代表了一套合同法原则和规则体系，这些原则和规则是现存各国法律体系中共通的部分，或者最能适应国际商事交易的特殊需要，所以当事人将有充分的理由明确选择《通则》作为管辖其合同的法律规则。当事人可以选择排他地适用《通则》，或与某一特定国内法一起结合适用，以该国内法补充调整《通则》未涵盖的事项（见序言第二段脚注中的示范条款）。

当事人若希望选择《通则》作为管辖合同的规则，建议最好将选择适用《通则》的条款与仲裁协议结合起来加以适用。

这样做的理由是：传统上当事人选择合同管辖法律的自由仅限于选择国内法。因此，当事人对《通则》的选择适用通常会被认为是仅同意将《通则》并入合同，而管辖合同的法律仍须依据法院地的国际私法规则加以确定。结果是，《通则》只在不影响当事人不得减损的适用法规则的范围内才能约束当事人（参见第1.4条注释3）。

如果当事人约定将合同项下产生的争议提交仲裁，情况就会有所不同。仲裁员并不当然受某一特定国内法的约束。如果当事人授权仲裁员作为友好的调解者行事或公正行事，这一点尤其不言自明。但即使在没有这种授权，一般也允许当事人选择国内法以外的"法律规则"作为仲裁员裁决的依据（详见1985年联合国国际贸易法委员会《国际商事仲裁示范法》第28条第(1)款，以及1965年《关于解决一国与他国国民投资争端公约》（《华盛顿公约》）第42条第(1)款）。

根据这种方法，当事人可自由选择以《通则》作为仲裁员据以裁决争议的"法律规则"。因此，除了那些无论哪一法律管辖合同，强制性的国内法规则均适用的情况下,《通则》将排除任何特定国家法律而

irrespective of which law governs the contract (see Comment 4 on Article 1.4).

In disputes falling under the ICSID Convention, the Principles might even be applicable to the exclusion of any domestic rule of law.

b. *The Principles applied as a manifestation of "general principles of law", the "lex mercatoria" or the like referred to in the contract*

Parties to international commercial contracts who cannot agree on the choice of a particular domestic law as the law applicable to their contract sometimes provide that it shall be governed by the "general principles of law", by the "usages and customs of international trade", by the *lex mercatoria*, etc.

Hitherto, such reference by the parties to not better identified principles and rules of a supranational or transnational character has been criticised, among other grounds, because of the extreme vagueness of such concepts. In order to avoid, or at least to reduce considerably, the uncertainty accompanying the use of such rather vague concepts, it might be advisable, in order to determine their content, to have recourse to a systematic and well-defined set of rules such as the Principles.

c. *The Principles applied in the absence of any choice of law by the parties*

The Principles may however be applied even if the contract is silent as to the applicable law. If the parties have not chosen the law governing their contract, it has to be determined on the basis of the relevant rules of private international law. In the context of international commercial arbitration such rules are very flexible, permitting arbitral tribunals to apply "the rules of law which they determine to be appropriate" (see e.g. Article 17(1) of the *1998 Rules of Arbitration of the International Chamber of Commerce*; Article 24(1) of the *Rules of the Arbitration Institute of the Stockholm Chamber of Commerce*). Normally arbitral tribunals will apply a particular domestic law as the proper law of the contract, yet exceptionally they may resort to a-national or supra-national rules such as the Principles. This may occur when it can be inferred from the circumstances that the parties intended to exclude the application of any domestic law (e.g. where one of the parties is a State or a government agency and both parties have made it clear that neither would accept the application of the other's domestic law or that of a third country), or when the contract presents connecting factors with

得以适用（参见第 1.4 条注释 4）。

对属《华盛顿公约》范畴的争议，《通则》甚至可以排除任何国内法规则得以适用。

b.《通则》作为合同所指的"一般法律原则"、"商人习惯法"或类似规范的明示化加以适用

国际商事合同的当事人若不能就选择某一特定国内法作为合同适用法达成一致意见，有时会规定合同受"一般法律原则"，或"国际贸易习惯和惯例"，或"商人习惯法"等管辖。

迄今，当事人引用这种不甚明确的超国家的或跨国性质的规则和原则的做法一直遭受批评，其中一个原因是这些概念极其模糊。为了避免或至少大幅减少使用此类模糊概念所带来的不确定性，求助于一套系统且界定清晰的规则体系，例如《通则》，以确定其内容是可取的。

c.《通则》在当事人未选择任何法律的情况下适用

即使在合同没有就适用法做出任何规定的情况下，《通则》也可以适用。如果当事人没有为合同选择适用法，那么，只得根据国际私法的相关规则确定。在国际商事仲裁中，这样的规则是很灵活的，允许仲裁庭适用"他们认为适当的法律规则"（参见 1998 年《国际商会仲裁规则》第 17 条第(1)款；《斯德哥尔摩商会仲裁院仲裁规则》第 24 条第(1)款）。仲裁庭通常适用某一特定国内法作为合同的适用法，但例外情况下，他们也求助于国内或超国家规则比如《通则》。例如，从有关情况可以推断出当事人意图排除适用任何国内法（比如，当事人一方是国家或政府机构，且双方当事人已经明确表示任何一方都不接受适用另一方的国内法或第三国的国内法），或合同呈现出与多

many countries none of which is predominant enough to justify the application of one domestic law to the exclusion of all the others.

5. The Principles as a means of interpreting and supplementing international uniform law instruments

International uniform law instruments may give rise to questions concerning the precise meaning of their individual provisions and may present gaps.

Traditionally international uniform law has been interpreted on the basis of, and supplemented by, principles and criteria of domestic law, be it the law of the forum or that which would, according to the relevant rules of private international law, be applicable in the absence of an international uniform law.

Recently, both courts and arbitral tribunals have increasingly abandoned such a "conflictual" approach, seeking instead to interpret and supplement international uniform law by reference to autonomous and internationally uniform principles and criteria. This approach, expressly sanctioned in recent conventions (see, e.g., Art. 7 of the *1980 UN Convention on Contracts for the International Sale of Goods (CISG)*), is based on the assumption that international uniform law, even after its incorporation into the various national legal systems, only formally becomes an integrated part of the latter, whereas from a substantive point of view it does not lose its original character of a special body of law autonomously developed at international level and intended to be applied in a uniform manner throughout the world.

Until now, such autonomous principles and criteria for the interpretation and supplementing of international uniform law instruments have had to be found in each single case by the judges and arbitrators themselves on the basis of a comparative survey of the solutions adopted in the different national legal systems. The Principles could considerably facilitate their task in this respect.

6. The Principles as a means of interpreting and supplementing domestic law

The Principles may also be used to interpret and supplement domestic law. In applying a particular domestic law, courts and arbitral tribunals may be faced with doubts as to the proper solution to be adopted under that law, either because different alternatives are available or because there seem to be no specific solutions at all. Especially where the dispute relates to an international commercial contract, it may be advisable to resort to the Principles as a source of

个国家具有关联，但与其中任一国家间的关联程度都没有强到足以要求适用一国的国内法而排除所有其他国家的国内法。

5.《通则》作为解释和补充国际统一法律文件的工具

国际统一法文件可能就单个条款的准确含义产生问题，并可能出现漏洞。

传统上，国际统一法是根据国内法的原则和标准加以解释和补充，这种国内法可能是法院地法，在没有国际统一法的情况下也可能是根据相关国际私法规则确定的适用法。

最近，法院和仲裁庭逐渐摒弃了这种"冲突"的方法，取而代之的是通过自成一体的和国际统一原则和标准来寻求解释和补充国际统一法。最近制定的一些公约已明示认可了这种方法（参见 1980 年《联合国国际货物销售合同公约》第 7 条）。这种方法基于如下假设，即国际统一法即使经并入国内法律体系，也仅在形式上成为后者的一部分，但从实体上来说，它并未失去其原有性质，即它是一个在国际层面上自足发展并旨在世界范围以统一方式适用的特殊法律体系。

迄今，这种解释和补充国际统一法律文件的自足的原则和标准，必须由法官和仲裁员在个案中通过比较考察不同国家法律体系采纳的解决方案分析得出。《通则》在这方面将大大方便他们的工作。

6.《通则》作为解释和补充国内法的工具

《通则》也可用于解释和补充国内法。在适用特定的国内法时，由于存在多个可用的解决方案，或者似乎根本不存在具体解决方案，法院和仲裁庭可能对在该法律之下应采用何种解决方案存在疑惑。特别是当争议涉及国际商事合同时，作为灵感源泉求助于《通则》应该是

inspiration. By so doing the domestic law in question would be interpreted and supplemented in accordance with internationally accepted standards and/or the special needs of cross-border trade relationships.

7. The Principles as a model for national and international legislators

In view of their intrinsic merits the Principles may in addition serve as a model to national and international law-makers for the drafting of legislation in the field of general contract law or with respect to special types of transaction. At a national level, the Principles may be particularly useful to those countries which lack a developed body of legal rules relating to contracts and which intend to update their law, at least with respect to foreign economic relationships, to current international standards. Not too different is the situation of those countries with a well-defined legal system, but which after the recent dramatic changes in their socio-political structure have an urgent need to rewrite their laws, in particular those relating to economic and business activities.

At an international level the Principles could become an important term of reference for the drafting of conventions and model laws.

So far the terminology used to express the same concept differs considerably from one instrument to another, with the obvious risk of misunderstandings and misinterpretations. Such inconsistencies could be avoided if the terminology of the Principles were to be adopted as an international uniform glossary.

8. Other possible uses of the Principles

The list set out in the Preamble of the different ways in which the Principles may be used is not exhaustive.

Thus, the Principles may also serve as a guide for drafting contracts. In particular the Principles facilitate the identification of the issues to be addressed in the contract and provide a neutral legal terminology equally understandable by all the parties involved. Such a use of the Principles is enhanced by the fact that they are available in a large number of languages.

The Principles may also be used as a substitute for the domestic law otherwise applicable. This is the case whenever it proves impossible or extremely difficult to establish the relevant rule of that particular domestic law with respect to a specific issue, i.e. it would entail disproportionate efforts and/or costs. The reasons for this

可取的。这样做可以保证根据国际上接受的标准和/或跨界贸易关系的特殊需要来解释和补充所涉的国内法律。

7.《通则》作为国内和国际立法的范本

鉴于《通则》的固有优点，国内和国际立法者在一般合同法领域或是针对特殊类型的交易起草立法时，《通则》还可作为范本使用。就国内立法而言，《通则》对于如下国家可能特别有用：他们缺乏完善的合同相关的法律规则体系，并且计划按照当前的国际标准修改他们的法律，至少在对外经济关系方面与现代国际水准接轨。《通则》对于如下拥有完善法律体系的国家也有用：最近经历了社会和政治结构的急剧变化，迫切需要更新自己的法律，特别是经济和商务行为相关的法律。

就国际立法而言，《通则》能够成为起草公约和示范法的重要参考资料。

迄今，不同法律文件用以表述同一概念的术语很不相同，存在着被误解和被错误解释的明显风险。如果《通则》所用的术语能被采纳为国际统一的术语，将能够避免术语不一致问题。

8.《通则》的其他可能用途

序言所列的用途，并没有穷尽《通则》的用法。

因此，《通则》还可以用作起草合同的指导。特别是，《通则》有助于提示当事人应在合同中对什么事项作出规定并提供了所有当事人都可理解的中立的法律术语。《通则》存在多种语言版本，这也加强了《通则》在这方面的作用。

《通则》也可以用作本应适用国内法的替代。例如，就某一特定问题要确定特定国内法的相关规则有时是不可能的或非常困难的，也即，它需要不成比例的努力和（或）成本。这时《通则》就可替代使用。

generally lie in the special character of the legal sources of the domestic law in question and/or the cost of accessing them.

Furthermore, the Principles may be used as course material in universities and law schools, thereby promoting the teaching of contract law on a truly comparative basis.

其原因通常在于相关国内法法律渊源的特性和（或）使用他们的成本。

　　此外，《通则》可以用作大学和法学院的教材，以此促进真正的比较合同法的教学。

CHAPTER 1

GENERAL PROVISIONS

ARTICLE 1.1
(Freedom of contract)

**The parties are free to enter into a contract
and to determine its content.**

COMMENT

1. Freedom of contract as a basic principle in the context of international trade

The principle of freedom of contract is of paramount importance in the context of international trade. The right of business people to decide freely to whom they will offer their goods or services and by whom they wish to be supplied, as well as the possibility for them freely to agree on the terms of individual transactions, are the cornerstones of an open, market-oriented and competitive international economic order.

2. Economic sectors where there is no competition

There are of course a number of possible exceptions to the principle laid down in this Article.

As concerns the freedom to conclude contracts with any other person, there are economic sectors which States may decide in the public interest to exclude from open competition. In such cases the goods or services in question can only be requested from the one available supplier, which will usually be a public body, and which may or may not be under a duty to conclude a contract with whoever makes a request, within the limits of the availability of the goods or services.

3. Limitation of party autonomy by mandatory rules

With respect to the freedom to determine the content of the contract, in the first instance the Principles themselves contain provisions from which the parties may not derogate (see Article 1.5).

第一章

总　则

第 1.1 条

（缔约自由）

当事人可自由订立合同并确定合同的内容。

注释：

1. 缔约自由是国际贸易中的一项基本原则

缔约自由原则在国际贸易中极为重要。经营者有权自主决定向谁或者希望由谁提供货物或服务，并且可以自由商定具体交易条件，这种权利及其可能性是开放的、市场导向的和竞争性的国际经济秩序的基石。

2. 不允许竞争的经济部门

本条所确定的缔约自由原则当然存在很多可能的例外。

就与任何其他人缔约的自由而言，在某些经济部门，出于公共利益的考虑政府可能决定排除公开竞争。在这种情况下，所需要的商品或服务只能向唯一的供应商请求，该供应商通常是一公共机构，它可能承担也可能不承担如下义务，即在可得的商品或服务范围内同任何需求者订立合同。

3. 强制性规则对当事人意思自治的限制

就确定合同内容的自由而言，首先，《通则》本身包含了一些当事人不得减损的规定（参见第 1.5 条）。

Moreover, there are mandatory rules, whether of national, international or supra-national origin, which, if applicable in accordance with the relevant rules of private international law, prevail over the provisions contained in the Principles and from which the parties cannot derogate (see Article 1.4).

ARTICLE 1.2

(No form required)

Nothing in these Principles requires a contract, statement or any other act to be made in or evidenced by a particular form. It may be proved by any means, including witnesses.

COMMENT

1. Contracts as a rule not subject to formal requirements

This Article states the principle that the conclusion of a contract is not subject to any requirement as to form. The same principle also applies to the subsequent modification or termination of a contract by agreement of the parties.

The principle, which is to be found in many, although not in all, legal systems, seems particularly appropriate in the context of international trade relationships where, thanks to modern means of communication, many transactions are concluded at great speed and by a mixture of conversations, telefaxes, paper contracts, e-mail and web communication.

The first sentence of the Article takes into account the fact that some legal systems regard requirements as to form as matters relating to substance, while others impose them for evidentiary purposes only. The second sentence is intended to make it clear that to the extent that the principle of freedom of form applies, it implies the admissibility of oral evidence in judicial proceedings.

2. Statements and other unilateral acts

The principle of no requirement as to form applies also to statements and other unilateral acts. The most important such acts are statements of intent made by parties either in the course of the formation or performance of a contract (e.g. an offer, acceptance of an offer, confirmation of the contract by the party entitled to avoid it,

另外，强制性规则，无论是一国的、国际的，还是超国家的，如果根据国际私法的相关规则得以适用，则它们优先于《通则》的规定，并且当事人不得减损该等规则（参见第1.4条）。

第1.2条

（无形式要求）

通则不要求合同、声明或其他任何行为必须以特定形式做出或以特定形式证明。合同、声明或行为可通过包括证人在内的任何形式证明。

注释：

1. 作为规则合同不受形式要求的约束

本条阐述了这样一个原则：合同的订立不以任何形式方面的要求为条件。相同的原则也适用于合同订立后当事人依约定修改或终止合同的行为。

很多（尽管不是所有）法律体系都采纳了这一原则，它尤其适合国际贸易关系，因为在这一领域，得益于各种现代化的通信方式，许多交易都是非常迅速地通过交谈、电传、纸面合同、电子邮件和网络通信等混合方式达成的。

本条的第一句考虑到这样一个事实，即一些法律体系把形式要求看做与实体相关的事项，而其另一些法律体系则仅为证明目的作此要求。本条第二句旨在表明：在采用形式自由原则的限度内，该原则意味着口头证据在司法程序中具有可采性。

2. 陈述和其他单方行为

无形式要求原则也适用于陈述和其他单方行为。最重要的该等行为是在合同订立或履行过程中所作的意思表示（比如，要约、要约的承诺、有权撤销合同的当事人对合同的确认、一方当事人确定价格

determination of the price by one of the parties, etc.), or in other contexts (e.g. the grant of authority by a principal to an agent, the ratification by a principal of an act performed by an agent without authority, the obligor's acknowledgement of the obligee's right before the expiration of the general limitation period, etc.).

3. Possible exceptions under the applicable law

The principle of no requirement as to form may of course be overridden by the applicable law (see Article 1.4). National laws as well as international instruments may impose special requirements as to form with respect either to the contract as a whole or to individual terms (e.g. arbitration agreements; choice of court agreements).

4. Form requirements agreed by the parties

Moreover, the parties may themselves agree on a specific form for the conclusion, modification or termination of their contract or for any other statement they may make or unilateral act they may perform in the course of the formation or performance of their contract or in any other context. In this connection see, in particular, Articles 2.1.13, 2.1.17 and 2.1.18.

ARTICLE 1.3

(Binding character of contract)

A contract validly entered into is binding upon the parties. It can only be modified or terminated in accordance with its terms or by agreement or as otherwise provided in these Principles.

等），或在其他情况下所作的意思表示（比如，本人对代理人的授权，本人对无权代理人行为的追认，债务人在一般时效届满前对债权人权利的承认等）。

3. 适用法中可能的例外

当然，无形式要求原则可以被适用法的规定取代（参见第 1.4 条）。国内法以及国际法律文件可以对整个合同或对合同的单个条款提出特别的形式要求（例如仲裁协议、选择法院的协议）。

4. 当事人约定的形式要求

另外，当事人可能就合同的成立、修改或终止，或者就合同订立或合同履行过程中及其他情况下可能做出的任何其他陈述和所作的单方作为，约定某一特定形式。在这方面详见第 2.1.13 条、第 2.1.17 条、第 2.1.18 条。

第 1.3 条

（合同的约束性）

有效订立的合同对当事人具有约束力。当事人仅能根据合同的条款，或通过协议，或根据通则的规定修改或终止合同。

COMMENT

1. The principle *pacta sunt servanda*

This Article lays down another basic principle of contract law, that of *pacta sunt servanda.*

The binding character of a contractual agreement obviously presupposes that an agreement has actually been concluded by the parties and that the agreement reached is not affected by any ground of invalidity. The rules governing the conclusion of contractual agreements are laid down in Chapter 2 Section 1 of the Principles, while the grounds of invalidity are dealt with in Chapter 3, as well as in individual provisions in other Chapters (see, e.g., Articles 7.1.6 and 7.4.13(2)). Additional requirements for the valid conclusion of contracts may be found in the applicable national or international mandatory rules.

2. Exceptions

A corollary of the principle of *pacta sunt servanda* is that a contract may be modified or terminated whenever the parties so agree. Modification or termination without agreement are on the contrary the exception and can therefore be admitted only when in conformity with the terms of the contract or when expressly provided for in the Principles (see Articles 3.2.7(2), 3.2.7(3), 3.2.10, 5.1.8, 6.1.16, 6.2.3, 7.1.7, 7.3.1 and 7.3.3).

3. Effects on third persons

By stating the principle of the binding force of the contract between the parties, this Article does not intend to prejudice any effect which that contract may have vis-à-vis third persons under the applicable law. Thus, a seller may in some jurisdictions be under a contractual duty to protect the physical integrity and property not only of the buyer, but also of accompanying persons during their presence on the seller's premises.

Similarly the Principles do not deal with the effects of avoidance and termination of a contract on the rights of third persons.

With respect to cases where the agreement between the parties by its very nature is intended to affect the legal relations of other persons, see Section 2 of Chapter 2 on "Authority of Agents", Section 2 of Chapter 5 on "Third Party Rights", Chapter 9 on "Assignment of Rights, Transfer of Obligations, Assignment of Contracts" and Chapter 11 on "Plurality of Obligors and Obligees".

注释:

1. "协议必须遵守"原则

本条规定了合同法的另一项基本原则,即"协议必须遵守"。

合同协议具有约束力明显预设了如下事实,即当事人事实上已经达成了一个协议,并且所达成的协议不受任何合同无效原因的影响。调整合同协议订立的规则规定在《通则》第二章第一节中,而合同无效的原因规定在第三章和其他章节的个别条款中(比如,参见第7.1.6条和第7.4.13条第(2)款)。有关合同有效缔结的其他要求可在适用的国内或国际强制性规则中找到。

2. 例外

从"协议必须遵守"原则可得出这样的结论,即当事人可随时协议修改或终止合同。相反,非经当事人协议的修改或终止则属例外情况,只有在符合合同条款的规定或《通则》有明文规定时才能得以承认(参见第 3.2.7 条(2)款、第 3.2.7 条(3)款、第 3.2.10 条、第 5.1.8 条、第 6.1.16 条、第 6.2.3 条、第 7.1.7 条、第 7.3.1 条和第7.3.3条)。

3. 合同对第三人的效力

本条规定合同在当事人之间具有约束力的原则,但它无意减损根据适用法合同可能对第三人产生的任何效力。因此,在一些法域中,卖方在其经营场所不但有义务保护买方的人身及财产安全,而且有义务保护买方随行人员的人身和财产安全。

同样,《通则》也不调整涉及因合同无效和终止对第三人权利产生的影响。

当事人之间的合同依其性质本意旨在影响另一人法律关系的情形,参见第二章第二节"代理人的权限",第五章第二节"第三方权利"、第九章"权利的转让、债务的转移、合同的转让"以及第十一章"多个债务人与多个债权人"。

A<small>RTICLE</small> 1.4

(Mandatory rules)

Nothing in these Principles shall restrict the application of mandatory rules, whether of national, international or supranational origin, which are applicable in accordance with the relevant rules of private international law.

C<small>OMMENT</small>

1. Mandatory rules prevail

Given the particular nature of the Principles as a non-legislative instrument, neither the Principles nor individual contracts concluded in accordance with the Principles, can be expected to prevail over mandatory rules of domestic law, whether of national, international or supranational origin, that are applicable in accordance with the relevant rules of private international law. Mandatory rules of national origin are those enacted by States autonomously (e.g. particular form requirements for specific types of contracts; invalidity of penalty clauses; licensing requirements; environmental regulations; etc.), while mandatory rules of international or supranational origin are those derived from international conventions or general public international law (e.g. *Hague-Visby Rules*; *UNIDROIT Convention on Stolen or Illegally Exported Cultural Objects*; *United Nations Convention against Corruption; United Nations Universal Declaration of Human Rights*, etc.) or adopted by supranational organisations (e.g. European Union competition law, etc.).

2. Broad notion of "mandatory rules"

The mandatory rules referred to in this Article are predominantly laid down by specific legislation, and their mandatory nature, may either be expressly stated or inferred by way of interpretation. However, in the various national legal systems restrictions on freedom of contract may also derive from general principles of public policy, whether of national, international or supranational origin (e.g. prohibition of commission or inducement of crime; prohibition of corruption and collusive bidding; protection of human dignity; prohibition of discrimination on the basis of gender, race or religion; prohibition of undue restraint of trade; etc). For the purpose of this Article the notionof "mandatory rules"

第1.4条

（强制性规则）

通则的任何规定均不应限制根据有关国际私
法规则所导致的对强制性规则的适用，不论这些
强制性规则是源于一国的、国际的还是超国家的。

注释：

1. 强制性规则优先

鉴于《通则》是一种非立法性文件这一特殊性质，我们不应该期望
《通则》或者根据《通则》订立的合同优于国内法的强制性规则，无论是
源于一国的、国际的还是超国家的，根据有关国际私法规则应予适用
的强制性规则。源于一国的强制性规则是指由国家自主颁发的该等规
则（例如对特定类型合同的特殊形式要求、罚金条款无效、许可要求、
环境规定等）；而国际的或超国家的强制性规则是指来源于国际公约或
一般国际公法的该等规则（例如《海牙—维斯比规则》、《国际统一私
法协会关于被盗或非法出口文物的公约》、《联合国反腐败公约》、《联
合国世界人权宣言》等），或者由超国家组织通过的该等规则（例如欧
盟竞争法等）。

2. 宽泛的"强制性规则"概念

本条所称强制性规则主要是指由具体立法机关规定的该等规则，
其强制性质或通过明示陈明，或者通过解释推导而出。然而在很多国
内法律体系中，对合同自由的限制也可能源于公共政策的一般原则，
这些原则可能是一国的、国际的或者超国家的（例如禁止从事或引诱
犯罪；禁止行贿和投标舞弊；保护人类尊严；禁止性别、种族或宗教
歧视；禁止不当限制贸易等）。在本条范围内，"强制性规则"概念应

is to be understood in a broad sense, so as to cover both specific statutory provisions and general principles of public policy.

3. Mandatory rules applicable in case of incorporation of the Principles as terms of contract

Where, as is the traditional and still prevailing approach adopted by domestic courts with respect to soft law instruments, the parties' reference to the Principles is considered to be merely an agreement to incorporate them in the contract (see Comment 4 lit. (a), third paragraph, to the Preamble), the Principles and the individual contracts concluded in accordance with the Principles will first of all encounter the limit of the principles and rules of the domestic law that govern the contract from which parties may not contractually derogate (so-called "ordinary" or "domestically mandatory" rules). Moreover, the mandatory rules of the forum State, and possibly of other countries, may also apply if the mandatory rules claim application irrespective of what the law governing the contract is, and, in the case of the mandatory rules of other countries, there is a sufficiently close connection between those countries and the contract in question (so-called "overriding" or "internationally mandatory" rules).

4. Mandatory rules applicable in case of reference to the Principles as law governing the contract

Where, as may be the case if the dispute is brought before an arbitral tribunal, the Principles are applied as the law governing the contract (see Comment 4 lit. (a), fourth paragraph, to the Preamble), they no longer encounter the limit of the ordinary mandatory rules of any domestic law. As far as the overriding mandatory rules of the forum State or of other countries are concerned, their application basically depends on the circumstances of the case. Generally speaking, since in international arbitration the arbitral tribunal lacks a predetermined *lex fori*, it may, but is under no duty to, apply the overriding mandatory rules of the country on the territory of which it renders the award. In determining whether to take into consideration the overriding mandatory rules of the forum State or of any other country with which the case at hand has a significant connection, the arbitral tribunal, bearing in mind its task to "make every effort to make sure that the Award is enforceable at law" (so expressly e.g. Article 35 of the *1998 ICC Arbitration Rules*), may be

作宽泛解释，以便同时涵盖具体的制定法的规定和公共政策的一般原则。

3.《通则》被并入合同条款之中时应适用强制性规则

如果将当事人引用《通则》仅仅视为是《通则》并入到合同之中的一项约定（参见序言注释 4 之 (a) 项第 3 段）——这是国内法院针对软法文件传统上，也是当前依然采取的主要方法，此时，《通则》及根据《通则》订立的合同首先会面临着一项限制，即当事人不得通过合同约定减损管辖该合同的国内法律规则的限制（所谓的"一般"或"国内强制性"规则）。另外，法院地国家、还可能包括其他国家的强制性规则也可能适用，如果该强制性规则主张无论管辖合同的法律是什么，自己均应得以适用；对于其他国家的强制性规则而言，该国与相关合同之间存在足够紧密的联系（所谓的"优先"或"国际强制性"规则）。

4.《通则》作为合同管辖法时应适用的强制性规则

在争端提交仲裁解决的情况下，如果《通则》作为管辖合同的法律得以适用（参见序言注释 4 之 (a) 项第 4 段），则《通则》不再受任何国内法之一般强制性规则的限制。至于法院地国家或其他有关国家的优先强制性规则，其适用基本取决于个案具体情况。一般来说，由于在国际仲裁中不存在一个预先确定的法院地法，仲裁庭可以，但并没有义务适用仲裁裁决作出地国家的优先强制性规则。在决定是否考虑法院地国或与争议案件具有重要联系的其他国家的优先强制性规则时，仲裁庭在铭记其"尽一切努力确保裁决能够依法执行"（1998 年《国际商会国际仲裁院仲裁规则》第35条如此明确地规定）之任务的情况下，会

expected to pay particular attention to the overriding mandatory rules of those countries where enforcement of the award is likely to be sought. Moreover, the arbitral tribunal may consider it necessary to apply those overriding mandatory rules that reflect principles widely accepted as fundamental in legal systems throughout the world (so-called "transnational public policy" or "*ordre public transnational*").

5. Recourse to rules of private international law relevant in each given case

In view of the considerable differences in the ways in which domestic courts and arbitral tribunals determine the mandatory rules applicable to international commercial contracts, this Article deliberately refrains from stating which mandatory rules apply and the Article refers instead to the relevant rules of private international law for the solution in each given case (see e.g. Article 9 of *EC Regulation No. 593/2008 (Rome I)* (replacing Article 7 of the *1980 Rome Convention on the Law applicable to Contractual Obligations*); Article 11 of the *1994 Inter-American Convention on the Law Applicable to International Contracts*; Articles 28, 34 and 36 of the *UNCITRAL Model Law on International Commercial Arbitration;* and Article V of the *New York Convention on the Recognition and Enforcement of Foreign Arbitral Awards*).

ARTICLE 1.5

(Exclusion or modification by the parties)

The parties may exclude the application of these Principles or derogate from or vary the effect of any of their provisions, except as otherwise provided in the Principles.

COMMENT

1. The non-mandatory character of the Principles

The rules laid down in the Principles are in general of a non-mandatory character, i.e. the parties may in each individual case either simply exclude their application in whole or in part or modify their content so as to adapt them to the specific needs of the kind of

被期特别关注需要在那些境内寻求执行仲裁裁决之国家的优先强制性规则。另外，仲裁庭可能认为有必要适用那些体现全世界各法律体系广泛接受之基本原则（所谓的"跨国公共政策"）的优先强制性规则。

5. 在个案中求助于国际私法规则

鉴于国内法院和仲裁庭在决定哪些强制性规则适用于国际商事合同的方法上存在重大差异，本条故意未规定哪些强制性规则应予适用，而是指出应在个案中根据相关国际私法规则找出解决办法（参见欧共体第 593/2008 号条例（罗马第一条例）第 9 条（取代《1980 年欧共体合同之债准据法公约》第 7 条）；《1994 年美洲际合同准据法公约》第 11 条；《联合国国际贸易法委员会国际商事仲裁示范法》第 28 条、第 34 条和第 36 条，以及《承认和执行外国仲裁裁决纽约公约》第 5 条）。

第 1.5 条

（当事人的排除或修改）

除通则另有规定外，当事人可以排除通则的适用或减损或改变通则任何条款的效力。

注释：

1.《通则》的非强制性

《通则》所规定的规则总体上是非强制性的，即当事人在个案中简单地全部或部分排除《通则》的适用，或修改其内容，使之符合所涉交

transaction involved (see the Model Clause in the footnote to the second paragraph of the Preamble).

2. Exclusion or modification may be express or implied

The exclusion or modification of the Principles by the parties may be either express or implied. There is an implied exclusion or modification when the parties expressly agree on contract terms which are inconsistent with provisions of the Principles and it is in this context irrelevant whether the terms in question have been negotiated individually or form part of standard terms incorporated by the parties in their contract.

If the parties expressly agree to the application of some only of the Chapters of the Principles (e.g. "As far as the performance and non-performance of this contract is concerned, the UNIDROIT Principles shall apply"), it is presumed that the Chapters concerned will be applied together with the general provisions of Chapter 1.

3. Mandatory provisions to be found in the Principles

A few provisions of the Principles are of a mandatory character, i.e. their importance in the system of the Principles is such that parties should not be permitted to exclude or to derogate from them as they wish. It is true that given the particular nature of the Principles the non-observance of this precept may have no consequences. On the other hand, it should be noted that the provisions in question reflect principles and standards of behaviour which are of a mandatory character under most domestic laws also.

Those provisions of the Principles which are mandatory are normally expressly indicated as such. This is the case with Article 1.7 on good faith and fair dealing, with the provisions of Chapter 3 on substantive validity, except in so far as they relate or apply to mistake and to initial impossibility (see Article 3.1.4), with Article 5.1.7(2) on price determination, with Article 7.4.13(2) on agreed payment for non-performance and Article 10.3(2) on limitation periods. Exceptionally, the mandatory character of a provision is only implicit and follows from the content and purpose of the provision itself (see, e.g., Articles 1.8 and 7.1.6).

易类型的特殊需要（参见序言第二段脚注中的示范条款）。

2. 排除或修改既可明示也可默示

当事人对《通则》所做的排除或修改既可以是明示的，也可以是默示的。若当事人明确约定了与《通则》规定不一致的合同条款，不论这些条款是否经单独的磋商还是构成被并入合同的标准条款的一部分，即被视为是对《通则》的默示排除或修改。

如果当事人仅明确同意适用《通则》的某些章节（如"就本合同的履行和不履行，适用《国际统一私法协会国际商事合同通则》"），则推定当事相关章节应与第一章"总则"一并适用。

3.《通则》中的强制性规定

《通则》中的少数规定具有强制性，即这些规定在《通则》的整个体系中至关重要，不允许当事人随意对此进行排除或减损。当然由于《通则》的特性，不遵守这些规则可能不会导致什么结果。另一方面，应该指出的是，这些规定反映的行为标准和准则在大多数国内法中也同样具有强制性。

《通则》中具有强制性的规定通常都明确表明了这种情况，如第1.7条关于"诚实信用和公平交易"的规定，第三章关于实质效力的规定，但那些关于或适用于自始不能或错误的规定除外（见第3.1.4条），第5.1.7条第(2)款关于确定价格的规定，第7.4.13条第(2)款关于不履行约定付款的规定，以及第10.3条第(2)款关于时效的规定。但例外情况下，某一规定的强制性特征只是默示的，只能从该规定本身的内容和意图推出（参见第1.8条和第7.1.6条）。

ARTICLE 1.6

(Interpretation and supplementation of the Principles)

(1) In the interpretation of these Principles, regard is to be had to their international character and to their purposes including the need to promote uniformity in their application.

(2) Issues within the scope of these Principles but not expressly settled by them are as far as possible to be settled in accordance with their underlying general principles.

C<small>OMMENT</small>

1. Interpretation of the Principles as opposed to interpretation of the contract

The Principles, like any other legal text, be it of a legislative or of a contractual nature, may give rise to doubts as to the precise meaning of their content. The interpretation of the Principles is however different from that of the individual contracts to which they apply. Even if the Principles are considered to bind the parties only at contractual level, i.e. their application is made dependent on their incorporation in individual contracts, they remain an autonomous set of rules worked out with a view to their application in a uniform manner to an indefinite number of contracts of different type entered into in various parts of the world. As a consequence they must be interpreted in a different manner from the terms of each individual contract. The rules for the interpretation of contracts (as well as of statements by or other conduct of the parties) are laid down in Chapter 4. This Article deals with the manner in which the Principles as such are to be interpreted.

2. Regard to the international character of the Principles

The first criterion laid down by this Article for the interpretation of the Principles is that regard is to be had to their "international character". This means that their terms and concepts are to be interpreted autonomously, i.e. in the context of the Principles themselves and not by reference to the meaning which might traditionally be attached to them by a particular domestic law.

第1.6条

（通则的解释和补充）

（1）在解释通则时，应考虑通则的国际性及其目的，包括促进其统一适用的需要。

（2）凡属于通则范围之内，但通则又未做出明确规定的事项，应尽可能地根据通则确定的一般基本原则来处理。

注释：

1.《通则》的解释与合同的解释之比较

同其他法律文件一样，《通则》不论具有立法性还是具有合同性，都可能就其内容的准确含义产生疑义。然而，对《通则》的解释不同于对适用《通则》的某个具体合同的解释。尽管《通则》被认为仅在合同层面上约束当事人，即其适用依赖于将《通则》引入具体合同中，但为了使它们以统一的方式适用于世界范围内订立的无数的不同类型合同，它仍有其独立的规则体系。因此，对这些规则的解释应采用不同于解释具体合同条款的方式。有关解释合同（以及当事人做出的声明或其他行为）的规则具体规定在《通则》第四章中。本条规定的是解释《通则》本身的方式。

2. 关于《通则》的国际性

本条规定的关于解释《通则》的第一标准是必须考虑其"国际性"。这意味着应对《通则》的条文和概念作自主的解释，即在《通则》自身的语境中，而非参照某一特定国内法传统上赋予该等条文或概念的含义。

Such an approach becomes necessary if it is recalled that the Principles are the result of thorough comparative studies carried out by lawyers coming from totally different cultural and legal backgrounds. When drafting the individual provisions, these experts had to find sufficiently neutral legal language on which they could reach a common understanding. Even in the exceptional cases where terms or concepts peculiar to one or more national laws are employed, the intention was never to use them in their traditional meaning.

3. Purposes of the Principles

By stating that in the interpretation of the Principles regard is to be had to their purposes, this Article makes it clear that they are not to be construed in a strict and literal sense but in the light of the purposes and the rationale underlying the individual provisions as well as the Principles as a whole. The purpose of the individual provisions can be ascertained both from the text itself and from the comments thereon. As to the purposes of the Principles as a whole, this Article, in view of the fact that the Principles' main objective is to provide a uniform framework for international commercial contracts, expressly refers to the need to promote uniformity in their application, i.e. to ensure that in practice they are to the greatest possible extent interpreted and applied in the same way in different countries. As to other purposes, see the remarks contained in the Introduction. See further Article 1.7 which, although addressed to the parties, may also be seen as an expression of the underlying purpose of the Principles as such to promote the observance of good faith and fair dealing in contractual relations.

4. Supplementation of the Principles

A number of issues which would fall within the scope of the Principles are not settled expressly by them. In order to determine whether an issue is one that falls within the scope of the Principles even though it is not expressly settled by them, or whether it actually falls outside their scope, regard is to be had first to what is expressly stated either in the text or in the Comments (see, e.g., Comment 3 on Article 1.3; Comment 5 on Article 1.4; Article 2.2.1(2) and (3) and Comment 5 on Article 2.2.1; Comment 5 on Article 2.2.7; Comment 5 on Article 2.2.9; Comment 1 on Article 2.2.10; Article 3.1.1; Comment 1 on Article 6.1.14; Article 9.1.2; Article 9.2.2; Article 9.3.2). A useful additional guide in this respect is the subject-matter index of the Principles.

如果考虑到《通则》是由来自具有完全不同文化和法律背景的法律专家们通过全面的比较研究而制定的这一事实，那么，使用这种自主的解释方法是非常必要的。在起草每一具体条文时，专家们不得不使用足够中性的法律语言，以求达成共同的理解。即便个别情况下使用了某一个或几个国家法律所特有的条款或概念，也绝无意使用其传统意义。

3.《通则》的目的

本条规定解释《通则》应考虑其目的，此举旨在说明不能依严格的字面意思解释《通则》，而应根据《通则》的目的以及具体条款和整个《通则》背后的原理加以解释。具体条款的目的可以通过文本本身内容及其注释加以确定。至于整个《通则》的目的，鉴于《通则》的主要目标是为国际商事合同提供一个统一框架，本条明确提及促进《通则》统一适用的需要，即在实践中应确保《通则》在不同国家最大限度地以同种方式解释并适用。至于其他目的，可以参见本书"导言"中的评论。还可进一步参见第1.7条，该条虽然是针对当事人提出的，但也可视为《通则》基本目的一种表述，即促进在合同关系中恪守"诚实信用和公平交易"的原则。

4.《通则》的补充

《通则》对其调整范围内的许多问题未予明确规定。为了确定某一问题是否属于《通则》的范畴，即便《通则》对此未予明确规定，或是要确定某一问题是否超出《通则》调整范围，首先应考虑《通则》的条文或其注释明确表达的内容（比如，参见第1.3条的注释3；第1.4条的注释5；第2.2.1条第(2)款和第(3)款和第2.2.1条注释5；第2.2.7条注释5；第2.2.9条注释5；第2.2.10条注释1；第3.1条；第6.1.14条注释1；第9.1.2条、第9.2.2条、第9.3.2条）。关于这一问题另外有用的指导是《通则》的主题索引。

The need to promote uniformity in the application of the Principles implies that when such gaps arise a solution should be found, whenever possible, within the system of the Principles itself before resorting to domestic laws.

The first step is to attempt to settle the unsolved question through an application by analogy of specific provisions. Thus, Article 6.1.6 on place of performance should also govern restitution. Similarly, the rules laid down in Article 6.1.9 with respect to the case where a monetary obligation is expressed in a currency other than that of the place for payment may also be applied when the monetary obligation is expressed by reference to units of account such as the Special Drawing Right (SDR). If the issue cannot be solved by a mere extension of specific provisions dealing with analogous cases, recourse must be made to their underlying general principles, i.e. to the principles and rules which may be applied on a much wider scale because of their general character. Some of these fundamental principles are expressly stated in the Principles (see, e.g., Articles 1.1, 1.3, 1.5, 1.7 and 1.8). Others have to be extracted from specific provisions, i.e. the particular rules contained therein must be analysed in order to see whether they can be considered an expression of a more general principle, and as such capable of being applied also to cases different from those specifically regulated.

Parties are of course always free to agree on a particular national law to which reference should be made for the supplementing of the Principles. A provision of this kind could read "This contract is governed by the UNIDROIT Principles supplemented by the law of Country X", or "This contract shall be interpreted and executed in accordance with the UNIDROIT Principles. Questions not expressly settled therein shall be settled in accordance with the law of Country X" (see the Model Clause in the footnote to the second paragraph of the Preamble).

ARTICLE 1.7

(Good faith and fair dealing)

(1) Each party must act in accordance with good faith and fair dealing in international trade.

(2) The parties may not exclude or limit this duty.

促进《通则》统一适用的需要意味着：当出现规范漏洞时，应在诉诸国内法之前，尽可能在《通则》自身的体系中寻找解决办法。

第一步是尝试通过具体条文的类推适用来解决未决的问题。因此，第6.1.6条关于履行地的规定也适用于返还义务。同样，第6.1.9条有关金钱债务以非付款地货币表示的规则，也可适用于以诸如特别提款权（SDR）货币单位表示的付款义务。如果仅通过扩展处理类似情况的具体条款还解决不了问题，就必须借助这些规定背后的一般原则，即因其一般性能在更大范围内适用的原则和规则。有一些此类基本原则在《通则》中有明确的规定（比如，参见第1.1条、第1.3条、第1.5条、第1.7条和第1.8条）。另外一些此类原则必须从具体条文中提炼出来，也即必须对具体条款包含的具体规则加以分析，才能确定它们是否能被视为一种更普遍的原则的表达，从而也能适用于那些与具体规定情况不同的其他情况。

当然，当事人总是可以自由约定以某一特定国内法作为对《通则》的补充。这种条款可表述为："本合同适用《国际统一私法协会国际商事合同通则》，并以 X 国法律作为《国际统一私法协会国际商事合同通则》之补充"，或是："本合同的解释和履行依《国际统一私法协会国际商事合同通则》之规定，《国际统一私法协会国际商事合同通则》没有明确规定的问题，依据 X 国法律确定"（参见序言第二段脚注的示范条款）。

第1.7条

（诚实信用和公平交易）

（1）每一方当事人应依据国际贸易中的诚实信用和公平交易原则行事。
（2）当事人不能排除或限制此项义务。

COMMENT

1. "Good faith and fair dealing" as a fundamental idea underlying the Principles

There are a number of provisions throughout the different Chapters of the Principles which constitute a direct or indirect application of the principle of good faith and fair dealing. See above all Article 1.8, but see also for instance, Articles 1.9(2); 2.1.4(2)(b), 2.1.15, 2.1.16, 2.1.18 and 2.1.20; 2.2.4(2), 2.2.5(2), 2.2.7 and 2.2.10; 3.2.2, 3.2.5 and 3.2.7; 4.1(2), 4.2(2), 4.6 and 4.8; 5.1.2 and 5.1.3; 5.2.5; 5.3.3 and 5.3.4; 6.1.3, 6.1.5, 6.1.16(2) and 6.1.17(1); 6.2.3(3)(4); 7.1.2, 7.1.6 and 7.1.7; 7.2.2(b)(c); 7.4.8 and 7.4.13; 9.1.3, 9.1.4 and 9.1.10(1). This means that good faith and fair dealing may be considered to be one of the fundamental ideas underlying the Principles. By stating in general terms that each party must act in accordance with good faith and fair dealing, paragraph (1) of this Article makes it clear that even in the absence of special provisions in the Principles the parties' behaviour throughout the life of the contract, including the negotiation process, must conform to good faith and fair dealing.

Illustrations

1.   A grants B forty-eight hours as the time within which B may accept its offer. When B, shortly before the expiry of the deadline, decides to accept, it is unable to do so: it is the weekend, the fax at A's office is disconnected and there is no telephone answering machine which can take the message. When on the following Monday A refuses B's acceptance A acts contrary to good faith since when it fixed the time-limit for acceptance it was for A to ensure that messages could be received at its office throughout the forty-eight hour period.

2.   A contract for the supply and installation of a special production line contains a provision according to which A, the seller, is obliged to communicate to B, the purchaser, any improvements made by A to the technology of that line. After a year B learns of an important improvement of which it had not been informed. A is not excused by the fact that the production of that particular type of production line is no longer its responsibility but that of C, a wholly-owned affiliated company of A. It would be against good faith for A to invoke the separate entity of C, which was specifically set up to take over this production in order to avoid A's contractual obligations vis-à-vis B.

3.   A, an agent, undertakes on behalf of B, the principal, to promote the sale of B's goods in a given area. Under the contract A's right to compensation arises only after B's approval of the contracts procured

注释：

1. "诚实信用和公平交易"是《通则》的一项基本理念

《通则》的许多章节中都有大量的条款都是"诚实信用和公平交易"原则的直接或间接适用,首先参见第1.8条,也可参见如第1.9条第(2)款;第2.1.4条第(2)款(b)项、第2.1.15条、第2.1.16条、第2.1.18条和第2.1.20条;第2.2.4条第(2)款、第2.2.5条第(2)款、第2.2.7条和第2.2.10条;第3.2.2条、第3.2.5条、第3.2.7条;第4.1条第(2)款、第4.2条第(2)款、第4.6条、第4.8条;第5.1.2条、第5.1.3条;第5.2.5条;第5.3.3条和第5.3.4条;第6.1.3条、第6.1.5条、第6.1.16条第(2)款、第6.1.17条第(1)款;第6.2.3条第(3)款和第(4)款;第7.1.2条、第7.1.6条、第7.1.7条;第7.2.2条(b)和(c)项;第7.4.8条和第7.4.13条;第9.1.3条、第9.1.4条和第9.1.10条(1)款。这表明"诚实信用和公平交易"是《通则》的一项基本理念。通过以一般条款规定每一方当事人应按照诚实信用和公平交易原则行事,本条第(1)款明确了即使在没有《通则》具体条款的规定的情况下,在整个合同期间,包括协商过程,当事人的行为都必须遵循这一原则。

示例：

1. A同意B在48小时内决定是否接受其要约。B在最后期限临近届满时决定接受,却无法告知A,因为此时正值周末,A办公室里的传真机未开通,也没有能接收消息的电话答录机。在紧接着的周一,A拒绝了B的承诺。A的这种做法违背了诚实信用原则,因为当A确定承诺时限时,必须确保其办公室在整个48小时内均能接收信息。

2. 在一份关于供应和安装某一特殊生产线的合同中含有这样一条规定：卖方A有义务将对该生产线技术所做的任何技术改进告知买方B。一年后,B了解到A未通知一项重要技术改进。对此A不能以以下事实为自己开脱,即：这种特定型号生产线的生产已不再由A负责,而是转由A的全资附属公司C负责。A援引C为独立实体为自己开脱的做法违背了诚实信用原则,因为A正是为了规避对于B的合同义务,特意设立独立实体C,并由其来承担这种生产。

3. 代理商A代表委托人B在某一指定地区推销B的商品。合同规定,只有在A代办的合同得到B批准后,A才有

by A. While B is free to decide whether or not to approve the contracts procured by A, a systematic and unjustified refusal to approve any contract procured by A would be against good faith.

4.   Under a line of credit agreement between A, a bank, and B, a customer, A suddenly and inexplicably refuses to make further advances to B whose business suffers heavy losses as a consequence. Notwithstanding the fact that the agreement contains a term permitting A to accelerate payment "at will", A's demand for payment in full without prior warning and with no justification would be against good faith.

2. Abuse of rights

A typical example of behaviour contrary to the principle of good faith and fair dealing is what in some legal systems is known as "abuse of rights". It is characterised by a party's malicious behaviour which occurs for instance when a party exercises a right merely to damage the other party or for a purpose other than the one for which it had been granted, or when the exercise of a right is disproportionate to the originally intended result.

Illustrations

5.   A rents premises from B for the purpose of setting up a retail business. The rental contract is for five years, but when three years later A realises that business in the area is very poor, it decides to close the business and informs B that it is no longer interested in renting the premises. A's breach of contract would normally lead to B's having the choice of either terminating the contract and claiming damages or requesting specific performance. However, under the circumstances B would be abusing its rights if it required A to pay the rent for the remaining two years of the contract instead of terminating the contract and claiming damages from A for the rent it has lost for the length of time necessary to find a new tenant.

6.   A rents premises from B for the purpose of opening a restaurant. During the summer months A sets up a few tables out of doors, but still on the owner's property. On account of the noise caused by the restaurant's customers late at night, B has increasing difficulties finding tenants for apartments in the same building. B would be abusing its rights if, instead of requesting A to desist from serving out of doors late at night, it required A not to serve out of doors at all.

3. "Good faith and fair dealing in international trade"

The reference to "good faith and fair dealing in international trade" first makes it clear that in the context of the Principles the two concepts

权获得报酬。尽管 B 可自由决定是否批准 A 代办的合同，但是，系统性地和毫无理由地拒绝批准 A 代办的所有合同则有悖于诚实信用原则。

4. 在银行 A 和用户 B 商定的信贷协议有效期内，A 突然不加说明地拒绝向 B 继续提供贷款，致使 B 的生意遭受了重大损失。尽管协议中有允许 A "随意" 要求加快偿还款项的条款，但 A 这种没有事先警告和没有正当理由的全额还款要求则违背了诚实信用原则。

2. 权利的滥用

与诚实信用和公平交易原则相悖的一个典型例子是一些法律体系中所称的 "权利滥用"。它是以一方当事人的恶意行为为特征，比如，一方当事人行使权利仅仅是为了损害另一方当事人或者是为了达到不同于先前赋予的目的，或者是权利的行使与最初料想的结果是不成比例的。

示例：

5. 为了建立零售业务，A 向 B 租赁房屋。租赁合同为期五年，但三年后，A 意识到该区域内的业务很不好，于是决定终止经营并通知 B 不打算继续租用其房屋。A 的违约通常使 B 可以选择终止合同并要求赔偿或者要求实际履行。然而，如果 B 要求 A 支付合同期剩余两年的租金，而不是终止合同并要求 A 赔偿其在寻找新承租人的必要期间内的租金损失，B 就是在滥用权利。

6. 为了开办一餐馆，A 向 B 租赁房屋。在夏天的几个月，A 在门外放置了几张桌子，但依旧在房东的财产范围内。餐馆顾客在深夜制造很大噪音，致使 B 为同一建筑物内的公寓寻找承租人日益困难。如果 B 不是要求 A 停止深夜在门外营业，而是要求 A 根本不在门外营业，B 就是在滥用权利。

3. "国际贸易中的诚实信用和公平交易"

"国际贸易中的诚实信用和公平交易" 这一用语，首先表明在《通则》中，这两个概念不应该按照不同国内法体系中通常采用的一般标

are not to be applied according to the standards ordinarily adopted within the different national legal systems. In other words, such domestic standards may be taken into account only to the extent that they are shown to be generally accepted among the various legal systems. A further implication of the formula used is that good faith and fair dealing must be construed in the light of the special conditions of international trade. Standards of business practice may indeed vary considerably from one trade sector to another, and even within a given trade sector they may be more or less stringent depending on the socio-economic environment in which the enterprises operate, their size and technical skill, etc.

It should be noted that whenever the provisions of the Principles and/or the comments thereto refer only to "good faith and fair dealing", such references should always be understood as a reference to "good faith and fair dealing in international trade" as specified in this Article.

Illustrations

7. Under a contract for the sale of high-technology equipment the purchaser loses the right to rely on any defect in the goods if it does not give notice to the seller specifying the nature of the defect without undue delay after it has discovered or ought to have discovered the defect. A, a buyer operating in a country where such equipment is commonly used, discovers a defect in the equipment after having put it into operation, but in its notice to B, the seller of the equipment, A gives misleading indications as to the nature of the defect. A loses its right to rely on the defect since a more careful examination of the defect would have permitted it to give B the necessary specifications.

8. The facts are the same as in Illustration 7, except that A operates in a country where this type of equipment is so far almost unknown. A does not lose its right to rely on the defect because B, being aware of A's lack of technical knowledge, could not reasonably have expected A properly to identify the nature of the defect.

准加以适用。换句话说，这些国内标准只应在被各个不同法律体系普遍接受的范围内才予以考虑。该用法进一步表明，诚实信用和公平交易必须结合国际贸易的特殊情况加以解释。贸易实践的标准确实会因贸易领域的不同而存在相当大的差异，即使在同一贸易领域，其标准也会因企业的经营所处的社会经济环境、企业的规模和技能等因素而宽严不等。

应指出的是，当《通则》的条文和/或注释仅提及"诚实信用和公平交易"时，这些提法均应理解为本条所规定的"国际贸易中的诚实信用和公平交易"。

示例：

7. 一项高科技设备销售合同规定，如买方在发现或应该发现设备的瑕疵后，未及时通知卖方并说明瑕疵的性质，则买方丧失基于设备瑕疵而产生的权利。买方 A 的经营所在国这种设备使用很普遍，将设备投入运行后 A 发现该设备有瑕疵，但在给卖方 B 的通知中，对于该瑕疵的性质，A 却提供了一份令人误解的说明。A 因此丧失了基于该瑕疵而产生的权利，因为他本可以通过更谨慎细致的检测提供给 B 一份必要的说明。

8. 事实与示例 7 相同，不同的是，在 A 的经营所在国这种型号的设备迄今几乎鲜为人知。A 没有丧失基于瑕疵所产生的权利，因为 B 知道 A 缺乏技术知识，因此不能合理地期望 A 能恰当地判定该瑕疵的性质。

4. The mandatory nature of the principle of good faith and fair dealing

The parties' duty to act in accordance with good faith and fair dealing is of such a fundamental nature that the parties may not contractually exclude or limit it (paragraph (2)). As to specific applications of the general prohibition to exclude or limit the principle of good faith and fair dealing between the parties, see Articles 3.1.4, 7.1.6 and 7.4.13.

On the other hand, nothing prevents parties from providing in their contract for a duty to observe more stringent standards of behaviour (see, e.g., Article 5.3.3).

ARTICLE 1.8

(Inconsistent behaviour)

A party cannot act inconsistently with an understanding it has caused the other party to have and upon which that other party reasonably has acted in reliance to its detriment.

COMMENT

1. Inconsistent behaviour and "good faith and fair dealing"

This provision is a general application of the principle of good faith and fair dealing (Article 1.7). It is reflected in other more specific provisions of the Principles (see, for example, Articles 2.1.4(2)(b), 2.1.18, 2.1.20, 2.2.5(2) and Comment 3 on Article 10.4). It imposes a responsibility on a party not to occasion detriment to another party by acting inconsistently with an understanding concerning their contractual relationship which it has caused that other party to have and upon which that other party has reasonably acted in reliance.

The prohibition contained in this Article can result in the creation of rights and in the loss, suspension or modification of rights otherwise than by agreement of the parties. This is because the understanding relied upon may itself be inconsistent with the agreed or actual rights of the parties. The Article does not provide the only means by which a right might be lost or suspended because of one party's conduct (see, for example, Articles 3.2.9 and 7.1.4(3)).

4. 诚实信用和公平交易原则的强制性

当事人必须按照诚实信用和公平交易原则行事的义务具有这样一种基本特性，即当事人不得对这一原则通过合同加以排除或限制（第(2)款）。关于普遍禁止当事人排除或限制诚实信用和公平交易原则的具体适用，参见第3.1.4条、第7.1.6条和第7.4.13条的规定。

另一方面，不能阻止当事人在合同中约定遵守更加严格的行为标准的义务（比如参见第5.3.3条）。

第1.8条

（不一致行为）

> 如果一方当事人致使另一方当事人产生某种理解，且该另一方当事人信赖该理解合理行事并对自己造成不利，则该方当事人不得以与该理解不一致的方式行事。

注释：

1. 不一致行为和"诚实信用和公平交易"

本条是诚实信用和公平交易原则的一般性适用（第1.7条）。它反映在《通则》其他更为具体的条款中（比如参见第2.1.4条(2)款(b)项、第2.1.18条、第2.1.20条、第2.2.5条(2)款和第10.4条注释3）。一方当事人承担如下义务：如果其导致对方就合同关系产生某种理解，且该对方已合理依赖该理解行事，则不得通过与该理解不一致的方式行事导致对方蒙受侵害。

本条的禁止性规定可以导致权利的创设，或者权利的丧失、中止或修改，除非当事人另有约定。这是因为被信赖的理解本身可能与当事人的约定或真实的权利不一致。本条并非规定因一方当事人的行为而导致权利丧失或中止的唯一方法（比如参见第3.2.9条和第7.1.4条(3)款）。

2. An understanding reasonably relied upon

There is a variety of ways in which one party may cause the other party to have an understanding concerning their contract, its performance, or enforcement. The understanding may result, for example, from a representation made, from conduct, or from silence when a party would reasonably expect the other to speak to correct a known error or misunderstanding that was being relied upon.

So long as it relates in some way to the contractual relationship of the parties, the understanding for the purposes of this Article is not limited to any particular subject-matter. It may relate to a matter of fact or of law, to a matter of intention, or to how one or other of the parties can or must act.

The important limitation is that the understanding must be one on which, in the circumstances, the other party can and does reasonably rely. Whether the reliance is reasonable is a matter of fact in the circumstances having regard, in particular, to the communications and conduct of the parties, to the nature and setting of the parties' dealings and to the expectations they could reasonably entertain of each other.

Illustrations

1.   A has negotiated with B over a lengthy period for a contract of lease of B's land under which B is to demolish a building and construct a new one to A's specification. A communicates with B in terms that induce B reasonably to understand that their contract negotiations have been completed, and that B can begin performance. B then demolishes the building and engages contractors to build the new building. A is aware of this and does nothing to stop it. A later indicates to B that there are additional terms still to be negotiated. A will be precluded from departing from B's understanding.

2.   B mistakenly understands that its contract with A can be performed in a particular way. A is aware of this and stands by while B's performance proceeds. B and A meet regularly. B's performance is discussed but no reference is made by A to B's mistake. A will be precluded from insisting that the performance was not that which was required under the contract.

3.   A regularly uses B to do sub-contract work on building sites. That part of A's business and the employees involved in it are taken over by A1, a related business. There is no change in the general course of business by which B obtains its instruction to do work. B continues to provide sub-contract services and continues to bill A for work done believing the work is being done for A. A does not inform B of its mistake. A is precluded from denying that B's contract for work done is with it and must pay for the work done.

2. 合理信赖的理解

一方当事人可以多种方式使另一方当事人就合同及其履行或执行产生一种理解。比如，该理解可产生自当事人所作的陈述，产生自所作的行为，或者在一方当事人合理期待另一方当事人对被信赖的错误或误解予以纠正时，产生自对方的沉默。

就本条而言，理解只要在某些方面与当事人间的合同关系相关即可，不限于任何特定的事项。它可能与事实问题或法律问题、合同意图，或一方或另一方当事人可能或必须如何行事相关。

对理解的重要限制是，该理解必须是具体情况下另一方当事人可以合理信赖并事实上已经合理地信赖。信赖合理与否是一个具体情况下的事实问题，在作出判断时应考虑多种因素，特别是当事人间的联系与行为、交易的性质与背景和当事人双方彼此可抱有的合理期待。

示例：

1. A 与 B 就租赁 B 土地的事宜进行了长时间的磋商，按照约定，B 将拆除一建筑物，并按照 A 的指示建造一新建筑物。A 与 B 联络时所用的措辞致使 B 合理地认为他们之间的合同已经成立，并且 B 可以开始履行合同。随后 B 拆除了原建筑物并雇佣承包人建造新的建筑物。A 明知且未阻止。A 随后向 B 指出尚有合同条款需要协商。A 的行为不得与 B 的理解相背离。

2. B 错误地理解其与 A 订立的合同可以以某一方式履行。A 明知 B 的理解错误但在 B 的履行过程中并未提出任何异议。B 与 A 定期相见并且双方还讨论过 B 的履行，A 并没有指出 B 的错误。A 的行为排除其主张履行与合同不符合的权利。

3. A 经常性地使用 B 在建筑工地从事分包工作。A 的这部分业务及其所涉雇佣人员由关联企业 A1 经营。B 借以获得指示进行工作的总体工作流程并无变化。B 继续提供分包服务并向 A 发出账单，因为他相信自己是在为 A 工作。A 并未告知 B 的这一错误。A 不能否认，就已完成的工作而言，自己是合同的一方当事人，A 必须就已完成的工作支付报酬。

4.   Because of difficulties it is experiencing with its own suppliers, A is unable to make deliveries on time to B under their contract. The contract imposes penalties for late delivery. After being made aware of A's difficulties, B indicates it will not insist on strict compliance with the delivery schedule. A year later B's business begins to suffer from A's late deliveries. B seeks to recover penalties for the late deliveries to date and to require compliance with the delivery schedule for the future. It will be precluded from recovering the penalties but will be able to insist on compliance with the schedule if reasonable notice is given that compliance is required for the future.

5.   B is indebted to A in the sum of AUD 10,000. Though the debt is due A takes no steps to enforce it. B assumes in consequence that A has pardoned the debt. A has done nothing to indicate that such actually is the case. It later demands payment. B cannot rely on A's inaction to resist that demand.

3. Detriment and preclusion

The responsibility imposed by the Article is to avoid detriment being occasioned in consequence of reasonable reliance. This does not necessarily require that the party seeking to act inconsistently must be precluded from so doing. Preclusion is only one way of avoiding detriment. There may, in the circumstances, be other reasonable means available that can avert the detriment the relying party would otherwise experience if the inconsistent action were allowed as, for example, by giving reasonable notice before acting inconsistently (see Illustration 4), or by paying for costs or losses incurred by reason of reliance.

Illustrations

6.   A and B are parties to a construction contract which requires that additional works be documented in writing and be certified by the site architect. A's contract manager orally requests B to do specified additional work on a time and materials basis and assures B it will be documented appropriately in due course. B commissions design works for the additional work at which stage A indicates that the work is not required. The cost incurred in commissioning the design work is far less than the cost that would be incurred if the additional work were to be done. If A pays B the costs incurred by B for the design work, B cannot then complain of A's inconsistent behaviour.

4. 因为 A 的供应商面临困境，致使 A 不能按照合同及时向 B 完成交付。合同规定了迟延交付赔偿金。在知悉 A 的困境后，B 表示将不会坚持要求严格遵守交付期限。一年后，B 的业务开始蒙受由于 A 迟延交付造成的损失。B 试图就迄今发生的迟延交付要求支付赔偿金并要求将来遵守交付期限。B 无权要求迟延赔偿金，但如果发出通知要求将来遵守期限的合理通知，B 可以坚持要求遵守交付期限。

5. B 欠 A 总计 1 万澳大利亚元。虽然债务已到期，但 A 未采取任何措施要求行使债权。B 因此认为 A 已经解除了该项债务。但 A 并未有采取任何措施表明事实如此。后来 A 要求支付。B 不能以 A 的不作为为由拒绝 A 的请求。

3. 损害和排除

本条规定的责任是避免因合理信赖而导致损害。这并不必然要求排除试图以不一致方式行事的当事人如此行事的权利，排除只是避免损害的方法之一。此外还存在其他合理可行的方法，以避免如若允许不一致行为信赖方本会遭受的损害，比如，在不一致行为前发出合理通知（参见示例4），或补偿由于合理信赖造成的成本或损失。

示例：

6. A 与 B 是建筑合同的当事人，合同要求额外的工作应以书面形式记载并由工地建筑师核准。A 方合同经理口头要求 B 在时间和材料方面完成特定的额外工作，并向 B 保证将会适当及时地加以记载。B 为完成额外工作把设计工作进行了委托，此时，A 提出不需要该项工作。委托设计工作所发生的费用远远少于完成额外工作完成将会发生的费用。如果 A 支付 B 因设计工作所产生的费用，那么，B 就不能控告 A 的不一致行为。

7.   A fails to meet on time a prescribed milestone in a software development contract with B. B is entitled under the contract to terminate the contract because of that failure. B continues to require and pay for changes to the software and acts co-operatively with A in continuing the software development program. A's continued performance is based on B's conduct subsequent to the breach. B will in such circumstances be precluded from exercising its right to terminate for the failure to meet the milestone. However, under the Principles B will be able to allow A an additional period of time for performance (see Article 7.1.5) and to exercise its right to terminate if the milestone is not met in that period.

ARTICLE 1.9

(Usages and practices)

(1) The parties are bound by any usage to which they have agreed and by any practices which they have established between themselves.

(2) The parties are bound by a usage that is widely known to and regularly observed in international trade by parties in the particular trade concerned except where the application of such a usage would be unreasonable.

COMMENT

1. Practices and usages in the context of the Principles

This Article lays down the principle according to which the parties are in general bound by practices and usages which meet the requirements set forth in the Article. Furthermore, these same requirements must be met by practices and usages for them to be applicable in the cases and for the purposes expressly indicated in the Principles (see, for instance, Articles 2.1.6(3), 4.3, and 5.1.2).

2. Practices established between the parties

A practice established between the parties to a particular contract is automatically binding, except where the parties have expressly excluded its application. Whether a particular practice can be deemed to be "established" between the parties will naturally depend on the

7. A 未能按时完成与 B 订立的软件开发合同中所规定的进度。按照合同规定，因为 A 的履行不能，B 有权终止合同。B 继续要求 A 开发且支付软件的改进费用，并在继续软件开发项目方面与 A 进行合作。A 之所以继续履行是基于自己违约后 B 的这些行为。在这样的情况下，B 因 A 未按时完成进度而终止合同的权利被排除。然而，根据《通则》的规定，B 可给予 A 一定的额外履行期间（参见第7.1.5条），如果在此期间内 A 依然不能完成进度，则 B 有权终止合同。

第1.9条

（惯例和习惯做法）

（1）当事人各方受其约定的任何惯例和其相互之间建立的任何习惯做法的约束。
（2）合同当事人应受国际贸易中从事相关特定贸易之人广泛知悉并惯常遵守之惯例的约束，除非适用该惯例是不合理。

注释：

1.《通则》中的习惯做法和惯例

本条规定了这样一项原则，根据该原则当事人应普遍受符合本条要求的习惯做法和惯例的约束。另外，在《通则》明确指明的情况中以及为了《通则》明确指明的目的而适用习惯做法和惯例时，也必须符合本条规定要求（参见第2.1.6条第（3）款、第4.3条和第5.1.2条的有关规定）。

2. 当事人之间确立的习惯做法

某一特定合同当事人之间确立的习惯做法自动具有约束力，除非当事人已明示排除其适用。能否认定某一特定习惯做法已在当事人间"建立"，自然取决于个案的具体情况，但在当事人之间唯一一次先前

circumstances of the case, but behaviour on the occasion of only one previous transaction between the parties will not normally suffice.

Illustration

1. A, a supplier, has repeatedly accepted claims from B, a customer, for quantitative or qualitative defects in the goods as much as two weeks after their delivery. When B gives another notice of defects after a fortnight, A cannot object that it is too late since the two-weeks' notice amounts to a practice established between A and B which will as such be binding on A.

3. Agreed usages

By stating that the parties are bound by usages to which they have agreed, paragraph (1) of this Article merely applies the general principle of freedom of contract laid down in Article 1.1. Indeed, the parties may either negotiate all the terms of their contract, or for certain questions simply refer to other sources including usages. The parties may stipulate the application of any usage, including a usage developed within a trade sector to which neither party belongs, or a usage relating to a different type of contract. It is even conceivable that the parties will agree on the application of what sometimes misleadingly are called usages, i.e. a set of rules issued by a particular trade association under the title of "Usages", but which only in part reflects established general lines of conduct.

4. Other applicable usages

Paragraph (2) lays down the criteria for the identification of usages applicable in the absence of a specific agreement by the parties. The fact that the usage must be "widely known to and regularly observed [...] by parties in the particular trade concerned" is a condition for the application of any usage, be it at international or merely at national or local level. The additional qualification "in international trade" is intended to avoid usages developed for, and confined to, domestic transactions also being invoked in transactions with foreigners.

Illustration

2. A, a real estate agent, invokes a particular usage of the profession in its country vis-à-vis B, a foreign customer. B is not bound by such a usage if that usage is of a local nature and relates to a trade which is predominantly domestic in character.

交易中发生的行为通常将不足以构成习惯做法。

示例：

　　1. 供应商 A 已多次接受了顾客 B 在交货后两周内提出的货物存在数量或质量瑕疵的主张。B 在两周之后又发出一份货物瑕疵通知，A 不能以通知太迟为由予以拒绝，因为两周的通知构成 A 和 B 之间的一项习惯做法，它因此对 A 有约束力。

3. 当事人约定的惯例

本条第(1)款阐明当事人受约定的惯例的约束，因此它只不过是第 1.1 条所规定的缔约自由一般原则的一种应用。事实上，当事人既可协商合同的所有条款，也可就特定问题简单地转引包括惯例在内的其他渊源。当事人可以约定适用任何惯例，包括任何一方当事人都未涉足过的某一贸易领域发展来的惯例，或与其他类型的合同相关的某种惯例。甚至可以想象当事人约定适用一些有时误被称作惯例的做法，也即某一特定行业协会以"惯例"名义发布的一系列规则，但是这些规则只部分反映了已经确立的一般行为规范。

4. 其他可适用的惯例

本条第(2)款规定了在当事人未作特定约定的情况下查明可适用惯例的标准。惯例必须是"从事相关特定贸易之人广泛知悉并惯常遵守的"，这是任何惯例得以适用的一个条件，无论是国际惯例，还是国内的或地方性的惯例。"国际贸易中"这一附加限制，是为了避免把在国内交易中发展来的并限于在国内交易中使用的惯例也适用于与外国人的交易中。

示例：

　　2. 房地产代理商 A 对一外国顾客 B 援引使用其所在国本行业的某一惯例。如果该惯例只具有地方性，且只与性质上国内因素占主导地位的贸易相关，则 B 不受这一惯例的约束。

Only exceptionally may usages of a purely local or national origin be applied without any reference thereto by the parties. Thus, usages existing on certain commodity exchanges or at trade exhibitions or ports should be applicable provided that they are regularly followed with respect to foreigners as well. Another exception concerns the case of a businessperson who has already entered into a number of similar contracts in a foreign country and who should therefore be bound by the usages established within that country for such contracts.

Illustrations

> 3.   A, a terminal operator, invokes a particular usage of the port where it is located vis-à-vis B, a foreign carrier. B is bound by this local usage if the port is normally used by foreigners and the usage in question has been regularly observed with respect to all customers, irrespective of their place of business and of their nationality.
>
> 4.   A, a sales agent from Country X, receives a request from B, one of its customers in Country Y, for the customary 10% discount upon payment of the price in cash. A may not object to the application of such a usage on account of its being restricted to Country Y if A has been doing business in that country for a certain period of time.

5. Application of usage unreasonable

A usage may be regularly observed by the generality of business people in a particular trade sector but its application in a given case may nevertheless be unreasonable. Reasons for this may be found in the particular conditions in which one or both parties operate and/or the atypical nature of the transaction. In such cases the usage will not be applied.

Illustration

> 5.   A usage exists in a commodity trade sector according to which the purchaser may not rely on defects in the goods if they are not duly certified by an internationally recognised inspection agency. When A, a buyer, takes over the goods at the port of destination, the only internationally recognised inspection agency operating in that port is on strike and to call another from the nearest port would be excessively costly. The application of the usage in this case would be unreasonable and A may rely on the defects it has discovered even though they have not been certified by an internationally recognised inspection agency.

纯粹地方性或国内性的惯例，只能在例外情况下，可以不经当事人提及便得以适用。因此，在特定商品交易所、贸易展览或港口存在的惯例，如果针对外国人也惯常地得到遵守，则应予以适用。还有一种例外的情况是，一商人已经在某一外国订立了大量类似合同，因此应受该国针对此类合同形成的惯例的约束。

示例：

　　3. A 是一位码头经营人，对外国承运人 B 援引适用其所在港口的某一特定惯例。如果该港口通常由外国人使用，且所有客户不论其营业地和国籍如何都一贯遵守该惯例，则 B 应受该地方性惯例的约束。

　　4. X 国的销售代理商 A 接到 Y 国顾客 B 的一项要求，B 要求 A 对其现金付款给予 10% 的惯常折扣。如果 A 在 Y 国从事商业活动已有一段时间，则 A 不能以该惯例仅限于 Y 国为由而拒绝适用该惯例。

5. 适用惯例不合理

一项惯例可能被某一特定贸易领域的大部分商人普遍遵守，但在特定情况下它的适用却可能是不合理的。其原因可能在于一方或双方当事人经营中遭遇的特殊情况和/或所从事交易的特殊性。在这种情况下，该惯例不应适用。

示例：

　　5. 在某一商品贸易领域存在这样一项惯例，按照该惯例，如果商品瑕疵不能得到国际认可的商检机构的合法证明，则买方不能主张该商品有瑕疵。当买方 A 在目的港接收货物时，该港口经营的唯一一个国际认可的商检机构正在罢工，并且邀请在最近的港口经营的另外一家商检机构费用又太高。在这种情况下，适用该惯例就不合理。因此，即使商品没有得到国际认可商检机构的证明，A 也可以主张其所发现的商品瑕疵。

6. Usages prevail over the Principles

Both courses of dealing and usages, once they are applicable in a given case, prevail over conflicting provisions contained in the Principles. The reason for this is that they bind the parties as implied terms of the contract as a whole or of single statements or other conduct on the part of one of the parties. As such, they are superseded by any express term stipulated by the parties but, in the same way as the latter, they prevail over the Principles, the only exception being those provisions which are specifically declared to be of a mandatory character (see Comment 3 on Article 1.5).

ARTICLE 1.10

(Notice)

(1) Where notice is required it may be given by any means appropriate to the circumstances.

(2) A notice is effective when it reaches the person to whom it is given.

(3) For the purpose of paragraph (2) a notice "reaches" a person when given to that person orally or delivered at that person's place of business or mailing address.

(4) For the purpose of this Article "notice" includes a declaration, demand, request or any other communication of intention.

COMMENT

1. Form of notice

This Article first lays down the principle that notice or any other kind of communication of intention (declarations, demands, requests, etc.) required by individual provisions of the Principles are not subject to any particular requirement as to form, but may be given by any means appropriate in the circumstances. Which means are appropriate will depend on the actual circumstances of the case, in particular on the availability and the reliability of the various modes of communication, and the importance and/or urgency of the message to be delivered. For an electronic notice to be "appropriate to the circumstances"

6. 惯例优于《通则》

一旦习惯做法和惯例在既定的案件中可以适用，它们则优先于《通则》中与之相冲突的条款而得以适用。原因是这些习惯做法和惯例作为整个合同的默示条款，或者作为某一方当事人的单独声明或其他行为的默示条款而约束当事人。因此，它们可被当事人规定的任何明示条款所取代，但正如明示条款取代默示条款一样，它们优于《通则》，唯一的例外是被特别宣布为强制性条款的那些《通则》条款（见第 1.5 条注释3）。

第 1.10 条

（通知）

（1）在需要发出通知时，通知可按适合于具体情况的任何方式发出。

（2）通知于到达被通知人时生效。

（3）就第（2）款而言，通知于口头传达被通知人或递送到被通知人的营业地或通信地址时，为通知"到达"被通知人。

（4）就本条而言，通知包括声明、要求、请求或任何其他意思表述。

注释:

1. 通知的形式

本条首先规定了这样一个原则，即《通则》具体条款所要求的通知或者任何其他意思的表达（声明、要求、请求等）不受任何特定形式要求的约束，而是可以使用适合个案具体情况的任何方式。哪种方式是适当的取决于个案的具体情况，特别是不同通信方式的可用性和可靠性，以及拟发送信息的重要性和/或紧迫性。对于电子通知而言，要构成"适合个案具体情况"，收件人必须已明示或默示同意以发件人

the addressee must expressly or impliedly have consented to receive electronic communications in the way in which the notice was sent by the sender, i.e. of that type, in that format and to that address. The addressee's consent may be inferred from the addressee's statements or conduct, from practices established between the parties, or from applicable usages.

Illustrations

1. Seller A and buyer B have a longstanding business relationship in the course of which they have always negotiated and concluded their contracts by telephone. On discovering a defect in the goods supplied on one occasion, B immediately sends A notice thereof by e-mail. A, who does not regularly read its e-mail and had no reason to expect an e-mail from B, on discovering B's notice three weeks after it had been sent rejects it as being too late. B may not object that it had given prompt notice of the defects since the notice was not given by a means appropriate to the circumstances.

2. Seller A and buyer B have a longstanding business relationship in the course of which they have regularly communicated by electronic means. On discovering a defect in the goods supplied on one occasion, B immediately sends A notice thereof by e-mail to an e-mail address different from the one normally used. A, who had no reason to expect an e-mail from B at that address, on discovering B's notice three weeks after it had been sent rejects it as being too late. B may not object that it had given prompt notice of the defects since the notice was not given by a means appropriate to the circumstances.

2. Receipt principle

With respect to all kinds of notices the Principles adopt the so-called "receipt" principle, i.e. they are not effective unless and until they reach the person to whom they are given. For some communications this is expressly stated in the provisions dealing with them: see Articles 2.1.3(1), 2.1.3(2), 2.1.5, 2.1.6(2), 2.1.8(1) and 2.1.10; 9.1.10 and 9.1.11. The purpose of paragraph (2) of this Article is to indicate that the same will also be true in the absence of an express statement to this effect: see Articles 2.1.9, 2.1.11; 2.2.9; 3.2.10, 3.2.11; 6.1.16, 6.2.3; 7.1.5, 7.1.7; 7.2.1, 7.2.2; 7.3.2, 7.3.4; and 8.3.

3. Dispatch principle to be expressly stipulated

The parties are of course always free expressly to stipulate the application of the dispatch principle. This may be appropriate in

所用的发送方式接收电子通信，即发件人所用的通知类型、格式和收件地址。收件人的同意可以从收件人的声明或行为、当事人之间确立的习惯做法或可适用的惯例中推导出来。

示例：

1. 卖方 A 和买方 B 有长期的业务关系，他们一贯通过电话来协商和缔结合同。一次 B 发现 A 提供的货物有瑕疵，B 立即以电子邮件通知 A，而 A 并不是定期查看电子邮件且没有理由期待会收到 B 的电子邮件。在电子邮件发出三周后 A 才发现 B 的通知。A 以通知太迟为由拒绝了 B 的通知。因为通知不是以适合于具体情况的方式发出的，B 不能以已对瑕疵迅速发出了通知为由提出异议。

2. 卖方 A 和买方 B 有长期的业务关系，他们惯常通过电子方式进行沟通。一次 B 发现 A 提供的货物有瑕疵，B 立即通过电子邮件向 A 不经常使用的电邮地址发出通知，A 没有理由期待会在那个地址收到 B 的电子邮件。在电子邮件发出三个星期之后 A 才发现了 B 的通知并以通知太迟为由拒绝了 B 的请求。因为通知不是以适合于具体情况的方式发出的，B 不能以已对瑕疵迅速发出了通知为由提出异议。

2. 到达主义原则

关于各种形式的通知，《通则》采纳了所谓的"到达主义原则"，也就是除非和直至通知到达被通知人时才生效。对于某些意思表达，相关条款对此有明确的规定：见第 2.1.3 条第（1）款、第 2.1.3 条第（2）款、第 2.1.5 条、第 2.1.6 条第（2）款、第 2.1.8 条第（1）款和第 2.1.10 条；第 9.1.10 条和第 9.1.11 条。本条第（2）款的目的旨在表明：在《通则》未有具体条款对此做出明确规定的情况下，同样适用到达主义原则：见第 2.1.9 条、第 2.1.11 条、第 2.2.9 条、第 3.2.10 条、第 3.2.11 条、第 6.1.16 条、第 6.2.3 条、第 7.1.5 条、第 7.1.7 条、第 7.2.1 条、第 7.2.2 条、第 7.3.2 条、第 7.3.4 条和第 8.3 条。

3. 明示约定的投邮主义原则

当然，当事人总是能自由地明确约定适用投邮主义原则。这一点

particular with respect to the notice a party has to give in order to preserve its rights in cases of the other party's actual or anticipated non-performance when it would not be fair to place the risk of loss, mistake or delay in the transmission of the message on the former. This is all the more true if the difficulties which may arise at international level in proving effective receipt of a notice are borne in mind.

4. "Reaches"

It is important in relation to the receipt principle to determine precisely when the communications in question "reach" the addressee. In an attempt to define the concept, paragraph (3) of this Article draws a distinction between oral and other communications. The former "reach" the addressee if they are made personally to it or to another person authorised by it to receive them. The latter "reach" the addressee as soon as they are delivered either to the addressee personally or to its place of business or (electronic) mailing address. The particular communication in question need not come into the hands of the addressee or actually be read by the addressee. It is sufficient that it be handed over to an employee of the addressee authorised to accept it, or that it be placed in the addressee's mailbox, or received by the addressee's fax or telex machine, or, in the case of electronic communications when it becomes capable of being retrieved by the addressee at an electronic address designated by the addressee (see Article 10(2) of the 2005 United Nations Convention on the Use of Electronic Communications in International Contracts).

ARTICLE 1.11

(Definitions)

In these Principles
—   **"court" includes an arbitral tribunal;**
—   **where a party has more than one place of business the relevant "place of business" is that which has the closest relationship to the contract and its performance, having regard to the circumstances known to or contemplated by the parties at any time before or at the conclusion of the contract;**

特别适用于如下通知，即在当事人实际不履行或预期不履行的情况下，对方为保护自己的权利只得对其发出的通知，因为此时要求该对方承担信息在传递中发生的丢失、错误或延误的风险是不公平的。如考虑到在国际层面上证明通知有效到达所具有的特殊困难，那么此时适用投邮主义原则就更为合适。

4. "到达"

准确界定相关意思表达何时"到达"收件人，对到达主义原则来说非常重要。为了界定这一概念，本条第(3)款对口头和其他形式的通知作了区分。如果口头通知是由发出人亲自向收件人或收件人授权接收的其他人作出，则视为到达。其他形式的通知只要一经送到收件人或其营业地或（电子）通信地址，即视为到达。特定的通知无须送到收件人手中或者被收件人实际阅读，只要通知交给收件人授权接受的雇员，或是放进收件人的信箱，或由收件人的传真机、电传机接收，或者，在电子通信的情况下，在收件人指定的电子地址能够被收件人检取之时（参见《联合国国际合同使用电子通信公约》第 10 条第(2)款），即已充分到达。

第 1.11 条

（定义）

通则中：

——"法院"，包括仲裁庭；

——在当事人有一个以上的营业地时，考虑到在合同订立之前任何时候或合同订立之时各方当事人所知晓或期待的情况，相关的"营业地"是指与合同和其履行具有最密切联系的营业地；

>   –   "obligor" refers to the party who is to perform an obligation and "obligee" refers to the party who is entitled to performance of that obligation;
>   – "writing" means any mode of communication that preserves a record of the information contained therein and is capable of being reproduced in tangible form.

COMMENT

1. Courts and arbitral tribunals

The importance of the Principles for the purpose of the settlement of disputes by means of arbitration has already been stressed (see above the Comments on the Preamble). In order however to avoid undue heaviness of language, only the term "court" is used in the text of the Principles, on the understanding that it covers arbitral tribunals as well as courts.

2. Party with more than one place of business

For the purpose of the application of the Principles a party's place of business is of relevance in a number of contexts such as the place for the delivery of notices (see Article 1.10(3)); a possible extension of the time of acceptance because of a holiday falling on the last day (see Article 1.12); the place of performance (Article 6.1.6) and the determination of the party who should apply for a public permission (Article 6.1.14(a)).

With reference to a party with multiple places of business (normally a central office and various branch offices) this Article lays down the rule that the relevant place of business should be considered to be that which has the closest relationship to the contract and to its performance. Nothing is said with respect to the case where the place of the conclusion of the contract and that of performance differ, but in such a case the latter would seem to be the more relevant one. In the determination of the place of business which has the closest relationship to a given contract and to its performance, regard is to be had to the circumstances known to or contemplated by both parties at any time before or at the conclusion of the contract. Facts known only to one of the parties or of which the parties became aware only after the conclusion of the contract cannot be taken into consideration.

　　——"债务人"是指履行义务的一方当事人；"债权人"是指有权要求履行义务的一方当事人；

　　——"书面"是指能保存所含信息的记录，并能以有形方式复制的任何通信方式。

注释：

1. 法院和仲裁庭

前文已经强调过《通则》在通过仲裁处理争议过程中的重要性（参见序言的注释）。然而，为了避免语言上的烦琐，《通则》只使用了"法院"这一术语，它应被理解为包括仲裁庭和法院。

2. 当事人有一个以上的营业地

涉及《通则》的适用，当事人的营业地与许多内容相关联，比如通知送达地（第 1.10 条第(3)款），因最后一日适逢节假日而顺延承诺期限（第 1.12 条），履行地（第 6.1.6 条）和哪方当事人申请公共许可的决定（第 6.1.14 条(a)项）。

对于拥有多个营业地的当事人（通常是一个总部和几个分支机构），依本条规定，相关的营业地应被视为与合同及其履行有最密切联系的营业地。本条对于合同的缔结地与履行地不一致的情况未有任何规定，但后者应被视为更相关的地点。在确定与某一合同及其履行有最密切联系的营业地时，应考虑当事人双方在签订合同时或此前所知的或所考虑的情况。仅为一方当事人所知的情况或是双方当事人仅在合同签订后才知道的情况，不予考虑。

3. "Obligor" – "obligee"

Where necessary, to better identify the party performing and the party receiving performance of obligations the terms "obligor" and "obligee" are used, irrespective of whether the obligation is non-monetary or monetary.

4. "Writing"

In some cases the Principles refer to a "writing" or a "contract in writing" (see Articles 2.1.12, 2.1.17 and 2.1.18). The Principles define this formal requirement in functional terms. Thus, a writing includes not only a telegram and a telex, but also any other mode of communication, including electronic communications, that preserves a record and can be reproduced in tangible form. This formal requirement should be compared with the more flexible form of a "notice" (see Article 1.10(1)).

ARTICLE **1.12**

(Computation of time set by parties)

(1)   Official holidays or non-business days occurring during a period set by parties for an act to be performed are included in calculating the period.

(2)   However, if the last day of the period is an official holiday or a non-business day at the place of business of the party to perform the act, the period is extended until the first business day which follows, unless the circumstances indicate otherwise.

(3)   The relevant time zone is that of the place of business of the party setting the time, unless the circumstances indicate otherwise.

COMMENT

The parties may, either unilaterally or by agreement, fix a period of time within which certain acts must be done (see, e.g., Articles 2.1.7, 2.2.9(2) and 10.3).

3. "债务人"和"债权人"

必要情况下，为了更好区分履行义务的当事人和接受义务履行的当事人，《通则》使用了"债务人"和"债权人"这一术语，不论该义务是非金钱性的还是金钱性的。

4. "书面"

在某些情况下，《通则》提到了"书面"或"书面合同"。(参见第 2.1.12 条、2.1.17 条和第 2.1.18 条)。《通则》以功能性术语来界定这种形式要求。因此，"书面"不但包括电报和电传，还包括任何其他的保存记录并能以有形方式予以再现的通信方式，包括电子通信手段。请比较这种形式要求与更加灵活的"通知"形式（参见第 1.10 条第 (1) 款)。

第 1. 12 条

(当事人所定时间的计算)

(1) 发生在当事人规定的某一行为履行期间内的法定节假日或非工作日，应包括在该期间的计算之内。

(2) 然而，如果期间的最后一天在履行该行为之当事人的营业地是法定节假日或非工作日，该期间顺延至随后的第一个工作日，除非情况有相反的表示。

(3) 相关的时区是设定时间一方当事人营业地的时区，除非情况有相反的表示。

注释:

当事人可以单方规定或协议规定必须履行某行为的期限（比如参见第 2.1.7 条、第 2.2.9 条第(2)款和第 10.3 条)。

In fixing the time limit the parties may either indicate merely a period of time (e.g. "Notice of defects in the goods must be given within ten days after delivery") or a precise date (e.g. "Offer firm until 1 March").

In the first case the question arises of whether or not holidays or non-business days occurring during the period of time are included in calculating the period of time, and according to paragraph (1) of this Article the answer is in the affirmative.

In both of the above-mentioned cases, the question may arise of what the effect would be of a holiday or non-business day falling at the expiry of the fixed period of time at the place of business of the party to perform the act. Paragraph (2) provides that in such an eventuality the period is extended until the first business day that follows, unless the circumstances indicate otherwise.

Finally, whenever the parties are situated in different time zones, the question arises as to what time zone is relevant, and according to paragraph (3) it is the time zone of the place of business of the party setting the time limit, unless the circumstances indicate otherwise.

Illustrations

1.   A sales contract provides that buyer A must give notice of defects of the goods within 10 days after delivery. The goods are delivered on Friday 16 December. A gives notice of defects on Monday 2 January and seller B rejects it as being untimely. A may not object that the holidays and non-business days which occurred between 16 December and 2 January should not be counted when calculating the ten days of the time limit.

2.   Offeror A indicates that its offer is firm until 1 March. Offeree B accepts the offer on 2 March because 1 March was a holiday at its place of business. A may not object that the fixed time limit for acceptance had expired on 1 March.

3.   Offeror A sends an offer to offeree B by e-mail on a Saturday indicating that the offer is firm for 24 hours. If B intends to accept, it must do so within 24 hours, even though the time limit elapses on a Sunday, since under the circumstances the time limit fixed by A was to be understood as absolute.

4.   The facts are the same as in Illustration 2, except that A is situated in Frankfurt and B in New York, and the time limit fixed for acceptance is "by 5 p.m. tomorrow at the latest". B must accept by 5 p.m. Frankfurt time.

在确定期限时,当事人可仅规定一个期间(比如,"有关货物瑕疵的通知必须在货物交付后的十天内发出")或规定一个确切的日期(比如,"要约承诺的最后截止日期是 3 月 1 日")。

在第一种情况下会出现的问题是,发生在此期间内的法定节假日或非工作日是否应计算在该期间内。根据本条第(1)款的规定,答案是肯定的。

在上述两种情况下,均可能出现的问题是,如果在该行为履行方的营业地,所定期间的最后一日是法定节假日或非工作日,会有什么效果。根据本条第(2)款的规定,这种情况下,期间顺延至随后的第一个工作日,除非情况有相反的表示。

最后,当事人处于不同时区,必然会出现以哪一时区为准的问题。根据本条第(3)款的规定,这种情况下,应以规定期限一方当事人的营业地所在时区为准,除非情况有相反的表示。

示例:

1. 一买卖合同规定,买方 A 必须在货物交付后的十天内就货物瑕疵发出通知。货物在 12 月 16 日星期五交付。A 在 1 月 2 日星期一发出瑕疵通知,卖方 B 以通知不及时为由拒绝了 A 的通知。A 不能以以下理由对此提出异议,即发生在 12 月 16 日至 1 月 2 日之间的法定节假日或非工作日不应计算在十天期间内。

2. 要约人 A 表明其要约在 3 月 1 日之前有效。受要约人 B 在 3 月 2 日接受该要约,因为 3 月 1 日在其营业地适逢节假日。A 不能以承诺期间已于 3 月 1 日到期为由反对。

3. 要约人 A 在星期六通过电子邮件向受要约人 B 发出要约,指出要约在 24 小时内有效。如果 B 有意接受要约,必须在 24 小时内接受,即便该期间于星期日届满,因为按照本案的具体情况,A 所确定的时限是绝对的。

4. 事实与示例 2 相同,不同点是 A 在法兰克福而 B 在纽约,规定的承诺时限是"最迟于明天下午 5 点前"。B 必须于法兰克福时间下午 5 点前承诺。

5.   A charterparty concluded between owner A, situated in Tokyo, and charterer B, situated in Kuwait City, provides for payment of the freight by B at A's bank in Zurich, Switzerland, on a specific date by 5 p.m. at latest. The relevant time zone is neither that of A nor that of B, but that of Zurich where payment is due.

5. 位于东京的所有人 A 和位于科威特城的承租人 B 订立一租船合同，合同规定，B 最迟应于某一日下午 5 点前向 A 在瑞士苏黎世的银行账户支付运费。相关的时区既不是 A 所在的时区也不是 B 所在的时区，而是支付地苏黎世所在的时区。

CHAPTER 2

FORMATION AND AUTHORITY OF AGENTS

SECTION 1: FORMATION

ARTICLE 2.1.1
(Manner of formation)

A contract may be concluded either by the acceptance of an offer or by conduct of the parties that is sufficient to show agreement.

COMMENT

1. Offer and acceptance

Basic to the Principles is the idea that the agreement of the parties is, in itself, sufficient to conclude a contract (see Article 3.1.2). The concepts of offer and acceptance have traditionally been used to determine whether, and if so when, the parties have reached agreement. As this Article and this Chapter make clear, the Principles retain these concepts as essential tools of analysis.

2. Conduct sufficient to show agreement

In commercial practice contracts, particularly when related to complex transactions, are often concluded after prolonged negotiations without an identifiable sequence of offer and acceptance. In such cases it may be difficult to determine if and when a contractual agreement has been reached. According to this Article a contract may be held to be concluded even though the moment of its formation cannot be determined, provided that the conduct of the parties is sufficient to show agreement. In order to determine whether there is sufficient evidence of the parties' intention to be bound by a contract, their conduct has to be interpreted in accordance with the criteria set forth in Article 4.1 *et seq.*

第二章

合同的订立与代理人的权限

第一节　合同的订立

第2.1.1条

（订立方式）

**合同可通过对要约的承诺或通过能充分表明
合意的当事人各方的行为而订立。**

注释：

1. 要约和承诺

《通则》的基本观点是当事人的合意自身足以构成合同（见第
3.1.2条）。要约和承诺的概念传统上用于确定当事人间的协议是否已
经达成以及何时达成。正如本条和本章所表明的，《通则》保留这些概
念作为必要的分析工具。

2. 能充分表明合意的行为

在商业实践中，特别是在涉及复杂交易时，合同通常是经过长期
谈判达成的，在这一过程中并没有一个可识别的要约和承诺的顺序。
这种情况下，很难断定缔约合意是否已经达成以及何时达成。根据本
条的规定，即便不能确定订立的时间，只要当事人的行为足以表明合
意，合同也可成立。为了确定是否有足够的证据证明当事人愿意受合
同约束，当事人的行为必须根据第4.1条以下列明的标准去解释。

Illustration

1.   A and B enter into negotiations with a view to setting up a joint venture for the development of a new product. After prolonged negotiations without any formal offer or acceptance and with some minor points still to be settled, both parties begin to perform. When subsequently the parties fail to reach an agreement on these minor points, a court or arbitral tribunal may decide that a contract was nevertheless concluded since the parties had begun to perform, thereby showing their intention to be bound by a contract.

3. Automated contracting

The language of this Article is sufficiently broad to cover also cases of so-called automated contracting, i.e. where the parties agree to use a system capable of setting in motion self-executing electronic actions leading to the conclusion of a contract without the intervention of a natural person.

Illustration

2.   Automobile manufacturer A and components supplier B set up an electronic data interchange system which, as soon as A's stocks of components fall below a certain level, automatically generates orders for the components and executes such orders. The fact that A and B have agreed on the operation of such a system makes the orders and performances binding on A and B, even though they have been generated without the personal intervention of A and B.

ARTICLE 2.1.2
(Definition of offer)

A proposal for concluding a contract constitutes an offer if it is sufficiently definite and indicates the intention of the offeror to be bound in case of acceptance.

COMMENT

In defining an offer as distinguished from other communications which a party may make in the course of negotiations initiated with a view to concluding a contract, this Article lays down two requirements: the proposal must (i) be sufficiently definite to permit the conclusion of the contract by mere acceptance and (ii) indicate the intention of the offeror to be bound in case of acceptance.

示例：

1. A 和 B 举行谈判，拟建立一合资企业从事一种新产品的开发。经过没有任何正式要约或承诺的长期谈判后，在一些次要问题尚待确定的情况下，双方当事人开始履行。随后当双方当事人未能就这些次要问题达成合意时，法院或仲裁庭仍可以裁定合同成立，因为双方当事人已开始履行合同，以此表明了他们愿受合同约束的意向。

3. 自动缔约

本条的用语足以涵盖所谓的自动缔约情况，即当事人约定使用一种系统，它可以在没有自然人参与的情况下，触发导致合同成立的自动执行的电子操作。

示例：

2. 汽车生产商 A 和零部件供应商 B 建立了一个电子数据交换系统，该系统在 A 的零部件库存低于某个水平时，自动地生成零部件订单并执行此类订单。A 与 B 已经就这一系统的运作达成合意的事实使得订单和履行对 A 和 B 均具有拘束力，尽管订单和履行是在没有 A 和 B 的个人干预下生成的。

第2.1.2条

（要约的定义）

一项订立合同的建议,如果十分确定,并表明要约人在得到承诺时受其约束的意思,即构成一项要约。

注释：

为定义"要约"，以使其与当事人为订立合同而启动的谈判过程中可能表达的其他意思相区别，本条规定了两个要件，即提议必须：（1）足够明确表明一经承诺合同即可成立；（2）表明在得到承诺时要约人愿受其约束的意思。

1. Definiteness of an offer

Since a contract is concluded by the mere acceptance of an offer, the terms of the future agreement must already be indicated with sufficient definiteness in the offer itself. Whether a given offer meets this requirement cannot be established in general terms. Even essential terms, such as the precise description of the goods or the services to be delivered or rendered, the price to be paid for them, the time or place of performance, etc., may be left undetermined in the offer without necessarily rendering it insufficiently definite: all depends on whether or not the offeror by making the offer, and the offeree by accepting it, intend to enter into a binding agreement, and whether or not the missing terms can be determined by interpreting the language of the agreement in accordance with Articles 4.1 *et seq.,* or supplied in accordance with Articles 4.8 or 5.1.2. Indefiniteness may moreover be overcome by reference to practices established between the parties or to usages (see Article 1.9), as well as by reference to specific provisions to be found elsewhere in the Principles (e.g. Articles 5.1.6 (*Determination of quality of performance*), 5.1.7 (*Price determination*), 6.1.1 (*Time of performance*), 6.1.6 (*Place of performance*) and 6.1.10 (*Currency not expressed*)).

Illustration

1.   A has for a number of years annually renewed a contract with B for technical assistance for A's computers. A opens a second office with the same type of computers and asks B to provide assistance also for the new computers. B accepts and, despite the fact that A's offer does not specify all the terms of the agreement, a contract has been concluded since the missing terms can be taken from the previous contracts as constituting a practice established between the parties.

2. Intention to be bound

The second criterion for determining whether a party makes an offer for the conclusion of a contract, or merely opens negotiations, is that party's intention to be bound in the event of acceptance. Since such an intention will rarely be declared expressly, it often has to be inferred from the circumstances of each individual case. The way in which the proponent presents the proposal (e.g. by expressly defining it as

1. 要约的确定性

因为只需承诺要约，合同即可成立，因此要约自身对于将来即将达成的条款必须已经有足够明确的表述。一项具体的要约是否满足这一要件不能通过一般性的条款来确定。即使要约未确定实质性条款，如对所交付的商品或所提供的服务的准确描述、所支付的价格、履约时间或地点等，也不必然导致要约缺乏足够的确定性。一切都取决于要约人通过发出要约、受要约人通过作出承诺，是否有意达成一个有约束力的协议，以及缺少的条款是否能够根据《通则》第 4.1 条以下的规定解释协议的语言来确定，或根据第 4.8 条或第 5.1.2 条的规定进行补充。此外，要约的不确定性可以通过以下方式解决：参考当事人之间业已建立的交易习惯或参考惯例（见第 1.9 条），或者参考《通则》的其他具体规定（例如：第 5.1.6 条 "履行质量的确定"，第 5.1.7 条 "价格的确定"，第 6.1.1 条 "履行时间"，第 6.1.6 条 "履行地"，第 6.1.10 条 "未定明货币"）。

示例：

　　1. A 已连续多年续展与 B 的合同，由 B 为 A 的计算机提供技术服务。A 又设立了一个办公室，用的是同一型号的计算机，要求 B 为其新计算机也提供服务。B 做出了承诺，尽管 A 的要约并没有规定协议的所有条款，但因为空缺的条款可以从已经成为该当事人之间习惯做法的先前的合同中沿用，因此该合同成立。

2. 受约束的意思

确定一方当事人是发出了订立合同的要约还是仅仅开始谈判的第二条标准是：一经承诺当事人即受其约束的意思。因为这种意思很少明确表明，通常必须根据个案的具体情况去推断。提议人提出建议的方式（例如明确指明它为 "要约" 或仅作为 "意向声明"）对于查明

an "offer" or as a mere "declaration of intent") provides a first, although not a decisive, indication of possible intention. Of even greater importance are the content and the addressees of the proposal. Generally speaking, the more detailed and definite the proposal, the more likely it is to be construed as an offer. A proposal addressed to one or more specific persons is more likely to be intended as an offer than is one made to the public at large.

Illustrations

    2.   After lengthy negotiations the Executive Directors of two companies, A and B, lay down the conditions on which B will acquire 51% of the shares in company C which is totally owned by A. The "Memorandum of Agreement" signed by the negotiators contains a final clause stating that the agreement is not binding until approved by A's Board of Directors. There is no contract before such approval is given by them.

    3.   A, a Government agency, advertises for bids for the setting up of a new telephone network. Such an advertisement is merely an invitation to submit offers, which may or may not be accepted by A. If, however, the advertisement indicates in detail the technical specifications of the project and states that the contract will be awarded to the lowest bid conforming to the specifications, it may amount to an offer with the consequence that the contract will be concluded once the lowest bid has been identified.

A proposal may contain all the essential terms of the contract but nevertheless not bind the proponent in case of acceptance if it makes the conclusion of the contract dependent on the reaching of agreement on some minor points left open in the proposal (see Article 2.1.13).

ARTICLE 2.1.3
(Withdrawal of offer)

(1) An offer becomes effective when it reaches the offeree.

(2) An offer, even if it is irrevocable, may be withdrawn if the withdrawal reaches the offeree before or at the same time as the offer.

可能的意思提供了一个初步的但不是决定性的指示。更为重要的是建议的内容和接收人。一般而言，建议越详细和明确，越有可能被解释为一项要约。向一个或多个特定人发出的建议比向全体公众发出的建议，更可能意在作为一项要约。

示例：

2. 经过长时间的谈判，A 和 B 两家公司的执行董事就 B 公司收购 A 公司的全资子公司 C 的 51% 的股份的条件作出约定。由谈判人员签署的"协议备忘录"中有一条最终条款，规定该协议只有在得到 A 公司董事会批准后方具拘束力。因此，在 A 公司董事会批准之前合同不成立。

3. A 是一家政府机构，为建立一个新的电话网络刊登招标公告。这种公告仅仅是要约邀请，A 可以接受也可以不接受据此提交的要约。然而，如果该公告中详细说明了这个项目的技术规格，并表示合同将由符合技术规格的、报价最低的投标人获得，则该公告构成要约，其结果是，一旦查明报价最低的投标，合同即告成立。

一项建议可能包含了合同的所有实质条款，但如果它表明合同的订立以当事人就建议中未确定的一些次要问题达成一致为条件，那么即使得到承诺，该建议也不能约束提议人（参见第2.1.13条）。

第2.1.3条

（要约的撤回）

（1）要约于到达受要约人时生效。

（2）一项要约即使不可撤销，仍可撤回，但撤回通知要在要约到达受要约人之前，或与要约同时到达受要约人。

COMMENT

1. When an offer becomes effective

Paragraph (1) of this Article, which is taken literally from Article 15 CISG, provides that an offer becomes effective when it reaches the offeree (see Article 1.10(2)). For the definition of "reaches" see Article 1.10(3). The time at which the offer becomes effective is of importance as it indicates the precise moment as from which the offeree can accept it, thus definitely binding the offeror to the proposed contract.

2. Withdrawal of an offer

There is, however, a further reason why it may in practice be important to determine the moment at which the offer becomes effective. Indeed, up to that time the offeror is free to change its mind and to decide not to enter into the agreement at all, or to replace the original offer by a new one, irrespective of whether or not the original offer was intended to be irrevocable. The only condition is that the offeree is informed of the offeror's altered intentions before or at the same time as the offeree is informed of the original offer. By expressly stating this, paragraph (2) of this Article makes it clear that a distinction is to be drawn between "withdrawal" and "revocation" of an offer: before an offer becomes effective it can always be withdrawn whereas the question of whether or not it may be revoked (see Article 2.1.4) arises only after that moment.

ARTICLE 2.1.4
(Revocation of offer)

(1) Until a contract is concluded an offer may be revoked if the revocation reaches the offeree before it has dispatched an acceptance.

(2) However, an offer cannot be revoked

(a) if it indicates, whether by stating a fixed time for acceptance or otherwise, that it is irrevocable; or

(b) if it was reasonable for the offeree to rely on the offer as being irrevocable and the offeree has acted in reliance on the offer.

注释：

1. 要约生效的时间

本条第(1)款逐字引用了《联合国国际货物销售合同公约》第15条，规定要约于到达受要约人时生效（参见第1.10条第(2)款）。"到达"的定义参见第1.10条第(3)款。要约生效的时间非常重要，因为它指出受要约人能够承诺要约的准确时间，从而明确地使要约人受拟议合同的约束。

2. 要约的撤回

然而，在实践中确定要约生效的时间之所以重要，还有进一步的理由。事实上，在要约生效前，要约人可以自由地改变想法，决定根本不达成协议，或是以一个新的要约代替原要约，而不论原要约是否是不可撤销的。唯一的条件是，要约人改变后的意思必须在原要约送达受要约人之前或同时通知受要约人。通过明确表述这一点，本条第(2)款同时表明要区分要约的"撤回"和"撤销"：要约在其生效前均可撤回，而要约能否撤销的问题只发生在其生效以后（见第2.1.4条）。

第2.1.4条

（要约的撤销）

（1）在合同订立之前，要约得予撤销，如果撤销通知在受要约人发出承诺之前到达受要约人。

（2）但是，在下列情况下，要约不得撤销：

（a）要约写明承诺期限，或以其他方式表明要约是不可撤销的；或

（b）受要约人有理由信赖该项要约是不可撤销的，且受要约人已依赖该要约行事。

COMMENT

The problem of whether an offer is or is not revocable is traditionally one of the most controversial issues in the context of the formation of contracts. Since there is no prospect of reconciling the two basic approaches followed in this respect by the different legal systems, i.e. the common law approach according to which an offer is as a rule revocable, and the opposite approach followed by the majority of civil law systems, the only remaining possibility is that of selecting one approach as the main rule, and the other as the exception.

1. Offers as a rule revocable

Paragraph (1) of this Article, which is taken literally from Article 16 CISG, states that until the contract is concluded offers are as a rule revocable. The same paragraph, however, subjects the revocation of an offer to the condition that it reach the offeree before the offeree has dispatched an acceptance. It is thus only when the offeree orally accepts the offer, or when the offeree may indicate assent by performing an act without giving notice to the offeror (see Article 2.1.6(3)), that the offeror's right to revoke the offer continues to exist until such time as the contract is concluded. Where, however, the offer is accepted by a written indication of assent, so that the contract is concluded when the acceptance reaches the offeror (see Article 2.1.6(2)), the offeror's right to revoke the offer terminates earlier, i.e. when the offeree dispatches the acceptance. Such a solution may cause some inconvenience to the offeror who will not always know whether or not it is still possible to revoke the offer. It is, however, justified in view of the legitimate interest of the offeree in the time available for revocation being shortened.

As to the determination of the time of dispatch, see Article 2.1.8 and the Comment thereto.

2. Irrevocable offers

Paragraph (2) provides for two important exceptions to the general rule as to the revocability of offers: (i) where the offer contains an indication that it is irrevocable and (ii) where the offeree, having other good reasons to treat the offer as being irrevocable, has acted in reliance on that offer.

a. *Indication of irrevocability contained in the offer*

The indication that the offer is irrevocable may be made in different ways, the most direct and clear of which is an express statement to that

注释：

要约可否撤销一直是有关合同订立争议最多的一个问题。要协调不同法系在这个问题上的两种基本观点是不太可能的。普通法认为原则上要约可以撤销，而大陆法的多数国家持相反的观点。因此，唯一可能的解决方法是选择一种观点作为主要规则，以另一种为例外。

1. 要约原则上可以撤销

本条第(1)款逐字引用了《联合国国际货物销售合同公约》第 16 条，规定在合同订立之前要约原则上可撤销。但该款也规定了撤销的条件，即撤销要约的通知必须于受要约人发出承诺前送达受要约人。因此，只有在当事人口头承诺要约或是通过某种行为表示同意而无须通知要约人（见第 2.1.6 条第(3)款），要约人撤销要约的权利才可一直持续到合同订立之时。而要约以书面表示同意的方式承诺时，承诺到达要约人时合同才订立（见第 2.1.6 条第(2)款），要约人撤销要约的权利将提前到受要约人发出承诺时终止。此类解决方式可能造成要约人的某些不便，因为要约人并不总是知道要约是否仍然可以撤销。但是，从受要约人的合法利益角度看，这是公平的，因为可用于撤销要约的时间缩短了。

关于受要约人发出承诺时间的确定，参见第 2.1.8 条以及相关注释。

2. 不可撤销的要约

第(2)款对要约可撤销这一基本规则规定了两个重要例外：（1）要约中含有不可撤销的表示；（2）受要约人有充分的理由认为该要约不可撤销，并且已依赖该要约行事。

a. 要约所包含的不可撤销的表示

不可撤销的意思表示可以用不同的方式做出，最直接和最清楚的

effect by the offeror (e.g. "This is a firm offer"; "We shall stand by our offer until we receive your answer"). It may, however, simply be inferred from other statements by, or conduct of, the offeror. The indication of a fixed time for acceptance may, but need not necessarily, amount by itself to an implicit indication of an irrevocable offer. The answer must be found in each case through a proper interpretation of the terms of the offer in accordance with the various criteria laid down in the general rules on interpretation in Chapter 4. In general, if the offeror operates within a legal system where the fixing of a time for acceptance is considered to indicate irrevocability, it may be assumed that by specifying such a fixed time the offeror intends to make an irrevocable offer. If, on the other hand, the offeror operates in a legal system where the fixing of a time for acceptance is not sufficient to indicate irrevocability, the offeror will not normally have had such an intention.

Illustrations

1.   A, a travel agency, informs a client of a cruise in its brochure for the coming New Year holidays. It urges the client to book within the next three days, adding that after that date there will probably be no more places left. This statement by itself will not be considered to indicate that the offer is irrevocable during the first three days.

2.   A invites B to submit a written offer of the terms on which B is prepared to construct a building. B presents a detailed offer containing the statement "Price and other conditions are not good after 1 September". If A and B operate within a legal system where such a statement is considered to be an indication that the offer is irrevocable until the specified date, B can expect the offer to be understood as being irrevocable. The same may not necessarily be the case if the offeree operates in a legal system where such a statement is not considered as being sufficient to indicate that the offer is irrevocable.

b. *Reliance by offeree on irrevocability of offer*

The second exception to the general rule regarding the revocability of offers, i.e. where "it was reasonable for the offeree to rely on the offer as being irrevocable", and "the offeree has acted in reliance on the offer", is an application of the general principle prohibiting inconsistent behaviour laid down in Article 1.8. The reasonable reliance of the offeree may have been induced either by the conduct of the offeror, or by the nature of the offer itself (e.g. an offer whose acceptance

方式是由要约人对其效力做出一个明确声明（例："此要约为实盘要约"；"收到贵方回复前我方信守要约"）。但也可从要约人的其他表示或行为中作出此种推断。表明确定的承诺时间本身可以（但并非必然）构成要约不可撤销的默示表示。这应结合个案，根据第四章关于解释的一般规则所确立的各种标准对要约的条款进行适当的解释，进而作出判断。一般而言，如果依要约人经营所在的法律体系，将确定承诺时间视为要约不可撤销的表示，则可以推定要约人规定这种确定的时限意在使要约不可撤销。而如果依要约人经营所在的法律体系，确定承诺时间不足以表示要约不可撤销，则要约人通常并没有使要约不可撤销的意思。

示例：

　　1. A是一家旅行社。A在其发送的小册子中通知游客将组织新年度假旅游，并敦促游客在通知后三天内预订，否则过期可能会没有剩余的名额。这个声明本身不应视为在这三天内该要约不可撤销的表示。

　　2. A请B就B计划建设一栋大楼的条款提交一份书面要约。B提交了一份详细的要约，其中含有这样的声明："9月1日后价格和其他条件将失效。"如果在A和B经营地所在的法律体系下，这种声明被视为该要约在这个规定的日期前不可撤销的表示，那么B可以期望该要约被理解为不可撤销的要约。如果在受要约人经营地所在的法律体系，这种声明被视为不足以表示该要约不可撤销，则结果就未必如此。

b. 受要约人对要约不可撤销的信赖

对要约可撤销这一基本规则的第二种例外情况是："受要约人有理由信赖该项要约是不可撤销的"，且"受要约人已依赖该要约行事"。这一例外是第1.8条规定的禁止不一致行为原则的体现。受要约人的合理信赖既可源于要约人的行为，也可源于要约本身的性质（例如，对某一项要约承诺前需要受要约人进行广泛的、费用昂贵的调查，或

requires extensive and costly investigation on the part of the offeree or an offer made with a view to permitting the offeree in turn to make an offer to a third party). The acts which the offeree must have performed in reliance on the offer may consist in making preparations for production, buying or hiring of materials or equipment, incurring expenses etc., provided that such acts could have been regarded as normal in the trade concerned, or should otherwise have been foreseen by, or known to, the offeror.

Illustrations

3.   A, an antique dealer, asks B to restore ten paintings on condition that the work is completed within three months and that the price does not exceed a specific amount. B informs A that, so as to know whether or not to accept the offer, B finds it necessary to begin work on one painting and will then give a definite answer within five days. A agrees, and B, relying on A's offer, begins work immediately. A may not revoke the offer during those five days.

4.   A seeks an offer from B for incorporation in a bid on a project to be assigned within a stated time. B submits an offer on which A relies when calculating the price of the bid. Before the expiry of the date, but after A has made the bid, B informs A that it is no longer willing to stand by its offer. B's offer is irrevocable until the stated date since in making its bid A relied on B's offer.

ARTICLE **2.1.5**
(Rejection of offer)

An offer is terminated when a rejection reaches the offeror.

COMMENT

1. Rejection may be express or implied

An offer may be rejected either expressly or impliedly. A frequent case of implied rejection is a reply to an offer which purports to be an acceptance but which contains additions, limitations or other modifications (see Article 2.1.11(1)).

发出某一要约意在使受要约人进而可以向第三方发出要约)。受要约人依此信赖所做的行为，可以是为生产所做的准备、购买或租用材料或设备、发生费用，等等。只要这些行为在有关的贸易中被视为正常的，或者应是要约人所能预见或知悉的行为。

示例：

3. A是一个古董商。A要求B在三个月内完成修复十幅画的工作，价格不超过一具体金额。B告知A，为了决定是否承诺该要约，B认为有必要先对一幅画进行修复，然后在五天内给出一个明确的答复。A同意。基于对A要约的信赖，B马上开始工作。A在这五天内不得撤销要约。

4. A请B就合作参与一个在规定期限内定标的项目提出要约。对于B提出的要约，A在计算投标价格时予以了信赖。在规定的时限届满前且A已投标后，B通知A不愿意再遵守其要约。因为A在投标时信赖了B的要约，因此该要约在规定的时限届满前是不可撤销的。

第2.1.5条

(要约的拒绝)

要约于拒绝通知到达要约人时终止。

注释：

1. 拒绝可以是明示的也可以是默示的

对一项要约既可以明示拒绝也可以默示拒绝。默示拒绝的一种常见情况是，对要约的答复，声称是承诺，但却对要约做了添加、限制或其他修改（参见第2.1.11条第(1)款）。

In the absence of an express rejection the statements by, or the conduct of, the offeree must in any event be such as to justify the belief of the offeror that the offeree has no intention of accepting the offer. A reply on the part of the offeree which merely asks whether there would be a possible alternative (e.g. "Is there any chance of the price being reduced?", or "Could you deliver a couple of days earlier?") would not normally be sufficient to justify such a conclusion.

It should be recalled that a rejection will bring about the termination of any offer, irrespective of whether it was revocable or irrevocable according to Article 2.1.4.

Illustration

A receives an offer from B stating that the offer will be firm for two weeks. A replies by return of post asking for partially different conditions which B does not accept. A may no longer accept the original offer even though there are still several days left before the expiry of the two week period since by making a counter-offer A implicitly rejected the original offer.

2. Rejection only one cause of termination of an offer

Rejection by the offeree is only one of the causes of termination of an offer. Other causes are dealt with in Articles 2.1.4(1) and 2.1.7.

ARTICLE 2.1.6
(Mode of acceptance)

(1) A statement made by or other conduct of the offeree indicating assent to an offer is an acceptance. Silence or inactivity does not in itself amount to acceptance.

(2) An acceptance of an offer becomes effective when the indication of assent reaches the offeror.

(3) However, if, by virtue of the offer or as a result of practices which the parties have established between themselves or of usage, the offeree may indicate assent by performing an act without notice to the offeror, the acceptance is effective when the act is performed.

在没有明确拒绝的情况下，受要约人的陈述或行为，无论如何必须能使要约人确信受要约人无意承诺该要约时才构成默示拒绝。如果受要约人的答复仅仅是询问要约的条款是否有选择余地（如"价格有没有降低的可能"或"能否提前几天交货"），该答复通常不足以使要约人合理地得出要约被拒绝的结论。

需要强调的是，拒绝将使任何要约归于终止，不论根据第 2.1.4 条该要约是可撤销的还是不可撤销的。

示例：

A 收到 B 的要约，其中规定该要约两周内是不可撤销的。A 通过邮件回复提出了部分不同的条件，对此 B 不予接受。尽管离期限届满还有几天时间，A 也不能再承诺原要约，因为通过发出反要约，A 默示地拒绝了原要约。

2. 拒绝仅是要约终止的原因之一

受要约人的拒绝仅是要约终止的原因之一，其他原因规定在第 2.1.4 条第(1)款和第 2.1.7 条中。

第 2.1.6 条

（承诺的方式）

（1）受要约人做出的表示同意要约的声明或其他行为构成承诺。缄默或不行为本身不构成承诺。

（2）对一项要约的承诺于同意的表示到达要约人时生效。

（3）但是，如果根据要约本身，或依照当事人之间建立的习惯做法，或依照惯例，受要约人可以通过做出某种行为来表示同意，而无须向要约人发出通知，则承诺于做出该行为时生效。

COMMENT

1. Indication of assent to an offer

For there to be an acceptance the offeree must in one way or another indicate "assent" to the offer. The mere acknowledgement of receipt of the offer, or an expression of interest in it, is not sufficient. Furthermore, the assent must be unconditional, i.e. it cannot be made dependent on some further step to be taken by either the offeror (e.g. "Our acceptance is subject to your final approval") or the offeree (e.g. "We hereby accept the terms of the contract as set forth in your Memorandum and undertake to submit the contract to our Board for approval within the next two weeks"). Finally, the purported acceptance must contain no variation of the terms of the offer or at least none which materially alters them (see Article 2.1.11).

2. Acceptance by conduct

Provided that the offer does not impose any particular mode of acceptance, the indication of assent may either be made by an express statement or be inferred from the conduct of the offeree. Paragraph (1) of this Article does not specify the form such conduct should assume: most often it will consist in acts of performance, such as the payment of an advance on the price, the shipment of goods or the beginning of work at the site, etc.

3. Silence or inactivity

By stating that "[s]ilence or inactivity does not in itself amount to acceptance", paragraph (1) makes it clear that as a rule mere silence or inactivity on the part of the offeree does not allow the inference that the offeree assents to the offer. The situation is different if the parties themselves agree that silence shall amount to acceptance, or if there exists a course of dealing or usage to that effect. In no event, however, is it sufficient for the offeror to state unilaterally in its offer that the offer will be deemed to have been accepted in the absence of any reply from the offeree. Since it is the offeror who takes the initiative by proposing the conclusion of the contract, the offeree is free not only to accept or not to accept the offer, but also simply to ignore it.

Illustrations

1.   A requests B to set out the conditions for the renewal of a contract for the supply of wine, due to expire on 31 December. In its offer B includes a provision stating that "if we have not heard from you at the latest by the end of November, we will assume that you

注释：

1. 同意要约的意思表示

要做出承诺，受要约人必须以一定的方式向要约人表示对要约的"同意"。仅仅是承认已收到要约，或仅表示对要约有兴趣，这都不足以显示"同意"。进一步讲，这种同意必须是无条件的，它不能依赖于要约人的后继行为（如"我方的承诺需经你方最后批准"）或受要约方的后继行为（如"在此我方接受你方备忘录中规定的合同条款，并承诺在以后两周内将合同提请我方董事会批准"）。最后，所谓的"承诺"不得与要约的条款有差异，或至少不得对条款做实质性修改（见第2.1.11条）。

2. 以行为承诺

假若要约对承诺方式没有特定要求，同意的表示既可以明确的声明作出，也可由受要约人的行为来推断。本条第(1)款没有规定该种行为所采取的形式，但通常存在于履行行为中，诸如预付价款、装运货物或在工地上开始工作等。

3. 缄默或不行为

本条第(1)款规定"缄默或不行为本身不构成承诺"，这就明确了仅由受要约人的缄默或不行为，原则上不得推断受要约人同意要约。但如果双方当事人自己同意缄默构成要约，或是存在这样的交易过程或惯例，情况则不同。但在任何情况下，要约人在其要约中所作的如下单方面声明都不构成受要约人的承诺：如果受要约人未做答复，视为要约已接受。因为是要约人主动提议订立合同，所以受要约人对要约有承诺或不承诺的自由，也有不予理会的自由。

示例：

1. A和B之间的供酒合同将于12月31日到期，A要求B提出续展合同的条件。B在其要约中规定"最晚在11月底以前，如果我方未收到你方的答复，我方将推定你方同意按

have agreed to renew the contract on the conditions indicated above". A finds the proposed conditions totally unacceptable and does not even reply. The former contract expires on the fixed date without a new contract having been agreed between the parties.

2. Under a long-term agreement for the supply of wine B regularly met A's orders without expressly confirming its acceptance. On 15 November A orders a large stock for New Year. B does not reply, nor does it deliver at the requested time. B is in breach since, in accordance with the practice established between the parties, B's silence in regard to A's order amounts to an acceptance.

4. When acceptance becomes effective

According to paragraph (2), an acceptance becomes effective at the moment the indication of assent reaches the offeror (see Article 1.10(2)). For the definition of "reaches" see Article 1.10(3). The reason for the adoption of the "receipt" principle in preference to the "dispatch" principle is that the risk of transmission is better placed on the offeree than on the offeror, since it is the former who chooses the means of communication, who knows whether the chosen means of communication is subject to special risks or delay, and who is consequently best able to take measures to ensure that the acceptance reaches its destination.

As a rule, an acceptance by means of mere conduct likewise becomes effective only when notice thereof reaches the offeror. It should be noted, however, that special notice to this effect by the offeree will be necessary only in cases where the conduct will not of itself give notice of acceptance to the offeror within a reasonable period of time. In all other cases, e.g. where the conduct consists in the payment of the price, or the shipment of the goods by air or by some other rapid mode of transportation, the same effect may well be achieved simply by the bank or the carrier informing the offeror of the funds transfer or of the consignment of the goods.

An exception to the general rule of paragraph (2) is to be found in the cases envisaged in paragraph (3), i.e. where "by virtue of the offer or as a result of practices which the parties have established between themselves or of usage, the offeree may indicate assent by performing an act without notice to the offeror". In such cases the acceptance is effective at the moment the act is performed, irrespective of whether or not the offeror is promptly informed thereof.

上述条件续展合同"。A 发现 B 所提议的条件完全不可接受，因此未予答复。这样，当事人间未能达成新的合同，先前的合同到期失效。

2. 在一项长期供酒协议中，B 惯常不经明确作出承诺而直接履行 A 的订单。11 月 15 日，A 为准备新年向 B 订一大批货。B 既没有答复，也没有按要求的时间发货。B 构成违约，因为根据当事人间业已建立的交易习惯，B 的缄默视同对 A 的订单的承诺。

4. 承诺生效的时间

根据本条第(2)款，对要约的承诺在同意的表示到达要约人时生效（见第1.10条第(2)款）。"到达"的定义参见第1.10条第(3)款。本款采用"到达原则"而非"投邮原则"的理由在于：由受要约人承担传递风险比由要约人承担更合理，因为选择通信方式的人是受要约人，他知道该方式是否容易出现特别风险或延误，因此他最能够采取有效措施以确保承诺到达目的地。

原则上，仅以行为作出的承诺同样只在承诺的通知到达要约人时生效。但应指出的是，只有在这种行为本身无法在合理期间内告知要约人承诺已作出的情况下，受要约人才有必要发出告知承诺的特别通知。在所有的其他情况下，例如相关行为是支付价款，或以航空或其他快捷的运输方式发货，银行或承运人向要约人发出的转账通知或发货通知就足以构成有效的承诺通知。

第(3)款规定的情况是第(2)款一般规则的一种例外，即"根据要约本身，或依照当事人之间建立的习惯做法或依照惯例，受要约人可以通过做出某种行为来表示同意，而无须向要约人发出通知"。这种情况下，无论要约人是否得到了及时的通知，承诺均于行为做出时生效。

Illustrations

> 3.   A asks B to write a special program for the setting up of a data bank. Without giving A notice of acceptance, B begins to write the program and, after its completion, insists on payment in accordance with the terms set out in A's offer. B is not entitled to payment since B's purported acceptance of A's offer never became effective as B never notified A of it.

> 4.   The facts are the same as in Illustration 3, except that in the offer B is informed of A's absence for the following two weeks, and that if B intends to accept the offer B should begin writing the program immediately so as to save time. The contract is concluded once B begins to perform, even if B fails to inform A thereof either immediately or at a later stage.

This Article corresponds to paragraphs (1), (2) first part and (3) of Article 18 CISG.

ARTICLE 2.1.7
(Time of acceptance)

An offer must be accepted within the time the offeror has fixed or, if no time is fixed, within a reasonable time having regard to the circumstances, including the rapidity of the means of communication employed by the offeror. An oral offer must be accepted immediately unless the circumstances indicate otherwise.

COMMENT

With respect to the time within which an offer must be accepted, this Article, which corresponds to the second part of paragraph (2) of Article 18 CISG, distinguishes between written and oral offers.

As concerns written offers, all depends upon whether or not the offer indicated a specific time for acceptance: if it did, the offer must be accepted within that time, while in all other cases the indication of assent must reach the offeror "within a reasonable time having regard to the circumstances, including the rapidity of the means of communication employed by the offeror".

示例:

　3. 为建立一数据库，A 要求 B 编写一套专门的程序。在没有向 A 发出承诺通知的情况下，B 开始编写程序，并在完成后要求 A 根据要约中所开列的条件付款。B 无权要求付款，因为 B 从未将承诺事实通知 A，所以 B 对要约的所谓"承诺"没有生效。

　4. 事实与示例 3 相同，不同的是，A 在要约中告知 B。随后两周内 A 不在，如果 B 有意承诺该要约，为节省时间，应立即着手编写程序。一旦 B 开始工作，合同即告成立，即便 B 未将承诺立即通知 A 或在以后阶段通知 A。

本条与《联合国国际货物销售合同公约》第 18 条第(1)款、第(2)款的第一部分及第(3)款的内容一致。

第 2.1.7 条

(承诺的时间)

要约必须在要约人规定的时间内承诺，或者如果未规定时间，应在考虑到交易的具体情况，包括要约人所使用的通信方法的快捷程度，在一段合理的时间内作出承诺。对口头要约必须立即作出承诺，除非情况有相反的表示。

注释:

　关于承诺要约的时间，本条与《联合国国际货物销售合同公约》第 18 条第(2)款第二部分相一致，对口头要约和书面要约作了区分。

　书面要约的承诺时间，完全取决于要约是否规定了承诺的确定期限:如果规定了确定的期限，则必须在该期限内承诺要约。在其他情况下，承诺要约的表示必须在"考虑到交易的具体情况，包括要约人所使用的通信方法的快捷程度，在一段合理的时间内"送达要约人。

Illustrations

1.   A sends B an offer on Monday indicating that if B intends to accept, it must do so by Friday at the latest. B's acceptance reaches A on the Monday of the following week. A may reject B's acceptance as being too late.

2.   A sends B an offer on Monday morning by e-mail, urging B to reply "as soon as possible". Although on previous occasions A and B had already communicated by e-mail, B accepts A's offer by letter which reaches A on Thursday. B's acceptance is too late since under the circumstances an acceptance by a letter which reaches A three days after its e-mail was not made "as soon as possible".

Oral offers must be accepted immediately unless the circumstances indicate otherwise. An offer is to be considered oral not only when made in the presence of the offeree, but whenever the offeree can respond immediately. This is the case of an offer made over the phone or communicated electronically in real time.

It is important to note that the rules laid down in this Article also apply to situations where, in accordance with Article 2.1.6(3), the offeree may indicate assent by performing an act without notice to the offeror: in these cases it is the act of performance which has to be accomplished within the respective periods of time.

For the determination of the precise starting point of the period of time fixed by the offeror, see Article 2.1.8; as to the calculation of holidays falling within that period of time, see Article 1.12; as to cases of late acceptance and of delay in transmission, see Article 2.1.9.

ARTICLE 2.1.8
(Acceptance within a fixed period of time)

A period of acceptance fixed by the offeror begins to run from the time that the offer is dispatched. A time indicated in the offer is deemed to be the time of dispatch unless the circumstances indicate otherwise.

COMMENT

Whenever an offeror fixes a period of time for acceptance the question arises of when the period begins to run. According to this Article it begins to run from the moment the offer is dispatched, i.e.

示例：

1. A 在周一向 B 发出一要约，表示如果 B 意欲接受，必须最迟在周五承诺。B 的承诺在下周一到达 A。A 可以承诺太迟为由拒绝 B 的承诺。

2. A 在周一上午通过电子邮件向 B 发出一要约，要求 B "尽快"答复。虽然 A 与 B 之前曾用电子邮件联络过，但 B 这次却以书信的方式接受 A 的要约，该书信于周四到达 A。B 的承诺太迟了，因为在本案的情况下，以书信作出承诺比通过电子邮件作出承诺晚三天，并没有做到"尽快"。

口头要约必须立即承诺，除非情况另有表明。并非只有在受要约人面前提出的要约才被视为口头要约，受要约人可以立即承诺的要约均被视为口头要约。例如，通过电话作出的要约或通过电子系统实时发送的要约。

很重要的一点是，本条规定的规则也适用第 2.1.6 条第（3）款规定的情况，即受要约人可以通过做出某一行为来表示同意，而无须通知要约人；在这些情况下，履行行为必须在各自的期限内完成。

确定要约人所规定的期限的起算点的方法见第 2.1.8 条；计算该规定期限内节假日的方法见第 1.12 条；有关逾期承诺和传递迟延的情况见第 2.1.9 条。

第2.1.8条

（规定期限内的承诺）

要约人规定的承诺期限自要约发出时起算。
要约中显示的时间应被视为是要约发出的时间，
除非情况有相反的表示。

注释：

如果要约人规定了承诺期限，就会产生期间何时起算的问题。根据本条的规定,该期间自要约发出,即脱离要约人的控制范围时起算。

has left the sphere of control of the offeror. As to when this occurs there is a presumption that the time of dispatch is the time indicated in the offer. For instance, in the case of a letter, the date of despatch will be the date shown on the letter; in the case of an e-mail, it will be the time indicated as the sending time by the offeror's server; etc. However, the presumption may be rebutted if in a given case the circumstances indicate otherwise. Thus, if the date shown on a fax letter is prior to the sending date printed by the fax machine, the latter date should prevail. Likewise, if the date shown on a letter is later than the delivery date of the letter, it is clear that the latter was written in by mistake and should therefore be disregarded.

ARTICLE 2.1.9

(Late acceptance. Delay in transmission)

(1) A late acceptance is nevertheless effective as an acceptance if without undue delay the offeror so informs the offeree or gives notice to that effect.

(2) If a communication containing a late acceptance shows that it has been sent in such circumstances that if its transmission had been normal it would have reached the offeror in due time, the late acceptance is effective as an acceptance unless, without undue delay, the offeror informs the offeree that it considers the offer as having lapsed.

COMMENT

1. Late acceptance normally ineffective

According to the principle laid down in Article 2.1.7, for an acceptance to be effective it must reach the offeror within the time fixed by the latter or, if no time is fixed, within a reasonable time. This means that as a rule an acceptance which reaches the offeror thereafter is without effect and may be disregarded by the offeror.

至于何时为要约发出之时，要约中显示的时间推定为要约发出的时间。例如，以信件方式发出的，发出日期是显示在信件上的日期；以电子邮件方式发出的，要约人服务器显示的寄送时间等。但是，如果情况另有表明，则可以推翻这项推定。因此，如果传真文件上显示的日期早于传真机打印的发送时间，应当适用后一日期。同样，如果信件上显示的日期晚于信件寄送日期，很明显信件上较晚的日期是书写错误，应当不予理会。

第2.1.9条

（逾期承诺与传递迟延）

　　（1）逾期承诺仍应具有承诺的效力，但要约人应毫不迟延地告知受要约人该承诺具有效力，或向受要约人发出具此效力之通知。
　　（2）如果载有逾期承诺的信息表明它是在如果传递正常即能及时到达要约人的情况下发出的，则该逾期承诺仍具有承诺的效力，除非要约人毫不迟延地通知受要约人此要约已失效。

注释：

1. 逾期承诺通常无效

　　根据第2.1.7条规定的原则，承诺生效的时间条件是，承诺在要约人规定的时间内到达要约人，如未规定时间，则须在合理的时间内到达要约人。这就意味着，原则上，承诺逾期到达要约人则无效，要约人可不予理会。

2. Offeror may nevertheless "accept" late acceptance

Paragraph (1) of this Article, which corresponds to Article 21 CISG, states that the offeror may nevertheless consider a late acceptance as having arrived in time and thus render it effective, provided that the offeror "without undue delay [...] so informs the offeree or gives notice to that effect". If the offeror takes advantage of this possibility, the contract is to be considered as having been concluded as soon as the late acceptance reaches the offeror and not when the offeror informs the offeree of its intention to consider the late acceptance effective.

Illustration

> 1.   A indicates 31 March as the deadline for acceptance of its offer. B's acceptance reaches A on 3 April. A, who is still interested in the contract, intends to "accept" B's late acceptance, and immediately informs B of its intention. Notwithstanding the fact that this notice only reaches B on 5 April the contract is concluded on 3 April.

3. Acceptance late because of delay in transmission

As long as the acceptance is late because the offeree did not send it in time, it is natural to consider it as having no effect unless the offeror expressly indicates otherwise. The situation is different when the offeree has replied in time, but the acceptance reaches the offeror late because of an unexpected delay in transmission. In such a case the reliance of the offeree on the acceptance having arrived in time deserves protection, with the consequence that the late acceptance is considered to be effective unless the offeror objects without undue delay. The only condition required by paragraph (2) is that the communication containing the late acceptance show that it was sent in such circumstances that, had its transmission been normal, it would have reached the offeror in due time.

Illustrations

> 2.   The facts are the same as in Illustration 1, except that B, knowing that the normal time for transmission of letters by mail to A is three days, sends its letter of acceptance on 25 March. Owing to a strike of the postal service in A's country the letter, which shows the date of its mailing on the envelope, only arrives on 3 April. B's acceptance, though late, is nevertheless effective unless A objects without undue delay.

2. 要约人仍可"接受"逾期承诺

本条第(1)款的规定与《联合国国际货物销售合同公约》第 21 条一致，规定要约人仍可将逾期承诺的视为是及时到达的，从而使其成为有效承诺，条件是要约人"毫不迟延地告知受要约人该承诺具有效力或向受要约人发出具此效力之通知"。如果要约人接受逾期承诺，则合同被视为成立的时间是逾期承诺到达要约人时，而不是在要约人将其认为该逾期承诺有效的意思通知受要约人时。

示例：

1. A 指定 3 月 31 日为承诺其要约的最后期限。B 的承诺于 4 月 3 日到达 A，A 对该合同仍有兴趣，愿意"接受"B 的逾期承诺，并立即将此意思通知了 B。尽管该通知于 4 月 5 日到达 B，但合同于 4 月 3 日成立。

3. 传递迟延造成的逾期

只要承诺是因受要约人未及时发送而逾期，自然应认定其是无效的，除非要约人有明确相反的表示。但如受要约人已及时答复，只是因为预料之外的传递迟延才导致承诺逾期到达要约人，情况则不同。在这种情况下，受要约人对于承诺能够及时到达的信赖应该得到保护，因此逾期承诺视为有效，除非要约人毫不迟延地拒绝。本条第(2)款所要求的唯一条件是，载有逾期承诺的沟通材料表明如果传递正常，本来能够及时到达要约人。

示例：

2. 事实与示例 1 相同，不同的是 B 知道信件传递到 A 的正常时间是三天，B 于 3 月 25 日发出了附有承诺的信件。由于 A 国邮政部门罢工，信封上盖有邮寄日期的信件 4 月 3 日才到。B 的承诺虽然逾期，但仍有效，除非 A 毫不迟延地拒绝。

3.   The facts are the same as in Illustration 1, except that B, after receiving A's offer, accepts it on 30 March by e-mail. Due to technical problems at A's server, the e-mail reaches A only on 1 April. B's acceptance, though late, is nevertheless effective unless A objects without undue delay.

ARTICLE 2.1.10
(Withdrawal of acceptance)

An acceptance may be withdrawn if the withdrawal reaches the offeror before or at the same time as the acceptance would have become effective.

COMMENT

With respect to the withdrawal of an acceptance this Article lays down the same principle as that contained in Article 2.1.3 concerning the withdrawal of an offer, i.e. that the offeree may change its mind and withdraw the acceptance provided that the withdrawal reaches the offeror before or at the same time as the acceptance.

It should be noted that while the offeror is bound by the offer and may no longer change its mind once the offeree has dispatched the acceptance (see Article 2.1.4(1)), the offeree looses its freedom of choice only at a later stage, i.e. when the notice of acceptance reaches the offeror.

This Article corresponds to Article 22 CISG.

ARTICLE 2.1.11
(Modified acceptance)

(1) A reply to an offer which purports to be an acceptance but contains additions, limitations or other modifications is a rejection of the offer and constitutes a counter-offer.

3. 事实与示例 1 相同，不同的是 B 收到 A 的要约后，于 3 月 30 日通过电子邮件承诺了该要约。由于 A 服务器的技术问题，该电子邮件于 4 月 1 日才到达 A。B 的承诺虽然逾期，但仍有效，除非 A 毫不迟延地拒绝。

第 2. 1. 10 条

（承诺的撤回）

承诺可以撤回，但撤回通知要在承诺本应生效之前或同时送达要约人。

注释：

对于承诺的撤回，本条规定了与第 2. 1. 3 条 "要约的撤回" 相同的原则，即受要约人可以改变其想法并撤回承诺，只要撤回通知在承诺到达要约人之前或同时送达要约人。

应该指出的是，一旦受要约人发出承诺，要约人将受其要约的约束，且再也不得改变主意（参见第 2. 1. 4 条第（1）款），但受要约人之时在之后的阶段才失去选择的自由，即承诺通知到达要约人之时。

本条的规定与《联合国国际货物销售合同公约》第 22 条一致。

第 2. 1. 11 条

（变更的承诺）

（1） 对要约意在表示承诺但载有添加、限制或其他变更的答复，即为对要约的拒绝，并构成反要约。

(2) However, a reply to an offer which purports to be an acceptance but contains additional or different terms which do not materially alter the terms of the offer constitutes an acceptance, unless the offeror, without undue delay, objects to the discrepancy. If the offeror does not object, the terms of the contract are the terms of the offer with the modifications contained in the acceptance.

COMMENT

1. Acceptance with modifications normally to be considered a counter-offer

In commercial dealings it often happens that the offeree, while signifying to the offeror its intention to accept the offer ("acknowledgement of order"), nevertheless includes in its declaration terms additional to or different from those of the offer. Paragraph (1) of this Article provides that such a purported acceptance is as a rule to be considered a rejection of the offer and that it amounts to a counter-offer by the offeree, which the offeror may or may not accept either expressly or impliedly, e.g. by an act of performance.

2. Modifications which do not alter the nature of the acceptance

The principle according to which the acceptance must be the mirror image of the offer implies that even unimportant differences between the offer and the acceptance permit either party at a later stage to question the existence of the contract. In order to avoid such a result, which a party may well seek merely because market conditions have changed unfavourably, paragraph (2) provides for an exception to the general rule laid down in paragraph (1) by stating that if the additional or modified terms contained in the acceptance do not "materially" alter the terms of the offer, the contract is concluded with those modifycations unless the offeror objects without undue delay.

What amounts to a "material" modification cannot be determined in the abstract but will depend on the circumstances of each case. Additional or different terms relating to the price or mode of payment, place and time of performance of a non-monetary obligation, the extent of one party's liability to the other or the settlement of disputes, will normally, but need not necessarily, constitute a material modification

　　（2）但是，对要约意在表示承诺但载有添加或不同条件的答复，如果所载的添加或不同条件没有实质性地改变要约的条件，则除非要约人毫不迟延地表示拒绝这些不符，此答复仍构成承诺。如果要约人不做出拒绝，则合同的条款应以该要约的条款以及承诺所载有的变更为准。

注释：

1. 变更的承诺一般被视为反要约

　　在商事交易中常常出现这种情况，即受要约人向要约人表示有意承诺要约（"订单确认书"），但同时在其声明中对要约条款有所添加或是载有与要约条款不同的内容。本条第（1）款规定，原则上，这种所谓的承诺被视为对要约的拒绝，并构成受要约人的反要约，要约人对此可以明示或默示（比如履行行为）接受或不接受。

2. 未改变承诺性质的变更

　　承诺必须与要约完全一致，这一原则表明要约和承诺之间即便只存在不重要的差异，也允许任何一方当事人都可在以后的阶段对合同的成立提出质疑。为了避免一方当事人仅因市场情况出现不利变化就试图质疑合同是否成立，本条第（2）款对第（1）款的一般规则规定了一项例外，即如果承诺所载的添加或变更条款没有对要约做"实质性"的变更，则合同按变更后的内容成立，除非要约人毫不迟延地拒绝。

　　对于什么构成"实质性"变更，无法抽象确定，必须视个案的具体情况而定。如果添加或不同条款的内容涉及价格或支付方式、非金钱债务的履行地点和时间、一方当事人对对方当事人承担责任的限度或争议的解决方式等问题，则通常（但不是必然）构成对要约的实质

of the offer. An important factor to be taken into account in this respect is whether the additional or different terms are commonly used in the trade sector concerned and therefore do not come as a surprise to the offeror.

Illustrations

1.   A orders a machine from B to be tested on A's premises. In its acknowledgement of order B declares that it accepts the terms of the offer, but adds that it wishes to be present at the testing of the machine. The additional term is not a "material" modification of the offer and will therefore become part of the contract unless A objects without undue delay.

2.   The facts are the same as in Illustration 1, except that in its acknowledgement of order B adds an arbitration clause. Unless the circumstances indicate otherwise, such a clause amounts to a "material" modification of the terms of the offer, with the result that B's purported acceptance would constitute a counter-offer.

3.   A orders a stated quantity of wheat from B. In its acknowledgement of order B adds an arbitration clause which is standard practice in the commodity sector concerned. Since A cannot be surprised by such a clause, it is not a "material" modification of the terms of the offer and, unless A objects without undue delay, the arbitration clause becomes part of the contract.

ARTICLE 2.1.12
(Writings in confirmation)

If a writing which is sent within a reasonable time after the conclusion of the contract and which purports to be a confirmation of the contract contains additional or different terms, such terms become part of the contract, unless they materially alter the contract or the recipient, without undue delay, objects to the discrepancy.

COMMENT

1. "Writings in confirmation"

This Article deals with the situation where a contract has already been concluded either orally or by the exchange of written communications limited to the essential terms of the agreement, and

性变更。在这方面应予考虑的一个重要因素是，添加或不同条款在相关贸易领域中是否广泛使用，因而不出乎要约人的意料之外。

示例：

1. A 向 B 订购一台机器，并提出在 A 的工地上调试。在订单确认书中，B 声明接受要约的条款，但增加了 B 希望参加检验机器的条款。该添加条款不是对要约的"实质性"变更，因此它将作为合同内容的一部分，除非 A 毫不迟延地拒绝。

2. 事实与示例 1 相同，不同的是在订单确认书中，B 增加了仲裁条款。除非情况有相反的表示，这一条款构成了对要约的"实质性"变更，其结果是 B 的所谓承诺构成反要约。

3. A 向 B 订购一定数量的小麦。在订单确认书中，B 增加了一项仲裁条款，该条款是相关商品交易中的标准做法。因为 A 对这种条款不会感到意外，因此它不构成对要约的"实质性"变更。除非 A 毫不迟延地拒绝，该仲裁条款构成合同的一部分。

第 2.1.12 条

（书面确认）

在合同订立后一段合理时间内发出的、意在确认合同的书面文件，如果载有添加或不同的条款，除非这些添加或不同条款实质性地变更了合同，或者接收方毫不迟延地拒绝了这些不符，则这些条款应构成合同的一个组成部分。

注释：

1. "书面确认"

本条要解决的是这样一种情况：基于当事人对协议必要条款的口头协商或书面交流，合同已经成立，一方当事人随后给另一方发去一

one party subsequently sends the other a document intended simply to confirm what has already been agreed upon, but which in fact contains terms which are additional to or different from those previously agreed by the parties. In theory, this situation clearly differs from that envisaged in Article 2.1.11, where a contract has not yet been concluded and the modifying terms are contained in the offeree's purported acceptance. Yet, since in practice it may be very difficult if not impossible to distinguish between the two situations, this Article adopts with respect to modifying terms contained in a writing in confirmation the same solution as that envisaged in Article 2.1.11. In other words, just as for the modifications contained in an acknowledgement of order, it is provided that terms additional to or different from those previously agreed by the parties contained in a writing in confirmation become part of the contract, provided that they do not "materially" alter the agreement and that the recipient of the document does not object to them without undue delay.

It goes without saying that also in the context of writings in confirmation the question of which of the new terms "materially" alter the terms of the previous agreement can be answered definitely only in the light of the circumstances of each individual case. On the other hand, this Article clearly does not apply to cases where the party sending the writing in confirmation expressly invites the other party to return it duly counter-signed for acceptance. In such circumstances it is irrelevant whether the writing contains modifications, and if so whether or not these modifications are "material" since the writing must in any case be expressly accepted by the addressee if there is to be a contract.

Illustrations

1. A orders by telephone a machine from B, who accepts the order. The following day A receives a letter from B confirming the terms of their oral agreement but adding that B wishes to be present at the testing of the machine on A's premises. The additional term is not a "material" modification of the terms previously agreed between the parties and will therefore become part of the contract unless A objects without undue delay.

2. The facts are the same as in Illustration 1, except that the modification contained in B's writing in confirmation consists in the addition of an arbitration clause. Unless the circumstances indicate otherwise such a clause amounts to a "material" modification of the terms previously agreed between the parties with the result that it will not become part of the contract.

份文件，仅想以此确认先前约定的内容，但实际上其中含有添加条款或与当事人先前约定不一致的内容。理论上，这种情况与第2.1.11条所设定的情况显然不同，因为在后一种情况中合同还没有成立，变更条款包含在受要约人的所谓承诺中。但在实践中要区分这两种情况虽然并非不可能，但却很困难，因此本条对于书面确认文件中含有的变更条款采用了与第2.1.11条相同的解决方法。换句话说，正如对订单确认书中所载的变更条款所作的处理一样，书面确认文件中所含有的添加条款或与当事人先前商定不一致的条款，只要没有"实质性"地变更协议，且接收方没有毫不迟延地拒绝，则应成为合同的一部分。

不用说，涉及书面确认文件，哪些新条款"实质性"地变更了先前的约定这一问题，也只能结合个案具体情况才能作出确定的回答。另一方面，若发出书面确认文件的一方明确邀请另一方作出有效的承诺附签并退回发出方，则本条显然不适用。在这种情况下，书面确认文件是否含有变更以及变更是否是"实质性"的并不重要，因为无论如何，只有该书面确认文件必须得到接收方明确的承诺，合同才能成立。

示例：

1. A通过电话向B订购一台机器，B接受订单。第二天，A收到B一封信，确认他们的口头协议，并同时提出希望参加在A工地进行的机器检验。该增加条款未对当事人先前的协议构成"实质性"变更，因此构成合同的一部分，除非A毫不迟延地拒绝。

2. 事实与示例1相同，不同的是B的书面确认文件中增加了仲裁条款。除非有相反情况，该条款构成了对当事人先前协议的"实质性"变更，因此不构成合同的一部分。

3.   A orders by e-mail a stated quantity of wheat and B accepts immediately by e-mail. Later on the same day B sends a letter to A confirming the terms of their agreement but adding an arbitration clause which is standard practice in the commodity sector concerned. Since A cannot be surprised by such a clause, it is not a "material" modification of the terms previously agreed and, unless A objects without undue delay, the arbitration clause becomes part of the contract.

2. Writing in confirmation to be sent within a reasonable time after conclusion of the contract

The rule according to which silence on the part of the recipient amounts to acceptance of the content of the writing in confirmation, including any non-material modifications of the terms previously agreed, presupposes that the writing is sent "within a reasonable time after the conclusion of the contract". Any writing of this kind sent after a period of time which, in the circumstances, appears to be unreasonably long, loses any significance, and silence on the part of the recipient may therefore no longer be interpreted as acceptance of its content.

3. Invoices

For the purposes of this Article, the term "writing in confirmation" is to be understood in a broad sense, i.e. as covering also those cases where a party uses the invoice or another similar document relating to performance to specify the conditions of the contract concluded either orally or by informal correspondence, provided that such use is customary in the trade sector and/or country concerned.

ARTICLE 2.1.13
*(Conclusion of contract dependent on agreement on
specific matters or in a particular form)*

Where in the course of negotiations one of the parties insists that the contract is not concluded until there is agreement on specific matters or in a particular form, no contract is concluded before agreement is reached on those matters or in that form.

3. A 通过电子邮件订购一定数量的小麦，B 立即以电子邮件承诺。同一天的晚些时候，B 给 A 发了一封信件，确认他们已达成的条款，但 B 增加了一条仲裁条款，该条款是相关商品交易中的标准做法。因为 A 不会对这种条款感到意外，所以它不构成对先前协议的"实质性"变更，构成合同的一部分，除非 A 毫不迟延地拒绝。

2. 书面确认文件须在合同订立后的合理期限内发出

接收方的缄默构成对书面确认文件所载内容（包括对先前协议的非实质性变更）的接受。这一规则预设了一个前提，即该书面确认文件应"在合同订立后一段合理时间内"发出。任何这种书面文件，若是经过显然是不合理的长时间后才发出，就失去了任何意义，因此接收方的缄默不能解释为构成对其内容的接受。

3. 发票

为本条之目的，对"书面确认文件"一词应做广义的理解，也就是说，还应涵盖如下情况，即一方当事人使用发票或其他与履行相关的类似单据，对以口头方式或非正式沟通方式达成的合同之条款加以记载，只要这种做法在相关的贸易领域和/或相关的国家是习惯做法。

第 2. 1. 13 条

（合同订立取决于特定事项或特定形式达成协议）

在谈判过程中，凡一方当事人坚持合同的订立以对特定事项或以特定形式达成协议为条件的，则在对该等特定事项或以该等特定形式达成协议之前，合同不能订立。

COMMENT

1. Conclusion of contract dependent on agreement on specific matters

As a rule, a contract is concluded if the parties reach agreement on the terms which are essential to the type of transaction involved, while minor terms which the parties have not settled may subsequently be implied either in fact or by law (see Comment 1 on Article 2.1.2 and also Articles 4.8 and 5.1.2).

Illustration

    1.   A agrees with B on all the terms which are essential to their intended contract for the distribution of A's goods. When the question subsequently arises of who should bear the costs of the publicity campaign, neither party may claim that no contract has come into existence by reason of the silence of the contract on this point, as the missing term is not essential to the type of transaction in question and will be implied in fact or by law.

Parties may, however, in a given case consider specific matters to be of such importance that they do not intend to enter into a binding agreement unless these matters are settled in a satisfactory manner. If the parties, or one only of them, make such an intention explicit, the contract as such does not come into existence without agreement on those matters. By using the word "insists", this Article makes it clear that it is not sufficient for the parties to manifest their intention to this effect simply in passing, but that it must be done unequivocally.

Illustration

    2.   The facts are the same as in Illustration 1, except that during the negotiations B repeatedly declares that the question of who should bear the cost of the publicity campaign must be settled expressly. Notwithstanding their agreement on all the essential terms of the contract, no contract has come into existence between A and B since B had insisted that the conclusion of the contract was dependent on agreement regarding that specific term.

2. Conclusion of contract dependent on agreement in a particular form

In commercial practice, particularly when transactions of considerable complexity are involved, it is quite frequent that after prolonged negotiations the parties sign an informal document called

注释：

1. 合同的订立取决于对特定事项达成一致

原则上，如果当事人已就相关类型交易的主要条款达成了协议，合同即告成立，尚未确定的次要条款可在随后以事实上的默示或法律上的默示加以补充（参见第 2.1.2 条注释 1 以及第 4.8 条和第 5.1.2 条）。

示例：

> 1. A 和 B 拟就销售 A 的产品的事宜订立合同，并已就合同主要条款达成一致。当后来出现由谁来负担宣传活动费用的问题时，任何一方当事人都不得以合同没有这方面的规定为由主张合同未成立。因为该空缺条款对于所涉及的这类交易并不重要，可以以事实上的默示或法律上的默示加以补充。

然而，在特定情况下，当事人可认为特定事项非常重要，如果不能满意地解决这些事项，他们将无意达成有约束力的协议。如果当事人双方或一方明确表达了这种意思，在未就这些事项达成一致的情况下，合同将不能成立。通过使用"坚持"一词，本条明确了当事人若只是顺带地表达了这种意思并不足以构成本条要求的意思，这种表达必须是非常明确的。

示例：

> 2. 事实与示例 1 相同，不同的是，在谈判过程中 B 反复声明，必须明确解决应由谁承担公共宣传费用的问题。虽然他们对合同的所有主要条款达成了一致，但 A 与 B 之间的合同并未成立，因为 B 坚持合同的成立取决于对该特定条款达成一致。

2. 合同的订立取决于以特定形式达成的协议

在商业实践中，特别是涉及相当复杂的交易时，在长时间的谈判之后，当事人往往签订一份非正式文件，例如"初步协议"、"谅解备

"Preliminary Agreement", "Memorandum of Understanding", "Letter of Intent" or the like, containing the terms of the agreement so far reached, but at the same time state their intention to provide for the execution of a formal document at a later stage ("Subject to Contract", "Formal Agreement to follow"). In some cases the parties consider their contract as already being concluded and the execution of the formal document only as confirmation of the already complete agreement. If, however, both parties, or only one of them, make it clear that they do not intend to be bound unless the formal document has been drawn up, there will be no contract until that time even if the parties have agreed on all the relevant aspects of their transaction.

Illustrations

3. After prolonged negotiations A and B sign a "Memorandum of Understanding" containing the terms of an agreement for a joint venture for the exploration and exploitation of the continental shelf of country X. The parties agree that they will at a later stage draw up the agreement in formal documents to be signed and exchanged at a public ceremony. If the "Memorandum" already contains all the relevant terms of the agreement and the subsequent documents are intended merely to permit the agreement to be properly presented to the public, it may be taken that the contract was already concluded when the first written document was signed.

4. The facts are the same as in Illustration 3, except that the "Memorandum of Understanding" contains a clause such as "Not binding until final agreement is executed" or the like. Until the signing and the exchange of the formal documents there is no binding contract.

ARTICLE 2.1.14
(Contract with terms deliberately left open)

(1) If the parties intend to conclude a contract, the fact that they intentionally leave a term to be agreed upon in further negotiations or to be determined by a third person does not prevent a contract from coming into existence.

(2) The existence of the contract is not affected by the fact that subsequently

(a) the parties reach no agreement on the term; or

忘录"、"意向书"等，该文件记载了迄今为止已达成协议的条款。但当事人同时也声明他们打算在晚些时候签署一份正式文件（"须签订合同"，"按照正式协议"）。在有些情况下，当事人认为他们的合同已成立，签署正式文件只不过是对已达成的协议进行确认。然而，如果当事人双方或一方明确了签订正式文件之前不受约束的意思，则在此之前合同不成立，即使当事人已就交易的所有方面达成一致。

示例：

3. 经过长时间的谈判，A 和 B 签订了一份"谅解备忘录"，记载了双方为就勘探和开发 X 国的大陆架成立合营企业一事达成的协议条款，该"备忘录"记载了双方已达成的条款。双方约定将在晚些时候起草协议的正式文件，并在公开仪式上签字并交换。如果该"备忘录"已经包含了协议的所有相关条款，后续文件仅是为了使协议能以适当的方式公开，则可认为在签署第一份书面文件时合同即已成立。

4. 事实与示例 3 相同，不同的是"谅解备忘录"中包含诸如"签署最后协议前无拘束力"这样的条款。这种情况下，在签署和交换正式文件前，合同未成立。

第 2.1.14 条

（特意待定之合同条款）

（1）如果当事人各方意在订立一项合同，但却有意将一项条款留待进一步谈判商定或由第三人确定，则这一事实并不妨碍合同的成立。

（2）考虑到当事人各方的意思，如果在具体情况下存在一种可选择的方法合理地确定此条款，则合同的存在亦不受此后发生的下列情况的影响：

（a）当事人各方未就该条款达成协议；或

(b) the third person does not determine the term,

provided that there is an alternative means of rendering the term definite that is reasonable in the circumstances, having regard to the intention of the parties.

COMMENT

1. Contract with terms deliberately left open

A contract may be silent on one or more issues because the parties simply did not think of them during the negotiations. Provided that the parties have agreed on the terms essential to the type of transaction concerned, a contract will nonetheless have been concluded and the missing terms will be supplied on the basis of Articles 4.8 or 5.1.2 (see Comment 1 on Article 2.1.2). Quite different is the case dealt with in this Article: here the parties intentionally leave open one or more terms because they are unable or unwilling to determine them at the time of the conclusion of the contract, and refer for their determination to an agreement to be made by them at a later stage, or to a third person.

This latter situation, which is especially frequent in, although not confined to, long-term transactions, gives rise in essence to two problems: first, whether the fact that the parties have intentionally left terms open prevents a contract from coming into existence and second, if this is not the case, what will happen to the contract if the parties subsequently fail to reach agreement or the third person fails to make the determination.

2. Open terms not in themselves an impediment to valid conclusion of contract

Paragraph (1) states that if the parties intended to conclude a contract, the fact that they have intentionally left a term to be agreed upon in further negotiations or to be determined by a third person does not prevent a contract from coming into existence.

In cases where it is not expressly stated, the parties' intention to conclude a contract notwithstanding the terms left open may be inferred from other circumstances, such as the non-essential character of the terms in question, the degree of definiteness of the agreement as a whole, the fact that the open terms relate to items which by their very nature can be determined only at a later stage, the fact that the agreement has already been partially executed, etc.

(b) 第三人未确定此条款。

注释：

1. 特意待定的合同条款

由于当事人在谈判中未考虑周全，合同可能对一个或多个事项未予明确。如果当事人已就该交易的主要条款达成了一致，合同即为成立，空缺条款将根据第 4.8 条或第 5.1.2 条予以补充（参见第 2.1.2 条注释 1）。本条所涉的情况非常不同：在此，当事人故意留下一个或多个条款待定，因为在合同订立时他们不能或不愿加以确定，而留待日后商定，或交由第三人确定。

后一种情况在长期交易中（但不限于）尤为常见。它会产生两个问题：第一，当事人故意留下一些条款待定是否妨碍合同成立？第二，如果不妨碍，若当事人日后未就待定条款达成一致或第三人未做出决定，对合同有何影响？

2. 待定条款本身不构成合同有效成立的障碍

第(1)款阐明如果当事人有意订立合同，特意将一项条款留待进一步谈判商定或由第三人确定，这一事实并不妨碍合同的成立。

在当事人订立合同的意图没有明确规定的情况下，尽管有待定条款，其仍可从其他情况来推断，例如待定条款的非重要性，整个协议的确定程度，待定条款所涉及的事项依其性质只能在以后决定的事实，协议已经部分履行的事实，等等。

Illustration

    1.   A, a shipping line, enters into a detailed agreement with B, a terminal operator, for the use of B's container terminal. The agreement fixes the minimum volume of containers to be discharged or loaded annually and the fees payable, while the fees for additional containers are left to be determined if and when the minimum volume is reached. Two months later A learns that B's competitor would offer better conditions and refuses to perform, claiming that the agreement with B never resulted in a binding contract because the question of the fees had not been settled. A is liable for non-performance because the detailed character of the agreement as well as the fact that both A and B began performance immediately indicate clearly that their intention was to enter into a binding agreement.

3. Failure of mechanism provided for by parties for determination of open terms

If the parties are unable to reach agreement on the open terms or the third person does not determine them, the question arises as to whether or not the contract comes to an end. According to paragraph (2) of this Article the existence of the contract is not affected "provided that there is an alternative means of rendering the term definite that is reasonable in the circumstances, having regard to the intention of the parties". A first alternative exists whenever the missing term can be supplied on the basis of Article 5.1.2; if the parties have deferred the determination of the missing term to a third person to be nominated by an instance such as the President of the Tribunal, or of the Chamber of Commerce, etc., it may also consist in the appointment of a new third person. The cases in which a given contract may be upheld by resorting to such alternative means will, however, be quite rare in practice. Few problems should arise as long as the term to be implemented is of minor importance. If, on the other hand, the term in question is essential to the type of transaction concerned, there must be clear evidence of the intention of the parties to uphold the contract: among the factors to be taken into account in this connection are whether the term in question relates to items which by their very nature can be determined only at a later stage, whether the agreement has already been partially executed, etc.

示例：

　　1. 海运承运人 A 与码头经营者 B 就使用 B 的集装箱码头达成了一份详细的协议。该协议确定了每年装卸集装箱的最小量和应支付的费用，超过最小容量后又增加的集装箱的费用待定。两个月后，A 了解到 B 的竞争对手可以提供更优惠的条件，因而拒绝履行协议，声称其与 B 的协议因为费用问题未解决根本不构成有约束力的合同。A 应对其不履行承担责任，因为协议的详实性质和 A、B 双方立即开始履行的事实清楚地表明，他们的意图是要订立一份有约束力的协议。

3. 当事人规定的确定待定条款的方式未能奏效

　　如果当事人未能就待定条款达成一致，或第三人未予确定，就产生了合同是否终止的问题。根据本条第(2)款，"考虑到当事人各方的意思，如果在具体情况下存在一种可选择的方法合理地确定此条款"，合同的存在将不受影响。如果空缺条款可根据第5.1.2条确定，这就是首要的可选择的方法；如果当事人约定交由第三人确定空缺条款，该第三人由诸如法庭庭长或商会主席来指定，则重新指定第三人也构成一种"可选择的方法"。但在实践中，一项合同要通过求助于这种可选择的方法得以维持效力的情况极为少见。只要待定的条款是次要的，就很少发生问题。另一方面，如果待定条款对这类相关交易至关重要，则必须有明确的证据证明当事人有维持合同效力的意思。此时所应考虑的相关因素包括，待定条款所涉及的事项依其性质是否只能在以后确定、协议是否已经部分履行，等等。

Illustration

2.   The facts are the same as in Illustration 1, except that when the minimum volume of containers to be loaded or unloaded is reached the parties fail to agree on the fees payable in respect of the additional containers. A stops performing, claiming that the contract has come to an end. A is liable for non-performance, since the fact that the parties have started performing without making future agreement on the missing term a condition for the continuation of their business relationship is sufficient evidence of their intention to uphold the contract even in the absence of such agreement. The fees for the additional containers will be determined according to the criteria laid down in Article 5.1.7.

ARTICLE 2.1.15
(Negotiations in bad faith)

(1) A party is free to negotiate and is not liable for failure to reach an agreement.

(2) However, a party who negotiates or breaks off negotiations in bad faith is liable for the losses caused to the other party.

(3) It is bad faith, in particular, for a party to enter into or continue negotiations when intending not to reach an agreement with the other party.

COMMENT

1. Freedom of negotiation

As a rule, parties are not only free to decide when and with whom to enter into negotiations with a view to concluding a contract, but also if, how and for how long to proceed with their efforts to reach an agreement. This follows from the basic principle of freedom of contract enunciated in Article 1.1, and is essential in order to guarantee healthy competition among business people engaged in international trade.

示例：

　　2. 事实与示例 1 相同，不同的是，当达到集装箱装卸最小量时，当事人未能就新增集装箱应付费用问题达成一致。A 停止履行，宣布合同终止。此时 A 应对其不履行承担责任，因为当事人已开始履行，且未将未来就缺漏条款达成一致作为继续业务关系的条件，这一事实足以证明当事人有即便无此协议合同仍然有效的意思，新增集装箱的应付费用根据第 5. 1. 7 条规定的标准确定。

第 2. 1. 15 条

（恶意谈判）

　　（1）当事人可自由进行谈判，并不因未达成协议而承担责任。
　　（2）但是，一方当事人如果恶意进行谈判或恶意终止谈判，则应对因此给另一方当事人所造成的损失承担责任。
　　（3）恶意，特别是指一方当事人在无意与对方达成协议的情况下，开始或继续进行谈判。

注释：

1. 谈判的自由

　　原则上，当事人为订立合同不仅可以自由决定何时谈判、与谁谈判，还可以自由决定如何进行谈判、以及为达成协议所付出的努力要持续多久。这条规则源于第 1. 1 条规定的"缔约自由"原则，对保证国际贸易经营者之间的健康竞争也至关重要。

2. Liability for negotiating in bad faith

A party's right freely to enter into negotiations and to decide on the terms to be negotiated is, however, not unlimited, and must not conflict with the principle of good faith and fair dealing laid down in Article 1.7. One particular instance of negotiating in bad faith which is expressly indicated in paragraph (3) of this Article is that where a party enters into negotiations or continues to negotiate without any intention of concluding an agreement with the other party. Other instances are where one party has deliberately or by negligence misled the other party as to the nature or terms of the proposed contract, either by actually misrepresenting facts, or by not disclosing facts which, given the nature of the parties and/or the contract, should have been disclosed. As to the duty of confidentiality, see Article 2.1.16.

A party's liability for negotiating in bad faith is limited to the losses caused to the other party (paragraph (2)). In other words, the aggrieved party may recover the expenses incurred in the negotiations and may also be compensated for the lost opportunity to conclude another contract with a third person (so-called reliance or negative interest), but may generally not recover the profit which would have resulted had the original contract been concluded (so-called expectation or positive interest).

Only if the parties have expressly agreed on a duty to negotiate in good faith, will all the remedies for breach of contract be available to them, including the remedy of the right to performance.

Illustrations

1. A learns of B's intention to sell its restaurant. A, who has no intention whatsoever of buying the restaurant, nevertheless enters into lengthy negotiations with B for the sole purpose of preventing B from selling the restaurant to C, a competitor of A's. A, who breaks off negotiations when C has bought another restaurant, is liable to B, who ultimately succeeds in selling the restaurant at a lower price than that offered by C, for the difference in price.

2. A, who is negotiating with B for the promotion of the purchase of military equipment by the armed forces of B's country, learns that B will not receive the necessary import licence from its own governmental authorities, a pre-requisite for permission to pay B's fees. A does not reveal this fact to B and finally concludes the contract, which, however, cannot be enforced by reason of the missing licences. A is liable to B for the costs incurred after A had learned of the impossibility of obtaining the required licence.

2. 恶意谈判的责任

然而，当事人自由地进行谈判、决定所谈判的条款，这一权利并非没有限制，它不得与第1.7条规定的"诚实信用和公平交易"原则相冲突。本条第(3)款明确指出了恶意谈判的一种具体情况，即一方当事人在无意与对方达成协议的情况下，开始或继续进行谈判。其他情况还包括，一方当事人故意或由于疏忽使对方当事人对所谈判合同的性质或条款产生误解，无论是通过实际上不陈述事实，还是通过隐瞒根据当事人和/或合同的性质应予披露的事实。有关保密义务参见第2.1.16条。

一方当事人对于恶意谈判所应承担的责任以给对方当事人造成的损失为限（第(2)款）。换句话说，受损害方可要求偿还谈判中发生的费用，还可要求就丧失与第三人订立合同的机会给予补偿（所谓的信赖利益或消极利益），但是一般不得要求赔偿若原合同订立可能产生的利益（所谓的预期利益或积极利益）。

只有当事人明确约定诚信谈判的义务，才有可能请求各种违约救济，包括实际履行的救济。

示例：

1. A了解到B有意转让餐馆。A根本没有打算购买该餐馆，但仅为阻止B将餐馆卖给竞争对手C，与B进行了长时间的谈判。C购买另一家餐馆之后，A中断了谈判，B最终以比C出价更低的价格将餐馆转让。A应向B偿付差价。

2. A为促进购买B所在国部队军事设备与B进行谈判，A了解到B将不能从其本国政府主管部门取得必要的进口许可证，而这是A获准向B付款的先决条件。A未向B披露这一事实，并最终与B签订了合同，但该合同由于B没有获得许可证不能执行。A应承担在其了解B不能取得许可证后B所发生的一切费用。

3.   A enters into lengthy negotiations for a bank loan from B's branch office. At the last minute the branch office discloses that it had no authority to sign and that its head office has decided not to approve the draft agreement. A, who could in the meantime have obtained the loan from another bank, is entitled to recover the expenses entailed by the negotiations and the profits it would have made during the delay before obtaining the loan from the other bank.

4.   Contractor A and supplier B enter into a pre-bid agreement whereby they undertake to negotiate in good faith for the supply of equipment in the event that A succeeds in becoming prime contractor for a major construction project. A is awarded the construction contract, but after preliminary contacts with B refuses to continue the negotiations. B may request enforcement of the duty to negotiate in good faith.

3. Liability for breaking off negotiations in bad faith

The right to break off negotiations also is subject to the principle of good faith and fair dealing. Once an offer has been made, it may be revoked only within the limits provided for in Article 2.1.4. Yet even before this stage is reached, or in a negotiation process with no ascertainable sequence of offer and acceptance, a party may no longer be free to break off negotiations abruptly and without justification. When such a point of no return is reached depends on the circumstances of the case, in particular the extent to which the other party, as a result of the conduct of the first party, had reason to rely on the positive outcome of the negotiations, and on the number of issues relating to the future contract on which the parties have already reached agreement.

Illustration

5.   A assures B of the grant of a franchise if B takes steps to gain experience and is prepared to invest USD 300,000. During the next two years B makes extensive preparations with a view to concluding the contract, always with A's assurance that B will be granted the franchise. When all is ready for the signing of the agreement, A informs B that the latter must invest a substantially higher sum. B, who refuses, is entitled to recover from A the expenses incurred with a view to the conclusion of the contract.

3. A 为从 B 的分支机构获得银行贷款与其进行了长时间的谈判。在最后时刻，该分支机构披露它无权签约，且其上级机构已经决定不批准该协议草案。在此期间，A 原本可以从另一家银行获得贷款。对于因谈判导致的费用支出，以及另从其他银行获得贷款前这段延误期内本可得到的收益，A 有权获得补偿。

4. 承包商 A 和供货商 B 达成了投标前协议，约定如果 A 成功成为一个重要建筑项目的主承包商，A 与 B 将就设备供应进行善意的谈判。A 获得了该建筑合同，但与 B 初步接触后拒绝继续谈判。B 可以请求执行诚信谈判的义务。

3. 恶意中断谈判的责任

中断谈判的权利同样应符合"诚实信用和公平交易"这一原则。要约一经做出，满足第 2.1.4 条规定的限制条件方可撤销。然而，即使在这一阶段之前或是在没有明确的要约和承诺顺序的谈判过程中，一方当事人也不得随意突然无正当理由地中断谈判。要确定从何时起要约或承诺不得撤销，得视具体情况而定，特别是一方当事人的行为导致另一方当事人在多大程度上有理由信赖谈判的积极结果，以及双方当事人已经达成一致的与拟订立合同有关事项的数量。

示例：

5. A 向 B 保证，如果 B 努力取得经验并准备投资 30 万美元，则向 B 授予专营许可。此后的两年间，B 为订立该合同做了大量的准备工作，且 A 一直保证会授予其专营许可。当订立协议的一切准备工作就绪时，A 通知 B 必须投资更多的金额。B 拒绝，并有权要求 A 补偿其为准备订立合同所发生的费用。

ARTICLE 2.1.16
(Duty of confidentiality)

Where information is given as confidential by one party in the course of negotiations, the other party is under a duty not to disclose that information or to use it improperly for its own purposes, whether or not a contract is subsequently concluded. Where appropriate, the remedy for breach of that duty may include compensation based on the benefit received by the other party.

COMMENT

1. Parties in general not under a duty of confidentiality

Just as there exists no general duty of disclosure, so parties, when entering into negotiations for the conclusion of a contract, are normally under no obligation to treat the information they have exchanged as confidential. In other words, since a party is normally free to decide which facts relevant to the transaction under negotiation to disclose, such information is as a rule to be considered non-confidential, i.e. information which the other party may either disclose to third persons or use for purposes of its own should no contract be concluded.

Illustration

1. A invites B and C, producers of air-conditioning systems, to submit offers for the installation of such a system. In their offers B and C also provide some technical details regarding the functioning of their respective systems, with a view to enhancing the merits of their products. A decides to reject B's offer and to continue negotiations only with C. A is free to use the information contained in B's offer in order to induce C to propose more favourable conditions.

2. Confidential information

A party may have an interest in certain information given to the other party not being divulged or used for purposes other than those for which it was given. As long as that party expressly declares that such information is to be considered confidential, the situation is clear,

第2.1.16条

（保密义务）

一方当事人在谈判过程中提供的保密性质的信息，无论此后是否达成合同，另一方当事人均不得泄露，也不得为自己的目的不适当地使用。在适当的情况下，违反该义务的救济可以包括根据另一方当事人所获得之利益，予以赔偿。

注释:

1. 当事人一般不负保密义务

正如不存在一般性的披露义务一样，在为订立合同进行谈判时，当事人通常也无义务将他们所交换的信息作为保密信息对待。换句话说，由于一方当事人通常可以自由地决定披露哪些与所谈交易相关的事实，这类信息原则上被认为是非保密信息，即如果合同没有达成，另一方当事人既可以向第三方披露，也可以用于自己的目的。

示例:

1. A 要安装空调系统，邀请空调系统生产商 B 和 C 发出要约。B 和 C 在其各自的要约中均提供了一些与其空调系统功能相关的技术细节，目的在于显示其产品的优点。A 决定拒绝 B 的要约，只与 C 继续谈判。A 可以自由地利用 B 要约中所含信息，以促使 C 提出更优惠的条件。

2. 保密信息

一方当事人对提供给对方当事人的某些信息可能具有如下利益，即不予披露，或不被用于提供之目的以外的其他目的。只要该当事人明确声明这种信息应该为保密信息，情况就很清楚了，因为另一方当

for by receiving the information the other party implicitly agrees to treat it as confidential. The only problem which may arise is that if the period during which the other party is not to disclose the information is too long, this might contravene the applicable laws prohibiting restrictive trade practices. Yet even in the absence of such an express declaration the receiving party may be under a duty of confidentiality. This is the case where, in view of the particular nature of the information or the professional qualifications of the parties, it would be contrary to the general principle of good faith and fair dealing for the receiving party to disclose it, or to use it for its own purposes after the breaking off of negotiations.

Illustrations

2. The facts are the same as in Illustration 1, except that in its offer B expressly requests A not to divulge certain technical specifications contained therein. A may not use this information in its negotiations with C.

3. A is interested in entering into a joint venture agreement with B or C, the two leading car manufacturers in country X. Negotiations progress with B in particular, and A receives fairly detailed information relating to B's plans for a new car design. Although B does not expressly request A to treat this information as confidential, because it is for a new car design. A may be under a duty not to disclose it to C, nor is A allowed to use those plans for its own production process should the negotiations not result in the conclusion of a contract.

3. Damages recoverable

The breach of confidentiality implies first liability in damages. The amount of damages recoverable may vary, depending on whether or not the parties entered into a special agreement for the non-disclosure of the information. Even if the injured party has not suffered any loss, it may be entitled to recover from the non-performing party the benefit the latter received by disclosing the information to third persons or by using it for its own purposes. If necessary, for example when the information has not yet been disclosed or has been disclosed only partially, the injured party may also seek an injunction in accordance with the applicable law.

事人接受这种信息就默示同意将其作为保密信息对待。唯一可能出现的问题是，如果另一方当事人不能公开该信息的期间过长，则可能会违反有关禁止限制性商业做法的法律规定。然而，即使没有这种明确的声明，信息的接受方也可能负有保密义务。例如，鉴于某种信息的特殊性质或因当事人的职业要求，接受方披露该信息或在中断谈判后用于自己的目的，有悖于"诚实信用和公平交易"原则。

示例：

2. 事实与示例 1 相同，不同的是，B 在其要约中明确要求 A 不得泄露要约所含的特定技术规格。则 A 不能在与 C 的谈判中使用该信息。

3. A 有意与 X 国两主要轿车生产商 B 和 C 中的一家达成一合资企业协议。特别是在与 B 的谈判过程中，A 收到了 B 关于一款新型车设计方案的详细资料。尽管 B 没有明确要求 A 将该信息作为保密信息对待，但因为这是一款新车型的设计方案，A 可能负有不向 C 披露该信息的义务，并且在未达成合同的情况下，A 也不得将该设计方案用于自己的生产程序。

3. 可求偿的损害赔偿

违反保密义务首先意味着要承担损害赔偿责任。根据当事人是否订有不披露信息的专门协议，可求偿的损害赔偿数额可能是不同的。即使受害方没有遭受任何实际损失，其仍有权就不履行方当事人因将信息披露给第三人或为自己所用而获取的收益取得赔偿。如有必要，例如在信息尚未泄露或只是部分泄露时，受害方当事人也可以依适用法寻求禁令保护。

ARTICLE 2.1.17
(Merger clauses)

A contract in writing which contains a clause indicating that the writing completely embodies the terms on which the parties have agreed cannot be contradicted or supplemented by evidence of prior statements or agreements. However, such statements or agreements may be used to interpret the writing.

COMMENT

If the conclusion of a contract is preceded by more or less extended negotiations, the parties may wish to put their agreement in writing and declare that document to constitute their final agreement. This can be achieved by an appropriately drafted "merger" or "integration" clause (e.g. "This contract contains the entire agreement between the parties"). However, the effect of such a clause is not to deprive prior statements or agreements of any relevance: they may still be used as a means of interpreting the written document (see also Article 4.3(a)).

A merger clause of course covers only prior statements or agreements between the parties and does not preclude subsequent informal agreements between them. The parties are, however, free to extend an agreed form even to future amendments (see Article 2.1.18).

This Article indirectly confirms the principle set out in Article 1.2 in the sense that, in the absence of a merger clause, extrinsic evidence supplementing or contradicting a written contract is admissible.

ARTICLE 2.1.18
(Modification in a particular form)

A contract in writing which contains a clause requiring any modification or termination by agreement to be in a particular form may not be otherwise modified or terminated. However, a party may be precluded by its conduct from asserting such a clause to the extent that the other party has reasonably acted in reliance on that conduct.

第2.1.17 条

（合并条款）

若一个书面合同中载有的一项条款，表明该合同包含了各方当事人已达成一致的全部条款，则此前的陈述或协议均不能作为证据对抗或补充该合同。但是，该等陈述或协议可用于解释该书面合同。

注释：

如果合同订立之前经历了或多或少漫长的谈判过程，当事人可能希望达成书面协议，并声明该协议构成他们的最后文本。这一目的可以通过草拟"合并条款"或"并入条款"实现（例如："本合同包括当事人间的全部协议"）。然而，这种条款的效力并不排除先前的任何有关陈述或协议，这些陈述或协议仍可用于解释该书面合同（参见第4.3 条(a)项）。

当然，合并条款仅包括当事人间先前的陈述或协议，并不排除当事人后来达成的非正式协议。但当事人甚至有权将原定的形式扩展适用于未来的修改（参见第2.1.18 条）。

本条间接地确认了第1.2 条确立的原则，即如果没有合并条款，则允许用外部证据补充或对抗书面合同。

第2.1.18 条

（特定形式修改）

如果书面合同中载有的一项条款，要求任何协议修改或协议终止必须以特定形式做出，则该合同不得以其他形式修改或终止。但是，如果一方当事人的行为导致另一方当事人信赖并合理行事，则在此限度内，该一方当事人因其行为不得主张该条款。

COMMENT

Parties concluding a written contract may wish to ensure that any modification or termination by agreement will also be in writing or otherwise in a particular form and to this end include a special clause in the contract (e.g. "Any modification of this Contract may be made only by a writing signed by both Parties"; "Alterations to the above-indicated Time-schedule must be confirmed in writing by the Engineer's representative on site").

This Article states that as a rule such a clause renders ineffective any modification or termination by agreement not in the particular form required.

Illustration

> 1. Contractor A contracts with purchaser B for the construction of a building. The contract provides that any modification to the work schedule must be in writing and the document must be signed by both parties. In the course of construction, A sends B an e-mail asking B to agree to the extension of a particular deadline. B accepts by return of e-mail. The modification is ineffective since there is no single document bearing both parties' signature.

Yet there is an exception to the general rule. In application of the general principle prohibiting inconsistent behaviour (see Article 1.8), this Article specifies that a party may be precluded by its conduct from invoking the clause requiring any modification or termination to be in a particular form to the extent that the other party has reasonably acted in reliance on that conduct.

Illustration

> 2. A, a contractor, contracts with B, a school board, for the construction of a new school building. The contract provides that the second floor of the building is to have sufficient bearing capacity to support the school library. Notwithstanding a "no oral modification" clause in the same contract, the parties orally agree that the second floor of the building should be of non-bearing construction. A completes construction according to the modification and B, who has observed the progress of the construction without making any objections, only at this point objects to how the second floor has been constructed. A court may decide that B is not entitled to invoke the "no oral modification" clause as A reasonably relied on the oral modification, and is therefore not liable for non-performance.

注释：

当事人订立书面合同，可能是希望确保任何协议修改或协议终止也都以书面方式或其他特定的形式进行，并为此目的在合同中订立一项特别条款（例如，"本合同的任何修改均须以双方签署的书面文件做出"；"前述时间表的改变必须经工程师的现场代表书面确认"）。

本条规定，原则上，此种条款使不符合特定形式要求的协议修改或协议终止归于无效。

示例：

1. 承包商 A 与购买者 B 就建筑一栋房屋订立合同。合同规定，对工作进度表的任何修改必须以书面形式做出并且该书面文件必须由双方签字。在施工过程中，A 发给 B 一封电子邮件请求 B 同意延展某一期限。B 以电子邮件回复表示接受。这一修改是无效的，因为没有一份载有双方签字的文件。

然而，这一一般规则也存在一个例外。在适用禁止不一致行为的一般原则（参见第 1.8 条）时，该条规定，如果一方因合理信赖对方的行为而行事，则后者将因其行为而不得援引要求以特定形式做出修改或终止的条款。

示例：

2. A 是一位承包商，B 是某学校的董事会。A 和 B 签订了一份建一栋新教学楼的合同。合同规定，该教学楼第二层的承重能力必须足以使该层作图书馆之用。尽管在该合同载有"非口头变更"条款，当事人仍口头同意了该楼的第二层应为非承重结构。A 依变更后的合同完成了施工，B 也看到了施工的过程，并未提出任何反对意见。但在完工时 B 却对第二层的建筑方式提出反对。法庭可以裁定 B 无权援引"非口头变更"条款，因为 A 合理信赖了口头变更，因此不承担不履行的责任。

ARTICLE 2.1.19
(Contracting under standard terms)

(1) Where one party or both parties use standard terms in concluding a contract, the general rules on formation apply, subject to Articles 2.1.20 – 2.1.22.

(2) Standard terms are provisions which are prepared in advance for general and repeated use by one party and which are actually used without negotiation with the other party.

COMMENT

1. Contracting under standard terms

This Article is the first of four articles (Articles 2.1.19 – 2.1.22) which deal with the special situation where one or both parties use standard terms in concluding a contract.

2. Notion of "standard terms"

"Standard terms" are to be understood as those contract provisions which are prepared in advance for general and repeated use by one party and which are actually used without negotiation with the other party (paragraph (2)). What is decisive is not their formal presentation (e.g. whether they are contained in a separate document or in the contract document itself; whether they have been issued on pre-printed forms or are only contained in an electronic file, etc.), nor who prepared them (the party itself, a trade or professional association, etc.), nor their volume (whether they consist of a comprehensive set of provisions covering almost all the relevant aspects of the contract, or of only one or two provisions regarding, for instance, exclusion of liability and arbitration). What is decisive is the fact that they are drafted in advance for general and repeated use and that they are actually used in a given case by one of the parties without negotiation with the other party. This latter requirement obviously relates only to the standard terms as such, which the other party must accept as a whole, while the other terms of the same contract may well be the subject of negotiation between the parties.

第 2.1.19 条

（按标准条款订立合同）

（1）一方或双方当事人使用标准条款订立合同的，适用订立合同的一般规则，但应受第 **2.1.20 条至第 2.1.22 条**的约束。

（2）标准条款是指一方当事人为通常和重复使用的目的而预先准备的、在实际使用时未与对方谈判的条款。

注释：

1. 按标准条款订立合同

第 2.1.19 条至第 2.1.22 条对一方或双方当事人使用标准条款订立合同这种特殊情况做了规定，本条是这四条中的第一条。

2. "标准条款"的概念

"标准条款"应理解为：一方当事人为通常和重复使用的目的而预先准备的、在实际使用时未与对方谈判的条款（第（2）款）。关键并不在于这种条款表现为何种形式（如，不论是单独作为一份文件还是包含在合同文件之中，也不论这些条款是以事先印好的格式发出，还是仅存于电子文档之中）、由谁拟定（当事人自己、某一行业协会或专业协会等）、内容广度如何（不论是几乎包括合同所有相关方面的综合性规定，还是仅仅涉及某方面的一两个条文，如责任的免除和仲裁）。关键在于这些条款为了通常和重复使用的目的而预先准备，一方当事人在实际使用时未与对方谈判。后一项要求显然只与标准条款本身有关，对方当事人必须全部接受，而当事人对合同中的其他条款则可能是当事人协商的主题。

3. General rules on formation apply

Usually, the general rules on formation apply irrespective of whether or not one or both parties use standard terms (paragraph (1)). It follows that standard terms proposed by one party bind the other party only on acceptance, and that it depends upon the circumstances of the case whether the two parties must refer to the standard terms expressly or whether the incorporation of such terms may be implied. Thus, standard terms contained in the contract document itself will normally be binding upon the mere signature of the contract document as a whole, at least as long as they are reproduced above that signature and not, for instance, on the reverse side of the document. On the other hand, standard terms contained in a separate document or electronic file will normally have to be referred to expressly by the party intending to use them. Implied incorporation may be admitted only if there exists a practice established between the parties or usage to that effect (see Article 1.9).

Illustrations

1. A intends to conclude an insurance contract with B covering the risk of liability for accidents of A's employees at work. The parties sign a model contract form presented by B after filling in the blank spaces relating, among other matters, to the premium and to the maximum amount insured. By virtue of its signature, A is bound not only by the terms which it has individually negotiated with B, but also by the General Conditions of the National Insurers' Association, which are printed on the form.

2. A normally concludes contracts with its customers on the basis of its own standard terms which are printed as a separate document. When making an offer to B, a new customer, A fails to make an express reference to the standard terms. B accepts the offer. The standard terms are not incorporated in the contract unless A can prove that B knew or ought to have known of A's intention to conclude the contract only on the basis of its own standard terms, e.g. because the same standard terms had regularly been adopted in previous transactions.

3. A intends to buy grain on the commodity exchange in London. In the contract concluded between A and B, a broker on that exchange, no express reference is made to the standard terms which normally govern brokerage contracts concluded at the exchange in question. The standard terms are nevertheless incorporated in the contract because their application to the kind of contract in question amounts to a usage.

3. 适用订立合同的一般规则

通常，不论当事人一方或双方是否使用标准条款，都应该适用订立合同的一般规则（第(1)款）。因此，一方当事人所提议的标准条款只有经对方接受才有约束力，并且当事人是否须明确引用标准条款还是可以默示纳入该等条款，则取决于具体情况。因此，合同本身所载有的标准条款通常只有对合同文件作为整体签署才产生拘束力，至少该等标准条款被复制于签字上方而非（如）文件背面。另一方面，记载于单独文件或电子文档中的标准条款，通常必须得到有意使用一方的明确引用方能生效。只有在当事人间存在某种习惯做法或惯例时，默示采用才能被承认为有效（参见第 1.9 条）。

示例：

1. A 有意与 B 订立一份保险合同，为其雇员工作中发生的意外事故责任险投保。双方在 B 提供的格式合同表空白处填写了有关保险费和承保上限等内容。一经签字，A 不仅要受与 B 个别商谈的条款的约束，而且要受印在格式合同表上的《全国保险机构协会一般条件》的约束。

2. A 通常在其自己的标准条款基础上与用户订立合同，这些条款印成一份单独的文件。当 A 向新用户 B 发出要约时，未明确引用标准条款。B 承诺了该要约。这些标准条款未纳入合同，除非 A 能证明 B 知道或应该知道 A 只打算以其标准条款为基础订立合同，例如因为这些条款在以前交易中已被惯常地采用。

3. A 想在伦敦商品交易所购买粮食。B 是在该交易所开展业务的经纪人。A 和 B 订立的合同，并未明确引用惯常适用于在此交易所达成的经纪合同的标准条款。但这些条款已被纳入该合同，因为这些标准条款适用于此类合同构成一项惯例。

ARTICLE 2.1.20
(Surprising terms)

(1) No term contained in standard terms which is of such a character that the other party could not reasonably have expected it, is effective unless it has been expressly accepted by that party.

(2) In determining whether a term is of such a character regard shall be had to its content, language and presentation.

COMMENT

1. Surprising terms in standard terms not effective

A party which accepts the other party's standard terms is in principle bound by them irrespective of whether or not it actually knows their content in detail or fully understands their implications. An important exception to this rule is, however, laid down in this Article which states that, notwithstanding its acceptance of the standard terms as a whole, the adhering party is not bound by those terms which by virtue of their content, language or presentation are of such a character that it could not reasonably have expected them. The reason for this exception is the desire to avoid a party which uses standard terms taking undue advantage of its position by surreptitiously attempting to impose terms on the other party which that party would scarcely have accepted had it been aware of them. For other articles intended to protect the economically weaker or less experienced party, see Articles 3.2.7 and 4.6.

2. Terms "surprising" by virtue of their content

A particular term contained in standard terms may come as a surprise to the adhering party first by reason of its content. This is the case whenever the content of the term in question is such that a reasonable person of the same kind as the adhering party would not have expected it in the type of standard terms involved. In determining whether or not a term is unusual, regard must be had on the one hand to the terms which are commonly to be found in standard terms generally used in the trade sector concerned, and on the other to the individual negotiations between the parties. Thus, for example, a term excluding or limiting the contractual   liability   of   the   proponent   may   or   may   not   be

第 2.1.20 条

（意外条款）

（1）如果标准条款中含有的条款，依其性质，另一方当事人不能合理预见，则除非该另一方当事人明示地表示接受，否则该条款无效。
（2）在确定某一条款是否具有这种性质时，应考虑到该条款的内容、语言和表现形式。

注释：

1. 标准条款中的意外条款无效

原则上，一方当事人一旦接受了对方的标准条款，就要受之约束，无论其是否实际知道这些条款的详细内容，或是否完全理解其含义。然而，本条对这一规则规定了一项重要的例外，即标准条款虽然整体上被接受，但如果其中某些条款由于其内容、语言和表现形式的特性使得附和方不能合理预见，则附和方不受此类条款约束。理由在于：要防止使用标准条款的一方当事人过分利用其有利地位，秘密地将某些条款强加于对方当事人。而对这些条款，如果对方当事人了解的话，几乎不可能接受。其他意在保护经济上处于弱势地位或缺乏经验的当事人的条款，参见第 3.2.7 条和第 4.6 条。

2. 内容致使条款"意外"

附和方之所以对标准条款中某一特定条款感到意外，第一种原因是该条款的内容。如果该条款的内容具有如下性质，就属于这种情况，即一个与附和方一样的通情达理的人在所涉类型的标准条款中不会预见到它。要确定某一条款是否不同寻常，一方面必须考虑相关贸易领域中广泛使用的标准条款中常见的条款，另一方面还要考虑当事人之间的单独的谈判。例如，一项免除或限制提出标准条款一方合同责任

considered to be "surprising", and in consequence ineffective in a particular case, its effectiveness depending on whether or not terms of that kind are common in the trade sector concerned, and are consistent with the way in which the parties conducted their negotiations.

Illustration

1.   A, a travel agency, offers package tours for business trips. The terms of the advertisement give the impression that A is acting as a tour operator who undertakes full responsibility for the various services comprising the package. B books a tour on the basis of A's standard terms. Notwithstanding B's acceptance of the terms as a whole, A may not rely on a term stating that, with respect to the hotel accommodation, it is acting merely as an agent for the hotelkeeper, and therefore declines any liability.

3. Terms "surprising" by virtue of their language or presentation

Other reasons for a particular term contained in standard terms being surprising to the adhering party may be the language in which it is couched, which may be obscure, or the way in which it is presented typographically, for instance in minute print. In order to determine whether or not this is the case, regard is to be had not so much to the formulation and presentation commonly used in the type of standard terms involved, but more to the professional skill and experience of persons of the same kind as the adhering party. Thus, a particular wording may be both obscure and clear at the same time, depending on whether or not the adhering party belongs to the same professional category as the party using the standard terms.

The language factor may also play an important role in the context of international transactions. If the standard terms are drafted in a foreign language it cannot be excluded that some of its terms, although fairly clear in themselves, will turn out to be surprising for the adhering party who could not reasonably have been expected fully to appreciate all their implications.

Illustrations

2.   A, an insurance company operating in country X, is an affiliate of B, a company incorporated in country Y. A's standard terms comprise some 50 terms printed in small type. One of the terms designates the law of country Y as the applicable law. Unless this term is presented in bold letters or in any other way apt to attract the attention of the adhering party, it will be without effect

的条款，在特定情况下可能被视为"意外"而无效，其效力取决于相关贸易领域中此类条款是否常用，是否与当事人进行谈判的方式相一致。

示例：

> 1. A是一家旅行社，提供一揽子商务旅行服务。A所做的广告给人的印象是A作为一家旅行经营机构，对一揽子服务中的各项目负完全责任。基于A的标准条款，B预订了一趟旅行。虽然B对标准条款做了整体的接受，但A仍不得援引其中一项条款拒绝承担任何责任，该条款规定对于旅馆住宿服务A只是作为旅馆经营人的代理人行事。

3. 语言或表现形式致使条款"意外"

标准条款中某一特定条款令附和方感到意外的其他原因可以是该条款的语言含糊不清，或条款印制的方式，如所用的字体极小。要确定是否属于这类情况，应考虑在此类标准条款中是否通常使用这种表述方式和表现形式，还应更多地考虑与附和方同类人的职业技能和经验。因此，某一措辞有可能同时既含糊又清楚，关键要看附和方与使用标准条款的一方当事人是否属于同一职业范畴。

在国际交易中，语言因素也非常重要。如果标准条款是以外国语言拟就的，则不排除这样一种可能性，即一部分条款虽然本身很清楚，但可能会使附和方感到意外，因为不能合理地期望附和方能完全领会这些条款的含义。

示例：

> 2. A是在X国经营业务的一家保险公司，B是在Y国注册成立的一家公司，A是B的关联公司。A的标准条款包括50个条款并以小字体印刷，其中有一条规定以Y国法律为准据法。除非该条款以粗字体或以其他任何能吸引附和方注意力的方式印刷，否则它没有效力。因为X国的投保人不可能

since customers in country X would not reasonably expect to find a choice-of-law clause designating a foreign law as the law governing their contracts in the standard terms of a company operating in their own country.

3.   A, a commodity dealer operating in Hamburg, uses in its contracts with its customers standard terms containing, among others, a provision stating "Hamburg – Freundschaftliche Arbitrage". In local business circles this clause is normally understood as meaning that possible disputes are to be submitted to a special arbitration governed by particular rules of procedure of local origin. In contracts with foreign customers this clause may be held to be ineffective, notwithstanding the acceptance of the standard terms as a whole, since a foreign customer cannot reasonably be expected to understand its exact implications, and this irrespective of whether or not the clause has been translated into the foreign customer's own language.

4. Express acceptance of "surprising" terms

The risk of the adhering party being taken by surprise by the kind of terms so far discussed clearly no longer exists if in a given case the other party draws the adhering party's attention to them and the adhering party accepts them. This Article therefore provides that a party may no longer rely on the "surprising" nature of a term in order to challenge its effectiveness, once it has expressly accepted the term.

ARTICLE 2.1.21
*(Conflict between standard terms
and non-standard terms)*

In case of conflict between a standard term and a term which is not a standard term the latter prevails.

COMMENT

Standard terms are by definition prepared in advance by one party or a third person and incorporated in an individual contract without their content being discussed by the parties (see Article 2.1.19(2)). It is therefore logical that whenever the parties specifically negotiate and agree on particular provisions of their contract, such provisions will prevail over conflicting provisions contained in the standard terms

合理预见在其自己国家经营的公司的标准条款中会有一个法律选择条款，指定外国法律为合同准据法。

3. A 是在汉堡开展业务的一位大宗商品经销商，在与客户订立的合同中使用标准条款，其中有一条规定："汉堡友好仲裁"。在当地商业界，这一条款通常被理解为：可能发生的争议应提交特别仲裁，该仲裁按源于当地的特定程序规则进行。在与外国客户订立的合同中，尽管该条款整体被接受，该条款仍可能被认定为不具效力，因为不能合理地期望外国用户能够理解其确切含义，不论该条款是否已翻译成该客户的本国语言。

4. 对"意外"条款的明确接受

在某一交易中，如果一方当事人已经提醒附和方注意"意外"条款，而附和方接受该等条款，则前述这类条款令附和方大感意外的风险显然将不复存在。因此，本条规定：一旦一方当事人明确接受一个条款，则该当事人就不得再以该条款具有"意外"性质为由，对其有效性提出质疑。

第 2.1.21 条

（标准条款与非标准条款的冲突）

若标准条款与非标准条款发生冲突，以非标准条款为准。

注释：

依定义，标准条款是由一方当事人或第三人预先准备的，并且在未经双方当事人讨论其内容的情况下并入某一合同（参见第 2.1.19 条第（2）款）。因此，很显然，一旦当事人就合同中某些具体条款进行了专门协商并达成一致，则该等具体条款的效力优于与之相冲突的标

since they are more likely to reflect the intention of the parties in the given case.

The individually agreed provisions may appear in the same document as the standard terms, but may also be contained in a separate document. In the first case they may easily be recognised on account of their being written in characters different from those of the standard terms. In the second case it may be more difficult to distinguish between the provisions which are standard terms and those which are not, and to determine their exact position in the hierarchy of the different documents. To this effect the parties often include a contract provision expressly indicating the documents which form part of their contract and their respective weight. Special problems may however arise when the modifications to the standard terms have only been agreed upon orally, without the conflicting provisions contained in the standard terms being struck out, and those standard terms contain a provision stating the exclusive character of the writing signed by the parties, or that any addition to or modification of their content must be in writing. For these cases see Articles 2.1.17 and 2.1.18.

ARTICLE 2.1.22
(Battle of forms)

Where both parties use standard terms and reach agreement except on those terms, a contract is concluded on the basis of the agreed terms and of any standard terms which are common in substance unless one party clearly indicates in advance, or later and without undue delay informs the other party, that it does not intend to be bound by such a contract.

COMMENT

1. Parties using different standard terms

It is quite frequent in commercial transactions for both the offeror when making the offer, and the offeree when accepting it, each to refer to its own standard terms. In the absence of express acceptance by the offeror of the offeree's standard terms, the problem arises as to whether a contract is concluded at all and if so, which, if either, of the two conflicting sets of standard terms should prevail.

准条款的效力，因为它们更能反映双方当事人在具体交易中的意图。

单独商定的条款可以与标准条款载于同一文件，也可以载于一个单独的文件。在第一种情况下，因为它们使用与标准条款不同的书写字体，因此很容易看出这些条款。而在第二种情况下，则很难区分标准条款与非标准条款，并很难确定它们在由不同文件组成的阶层中所处准确位置。为此，当事人常常在合同中载入一项条款，明确指明哪些文件构成合同的组成部分以及这些文件各自的分量如何。然而，如果仅以口头方式对标准条款进行了修改，但标准条款中包含的不一致规定并没有删除，标准条款又有这样一项规定，即经双方当事人签署的书面文件具有排他性，或规定对标准条款的任何添加或修改都必须以书面形式做出，在这种情况下则可能出现特殊问题。有关这方面的情况，参见第2.1.17条和第2.1.18条。

第2.1.22条

（格式之争）

如果双方当事人均使用标准条款并对标准条款以外的条款达成一致，则合同应根据已达成一致的条款以及在实体内容上相同的标准条款订立，除非一方当事人已事先明确表示或事后毫不迟延地通知另一方当事人其不愿受这种合同的约束。

注释：

1. 当事人使用不同的标准条款

在商事交易中，经常发生的情况是，要约人发出要约时和受要约人承诺要约时各自使用自己的标准条款。如果要约人未明确承诺受要约人的标准条款，就会产生诸如合同是否已订立，以及如果合同已订立，两套相互冲突的标准条款中何者优先等问题。

2. "Battle of forms" and general rules on offer and acceptance

If the general rules on offer and acceptance were to be applied, there would either be no contract at all since the purported acceptance by the offeree would, subject to the exception provided for in Article 2.1.11(2), amount to a counter-offer, or if the two parties have started to perform without objecting to each other's standard terms, a contract would be considered to have been concluded on the basis of those terms which were the last to be sent or to be referred to (the "last shot").

3. The "knock-out" doctrine

The "last shot" doctrine may be appropriate if the parties clearly indicate that the adoption of their standard terms is an essential condition for the conclusion of the contract. Where, on the other hand, the parties, as is very often the case in practice, refer to their standard terms more or less automatically, for example by exchanging printed order and acknowledgement of order forms with the respective terms on the reverse side, they will normally not even be aware of the conflict between their respective standard terms. There is in such cases no reason to allow the parties subsequently to question the very existence of the contract or, if performance has commenced, to insist on the application of the terms last sent or referred to.

It is for this reason that this Article provides, notwithstanding the general rules on offer and acceptance, that if the parties reach an agreement except on their standard terms, a contract is concluded on the basis of the agreed terms and of any standard terms which are common in substance ("knock-out" doctrine).

Illustration

1.   A orders a machine from B indicating the type of machine, the price and terms of payment, and the date and place of delivery. A uses an order form with its "General Conditions for Purchase" printed on the reverse side. B accepts by sending an acknowledgement of order form on the reverse side of which appear its own "General Conditions for Sale". When A subsequently seeks to withdraw from the deal it claims that no contract was ever concluded as there was no agreement as to which set of standard terms should apply. Since, however, the parties have agreed on the essential terms of the contract, a contract has been concluded on those terms and on any standard terms which are common in substance.

A party may, however, always exclude the operation of the "knock-out" doctrine by clearly indicating in advance, or by later and without undue delay informing the other, that it does not intend to be bound by a

2. "格式之争"和关于要约与承诺的一般规则

若适用关于要约和承诺的一般规则，则可能根本不存在合同，因为根据第 2.1.11 条第(2)款所规定的例外，因为受要约人所谓的承诺构成对要约人的反要约；或者，如果双方当事人未对彼此的标准条款提出反对就开始履行，则视为依最后发出或被引用的标准条款成立合同("最后确定"原则)。

3. "排除异意"原则

如果当事人明确表示采用其标准条款是合同订立的一个基本条件，则"最后确定"原则可能是适宜的。但实践中经常出现的另一种情况是，当事人或多或少只是自动引用他们的标准条款，例如双方当事人交换印制好的订单和订单确认书格式，背面附有各自的条款。当事人通常甚至不会注意到他们的标准条款之间存在冲突。在这种情况下，没有理由允许当事人事后质疑合同的存在，或者，合同开始履行后坚持适用最后发出或引用的条款。

基于这种理由，本条规定：尽管关于要约和承诺有一般规则，但如果当事人就标准条款以外的事项达成协议，则合同应根据已达成一致的条款和实质相同的标准条款订立("排除异意"原则)。

示例：

> 1. A 向 B 订购一台机器，并在订单中指明了机器的型号、价格、支付条款以及交货时间和地点。A 所用的订单格式背面印着 A 的"一般购买条件"。B 发出订单确认书格式予以承诺，确认书格式背面印有 B 的"一般销售条件"。A 事后试图撤出该交易，声称双方从未订立任何合同，因为他们对适用何种标准条款未达成协议。但是，因为双方当事人已就合同的主要条款达成一致，根据已约定的条款以及实质相同的标准条款，合同已经订立。

当然，一方当事人总是可以通过以下方式排除"排除异意"原则的适用：事先明确表示，或在事后毫不迟延地通知对方，自己不愿受

contract which is not based on its own standard terms. What will in practice amount to such a "clear" indication cannot be stated in absolute terms but the inclusion of a clause of this kind in the standard terms themselves will not normally be sufficient since what is necessary is a specific declaration by the party concerned in its offer or acceptance.

Illustrations

2. The facts are the same as in Illustration 1, except that A claims that the contract was concluded on the basis of its standard terms since they contain a clause which states that "Deviating standard terms of the party accepting the order are not valid if they have not been confirmed in writing by us". The result will be the same as in Illustration 1, since merely by including such a clause in its standard terms A does not indicate with sufficient clarity its determination to conclude the contract only on its own terms.

3. The facts are the same as in Illustration 1, except that the non-standard terms of A's offer contain a statement to the effect that A intends to contract only on its own standard terms. The mere fact that B attaches its own standard terms to its acceptance does not prevent the contract from being concluded on the basis of A's standard terms.

非依据自己的标准条款订立的合同的约束。在实践中，究竟什么能构成上述"明确"表示，不能用确切的术语表述出来，但仅在标准条款中包含此种条款通常是不够的，因为在这种情况下必须由有关当事人在其要约或承诺中做出具体的声明。

示例：

2. 事实与示例 1 相同，不同的是，A 声称合同是依据其标准条款订立的，因为其标准条款中有一条规定："如未经我方书面确认，接受订单者所做承诺中与我方标准条款相冲突的内容视为无效。"本例结果与示例 1 相同，合同应为订立，因为仅由标准条款中包含这一条款，A 并不能充分表明他只愿意依自己的标准条款订立合同。

3. 事实与示例 1 相同，不同的是，A 在其要约的非标准条款中有一声明，即 A 仅愿依自己的标准条款订立合同。B 在承诺中附有自己的标准条款，但仅这一事实并不能妨碍该合同依据 A 的标准条款订立。

SECTION 2: AUTHORITY OF AGENTS

ARTICLE 2.2.1
(Scope of the Section)

(1) This Section governs the authority of a person ("the agent") to affect the legal relations of another person ("the principal") by or with respect to a contract with a third party, whether the agent acts in its own name or in that of the principal.

(2) It governs only the relations between the principal or the agent on the one hand, and the third party on the other.

(3) It does not govern an agent's authority conferred by law or the authority of an agent appointed by a public or judicial authority.

COMMENT

1. Scope of the Section

This Section governs the authority of an agent to affect the legal relations between its principal and a third party. In other words, it focuses on the external relations between the principal or the agent on the one hand and the third party on the other and is not concerned with the internal relations between the principal and the agent. Even those provisions which deal with issues affecting both the internal and the external relations (see, e.g., Articles 2.2.2 and 2.2.10 on the establishment and termination of the agent's authority, Article 2.2.7 on conflict of interests and Article 2.2.8 on sub-agency), consider those issues only with respect to their effects on the third party.

The rights and duties as between principal and agent are governed by their agreement and the applicable law which, with respect to specific types of agency relationships such as those concerning so-called "commercial agents", may provide mandatory rules for the protection of the agent.

2. Authority to contract

The Section deals only with agents who have authority to conclude contracts on behalf of their principals. Intermediaries whose task it is

第二节　代理人的权限

第 2.2.1 条

（本节的范围）

（1）本节调整某人（代理人）通过订立合同或与合同相关行为，影响另一人（本人）与第三方之间法律关系的权限，而不论代理人是以自己的名义还是以本人的名义行事。

（2）本节仅调整以本人或代理人为一方当事人，以第三方为另一方当事人之间的关系。

（3）本节并不调整由法律赋予代理人的权限，或由公共或司法机构指定的代理人的权限。

注释：

1. 本节的范围

本节调整代理人影响本人和第三方之间法律关系的权限。换句话说，它关注的是本人或代理人与第三方之间的外部关系，而并不关注本人和代理人之间的内部关系。即使某些条款涉及到对内部和外部关系都有影响的事项（例如，参见关于代理人权限的设立和终止的第2.2.2条和第2.2.10条，关于利益冲突的第2.2.7条以及关于次代理的第2.2.8条），仅考虑这些事项对第三方有影响的方面。

本人和代理人之间的权利义务由他们之间的合同和适用法调整，就某些类型的代理关系，例如那些涉及所谓"商事代理"的代理关系，适用法可能规定了保护代理人的强制性规定。

2. 缔约的权限

本节仅调整有权代表本人缔约的代理人。那些仅介绍双方当事人

merely to introduce two parties to one another with a view to their concluding a contract (e.g. real estate agents), or to negotiate contracts on behalf of a principal but who have no authority to bind the principal (as may be the case of commercial agents) are outside the scope of the Section.

On the other hand, the wording "the authority [...] to affect the legal relations of [...] the principal by or with respect to a contract with a third party" used in paragraph (1) is to be understood in a broad sense, so as to comprise any act by the agent aimed at concluding a contract or which relates to its performance, including giving a notice to, or receiving it from, the third party.

3. Irrelevant whether agent acts in its own name or in that of its principal

Contrary to a number of legal systems that distinguish between "direct representation" and "indirect representation" depending on whether the agent acts in the principal's name or in its own name, no such distinction is made in this Section. As to the distinction between "disclosed" and "undisclosed" agency, see Articles 2.2.3 and 2.2.4.

4. Voluntary nature of the relationship between principal and agent

A further condition for the application of this Section is the voluntary nature of the relationship between principal and agent. Cases where the agent's authority is conferred by law (e.g. in the field of family law, matrimonial property and succession), or is derived from judicial authorisation (e.g. acting for a person without capacity to act), are outside the scope of this Section.

5. Agents of companies

The authority of organs, officers or partners of a corporation, partnership or other entity, with or without legal personality, is traditionally governed by special rules, sometimes even of a mandatory character, which by virtue of their specific scope necessarily prevail over the general rules on the authority of agents laid down in this Section. Thus, for instance, if under the special rules governing the authority of its organs or officers a corporation is prevented from invoking any limitation to their authority against third parties, that corporation may not rely on Article 2.2.5(1) to claim that it is not bound by an act of its organs or officers that falls outside the scope of their authority.

结识以促进其缔约的中介人（如房地产经纪），或仅代表本人谈判合同但无权拘束本人的中介人（如商事代理），不属本节的调整范围。

另一方面，第(1)款的表述："通过订立合同或与合同相关行为，影响本人法律关系的权限"，应从广义上理解，以致包括代理人的任何旨在缔约的行为或与其履行相关的行为，包括向第三方发出通知，或从第三方接受通知。

3. 不论代理人以自己的名义还是以本人名义行事

许多法律体系根据代理人是以本人名义还是以自己名义行事区分"直接代理"和"间接代理"。与这些法律体系不同，本节并未做出此类区分。至于"显名"和"隐名"代理的区分，参见第 2.2.3 条和第 2.2.4 条。

4. 本人和代理人之间关系的意定性

本节的另一项适用条件是本人和代理人之间关系的意定性。代理人权限来自法律授予（例如，在家事法、婚姻财产和继承领域）或来自司法授权（例如，代表无行为能力人行事）的情况不属本节的调整范围。

5. 公司的代理人

公司、合伙或其他实体（无论是否具有法人资格）的机构、主管或合伙人的权限通常由特殊规则调整，它们有时甚至具有强制性。由于其特定的适用范围，这些特殊规则必然较本节规定的关于代理人权限的一般规则优先适用。因此，例如，若根据调整公司机构或主管权限的特殊规则，公司不得援引任何针对该等机构或人员的权限限制对抗第三人，那么公司也不能依第 2.2.5 条第(1)款主张其不受其机构或主管超越权限范围的行为约束。

On the other hand, as long as the general rules laid down in this Section do not conflict with the above-mentioned special rules on the authority of organs, officers or partners, they may well be applied in lieu of the latter. Thus, for instance, a third party seeking to demonstrate that the contract it has concluded with an officer of a corporation binds that corporation, may invoke either the special rules governing the authority of that corporation's organs or officers or, as the case may be, the general rules on apparent authority laid down in Article 2.2.5(2).

Illustrations

1. A, a Chief Executive Officer of company B incorporated in country X, has under the company's articles authority to carry out all transactions falling within the company's ordinary course of business. A enters into a contract with C that clearly falls outside the scope of B's ordinary business. According to Section 35A of the Companies Act of country X, "[i]n favour of a person dealing with a company in good faith, the power of the Board of Directors to bind the company, or authorise others to do so, shall be deemed to be free of any limitation under the company's constitution" and "[...] a person shall not be regarded as acting in bad faith by reason only of that person's knowing that an act is beyond the powers of the directors under the company's constitution [...]". B is bound by the contract between A and C even if C knew or ought to have known of the limitations to A's authority, and B may not rely on Article 2.2.5(1) to claim the contrary.

2. A, Managing Director of company B incorporated in country X, has been given by the Board of Directors of the company the authority to carry out all transactions falling within the company's ordinary course of business except the hiring and dismissal of employees. A hires C as the new accountant of B's branch in country Y. B refuses to be bound by this appointment on account of A's lack of authority to hire employees. C may overcome B's objection by invoking Section 35A of the Companies Act of country X. Yet C, who as a national of country Y may not be familiar with that special provision of the Companies Act of country X, may equally rely on the general rule on apparent authority laid down in Article 2.2.5(2) and claim that, in view of A's position as Managing Director of B, it was reasonable for C to believe that A had the authority to hire employees.

另一方面，只要不与上文提及的关于机构、主管或合伙人权限的特殊规则相冲突，本节规定的一般规则就可以与这些特殊规则择一适用。因此，比如寻求证明其与公司主管签订的合同对该公司有拘束力的第三方，可以援引规范公司机构或主管权限的特殊规则，也可以根据情形援引第 2.2.5 条(2)款关于表见代理的一般规则。

示例：

　　1. 作为 X 国公司 B 的首席执行官，A 根据公司章程有权处理属于公司日常经营活动范围内的所有交易。A 与 C 达成一项明显超出 B 日常经营活动范围的合同。根据 X 国公司法第 35A 节，"为维护与公司善意交易之人的利益，董事会约束公司的权限或其授权其他人约束公司的权限，应视为不受公司章程的任何限制性规定的限制"，并且"……不能仅因知晓根据公司章程一行为超出董事权限而视该人恶意行事……"。即使 C 已知或应知 A 的权限，B 仍应受 A 与 C 所签合同的约束，不得依第 2.2.5 条(1)款提出相反主张。

　　2. 作为 X 国公司 B 的管理董事，A 被董事会授权处理除雇员聘用、辞退之外的所有属于公司日常经营活动范围内的所有交易。A 雇佣 C 作为 B 在 Y 国分支机构的会计。B 以 A 没有聘用雇员的权限为由拒绝接受这一任命。C 可通过援引 X 国公司法 35A 节对抗 B 的主张。然而作为 Y 国国民，C 可能并不熟悉 X 国公司法的这一特殊规定，因此其也可依赖第 2.2.5 条第(2)款关于表见代理的一般规则，主张因 A 为 B 的管理董事，C 可以合理地认为 A 有权聘用雇员。

ARTICLE 2.2.2
*(Establishment and scope of the
authority of the agent)*

**(1) The principal's grant of authority to an
agent may be express or implied.**

**(2) The agent has authority to perform all
acts necessary in the circumstances to achieve the
purposes for which the authority was granted.**

COMMENT

1. Express or implied grant of authority

Paragraph (1) makes it clear that the granting of authority to the
agent by the principal is not subject to any particular requirement of
form and that it may be either express or implied.

The most common case of express authority is a power of attorney,
but the principal may also confer authority on the agent in an oral
statement or written communication or, in the case of a corporate entity,
in a resolution by its board of directors. The granting of express
authority in writing has the obvious advantage of providing clear
evidence of the existence and precise scope of the agent's authority to
all parties concerned (principal, agent and third parties).

An implied authority exists whenever the principal's intention to
confer authority on an agent can be inferred from the principal's
conduct (e.g. the assigning of a particular task to the agent) or other
circumstances of the case (e.g. the terms of the express authorisation, a
particular course of dealing between the two parties or a general trade
usage).

Illustration

    1.   B appoints A as Manager of B's apartment building. A has
implied authority to conclude short term lease contracts relating to
the individual apartments.

2. Scope of the authority

The broader the mandate conferred on the agent, the broader the
scope of its authority. Accordingly, paragraph (2) makes it clear that the
agent's authority, unless otherwise provided by the principal in its
authorisation, is not limited to its express terms, but extends to all acts

第2.2.2条

（代理人权限的设立和范围）

（1）本人对代理人权限的授予既可以是明示的，也可以是默示的。

（2）代理人为实现授权之目的，有权采取情况所需的所有行为。

注释：

1. 明示或默示授权

第（1）款明确了本人授予代理人权限的行为无须满足任何特定的形式要求，授权可以是明示或默示的。

最常见的明示授权形式是授权委托书，但是本人也可以通过口头陈述或书面呈述，或在本人为公司实体的情况下以董事会决议的方式授予代理人权限。以书面方式明示授予代理权有明显的好处，即能向所有利害关系方（本人、代理人和第三方）提供代理人权限存在及其确切范围的清晰证据。

默示授予代理权存在于以下情况，即从本人的行为（例如，委派给代理人特定的任务）或其他情况（例如，明示授权的条款，当事人间的特定交易过程或通用贸易惯例）中推断出本人授予代理人权限的意图。

示例：

> 1. B任命A作为B一栋公寓大楼的管理人，A拥有就单个公寓达成短期租赁合同的默示授权。

2. 权限范围

委托代理人的职责越广泛，其权限范围越大。因此，第（2）款明确规定,除非本人在授权中另有规定,代理人的权限不限于其明示的条

necessary in the circumstances to achieve the purposes for which the authority was granted.

Illustration

> 2. Owner B consigns to shipmaster A a cargo to be carried to country X within 10 days. With only three days of navigation left, the ship is damaged and must stop in the nearest port for repairs. A has implied authority to unload the cargo and consign it to another shipmaster to be carried to destination on another ship.

ARTICLE 2.2.3
(Agency disclosed)

(1) Where an agent acts within the scope of its authority and the third party knew or ought to have known that the agent was acting as an agent, the acts of the agent shall directly affect the legal relations between the principal and the third party and no legal relation is created between the agent and the third party.

(2) However, the acts of the agent shall affect only the relations between the agent and the third party, where the agent with the consent of the principal undertakes to become the party to the contract.

COMMENT

1. "Disclosed" agency

With respect to the effects of the acts of the agent, this Section distinguishes between two basic situations: one in which the agent acts on behalf of a principal and within the scope of its authority and the third party knows or ought to know that the agent is acting as an agent, and the other in which the agent acts on behalf of a principal within the scope of its authority but the third party neither knows nor ought to know that the agent is acting as an agent. The first situation, which is the normal one, may be referred to as "disclosed" agency and is dealt with in this Article.

款，而是扩及为实现授权目的的情况下所有必要的行为。

示例：

　　2. 货主 B 委托船东 A 在 10 天内运送一批货物到 X 国。在只剩三天航程时，船舶受损，必须停靠最近的港口修理。A 有卸下货物并委托另一船东用另一艘船运至目的地的默示授权。

第 2.2.3 条

（显名代理）

　　（1）如当代理人在其权限范围内行事，且第三方已知或应知其以代理身份行事，则代理人的行为直接影响本人和第三方之间的法律关系，在代理人和第三方之间不创设任何法律关系。
　　（2）但是，当代理人经本人同意成为合同一方当事人，则代理人的行为应仅影响代理人和第三方之间的关系。

注释：

1. "显名"代理

　　就代理人行为效果而言，本节区分了两种基本情况：一种是代理人在其权限范围内代表本人行事，并且第三方已知或应知其以代理人身份行事；另一种是代理人在其权限范围内代表本人行事，但第三方不知也不应知其以代理人身份行事。第一种是正常情况，可称为"显名"代理，由本条调整。

2. Agent's acts directly affect legal relations between principal and third party

In the case of a "disclosed" agency, the rule is that the agent's acts directly affect the principal's legal position vis-à-vis the third party (paragraph (1)). Thus, a contract made by the agent directly binds the principal and the third party to each other. Likewise, any communication of intention that the agent makes to, or receives from, the third party affects the principal's legal position as if the principal itself had made or received it.

Illustrations

1. A, a sales representative for computer manufacturer B, accepts the order placed by university C for the purchase of a certain number of computers. The sales contract directly binds B vis-à-vis C with the result that it is B, and not A, who is under an obligation to deliver the goods to C and who is entitled to payment by C.

2. The facts are the same as in Illustration 1, except that one of the computers delivered is defective. The notice of such defects given by C to A directly affects B.

3. Acting in the principal's name not necessary

For the establishment of a direct relationship between the principal and the third party it is sufficient that the agent acts within the scope of its authority and that the third party knows or ought to know that the latter acts on behalf of another person. By contrast, it is as a rule not necessary for the agent to act in the principal's name (see also Article 2.2.1(1)).

In practice, however, there might be cases in which it is in the agent's own interest to indicate expressly the identity of the person on whose behalf it is acting. Thus, whenever the contract requires the signature of the parties, the agent is well advised not simply to sign in its own name, but to add language such as "for and on behalf of" followed by the principal's name, so as to avoid any risk of being held personally liable under the contract.

Illustrations

3. The facts are the same as in Illustration 1. For the sales contract to directly bind B vis-à-vis C it is irrelevant whether A, when accepting C's order over the telephone, acts in its own name or expressly states that it is accepting in the name of B.

4. Computer specialist A is contacted by research centre C with a view to creating a computer programme for a special database on

2. 代理人的行为直接影响本人和第三方之间的法律关系

在"显名"代理的情况下，规则是代理人的行为直接影响本人相对于第三方的法律地位（第（1）款）。因此，代理人订立的合同直接约束本人和第三方。同样，代理人向第三方做出或从第三方收到的任何意思沟通，如同本人自己做出或收到的一样影响本人的法律地位。

示例：

1. A作为计算机生产商B的销售代表接受了C大学购买一定数量计算机的订单。销售合同直接约束B和C，其结果是B而不是A有义务发货给C，并有权得到C的支付。

2. 事实同示例1一样，区别是交付的一台计算机有缺陷，C就此缺陷向A发出的通知直接影响B。

3. 并不必须以本人的名义行事

为在本人和第三方之间设立直接关系，代理人在其权限范围内行事并且第三方已知或应知代理人代表另一人行事足矣。相比之下，原则上，代理人并不必须以本人的名义行事（也可参见第2.2.1条第（1）款）。

但在实践中，在某些情况下，代理人明确指出其所代表之人的身份，可能符合代理人自身利益。因此，当合同要求双方签字时，建议代理人最好不要仅以自己的名义签字，而且附加例如"为……和代表……"用语并在之后紧跟本人姓名，以避免合同项下的个人责任风险。

示例：

3. 事实同示例1。对于直接约束B和C的销售合同，A在通过电话接受C订单时是以自己名义还是明确说明是以B的名义接受的，都无关紧要。

4. 计算机专家A与研究中心C订立合同，由A为关于国际案例法的特别数据库开发计算机程序。A以软件公司之B雇

international case law. A, when signing the contract in its capacity as employee of software company B, should expressly state that it is acting on behalf of B. If A merely signs the contract without indicating B, C may hold A personally liable under the contract

4. Agent undertakes to become party to the contract

An agent, though openly acting on behalf of a principal, may exceptionally itself become party to the contract with the third party (paragraph (2)). This is the case, in particular, where a principal, who wants to remain anonymous, instructs the agent to act as a so-called "commission agent", i.e. to deal with the third party in its own name without establishing any direct relation between the principal and the third party. This is also the case where the third party makes it clear that it does not intend to contract with anyone other than the agent and the agent, with the consent of the principal, agrees that it alone and not the principal will be bound by the contract. In both cases it will follow from the terms of the agreement between the principal and the agent that, once the agent has acquired its rights under the contract with the third party, it will transfer them to the principal.

Entirely different is the case where the agent steps in and, in violation of its agreement with the principal, decides to become party to the contract with the third party. In so doing the agent no longer acts as an agent, and this case therefore falls outside the scope of this Section.

Illustrations

5.   Dealer B, expecting a substantial increase in the price of wheat, decides to purchase a large quantity of wheat. B, wishing to remain anonymous, entrusts commission agent A with this task. Even though supplier C knows that A is purchasing on behalf of a principal, the purchase contract is binding on A and C and does not directly affect B's legal position.

6.   Confirming house A, acting on behalf of overseas buyer B, places an order with supplier C for the purchase of certain goods. Since C, who does not know B, insists on A's confirmation of B's order, A accepts to be held liable itself vis-à-vis C. Even though C knows that A is purchasing on behalf of B, the purchase contract is binding on A and C and does not directly affect B's legal position.

员的身份签约时，应明确告知他代表 B 行事。如果 A 签订合同时未披露 B，C 可能要求 A 在合同项下承担个人责任。

4. 代理人成为合同的一方

尽管公开代表本人行事，代理人可能例外地成为与第三方之间合同的一方当事人（第(2)款）。这种情况特别发生在本人想要保持匿名，指示代理人作为所谓的"佣金代理人"行事的情形，即代理人以自己名义与第三方交易，而在本人和第三方之间不设立任何直接关系。类似的情况是，第三方明确表示他无意愿同代理人之外的其他人订立合同，且代理人经本人允许，同意由他自己而不是本人将受合同约束。在这两种情况下，根据本人和代理人之间协议的规定，一旦代理人获得其在与第三方的合同项下的权利，其将把这权利转让给本人。

完全不同的情况是，代理人介入，并违背其与本人之间的协议，决定成为与第三方合同的当事方。此时，代理人不再是以代理人身份行事，因此这种情况不属于本节的调整范围。

示例：

5. 交易商 B 预计小麦价格将大幅上涨，决定购买大量小麦。B 希望保持匿名，委托佣金代理人 A 从事这一交易。即使供货商 C 知道 A 代表本人购买，购买合同也仅约束 A 和 C，并不直接影响 B 的法律地位。

6. 保兑公司 A 代表海外买方 B 向供货商 C 定购了某些货物。C 不知道 B，由于 C 坚持要求 A 确认 B 的订单，A 同意对 C 承担个人责任。即使 C 知道 A 代表 B 购买，购买合同也只约束 A 和 C，并不直接影响 B 的法律地位。

7.   Dealer B instructs agent A to purchase a certain quantity of oil on its behalf. When A is about to conclude the contract with supplier C, the news arrives that the oil producing countries intend to reduce production substantially. A, expecting a rise in oil prices, decides to purchase the oil on its own behalf and enters into the contract with C as the only other party. In so doing A has ceased to act as agent for the principal and the consequences of its acts are no longer governed by this Section.

ARTICLE 2.2.4
(Agency undisclosed)

(1) Where an agent acts within the scope of its authority and the third party neither knew nor ought to have known that the agent was acting as an agent, the acts of the agent shall affect only the relations between the agent and the third party.

(2) However, where such an agent, when contracting with the third party on behalf of a business, represents itself to be the owner of that business, the third party, upon discovery of the real owner of the business, may exercise also against the latter the rights it has against the agent.

COMMENT

1. "Undisclosed" agency

This Article deals with what may be referred to as "undisclosed" agency, i.e. the situation where an agent acts within the scope of its authority on behalf of a principal but the third party neither knows nor ought to know that the agent is acting as an agent.

2. Agent's acts directly affect only the relations between agent and third party

Paragraph (1) provides that in the case of an "undisclosed" agency the agent's acts affect only the relations between the agent and the third party and do not directly bind the principal vis-à-vis the third party.

7. 交易商 B 指示代理人 A 代表其购买一定数量的石油。但 A 即将与供货商 C 达成合同时，有消息称，石油生产国意图大幅减产。A 预期油价上升，决定以自己的名义购买石油，并作为唯一的合同另一方与 C 达成合同。由此，A 已经停止作为本人的代理人行事，其行为的后果不再受本节调整。

第2.2.4条

（隐名代理）

（1）当代理人在其权限范围内行事，但第三方既不知道也不应知道代理人是以代理人身份行事，则代理人的行为仅影响代理人与第三方之间的关系。

（2）然而，如果代理人代表一个企业与第三方达成合同，并声称是该企业的所有人，则第三方在发现该企业的真实所有人后，亦可以向后者行使其对代理人的权利。

注释：

1."隐名"代理

本条涉及的情况是"隐名"代理，即代理人在权限范围内代表本人行事，但第三方不知也不应知代理人以代理人身份行事。

2. 代理人的行为仅直接影响代理人和第三方之间的关系

第(1)款规定，在"隐名"代理情况下，代理人的行为仅影响代理人和第三方之间的关系，并不直接约束本人和第三方。

Illustration

> 1. Art dealer A purchases a painting from artist C. When entering into the contract A does not disclose the fact that it is acting on behalf of client B, nor has C any reason to believe that A is not acting on its own behalf. The contract is binding on A and C only, and does not give rise to a direct relationship between B and C.

3. Third party's right of action against principal

Notwithstanding the rule laid down in paragraph (1), the third party may exceptionally have a right of direct action also against the principal. More precisely, according to paragraph (2), if the third party believes that it is dealing with the owner of a business while in fact it is dealing with the owner's agent, it may, upon discovery of the real owner, exercise also against the owner the rights it has against the agent.

Illustration

> 2. Manufacturer A, after having transferred its assets to a newly formed company C, continues to contract in its own name without disclosing to supplier B that it is in fact acting only as the Managing Director of C. Upon discovery of the existence of C, B has a right of action also against that company.

ARTICLE 2.2.5
(Agent acting without or exceeding its authority)

(1) Where an agent acts without authority or exceeds its authority, its acts do not affect the legal relations between the principal and the third party.

(2) However, where the principal causes the third party reasonably to believe that the agent has authority to act on behalf of the principal and that the agent is acting within the scope of that authority, the principal may not invoke against the third party the lack of authority of the agent.

示例:

> 1. 艺术品交易商 A 向艺术家 C 购买一幅画。在订立合同时,A 并未披露自己代表客户 B 行事的事实,C 也没有任何理由认为 A 不是在以自己的身份行事。合同仅约束 A 和 C,并不在 B 和 C 之间产生直接关系。

3. 第三方对抗本人的诉权

尽管第(1)款规定了上述规则,但例外情况下,第三方也可以有直接的诉权对抗本人。更确切地说,根据第(2)款,如果第三方认为交易对方是一企业组织的所有者,而事实上是与所有者的代理人进行交易,在发现真实所有者后,第三方也可向所有者行使其对抗代理人的权利。

示例:

> 2. 制造商 A,在将其资产转给新设立的 C 公司后,继续以自己的名义订立合同,而没有向供货商 B 披露自己只是作为 C 公司的管理董事行事的事实。在发现 C 公司的存在后,B 也有对抗该公司的诉权。

第2.2.5条

(代理人无权或越权行事)

(1) 代理人没有代理权或超越代理权行事时,其行为不影响本人和第三方之间的法律关系。

(2) 但是,如果本人造成第三方合理相信代理人有权代表本人行事并且是在授权范围内行事,则本人不得以代理人无代理权为由对抗第三方。

COMMENT

1. Lack of authority

Paragraph (1) expressly states that where an agent acts without authority, its acts do not bind the principal and the third party to each other. The same applies to the case where the agent has been granted authority of limited scope and acts exceeding its authority.

As to the liability of the false agent vis-à-vis the third party, see Article 2.2.6.

Illustration

1.   Principal B authorises agent A to buy on its behalf a specific quantity of grain but without exceeding a certain price. A enters into a contract with seller C for the purchase of a greater quantity of grain and at a higher price than that authorised by B. On account of A's lack of authority, the contract between A and C does not bind B, nor does it become effective between A and C.

2. Apparent authority

There are two cases in which an agent, though acting without authority or exceeding its authority, may bind the principal and the third party to each other.

The first case occurs whenever the principal ratifies the agent's act and is dealt with in Article 2.2.9.

The second case is that of so-called "apparent authority" and is dealt with in paragraph (2) of this Article. According to this provision a principal, whose conduct leads a third party reasonably to believe that the agent has authority to act on its behalf, is prevented from invoking against the third party the lack of authority of the agent and is therefore bound by the latter's act.

Apparent authority, which is an application of the general principle of good faith (see Article 1.7) and of the prohibition of inconsistent behaviour (see Article 1.8), is especially important if the principal is not an individual but an organisation. In dealing with a corporation, partnership or other business association a third party may find it difficult to determine whether the persons acting for the organisation have actual authority to do so and may therefore prefer, whenever possible, to rely on their apparent authority. For this purpose the third party only has to demonstrate that it was reasonable for it to believe that the person purporting to represent the organisation was authorised

注释：

1. 无权代理

第(1)款明确规定，当代理人没有权限行事时，其行为不约束本人和第三方。这同样也适用于代理人被授予有限代理权但超越代理权限行事的情况。

至于无权代理人对第三方的责任，参见第2.2.6条。

示例：

> 1. 本人B授权代理人A代表其在不超过某确定价格的情况下，购买一定数量的谷物。A与卖方C达成合同，但购买谷物的数量和价格均超过了B的代理权范围。因为A为无权代理，所以A和C之间的合同并不约束B，在A和C之间也不生效。

2. 表见代理权

在两种情况下，代理人尽管没有代理权或超越代理权行事，其行为仍可约束本人和第三方。

第一种情况是，本人追认了代理人的行为，第2.2.9条中对此作了规定。

第二种情况是所谓的"表见代理权"，本条第(2)款对此作了规定。根据这一规定，本人的行为导致第三方合理相信代理人有权代表本人行事时，本人不能以代理人无权代理对抗第三方，而应受代理人行为的约束。

作为诚实信用一般原则（参见第1.7条）和禁止不一致行为之规定（参见第1.8条）的适用，表见代理在本人不是个人而是组织时尤为重要。在与公司、合伙或其他商业组织交易时，第三方很难确定代表该组织行事的人是否有实际代理权，因此会尽可能倾向于依赖他们的表见代理权。出于这一目的，第三方只须证明他合理相信自称该组织的人被授权行事，并且这一信赖是由实际有权代表该组织的人（董

to do so, and that this belief was caused by the conduct of those actually authorised to represent the organisation (Board of Directors, executive officers, partners, etc.). Whether or not the third party's belief was reasonable will depend on the circumstances of the case (position occupied by the apparent agent in the organisation's hierarchy, type of transaction involved, acquiescence of the organisation's representatives in the past, etc.).

Illustrations

> 2.   A, a manager of one of company B's branch offices, though lacking actual authority to do so, engages construction company C to redecorate the branch's premises. In view of the fact that a branch manager normally would have authority to enter into such a contract, B is bound by the contract with C since it was reasonable for C to believe that A had actual authority to enter into the contract.

> 3.   A, Chief Financial Officer of company B, though lacking authority to do so, has, with the acquiescence of the Board of Directors, repeatedly entered into financial transactions with bank C on behalf of B. On the occasion of a new transaction which proves to be disadvantageous to B, B's Board of Directors raises against C the objection of A's lack of authority. C may defeat this objection by claiming that B is bound by A's apparent authority to enter into the financial transaction on B's behalf.

A<small>RTICLE</small> **2.2.6**
*(Liability of agent acting without or
exceeding its authority)*

(1) An agent that acts without authority or exceeds its authority is, failing ratification by the principal, liable for damages that will place the third party in the same position as if the agent had acted with authority and not exceeded its authority.

(2) However, the agent is not liable if the third party knew or ought to have known that the agent had no authority or was exceeding its authority.

事会成员、执行主管、合伙人等）的行为造成的。第三方的信赖是否合理将取决于具体情形（表见代理人在组织等级中的地位，所涉交易的类型，组织代表人以前的默许，等等）。

示例：

2. A作为B公司一家分支机构的经理，尽管没有相关的实际代理权，与建筑公司C就分支机构办公场所的重新装修缔约。鉴于分支机构经理通常有权订立此类合同的事实，C可以合理地相信A有订立合同的实际代理权，B应受该合同的约束。

3. A作为B公司的首席财务官，尽管没有相关的实际代理权，在董事会默许下一直代表B与C银行进行金融交易。当一项新交易表明对B不利时，B董事会以A无权代理而向C提出异议。C可主张B受A有代表B进行金融交易的表见代理权的约束，从而击败这一异议。

第2.2.6条

（代理人无权或越权行事的责任）

（1）没有代理权或超越代理权行事的代理人，如未经本人追认，则应对第三方承担将其恢复至如同代理人有代理权或未超越代理权行事时第三方所处同等状况的损害赔偿责任。

（2）但是，如果第三方已知或应知代理人没有代理权或超越代理权，则代理人不承担责任。

COMMENT

1. Liability of false agent

It is generally recognised that an agent acting without authority or exceeding its authority shall, failing ratification by the principal, be liable for damages to the third party. Paragraph (1), in stating that the false agent shall be liable to pay the third party such compensation as will place the third party in the same position as it would have been in if the agent had acted with authority, makes it clear that the liability of the false agent is not limited to the so-called reliance or negative interest, but extends to the so-called expectation or positive interest. In other words, the third party may recover the profit that would have resulted if the contract concluded with the false agent had been a valid one.

Illustration

1.   Agent A, without being authorised by principal B, enters into a contract with third party C for the sale of a cargo of oil belonging to B. Failing B's ratification of the contract, C may recover from A the difference between the contract price and the current market price.

2. Third party's knowledge of agent's lack of authority

The false agent is liable to the third party only to the extent that the third party, when entering into the contract with the false agent, neither knew nor ought to have known that the latter was acting without authority or exceeding its authority.

Illustration

2.   A, a junior employee of company B, without having authority to do so engages construction company C to redecorate B's premises. B refuses to ratify the contract. Nevertheless C may not request damages from A since it should have known that an employee of A's rank normally has no authority to enter into such a contract.

注释：

1. 无权代理的责任

通常认为，没有代理权或超越代理权行事的代理人，如未经本人追认，则应对第三方受到的损害承担责任。第(1)款规定无权代理人有责任补偿第三方以使其恢复至代理人若有权行事其本应所处的状况。这一规定明确了无权代理人的责任不限于所谓的信赖利益或消极利益，而且扩及所谓的预期利益或积极利益。换句话说，第三方可以求偿若与无权代理人订立的合同有效所会产生的利润。

示例：

  1. 代理人 A 未经本人 B 授权，与第三方 C 订立合同出售一批属于 B 的石油。除非 B 追认该合同，否则 C 可向 A 求偿合同价与目前市场价之间的差价。

2. 第三方知晓代理人无权代理

只有在第三方与无权代理人订立合同时不知且不应知后者没有代理权或超越代理权行事时，无权代理人才对第三方承担责任。

示例：

  2. A 作为 B 公司的低级雇员，在无相关权限的情况下，同建筑公司 C 就重新装修 B 办公场所订立合同。B 拒绝追认该合同。C 不得向 A 请求损害赔偿，因为他应知 A 所处地位的雇员无权订立此类合同。

ARTICLE 2.2.7
(Conflict of interests)

(1) If a contract concluded by an agent involves the agent in a conflict of interests with the principal of which the third party knew or ought to have known, the principal may avoid the contract. The right to avoid is subject to Articles 3.2.9 and 3.2.11 to 3.2.15.

(2) However, the principal may not avoid the contract

(a) if the principal had consented to, or knew or ought to have known of, the agent's involvement in the conflict of interests; or

(b) if the agent had disclosed the conflict of interests to the principal and the latter had not objected within a reasonable time.

COMMENT

1. Conflict of interests between agent and principal

It is inherent in any agency relationship that the agent, in fulfilling its mandate, will act in the interest of the principal and not in its own interest or in that of anyone else if there is a conflict between such an interest and that of the principal.

The most frequent cases of potential conflict of interests are those where the agent acts for two principals and those where the agent concludes the contract with itself or with a firm in which it has an interest. However, in practice even in such cases a real conflict of interests may not exist. Thus, for instance, the agent's acting for two principals may be in conformity with the usages of the trade sector concerned, or the principal may have conferred on the agent a mandate which is so stringent as to leave it no margin for manoeuvre.

2. Conflict of interests as grounds for avoidance of the contract

Paragraph (1) of this Article lays down the rule that a contract concluded by an agent acting in a situation of real conflict of interests may be avoided by the principal, provided that the third party knew or ought to have known of the conflict of interests.

The requirement of the actual or constructive knowledge of the third party is intended to protect the innocent third party's interest in

第 2.2.7 条

（利益冲突）

（1）如果代理人订立的合同涉及代理人与本人之间的利益冲突，而且第三方已知或应知这一情况，则本人可宣告合同无效。宣告无效的权利由第 3.2.9 条和第 3.2.11 条至第 3.2.15 条调整。

（2）但是，在以下情况下，本人不得宣告合同无效：

（a）本人已经同意，或已知或应知代理人涉及利益冲突；或

（b）代理人已经向本人披露该利益冲突，但本人在合理时间内并未提出反对。

注释：

1. 代理人和本人间的利益冲突

在任何代理关系中都内含着一项要求，即代理人在履行职责时，如果其自身利益或任何他人的利益与本人利益发生冲突时，其应该代表本人利益而不是代表自己或其他人的利益行事。

最常见的可能的利益冲突情况是，代理人代表两个本人行事和代理人与自己或与自己有利益关系的公司缔约。但是，实践中即使在这些情况下，也并不一定存在真正的利益冲突。例如，代理人代表两个本人行事可能符合所涉贸易部门的惯例，或者本人可能曾授予代理人非常严格的命令，使其没有自行操作的余地。

2. 利益冲突作为宣告合同无效的根据

本条第（1）款规定，在有真实利益冲突的情况下，只要第三方已知或应知该等利益冲突，本人可宣告代理人订立的合同无效。

对第三方实际或推断性知悉的要求意在保护善意第三方对于维持

preserving the contract. This requirement is obviously no longer relevant where the agent concludes the contract with itself and is therefore at one and the same time agent and third party.

Illustrations

1.   Solicitor A is requested by foreign client B to purchase on its behalf an apartment in A's city. A buys an apartment client C has requested A to sell on its behalf. B may avoid the contract if it can prove that C knew or ought to have known of A's conflict of interests. Likewise, C may avoid the contract if it can prove that B knew or ought to have known of A's conflict of interests.

2.   Sales agent A, requested by retailer B to purchase certain goods on its behalf, purchases the goods from company C in which A is a majority shareholder. B may avoid the contract if it can prove that C knew or ought to have known of A's conflict of interests.

3.   Client B instructs bank A to buy on its behalf one thousand shares of company C at the closing price of day M on the stock exchange of city Y. Even if A sells B the requested shares from out of those it has in its own portfolio, there can be no conflict of interests because B's mandate leaves A no margin for manoeuvre.

4.   A, Chief Executive Officer of company B, has authority to appoint the company's counsel in the event of a law suit being brought by or against B. A appoints itself as B's counsel. B may avoid the contract.

3. Procedure for avoidance

As to the procedure for avoidance, the provisions laid down in Articles 3.2.9 (*Confirmation*), 3.2.11 (*Notice of avoidance*), 3.2.12 (*Time limits*), 3.2.13 (*Partial avoidance*), 3.2.14 (*Retroactive effect of avoidance*) and 3.2.15 (*Restitution*) apply.

4. Avoidance excluded

According to paragraph (2), the principal loses its right to avoid the contract if it has given its prior consent to the agent's acting in a situation of conflict of interests, or at any rate knew or ought to have known that the agent would do so. The right of avoidance is likewise excluded if the principal, having been informed by the agent of the contract it has concluded in a situation of conflict of interests, raises no objection.

合同所具有的利益。在代理人同自己缔约，即代理人同时是代理人和第三方的情况下，这一要求很明显没有意义。

示例：

1. A 律师应外国客户 B 要求，代表 B 在 A 所在的城市购买一套公寓。A 所买的公寓是客户 C 要求 A 代表 C 出售的。如果 B 能证明 C 已知或应知 A 的利益冲突，就可以宣告合同无效。同样，如果 C 能证明 B 已知或应知 A 的利益冲突，也可以宣告合同无效。

2. 销售代理 A 应零售商 B 请求代表 B 购买某些商品，A 向 C 公司购买了该货物，同时 A 是 C 的大股东。如果能证明 C 已知或应知 A 的利益冲突，B 可以宣告合同无效。

3. 客户 B 指示银行 A 代表其在 Y 城的股票交易所以 M 日的收盘价购买 1000 股 C 公司股票。即使 A 将自己持有的该股票出售给 B，也不存在利益冲突，因为 B 的委托没有给 A 留下自主操作的空间。

4. B 公司首席执行官 A 有权在由 B 提起或向 B 提起的法律诉讼中任命公司律师。A 任命自己为公司律师。B 可以宣告该合同无效。

3. 宣告合同无效的程序

宣告合同无效的程序适用第 3.2.9 条（确认）、第 3.2.11 条（宣告合同无效的通知）、第 3.2.12 条（时间期限）、第 3.2.13 条（部分无效）、第 3.2.14 条（宣告合同无效的追溯力）以及第 3.2.15 条（恢复原状）。

4. 排除宣告合同无效

根据第（2）款，如果本人事先同意代理人在利益冲突的情况下行事，或无论如何已知或应知代理人将如此行事，本人丧失宣告合同无效的权利。如果代理人已告知本人其在利益冲突情况下订立的合同，但本人并未提出异议，则宣告合同无效的权利同样被排除。

Illustration

> 5. The facts are the same as in Illustration 1, except that before concluding the contract A duly informs B that it is acting as agent also for C. If B does not object B loses its right to avoid the contract. Likewise, if A duly informs C that it is acting as agent also for B and C does not object, C loses its right to avoid the contract.

5. Issues not covered by this Article

In conformity with the scope of this Section set out in Article 2.2.1, this Article addresses only the impact that the agent's involvement in a conflict of interests situation may have on the external relationship. Issues such as the agent's duty of full disclosure vis-à-vis the principal and the principal's right to damages from the agent may be settled on the basis of other provisions of the Principles (see Articles 1.7, 3.2.16, 7.4.1 *et seq.*) or are otherwise governed by the law applicable to the internal relationship between principal and agent.

ARTICLE **2.2.8**
(Sub-agency)

An agent has implied authority to appoint a sub-agent to perform acts which it is not reasonable to expect the agent to perform itself. The rules of this Section apply to the sub-agency.

COMMENT

1. Role of sub-agents

In carrying out the mandate conferred on it by the principal, an agent may find it convenient or even necessary to avail itself of the services of other persons. This is the case, for instance, where certain tasks are to be performed in a place distant from the agent's place of business, or if a more efficient performance of the agent's mandate requires distribution of work.

2. Implied authority to appoint sub-agents

Whether or not the agent is authorised to appoint one or more sub-agents depends on the terms of the authority granted by the principal.

示例:

　　5. 事实同示例1,不同点是在合同订立前,A 适时告知 B 他也作为 C 的代理人行事。如 B 未提出异议,即丧失宣告合同无效的权利。同样,如果 A 适时告知 C 他作为 B 的代理人行事,且 C 未提异议,C 丧失宣告合同无效的权利。

5. 本条不涵盖的问题

与第2.2.1条中列明的范围一致,本条仅解决代理人涉及利益冲突可能对外部关系产生的影响。代理人向本人承担的全面披露的义务以及本人要求代理人损害赔偿权利等问题,可根据《通则》其他条款解决(参见第1.7条、第3.2.16条、第7.4.1条及其以下条款,等等)或由适用于本人与代理人之间内部关系的法律调整。

第2.2.8条

(次代理)

对于不应合理期待代理人亲自履行的行为,代理人具有指定次代理人履行的默示权力。本节的规则适用于次代理。

注释:

1. 次代理的作用

在执行本人指令时,代理人可能发现利用他人的服务更方便甚至是必须的。比如,某任务的履行地远离代理人营业地,或者为了更有效地履行代理人的指令需要分配工作。

2. 指定次代理人的默示授权

代理人是否被授予指定一个或多个次代理人的权限,取决于本人授予代理权的条款。因此,本人可以明示排除指定次代理人或规定以

Thus, the principal may expressly exclude the appointment of sub-agents or make it conditional upon its prior approval. If nothing is said in the authorisation as to the possibility of appointing sub-agents and the terms of the authority granted are not otherwise inconsistent with such a possibility, the agent has the right under this Article to appoint sub-agents. The only limitation is that the agent may not entrust the sub-agent(s) with tasks that it is reasonable to expect the agent itself to perform. This is the case in particular of acts requiring the agent's personal expertise.

Illustrations

1. Chinese museum B instructs a London-based art dealer A to buy a particular piece of Greek pottery on sale at a private auction in Germany. A has implied authority to appoint German sub-agent S to purchase that piece of pottery at the auction in Germany and to send it to B.

2. The facts are the same as in Illustration 1, except that B does not specify the particular piece of Greek pottery to be acquired at the auction in Germany as it relies on A's expertise to choose the most suitable item offered for sale. A is expected to make the purchase at the auction itself, but once it has purchased the piece of pottery, it may appoint sub-agent S to send it to B.

3. Effects of a sub-agent's acts

This Article expressly states that the rules of this Section apply to the sub-agency. In other words, the acts of a sub-agent legitimately appointed by the agent bind the principal and the third party to each other, provided that those acts are within both the agent's authority and the authority conferred on the sub-agent by the agent, which may be more limited.

Illustration

3. The facts are the same as in Illustration 1. The purchase of the piece of Greek pottery by S directly binds B provided that it is within both the authority that B has granted to A and the authority that A has granted to S.

获得其事先批准为条件。如果在授权中没有提及指定次代理的可能性，且授权条款与此可能性也不存在冲突，则根据本条代理人有权指定次代理人。唯一的限制是代理人不可以委托次代理人从事合理预期由代理人自己履行的任务，特别是需要代理人个人专业技能的情况下。

示例：

1. 中国博物馆 B 指示一家设在伦敦的艺术品交易商 A，购买在德国一私人拍卖会中出售的某一件特定的希腊陶器。A 有指定德国次代理人 S 在德国的拍卖会上购买该陶器并交给 B 的默示代理权。

2. 事实同示例1，不同之处是 B 并未特别指定在德国拍卖会上将要购买哪一件希腊陶器，因为它依赖 A 的专业技能挑选最适合的商品。A 被预期会亲自参加拍卖并购买，但一旦购买了某件陶器，他可以指定次代理人 S 去交给 B。

3. 次代理人行为的效果

本条明确本节规则适用于次代理。换句话说，代理人合法指定的次代理人的行为约束本人和第三方，只要其行为在代理人的权限以及在代理人授予次代理人的可能更狭窄的代理权限范围内。

示例：

3. 事实同示例1，S 购买希腊陶器的行为直接约束 B，只要该行为同时在 B 授予 A 的权限范围内和 A 授予 S 的权限范围内。

ARTICLE 2.2.9
(Ratification)

(1) **An act by an agent that acts without authority or exceeds its authority may be ratified by the principal. On ratification the act produces the same effects as if it had initially been carried out with authority.**

(2) **The third party may by notice to the principal specify a reasonable period of time for ratification. If the principal does not ratify within that period of time it can no longer do so.**

(3) **If, at the time of the agent's act, the third party neither knew nor ought to have known of the lack of authority, it may, at any time before ratification, by notice to the principal indicate its refusal to become bound by a ratification.**

COMMENT

1. Notion of ratification

This Article lays down the generally accepted principle whereby acts which have no effect on the principal because they have been carried out by an agent holding itself out to have authority but actually without authority or exceeding its authority, may be authorised by the principal at a later stage. Such subsequent authorisation is known as "ratification".

Like the original authorisation, ratification is not subject to any requirement as to form. As it is a unilateral manifestation of intent, it may be either express or implied from words or conduct and, though normally communicated to the agent, to the third party, or to both, it need not be communicated to anyone, provided that it is manifested in some way an d can therefore be ascertained by probative material.

Illustration

Agent A purchases on behalf of principal B goods from third party C at a price higher than that which A is authorised to pay. Upon receipt of C's bill, B makes no objection and pays it by bank transfer. The payment amounts to ratification of A's act even if B does not expressly declare its intention to ratify, fails to inform

第2.2.9条

（追认）

（1）代理人没有代理权或超越代理权的行为可由本人追认。经追认的行为与代理人自始依代理权行事产生同样的效力。

（2）第三方可以通知本人在规定的一段合理的时间内追认。本人如未在该时间内追认，则不能再予追认。

（3）如果在代理人行事时，第三方既不知道也不应知道代理人无权代理，则第三方可在本人追认前，随时通知本人表示拒绝受追认的约束。

注释：

1. 追认的概念

本条规定了一项普遍接受的原则，即，在代理人虽自己表示有代理权但实际无代理权或超越代理权的情况下做出的行为对本人无效，但本人可在事后予以授权。此类事后的授权即为"追认"。

同原始授权一样，追认不受任何形式的约束。因为它是单方的意思表示，可以是以文字或行为的方式明示或默示做出。尽管这种意思表示通常都通知给代理人或者第三方，或者同时通知二者，然而也无须通知任何人，只要这种意思能以某种方式表示出来，并能以证据确认。

示例：

代理人A代表本人B从第三方C处以高于A被授权的购买价格购买了货物。在收到C的账单后，B并未反对，而是通过银行转账付款。即使B并未明确宣称其追认的意思，也

both A and C of the payment and C is only subsequently informed of the payment by its bank.

2. Effects of ratification

On ratification the agent's acts produce the same effects as if they had been carried out with authority from the outset (paragraph (1)). It follows that the third party may refuse partial ratification of the agent's acts by the principal as it would amount to a proposal by the principal to modify the contract that the third party has concluded with the agent. In turn, the principal may not revoke ratification after it has been brought to the attention of the third party. Otherwise the principal would be in a position to withdraw unilaterally from the contract with the third party.

3. Time of ratification

The principal may in principle ratify at any time. The reason for this is that normally the third party does not even know that it has contracted with an agent who did not have authority or who exceeded its authority. However, even if the third party knows from the outset, or subsequently becomes aware, that the agent was a false agent, it will have a legitimate interest not to be left in doubt indefinitely as to the ultimate fate of the contract concluded with the false agent. Accordingly, paragraph (2) grants the third party the right to set a reasonable time limit within which the principal must ratify if it intends to do so. It goes without saying that in such a case ratification must be notified to the third party.

4. Ratification excluded by third party

A third party, who when dealing with the agent neither knew nor ought to have known of that agent's lack of authority, may exclude ratification by giving the principal notice to this effect any time before ratification by the latter. The reason for granting the innocent third party such a right is to avoid that the principal is the only one in a position to speculate and to decide whether or not to ratify depending on market developments.

5. Third persons' rights not affected

This Article deals only with the effects of ratification on the three parties directly involved in the agency relationship, i.e. the principal, the agent and the third party. In accordance with the scope of this Section as defined in Article 2.2.1, the rights of other third persons are

未将付款事宜告知 A 和 C，C 只是随后由银行处得知此事，B 的支付行为即等于追认了 A 的行为。

2. 追认的效果

经追认的代理人的行为与自始就依授权行事产生同样的效果（第(1)款）。因此，第三方可拒绝本人对代理人行为的部分追认，因为这相当于本人提出的修改第三方已和代理人达成的合同的提议。进而，本人不可以在追认已经提请第三方注意后撤销追认。否则，本人就能够单方解除与第三方订立的合同。

3. 追认的时间

原则上，本人可在任何时间追认。理由是，通常第三方甚至不知道与自己订立合同的代理人没有代理权或超越代理权。但是，即使第三方自始知道，或随后知道代理人是个无权代理人，对于其与无权代理人达成合同的最终命运如何，第三人具有合法权利不使自己无限期地处于不确定的疑惑之中。因此，第(2)款授权第三方可设定一合理期限，要求本人在该期限内予以追认。在这种情况下，追认当然还必须通知第三方。

4. 第三方排除追认

第三方如在同代理人交易时既不知也不应知代理人为无权代理，可在本人追认前的任何时间告知本人拒绝接受追认从而排除追认。授予善意第三方此项权利的原因是为避免本人成为唯一能根据市场变化推测并决定是否追认的情况。

5. 第三人的权利不受影响

本条仅调整追认对代理关系中所直接涉及的三方，即本人、代理人、第三方的影响。根据第2.2.1条界定的本节的适用范围，其他第

not affected. For instance, if the same goods have been sold first by the false agent to C, and subsequently by the principal to another person D, the conflict between C and D as a result of the principal's subsequent ratification of the first sale will have to be solved by the applicable law.

ARTICLE 2.2.10

(Termination of authority)

(1) Termination of authority is not effective in relation to the third party unless the third party knew or ought to have known of it.

(2) Notwithstanding the termination of its authority, an agent remains authorised to perform the acts that are necessary to prevent harm to the principal's interests.

COMMENT

1. Grounds for termination not covered by this Article

There are several grounds on which the agent's authority may be terminated: revocation by the principal, renunciation by the agent, completion of the act(s) for which authority had been granted, loss of capacity, bankruptcy, death or cessation of the existence of the principal or the agent, etc. What exactly constitutes a ground for termination and the way it operates as between the principal and the agent falls outside the scope of this Article and is to be determined in accordance with the applicable laws (e.g. the law governing the internal relations between principal and agent, the law governing their legal status or personality, the law governing bankruptcy, etc.) which may vary considerably from one country to another.

2. Termination effective vis-à-vis third party

Whatever the grounds for termination of the agent's authority, in relation to the third party termination is not effective unless the third party knew or ought to have known of it (paragraph (1)). In other words, even if the agent's authority has been terminated for one reason or another, the agent's acts continue to affect the legal relationship between the principal and the third party as long as the third party is

三人的权利不受影响。例如，如果同一批货物，先由无权代理人卖给C，随后由本人卖给另一人 D，因本人随后对第一次销售追认所产生的 C 与 D 之间的冲突，只能由适用法解决。

第2.2.10条

（代理权终止）

　　（1）代理权的终止对第三方不产生效力，除非第三方已知或应知这一情况。
　　（2）尽管代理权终止，但代理人仍有权为防止本人利益蒙受损害而采取必要的行为。

注释：

1. 本条不涉及终止的理由

　　代理权可基于某些理由终止：本人取消委托、代理人辞去委托、授权代理事务完成、丧失行为能力、破产、本人或代理人死亡或不再存续等。关于什么构成终止的确切理由，以及其在本人与代理人之间运作的方式不属于本条的调整范围，应根据适用法加以确定（例如，规范本人和代理人内部关系的法律，规范他们法律地位和法律人格的法律，规范破产的法律，等等），这些适用法可能在国与国之间差异很大。

2. 终止对第三方的效力

　　无论代理权终止的理由是什么，除非第三方已知或应知代理权终止，否则对第三方不产生效力（第（1）款）。换句话说，即使代理权已经由于某个理由终止，代理人的行为仍将继续影响本人和第三方之

neither aware of nor ought to know that the agent no longer has authority.

Obviously the situation is clear whenever either the principal or the agent gives the third party notice of the termination. In the absence of such notice it will depend on the circumstances of the case whether the third party ought to have known of the termination.

Illustrations

1. Principal B opens a branch office in city X. An advertisement published in the local newspaper indicates Managing Director A as having full authority to act on behalf of B. When B subsequently revokes A's authority, a similar notice thereof in the same newspaper is sufficient to make the termination effective vis-à-vis B's customers in city X.

2. Retailer C has repeatedly placed orders with sales represent-ative A for the purchase of goods sold by principal B. A continues to accept orders from C even after its authority has been terminated on account of B's bankruptcy. The mere fact that the bankruptcy proceedings were given the publicity required by the applicable law is not sufficient to make the termination effective vis-à-vis C.

3. Authority of necessity

Even after termination of the agent's authority the circumstances of the case may make it necessary for the agent to perform additional acts in order to prevent the principal's interests from being harmed.

Illustration

3. Agent A has authority to purchase a certain quantity of perishable goods on behalf of principal B. After the purchase of the goods A is informed of B's death. Notwithstanding the termination of its authority, A continues to be authorised either to resell the goods or to store them in a suitable warehouse.

4. Restriction of authority also covered

The rules of this Article apply not only to termination but, with appropriate modifications, also to subsequent restrictions of an agent's authority.

间的法律关系，只要第三方既不知道也不应知道代理人不再有权限。

本人或代理人应向第三方发出终止通知，情况当然会很清楚。在没有此类通知的情况下，则取决于个案具体情况下第三方是否应当知道代理权已终止。

示例：

> 1. 本人 B 在 X 城开办了一家分支机构。当地报纸刊登的广告表明，管理董事 A 有权全权代表 B 行事。当随后 B 撤销 A 的代理权时，在相同的报纸刊登相似的通知足以使代理权终止对 X 城的 B 的客户生效。

> 2. 零售商 C 一直向销售代表 A 订购本人 B 出售的商品。A 甚至在其代理权已经因 B 破产而终止后仍继续接受 C 的订单。根据适用法的要求已完成了破产公告程序，这一唯一事实并不足以使代理权终止对 C 生效。

3. 必要的代理权

即使在代理权终止后，个案的具体情况仍可能使代理人需要采取额外的行为以防止本人利益受到损害。

示例：

> 3. 代理人 A 有权代表本人 B 购买一定数量易腐烂的货物。在购买货物后，得知 B 的死讯。虽然代理权终止，但是 A 仍有权转售货物或在合适的仓库内存放这些货物。

4. 也调整对代理权的限制

本条规则不仅适用于代理权的终止，经适当修改后，也适用于事后对代理人权限的限制。

CHAPTER 3

VALIDITY

SECTION 1: GENERAL PROVISIONS

ARTICLE 3.1.1
(Matters not covered)

This Chapter does not deal with lack of capacity.

COMMENT

This Article makes it clear that not all the grounds of invalidity of a contract to be found in the various national legal systems fall within the scope of the Principles. This is in particular the case of lack of capacity. The reason for its exclusion lies in both the inherent complexity of questions of status and the extremely diverse manner in which these questions are treated in domestic law. In consequence, matters such as *ultra vires* will continue to be governed by the applicable law.

As to the authority of organs, officers or partners of a corporation, partnership or other entities to bind their respective entities, see Comment 5 on Article 2.2.1.

ARTICLE 3.1.2
(Validity of mere agreement)

A contract is concluded, modified or terminated by the mere agreement of the parties, without any further requirement.

第三章
合同的效力

第一节　一般规定

第3.1.1条

（未涉及事项）

本章不处理无行为能力问题。

注释：

　　本条清楚表明不同国家法律制度下导致合同无效的原因未必都在《通则》的调整范围之内，尤其是涉及无行为能力的情况。将其排除在《通则》调整范围之外的原因有二：一方面在于身份问题的内在复杂性，另一方面在于不同国内法对这类问题的处理方式截然不同。因此，例如越权行为的问题将继续受适用法管辖。

　　关于公司、合伙企业或其他实体的机构、主管或合伙人约束各自实体的权限，参见第2.2.1条注释5。

第3.1.2条

（效力仅凭协议）

　　合同仅凭当事人的协议订立、修改或终止，除此别无其他要求。

COMMENT

The purpose of this Article is to make it clear that the mere agreement of the parties is sufficient for the valid conclusion, modification or termination by agreement of a contract, without any of the further requirements which are to be found in some domestic laws.

1. No need for consideration

In common law systems, "consideration" is traditionally seen as a prerequisite for the validity or enforceability of a contract, as well as for the modification or termination of a contract by the parties.

However, in commercial dealings this requirement is of minimal practical importance since in that context obligations are almost always undertaken by both parties. It is for this reason that Article 29(1) CISG dispenses with the requirement of consideration in relation to the modification and termination by the parties of contracts for the international sale of goods. The fact that this Article extends this approach to the conclusion, modification and termination by the parties of international commercial contracts in general can only bring about greater certainty and reduce litigation.

2. No need for *cause*

This Article also excludes the requirement of *"cause"* which exists in some civil law systems and is in certain respects functionally similar to the common law "consideration".

Illustration

> 1.   At the request of its French customer A, bank B in Paris issues a guarantee on first demand in favour of C, a business partner of A in England. Neither B nor A can invoke the possible absence of consideration or *cause* for the guarantee.

It should be noted, however, that this Article is not concerned with the effects which may derive from other aspects of *cause*, such as its illegality (see Comment 2 on Article 3.1.3).

3. All contracts consensual

Some civil law systems have retained certain types of "real" contract, i.e. contracts concluded only upon the actual handing over of the goods concerned. These rules are not easily compatible with modern business perceptions and practice and are therefore excluded by this Article.

注释：

本条的目的在于表明，只要有合同当事人的协议就足以有效订立、修改或终止合同，而不考虑某些国内法中规定的任何其他要求。

1. 无须对价

在普通法系，传统上将"对价"视为合同有效或可强制执行的前提，同时也是当事人修改或终止合同的前提。

但在商业交往中，由于合同项下的义务几乎总是由合同双方当事人来承担，这种"对价"要求的实际意义不大。正是基于这一理由，《联合国国际货物销售合同公约》第 29 条第(1)款规定，国际货物买卖合同当事人修改或终止合同内容时，免除"对价"这项条件。本条把这一条规定一般性地扩展适用于国际商事合同的订立、修改和终止，这有利于提升确定性，并能减少诉讼。

2. 无须约因

本条也排除某些大陆法系国家中存在的有关约因的要求，在某些方面约因与普通法系中的对价具有相似的功能。

示例：

> 1. 巴黎的银行 B 根据其法国客户 A 的要求，向 C 出具了一份见索即付保函，C 是 A 在英国的商业合作伙伴。无论 A 还是 B 都不能主张保函可能缺少对价或约因。

然而必须注意的是，本条不涉及约因其他方面可能产生的效力，比如非法性（参见第 3.1.3 条注释 2）。

3. 所有合同只须双方同意

一些大陆法系国家仍然保留了某些类型的"要物"合同，即只有实际交付相关货物才能有效成立的合同。这些规则很难与现代商业理念和实践相一致，因此被本条规定排除。

Illustration

2.   Two French businessmen, A and B, agree with C, a real estate developer, to lend C EUR 300,000 on 2 July. On 25 June, A and B inform C that, unexpectedly, they need the money for their own business. C is entitled to receive the loan, although the loan is generally considered a "real" contract in France.

ARTICLE 3.1.3
(Initial impossibility)

(1) The mere fact that at the time of the conclusion of the contract the performance of the obligation assumed was impossible does not affect the validity of the contract.

(2) The mere fact that at the time of the conclusion of the contract a party was not entitled to dispose of the assets to which the contract relates does not affect the validity of the contract.

COMMENT

1. Performance impossible from the outset

Contrary to a number of legal systems which consider a contract of sale void if the specific goods sold have already perished at the time of conclusion of the contract, paragraph (1) of this Article, in conformity with the most modern trends, states in general terms that the mere fact that at the time of the conclusion of the contract the performance of the obligation assumed was impossible does not affect the validity of the contract.

A contract is valid even if the assets to which it relates have already perished at the time of contracting, with the consequence that initial impossibility of performance is equated with impossibility occurring after the conclusion of the contract. The rights and duties of the parties arising from one party's (or possibly even both parties') inability to perform are to be determined according to the rules on non-performance. Under these rules appropriate weight may be attached, for example, to the fact that the obligor (or the obligee) already knew of the impossibility of performance at the time of contracting. The rule laid down in paragraph (1) also removes possible doubts as to the validity of contracts for the delivery of future goods.

示例：

2. 两个法国商人 A 和 B，与房地产开发商 C 缔结协议，同意于 7 月 2 日借给 C 30 万欧元，但是 6 月 25 日，A 和 B 通知 C，由于意外原因，他们自己的公司也需要这笔资金，所以不打算履行借款合同。在这种情况下，尽管在法国借款合同通常被认为是"要物"合同，但依据《通则》C 有权得到这笔贷款。

第3.1.3条

（自始不能）

（1）合同订立时不能履行所承担之义务的事实本身，并不影响合同的效力。

（2）合同订立时一方当事人无权处置与该合同相关联之财产的事实本身，并不影响合同的效力。

注释：

1. 自始履行不能

许多法系都规定，如果在合同订立时，待售的具体货物已灭失，则该买卖合同无效，而第(1)款的规定恰好与此相反，该款一般性地规定，合同订立时即不能履行所承担义务的事实本身并不影响合同的效力。这一规定符合现代合同法发展的趋势。

即使合同项下的相关财产在合同订立时已灭失，合同也仍然有效，自始履行不能和合同缔结后发生的不能是同样的。因此，当事人一方（或者甚至是双方）就不能履行合同所产生的权利和义务，应当根据有关不履行的规则来确定。根据这些关于不履行的规则，可以对有关事实给予适当的考虑，比如，债务人（或债权人）在订立合同时是否已经知道履行不能。本条第(1)款的规则也排除了对于将来交付货物合同的效力可能产生的疑问。

If an initial impossibility of performance is due to a legal prohibition (e.g. an export or import embargo), the validity of the contract depends upon whether under the law enacting the prohibition the latter is intended to invalidate the contract or merely to prohibit its performance.

Paragraph (1) moreover departs from the rule to be found in some civil law systems according to which the object (*objet*) of a contract must be possible.

The paragraph also deviates from the rule of the same systems which requires the existence of a *cause*, since, in a case of initial impossibility, the *cause* for a counter-performance is lacking (see Article 3.1.2).

2. Lack of legal title or power

Paragraph (2) of this Article deals with cases where the party promising to transfer or deliver assets was not entitled to dispose of the assets because it lacked legal title or the right of disposition at the time of the conclusion of the contract.

Some legal systems declare a contract of sale concluded in such circumstances to be void. Yet, as in the case with initial impossibility, and for even more cogent reasons, paragraph (2) of this Article considers such a contract to be valid. Indeed, a contracting party may, and often does, acquire legal title to, or the power of disposition over, the assets in question after the conclusion of the contract. Should this not occur, the rules on non-performance will apply.

Cases where the power of disposition is lacking must be distinguished from those of lack of capacity. The latter relate to certain disabilities of a person which may affect all or at least some types of contract concluded by it, and falls outside the scope of the Principles (see Article 3.1.1).

如果自始不能是因为法律的禁止（比如出口或进口禁令），则合同的效力取决于规定该禁令的法律的意图，即它是想使合同归于无效还是仅仅想禁止履行。

而且，本条第(1)款的规定也不同于一些大陆法系国家的如下规则，即合同的标的必须是可能的。

这一款规定也不同于要求存在某项约因的大陆法系国家的规则，因为在自始不能的情况下，缺少对等履行的约因（参见第 3.1.2 条）。

2. 没有合法的所有权或权力

本条第(2)款所调整的情况是，承诺转让或移交货物的当事人无权处分该财产，因为其在订立合同时没有合法的所有权或处分权。

一些法律体系宣称在此情况下订立的买卖合同无效。但是，正如自始不能的情况一样，并且因为其他更为正当的理由，本条第(2)款将这种合同视为有效。事实上，合同当事人可能并且事实上经常在合同订立之后取得对合同所涉财产的合法所有权或处分权。如果合同当事人事后没有取得这些权利（所有权或处分权），则适用不履行的规则。

应该将没有处分权和没有行为能力两种情形区分开来。后者是指某人的身体缺陷可能影响到其订立所有合同的效力或至少是某些类型合同的效力，这种情况不受《通则》调整（参见第 3.1.1 条）。

ARTICLE 3.1.4
(Mandatory character of the provisions)

The provisions on fraud, threat, gross disparity and illegality contained in this Chapter are mandatory.

COMMENT

The provisions of this Chapter relating to fraud, threat, gross disparity and illegality are of a mandatory character. It would be contrary to good faith for the parties to exclude or modify these provisions when concluding their contract. However, nothing prevents the party entitled to avoidance for fraud, threat and gross disparity to waive that right once that party learns of the true facts or is able to act freely.

On the other hand, the provisions of this Chapter relating to the binding force of a mere agreement, to initial impossibility or to mistake are not mandatory. Thus the parties may reintroduce special requirements of domestic law, such as consideration or *cause*. They may likewise agree that their contract shall be invalid in case of initial impossibility, or that mistake by one of the parties is not a ground for avoidance.

第 3.1.4 条

（强制性条文）

本章关于欺诈、胁迫、重大失衡及非法之规定均属强制性条款。

注释：

　　本章有关欺诈、胁迫、重大失衡及违法的条文均属于强制性条款。当事人在订立合同时排除或修改这些条文，将构成违反诚实信用。然而，本章并不阻止有权以欺诈、胁迫和重大失衡为由宣告合同无效的当事人，在得知事实真相或者能够自由行事之后，放弃该权利。

　　另一方面，本章条文就有关协议本身的拘束力、自始不能，或错误的条款，不具强制力。因此，当事人可以再引入国内法的要求，例如对价或约因。同样，他们可以约定他们之间的合同在自始不能的情况下无效，也可以约定一方当事人的错误不构成宣告合同无效的事由。

SECTION 2: GROUNDS FOR AVOIDANCE

ARTICLE 3.2.1
(Definition of mistake)

Mistake is an erroneous assumption relating to facts or to law existing when the contract was concluded.

COMMENT

1. Mistake of fact and mistake of law

This Article equates a mistake relating to facts with a mistake relating to law. Identical legal treatment of the two types of mistake seems justified in view of the increasing complexity of modern legal systems. For cross-border trade the difficulties caused by this complexity are exacerbated by the fact that an individual transaction may be affected by foreign and therefore unfamiliar legal systems.

2. Decisive time

This Article indicates that a mistake must involve an erroneous assumption relating to the factual or legal circumstances that exist at the time of the conclusion of the contract.

The purpose of fixing this time element is to distinguish cases where the rules on mistake with their particular remedies apply from those relating to non-performance. Indeed, a typical case of mistake may, depending on the point of view taken, often just as well be seen as one involving an obstacle which prevents or impedes the performance of the contract. If a party has entered into a contract under a misconception as to the factual or legal context and therefore misjudged its prospects under that contract, the rules on mistake will apply. If, on the other hand, a party has a correct understanding of the surrounding circumstances but makes an error of judgment as to its prospects under the contract, and later refuses to perform, then the case is one of non-performance rather than mistake.

第二节 宣告合同无效的根据

第3.2.1条

（错误的定义）

错误是指在合同订立时，就已经存在的事实或法律所做的不正确的假设。

注释：

1. 事实错误和法律错误

本条将事实错误和法律错误做相同处理。考虑到日益复杂的现代法律体系，对这两种类型的错误采取相同的法律对待似乎是正当的。对于跨境贸易来说，因为每一交易都可能受到不熟悉的外国法律制度的影响，从而使得由法律体系的复杂性所产生的困难进一步加大。

2. 决定性时间

本条表明，错误是指对合同订立时已经存在的事实或法律情况所做的不正确的假设。

设定该时间要素的目的在于将适用有关错误的规则及其特殊救济的规则的案件与涉及不履行的案件区分开来。实际上，从这一观点来看，一个典型的错误通常可以被认为是妨碍或阻止合同履行的一种障碍。如果一方当事人基于对事实或法律情况的错误理解而订立了合同，并根据该合同对其前景做出了错误的判断，那么就应适用关于错误的规则。另一方面，如果一方当事人对相关情况有正确的理解，但是却根据合同对其前景做出了错误的判断，并且后来又拒绝履行合同，那么这就是"不履行"的情形而不是"错误"的情形。

ARTICLE 3.2.2
(Relevant mistake)

(1) A party may only avoid the contract for mistake if, when the contract was concluded, the mistake was of such importance that a reasonable person in the same situation as the party in error would only have concluded the contract on materially different terms or would not have concluded it at all if the true state of affairs had been known, and

(a) the other party made the same mistake, or caused the mistake, or knew or ought to have known of the mistake and it was contrary to reasonable commercial standards of fair dealing to leave the mistaken party in error; or

(b) the other party had not at the time of avoidance reasonably acted in reliance on the contract.

(2) However, a party may not avoid the contract if

(a) it was grossly negligent in committing the mistake; or

(b) the mistake relates to a matter in regard to which the risk of mistake was assumed or, having regard to the circumstances, should be borne by the mistaken party.

COMMENT

This Article states the conditions necessary for a mistake to be relevant with a view to avoidance of the contract. The introductory part of paragraph (1) determines the conditions under which a mistake is sufficiently serious to be taken into account; sub-paragraphs (a) and (b) of paragraph (1) add the conditions regarding the party other than the mistaken party; paragraph (2) deals with the conditions regarding the mistaken party.

1. Serious mistake

To be relevant, a mistake must be serious. Its weight and importance are to be assessed by reference to a combined objective/subjective standard, namely what "a reasonable person in the same situation as

第 3.2.2 条

（相关错误）

（1） 一方当事人仅可在下列情况下以错误为由宣告合同无效，该错误在订立合同时如此之重大，以至于一个通情达理的人处在与发生错误之当事人相同情况下，如果知道事实真相，就会按实质不同的条款订立合同，或根本不会订立合同，并且

（a） 另一方当事人发生了相同的错误；或造成该错误；或者另一方当事人知道或理应知道该错误并且有悖于公平交易的合理商业标准，使发生错误方一直处于错误状态之中；或者

（b） 在宣告合同无效时，另一方当事人尚未依其对合同的信赖而合理行事。

（2） 但在如下情况下，一方当事人不能宣告合同无效：

（a） 该当事人由于重大疏忽而发生此错误；或者

（b） 对于该错误所涉及之事项，其发生错误之风险已由发生错误方承担，或者考虑到相关情况，应当由发生错误方承担。

注释：

本条阐明了要以错误为由宣告合同无效应满足的条件。第（1）款的引言部分规定了一个应加以考虑的足够严重的错误需满足的条件；第（1）款的（a）项和（b）项增加了与非错误方有关的一些条件，第（2）款规定了一些与错误方相关的条件。

1. 严重错误

要想成为宣告合同无效的理由，错误必须是严重的。错误的分量和重要性应综合参照主观和客观两方面的标准进行衡量，也即，在订立合同时"一个通情达理的人处在与发生错误之当事人相同情况下"，

the party in error" would have done if it had known the true circumstances at the time of the conclusion of the contract. If it would not have contracted at all, or would have done so only on materially different terms, then, and only then, is the mistake considered to be serious.

In this context the introductory part of paragraph (1) relies on an open-ended formula, rather than indicating specific essential elements of the contract to which the mistake must relate. This flexible approach allows full account to be taken of the intentions of the parties and the circumstances of the case. In ascertaining the parties' intentions, the rules of interpretation laid down in Chapter 4 must be applied. General commercial standards and relevant usages will be particularly important.

Normally in commercial transactions certain mistakes, such as those concerning the value of goods or services or mere expectations or motivations of the mistaken party, are not considered to be relevant. The same is true of mistakes as to the identity of the other party or its personal qualities, although special circumstances may sometimes render such mistakes relevant (e.g. when services to be rendered require certain personal qualifications or when a loan is based upon the credit-worthiness of the borrower).

The fact that a reasonable person would consider the circumstances erroneously assumed to be essential is however not sufficient, since additional requirements concerning both the mistaken and the other party must be met if a mistake is to become relevant.

2. Conditions concerning the party other than the mistaken party

A mistaken party may avoid the contract only if the other party satisfies one of four conditions laid down in paragraph (1).

The first three conditions indicated in sub-paragraph (a) have in common the fact that the other party does not deserve protection because of its involvement in one way or another with the mistaken party's error.

The first condition is that both parties laboured under the same mistake.

Illustration

1. A and B, when concluding a contract for the sale of a sports car, were not and could not have been aware of the fact that the car had in the meantime been stolen. Avoidance of the contract is admissible.

However, if the parties erroneously believe the object of the contract to be in existence at the time of the conclusion of the contract, while in

如果已经知道了当时的真实情况可能做出的行为。如果他因此将根本不会订立合同或仅会订立实质条款不同的合同，那么此时，也只有在此时，才认为错误是严重的。

在此背景下，第(1)款的引言部分设定了一个开放式的公式，未指明必须与错误相关的合同的特定基本要素。这种灵活的规定允许全面考虑当事人的意图和案件具体情况。在确定当事人的意图时，应适用第四章有关解释规则的规定。一般商事标准和相关的商业惯例尤为重要。

在商业交易中，某些错误通常不被认为是与宣告合同无效相关的错误，如关于商品或服务价值，或者仅关于发生错误方的期望或动机的错误。有关另一方当事人身份或其个人品质方面的认识错误也不是相关的错误，尽管在特殊情况下，有时也可能成为相关错误（比如，所提供的服务要求具有某种个人资格或贷款是基于借款人良好的信用）。

然而，仅仅是一个通情达理的人认为被错误假定的情况是重要的，这还不够。因为一个错误要成为相关错误，还必须同时满足本条针对错误方和非错误方当事人所规定的其他附加条件。

2. 关于非错误方当事人的条件

只有当另一方当事人满足第(1)款规定的四个条件之一时，发生错误方当事人才能宣告合同无效。

第(1)款(a)项中规定的前三个条件是基于以下相同的事实，即另一方当事人以这样或那样的方式与发生错误方当事人的错误相关联，所以该当事人不受保护。

第一个条件是双方当事人都犯了同样的错误。

示例：

> 1. A 和 B 订立一赛车买卖合同，他们没有也不可能了解到就在他们订立合同时该赛车被盗。宣告合同无效是可以接受的。

然而，如果合同的双方当事人在订立合同时错误地认为合同的标

reality it had already been destroyed, Article 3.1.3 has to be taken into account.

The second condition is that the error of the mistaken party is caused by the other party. This is the case whenever the error can be traced to specific representations made by the latter party, be they express or implied, negligent or innocent, or to conduct which in the circumstances amounts to a representation. Even silence may cause an error. A mere "puff" in advertising or in negotiations will normally be tolerated.

If the error was caused intentionally, Article 3.2.5 applies.

The third condition is that the other party knew or ought to have known of the error of the mistaken party and that it was contrary to reasonable commercial standards of fair dealing to leave the mistaken party in error. What the other party ought to have known is what should have been known to a reasonable person in the same situation as that party. In order to avoid the contract the mistaken party must also show that the other party was under a duty to inform it of its error.

The fourth condition is laid down in sub-paragraph (b) and is that the party other than the mistaken party had not, up to the time of avoidance, reasonably acted in reliance on the contract. For the time of avoidance, see Articles 3.2.12 and 1.10.

3. Conditions concerning the mistaken party

Paragraph (2) of this Article mentions two cases in which the mistaken party may not avoid the contract.

The first of these, dealt with in sub-paragraph (a), is that the error is due to the gross negligence of the mistaken party. In such a situation it would be unfair to the other party to allow the mistaken party to avoid the contract.

Sub-paragraph (b) contemplates the situation where the mistaken party either has assumed the risk of mistake or where this risk should in the circumstances be borne by it. An assumption of the risk of mistake is a frequent feature of speculative contracts. A party may conclude a contract in the hope that its assumption of the existence of certain facts will prove to be correct, but may nevertheless undertake to assume the risk of this not being so. In such circumstances it will not be entitled to avoid the contract for its mistake.

的物存在，但事实上该标的物已经灭失，则必须考虑第 3.1.3 条的规定。

第二个条件是发生错误方当事人的错误是由另一方当事人造成的。只要这种错误能追溯到后者所做的具体陈述（不论这些陈述是明示的还是默示的，是基于疏忽而为还是无过失而为），或者能追溯到在具体情况下构成陈述的行为，都属于第二个条件规定的情况。即使沉默也可能造成错误。至于在广告或谈判中"夸大其词"通常可以接受。

如果错误是故意造成的，则适用第 3.2.5 条的规定。

第三个条件是另一方当事人知道或应当知道错误方当事人的错误，并且有悖于公平交易的合理商业标准，使发生错误方一直处于错误状态之中。另一方当事人应当知道的情况是指，与该当事人处于相同情况下的任一通情达理的人应当知道的情况。为宣告合同无效，发生错误方当事人还必须证明另一方当事人负有告知其错误的义务。

第四个条件规定在第(1)款(b)项中，是指在宣告合同无效时，合同的非错误当事人尚未依其对合同的信赖行事。关于宣告合同无效的时间，参见第 3.2.12 条和第 1.10 条。

3. 关于错误方当事人的条件

本条第(2)款规定了发生错误方当事人不能宣告合同无效的两种情况。

(a)项规定了第一种情况，即错误是由错误方当事人的重大过失造成的。在此情况下，如果允许错误方当事人宣告合同无效，则对另一方当事人不公平。

(b)项适用的情况是，发生错误方当事人已承担了这种错误的风险或者在具体情况下，这种风险应该由错误方当事人来承担。承担错误风险是投机合同的常见特征。当事人订立合同可以是基于他期望对某一事实所作的假设是正确的，但他可能也承担了事实并非如他所愿的风险。在此情况下，错误方当事人则无权以其错误为由宣告合同无效。

Illustration

> 2. A sells to B a picture "attributed" to the relatively unknown painter C at a fair price for such paintings. It is subsequently discovered that the work was painted by the famous artist D. A cannot avoid its contract with B on the ground of its mistake, since the fact that the picture was only "attributed" to C implied the risk that it might have been painted by a more famous artist.

Sometimes both parties assume a risk. However, speculative contracts involving conflicting expectations of future developments, e.g. those concerning prices and exchange rates, may not be avoided on the ground of mistake, since the mistake would not be one as to facts existing at the time of the conclusion of the contract.

ARTICLE 3.2.3
(Error in expression or transmission)

An error occurring in the expression or transmission of a declaration is considered to be a mistake of the person from whom the declaration emanated.

COMMENT

This Article equates an error in the expression or transmission of a declaration with an ordinary mistake of the person making the declaration or sending it and thus the rules of Article 3.1.4, Article 3.2.2 and Articles 3.2.9 to 3.2.16 apply also to these kinds of error.

1. Relevant mistake

If an error in expression or transmission is of sufficient magnitude (especially if it has resulted in the misstatement of figures), the receiver will be, or ought to be, aware of the error. Since nothing in the Principles prevents the receiver/offeree from accepting the erroneously expressed or transmitted offer, it is for the sender/offeror to invoke the error and to avoid the contract provided that the conditions of Article 3.2.2 are met, in particular that it was contrary to reasonable commercial standards of fair dealing for the receiver/offeree not to inform the sender/offeror of the error.

示例:

　　2. A 向 B 出售一幅画,这幅画"被认为"是不出名的画家 C 的作品,出售价格是这类画的公平价格。但是后来发现这幅画是著名画家 D 的作品。这种情况下,A 不得以其发生错误为由宣告与 B 订立的合同无效。因为该画仅仅"被认为"是 C 所作已经暗示了某种风险,即该画有可能是一著名画家的作品。

　　有时,双方当事人都承担风险,然而,包含对未来发展有不同预期的投机合同,比如关于价格和汇率的预期,当事人不能以错误为由而宣告合同无效。因为这种错误与合同订立时存在的事实无关。

第 3.2.3 条

（表述或传达中的错误）

在表述或传达一项声明过程中发生的错误应视为作出该声明之人的错误。

注释:

　　本条将在表述或传达一项声明过程中所发生的错误等同于作出或发出该声明之人的一般错误,因此,第 3.1.4 条、第 3.2.2 条和第 3.2.9 条至第 3.2.16 条的规则也适用于这类错误。

1. 相关错误

　　如果表述或传达中的错误相当严重（尤其是在数字方面的错误）,则接收人将知道或应当知道该错误。因为《通则》没有任何规定阻止接收人/受要约人接受表述或传达错误的要约,那么在符合第 3.2.2 条规定的条件下,发送人/要约人可以以错误为由宣告合同无效,尤其是当接收人/受要约人不告知对方表述或传达中存在错误的情况,则显然有悖于公平交易的合理商业标准时。

In some cases the risk of the error may have been assumed by, or may have to be imposed upon, the sender if it uses a method of transmission which it knows or ought to know to be unsafe either in general or in the special circumstances of the case.

2. Mistakes on the part of the receiver

Transmission ends as soon as the message reaches the receiver (see Article 1.10).

If the message is correctly transmitted, but the receiver misunderstands its content, the case falls outside the scope of this Article.

If the message is correctly transmitted to the receiver's machine which, however, due to a technical fault, prints out a mutilated text, the case is again outside the scope of this Article. The same is true if, at the receiver's request, a message is given orally to the receiver's messenger who misunderstands it or transmits it wrongly.

In the two above-mentioned situations the receiver may however be entitled to invoke its own mistake in accordance with Article 3.2.2, if it replies to the sender and bases its reply upon its own misunderstanding of the sender's message and if all the conditions of Article 3.2.2 are met.

ARTICLE 3.2.4

(Remedies for non-performance)

A party is not entitled to avoid the contract on the ground of mistake if the circumstances on which that party relies afford, or could have afforded, a remedy for non-performance.

COMMENT

1. Remedies for non-performance preferred

This Article is intended to resolve the conflict which may arise between the remedy of avoidance for mistake and the remedies for non-performance. In the event of such a conflict, preference is given to the remedies for non-performance since they seem to be better suited and are more flexible than the radical solution of avoidance.

某些情况下，如果发送人知道或应当知道其所使用的传达方式，无论是在一般情况下还是特殊情况下，都是不安全的，那么发送人可能承担了或者可能必须承担由此而造成的"错误"的风险。

2. 接收人的错误

接收人一收到信息，传递即告结束（参见第 1.10 条）。

如果信息传递正确，但接收人却误解了信息的内容，那么这种情形不受本条规定调整。

如果信息正确地传达到了接收人的机器，但因为该机器有技术故障，打印出来的内容不完整，这种情形也不受本条规定调整。如果应接收人的要求，信息以口头方式传达给接收人的信使，但是信使却误解了信息的内容或做出错误的传达，这种情形也不受本条规定调整。

在上述两种情形下，如果接收人依据其对发送方所发信息的错误理解答复发送方，并且符合第 3.2.2 条规定的所有条件，则接收人有权依据第 3.2.2 条的规定援引错误规则。

第 3.2.4 条

（对不履行的救济）

如果一方当事人所依赖的情况，存在或本来就存在基于不履行的救济，则该方当事人无权以错误为由宣告合同无效。

注释：

1. 对不履行的救济优先

本条旨在解决以错误为由宣告合同无效这种救济措施和对不履行合同而提供的救济措施之间所可能产生的冲突。在出现这种冲突的情况下，对不履行的救济措施优先于以错误为由宣告合同无效这种救济措施，因为这些救济措施看起来比宣告合同无效这种激烈的解决方案更合适、更灵活。

2. Actual and potential conflicts

An actual conflict between the remedies for mistake and those for non-performance arises whenever the two sets of remedies are invoked in relation to what are essentially the same facts.

Illustration

> A, a farmer, who finds a rusty cup on the land sells it to B, an art dealer, for EUR 10,000. The high price is based upon the assumption of both parties that the cup is made of silver (other silver objects had previously been found on the land). It subsequently turns out that the object in question is an ordinary iron cup worth only EUR 1,000. B refuses to accept the cup and to pay for it on the ground that it lacks the assumed quality. B also avoids the contract on the ground of mistake as to the quality of the cup. B is entitled only to the remedies for non-performance.

It may be that the conflict between the two sets of remedies is only potential, since the mistaken party could have relied upon a remedy for non-performance, but is actually precluded from doing so by special circumstances, for example because a statutory limitation period has lapsed. Even in such a case this Article applies with the consequence that the remedy of avoidance for mistake is excluded.

ARTICLE 3.2.5
(Fraud)

A party may avoid the contract when it has been led to conclude the contract by the other party's fraudulent representation, including language or practices, or fraudulent non-disclosure of circumstances which, according to reasonable commercial standards of fair dealing, the latter party should have disclosed.

COMMENT

1. Fraud and mistake

Avoidance of a contract by a party on the ground of fraud bears some resemblance to avoidance for a certain type of mistake. Fraud may be regarded as a special case of mistake caused by the other

2. 现实冲突和潜在冲突

如果对实质上相同的事实同时援引对错误的救济和对不履行的救济两种救济方法，就会产生现实的冲突。

示例：

> A 是一个农民，B 是一个艺术品经销商，A 在其土地上发现了一只古旧的杯子，并以 1 万欧元的价格将这只杯子卖给了 B。这只杯子之所以能卖这么高的价钱，是因为双方都认为这只杯子是银制的（在此之前，这块土地上曾经发现过其他银制品），但最后却证明这只杯子只不过是一只普通的铁杯，仅仅值 1,000 欧元。B 以这只杯子不具有预想的品质为由拒绝接受交付并拒绝付款。B 还以对杯子品质的错误认识为由主张合同无效。B 仅仅有权援引适用于不履行的救济方法。

两类救济之间也可能只存在潜在的冲突，因为错误方当事人可能依赖了对不履行的救济方法，但实际上可能因特殊情况的存在又不可能获得这类救济，比如法定时效已过。但是即使这样，本条依然适用，排除适用因错误而宣告合同无效这一救济方法。

第 3.2.5 条

（欺诈）

> 如果一方当事人订立合同是基于另一方当事人的欺诈性陈述，包括欺诈性的语言或做法，或按照公平交易的合理商业标准，另一方当事人对应予披露的情况欺诈性地未予披露，则该一方当事人可宣告合同无效。

注释：

1. 欺诈与错误

一方当事人以欺诈为由宣告合同无效和因某种错误而宣告合同无效具有某些相似之处。欺诈可以被视为是由另一方当事人导致的错误

party. Fraud, like mistake, may involve either representations, whether express or implied, of false facts or non-disclosure of true facts.

2. Notion of fraud

The decisive distinction between fraud and mistake lies in the nature and purpose of the defrauding party's representations or non-disclosure. What entitles the defrauded party to avoid the contract is the "fraudulent" representation or non-disclosure of relevant facts. Such conduct is fraudulent if it is intended to lead the other party into error and thereby to gain an advantage to the detriment of the other party. The reprehensible nature of fraud is such that it is a sufficient ground for avoidance without the need for the presence of the additional conditions laid down in Article 3.2.2 for the mistake to become relevant.

A mere "puff" in advertising or negotiations does not suffice.

ARTICLE 3.2.6
(Threat)

A party may avoid the contract when it has been led to conclude the contract by the other party's unjustified threat which, having regard to the circumstances, is so imminent and serious as to leave the first party no reasonable alternative. In particular, a threat is unjustified if the act or omission with which a party has been threatened is wrongful in itself, or it is wrongful to use it as a means to obtain the conclusion of the contract.

COMMENT

This Article permits the avoidance of a contract on the ground of threat.

1. Threat must be imminent and serious

Threat of itself is not sufficient. It must be of so imminent and serious a character that the threatened person has no reasonable alternative but to conclude the contract on the terms proposed by the

的一种特例。与错误一样，欺诈既可以是（明示或默示的）对虚假事实的陈述，也可以是对真实情况不披露。

2. 欺诈的概念

欺诈和错误之间的决定性差别在于欺诈方的陈述或不披露行为的性质和目的。使受欺诈方有权宣告合同无效的事实是"欺诈性"的陈述或不披露相关事实的行为。欺诈行为是指意欲诱导另一方犯错误，并因此从另一方的损失中获益的行为。鉴于欺诈所具有的应受谴责的性质，其已构成宣告合同无效的充分条件，无须满足第 3.2.2 条中规定的有关"相关错误"的附加条件。

仅仅是在广告或谈判中"夸大其词"不构成欺诈。

第 3.2.6 条

（胁迫）

如果一方当事人订立合同是基于另一方当事人的不正当胁迫，而且考虑到相关情况，该胁迫是如此急迫、严重，以至于使第一方当事人无其他的合理选择，则该一方当事人可宣告合同无效。尤其是当使一方当事人受到胁迫的作为或不作为本身属于非法时，或者以其作为手段来获取合同的订立属非法时，均构成不正当的胁迫。

注释：

本条允许以胁迫为由宣告合同无效。

1. 胁迫必须是急迫和严重的

仅有胁迫本身是不够的。胁迫必须非常急迫、严重以致受胁迫人除了按照对方所提出的条款订立合同外，别无其他合理的选择。胁迫

other party. The imminence and seriousness of the threat must be evaluated by an objective standard, taking into account the circumstances of the individual case.

2. Unjustified threat

The threat must in addition be unjustified. The second sentence of this Article sets out, by way of illustration, two examples of an unjustified threat. The first envisages a case where the act or omission with which the contracting party has been threatened is wrongful in itself (e.g. a physical attack). The second refers to a situation where the threatened act or omission is in itself lawful, but the purpose to be achieved is wrongful (e.g. the bringing of a court action for the sole purpose of inducing the other party to conclude the contract on the terms proposed).

Illustration

> 1.   A, who is in default with the repayment of a loan, is threatened by B, the lender, with proceedings for the recovery of the money. The only purpose of this threat is to obtain on particularly advantageous terms a lease of A's warehouse. A signs the lease, but is entitled to avoid the contract.

3. Threat affecting reputation or economic interests

For the purpose of the application of this Article, threat need not necessarily be made against a person or property, but may also affect reputation or purely economic interests.

Illustration

> 2.   Faced with a threat by the players of a basketball team to go on strike unless they receive a much higher bonus than had already been agreed for winning the four remaining matches of the season, the owner of the team agrees to pay the requested bonus. The owner is entitled to avoid the new contract with the players, since the strike would have led automatically to the team being relegated to a minor league and therefore represented a serious and imminent threat to both the reputation and the financial position of the club.

的急迫性和严重性必须考虑个案的具体情况，以客观标准衡量。

2. 不正当胁迫

胁迫还必须是不正当的。本条第二句以举例说明的方式列出了两种不正当胁迫的例子。第一种情况是指使合同当事人受到胁迫的作为或不作为本身就是不正当的（如人身攻击）。第二种情况是指使合同当事人受到胁迫的作为和不作为本身是合法的，但是其所要达到的目的却是不正当的（如仅为迫使另一方当事人按拟定条款订立合同而提起诉讼）。

示例：

　　1. A未偿还借款，出借人B威胁A要提起返还借款之诉。而其唯一目的在于要以特别优惠的条件租用A的仓库。A被迫订立了租借仓库的合同，但有权宣告合同无效。

3. 胁迫影响声誉或经济利益

本条的适用不一定要求胁迫必须针对某一人或某一项财产，胁迫也可以是影响声誉或单纯经济利益。

示例：

　　2. 某篮球队球员威胁说，除非他们赢得本赛季剩下的四场比赛获得的奖金远远高于原来商定的金额，否则他们将罢赛。球队的老板同意了他们要求增加奖金的要求。但该老板有权宣布他与这些球员订立的新合同无效，因为罢赛将会致球队自动降级，这构成了对球队俱乐部声誉和财务状况的急迫且严重的威胁。

ARTICLE 3.2.7
(Gross disparity)

(1) A party may avoid the contract or an individual term of it if, at the time of the conclusion of the contract, the contract or term unjustifiably gave the other party an excessive advantage. Regard is to be had, among other factors, to

(a) the fact that the other party has taken unfair advantage of the first party's dependence, economic distress or urgent needs, or of its improvidence, ignorance, inexperience or lack of bargaining skill, and

(b) the nature and purpose of the contract.

(2) Upon the request of the party entitled to avoidance, a court may adapt the contract or term in order to make it accord with reasonable commercial standards of fair dealing.

(3) A court may also adapt the contract or term upon the request of the party receiving notice of avoidance, provided that that party informs the other party of its request promptly after receiving such notice and before the other party has reasonably acted in reliance on it. Article 3.2.10(2) applies accordingly.

COMMENT

1. Excessive advantage

This provision permits a party to avoid a contract in cases where there is gross disparity between the obligations of the parties, which gives one party an unjustifiably excessive advantage.

The excessive advantage must exist at the time of the conclusion of the contract. A contract which, although not grossly unfair when entered into, becomes so later may be adapted or terminated under the rules on hardship contained in Chapter 6, Section 2.

As the term "excessive" advantage denotes, even a considerable disparity in the value and the price or some other element which upsets the equilibrium of performance and counter-performance is not

第 3.2.7 条

（重大失衡）

（1）　如果一方当事人在订立合同时，合同或其个别条款不正当地对另一方当事人过分有利，则该一方当事人可宣告该合同或该个别条款无效。除其他因素外，应考虑下列各项：

（a）　该另一方当事人不公平地利用了对方当事人的依赖、经济困境或紧急需要，或不公平地利用了对方当事人的缺乏远见、无知、无经验或缺乏谈判技巧，以及

（b）　合同的性质和目的。

（2）　依有权宣告合同无效的一方当事人的请求，法院可以调整该合同或其条款，以使其符合公平交易的合理商业标准。

（3）　依收到宣告合同无效通知的一方当事人的请求，法院亦可调整合同或其条款，只要该方当事人在收到此项通知后，且在对方当事人信赖该通知合理行事前，立即将其请求告知对方当事人。此时，本章第 3.2.10 条第(2)款的规定应予适用。

注释：

1. 过分利益

如果当事人间的义务存在重大失衡，以致一方当事人获得不正当的过分的利益，本条允许另一方当事人依此情况宣告合同无效。

过分利益在合同订立时就必须存在。如果一份合同虽在订立时并未过分不公平，但后来却变得过分不公平，则该合同可以根据第六章第二节有关艰难情形的规定予以调整或终止。

"过分"利益一词表明，即使价值和价格或者扰乱履行与对等履行之间平衡的某一因素发生明显失衡，亦不足以允许依本条宣告合同无

sufficient to permit the avoidance or the adaptation of the contract under this Article. What is required is that the disequilibrium is in the circumstances so great as to shock the conscience of a reasonable person.

2. Unjustifiable advantage

Not only must the advantage be excessive, it must also be unjustifiable. Whether this requirement is met will depend upon an evaluation of all the relevant circumstances of the case. Paragraph (1) of this Article refers in particular to two factors which deserve special attention in this connection.

a. *Unequal bargaining position*

The first factor is that one party has taken unfair advantage of the other party's dependence, economic distress or urgent needs, or its improvidence, ignorance, inexperience, or lack of bargaining skill (sub-paragraph (a)). As to the dependence of one party vis-à-vis the other, superior bargaining power due to market conditions alone is not sufficient.

Illustration

> A, the owner of an automobile factory, sells an outdated assembly line to B, a Governmental agency from a country eager to set up its own automobile industry. Although A makes no representations as to the efficiency of the assembly line, it succeeds in fixing a price which is manifestly excessive. B, after discovering that it has paid an amount which corresponds to that of a much more modern assembly line, is entitled to avoid the contract.

b. *Nature and purpose of the contract*

The second factor to which special regard must be had is the nature and purpose of the contract (sub-paragraph (b)). There are situations where an excessive advantage is unjustifiable even if the party who will benefit from it has not abused the other party's weak bargaining position.

Whether this is the case will often depend upon the nature and purpose of the contract. Thus, a contract term providing for an extremely short period for giving notice of defects in goods or services to be supplied may or may not be excessively advantageous to the seller or supplier, depending on the character of the goods or services in question.

效或调整合同。这种不平衡必须非常严重，以至于震动了通情达理的人的良心。

2. 不正当利益

利益不但要过分还必须是不正当的。是否满足这一条件要依据所有的相关情况来衡量。本条第(1)款特别指出了两个应当特别关注的因素：

a. 不平等的谈判地位

第一个因素是一方当事人不公平地利用对方当事人的依赖、经济困境或紧急需要，或不公平地利用对方当事人缺乏远见、无知、无经验或不懂谈判技巧的事实（参见第(1)款(a)项）。至于一方当事人对另一方当事人的依赖，仅由于市场情况而产生的谈判优势是不够的。

示例：

> A 是一个汽车制造厂的所有人，B 是某国的一个政府机构，其国家迫切希望建立本国自己的汽车工业，A 向 B 出售了一条过时的汽车生产线。虽然 A 对生产线的效率未做任何表述，但成功地确定了明显过高的价格。B 在发现其所支付的价款相当于购买一条先进得多的生产线的价格之后，有权宣告该合同无效。

b. 合同的性质和目的

第二个应予特别考虑的因素是合同的性质和目的（参见第(1)款(b)项）。即使从中获益的一方当事人并未利用另一方当事人的谈判劣势，也可能会出现存在过分利益不正当的情形。

是否属于此类情况，往往取决于合同的性质和目的。因此，若某合同条款对所供货物或服务中存在的瑕疵只规定了极短的通知时间，该合同条款对货物的卖方或服务的提供者是否构成过分优势，主要取决于所涉及的货物或服务的性质。同样，在依据所售货物或所提供服

Equally, an agent's fee expressed in terms of a fixed percentage of the price of the goods or services to be sold or rendered, although justified in the event of the agent's contribution to the conclusion of the transaction being substantial and/or the value of the goods or services concerned not being very high, may well turn out to confer an excessive advantage on the agent if the latter's contribution is almost negligible and/or the value of the goods or services are extraordinarily high.

c. *Other factors*

Other factors may need to be taken into consideration, for example the ethics prevailing in the business or trade.

3. Avoidance or adaptation

The avoidance of the contract or of any of its individual terms under this Article is subject to the general rules laid down in Articles 3.2.11 to 3.2.16.

However, according to paragraph (2) of this Article, at the request of the party who is entitled to avoidance, the court may adapt the contract in order to bring it into accord with reasonable commercial standards of fair dealing. Similarly, according to paragraph (3) the party receiving notice of avoidance may also request such adaptation provided it informs the avoiding party of its request promptly after receiving the notice of avoidance, and before the avoiding party has reasonably acted in reliance on that notice.

After such a request by the other party, the party entitled to avoidance looses its right to avoid the contract and any earlier notice of avoidance becomes ineffective (see Article 3.2.10(2)).

If the parties are in disagreement as to the procedure to be adopted, it will be for the court to decide whether the contract is to be avoided or adapted and, if adapted, on which terms.

ARTICLE 3.2.8
(Third persons)

(1) Where fraud, threat, gross disparity or a party's mistake is imputable to, or is known or ought to be known by, a third person for whose acts the other party is responsible, the contract may be avoided under the same conditions as if the behaviour or knowledge had been that of the party itself.

务的价格的一定百分比来确定代理费的情况下，如代理人的作用对成交至关重要，且/或所涉货物或服务的价格不是很高，代理费可能是合理的；但如果代理人在交易中的作用微不足道，且/或所涉货物或服务的价格太高，则该代理费也可能因对代理人过分有利而不合理。

c. 其他因素

可能还需要考虑其他因素，比如商业或贸易之中通行的道德标准。

3. 宣告合同无效或修改合同

依本条关于宣告合同无效或宣告合同任何个别条款无效时，还必须遵守第3.2.11条至第3.2.16条规定的一般规则。

然而，根据本条第(2)款，应有权宣告合同无效的一方当事人的请求，法院可以调整合同，以使其符合公平交易的合理商业标准。同样，根据本条第(3)款，收到宣告合同无效通知的一方当事人也可以要求调整合同，只要该方当事人在收到此项通知后，且在另一方当事人信赖该项通知合理行事前，立即将其请求告知另一方当事人。

在另一方提出该等请求后，有权宣告合同无效的一方丧失宣告无效权，并且先前的任何宣告无效通知均归于失效（参见第3.2.10条第(2)款）。

如果当事人未能就所要采用的程序达成一致，则由法院决定合同是否应该被宣告无效或修改，如果修改应改哪些条款。

第3.2.8条

（第三人）

（1）如果欺诈、胁迫、重大失衡或一方当事人的错误可归因于某第三人，或者该第三人知道或应当知道这些情况，而该第三人的行为由另一方当事人负责，则可按如同该另一方当事人本身之行为或知悉的相同条件，宣告该合同无效。

(2) Where fraud, threat or gross disparity is imputable to a third person for whose acts the other party is not responsible, the contract may be avoided if that party knew or ought to have known of the fraud, threat or disparity, or has not at the time of avoidance reasonably acted in reliance on the contract.

COMMENT

This Article deals with situations, frequent in practice, in which a third person has been involved or has interfered in the negotiation process, and the ground for avoidance is in one way or another imputable to that person.

1. Third person for whom a party is responsible

Paragraph (1) is concerned with cases in which fraud, threat, gross disparity or a party's mistake is caused by a third person for whose acts the other party is responsible, or cases in which, without causing the mistake, the third person knew or ought to have known of it. A party is responsible for the acts of a third person in a variety of situations ranging from those in which that person is an agent of the party in question to those where the third person acts for the benefit of that party on its own initiative. In all such cases it seems justified to impute to that party the third person's acts or its knowledge, whether actual or constructive, of certain circumstances, and this irrespective of whether the party in question knew of the third person's acts.

2. Third person for whom a party is not responsible

Paragraph (2) deals with cases where a party is defrauded, threatened or otherwise unduly influenced by a third person for whom the other party is not responsible. Such acts may be imputed to the latter party only if it knew or ought to have known of them.

There is however one exception to this rule: the defrauded, threatened or otherwise unduly influenced party is entitled to avoid the contract, even if the other party did not know of the third person's acts, whenever the other party has not reasonably acted in reliance on the contract before the time of avoidance. This exception is justified because in this situation the other party is not in need of protection.

（2）如果欺诈、胁迫或重大失衡可归因于第三人，而该第三人的行为不由另一方当事人负责，则若该另一方当事人知道或理应知道此欺诈、胁迫或重大失衡，或在宣告合同无效时尚未信赖该合同而合理行事，该合同可被宣告无效。

注释：

本条处理的是实践中常见的问题，即第三人参加或介入了谈判过程，且宣告合同无效的原因以某种方式归因于该第三人。

1. 第三人的行为由一方当事人负责

第（1）款处理的情况是第三人造成欺诈、胁迫、重大失衡或当事人的错误，且该第三人的行为应由另一方当事人负责的；或虽然第三人没有造成错误，但是第三人知道或应当知道会发生错误。在许多情形下，一方当事人都要对第三人的行为负责，例如第三人是该方当事人的代理人，或者第三人主动为该方当事人的利益行事。在所有这些情形下，将该第三人的行为或其对情况的知悉（无论是实际的还是推断的）归因于该方当事人都是合理的，不论该当事人是否知道第三人的行为。

2. 第三人的行为不由一方当事人负责

第（2）款处理的情况是一方当事人受到第三人的欺诈、胁迫或其他不当影响，但该第三人的行为不由另一方当事人负责。只有该另一方当事人知道或应当知道第三人的行为时，才有可能将该第三人的行为后归于该另一方当事人。

但是本条规则还有一种例外情形：即使另一方当事人不知道第三人的行为，受欺诈、胁迫或受其他不当影响的一方当事人仍有权宣告合同无效，只要另一方当事人在宣告合同无效前没有依照对合同的信赖合理行事。这一例外的合理之处在于，在这种情形下另一方当事人不需要保护。

ARTICLE 3.2.9
(Confirmation)

If the party entitled to avoid the contract expressly or impliedly confirms the contract after the period of time for giving notice of avoidance has begun to run, avoidance of the contract is excluded.

COMMENT

This Article lays down the rule according to which the party entitled to avoid the contract may either expressly or impliedly confirm the contract.

For there to be an implied confirmation it is not sufficient, for example, for the party entitled to avoid the contract to bring a claim against the other party based on the latter's non-performance. A confirmation can only be assumed if the other party acknowledges the claim or if a court action has been successful.

There is also confirmation if the party entitled to avoidance continues to perform the contract without reserving its right to avoid the contract.

ARTICLE 3.2.10
(Loss of right to avoid)

(1) If a party is entitled to avoid the contract for mistake but the other party declares itself willing to perform or performs the contract as it was understood by the party entitled to avoidance, the contract is considered to have been concluded as the latter party understood it. The other party must make such a declaration or render such performance promptly after having been informed of the manner in which the party entitled to avoidance had understood the contract and before that party has reasonably acted in reliance on a notice of avoidance.

(2) After such a declaration or performance the right to avoidance is lost and any earlier notice of avoidance is ineffective.

第 3.2.9 条

（确认）

有权宣告合同无效的一方当事人如果在应该发出合同无效通知的期间开始计算后，明示或默示地确认合同，则该方当事人不得再宣告合同无效。

注释：

根据本条规则，有权宣告合同无效的一方当事人，既可以明示也可以默示地确认合同。

但仅有默示确认还是不够的，比如，有权宣告合同无效的一方当事人以另一方当事人不履行合同为由提起诉讼请求。只有在另一方当事人承认该诉讼请求或在诉讼中胜诉的情况下，才构成默示确认。

如果有权宣告合同无效的一方当事人在没有保留其宣告合同无效的权利的前提下继续履行合同，也可以构成对合同的确认。

第 3.2.10 条

（宣告无效权的丧失）

（1）如果一方当事人有权以错误为由宣告合同无效，而另一方当事人声明将愿意或他已实际按照有权宣告合同无效的一方当事人对合同的理解履行合同，则该合同应视为按照宣告合同无效的一方当事人的理解订立。另一方当事人必须在收到有权宣告合同无效一方当事人对合同的理解方式的通知后，且在该方当事人依赖宣告合同无效通知合理行事之前，立即作出此种声明或进行此种履行。

（2）做出此种声明或履行之后，宣告合同无效的权利即行丧失，任何以前宣告合同无效的通知均丧失效力。

COMMENT

1. Performance of the contract as understood by the mistaken party

According to this Article a mistaken party may be prevented from avoiding the contract if the other party declares itself willing to perform or actually performs the contract as it was understood by the mistaken party. The interest of the other party in so doing may lie in the benefit to be derived from the contract, even in its adapted form.

Such regard for the interests of the other party is only justified in the case of mistake and not in other cases of defective consent (threat and fraud) where it would be extremely difficult to expect the parties to keep the contract alive.

2. Decision to be made promptly

The other party has to declare its decision to perform or actually to perform the contract in its adapted form promptly after having been informed of the manner in which the mistaken party had understood the contract. How the other party is to receive the information about the erroneous understanding of the terms of the contract will depend on the circumstances of the case.

3. Loss of right to avoid

Paragraph (2) expressly states that after the other party's declaration or performance the right of the mistaken party to avoid the contract is lost and that any earlier notice of avoidance becomes ineffective.

Conversely, the other party is no longer entitled to adapt the contract if the mistaken party has not only given notice of avoidance but has also reasonably acted in reliance on that notice.

4. Damages

The adaptation of the contract by the other party does not preclude the mistaken party from claiming damages in accordance with Article 3.2.16 if it has suffered loss which is not compensated by the adaptation of the contract.

注释：

1. 按发生错误方当事人对合同的理解履行合同

依据本条，如果另一方当事人声明其愿意或实际上已经按照发生错误方当事人对合同的理解来履行合同，则可以阻止发生错误方当事人宣告合同无效。另一方当事人这样做的原因在于其可以从该合同中获益，即便经过如此调整。

对另一方当事人利益的这种考虑只是在出现错误的情况下才合理；在其他瑕疵同意的情况下（胁迫和欺诈）则是不合理的，因为在此情形下指望当事人继续维系合同将非常困难。

2. 立即做出决定

另一方当事人必须在收到有关发生错误方当事人对合同理解方式的通知后，立即宣布自己愿意按照调整后的形式履行合同或者实际已经开始如此履行。至于另一方当事人如何收到关于对合同条款错误理解的通知，则取决于具体情况。

3. 丧失宣告合同无效的权利

第(2)款明确表示，在另一方当事人作出声明或履行之后，发生错误方当事人即丧失宣告合同无效的权利，且此前发出的任何宣告合同无效的通知均告无效。

相反，如果发生错误方当事人不仅发出了宣告合同无效的通知，而且已经依对该通知的信赖合理行事，则另一方当事人无权再调整合同。

4. 损害赔偿

如果调整合同不能补偿发生错误方当事人因合同错误而遭受的损失，则另一方当事人对合同的调整并不能剥夺发生错误方当事人根据第 3.2.16 条的规定请求损害赔偿的权利。

ARTICLE 3.2.11
(Notice of avoidance)

**The right of a party to avoid the contract is
exercised by notice to the other party.**

COMMENT

1. The requirement of notice

This Article states the principle that the right of a party to avoid the contract is exercised by notice to the other party without the need for any intervention by a court.

2. Form and content of notice

No provision is made in this Article for any specific requirement as to the form or content of the notice of avoidance. It follows that, in accordance with the general rule laid down in Article 1.10(1), the notice may be given by any means appropriate to the circumstances. As to the content of the notice, it is not necessary that the term "avoidance" actually be used, or that the reasons for avoiding the contract be stated expressly. However, for the sake of clarity a party would be well advised to give some reasons for the avoidance in its notice, although in cases of fraud or gross disparity the avoiding party may assume that those reasons are already known to the other party.

Illustration

> A, B's employer, threatens B with dismissal if B does not sell A a Louis XVI chest of drawers. B ultimately agrees to the sale. Two days later A receives a letter from B announcing B's resignation and stating that B has sold the chest of drawers to C. B's letter is sufficient notice of avoidance of the contract of sale with A.

3. Notice must be received

The notice of avoidance becomes effective when it reaches the other party (see Article 1.10(2)).

第 3.2.11 条

（宣告合同无效的通知）

**一方当事人通过向另一方当事人发出通知来
行使其宣告合同无效的权利。**

注释：

1. 通知的要求

本条规定的原则是一方当事人以向另一方当事人发出通知的方式行使其宣告合同无效的权利，无须法院介入。

2. 通知的形式和内容

本条对宣告合同无效的通知的形式或内容未作任何特殊的要求。因此，依据第 1.10 条第(1)款的一般规则，通知可以用适合于具体情况的任何方式发出。至于通知的内容，不必实际使用"宣告合同无效"的表述，也不必明确表述宣告合同无效的理由。但是，为了清楚起见，当事人最好在其宣告合同无效的通知中给出宣告无效的理由，尽管在欺诈或重大失衡的情况下，宣告合同无效的一方当事人可以认为另一方当事人已经知道了那些理由。

示例：

> A 是 B 的老板。A 威胁 B，要求 B 将一个路易十六的衣柜卖给他，否则要开除 B。B 最终同意做这笔买卖。两天后，A 收到 B 的一封信，信中 B 宣布辞职，且表明其已经将那个路易十六的衣柜卖给了 C。B 的这封信足以构成宣告其与 A 之间买卖合同无效的通知。

3. 通知必须被收到

宣告合同无效的通知于到达另一方当事人时生效（参见第 1.10 条第(2)款）。

ARTICLE 3.2.12
(Time limits)

(1) Notice of avoidance shall be given within a reasonable time, having regard to the circumstances, after the avoiding party knew or could not have been unaware of the relevant facts or became capable of acting freely.

(2) Where an individual term of the contract may be avoided by a party under Article 3.2.7, the period of time for giving notice of avoidance begins to run when that term is asserted by the other party.

COMMENT

According to paragraph (1) of this Article notice of avoidance must be given within a reasonable time after the avoiding party became aware or could not have been unaware of the relevant facts or became capable of acting freely. More precisely, the mistaken or defrauded party must give notice of avoidance within a reasonable time after it became aware or could no longer be unaware of the mistake or fraud. The same applies in cases of gross disparity which result from an abuse of the innocent party's ignorance, improvidence or inexperience. In cases of threat or abuse of the innocent party's dependence, economic distress or urgent needs the period runs from the time the threatened or abused party becomes capable of acting freely.

In case of avoidance of an individual term of the contract in accordance with Article 3.2.7, paragraph (2) of this Article states that the period of time for giving notice begins to run when that term is asserted by the party.

ARTICLE 3.2.13
(Partial avoidance)

Where a ground of avoidance affects only individual terms of the contract, the effect of avoidance is limited to those terms unless, having regard to the circumstances, it is unreasonable to uphold the remaining contract.

第 3.2.12 条

（时间期限）

（1）宣告合同无效的通知，应在宣告合同无效的一方当事人已知或不可能不知道有关事实之后，或者在其可以自由行事之后，考虑到相关情况，在合理时间内做出。

（2）如果一方当事人根据第 3.2.7 条的规定有权宣告合同中的个别条款无效，则发出宣告无效通知的期限自另一方当事人主张该条款之时起算。

注释：

根据本条第（1）款，宣告合同无效的通知应该在有权宣告合同无效的当事人知道或不可能不知道相关事实或者能自由行事后的一段合理时间内发出。更准确地说，发生错误或受欺诈方当事人应该在其知道或不可能不知道存在错误或欺诈后的一段合理时间内发出宣告合同无效的通知。这一规则也同样适用于因滥用无辜当事人的无知、缺乏远见或无经验而导致重大失衡的情形。在胁迫或滥用无辜当事人的依赖、经济困境或紧急需要的情况下，宣告合同无效的期间自受胁迫或被利用的当事人可以自行事时起计算。

若根据第 3.2.7 条宣告合同个别条款无效，本条第（2）款规定发出通知的期限自另一方当事人主张该条款时起算。

第 3.2.13 条

（部分无效）

如果宣告合同无效的理由仅影响合同的个别条款，则宣告合同无效的效力仅限于这些条款，除非考虑到相关情况，维持合同的其余部分是不合理的。

COMMENT

This Article deals with situations where the grounds of avoidance affect only individual terms of the contract. In such cases the effects of avoidance will be limited to the terms affected unless it would in the circumstances be unreasonable to uphold the remaining contract. This will generally depend upon whether or not a party would have entered into the contract had it envisaged that the terms in question would have been affected by grounds of avoidance.

Illustrations

1.   A, a contractor, agrees to build two houses on plots of land X and Y for B, one of which B intends to live in and the other to let. B was mistaken in assuming that it had a licence to build on both plots, since in fact the licence covered only plot X. Unless the circumstances indicate otherwise, notwithstanding the avoidance of the contract concerning the building of the house on plot Y, it would be reasonable to uphold the remaining contract concerning the building of the house on plot X.

2.   The situation is the same as in Illustration 1, except that a school was to be built on plot X and living quarters for the students on plot Y. Unless the circumstances indicate otherwise, after the avoidance of the contract concerning the building of the living quarters on plot Y it would not be reasonable to uphold the remaining contract for the building of the school on plot X.

ARTICLE 3.2.14
(Retroactive effect of avoidance)

Avoidance takes effect retroactively.

COMMENT

This Article states the rule that avoidance takes effect retroactively. In other words, the contract is considered never to have existed. In the case of a partial avoidance under Article 3.2.13 the rule applies only to the avoided part of the contract.

There are however individual terms of the contract which may survive even in cases of total avoidance. Arbitration, jurisdiction and choice-of-law clauses are considered to be different from the other terms of the contract and may be upheld notwithstanding the avoidance of the contract in whole or in part. Whether in fact such clauses remain operative is to be determined by the applicable domestic law.

注释：

本条调整的是宣告合同无效的理由仅影响合同的个别条款的情况。在此情况下，宣告合同无效的效力仅限于受影响的条款，除非在具体情况下维持合同其余部分不合理。一般来说，这取决于如果一方当事人曾想象到所涉条款会受到宣告合同无效的理由的影响，其是否还会订立合同。

示例：

1. 一承包商 A 与业主 B 就在 X 和 Y 两块土地上盖两幢房子达成协议。B 打算一幢自己住，另一幢用来出租。B 错误地认为自己拥有了这两块土地上盖房的许可证，而实际上他只有在 X 土地上建房的许可证。除非情况另有所示，尽管合同中关于在 Y 地上修建房屋的部分被宣告无效，关于在 X 地上修建房屋的部分应保持有效。

2. 情况与示例1相同，不同的是，在 X 地上要建的是一所学校，而在 Y 地上要建的是学生生活区。那么除非情况另有所示，当合同中关于在 Y 地上建学校生活区的部分被宣告无效后，继续维持合同中在 X 地上建学校的部分是不合理的。

第3.2.14条

（宣告合同无效的追溯力）

宣告合同无效具有追溯力。

注释：

本条规定宣告合同无效具有追溯力。换句话说，合同将被视为自始不存在。在依照第3.2.13条宣告部分无效的情况下，这一规定仅适用于合同中被宣告无效的部分。

然而，即使在整个合同被宣告无效的情况下，合同中的个别条款仍可能继续有效。仲裁、管辖和法律选择条款就与合同中的其他条款不同，即使合同整体或部分无效，这些条款仍具有效力。但实践中，这些条款是否仍然有效，应由所适用的国内法来确定。

ARTICLE 3.2.15
(Restitution)

(1) On avoidance either party may claim restitution of whatever it has supplied under the contract, or the part of it avoided, provided that such party concurrently makes restitution of whatever it has received under the contract, or the part of it avoided.

(2) If restitution in kind is not possible or appropriate, an allowance has to be made in money whenever reasonable.

(3) The recipient of the performance does not have to make an allowance in money if the impossibility to make restitution in kind is attributable to the other party.

(4) Compensation may be claimed for expenses reasonably required to preserve or maintain the performance received.

COMMENT

1. Right of parties to restitution on avoidance

According to paragraph (1) of this Article either party may claim restitution of what the party has supplied under the contract or the part of it avoided. The only condition is that each party makes restitution of whatever the party has received under the contract or the part of it avoided.

Illustration

1. In the process of a takeover of a company, the controlling shareholder A agrees to sell and transfer to B shares for GBP 100,000. After discovering that A had fraudulently misstated the profits the company was earning, B avoids the contract. B can claim back the purchase price of GBP 100,000. At the same time, B has to return the shares received from A.

As regards the costs involved in making restitution, Article 6.1.11 applies.

第 3.2.15 条

（恢复原状）

（1）宣告合同无效后，任何一方当事人均可要求返还其根据已被宣告无效或部分被宣告无效的合同已提供的一切，但要以该方当事人也同时返还其根据已被宣告无效或部分被宣告无效的合同已得到的一切为条件。

（2）如果返还实物不可能或不适当，只要合理，应折价补偿。

（3）如果不能进行实物返还之原因归咎于对方当事人，则接收履行的当事人无须折价补偿。

（4）对于为保存或维护已接收的履行而合理发生的费用，可请求赔偿。

注释：

1. 宣告合同无效时当事人请求返还的权利

根据本条第(1)款，当合同被整体或部分宣告无效时，任何一方当事人均可请求返还其据此已提供的一切。唯一的条件是他必须同时返还其根据被宣告无效的合同或条款已收到的一切。

示例：

1. 在某起公司收购过程中，公司控股股东 A 同意以 10 万英镑的价格向 B 出售股票。在发现 A 对公司的盈利状况作了欺诈性不实陈述之后，B 宣告合同无效。B 可以请求返还 10 万英镑的购买价款，与此同时必须返还从 A 处取得的股票。

有关返还过程中所发生的费用，适用第 6.1.11 条。

2. Restitution in kind not possible or appropriate

Restitution must normally be in kind. There are, however, instances where instead of restitution in kind, an allowance in money has to be made. This is the case, first of all, where restitution in kind is not possible. The allowance will normally amount to the value of the performance received.

Illustration

> 2.   A commissions B to paint A's factory. B had fraudulently induced A to conclude the contract at a price that is much higher than the market price. After having discovered the fraud, A avoids the contract. A can reclaim the purchase price from B while A is itself under a duty to pay for the value of having had its factory painted.

An allowance is further envisaged by paragraph (2) of this Article whenever restitution in kind would not be appropriate. This is so in particular when returning the performance in kind would cause unreasonable effort or expense. The standard, in that respect, is the same as under Article 7.2.2(b).

Illustration

> 3.   Antiquarian A fraudulently induces antiquarian B to buy a collection of gold coins. The gold coins are reloaded onto one of B's ships. In a heavy storm the ship sinks. B subsequently discovers the fraud and avoids the contract. B can recover the price that it has paid, while itself having to make an allowance representing the value of the gold coins. This is in view of the fact that recovery of the gold coins from the sunken ship would involve expenses vastly exceeding their value.

The purpose of specifying that an allowance has to be made in money "whenever reasonable" is to make it clear that an allowance only has to be made if, and to the extent that, the performance received constitutes a benefit for the recipient.

Illustration

> 4.   A has undertaken to decorate the entrance hall of B's business centre. After A has completed about half of the decorations B discovers that A is not the well-known decorator A has pretended to be. B avoids the contract. Since the decorations so far made cannot be returned and if they have no value for B, A is not entitled to any allowance for the work done.

2. 实物返还不可能或不适当

返还通常必须是对实物的返还。但在某些情况下，只能以折价返还的方式代替实物返还。第一种情况是，不可能返还实物。此时，折价金额通常等于已收到履行之价值。

示例：

2. A 委托 B 为其工厂刷漆。B 以欺诈方式引诱 A 以远高于市场价格的价格订立合同。在发现欺诈情况后，A 宣告合同无效。A 可以向 B 索回购买价款，但 A 同时有义务支付工厂已被刷漆部分的价值。

本条第(2)款考虑到的另一种折价补偿情况是，实物返还不适当。例如，实物返还将导致不合理的费用，或需付出不合理的努力就属这种情况。适用这种情况的标准同第 7.2.2 条(b)项之规定。

示例：

3. 古董商 A 以欺诈方式引诱古董商 B 购买一批金币。这些金币已经装载到 B 的一艘船上。该船因遭遇大风暴沉没。随后 B 发现 A 的欺诈情形并宣告合同无效。B 可以请求返还已支付的价款，但同时自己必须对代表这些金币的价值做折价返还。这是考虑到从沉船中找回金币会发生大大超过金币价值的费用。

该条规定"只要合理"就要折价补偿的目的，在于明确只要收到的履行对接收方构成一种利益，而且在此利益范围内，就要折价补偿。

示例：

4. A 承诺为 B 装饰其商业中心之大堂入口。在装饰工作进行到一半时，B 发现 A 并非是他所冒充的那位著名的装饰专家。B 宣告合同无效。已完成的装饰部分无法返还，如果完成的装饰部分对 B 毫无价值，A 无权要求对所做的工作给予任何折价补偿。

3. The allocation of risk

The rule contained in paragraph (2) implies an allocation of risk: it imposes a liability on the recipient of the performance to make good the value of that performance if it is unable to make restitution in kind. The rule in paragraph (2) applies irrespective of whether the recipient was responsible for the deterioration or destruction of what it had received. This allocation of the risk of deterioration or destruction is justified, in particular, because the risk should lie with the person in control of the performance. On the contrary, there is no liability to make good the value if the deterioration or destruction is attributable to the other party, either because it was due to the other party's fault, or because it was due to a defect inherent in the performance. Hence the rule in paragraph (3).

Illustration

> 5. Art dealer A buys from art dealer B a painting which both of them believe to be a genuine Constable. Subsequently doubts arise about the authenticity of the painting. B undertakes to obtain an expert opinion by the well-known expert C. C confirms that the painting actually is from a much less well-known painter living at the time of Constable. Due to B's negligence, the painting is destroyed on the way back from C to A. A avoids the contract on the ground of a relevant mistake under Article 3.2.2. A can claim back the purchase price but does not have to make an allowance for the value of the painting.

The recipient's liability to pay the value of the performance received is not excluded in cases where the deterioration or destruction would also have occurred had the performance not been rendered.

Illustration

> 6. Company A sells and transfers earth-moving equipment to company B. The equipment is subsequently destroyed by a hurricane that floods the properties of both A and B. B avoids the contract because of a relevant mistake under Article 3.2.2. B can reclaim the purchase price but, at the same time, B has to make an allowance for the value of the earth-moving equipment.

Nor is the recipient's liability to make good the value of the performance excluded in cases where it has been led to conclude the contract by the other party's fraudulent representation.

3. 风险分配

第(2)款的规定默示一种风险分配：收到履行一方如果不能实物返还，有责任补偿该履行所具有的价值。不管接收方对其收到的东西所发生的贬值或损坏是否负责，该款的规则均应适用。这样分配贬值或损坏之风险是有道理的：风险应该由控制该履行的一方承担。相反，如果贬值或损坏是由另一方造成的，无论是因为其过错，还是因为履行的内在缺陷，则均不存在收到履行一方补偿履行价值的责任。于是就有了第(3)款的规则。

示例：

　　5. 艺术品交易商 A 向艺术品交易商 B 购买一幅油画，双方均认为它是康斯特勃尔的真品，后来，对该画的真伪发生了怀疑。B 聘请著名专家 C 出具专家鉴定意见，C 确认该画事实上是由康斯特勃尔同时期的一个远没有他知名的画家所作。由于 B 的疏忽，该画在从 C 运回 A 的过程中被毁。A 以第3.2.2 条规定的相关错误为由宣告合同无效。A 可以请求返还购买价款，但无须对该画的价值给予折价补偿。

即便未发生履行，如果照样会发生贬值或损坏，接收方并不能因此被免除补偿所收到履行之价值的义务。

示例：

　　6. A 公司向 B 公司出售并转让一台挖土设备。随后该设备在飓风中被毁，该飓风同时破坏了 A 和 B 的场地。B 以第3.2.2 条规定的相关错误为由宣告合同无效。B 可以请求返还购买价款，但同时必须折价补偿该挖土设备的价值。

如果收到履行方因另一方的欺诈性陈述而订立合同，其也不能免除补偿履行之价值的义务。

Illustration

> 7.   Antique dealer A has fraudulently induced garage owner B to swap A's ramshackle car against a valuable ancient Greek vase belonging to B. The car is accidentally destroyed while standing in B's garage. If B avoids the contract under Article 3.2.5, B can claim the vase back but has to make good the value of the car.

While Article 3.2.5 is intended to make sure that B is not bound by the contract that it has entered into (hence the right of avoidance) and that B is not saddled with the consequences of a bad bargain that A has induced B to make (hence the right to restitution), Article 3.2.5. does not protect B against accidents.

The question of the recipient's liability to pay the value of the performance only arises in cases where the deterioration or destruction occurs before avoidance of the contract. If what has been performed deteriorates or is destroyed after avoidance of the contract, the recipient of the performance is under a duty to return what the recipient has received. Any non-performance of that duty gives the other party a right to claim damages according to Article 7.4.1, unless the non-performance is excused under Article 7.1.7.

Illustration

> 8.   Art dealer A buys from art dealer B a painting which both parties believe to be a genuine Constable. After it has become apparent that the painting actually is from a much less well-known painter living at the time of Constable, A avoids the contract on the ground of a relevant mistake under Article 3.2.2. As a result, A can reclaim the purchase price but is under a duty to return the painting. Before A can return the painting it is stolen by burglars. Whether B can claim damages depends on whether the burglary can be regarded as *force majeure* (see Article 7.1.7).

4. Compensation for expenses

If the recipient of a performance has incurred expenses for the preservation or maintenance of the object of the performance, it is reasonable to allow the recipient to claim compensation for these expenses in cases where the contract has been avoided and where, therefore, the parties have to return what they have received.

示例：

　　7. 古董交易商 A，欺诈性地引诱汽车修理厂老板 B，用 A 的古董车交换 B 拥有的一个贵重的古希腊花瓶。该车在 B 的车库中意外被毁。如果 B 依第 3.2.5 条宣告合同无效，其可以请求要回花瓶，但必须补偿该车的价值。

第 3.2.5 条旨在确保 B 不受其订立的合同的约束（即宣告合同无效权），并且不会深陷 A 引诱其达成糟糕交易的后果之中（即恢复原状权），但该条并不保护 B 免受意外事件的后果。

接收方补偿履行价值的义务，只有在宣告合同无效之前发生贬值或损坏，才会产生。如果履行贬值或损坏发生在宣告合同无效之后，收到履行方有义务退还其所收到的一切。如果不履行该义务，另一方当事人有权根据第 7.4.1 条请求损害赔偿，除非根据 7.1.7 条该不履行可以免责。

示例：

　　8. 艺术品交易商 A 向艺术品交易商 B 购买一幅油画，双方均认为其是康斯特勃尔的真品。在发现该画实际出自康斯特勃尔同时期的一个远没有他知名的画家之手后，A 以第 3.2.2 条规定的相关错误为由宣告合同无效。A 有权请求返还购买价款但同时有义务返还油画。在 A 返还之前，油画被盗。B 能否请求损害赔偿取决于该盗窃是否可以被视为不可抗力（参见第 7.1.7 条）。

4. 补偿费用

如果收到履行方为保存或维护履行标的发生了费用，在合同被宣告无效，且双方当事人因此必须返还各自所收到的东西情况下，允许收到履行方请求补偿该等费用是合理的。

Illustration

> 9.   Company A has sold and delivered a race horse to company B. After some time B realizes that A has fraudulently concealed from him the true parentage of that horse. B avoids the contract. B can claim compensation for the costs incurred in feeding and caring for the horse.

This rule applies only to reasonable expenses. What is reasonable depends on the circumstances of the case. In Illustration 9 it would matter whether the horse had been sold as a race horse or as an ordinary farm horse.

Compensation cannot be claimed for expenses which are not required to preserve or maintain the performance received, even if they are reasonable.

Illustration

> 10.   Company A has sold and delivered a software package to company B which both parties believe to possess a certain functionality. When B discovers that this is not the case, B asks C to check whether that functionality can still be implemented. Since that turns out not to be possible, B avoids the contract for relevant mistake under Article 3.2.2. B cannot recover from A the fee paid to C as expenses under paragraph (4).

5. Benefits

The Principles do not take a position concerning benefits that have been derived from the performance, or interest that has been earned. In commercial practice it will often be difficult to establish the value of the benefits received by the parties as a result of the performance. Furthermore, often both parties will have received such benefits.

ARTICLE 3.2.16
(Damages)

Irrespective of whether or not the contract has been avoided, the party who knew or ought to have known of the ground for avoidance is liable for damages so as to put the other party in the same position in which it would have been if it had not concluded the contract.

示例：

> 9. A 公司向 B 公司出售并交付一匹赛马。一段时间后 B 发现 A 欺诈性地对其隐瞒了马的真实品种。B 宣告合同无效。B 可以请求补偿为饲养和看护马匹所发生的费用。

该规则仅适用于合理费用。何谓合理则取决于个案具体情况。在本示例 9 中，该马匹是作为赛马还是普通耕作马匹出售，至关重要。

不是为了需要保存或维护收到的履行所发生的费用，即便该费用合理，也不能请求补偿。

示例：

> 10. A 公司向 B 公司出售并交付一套软件包，双方均认为其具有某项功能。在发现该软件包不具有该功能后，B 请求 C 检查是否可以实施该功能。在 C 发现不可能之后，B 以第 3.2.2 条规定的相关错误为由宣告合同无效。B 不得根据第 (4) 款请求 A 补偿其向 C 支付的费用。

5. 利益

对于从履行中取得的利益，或者从履行中所获得的利息，《通则》未做规定。商业实践中通常难以确定当事人因履行而取得的利益之价值。另外，通常双方均取得了该种好处。

第 3.2.16 条

（损害赔偿）

无论是否宣告合同无效，已知或应该知道合同无效原因的一方当事人应承担损害赔偿的责任，以使另一方当事人处于如同其未订立合同时所应处的状况。

COMMENT

1. Damages if ground for avoidance known to the other party

This Article provides that a party which knew or ought to have known of a ground for avoidance is liable for damages to the other party. The right to damages arises irrespective of whether or not the contract has been avoided.

2. The measure of damages

Unlike the damages in case of non-performance under Chapter 7, Section 4, the damages contemplated by this Article are intended simply to put the other party in the position it would have been in if it had not concluded the contract.

Illustration

> Company A sells software to company B and could not have been unaware of B's mistake as to its appropriateness for the use intended by B. Irrespective of whether or not B avoids the contract, A is liable to B for all the expenses incurred by B in training its personnel in the use of the software, but not for the loss suffered by B as a consequence of the impossibility to use the software for the intended purpose.

ARTICLE 3.2.17
(Unilateral declarations)

The provisions of this Chapter apply with appropriate adaptations to any communication of intention addressed by one party to the other.

COMMENT

This Article takes account of the fact that, apart from the contract itself, the parties, either before or after the conclusion of the contract, often exchange a number of communications of intention which may likewise be affected by invalidity

In a commercial setting, the most important example of unilateral communications of intention that are external, but preparatory, to a contract are bids for investment, works, delivery of goods or provision

注释：

1. 知悉合同无效的理由时对另一方当事人的损害赔偿

本条规定，知道或应当知道合同无效理由的一方当事人应承担向另一方当事人赔偿损失的责任。不管合同是否被宣告无效，另一方当事人都有主张损害赔偿的权利。

2. 损害赔偿的计算

与第七章第四节规定的针对不履行的损害赔偿不同，本条规定的损害赔偿只是意在使另一方当事人处于如同其未订立合同时所应处的状况。

示例：

> A 公司向 B 公司出售软件，并且不可能不知道 B 错误地认为该软件适合其所需要的用途。无论 B 是否宣告合同无效，A 都应当赔偿 B 为培训其员工使用该软件而支出的费用，但不赔偿 B 因不能按其预定的目的使用该软件而遭受的损失。

第 3.2.17 条

（单方声明）

本章各项规定经适当调整后，亦适用于一方当事人向另一方当事人传达的任何意思表示。

注释：

本条考虑的是这样一种情况，即除合同本身以外，当事人在订立合同之前或之后，通常会交换许多意思表示，而这些意思表示同样也会受到合同无效的影响。

在商务实践中，合同之外但属准备性的单方意思表示传达之中，最重要的例子就是有关投资、工程、交付货物，或提供服务的投标。

of services. Communications of intention made after the conclusion of a contract take a variety of forms, such as notices, declarations, demands and requests. In particular, waivers and declarations by which a party assumes an obligation may be affected by a defect of consent.

合同订立后所进行的意思表示传达可采用多种形式，比如通知、声明、要求和请求。特别是弃权，以及当事人承担某种义务的的声明，可能会受到瑕疵同意的影响。

SECTION 3: ILLEGALITY

ARTICLE 3.3.1
(Contracts infringing mandatory rules)

(1) Where a contract infringes a mandatory rule, whether of national, international or supranational origin, applicable under Article 1.4 of these Principles, the effects of that infringement upon the contract are the effects, if any, expressly prescribed by that mandatory rule.

(2) Where the mandatory rule does not expressly prescribe the effects of an infringement upon a contract, the parties have the right to exercise such remedies under the contract as in the circumstances are reasonable.

(3) In determining what is reasonable regard is to be had in particular to:

(a) the purpose of the rule which has been infringed;

(b) the category of persons for whose protection the rule exists;

(c) any sanction that may be imposed under the rule infringed;

(d) the seriousness of the infringement;

(e) whether one or both parties knew or ought to have known of the infringement;

(f) whether the performance of the contract necessitates the infringement; and

(g) the parties' reasonable expectations.

COMMENT

1. Scope of the Section

Despite its paramount importance (see Article 1.1), under the Principles freedom of contract is not without limit. Not only must parties conclude the contract without error and without constraints, also the contract must not violate the applicable mandatory rules. While defects of consent are dealt with in Section 2 of this Chapter, this

第三节 违 法

第 3.3.1 条

（违反强制性规则之合同）

（1） 如果合同违反了依本通则第 **1.4** 条所适用的强制性规则，无论其是源于一国的、国际的，还是超国家的，当该强制性规则对违反行为于合同效力有明确规定时，从其规定。

（2） 当强制性规则未对违反行为于合同效力做出明示规定时，当事人有权依据合同，按合理的情况行使救济。

（3） 在确定何谓合理时，尤其应考虑以下各项因素：

（a） 被违反之规则的宗旨；

（b） 该规则旨在保护的人群之类别；

（c） 依被违反之规则可以施加的制裁措施；

（d） 违反的严重程度；

（e） 当事人一方或双方是否知道或应该知道该项违反；

（f） 是否合同的履行必然导致该违反行为；而且

（g） 当事人的合理期待。

注释：

1. 本节的适用范围

合同自由在《通则》项下尽管至关重要（参见第 1.1 条），但并非没有边际。不但合同当事人必须订立不带有错误或强制的合同，而且合同也不得违反应适用的强制性规则。本章第二节是对合意缺陷做出了规

Section is concerned with a contract that infringes mandatory rules, whether by its terms, performance, purpose or otherwise. More precisely, this Section deals with the effects of that infringement on the contract by laying down the criteria to be followed in determining whether, despite the infringement, parties may still be granted remedies, and if so, whether there will be remedies under the contract (Article 3.3.1) or restitution (Article 3.3.2).

2. Only mandatory rules applicable under Article 1.4 relevant

For the purpose of this Section, only mandatory rules, whether of national, international or supranational origin, that are applicable under Article 1.4 are relevant (see Comments 1 and 2 on Article 1.4). In other words, this Section is concerned only with a contract infringing mandatory rules, be they specific statutory provisions or unwritten general principles of public policy, which are applicable in accordance with the relevant rules of private international law. Which mandatory rules will be applicable in a given case basically depends on whether the dispute is pending before a domestic court or an arbitral tribunal, and on whether the parties' reference to the Principles is considered to be only an agreement to incorporate them in the contract or whether the Principles are applied as the law governing the contract (see Comments 3, 4 and 5 on Article 1.4). Note that the Illustrations below do not address these questions and are based on the assumption that the mandatory rules referred to apply in the cases illustrated.

3. Ways in which a contract may infringe mandatory rules

A contract may infringe mandatory rules first of all by its very terms. As shown by the following Illustrations concerning corruption and collusive bidding, mandatory rules may be specific statutory provisions or unwritten general principles of public policy.

Illustrations

1. Contractor A of country X enters into an agreement with agent B ("the Commission Agreement") under which B, for a fee of USD 1,000,000, would pay USD 10,000,000 to C, a high-ranking procurement advisor of D, the Minister of Economics and Development of country Y, in order to induce D to award A the contract for the construction of a new power plant in country Y ("the Contract"). In both countries X and Y bribery of public officials is prohibited by statute. The Commission Agreement infringes the statutory prohibitions in question by its terms. As to the Contract for the construction of the power plant, see Illustration 7.

定，本节则是处理那些违反强制性规则的合同，而不管这种违反是条文上的违反，履行导致的违反，还是目的上的违反，或其他方式的违反。更确切地讲，本节是通过制定标准来调整违法行为对合同所产生的影响。这些标准，尽管由于发生了违法行为，在确定当事人是否仍旧能够获得救济，以及如果可以，是否可以获得合同项下的救济（第 3.3.1 条），或者恢复原状救济（第 3.3.2 条）时，应予遵守。

2. 只有依第 1.4 条适用的强制性规则是相关的

在本节项下，只有根据第 1.4 条适用的强制性规则，无论是一国的、国际的还是超国家的，才是相关的强制性规则（参见第 1.4 条注释 1 和 2）。易言之，本节仅涉及一项合同违反根据相关国际私法规则应予适用的具体法定条文，或是不成文的公共政策的一般原则的强制性规则。个案中应该适用何种强制性规则，基本取决于：争议由国内法院还是由仲裁庭受理；当事人对通则的援引仅被视为是将通则并入合同中之约定，还是将通则作为管辖合同的法律加以适用（参见第 1.4 条注释 3、4 和 5）。请注意下文举例不涉及这一问题，而是假定各个例子中提及的强制性规则应予适用。

3. 合同违反强制性规则的方式

首先，一项合同可能在条文上违反强制性规则。正如下文有关腐败和投标舞弊的例子所示，强制性规则可以是具体的制定法条文，也可以是不成文的公共政策的一般原则。

示例：

1. X 国的承包商 A 与代理人 B 订立一项协议（"代理协议"），规定 A 向 B 支付 100 万美元，并由 B 向 C——Y 国经济和发展部部长 D 的高级采购顾问，支付 1,000 万美元，以引诱 D 将在 Y 国建设的一个新发电厂合同（"合同"）授予 A 承包。在 X 国和 Y 国向公共官员行贿皆为法律所禁止。代理协议在条文上即违反了相关法律的禁止性规定。至于建设发电厂的合同的效力参见示例 7。

2.   Contractor A of country X enters into an agreement with agent B ("the Commission Agreement") to pay EUR 100,000 to C, a high ranking officer of company D of country Y, in order to induce D to award A the contract for the installation of a sophisticated IT system. Neither in country X nor in country Y is bribery in the private sector prohibited by statute but in both countries it is considered contrary to public policy. The Commission Agreement violates these principles of public policy by its terms.

3.   Bidders A and B of countries X and Y respectively enter into an agreement ("the Collusive Bidding Agreement") according to which in a series of public tendering proceedings for the procurement of construction contracts in country Z, they would collude so that A would get some of the contracts and B the others. A statutory regulation of country Z prohibits collusive bidding in public tendering proceedings. The Collusive Bidding Agreement infringes the statutory prohibition by its terms.

4.   Bidders A and B of countries X and Y respectively enter into an agreement ("the Collusive Bidding Agreement") according to which in a series of public tendering proceedings for the procurement of construction contracts in country Z, they would collude so that A would get some of the contracts and B the others. In country Z there is no statutory regulation prohibiting collusive bidding in public tendering proceedings but collusive bidding is considered contrary to public policy. The Collusive Bidding Agreement violates this principle of public policy by its terms.

A contract may also by its performance infringe mandatory rules.

Illustrations

5.   A, a large-scale retailer in country X, enters into an agreement with B, a manufacturer in country Y, for the manufacture of toys according to its specifications ("the Manufacture Agreement"). A knew or ought to have known that the toys ordered would be manufactured by child labourers. In both country X and country Y child labour is considered contrary to public policy. The Manufacture Agreement violates these principles of public policy by its performance.

6.   Importer A from country X enters into an agreement with exporter B from country Y for the supply of equipment. After the conclusion of the contract, the United Nations imposes an embargo on the importation of such type of equipment into country X. B nevertheless delivers the equipment in violation of

2. X 国的承包商 A 与代理人 B 订立一项协议（"代理协议"），规定 B 向 Y 国 D 公司的高级管理人员 C 支付 10 万欧元，以引诱 D 将安装一套精密 IT 系统的合同（"合同"）授予 A 承包。X 国和 Y 国均无成文法禁止向私营部门行贿，但在两国该种行为均被认为违反公共政策。故代理协议在条文上属违反了该公共政策原则。

3. 分别来自 X 国和 Y 国的投标人 A 和 B 订立一项协议（"共谋投标协议"），约定在 Z 国就一系列建筑合同采购举行的公开招标程序中进行共谋，即由 A 获得某些合同而 B 获得另外一些合同。Z 国一项制定法条文禁止在公开招标程序中共谋投标。共谋投标协议在条文上违反了该制定法的禁止性规定。

4. 分别来自 X 国和 Y 国的投标人 A 和 B 订立一项协议（"共谋投标协议"），约定在 Z 国举行的一系列建筑合同采购公开招标活动中，进行共谋，即由 A 获得某些合同而 B 获得另外一些合同。Z 国对在公开招标程序中共谋投标并无禁止性法律规定，但该行为被认为违反公共政策。故该共谋投标协议条款违反了该公共政策原则。

合同还可能因履行而违反强制性规则。

示例：

5. 位于 X 国的大型零售商 A 与位于 Y 国的 B 公司订立一项协议，约定由 B 按照 A 的规格制造玩具（"制造协议"）。A 知道或者应当知道这些定做的玩具将交由童工生产。在 X 国和 Y 国使用童工都被视为违反公共政策。该制造协议因履行而违反了公共政策原则。

6. X 国的进口商 A 与 Y 国的出口商 B 订立一项设备供应协议。合同订立后，联合国对该等设备进口至 X 国实施了禁

the embargo. The agreement between A and B violates the embargo by its performance.

Moreover, a contract may also infringe mandatory rules in other ways, for example by the way in which it is formed or by its purpose.

Illustrations

> 7. The facts are the same as in Illustration 1, except that B pays C the USD 10,000,000 bribe and D awards the Contract to A. The Contract violates the statutes prohibiting corruption by the way in which it is formed.
>
> 8. A, a manufacturer of plastic explosives situated in country X, enters into an agreement with B, a trading company situated in country Y, for the supply of quantities of semtex, a material useful for peaceful purposes as well as for the manufacture of bombs ("the Supply Agreement"). A knew or ought to have known that B would ultimately forward the goods to a terrorist organisation. The Supply Agreement violates the fundamental principle of public policy prohibiting the support of terrorist activities by its purpose.

4. Effects of infringement expressly prescribed by the mandatory rule infringed

Sometimes the mandatory rule itself expressly states which contractual or restitutionary remedies, if any, are available to the parties in case of its infringement. Thus, for instance, Article 101(2) of the Treaty on the European Union (former Article 85(2) of the Treaty of Rome) expressly states that anti-competitive agreements between enterprises which may affect trade between member States of the European Union prohibited under Article 101(1) "shall be automatically void". Similarly the UNIDROIT Convention on Stolen or Illegally Exported Cultural Objects provides that "[a] Contracting State may request […] the return of a cultural object illegally exported from the territory of the requesting State" (Article 5) and that "[t]he possessor of a cultural object who acquired the object […] illegally exported shall be entitled […] to payment by the requesting State of fair and reasonable compensation, provided that [it] neither knew nor ought reasonably to have known at the time of acquisition that the object had been illegally exported" (Article 6).

运。B 依然违反禁运交付了设备。A 和 B 之间的协议因履行而违反禁运。

另外，合同还可能以其他方式违反强制性规则，例如合同的订立方式或者合同的目的。

示例：

7. 事实同示例 1，但 B 向 C 支付了 1,000 万美元的贿金，D 将合同授予 A。合同因订立方式而违反禁止腐败的制定法。

8. 位于 X 国的塑料炸药生产商 A 与位于 Y 国的贸易公司 B 订立了一份供应一定数量塞姆汀塑胶炸药的协议（"供应协议"）。塞姆汀塑胶炸药是一种既可用于民用目的，亦可用于制造炸弹的材料。A 知道或者应当知道 B 最终将会把这批货物转交一个恐怖组织。供应协议在目的上违反了禁止支持恐怖主义活动的基本公共政策原则。

4. 被违反之强制性规则明示规定的违法后果

有时强制性规则本身明示规定了当出现违法时，当事人可获得何种合同救济或恢复原状救济。例如，《欧盟条约》第 101 条第（2）款（前《罗马条约》第 85 条第（2）款）明确规定，被第 101 条第（1）款所禁止的、经营者之间订立的可能影响欧盟成员国之间贸易的反竞争协议"应自动无效"。同样，《国际统一私法协会关于被盗或非法出口文物的公约》也规定，"一个缔约国可以要求……归还从要求国领土被非法出口的文物"（第 5 条），而且规定"获得该非法出口文物的占有人，如果在其获得该物品时不知道或者理应不知道这一物品是非法出口的，则有权……得到要求国公平、合理的赔偿"（第 6 条）。

5. Effects of infringement to be determined according to what is reasonable in the circumstances

If the mandatory rule does not expressly provide for the effects of its infringement upon the contract, paragraph (2) provides that the parties may exercise "such remedies under the contract as in the circumstances are reasonable". The formula used is sufficiently broad to permit a maximum of flexibility. Thus, notwithstanding the infringement of the mandatory rule, one or both of the parties may, depending on the circumstances of the case, be granted the ordinary remedies available under a valid contract (including the right to performance), or other remedies such as the right to treat the contract as being of no effect, the adaptation of the contract or its termination on terms to be fixed. The latter kind of remedies may be particularly appropriate where as a consequence of the infringement only part of the contract becomes ineffective. As to the granting of restitution of the performances rendered under a contract infringing a mandatory rule, see Article 3.3.2.

6. Criteria for determining what is reasonable in the circumstances

Given the great variety of mandatory rules which may be relevant under this Article, ranging from regulations of a merely technical nature to prohibitions for the purpose of preventing grave social harm, paragraph (3) provides a list of criteria to determine the contractual remedies available in the circumstances, if any. The list is not exhaustive. In many cases more than one of the criteria will be relevant and the decision will involve a weighing of these criteria.

a. *Purpose of the rule infringed*

Among the most important factors to be taken into consideration is the purpose of the mandatory rule and whether the attaining of its purpose would or would not be affected by granting at least one of the parties a remedy under the contract.

Illustrations

> 9.   The facts are the same as in Illustration 1, except that even though B paid C A's bribe, D does not award the Contract to A. Since the purpose of the relevant statutory prohibition of bribery would be frustrated by granting A and B any remedy under the Commission Agreement, B may not request the payment of the USD 1,000,000 fee from A, nor may A recover from B the USD 10,000,000 B has paid to C.

5. 依情况合理确定违法之后果

如果强制性规则本身未明示规定违反该规则对合同所产生的影响，第(2)款规定当事人可行使"在相关情况下合理的、合同项下的救济"。这里运用的模式十分宽泛，允许最大程度的灵活性。因此，尽管违反了强制性规则，依个案具体情况，一方或双方当事人仍然可能被准予获得有效合同项下可获得的一般救济（包括履行权），或者其他救济，包括将合同作为无效处理的权利，调整合同的权利，或者按规定条款终止合同的权利。在违反后果仅导致合同部分无效的情况下，后几种救济方式尤为适当。至于准予根据违反强制性规则的合同对已履行之恢复原状问题，参见第 3. 3. 2 条。

6. 确定相关情况下合理救济之标准

鉴于本条项下相关的强制性规则可能种类繁多，从纯技术性的规章到以阻止严重社会损害为目的的禁止性规定，第(3)款提供了一个在确定相关情况下获得合同救济时，需考察的标准清单。该清单不是穷尽性的。许多情况下，一个以上的标准可能是相关的，因此，在做出决定时涉及对这些标准的权衡。

a. 被违反规则之目的

需要考虑的最重要的因素之一是被违反之规则的目的，以及给予至少一方当事人合同规定的救济，是否会还是不会影响该目的的实现。

示例：

9. 事实同示例 1，但是尽管 B 向 C 支付了 A 的贿金，D 却没有把合同授予 A。如果给予 A 和 B 委托协议规定的任何救济，将会导致禁止贿赂的制定法目的落空，因此 B 不得向 A 索回 100 万美元的代理费，A 也不得向 B 索回 B 已经支付给 C 的 1,000 万美元。

10. A, an aircraft manufacturer in country X, knowing that C, the Ministry of Defence of country Y, intends to purchase a number of military aircraft, enters into an agreement with B, a consultancy firm located in country Y, by which B is to negotiate the possible purchase by C of the aircraft manufactured by A ("the Agency Agreement"). A statutory regulation of country Y prohibits the employment of intermediaries in the negotiation and conclusion of contracts with governmental agencies. Since the purpose of the statutory prohibition of the employment of intermediaries is to fight corruption, neither A nor B should be granted any remedy under the Agency Agreement.

11. The facts are the same as in Illustration 6. Since the purpose of the embargo is to impose a sanction on country X following X's violation of international law, the attaining of that purpose requires that all contracts concluded or performed in violation of the embargo have no effect and that parties be denied any remedy under such contracts.

b. *Category of persons to be protected by the rule infringed*

Another important factor to be taken into consideration is whether the mandatory rule that is infringed is aimed at protecting the interests of the public in general or those of a specific category of persons. Licensing requirements are often of the latter type, i.e. are imposed by law on those carrying out certain activities for the protection of their customers or clients. If a contract is entered into by an unlicensed party it might be reasonable to grant its customer or client at least some remedies under the contract such as damages.

Illustration

12. Company A in country X enters into an agreement with engineer B in country Y for the preparation of plans for the restructuring of A's factory ("the Engineering Contract"). A statutory regulation of country X requires that only licensed engineers carry out this activity. B, who does not have the necessary license, delivers plans that are in part based on erroneous calculations causing a delay in the restructuring work. Requested by A to pay damages for the loss caused by the delay, B refuses to pay on the ground that the Engineering Contract was invalid as B lacked the required license. Since the purpose of the license requirement is the protection of the clients, A may be granted the right to damages.

10. 位于 X 国的飞机制造商 A，得知 Y 国国防部 C 打算购买一批军用飞机。于是 A 与位于 Y 国的咨询公司 B 订立一项协议，约定由 B 就 C 可能购买 A 制造的飞机之事宜进行谈判（"代理协议"）。Y 国的一项制定法禁止在与政府机构谈判和订立合同过程中聘用中介。由于禁止雇佣中介的制定法旨在打击腐败行为，A 和 B 均无权获得代理协议规定的任何救济。

11. 事实同示例 6。由于该禁运目的是在 X 违反国际法之后，对其实施的制裁，实现该目的就要求对违反该禁运所订立或履行的所有合同均属无效，当事人亦无权获得合同项下的任何救济。

b. 被违反规则旨在保护的人群

另一项需要考虑的重要因素是，被违反的强制性规则是旨在保护一般公众的利益，还是旨在保护某一特定人群的利益。许可要求往往属于后者，是为了保护客户的利益而对履行某些活动的人所施加的要求。如果未得到许可，一个人却订立了一项合同，比较合理的作法是给予其顾客，或客户合同项下的某些起码救济，例如损害赔偿。

示例：

12. 位于 X 国的 A 公司与位于 Y 国的工程师 B 订立一项协议，规定由 B 为 A 的工厂改造工作编制计划（"工程合同"）。X 国的一项制定法要求只有获得许可的工程师才可以实施这类工程。B 未获得必要的许可，其向 A 交付的计划存在部分错误计算，导致改造工作延期。A 就延误导致的损失提出损害赔偿，B 拒绝支付，理由是 B 缺少必要的许可因此工程合同无效。由于许可要求的目的是为了保护客户，可以赋予 A 损害赔偿的权利。

c. *Any sanction that may be imposed under the rule infringed*

Statutory regulations prohibiting certain activities or imposing limitations to certain activities often provide criminal or administrative sanctions. As noted in Comment 4, when such a regulation expressly states the effect of violation on contractual rights or remedies, that statement controls. When the regulation is silent as to that effect, however, the existence and nature of the criminal or administrative sanctions can provide important insight into the purpose of the rule that has been violated, the category of persons for whose protection the rule exists, and the seriousness of the violation. Accordingly, the existence and nature of these sanctions should be taken into consideration in determining the effect of such a violation on contractual rights and remedies.

Illustration

> 13. A, an exporter in country X, enters into a contract of carriage with B, a ship-owner in country Y, to carry goods by sea from country X to country Y ("the Contract"). A statutory regulation in country X imposes limits on the loads that ships may carry. The statutory regulation provides for a fine in the case of its violation but it says nothing about the effects a violation would have on the individual contracts of carriage. B overloads the ship and A, claiming the invalidity of the Contract, refuses to pay the freight notwithstanding the fact that the goods had arrived safely. Since the purpose of the statutory regulation is to prevent, in the interests of the safety of the ship and its crew, overloading and not to prohibit contracts, and this purpose is sufficiently achieved by the fining of B, B may be granted the right to be paid the agreed freight for the carriage of the goods.

d. *Seriousness of infringement*

Another factor to be taken into consideration is the seriousness of the infringement. Thus, remedies under the contract may be granted where the mandatory rule is of a purely technical nature and its infringement has no impact on the other party.

Illustrations

> 14. Cattle farmer A in country X sells cattle to cattle farmer B in country Y. A statutory regulation in country Y requires incoming cattle to be properly tagged and that the information contained on the tags also be set out in accompanying documents. The cattle delivered is properly tagged but the accompanying documents are

c. 被违反之规则规定的制裁措施

禁止或限制某些行为的制定法条文往往会规定相应的刑事或行政制裁。正如注释 4 指明的，如果该条文就违法行为对合同权利或合同救济所产生的影响做出了明示规定，应从其规定。然而，如果该条文没有对该影响做出规定，刑事或行政制裁措施的存在及其性质可以对被违反之规则之目的，对该规则旨在保护的人群，以及对违法行为的严重性，提供重要的认识。因此，在决定该违法行为对合同权利和救济产生的影响时，应该考虑制裁措施的存在和性质。

示例：

13. 位于 X 国的出口商 A 与位于 Y 国的船东 B 订立一项货运合同，约定由 B 通过海运从 X 国向 Y 国运输货物（"合同"）。X 国的一项制定法对货船装载量规定了一定的限制。该制定法对违反该规定的行为规定了罚金，但并未就违反行为对具体货运合同的效力影响做出任何规定。B 超载，A 主张合同无效并拒绝支付运费，尽管货物已安全到达目的地。由于该制定法是为了保护货船及其船员的安全而禁止超载，而不是为了禁止合同，该目的通过对 B 实施罚款即可充分实现，因此，可以授予 B 就所运货物获得约定运费的权利。

d. 违反的严重程度

另外一项需要考虑的因素是违法行为的严重性。因此如果强制性规则属于纯技术性的，并且违反该规则不会对另一方当事人产生影响，则可以给予合同项下的救济。

示例：

14. 位于 X 国的肉牛养殖户 A 向位于 Y 国的肉牛养殖户 B 出售一批肉牛。Y 国的一项制定法要求必须对进口肉牛贴上适当的标签，并且标签上的内容必须同时记载于交付的文件之中。这批肉牛贴有适当的标签，但相关文件记载不完整。A

incomplete. A may nevertheless be granted the right to payment of the price.

15.   A, an exporter in country X, enters into a contract with B, a carrier from country Y, for the carriage of dangerous goods from country X to country Y ("the Contract"). Country X has a statutory regulation requiring goods of the kind in question to be carried on a vehicle with particular safety requirements. The statutory regulation provides a criminal sanction in case of violation but says nothing about the effects a violation would have on the individual contracts of carriage. B carries the goods on a vehicle that does not meet the prescribed safety requirements. A, claiming the invalidity of the Contract, refuses to pay the freight notwithstanding the fact that the goods arrived safely. Since the purpose of the statutory regulations is the prevention of injury to third persons or damage to the environment, B, irrespective of the imposition of the criminal sanction, should not be granted the right to be paid the agreed freight.

e.   *Whether one or both parties knew or ought to have known of the infringement*

Granting remedies under the contract may also depend on whether one or even both of the parties knew or ought to have known of the mandatory rule or of its infringement.

Illustrations

16.   The facts are the same as in Illustration 1, except that B has paid the bribe to C and D, who neither knew nor ought to have known of the bribe to C, awarded the Contract to A. If D subsequently becomes aware of the payment of the bribe, D may choose whether or not to treat the Contract as effective. If D chooses to treat the Contract as effective, A will be obliged to perform and D will have to pay the price, subject to an appropriate adjustment taking into consideration the payment of the bribe. If, on the other hand, D chooses to treat the Contract as being of no effect, neither of the parties has a remedy under the Contract. This is without prejudice to any restitutionary remedy that may exist.

17.   Contractor A of country X enters into negotiations with D, the Minister of Economics and Development of country Y, with a view to conclude an agreement on a large infrastructure project ("the Contract"). D requests the payment of a "commission" of 7.5% of the contract price in order to conclude the Contract. A pays the requested "commission" and the Contract is concluded. When A has already performed half of its obligations under the

可具有获得价款的权利。

　　15. 位于 X 国的出口商 A 与位于 Y 国的承运人 B 订立一项货运合同，约定由 B 通过海运从 X 国向 Y 国运输一批危险货物（"合同"）。X 国的一项制定法要求该等货物必须使用符合特殊安全要求的运输工具运输。该制定法对违反该规定的行为规定了一项刑事制裁，但未对该等违反行为于具体货运合同的效力影响做出规定。B 使用不符合安全要求的工具运输货物。A 主张合同无效并拒绝支付运费，尽管货物已安全到达目的地。由于该制定法旨在防止对第三人造成伤害，或对环境造成损害，无论是否对 B 进行刑事制裁，均不应授予 B 获得约定运费的权利。

e. 当事人一方或双方是否知道或应该知道该违反行为

　　是否授予合同项下救济，还取决于当事人一方甚或双方是否知道或应该知道该强制性规则，或对该规则的违反行为。

示例：

　　16. 事实同示例 1，但 B 已经将贿金支付给 C，D 不知道也没有理由知道 B 向 C 支付贿金的情况，并将合同授予了 A。如果 D 后来发现支付贿金的情况，其可以选择该合同是否视为有效合同。如果 D 选择合同有效，A 有义务履行合同，D 也有义务支付价款，但要考虑到支付贿金的情况并对价款做适当调整。而如果 B 选择合同无效，则双方当事人均无权获得合同项下的救济。但这不应影响到可能存在的任何恢复原状救济。

　　17. 位于 X 国的承包商 A 与 Y 国经济发展部长 D 就达成一项大型基础设施项目协议（"合同"）进行谈判。D 要求 A，如欲取得合同，需向其支付合同价款 7.5% 的"佣金"。A 支付了 D 要求的"佣金"，并取得了合同。当 A 履行完其在合

Contract, a new Government comes to power in country Y and the new Minister of Economics and Development, invoking the payment of the "commission", cancels the project and refuses to pay for the work already performed. A is not entitled to any remedy under the Contract. This is without prejudice to any restitutionary remedy that may exist.

f. *Whether the performance of the contract necessitates the infringement*

Another factor to be taken into consideration is whether the performance of the contract necessitates the infringement. Thus, if by its very terms the contract provides for, or even only implicitly involves, the violation of a statutory regulation it might be reasonable not to grant the parties any remedy under the contract.

Illustration

18. Company A of country X enters into a contract with company B of country Y for the construction of a chemical fertilizer production plant in country Y ("the Contract"). The Contract does not provide for the installation of the safety devices required by the environmental protection laws of country Y and the parties deliberately agree on a price insufficient to cover the costs of the installation of the devices in question. Neither A nor B should be granted any remedy under the contract.

g. *The parties' reasonable expectations*

If one of the parties on account of different legal or commercial culture could not have reasonably been aware of the infringement or, as is more often the case, one of the parties creates a legitimate expectation as to the enforceability of the contract or its individual terms and later invokes a statutory prohibition of its own law in order to nullify that expectation, it might be reasonable to grant the other party the remedies available under the contract or its individual terms.

Illustration

19. Company A of country X enters into an agreement with B, the Minister of Economics and Development of country Y, concerning an investment project in country Y ("the Agreement"). The Agreement contains a clause providing that all disputes arising out of the Agreement should be decided by arbitration to be held in country Z in accordance with the UNCITRAL Arbitration Rules. If a dispute subsequently arises and A commences arbitration proceedings, B, with a view to

同项下的一半义务时，Y 国新政府上台，新的经济发展部长以支付"佣金"为由，撤销了项目，并拒绝对已完成的工作支付价款。A 无权取得合同项下的任何救济。但这不影响可能存在的任何恢复原状救济。

f. 合同的履行是否必然导致该违反行为

另一项需要考虑的因素是，合同的履行是否必然导致该违反行为。因此，如果合同条款本身规定，甚或仅仅默示地涉及要违反一项制定法规定，合理的做法会是不给予当事人任何合同项下的救济。

示例：

> 18. 位于 X 国的 A 公司与位于 Y 国的 B 公司订立一项在 Y 国建设一座化肥厂的合同（"合同"）。合同未就安装 Y 国环保法要求的安全设备作任何规定，并且双方当事人故意约定一个不足以包括安装该设备成本的价款。A 和 B 均无权获得合同项下的任何救济。

g. 当事人的合理期待

如果另一方当事人由于法律或商务文化的不同，无法合理地知道该违法行为，或者更为常见的是，一方当事人导致另一方当事人对于合同或其个别条款的可强制执行性产生合理期待，但随后援引本国法律的禁止性规定否定该期待，合理的做法是给予该另一方当事人在合同或其个别条款项下可获得的救济。

示例：

> 19. 位于 X 国的 A 公司就在 Y 国进行一项投资项目与 Y 国经济发展部长 B 订立协议（"协议"）。协议中的一项条款规定，协议项下产生的所有争议均应在 Z 国按照联合国国际贸易法委员会仲裁规则以仲裁方式解决。如果随后发生争议，A

avoiding arbitration, cannot invoke a mandatory rule of country Y according to which the domestic courts of country Y have exclusive jurisdiction which may not be contractually excluded by an arbitration agreement for disputes relating to contracts of the type of the Agreement.

h. *Other criteria*

In addition to the criteria expressly listed in paragraph (3) of this Article, there are others which may be taken into consideration to determine the remedies available in the circumstances, if any. One criterion is the extent to which the contract infringes the mandatory rule. If the contract infringes the mandatory rule only in part, it may be reasonable to adapt the contract and grant the parties remedies under it.

Illustration

20. The facts are the same as in Illustration 5, except that only one specific type of toy ordered by A is manufactured by child labourers in their homes, while all the other types are manufactured by workers lawfully employed by B in its factory. Under the circumstances it may be reasonable to adapt the Manufacture Agreement accordingly and grant the parties the ordinary remedies under the adapted Manufacture Agreement.

Another factor is the timely withdrawal from the improper transaction. Thus, if a party to a contract infringing a mandatory rule repents of its action before the unlawful purpose of the contract has been achieved, that party may be granted the right to recover what it has performed.

Illustration

21. The facts are the same as in Illustration 1, except that A, after having paid B the agreed fee of USD 1,000,000, but before B pays C the USD 10,000,000 bribe, decides no longer to pursue the illegal purpose and withdraws from the Contract. A may be granted the right to recover the fee from B.

提请仲裁，B 此时不得为了避免仲裁而援引 Y 国的强制性规则，即 Y 国国内法院对于该协议类型合同相关的争议具有专属管辖权，并且当事人不得以仲裁协议方式协议排除该管辖权。

h. 其他标准

除了本条第(3)款明确列举的标准以外，在决定相关情况下可以获得的救济时，还可以考虑其他因素。其中一个标准是合同违反强制性规则的程度。如果合同仅属部分违反强制性规则，合理的做法是调整合同并给予当事人合同项下的救济。

示例：

20. 事实同示例 5，但 A 定做的玩具中只有某一特定类别的玩具是由童工在家中制作，其他所有类型的玩具都由 B 合法雇佣的工人在工厂中生产。在这种情况下，合理的做法是对生产协议做适当的调整，并按修改后生产协议项下给予双方当事人正常救济。

另一项因素是及时退出不适当的交易。因此，如果违反强制性规则的合同一方当事人在合同的非法目的实现之前及时悔悟，该当事人可以获得追回其已履行的权利。

示例：

21. 事实同示例 1，但在 A 向 B 支付了约定的 100 万美元代理费之后，在 B 向 C 支付 1,000 万美元贿金之前，A 决定不再追求非法目的并退出了合同。A 可以获得向 B 追回代理费的权利。

ARTICLE 3.3.2
(Restitution)

(1) Where there has been performance under a contract infringing a mandatory rule under Article 3.3.1, restitution may be granted where this would be reasonable in the circumstances.

(2) In determining what is reasonable, regard is to be had, with the appropriate adaptations, to the criteria referred to in Article 3.3.1(3).

(3) If restitution is granted, the rules set out in Article 3.2.15 apply with appropriate adaptations.

COMMENT

1. Restitution under contracts infringing mandatory rules to be granted where reasonable under the circumstances

Even where as a consequence of the infringement of a mandatory rule the parties are denied any remedies under the contract, it remains to be seen whether they may at least claim restitution of what they have rendered in performing the contract. According to Article 3.3.1(1), the answer first of all depends on the mandatory rule itself which may or may not expressly address the issue (see also Comment 4 on Article 3.3.1).

If the mandatory rule is silent on the issue, this Article, in line with the modern trend, adopts a flexible approach and provides that where there has been performance under a contract infringing a mandatory rule, restitution may be granted if this would be reasonable in the circumstances (paragraph 1). In other words, contrary to the traditional view that, at least where both parties were aware or ought to have been aware of the infringement of the mandatory rule, they should be left where they stand, i.e. should not even be entitled to recover the benefits conferred, under the Principles restitution may or may not be granted depending on whether it is more appropriate to allow the recipient to keep what it has received or to allow the performer to reclaim it.

第3.3.2条

（恢复原状）

（1）如果已履行的合同属于第3.3.1条规定的违反强制性规则的合同，在返还属合理情况时，可准许恢复原状。

（2）在确定何谓合理时，应考虑经适当调整的第3.3.1条第（3）款述及的各项标准。

（3）如果准许恢复原状，第3.2.15条的规则经适当调整后，应予适用。

注释：

1. 若在相关情况下合理，准许违反强制性规则之合同恢复原状

即便作为合同违反强制性规则的后果，当事人不能获得合同项下的任何救济，但仍然要考虑各当事方是否至少可以就其履行合同过程中已提供的东西请求恢复原状。根据第3.3.1条第（1）款之规定，答案首先取决于该强制性规则本身，它可能或明示或未明示地规定了该问题（参见第3.3.1条注释4）。

如果强制性规则就该问题未做明示规定，根据现代的趋势，本条采用了一种灵活方法，规定：如果违反强制性规则的合同已做了履行，而且具体情况显示准许恢复原状是合理的，则可准许恢复原状（第（1）款）。换言之，这与传统的观点不同。按照传统的观点，至少在双方当事人都知道或应当知道违反强制性规则的情况下，他们不应被给予任何救济，即不允许追回已给与另一方的利益。通则规定，是否准许恢复原状，取决于在让收到履行方保留收到的东西与允许履行方追回之间，哪一个更适当。

2. Criteria for determining whether granting of restitution reasonable

The same criteria laid down in paragraph (3) of Article 3.3.1 to determine if any contractual remedies are available in the circumstances, if any, apply to determine whether granting restitution under paragraph (1) of this Article is reasonable. However, since the contractual and restitutionary remedies are different, the same criteria may lead to different results under the same facts.

Illustrations

1.   The facts are the same as in Illustration 1 in the Comments on Article 3.3.1, except that A, having been awarded the Contract, had almost completed the construction of the power plant when in country Y a new Government comes to power which claims that the Contract is invalid because of corruption and refuses to pay the outstanding 50% of the price. Under the circumstances it would not be fair to let D have the almost completed power plant for half the agreed price. A may be granted an allowance in money for the work done corresponding to the value that the almost completed power plant has for D and D may be granted restitution of any payment it has made exceeding this amount.

2.   Contractor A of country X enters into negotiations with D, the Minister of Economics and Development of country Y, with a view of concluding an agreement on a large infrastructure project ("the Contract"). D requests the payment of a "commission" of 7.5% of the contract price in order to conclude the Contract. A pays the requested "commission" and the Contract is concluded. After A has fulfilled all of its obligations under the Contract, a new Government comes to power in country Y and the new Minister of Economics and Development, invoking the payment of the "commission", refuses to pay the remaining contract price. A may be granted an allowance in money for the work done corresponding to the value of the infrastructure project.

3.   The facts are the same as in Illustration 15 in the Comments on Article 3.3.1, except that B, given that the goods had arrived safely at destination, claims the recovery of at least the value of its service. Under the circumstances, i.e. in view of the seriousness of the violation and the necessity of preventing by all means the carriage of dangerous goods by vehicles lacking the required safety requirements, B may not even be granted the right to recover the value of its service.

2. 确定准许恢复原状是否合理的标准

第 3.3.1 条第(3)款规定了在相关情况下确定是否给予合同救济的标准。同样的标准，也适用于确定本条第(1)款项下准许恢复原状是否合理的情况。然而，由于合同救济和恢复原状救济的不同，同样的标准在相同事实情况下可能导致不同的结果。

示例：

　　1. 事实同第 3.3.1 条注释项下示例 1，但 A 在取得合同后，在 Y 国新政府上台声称存在腐败、合同无效，并拒绝支付剩余 50% 价款时，建设发电厂的工程几乎已经完工。在这种情况下，允许 D 以约定价款之一半的价格享有几乎完工的发电厂的利益，是不公平的。此时，A 可以就已完成的工作获得补偿，金额等于几近完工的发电厂对于 D 所具有的价值，而 D 可就其已支付的超过该金额部分的价款获得返还。

　　2. 位于 X 国的承包商 A 与 Y 国经济发展部长 D 就达成一项大型基础设施项目协议（"合同"）进行谈判。D 要求 A，如欲取得合同需向其支付合同价款 7.5% 作为"佣金"。A 支付了 D 要求的"佣金"，并订立了合同。当 A 履行完其在合同项下的所有义务时，Y 国新政府上台，新的经济发展部长以支付"佣金"为由，拒绝支付剩余的合同价款。A 可就已完成的工作获得补偿，金额等于已完成的基础设施项目的价值。

　　3. 事实同第 3.3.1 条注释示例 15，但是 B 主张，鉴于货物已安全到达目的地，其至少应获得其服务所具有的价值。在这种情况下，鉴于违法行为的严重性，以及需采取一切手段来阻止使用不符安全要求工具运输危险货物的必要性，B 连获取服务价值的权利都不应赋予。

3. Rules governing restitution if granted

If restitution is granted under this Article it is governed by the rules set out in Article 3.2.15 on restitution in the context of avoidance. These rules however need some adaptations, in the sense that in paragraph (1) of Article 3.2.15 the reference to avoidance is to be understood as a reference to the case where the contract becomes ineffective as a result of the infringement of a mandatory rule, and the reference to avoidance of part of the contract as a reference to the case where only part of the contract becomes ineffective as a result of the infringement of a mandatory rule. For further explanation of the rules on restitution referred to in this Article, see the Comments on Article 3.2.15.

3. 准许恢复原状时的调整规则

如果根据本条准许恢复原状，则恢复原状应适用第 3.2.15 条关于宣告合同无效时恢复原状的规则。但这些规则应做适当调整，即第 3.2.15 条第(1)款中所称的宣告合同无效应指合同因违反强制性规则而无效，所称的宣告合同部分无效应指合同因违反强制性规则而部分无效。关于对本条所称的恢复原状规则的进一步解释，参见第 3.2.15 条的注释。

CHAPTER 4

INTERPRETATION

ARTICLE 4.1
(Intention of the parties)

(1) A contract shall be interpreted according to the common intention of the parties.

(2) If such an intention cannot be established, the contract shall be interpreted according to the meaning that reasonable persons of the same kind as the parties would give to it in the same circumstances.

COMMENT

1. Common intention of the parties to prevail

Paragraph (1) of this Article lays down the principle that in determining the meaning to be attached to the terms of a contract, preference is to be given to the intention common to the parties. In consequence, a contract term may be given a meaning which differs both from the literal sense of the language used and from the meaning which a reasonable person would attach to it, provided that such a different understanding was common to the parties at the time of the conclusion of the contract.

The practical importance of the principle should not be over-estimated, firstly because parties to commercial transactions are unlikely to use language in a sense entirely different from that usually attached to it, and secondly because even if this were to be the case it would be extremely difficult, once a dispute arises, to prove that a particular meaning which one of the parties claims to have been their common intention was in fact shared by the other party at the time of the conclusion of the contract.

第四章

合同的解释

第4.1条

（当事人的意思）

（1）合同应根据当事人各方的共同意思予以解释。

（2）如果该意思不能确定，合同应根据一个与各方当事人具有同等资格的、通情达理的人处于相同情况下时，对该合同所应有的理解来解释。

注释：

1. 当事人的共同意思优先

本条第（1）款规定了一项原则，即在确定合同条款的含义时，应当优先考虑当事人各方的共同意思。因此，对于合同条款的解释既可能不同于合同用语的字面含义，也可能不同于一个通情达理的人所理解的含义，只要这种不同的理解是当事人各方在订立合同时所共同拥有的意思。

但不应该高估该原则在实践中的重要性。首先，商业交易的当事人在使用某一文字时，不可能采用一种与通常理解完全不同的含义；其次，即使当事人在合同中使用了该语言的特殊意义，一旦发生争议，当事人一方要证明其所主张的该种特定含义事实上就是订立合同时他与另一方共同拥有的意思，也是极其困难的。

2. Recourse to the understanding of reasonable persons

For those cases where the common intention of the parties cannot be established, paragraph (2) provides that the contract shall be interpreted in accordance with the meaning which reasonable persons of the same kind as the parties would give to it in the same circumstances. The test is not a general and abstract criterion of reasonableness, but rather the understanding which could reasonably be expected of persons with, for example, the same linguistic knowledge, technical skill, or business experience as the parties.

3. How to establish the common intention of the parties or to determine the understanding of reasonable persons

In order to establish whether the parties had a common intention and, if so, what that common intention was, regard is to be had to all the relevant circumstances of the case, the most important of which are listed in Article 4.3. The same applies to the determination of the understanding of reasonable persons when no common intention of the parties can be established.

4. Interpretation of standard terms

Both the "subjective" test laid down in paragraph (1) and the "reasonableness" test in paragraph (2) may not always be appropriate in the context of standard terms. Indeed, given their special nature and purpose, standard terms should be interpreted primarily in accordance with the reasonable expectations of their average users irrespective of the actual understanding which either of the parties to the contract concerned, or reasonable persons of the same kind as the parties, might have had. For the definition of "standard terms", see Article 2.1.19(2).

ARTICLE 4.2

(Interpretation of statements and other conduct)

(1) The statements and other conduct of a party shall be interpreted according to that party's intention if the other party knew or could not have been unaware of that intention.

2. 依据通情达理的人的理解来解释

第(2)款规定，当无法确定当事人的共同意思时，应当根据与各方当事人具有同等资格的通情达理的人在相同情况下对合同的理解来解释合同。这种标准并不是一种一般性的、抽象的合理标准，而是指与当事人具有相同语言知识、技术技能或商业经验等的人合理地可能具有的理解。

3. 怎样确定当事人的共同意思或怎样确定通情达理的人的理解

为了确定当事人是否具有共同意思，以及共同意思是什么，必须考虑案件的所有相关情况，第4.3条列举了其中最重要的几种。当事人的共同意思无法确定而采用通情达理的人的理解时，需要通过同样的方法来确定这种理解。

4. 标准条款的解释

第(1)款确定的"主观"标准和第(2)款确定的"合理"标准，用于确定标准条款的含义时并不总是合适的。实际上，鉴于标准条款所具有的特殊性质和目的，应按照标准条款通常使用者所具有的合理预期来解释，而不论系争合同的当事人或与其具有同等资格的通情达理的人所可能具有的实际理解如何。关于"标准条款"的定义，参见第2.1.19条第(2)款的规定。

第4.2条

（对陈述和其他行为的解释）

（1）一方当事人的陈述和其他行为应根据该当事人的意思来解释，但要以另一方当事人已知或不可能不知道该意思为条件。

(2) If the preceding paragraph is not applicable, such statements and other conduct shall be interpreted according to the meaning that a reasonable person of the same kind as the other party would give to it in the same circumstances.

COMMENT

1. Interpretation of unilateral acts

By analogy to the criteria laid down in Article 4.1 with respect to the contract as a whole, this Article states that in the interpretation of unilateral statements or conduct preference is to be given to the intention of the party concerned, provided that the other party knew (or could not have been unaware) of that intention, and that in all other cases such statements or conduct are to be interpreted according to the understanding that a reasonable person of the same kind as the other party would have had in the same circumstances.

In practice the principal field of application of this Article, which corresponds almost literally to Article 8(1) and (2) CISG, will be in the process of the formation of contracts where parties make statements and engage in conduct the precise legal significance of which may have to be established in order to determine whether or not a contract is ultimately concluded. There are however also unilateral acts performed after the conclusion of the contract which may give rise to problems of interpretation: for example, a notification of defects in goods, notice of avoidance or of termination of the contract, etc.

2. How to establish the intention of the party performing the act or to determine the understanding of a reasonable person

In applying both the "subjective" test laid down in paragraph (1) and the "reasonableness" test in paragraph (2), regard is to be had to all the relevant circumstances, the most important of which are listed in Article 4.3.

（2）如果前款不适用，该等陈述和其他行为应根据一个与另一方当事人具有同等资格的、通情达理的人处于相同情况下时，对该陈述和行为所应有的理解来解释。

注释：

1. 单方行为的解释

与第 4.1 条对于解释合同整体所规定的标准相似，本条规定，在解释一方当事人的单方陈述或单方行为时，应当优先考虑该当事人的意思，如果另一方当事人知道（或不可能不知道）该当事人的意思的话；在其余各种情况下，应当根据与对方当事人具有同等资格的通情达理的人在相同情况下对该陈述或行为的应有的理解来解释。

本条规定和《联合国国际货物销售合同公约》（CISG）第 8 条第（1）款和第（2）款的规定在文字表述上几乎相同。在实践中，本条主要适用于合同的订立过程，这个过程中，当事人往往作出某些陈述和行为；为了判断合同是否最终已经成立，需要确定这些陈述和行为的确切的法律含义。但是，合同订立后也会有一些单方行为引发合同解释的问题：比如，关于货物瑕疵的通知、宣告合同无效的通知或终止合同的通知，等等。

2. 怎样确定行为方当事人的意思或怎样确定通情达理的人的理解

在适用第（1）款规定的"主观"标准和第（2）款规定的"合理"标准时，都必须考虑所有相关的情况，第 4.3 条列举了其中最重要的几种。

ARTICLE 4.3
(Relevant circumstances)

In applying Articles 4.1 and 4.2, regard shall be had to all the circumstances, including

(a) preliminary negotiations between the parties;

(b) practices which the parties have established between themselves;

(c) the conduct of the parties subsequent to the conclusion of the contract;

(d) the nature and purpose of the contract;

(e) the meaning commonly given to terms and expressions in the trade concerned;

(f) usages.

COMMENT

1. Circumstances relevant in the interpretation process

This Article indicates circumstances which have to be taken into consideration when applying both the "subjective" test and the "reasonableness" test in Articles 4.1 and 4.2. The list mentions only those circumstances which are the most important and is in no way intended to be exhaustive.

2. "Particular" and "general" circumstances compared

Of the circumstances listed in this Article some relate to the particular relationship which exists between the parties concerned, while others are of a more general character. Although in principle all the circumstances listed may be relevant in a given case, the first three are likely to have greater weight in the application of the "subjective" test.

Illustrations

1. A contract for the writing of a book between A and B, a publisher, indicates that the book should consist of "about 300 pages". During their negotiations B had assured A that an approximate indication of the number of pages was necessary for administrative reasons and that A was not bound to stick precisely to that number of pages, but could exceed it, substantially if need

第4.3条

（相关情况）

　　适用第**4.1**条和第**4.2**条时，应考虑所有情况，包括：
　　（**a**）当事人之间的初期谈判；
　　（**b**）当事人之间已确立的习惯做法；
　　（**c**）合同订立后当事人的行为；
　　（**d**）合同的性质和目的；
　　（**e**）所涉交易中通常赋予合同条款和表述的含义；
　　（**f**）惯例。

注释：

1. 解释过程中相关的各种情况

　　本条意在表明，在适用第4.1条和第4.2条确定的"主观"标准和"合理"标准时，必须考虑的各种情况。不过，该清单仅仅列举了那些最重要的相关情况，并且绝对无意以此清单穷尽所有相关情况。

2. "具体"情况和"一般"情况的比较

　　在本条所列举的几种情况中，有一些情况涉及合同当事人间的具体关系，其余则是更具一般性的情况。虽然原则上讲，本条所列举的各种情况在具体案件中可能都是相关的，但是前三项情况可能在适用"主观"标准时更为重要。

示例：

　　1. A和出版商B就写作一本书的问题签订了一份合同，合同规定该书"大约300页"。在谈判中，B告诉A是出于行政管理的需要才对页数有大致的规定，A无须受该页数的严格限制，如果确有需要可以超过300页。A提交了一份500页

be. A submits a manuscript of 500 pages. In interpreting the meaning of "about 300 pages" due consideration should be given to these preliminary negotiations (see Article 4.3(a)).

2. A, a Canadian manufacturer, and B, a United States retailer, conclude a number of contracts for the delivery of optical lenses in which the price is always expressed in Canadian dollars. A makes B a new offer indicating the price in "dollars" without further specification, but intending to refer again to Canadian dollars. In the absence of any indication to the contrary, A's intention will prevail (see Article 4.3(b)).

The remaining circumstances listed in this Article, i.e. the nature and purpose of the contract, the meaning commonly given to terms and expressions in the trade concerned and usages, are important primarily, although not exclusively, in the application of the "reasonableness" test.

The criteria in sub-paragraphs (e) and (f) may at first sight appear to overlap. There is however a difference between them: while the "usages" apply only if they meet the requirements laid down in Article 1.9, the "meaning commonly given [...] in the trade concerned" can be relevant even if it is peculiar to a trade sector to which only one, or even neither, party belongs, provided that the expression or term concerned is one which is typical in that trade sector.

Illustrations

3. A and B conclude a contract for the sale of a cargo of oil at USD 80 per barrel. The parties subsequently disagree on the size of the barrel to which they had referred, A having intended a barrel of 42 standard gallons and B one of 36 Imperial gallons. In the absence of any indications to the contrary, A's understanding prevails, since in the international oil trade it is a usage to measure barrels in standard gallons (see Article 4.3(f)).

4. A, a shipowner, concludes a charterparty agreement with B for the carriage of grain containing the standard term "whether in berth or not" with respect to the commencement of the lay-time of the ship after its reaching the port of destination. When it subsequently emerges that the parties attached different meanings to the term, preference should, in the absence of any indication to the contrary, be given to the meaning commonly attached to it in the shipping trade since the term is typical in the shipping trade (see Article 4.3(e)).

的手稿。在解释"大约 300 页"的含义时，应该考虑这些初期谈判情况（参见第 4.3 条（a）项）。

2. 加拿大制造商 A 和美国零售商 B 签订了多份向 B 交付光学镜头的合同，这些合同一直是以加拿大元计价的。后来 A 又向 B 发出一份新的要约，以"元"计价，对"元"未作任何限定，但是其本意是继续用加拿大元计价。如果没有任何相反的表示，将采纳 A 的意思（参见第 4.3 条（b）项）。

本条所列举的其他情况，即合同的性质和目的、在相关行业通常赋予某些条款和表述的含义以及惯例，在适用"合理"标准时非常重要，尽管这并不是绝对的。

乍一看，（e）和（f）两项中的标准似乎有些重复。但它们之间有区别：惯例只有在满足第 1.9 条要求时才能适用；而"在所涉行业中，通常赋予［……］的含义"，即便这一含义是某一贸易行业所独有的，并且仅有一方当事人属于该行业甚或双方当事人均不属于该行业，它们也可以适用，只要该表述或合同条款是该贸易行业中典型的用法。

示例：

3. A 和 B 以每桶 80 美元的价格订立了一份销售一船石油的合同。后来，双方当事人就拟使用的油桶容量出现分歧，A 的意思是使用容量为 42 标准加仑的油桶，B 的意思是使用容量为 36 英国法定标准加仑的油桶。如果没有任何相反的表示，应当采纳 A 的理解，因为以标准加仑计量油桶容量是国际石油贸易中的惯例（参见第 4.3 条（f）项）。

4. B 与船东 A 签订了一份承运谷物的租船合同，关于船舶到达目的港后装卸期的起算时间，合同有一项格式条款规定："无论靠泊与否。"之后双方当事人就该款的含义出现分歧，在没有任何相反表示的情况下，应该优先适用该条款在租船贸易中的通常含义，因为在租船贸易中该条款非常典型（参见第 4.3 条（e）项）。

3. "Merger" clauses

Parties to international commercial transactions frequently include a provision indicating that the contract document completely embodies the terms on which they have agreed. For the effect of these so-called "merger" or "integration" clauses, in particular whether and to what extent they exclude the relevance of preliminary negotiations between the parties, albeit only for the purpose of the interpretation of the contract, see Article 2.1.17.

ARTICLE 4.4
(Reference to contract or statement as a whole)

Terms and expressions shall be interpreted in the light of the whole contract or statement in which they appear.

COMMENT

1. Interpretation in the light of the whole contract or statement

Terms and expressions used by one or both parties are clearly not intended to operate in isolation but have to be seen as an integral part of their general context. Consequently they should be interpreted in the light of the whole contract or statement in which they appear.

Illustration

A, a licensee, hears that, despite a provision in their contract granting A an exclusive licence, B, the licensor, has concluded a similar contract with C, one of A's competitors. A sends B a letter complaining of B's breach and ending with the words "your behaviour has clearly demonstrated that it was a mistake on our part to rely on your professional correctness. We hereby avoid the contract we have with you". Despite the use of the term "avoid", A's words interpreted in the light of the letter as a whole, must be understood as a notice of termination.

2. In principle no hierarchy among contract terms

In principle there is no hierarchy among contract terms, in the sense that their respective importance for the interpretation of the remaining part of the contract is the same regardless of the order in which

3. "合并"条款

国际商事合同的当事人常常规定这样一个条款,表明合同文本包括了双方当事人已经达成一致的全部条款。这些所谓"合并"条款或"并入"条款的效力,特别是出于解释合同的目的,它们能否以及何种程度上排除考虑当事人初期谈判情况,参见第 2.1.17 条的规定。

第 4.4 条

(参考整体合同或陈述)

合同条款和表述应根据其所属的整个合同或全部陈述予以解释。

注释:

1. 根据整个合同或全部陈述来解释

一方或双方当事人在使用某一条款或表述时,很显然无意孤立地使用其含义,而应该视其为上下文不可分割的一部分。因此,应当依据这些条款或表述所在的整个合同或全部陈述对其进行解释。

示例:

> 被许可方 A 和许可方 B 签订了一份合同,依据该合同,A 被授予独占许可。但是 A 听说 B 又与 A 的竞争对手 C 签订了一份类似的合同。所以,A 致函 B 表达了对 B 违约行为的不满,并在信的结尾处说:"你方的行为清楚地表明,我方对你方职业操守的信赖是一种错误。因此我方宣告与你方订立的合同无效。"虽然 A 使用了"宣告无效"一词,但依据这封信的全部内容来看,这应当被理解成是终止合同的通知。

2. 合同条款之间原则上没有等级区别

原则上,合同条款之间没有效力优劣之别,也即,无论每一条款在合同中出现的顺序如何,其对于解释合同其他部分时所具有的意义

they appear. There are, however, exceptions to this rule. Firstly, declarations of intent made in the preamble may or may not be of relevance for the interpretation of the operative provisions of the contract. Secondly, it goes without saying that, in cases of conflict, provisions of a specific character prevail over provisions laying down more general rules. Finally, the parties may themselves expressly establish a hierarchy among the different provisions or parts of their contract. This is frequently the case with complex agreements consisting of different documents relating to the legal, economic and technical aspects of the transaction.

ARTICLE 4.5
(All terms to be given effect)

Contract terms shall be interpreted so as to give effect to all the terms rather than to deprive some of them of effect.

COMMENT

It is to be expected that when drafting their contract parties do not use words to no purpose. It is for this reason that this Article lays down the rule that unclear contract terms should be interpreted so as to give effect to all the terms rather than to deprive some of them of effect. The rule however comes into play only if the terms in question remain unclear notwithstanding the application of the basic rules of interpretation laid down in Articles 4.1 to 4.3.

Illustration

A, a commercial television network, enters into an agreement with B, a film distributor, for the periodic supply of a certain number of films to be transmitted on A's network in the afternoon, when only those films that are admissible for all viewers may be transmitted. According to the contract the films submitted must "have passed the admission test" of the competent censorship commission. A dispute arises between A and B as to the meaning of this term. B maintains that it implies only that the films must have been released for circulation, even if they are X-rated, while A insists that they must have been classified as admissible for everybody. If it is not possible otherwise to establish the meaning to be attached to the term in question, A's understanding prevails since B's interpretation would deprive the provision of any effect.

都是一样的。但是这条规则也存在几个例外。首先，合同序言中有关意图的宣示，在解释合同正文条款时，可能有用也可能没用；其次，不言而喻，出现条文冲突时，特别性质的条文优于规定一般性规则的条文；最后，当事人自己可能明确规定合同不同条款或不同部分之间具有不同的等级，这种划分条款等级的做法在下列复杂协议中相当常见，即由对交易的法律、经济、技术等方面分别作出规定的不同文件组成的复杂协议。

第4.5条

（给予所有条款以效力）

解释合同条款时，应使全部条款均具有效力，而不是排除其中一些条款的效力。

注释：

按照一般的预期，当事人在起草合同时不会无故使用多余的词汇。为此，本条制定了这样一条规则：解释意思不清楚的合同条款时，应该力求让所有的条款都具有效力，而不是排除其中一些条款的效力。不过，只有在适用第4.1条至第4.3条规定的基本规则仍不能清楚地解释相关条款时，才能适用这一规则。

示例：

一家商业电视网A和一家电影发行商B缔结了一份协议，协议的内容是，B定期向A提供一定数量的影片以供A在其电视网的下午时段播放，这一时段只能播放准予向所有观众播放的影片。根据协议的规定，B所提交的影片"必须已经通过了"主管审查委员会的"许可审查"。A和B就这一条款的含义产生了争议。B坚持认为该条款表明影片即使是三级片也没有关系，只要该片是已经获准发行放映的就行，而A则坚持认为影片必须是准予向所有人播放的才行。如果无法通过其他途径确定争议条款的含义，应适用A的理解，因为B的解释剥夺了该条款的效力。

ARTICLE 4.6
(Contra proferentem rule)

If contract terms supplied by one party are unclear, an interpretation against that party is preferred.

COMMENT

A party may be responsible for the formulation of a particular contract term, either because that party has drafted it or otherwise supplied it, for example, by using standard terms prepared by others. Such a party should bear the risk of possible lack of clarity of the formulation chosen. It is for this reason that this Article states that if contract terms supplied by one party are unclear, there is a preference for their interpretation against that party. The extent to which this rule applies will depend on the circumstances of the case; the less the contract term in question was the subject of further negotiations between the parties, the greater the justification for interpreting it against the party who included it in the contract.

Illustration

> A contract between A, a contractor, and B for the construction of an industrial plant contains a provision drafted by A and not discussed further stating that "[t]he Contractor shall be liable for and shall indemnify the Purchaser for all losses, expenses and claims in respect of any loss of or damage to physical property (other than the works), death or personal injury caused by negligence of the Contractor, its employees and agents". One of A's employees plays around with some of B's equipment after working hours and damages it. A denies liability, contending that the provision in question covers only cases where A's employees act within the scope of their employment. In the absence of any indication to the contrary, the provision will be interpreted in the manner which is less favourable to A, i.e. as also covering cases where its employees are not acting within the scope of their employment.

第4.6条

（对条款提供人不利规则）

**如果一方当事人所提出的合同条款含义不清，
则应做出对该方当事人不利的解释。**

注释：

　　如果一方当事人起草了或以其他方式提供了某一合同条款（比如，使用其他人事先起草的格式条款），那么该当事人可能要对该条款的表述负责。该当事人应当承担因所用表述含义不清而导致的风险。正是基于这个原因，本条规定如果一方当事人所提供的合同条款含义不清，则应做出对该方当事人不利的解释。但是本规则适用的程度取决于案件的具体情况：该合同条款越是没有经过当事人之间的充分谈判，就越是有理由做出不利于将该条款写入合同的一方当事人的解释。

　　示例：

　　　　A 是一家承包商，A 和 B 就修建一座工厂订立了一份合同。合同中包含一项由 A 起草且未经双方进一步磋商的条款，该款规定："因承包商或其雇员或代理人的疏忽造成（除工厂以外的）有形财产损失或损害、人身伤害或死亡的，承包商应对由此带来的任何损失、费用和请求负责并赔偿买方。"A 的一个雇员在下班后玩弄 B 的设备，导致该设备毁损。A 拒绝承担责任，理由是上述规定仅仅适用于其雇员在其受雇范围内所为的行为。在没有任何相反表示的情况下，对该款应作不利于 A 的解释，也即，将该款解释为也包括 A 的雇员在受雇范围之外所为的行为。

ARTICLE 4.7
(Linguistic discrepancies)

Where a contract is drawn up in two or more language versions which are equally authoritative there is, in case of discrepancy between the versions, a preference for the interpretation according to a version in which the contract was originally drawn up.

COMMENT

International commercial contracts are often drawn up in two or more language versions which may diverge on specific points. Sometimes the parties expressly indicate which version shall prevail. If all versions are equally authoritative the question arises of how possible discrepancies should be dealt with. This Article does not lay down a hard and fast rule, but merely indicates that preference should be given to the version in which the contract was originally drawn up or, should it have been drawn up in more than one original language version, to one of those versions.

Illustration

> 1.   A and B, neither of them a native English speaker, negotiate and draw up a contract in English before translating it into their respective languages. The parties agree that all three versions are equally authoritative. In case of divergences between the texts, the English version will prevail unless circumstances indicate the contrary.

A situation where a different solution may be preferable could arise where the parties have contracted on the basis of internationally and widely known instruments such as INCOTERMS or the *Uniform Customs and Practices on Documentary Credits*. In case of divergencies between the different versions used by the parties it may be preferable to refer to yet another version if that version is much clearer than the ones used.

Illustration

> 2.   A contract between a company from country X and a company from country Y drawn up in three equally authoritative versions, the language of country X, the language of country Y and English,

第4.7条

（语言差异）

如果合同文本以两种或两种以上具有同等效力的文字起草，若各文本之间存在差异，应优先依据合同最初起草的文本予以解释。

注释：

国际商事合同经常采用两种或多种文字的文本订立，不同文本之间可能就某些具体问题产生分歧。有时候合同当事人明确指定某种文字的文本优先。但如果所有文字的文本具有同等效力，则可能产生如何处理不同文本之间潜在分歧的问题。本条对此并未作出硬性规定，只是规定应优先考虑合同最初起草的文本，或者如果最初是以多种文字起草的，则优先考虑其中的一种文本。

示例：

1. A 和 B 的母语都不是英语，他们以英语谈判和起草了一份合同，然后再将该合同翻译成各自的语言。当事人约定这三种不同语言的合同文本具有同等效力。如果对合同不同文本的内容产生分歧，除非当事人有相反表示，否则英文文本优先。

如果当事人根据国际通行并广为人知的文件（比如《国际贸易术语解释通则》或《跟单信用证统一惯例》）订立合同，则采用一种不同的解决方法可能更为可取。在当事人所使用的不同文本之间存在分歧时，如果还有一种文本比所采用的这些文本更清楚，则可以优先使用该文本。

示例：

2. 一家 X 国公司和一家 Y 国公司起草了一份合同，该合同有 X 国语、Y 国语和英语三个文本，并且这三种文本具有

contains a reference to INCOTERMS 2000. If the French version of INCOTERMS is much clearer than the other three on a point in dispute, that version might be referred to.

ARTICLE **4.8**

(Supplying an omitted term)

(1) Where the parties to a contract have not agreed with respect to a term which is important for a determination of their rights and duties, a term which is appropriate in the circumstances shall be supplied.

(2) In determining what is an appropriate term regard shall be had, among other factors, to

(a) the intention of the parties;

(b) the nature and purpose of the contract;

(c) good faith and fair dealing;

(d) reasonableness.

COMMENT

1. Supplying of omitted terms and interpretation

Articles 4.1 to 4.7 deal with the interpretation of contracts in the strict sense, i.e. with the determination of the meaning which should be given to contract terms which are unclear. This Article addresses a different though related issue, namely that of the supplying of omitted terms. Omitted terms or gaps occur when, after the conclusion of the contract, a question arises which the parties have not regulated in their contract at all, either because they preferred not to deal with it or simply because they did not foresee it.

2. When omitted terms are to be supplied

In many cases of omitted terms or gaps in the contract the Principles will themselves provide a solution to the issue (see, for example, Articles 5.1.6 (*Determination of quality of performance*), 5.1.7 (*Price determination*), 6.1.1 (*Time of performance*), 6.1.4 (*Order of performance*), 6.1.6 (*Place of performance*) and 6.1.10

同等效力。合同规定适用《2000 年国际贸易术语解释通则》。如果法文版的《国际贸易术语解释通则》就系争事项的规定比其他三种语言的版本更清楚，则可能适用法文版本。

第4.8条

（补充空缺条款）

（1）如果合同当事人各方就一项确定其权利和义务的重要条款未达成一致，应补充一项于相关情况下适当的条款。

（2）在决定何为适当条款时，除其他因素外，应考虑以下因素：

（a）各方当事人的意思；

（b）合同的性质和宗旨；

（c）诚实信用和公平交易原则；

（d）合理性。

注释：

1. 缺漏条款的补充与合同的解释

第4.1 条至第4.7 条所调整的是严格意义上的合同解释问题，也就是确定意思不清楚的合同条款的应有之意。本条规定是一个与此相关但又不同的问题，即缺漏条款的补充问题。如果合同订立后出现了一个问题，当事人在合同中对此未作任何规定可能是因为当事人故意不作出规定，也可能是因为当事人当时根本没有预见到，那么此时就产生了条款缺漏或空缺的问题。

2. 何时应该补充缺漏条款

对于很多合同缺漏条款或空缺的情况，《通则》本身提供了解决方法（如参见第5.1.6 条（履行质量的确定），第5.1.7 条（价格的确定），第6.1.1 条（履行时间），第6.1.4 条（履行顺序），第6.1.6 条

(*Currency not expressed*). See also, in general, Article 5.1.2 on implied obligations). However, even when there are such suppletive, or "stop-gap", rules of a general character they may not be applicable in a given case because they would not provide a solution appropriate in the circumstances in view of the expectations of the parties or the special nature of the contract. This Article then applies.

3. Criteria for the supplying of omitted terms

The terms supplied under this Article must be appropriate to the circumstances of the case. In order to determine what is appropriate, regard is first of all to be had to the intention of the parties as inferred from, among other factors, the terms expressly stated in the contract, prior negotiations or any conduct subsequent to the conclusion of the contract.

Illustration

1. The parties to a construction contract agree on a special interest rate to be paid by the purchaser in the event of delay in payment of the price. Before the beginning of the work, the parties decide to terminate the contract. When the constructor delays restitution of the advance payment the question arises of the applicable interest rate. In the absence of an express term in the contract dealing with this question, the circumstances may make it appropriate to apply the special interest rate agreed for delay in payment of the price by the purchaser also to delay in restitution by the constructor.

If the intention of the parties cannot be ascertained, the term to be supplied may be determined in accordance with the nature and purpose of the contract, and the principles of good faith and fair dealing and reasonableness.

Illustration

2. A distribution franchise agreement provides that the franchisee may not engage in any similar business for a year after the termination of the agreement. Although the agreement is silent on the territorial scope of this prohibition, it is, in view of the particular nature and purpose of the franchise agreement, appropriate that the prohibition be restricted to the territory where the franchisee had exploited the franchise.

（履行地）和第6.1.10条（未定明货币）。还可以一般地参见第5.1.2条关于默示义务的规定）。然而，即使有这类一般性的补充规则或"填补遗漏"的规则，但是鉴于当事人的期望或合同的特殊性质，它们也许并不能提供一个具体情况下适当的解决方法，因此个案中这些规则可能并不适用。这时应适用本条。

3. 补充缺漏条款的标准

根据本条规定所补充的条款必须是具体案件情况下适当的条款。为了确定何谓"适当的"，首先应该考虑的是当事人的意思，该意思可以通过某些因素推断出来，例如合同中的明示条款、初期谈判情况或者合同订立后的任何行为。

示例：

1. 一项建筑合同的双方当事人约定，在付款迟延的情况下，买方应按约定的特殊利率支付利息。在工程开始前，双方当事人决定终止合同。当承包商迟延返还预付款时，出现了适用何种利率的问题。合同没有规定解决这一问题的明示条款，但是根据本案的具体情况，将合同规定的买方迟延付款时应适用的特殊利率适用于承包商迟延返还预付款的情形，是适当的。

如果无法确定当事人的意思，确定补充条款时则应根据合同的性质和目的、诚实信用和公平交易原则以及合理性原则。

示例：

2. 一项分销特许经营协议规定，受特许人在该协议终止后一年内不得从事类似的商业活动。虽然该协议就该禁止规定适用的地域范围未作明确规定，但根据该协议的特殊性质和目的，将该禁止规定适用的地域范围限定在受特许人开发该特许经营的地域范围内是适当的。

CHAPTER 5

CONTENT, THIRD PARTY RIGHTS AND CONDITIONS

SECTION 1: CONTENT

ARTICLE 5.1.1
(Express and implied obligations)

The contractual obligations of the parties may be express or implied.

COMMENT

This provision restates the widely accepted principle according to which the obligations of the parties are not necessarily limited to that which has been expressly stipulated in the contract. Other obligations may be implicit (see Article 5.1.2, Comments and Illustrations).

Close links exist between this Article and some of the other provisions of the Principles. Thus Article 5.1.1 is a direct corollary of the rule according to which "[e]ach party must act in accordance with good faith and fair dealing in international trade" (Article 1.7). Insofar as the rules on interpretation (Chapter 4) provide criteria for filling lacunae (besides criteria for solving ambiguities), those rules may assist in determining the precise content of the contract and therefore in establishing the terms which must be considered as implied.

ARTICLE 5.1.2
(Implied obligations)

Implied obligations stem from
(a) the nature and purpose of the contract;
(b) practices   established   between   the parties and usages;
(c) good faith and fair dealing;
(d) reasonableness.

第五章

合同的内容、第三方权利与条件

第一节　合同的内容

第5.1.1条

（明示和默示义务）

当事人各方的合同义务可以是明示的，也可以是默示的。

注释：

本条重申了一项被广泛接受的原则，即，当事人的义务并不必然限于合同中明示规定的义务。其义务也可以是默示的（参见第5.1.2条及其注释和示例）。

本规则和《通则》其他一些条款有密切联系。因此，第5.1.1条是"在国际贸易中各方当事人都应依诚实信用和公平交易原则行事"（第1.7条）规则的一个直接的引申。第四章解释规则为补充空缺（以及解决含义不清条款）确定了标准，这些解释规则有助于确定合同的准确内容，从而也有助于确定哪些条款必须被视为默示条款。

第5.1.2条

（默示义务）

默示的义务源自于：

（a）合同的性质与宗旨；

（b）当事人各方之间确立的习惯做法，以及惯例；

（c）诚实信用和公平交易原则；

（d）合理性。

COMMENT

This Article describes the sources of implied obligations. Different reasons may account for the fact that they have not been expressly stated. The implied obligations may for example have been so obvious, given the nature or the purpose of the obligation, that the parties felt that the obligations "went without saying". Alternatively, they may already have been included in the practices established between the parties or prescribed by trade usages according to Article 1.9. Yet again, they may be a consequence of the principles of good faith and fair dealing and reasonableness in contractual relations.

Illustrations

1.   A rents a full computer network to B and installs it. The contract says nothing as to A's possible obligation to give B at least some basic information concerning the operation of the system. This may however be considered to be an implied obligation since it is obvious, and necessary for the accomplishment of the purpose of such a contract, that the provider of sophisticated goods should supply the other party with a minimum of information (see Article 5.1.2(a)).

2.   A broker who has negotiated a charterparty claims the commission due. Although the brokerage contract is silent as to the time when the commission is due, the usages of the sector can provide an implied term according to which the commission is due, for example, only when the hire is earned, or alternatively when the charterparty was signed, regardless of whether or not the hire will effectively be paid (see Article 5.1.2(b)).

3.   A and B, who have entered into the negotiation of a co-operation agreement, conclude an agreement concerning a complex feasibility study, which will be most time-consuming for A. Long before the study is completed, B decides that it will not pursue the negotiation of the co-operation agreement. Even though nothing has been stipulated regarding such a situation, good faith requires B to notify A of its decision without delay (see Article 5.1.2(c)).

ARTICLE 5.1.3
(Co-operation between the parties)

Each party shall cooperate with the other party when such co-operation may reasonably be expected for the performance of that party's obligations.

注释：

本条规定了默示义务的来源。导致合同对这些义务未加以明示规定的原因有多种。比如，鉴于其性质和目的，一项默示义务非常清楚，合同各方当事人都认为它是"不言而喻"的。或者，依第1.9条该默示义务已包含在当事人之间的习惯做法之中，或者行业惯例对此已作规定。此外，默示义务也可以是合同关系中诚实信用、公平交易和合理性原则的结果。

示例：

1. A向B出租一整套计算机网络系统，并且负责安装。合同对于A是否承担至少向B提供关于操作该系统的基本信息的义务未作规定，但是这可能被视为一项默示义务，因为高科技产品的供应商应该向产品使用者提供最起码的信息，这是不言而喻的，并且为实现该等合同的目的也是必须的（参见第5.1.2条(a)项）。

2. 某个经纪人在谈成一份租船合同后向委托人收取应付的佣金。虽然经纪合同中没有明确规定支付佣金的时间，但是该行业的惯例可以提供一个关于何时支付佣金的默示条款，比如，支付租金后委托人才支付佣金；或者租船合同成立时就应当支付佣金，而不管是否已实际支付租金（参见第5.1.2条(b)项）。

3. A和B就达成一项合作协议进行谈判。为此他们就一项复杂的可行性研究签订了一份协议，A需要花费大量时间才可能完成该可行性研究。但在该可行性研究远未完成之前，B决定终止该合作协议的谈判。即使协议对这种情形未作任何规定，根据诚实信用的原则，B也应该毫不迟延地将该决定通知A（参见第5.1.2条(c)项）。

第5.1.3条

（当事人之间的合作）

如果一方当事人在履行其义务时，可合理地期待对方当事人提供此类合作，则该对方当事人应提供此等合作。

COMMENT

A contract is not merely a meeting point for conflicting interests but must also, to a certain extent, be viewed as a common project in which each party must cooperate. This view is clearly related to the principle of good faith and fair dealing (see Article 1.7) which permeates the law of contract, as well as to the obligation to mitigate harm in the event of non-performance (see Article 7.4.8).

The duty of co-operation must of course be confined within certain limits (the provision refers to reasonable expectations), so as not to upset the allocation of duties in the performance of the contract. Although the principal concern of the provision is the duty not to hinder the other party's performance, there may also be circumstances which call for more active co-operation.

Illustrations

1.   A, after contracting with B for the immediate delivery of a certain quantity of oil, buys all the available oil on the spot market from another source. Such conduct, which will hinder B in performing its obligation, is contrary to the duty of co-operation.

2.   A, an art gallery in country X, buys a sixteenth century painting from B, a private collector in country Y. The painting may not be exported without a special authorisation and the contract requires B to apply for that permission. B, who has no experience of such formalities, encounters serious difficulties with the application whereas A is familiar with such procedures. In these circumstances, and notwithstanding the contractual provision, A can be expected to give at least some assistance to B.

ARTICLE 5.1.4
(Duty to achieve a specific result.
Duty of best efforts)

(1) To the extent that an obligation of a party involves a duty to achieve a specific result, that party is bound to achieve that result.

(2) To the extent that an obligation of a party involves a duty of best efforts in the performance of an activity, that party is bound to make such efforts as would be made by a reasonable person of the same kind in the same circumstances.

注释：

合同不仅仅是相互冲突的利益的交汇点，在某种程度上，也应当被视为需要当事人相互合作的共同项目。该观点明显涉及贯穿合同法始终的诚实信用和公平交易原则（参见第1.7条），以及不履行情况下减轻损害的义务（参见第7.4.8条）。

当然，合作的义务应当被限定在一定范围之内（本条提及合理期待），这样才不会阻挫合同履行过程中的义务分配。虽然本条主要规定了不妨碍另一方履约的义务，但是有时也要求更加积极的合作。

示例：

1. A与B签订了一份买卖合同，规定B立即向A交付一定数量的石油。但是合同订立后，A通过其他途径从现货市场上购买了所有能买到的石油。这一行为违反了A所承担的合作义务，因为这种行为将会妨碍B履行其合同项下的义务。

2. A是X国的一家艺术画廊，B是Y国的一个私人收藏家。A向B购买了一幅16世纪的油画。根据Y国法律，未经特殊许可，该画不得出口，而合同要求B申请这项特殊的出口许可。B在申请这种手续方面没有经验，在申请该许可过程中遇到了很大的困难，而A却非常熟悉这些手续。这种情况下，尽管合同对申请义务已作了规定，但可以期待A至少向B提供一些帮助。

第5.1.4条

（取得特定结果的义务、尽最大努力的义务）

（1）如果一方当事人在一定程度内承担取得某一特定结果之义务，则该方当事人在该程度内有义务取得此特定结果。

（2）如果一方当事人在一定程度内承担对履行某一项活动应尽最大努力之义务，则该方当事人在该程度内有义务尽一个具有同等资格的、通情达理的人在相同情况下所会付出的努力。

COMMENT

1. Distinction between the duty to achieve a specific result and the duty of best efforts

The degree of diligence required of a party in the performance of an obligation varies considerably depending upon the nature of the obligation incurred. Sometimes a party is bound only by a duty of best efforts. That party must then exert the efforts that a reasonable person of the same kind would exert in the same circumstances, but does not guarantee the achievement of a specific result. In other cases, however, the obligation is more onerous and such a specific result is promised.

The distinction between a "duty to achieve a specific result" and a "duty of best efforts" corresponds to two frequent and typical degrees of severity in the assumption of a contractual obligation, although it does not encompass all possible situations.

Obligations of both types may coexist in the same contract. For instance, a firm that repairs a defective machine may be considered to be under a duty of best efforts concerning the quality of the repair work in general, and under a duty to achieve a specific result as regards the replacement of certain spare parts.

2. Distinction provides criteria for determining whether a party has performed its obligations

Taken together, the two paragraphs of this Article provide judges and arbitrators with criteria by which correct performance can be evaluated. In the case of an obligation to achieve a specific result, a party is bound simply to achieve the promised result, failure to achieve which amounts in itself to non-performance, subject to the application of the force majeure provision (see Article 7.1.7). On the other hand, the assessment of non-performance of an obligation of best efforts calls for a less severe judgment, based on a comparison with the efforts a reasonable person of the same kind would have made in similar circumstances. This distinction signifies that more will be expected from a highly specialised firm selected for its expertise than from a less sophisticated partner.

Illustrations

1. A, a distributor, promises that it will reach a quota of 15,000 sales within a year in the contract zone. If at the end of the period A has sold only 13,000 items, it has clearly failed to perform its obligation (see Article 5.1.4(1)).

注释：

1. 取得特定结果的义务与尽最大努力的义务之间的区别

一方当事人在履行一项义务时需要付出的勤勉程度，因相关义务的性质的不同而异。有时候一方当事人仅负有尽最大努力的义务，该当事人只要做出一个与其具有同等资格的通情达理的人在相同情况下所会做出的努力即可，而无须保证一定取得某种特定的结果。相反，在某些情况下，当事人需要承担更多的责任，以保证取得一个特定的结果。

"取得特定结果的义务"与"尽最大努力的义务"的区分，与关于合同义务的承担的两个常用的和典型的严格层级相一致，尽管这种区分并不能涵盖所有可能的情况。

这两种类型的义务可能并存于同一合同之中。比如，一家工厂修理一部出问题的机器，则可以认为，对于修理工作的整体质量，该工厂负有尽最大努力的义务；而对于更换机器的某些零部件，则有义务取得特定的结果。

2. 上述区分为确定一方当事人是否履行其义务提供了判断标准

本条两款规定共同为法官和仲裁员提供了据以评判是否正确履约的标准。对于取得特定结果的义务，一方当事人必须取得承诺的结果；如果没有取得该结果，除非可以适用不可抗力条款（第7.1.7条），否则就构成不履行。另一方面，在评判当事人是否违反了尽最大努力的义务时，则只需要一个严格程度稍次的判断标准，即与一个具有同等资格的通情达理的人在相同情况下所可能作出的努力进行比较。这一区分表明，对于一个因其专长而被选为合同当事人的具有高度专业技能的公司，要比对一个并非如此精深的当事人会有更高的期待。

示例：

1. 分销商 A 承诺在合同规定的销售区内完成年销售15,000件货物的定额。如果一年期限届满时 A 只售出13,000件货物，A 明显未能履行其义务（参见第5.1.4条第(1)款）。

2.   B, another distributor, promises "to use our best efforts to expand the sales of the product" in the contract zone, without any stipulation that it must reach a minimum quantity. This provision creates an obligation of best efforts; it obliges B to take all the steps that a reasonable person, placed in similar circumstances (nature of the product, characteristics of the market, importance and experience of the firm, presence of competitors, etc.) would take to promote the sales (advertising, visits to customers, proper service, etc.). B does not promise the specific result of selling a certain number of items per year, but does undertake to do all that can be expected of it when acting as a reasonable person (see Article 5.1.4(2)).

ARTICLE 5.1.5
(Determination of kind of duty involved)

In determining the extent to which an obligation of a party involves a duty of best efforts in the performance of an activity or a duty to achieve a specific result, regard shall be had, among other factors, to
(a) the way in which the obligation is expressed in the contract;
(b) the contractual price and other terms of the contract;
(c) the degree of risk normally involved in achieving the expected result;
(d) the ability of the other party to influence the performance of the obligation.

C OMMENT

1. Criteria for determining the nature of the obligation

It is important to determine whether an obligation involves a duty to achieve a specific result or simply a duty of best efforts, as the obligation is more onerous in the former case. Such a determination may sometimes be difficult. This Article therefore establishes criteria which may offer guidance to parties, judges and arbitrators, although the list is not exhaustive. The problems involved are frequently matters of interpretation.

2. 另一个分销商 B 承诺在合同规定的销售区内"尽最大努力扩大产品的销售",但合同本身并未规定必须达到的最低销售数量。该规定就设定了一项尽最大努力的义务,该义务要求 B 采取一切可以采取的措施来履约,而且这些措施应该是一个通情达理的人在相同情况下(如产品的性质、市场的特点、公司的重要性和经验、竞争者的有无等)将会采取的促销措施(如做广告、访问客户、优质的售后服务等)。B 并没有承诺要达到每年销售一定数额的特定结果,但是 B 应当做到一个通情达理的人可被期待做到的一切(参见第5.1.4条第(2)款)。

第5.1.5条

(所涉义务类型的确定)

在确定一方当事人在多大程度内承担对履行某一项活动应尽最大努力或者应取得某一特定结果的义务时,除其他因素外,应考虑以下因素:

(a) 合同中表述该义务的方式;
(b) 合同价格以及合同的其他条款;
(c) 取得预期结果通常所涉及的风险程度;
(d) 另一方当事人影响义务履行的能力。

注释:

1. 确定义务性质的标准

确定所涉义务是取得特定结果的义务还是尽最大努力的义务非常重要,因为前者意味着更重的义务。但有时候义务的性质很难确定。为此,本条设立了判断标准,为当事人、法官和仲裁员提供指引,但这一清单并未穷尽列举所有考虑因素。涉及的问题通常都是解释问题。

2. Nature of the obligation as expressed by the contract

The way in which an obligation is expressed in the contract may often be of assistance in determining whether the parties intended to create a duty to achieve a specific result or a duty of best efforts.

Illustration

> 1.   A, a contractor, agrees to build storage facilities for B, who is most keen that the work be finished in an unusually short time. If A undertakes that "the work will be completed before 31 December", it assumes an obligation to achieve the specific result of meeting that deadline. If it merely undertakes "to try to complete the work before 31 December", its obligation involves a duty of best efforts to attempt to meet the deadline, but no guarantee that it will definitely be met (see Article 5.1.5(a)).

3. Price or other terms of the contract

The contractual price or other terms of the contract may also offer clues as to the nature of an obligation. An unusually high price or another particular non-monetary reciprocal obligation may indicate a duty to achieve a specific result in cases where a mere duty of best efforts would normally be assumed. Clauses linking payment of the price to the successful outcome of the operation, penalty clauses applicable if the result is not achieved and hardship clauses enabling a party to adapt the contract if circumstances make it too harsh to perform as initially agreed are other examples of contractual terms which may - in one way or another - assist in determining the nature of the obligation in question (see Article 5.1.5(b)).

4. Degree of risk in performance of an obligation

When a party's performance of an obligation normally involves a high degree of risk it is generally to be expected that that party does not intend to guarantee a result, and that the other party does not expect such a guarantee. The opposite conclusion will be drawn when the desired result can as a rule be achieved without any special difficulty (see Article 5.1.5(c)).

2. 合同表述方式指示义务的性质

合同表述某项义务的方式，往往有助于确定当事人是意图设立一项取得特定结果的义务，还是设立一项尽最大努力的义务。

示例：

> 1. 承包商 A 同意为 B 修建仓储设施，B 热切期望这项工作能在一个很短时间内完成。如果 A 承诺"将在 12 月 31 日之前完工"，它就承担了取得按时完工这一特定结果的义务。如果 A 仅承诺"将尽力在 12 月 31 日之前完工"，A 的义务就只涉及尽最大努力按时完工的义务，并未保证一定会按时完工（参见第 5.1.5 条(a)项）。

3. 合同价格或合同的其他条款

合同价格或其他条款也可以提供判断义务性质的线索。在通常只需承担尽最大努力义务的情况下，一个非同寻常的高价或一项具体的非金钱性互惠义务，可能表明这是一项取得特定结果的义务。有助于——通过这样或那样的方式——判断有关义务性质的其他条款，例如，将支付价款与实现成功结果相联系的条款，未取得结果时适用的罚金条款，以及在情势艰难致使合同无法按最初约定履行时授权一方当事人修改合同的艰难情形条款（参见第 5.1.5 条(b)项）。

4. 履行义务所包含的风险程度

如果一方当事人履行义务时通常包含较高程度的风险，一般就可以预期该方当事人不打算保证取得一个特定的结果，而另一方当事人也会不期望得到这种保证。但是当取得所期望的结果通常没有特殊困难时，结论则正好相反（参见第 5.1.5 条(c)项）。

Illustrations

> 2.   A space agency undertakes to put a telecommunication satellite into orbit, the rate of failure of past launchings having been 22%. The space agency cannot be expected to guarantee that the orbiting will be successful. The obligation is merely to observe the degree of diligence required for such launchings in view of the present state of technology.

> 3.   A promises to deliver 20 tons of steel to B on 30 June. Such a relatively simple operation is subject to no special risk. A is committed to the specific result of delivering the required quantity of steel on the date specified and not merely to attempting to do so.

5. Influence of obligee over performance of an obligation

In some situations one party may have a degree of influence over the performance of the other party's obligations. This fact may transform into duties of best efforts obligations which might otherwise be characterised as duties to achieve specific results.

Illustration

> 4.   A is prepared to provide B with the technical assistance necessary to apply a newly discovered chemical process, and it is agreed that B will send some of its engineers to attend training sessions organised by A. A cannot promise that the new process will be mastered by the other party, since that result depends in part on B's effectively sending its engineers to the training sessions, on those engineers' competence and on their attentiveness at the sessions (see Article 5.1.5(d)).

ARTICLE 5.1.6
(Determination of quality of performance)

Where the quality of performance is neither fixed by, nor determinable from, the contract a party is bound to render a performance of a quality that is reasonable and not less than average in the circumstances.

示例：

　　2. 某空间发射站承诺是将一颗通讯卫星送入轨道。过去从事此类发射业务的失败率在22%，因而不能期望该空间发射站会保证此次发射一定成功。该项义务仅仅要求达到在当前的技术水平下此类发射所需的勤勉程度。

　　3. A承诺在6月30日向B交付20吨钢材。由于这种相对简单的履行并没有什么特殊的风险，因而A承诺的是取得在规定的日期交付规定数量的钢材这一特定的结果，而不仅仅是争取取得这一结果。

5. 债权人对于履行义务的影响

在某些情况下，一方当事人对另一方当事人义务的履行可能具有一定程度的影响。这种情况可能会使一项取得特定结果的义务转化为尽最大努力的义务。

示例：

　　4. A准备向B提供必要的技术支持，以帮助B使用一项新发明的化学工序。双方约定，B将派其工程师参加由A组织的培训班。A无法保证对方一定能够通过培训班掌握该新化学程序，因为A履约的结果部分取决于，B有效地派遣其工程师参加培训班，参加培训班的工程师的个人能力以及他们是否认真学习培训内容（参见第5.1.5条(d)项）。

第5.1.6条

（履行质量的确定）

　　如果合同中未规定履行质量，而且根据合同也无法确定履行质量，则一方当事人有义务使其履行质量达到合理的标准，并且不得低于所涉情况的平均水准。

COMMENT

Standards have been set in Article 5.1.4 concerning the exercise of "best efforts", but quality of performance is a wider problem addressed by Article 5.1.6. If goods are to be supplied, or services rendered, it is not sufficient to supply those goods or to render those services; they must also be of a certain quality.

The contract will often be explicit as regards the quality due ("grade 1 oil"), or it will provide elements making that quality determinable. In other cases, the rule established by Article 5.1.6 is that the quality must be "reasonable and not less than average in the circumstances". Two criteria are thus combined.

Illustration

> 1. A undertakes to build a hotel next to a busy railway station. The contract provides for "adequate sound isolation", the quality of which is not more precisely determined. It is, however, determinable from the contract that the sound isolation must meet the high standards needed in view of the hotel's proximity to a railway station.

1. Performance must be of average quality

The minimum requirement is that of providing goods of average quality. The supplier is not bound to provide goods or services of superior quality if that is not required by the contract, but neither may it deliver goods or services of inferior quality. This average quality is determined according to the circumstances, which normally means that which is available on the relevant market at the time of performance (there may for example have been a recent technological advance). Other factors may also be of relevance, such as the specific qualifications for which the performing party was chosen.

Illustration

> 2. A buys 500 kgs. of oranges from B. If the contract says nothing more precise, and no other circumstances call for a different solution, those oranges may not be of less than average quality. Average quality will however suffice unless it is unreasonably defective.

注释：

第5.1.4条对于何谓尽"最大努力"确定了认定标准，履行质量是第5.1.6条调整的一个范围更广的问题。如果有提交货物或提供服务的义务，仅仅是提交了货物或者提供了服务还不够，它们还必须达到一定的质量标准。

合同通常都会对应该达到的质量标准作出明示的规定（比如"一级石油"），或者会提供可用以确定履行质量的各种要素。对于其他情况，第5.1.6条确立了一个规则，即必须"质量达到合理的标准，并且不得低于个案情况下的平均标准"。因而，这一规则糅合了两个标准。

示例：

1. A将在一个繁忙的火车站旁修建一座旅馆。合同只规定该旅馆应有"适当的隔音设施"，但是并未规定更明确的质量要求。然而，鉴于该旅馆临近火车站，所以根据合同可以确定该隔音设施必须达到必要的高级标准。

1. 履约必须达到平均质量标准

最低质量要求是，必须提供达到平均质量标准的货物。除非合同有规定，否则供应商没有义务提供优质的货物或服务（但是也不能提供劣质的货物或服务）。平均质量标准应根据具体情况确定，通常是指履约时相关市场上可达到的质量（比如可能出现了最新的技术进步）。还有一些因素也可能是相关的，比如，履行方被选中为交易对象时被看重的特殊资历。

示例：

2. A向B购买500公斤橙子。如果合同没有更明确的质量要求，其他情况也没有表明需要一个不同的解决方法，则这些橙子的质量应该不低于平均质量。不过，平均质量标准就足够了，除非它存在不合理的瑕疵。

2. Performance must be reasonable

The additional reference to reasonableness is intended to prevent a party from claiming that it has performed adequately if it has rendered an "average" performance in a market where the average quality is most unsatisfactory and is intended to give the judge or arbitrator an opportunity to raise those insufficient standards.

Illustration

> 3.   A company based in country X organises a banquet to celebrate its 50th anniversary. Since the cuisine in country X is mediocre, the company orders the meal from a renowned restaurant in Paris. In these circumstances the quality of the food provided must not be less than the average standards of the Parisian restaurant. It would clearly not be sufficient simply to meet the average standards of country X.

ARTICLE 5.1.7
(Price determination)

(1) Where a contract does not fix or make provision for determining the price, the parties are considered, in the absence of any indication to the contrary, to have made reference to the price generally charged at the time of the conclusion of the contract for such performance in comparable circumstances in the trade concerned or, if no such price is available, to a reasonable price.

(2) Where the price is to be determined by one party and that determination is manifestly unreasonable, a reasonable price shall be substituted notwithstanding any contract term to the contrary.

(3) Where the price is to be fixed by a third person, and that person cannot or will not do so, the price shall be a reasonable price.

(4) Where the price is to be fixed by reference to factors which do not exist or have ceased to exist or to be accessible, the nearest equivalent factor shall be treated as a substitute.

2. 履约必须合理

本条还提到了合理性要求。目的有二：一是在平均质量非常无法令人满意的市场上，防止一方当事人按照"平均"标准履约后声称已经充分履行。二是也给法官或仲裁员提供一个提高这些不充分标准的机会。

示例：

3. 总部位于 X 国的 A 公司筹办了一场 50 周年庆祝宴会。因为 X 国的烹饪水平很一般，该公司特意从巴黎一家著名餐馆订餐。这种情况下，该餐馆供应的食物的质量不得低于巴黎餐馆的平均标准；仅仅达到 X 国的平均标准，则显然不够。

第5.1.7条

（价格的确定）

（1）如果合同未规定价格，也无如何确定价格的规定，在没有任何相反表示的情况下，应视为当事人各方引用订立合同时相关贸易中可比较的情况下对比此类履行通常收取的价格，或者，若无此价格，应为合理的价格。

（2）如果价格应由一方当事人确定，而且此等确定又明显不合理，则不管合同中是否有任何条款的相反规定，均应以合理价格替代。

（3）如果价格应由一个第三人确定，而该第三人不能或不愿确定该价格，则应采用合理价格。

（4）如果确定价格需要参照的因素不存在，或已不复存在或已不可获得，则应以最相似的因素替代。

COMMENT

1. General rule governing price determination

A contract usually fixes the price to be paid, or makes provision for its determination. If however this is not the case, paragraph (1) of this Article presumes that the parties have made reference to the price generally charged at the time of the conclusion of the contract for such performance in comparable circumstances in the trade concerned. All these qualifications are of course significant. The provision also permits the rebuttal of the presumption if there is any indication to the contrary.

This Article is inspired by Article 55 CISG. The rule has the necessary flexibility to meet the needs of international trade.

It is true that in some cases the price usually charged on the market may not satisfy the reasonableness test which prevails elsewhere in this Article. Recourse would then have to be made to the general provision on good faith and fair dealing (see Article 1.7), or possibly to some of the provisions on mistake, fraud and gross disparity (see Chapter 3, Section 2).

Some international contracts relate to operations which are unique or at least very specific, in respect of which it is not possible to refer to the price charged for similar performance in comparable circumstances. According to paragraph (1) the parties are then deemed to have made reference to a reasonable price and the party in question will fix the price at a reasonable level, subject to the possible review by courts or arbitral tribunals.

Illustrations

1. A, a firm specialised in express mailing throughout the world, receives from B a parcel to be delivered as soon as possible from country X to country Y. Nothing is said as to the price. A should bill B with the price usually charged in the sector for such a service.

2. The next order which A receives from B is one to deliver another parcel as soon as possible to remote and not easily accessible country Z, where a team of explorers is in need of urgent supplies. Again, nothing is said as to price, but since no possible market comparison can be made A must act reasonably when fixing the price.

2. Determination of price by one party

In some cases the contract expressly provides that the price will be determined by one of the parties. This happens frequently in several sectors, for example the supply of services. The price cannot easily be

注释：

1. 确定价格的一般规则

合同通常都会对合同价款或者确定价款的方法作出规定。但如果没有上述规定，则适用本条第(1)款规定的方法，也即，推定当事人引用了合同订立时相关行业中可比较的情况下对此类履行通常收取的价格。所有的这些限定条件都非常重要。如果有任何相反表示，本条也允许当事人反驳这一推定。

本条规定借鉴了《联合国国际货物销售合同公约》第55条的规定。这条规则具有足够的灵活性，能够满足国际贸易的要求。

当然，在某些情况下，市场通行价格可能无法满足合理性标准的要求，本条其他规定都采用了合理性标准。此时只能援引诚实信用和公平交易这个一般性规定（参见第1.7条），也可能援引有关错误、欺诈和重大失衡的某些规定（参见第三章第二节）。

某些国际合同涉及的业务是独一无二的（至少非常特殊），对此，无法通过参照可比情况下的相似履行价格来确定价格。根据本条第(1)款，此时视为当事人各方参照了合理价格，因而相关当事方可以在合理水平上确定合同价格，并可能要受到法院或仲裁庭的审查。

示例：

1. 一家专门经营国际邮件快递业务的公司A，收到B投递的一个包裹，B要求尽快将该包裹从X国送到Y国。双方没有约定价格。A应该按该行业提供此种服务时通常收取的价格向B收取价款。

2. A又接到了B的另一个订单，要求A尽快将包裹送到偏远、难以到达的Z国，以满足某个考察队的紧急需要。双方同样没有约定价格。由于没有可比较的市场价格，所以A必须合理地确定一个价格。

2. 由一方当事人确定价格

有时，合同明确规定由某一方当事人确定合同的价格。这种情形经常发生在某些行业，比如服务业。在这些行业,价格不易事先确定,

determined in advance, and the performing party is in the best position to place a value on what it has done.

In those cases where the parties have made such a provision for determining the price, it will be enforced. To avoid possible abuses however, paragraph (2) enables judges or arbitrators to replace a manifestly unreasonable price by a reasonable one. This provision is mandatory.

3. Determination of price by third person

A provision that the price will be determined by a third person can give rise to serious difficulty if that third person is unable to accomplish the mission (not being the expert he or she was thought to be) or refuses to do so. Paragraph (3) provides that the price, possibly determined by judges or arbitrators, shall be reasonable. If the third person determines the price in circumstances that may involve fraud, gross disparity or threat, Article 3.2.8(2) may apply.

4. Determination of price by reference to external factors

In some situations the price is to be fixed by reference to external factors, typically a published index, or quotations on a commodity exchange. In cases where the reference factor ceases to exist or to be accessible, paragraph (4) provides that the nearest equivalent factor shall be treated as a substitute.

Illustration

3. The price of a construction contract is linked to several indexes, including the "official index of charges in the construction sector", regularly published by the local Government. Several instalments of the price still have to be calculated when that index ceases to be published. The Construction Federation, a private trade association, decides however to start publishing a similar index to replace the former one and in these circumstances the new index will serve as a substitute.

而且履约方当事人最有条件为其履约确定一个价格。

如果当事人规定采用这种方式确定价格，则该规定应得以执行。然而为了避免滥用定价权，本条第(2)款规定法官或仲裁员可以用一个合理的价格取代一个明显不合理的价格。这是一个强制性规定。

3. 由第三人确定价格

合同可能规定由第三人确定价格。如果该第三人不能胜任（他或她并不是当初所认为的专家）或者拒绝做这项工作，可能会造成非常严重的困难。本条第(3)款规定，此时的价格（有可能由法官或仲裁员确定）应当是一个合理价格。如果第三人在定价时涉及到欺诈、重大失衡或胁迫等问题，则适用第3.2.8条第(2)款的规定来处理。

4. 参照外部因素确定价格

有时通过参照外部因素来确定价格。典型的外部因素，如一项公布的指数或商品交易所的报价。但如果该参照的因素不复存在或已不可获得，本条第(4)款规定，应选择最相似的因素作为替代。

示例：

    3. 建筑合同的价格与若干个由地方政府定期发布的指数相关联，包括"建筑业价格官方指数"。该官方指数停止发布时，仍有几笔分期付款的价格需要计算。然而，一家非官方行业协会——建筑业联合会决定发布一个相似的指数来取代以前的官方指数，此时新指数将作为一个替代指数。

ARTICLE 5.1.8
(Contract for an indefinite period)

A contract for an indefinite period may be ended by either party by giving notice a reasonable time in advance.

COMMENT

The duration of a contract is often specified by an express provision, or it may be determined from the nature and purpose of the contract (e.g. technical expertise provided in order to assist in performing specialised work). However, there are cases when the duration is neither determined nor determinable. Parties can also stipulate that their contract is concluded for an indefinite period.

This Article provides that in such cases either party may end the contractual relationship by giving notice a reasonable time in advance. What a reasonable time in advance will be will depend on circumstances such as the period of time the parties have been cooperating, the importance of their relative investments in the relationship, the time needed to find new partners, etc.

The rule can be understood as a gap-filling provision in cases where parties have failed to specify the duration of their contract. More generally, it also relates to the widely recognised principle that contracts may not bind the parties eternally and that they may always opt out of such contracts provided they give notice a reasonable time in advance.

This situation is to be distinguished from the case of hardship which is covered by Articles 6.2.1 to 6.2.3. Hardship requires a fundamental change of the equilibrium of the contract, and gives rise, at least in the first instance, to renegotiations. The rule in this Article requires no special condition to be met, except that the duration of the contract be indefinite and that it permit unilateral cancellation.

Illustration

> A agrees to distribute B's products in country X. The contract is concluded for an indefinite period. Either party may cancel this arrangement unilaterally, provided that it gives the other party notice a reasonable time in advance.

第5.1.8条

（无固定期限的合同）

任何一方当事人均可通过预先在一段合理时间内发出通知，终止一个无固定期限的合同。

注释：

合同的期限通常都是以明示条款作出规定，或者可以根据合同的性质和目的加以确定（比如，为了帮助完成某项特殊工作而提供技术专长）。但是，有时候会出现没有规定也无法确定合同期限的情形。当事人也可以约定其合同是一个无限期的合同。

本条规定，在合同期限不确定的情况下，任何一方当事人都可以通过预先在一段合理时间内发出通知来终止合同关系。何谓"预先在一段合理时间内"，应视情况而定：比如当事人之间合作时间的长短；相互投资在其间关系中的重要性；寻找新的合作伙伴需要的时间，等等。

本条规则被视为一个补充空缺的条款，适用于当事人没有就合同期限作出规定的情况。从更宽泛的意义上讲，该规则还印证了一项被广泛接受的原则，即合同不得无限期地约束合同当事人，而可以通过预先在一段合理时间内发出通知来终止合同。

本条调整的这种情形应当与第6.2.1条至第6.2.3条规定的艰难情形相区别。艰难情形要求合同的均衡关系发生了根本性变化，导致重谈合同的后果（至少最初如此）。本条规则并不要求满足特殊的条件，只需合同期限不确定且允许单方面撤销合同即可。

示例：

A同意在X国销售B的产品。该合同是一个期限不确定的合同。任何一方当事人都可以单方面撤销该合同，只要撤销方预先在一段合理时间内通知了对方即可。

ARTICLE 5.1.9
(Release by agreement)

(1) An obligee may release its right by agreement with the obligor.

(2) An offer to release a right gratuitously shall be deemed accepted if the obligor does not reject the offer without delay after having become aware of it.

COMMENT

An obligee may wish to release the obligor from its obligation (or, in case the obligor owes more than one obligation, from more than one or from all its obligations). The release may either be a separate act, or constitute a part of a more complex transaction between the parties, e.g. a compromise which settles a dispute between them.

This Article provides that such renunciation of the obligee's right(s) requires an agreement between the parties, irrespective or whether the obligee renounces its right(s) for value or gratuitously.

In the latter case, while the obligor should not be compelled to accept a benefit against its will, it will normally consent to accepting the benefit. For this reason paragraph (2) provides that a gratuitous offer shall be deemed accepted if the obligor does not reject the offer without delay after having become aware of it.

Illustrations

1. Company A is in financial difficulties and needs the co-operation of its creditors in order to survive. Bank B is prepared to renounce 50% of its claim against A and the interest that has fallen due on condition that A pay an interest of 9% (instead of the 5% paid previously) on the remaining debt. B sends a notice to this effect on 15 January. By 22 January A has not reacted to the notice. B's renunciation will only be effective after A has accepted B's offer in accordance with Article 2.1.6 *et seq.*

2. Company A is in financial difficulties and needs the co-operation of its creditors in order to survive. Bank B is prepared to renounce 50% of its claim against A and the interest that has fallen due and sends A a notice to this effect on 15 January. By 22 January A has not reacted to the notice. B's offer is deemed to be accepted by A.

第5.1.9条

（通过协议放弃权利）

（1）债权人可以通过与债务人达成协议放弃其权利。

（2）一项无偿放弃权利的要约，若债务人在知晓该要约后未毫不迟延地拒绝，应视为被承诺。

注释：

债权人有时候可能希望免除债务人的义务（或者，在债务人承担不只一项义务的情况下，免除其多项义务或所有义务）。免除可能是一个独立的行为，也可能构成当事人之间一个较为复杂的交易的一部分，比如，解决其间争端的一项和解。

本条规定，债权人免除需要以当事人之间达成协议为条件，而不论债权人是有偿免除还是无偿免除。

在债权人无偿免除的情况下，虽不应强迫债务人接受某种利益，但债务人通常都会同意接受该利益。有鉴于此，本条第（2）款规定，如果债务人在知晓债权人的无偿弃权要约后没有立即表示拒绝，则视为承诺该要约。

示例：

1. 公司A陷入财务困境，为了生存，A需要其债权人的合作。银行B有意放弃其对A的50%债权以及已经到期的利息，条件是A对其余债务需按9%的利率支付利息（而不是原来约定的5%）。1月15日B就上述意向向A发出通知，但是直到1月22日，A也没有对该通知做出回应。按照第2.1.6条及其以下条款之规定，只有在A对B的要约作出承诺后，B的弃权才有效。

2. 公司A陷入财务困境，为了生存，A需要其债权人的合作。银行B有意放弃其对A的50%债权以及已经到期的利息。1月15日B就上述意向向给A发出通知，但是直到1月22日，A也没有对该通知做出回应。按照本条第（2）款的规定，则视为A已承诺B的要约。

SECTION 2: THIRD PARTY RIGHTS

ARTICLE 5.2.1
(Contracts in favour of third parties)

(1) The parties (the "promisor" and the "promisee") may confer by express or implied agreement a right on a third party (the "beneficiary").

(2) The existence and content of the beneficiary's right against the promisor are determined by the agreement of the parties and are subject to any conditions or other limitations under the agreement.

COMMENT

Usually contracts are intended by the parties to create rights and obligations between themselves. In such cases only the parties will acquire rights and duties under the contract. The mere fact that a third party will benefit from the performance of the contract does not in itself give that third party any rights under the contract.

Illustration

1. Professor A makes a contract with the University of country X under which he agrees to give forty one-hour lectures comparing the laws of contract of countries X and Y. A only appears for twenty lectures and does not mention the law of country Y in the lectures. T, a student, does not acquire rights under the contract between A and the University.

However, third parties are not always left without rights. The underlying principle is that of the autonomy of the parties, who, if they wish to create rights in a third party, should be free to do so. The parties may state expressly that this is their intention, but this is not essential since the intention to benefit the third party may be implicit in the contract. In cases where implied intention is alleged, the decision will turn on all the terms of the contract and the circumstances of the case.

The following are illustrations of implied intention.

第二节 第三方权利

第5.2.1条

(第三方受益的合同)

(1) 合同当事人（即允诺人和受诺人）可通过明示或默示协议对第三方（即受益人）设定权利。

(2) 受益人对允诺人享有权利的存在及其内容，由当事人之间的协议确定，并受该协议项下的任何条件或其他限制的约束。

注释：

通常当事人意欲通过合同为其自身创设权利和义务，这种情形下，只有当事人通过合同获得权利承担义务。第三方因合同履行而受益的这一事实本身并不足以赋予该第三方合同项下的任何权利。

示例：

1. 教授 A 和 X 国某大学签订了一份合同，约定教授 A 讲授 40 场一小时长的讲座，内容是比较 X 国和 Y 国合同法。但是教授 A 仅讲授了 20 个场次，并且在授课中也从未提及 Y 国法律。学生 T 不能根据 A 和该大学之间订立的合同获得该合同项下的权利。

然而第三方也不总是没有任何权利。根本原则是当事人自治，只要他们愿意，他们可以自由地为第三方创设权利。当事人可以明示其旨在为第三方创设权利，但这并不是必须的，使第三方受益的意思也可默示蕴藏于合同之中。在主张有此默示意思时，应根据所有合同条款及个案的具体情况来确定。

以下是存在默示意思的例子。

Illustrations

2.   A takes out a policy of insurance on its fleet of lorries which are regularly driven by its employees. The contract provides that the insurance company will cover anyone driving a lorry with A's consent. An employee, T, has an accident while driving the lorry. T is covered in respect of its liability for the accident.

3.   A sells his business to B on the terms that B will pay A GBP 1,000 a month for the rest of his life and will pay A's wife, T, GBP 500 a month if A predeceases her. A dies. B refuses to pay T anything. T is entitled to the GBP 500 a month.

4.   A, the International World University, wishes to build a new law library on land owned by the University. For legitimate tax reasons the contract for the erection of the library is made by B, a company wholly owned by the University, although the contractor well knows that when completed the library will be occupied and used by A. The building has been badly built and it will cost USD 5,000,000 to complete it satisfactorily. A can recover the cost of the remedial work.

5.   A, the developer of a shopping mall, concludes a contract with B, a security firm, to provide security at the mall. Both A and B know that the shops will be operated by tenants of A. These tenants are told that one of the major attractions of the mall will be the high level of security provided by B. It is a term of the contract between A and B that all employees of B working at the mall will be ex-policemen personally selected by B's chief executive. In fact, selection is delegated to a consultancy firm which recruits many unsuitable people. There are many thefts at the shops. Tenants who suffer losses will have contractual claims against B.

The following are illustrations where there is no such implied intention unless the circumstances clearly indicate otherwise.

Illustrations

6.   A goes to an expensive furrier and selects and buys a coat. A tells the assistant (truthfully) that it is for T, the wife of a visiting head of State. By the side of the coat is a prominent card saying "It looks like mink, it feels like mink but is guaranteed man made." A gives the coat to T. In fact, owing to a mistake by the furrier, the coat is a real mink coat and T is subjected to violent and hostile criticism by animal lovers in her country. T has no enforceable contract right.

示例：

2. A 为通常由其雇员驾驶的货车车队投保。保险合同规定保险公司的承包范围涵盖经 A 同意驾驶货车的任何人因事故而遭受的损失。A 的雇员 T 在驾驶货车时遭遇意外事故，T 因该意外事故而应承担的责任在承包范围之内。

3. A 向 B 出售其公司，条件是 B 在 A 去世前每个月向 A 支付 1,000 英镑，且如果 A 比妻子 T 先去世，则由 B 每个月向 T 支付 500 英镑。A 死亡。如果 B 拒绝向 T 支付，则 T 有权主张 B 每月应向其支付 500 英镑。

4. 国际大学 A 希望在其拥有的土地上新建一座法律图书馆。为了使税收合法化，该建筑合同由该大学全资所有的 B 公司签署。虽然该工程的承揽人完全了解该图书馆竣工后将由 A 占有和使用，但是施工质量极差，需要花费 500 万美元才能使该工程顺利完工。A 有权获得补救该工程所需要的费用。

5. 购物中心开发商 A，与保安公司 B 签订了一份合同，由 B 维护购物中心的安全。A 和 B 都知道商店将由 A 的商户经营使用。这些商户被告知该购物中心有吸引力的一个重要原因就是由 B 提供的高水平的保安服务。A 和 B 所签的合同有一条款规定，所有在该中心工作的 B 的保安人员必须从事过警察职业，且由 B 的首席执行官亲自挑选。但事实上，B 将选任工作委托给了一家咨询公司，该公司招收了许多不合格的保安人员。商店经常失窃。受损商户可依据合同向 B 提出索赔。

除非情况另有表明，以下是不存在默示意思的例子。

示例：

6. A 去一高档皮货商店选购大衣。A（如实地）告诉店员大衣是给一位来访的国家元首的妻子 T 购买的。这件大衣旁边挂有明显标牌，注明："看着像貂皮，感觉像貂皮，但保证是人工制品"。A 将这件大衣送给了 T。事实上，因为皮货商的错误，该大衣是真正的貂皮大衣，T 因而受到其本国动物保护者强烈的敌意的谴责。T 没有可强制执行的合同权利。

7. A, a company with a large factory, concludes a contract with a company operating the local sewage system. Under the contract, A is entitled to discharge its waste into the sewer but undertakes not to discharge certain types of waste. In breach of this undertaking, A discharges waste which blocks the sewer and causes damage to T, another user of the sewer. T has no enforceable contract right.

8. A, a company from country X, sells materials to B, a company from country Y. A knows that B plans to resell the materials to T, a pharmaceutical company from country Z, which will use the materials for the manufacture of a new drug under a contract which will effectively limit B's liability to T to USD 1,000,000. The materials are defective and T's losses greatly exceed USD 1,000,000. T has no enforceable contract right against A.

The application of this Article will often come up in the context of an associated claim in tort. This possibility is outside the scope of the Principles.

It follows from the scheme of this Article that an express statement that the parties do not intend to create rights in a third party will be effective. It also follows that the promisor and promisee enjoy broad powers to shape the rights created in favour of the beneficiary. In this context the word "rights" should be interpreted liberally. In principle, a third party beneficiary will have the full range of contractual remedies including the right to performance and damages.

ARTICLE 5.2.2
(Third party identifiable)

The beneficiary must be identifiable with adequate certainty by the contract but need not be in existence at the time the contract is made.

COMMENT

The parties may well wish to make a contract in which the identity of the third party is not known at the time the contract is made, but a mechanism is provided by which it will become known by the time performance is due. This might be by providing that the parties, or one of them, can identify the beneficiary at a later date, or by choosing a definition of the beneficiary, of which later circumstances will serve to make the identity clear.

7. A 是一家拥有大型工厂的公司，A 和负责当地污水处理系统的公司签订合同。根据合同，A 有权将其工厂污水排入污水管道，同时也承诺不排放某些类型的污物。但 A 违反该承诺排放了某些禁排的污物，导致污水管道堵塞，且给该污水管道的另一使用者 T 造成了损失。T 没有可强制执行的合同权利。

8. 一家 X 国公司 A 向一家 Y 国公司 B 出售原材料。A 知道 B 将把这批原材料转售给一家 Z 国制药公司 T，而 T 将用其生产一种新药。根据 B 和 T 之间的合同，B 向 T 承担的合同责任限额为 100 万美元。这批有缺陷的原材料致使 T 遭受的损失大大超过 100 万美元。T 对 A 没有可强制执行的合同权利。

在侵权之诉的附带诉讼请求中将经常适用本条的规定，但是其适用性不在《通则》的调整范围之内。

根据本条的安排，当事人无意为第三方创设权利的明示表述是有效的。同样，合同的允诺人与受诺人在为受益人创设什么样的权利方面享有广泛的自由。在这种语境下，对"权利"一词应作自由的解释。原则上，第三方受益人享有所有的合同救济手段，包括要求实际履行的权利和主张损害赔偿的权利。

第5.2.2条

（第三方的确定性）

受益人必须能够根据合同充分明确地加以确定，但其不必须在订立合同时就存在。

注释：

当事人可能希望订立这样一个合同，即订立合同时第三方的身份还不明确，但却规定一种在履行期届至时能够确定第三方身份的机制。例如规定：合同的双方当事人，或一方当事人可以在合同订立后确定受益人；或者选定一个受益人的定义，后续情况将明确其身份。

Illustrations

    1.   A, a married man with children but no grandchildren, makes a contract with the XYZ insurance company under which A pays GBP 10 a month to the insurance company and they promise to pay GBP 10,000 to each of his grandchildren on his death. Grandchildren born after the date of the contract but before A's death are entitled to GBP 10,000.

    2.   Company A launches a takeover bid for company B, a public company the shares of which are traded on leading stock exchanges. B engages C, a leading firm of accountants, to prepare a report on B for distribution to shareholders. The contract between B and C requires C to produce an honest, thorough and competent report. Owing to incompetence C produces a report that is much too favourable to B. As a result the majority of shareholders vote to reject A's offer. Some shareholders show copies of the report to friends who buy shares in B. The old shareholders can acquire rights under the contract between B and C but the new shareholders cannot.

ARTICLE 5.2.3

(Exclusion and limitation clauses)

    The conferment of rights in the beneficiary includes the right to invoke a clause in the contract which excludes or limits the liability of the beneficiary.

COMMENT

    Contractual provisions limiting or excluding liability of those who are not parties to the contract are very common, particularly in contracts of carriage, where they often form part of a settled pattern of insurance. Perhaps the best known example is the so-called Himalaya clause, which in some form is frequently to be found in bills of lading. In general the autonomy of the parties should be respected in this area too.

Illustration

    A, the owner of goods, makes a contract with a sea carrier to carry them from country X to country Y. The bill of lading is subject to the Hague-Visby Rules and purports to exclude the liability of (a) the master and crew; (b) stevedores employed in loading and unloading the cargo; and (c) the owners of ships onto which the goods may be transhipped. These exclusions will be effective.

示例：

    1. 有儿无孙的已婚男子A与XYZ保险公司签订了一份合同。根据合同，A每月向保险公司支付10英镑，保险公司则承诺在他去世后向他的每个孙子女给付1万英镑。那么，在该保险合同订立之后且在A去世之前出生的A的孙子女都有权获得1万英镑。

    2. A公司向B上市公司发出一收购要约，B公司的股票在多家著名证券交易所上市交易。B公司聘请著名会计师事务所C为其出具一份报告，以供向股东发布。B和C签订的合同要求C制作一真实、全面、合格的报告。但由于能力欠缺，C出具了一份对B过于有利的报告。结果，B公司的多数股东投票拒绝接受A公司的收购要约，一些股东还将这份报告副本出示给购买了B公司股票的朋友。原股东有权依据B和C签订的合同对C请求赔偿，但是新股东却无此权利。

第5.2.3条

（排除和限制条款）

为受益人设定的权利，包括受益人援引合同中排除或限制其责任的条款的权利。

注释：

    合同中限制或排除非合同当事人责任的条款非常普遍，特别是在运输合同中，这些条款往往构成保险合同条款的一部分。众所周知的例子就是所谓的"喜马拉雅条款"，它经常以某种形式出现在提单中。一般来说，当事人在这方面的自治权也应受到尊重。

    示例：

    货主A和一个海运承运人签订了一份将货物从X国运往Y国的合同。提单受《海牙—维斯比规则》调整且声称排除以下人员的责任：（a）船长和船员；（b）受雇装卸货的搬运工人；以及（c）转运货物到其船上的其他船东。这些免责条款都是有效的。

Another situation which would be covered by this Article arises where the promisor and promisee agree that the beneficiary shall be released from an obligation which it owed the promisor.

ARTICLE 5.2.4
(Defences)

The promisor may assert against the beneficiary all defences which the promisor could assert against the promisee.

COMMENT

Under Article 5.2.1 the content of the beneficiary's right may be made subject to any conditions or limitations devised by the parties. The promisor and promisee may devise a contract in which the position of the beneficiary is significantly different from that of the promisee. The parties' autonomy is in principle unlimited but they may well not provide expressly for all possibilities. The normal default rule will therefore be as stated in this Article.

Illustrations

1.   A takes out a policy of life insurance with insurance company B in favour of C. The contract provides for the payment of premiums for 25 years but after 5 years A stops paying premiums. The position of C will be modelled on that of A if the policy had been in A's favour. Such policies do not usually deny all return on the premiums paid. If, however, the policy had been liable to be set aside by the insurance company, for instance because A had not made material disclosure, then B would normally be entitled to raise this defence against C.

2.   Company A takes out a policy of fidelity insurance with insurance company B to cover dishonest employees. The insurance policy provides that B will indemnify in full customers who are defrauded by employees of A and that it will indemnify A only if A has not been negligent in the selection or supervision of the employees. Clearly in such a contract B will have defences against A which it cannot raise against the customers.

受本条调整的另一种情况是：允诺人和受诺人约定免除受益人对允诺人承担的责任。

第5.2.4条

（抗辩）

允诺人可以向受益人主张其可以向受诺人主张的所有抗辩。

注释：

依据第5.2.1条的规定，受益人权利的内容可能受合同当事人设定的任何条件或限制的约束。允诺人和受诺人可以设计这样一个合同，在该合同中，受益人的地位完全不同于受诺人的地位。原则上，当事人的自治权是没有限制的，但是他们不可能对所有可能出现的情况都作出规定。因此正常的缺省规则应如本条规定。

示例：

1. A向保险公司B办理了一份以C为受益人的寿险保单。合同规定A应支付25年的保险费，但五年之后，A停止支付该保险费。C的地位应与若投保人A自己为受益人时A的地位相同。此类保单通常并不完全拒绝返还已支付的保险费。但是如果该保单存在可能被保险公司宣告无效的事由，比如在投保时A对重大事实没有披露，则B通常有权向C主张该抗辩。

2. 公司A向保险公司B办理了一份忠诚保单，以承保不忠诚雇员造成的损失。保单规定全额赔偿受到A的雇员欺诈的顾客，并规定只有当A在选任监督雇员方面不存在过失时才赔偿A。很明显，在本合同中，B可以向A主张抗辩但是却不能向顾客主张抗辩。

ARTICLE 5.2.5
(Revocation)

The parties may modify or revoke the rights conferred by the contract on the beneficiary until the beneficiary has accepted them or reasonably acted in reliance on them.

COMMENT

It might be the rule that the promisor and promisee are free to revoke the third party's rights at any time or, contrariwise, that the third party's rights are immutable once the contract is concluded. It appears that few systems adopt either of these extreme positions. The solution adopted is that the third party's rights become irrevocable once the third party has either accepted the rights or has reasonably acted in reliance on them. It will, of course, be open to the parties to provide for a different regime in the contract either by making the beneficiary's rights irrevocable sooner, or by preserving a right of revocation even after the beneficiary has acted in reliance on the rights. There may well be situations where a right of revocation is given only to one party. For example, in a contract of life insurance it might be provided that the insured can change the beneficiary. There might be relevant usages which limit the possibility of revocation.

Illustration

A, the main contractor on a major construction contract, takes out a policy of insurance with insurance company B to cover damage to the work in progress. The policy is expressed to cover the interests of all sub-contractors involved in the contract and the sub-contractors are all told of the policy. C, a sub-contractor, does not take out any insurance itself, but does not tell A or B. Absent clear words to the contrary, C's reliance makes the contract between A and B irrevocable.

第5.2.5条

（撤销）

**在受益人接受合同为其设定的权利或已信赖
该权利合理行事之前，合同当事人可以修改或者
撤销该权利。**

注释：

可能存在两条相反的规则，即允诺人和受诺人可随时自由撤销为
第三方设定的权利，或者反之，一旦合同订立第三方权利便不可撤销。
似乎很少有法律体系采纳这两种极端情形中的任何一种。《通则》所采
纳的解决方式是：一旦第三方接受权利或已信赖该权利合理行事，第
三方的权利就成为不可撤销的。当然，合同当事人也可以在合同中规
定一种完全不同的方式，例如规定受益人的权利更早成为不可撤销的，
或者保留即使在受益人已经依据授予的权利合理行事后仍可撤销的权
利。还有种情形是仅仅将撤销权赋予一方当事人。比如，一份寿险合
同规定被保险人可以变更受益人。另外，还可能存在限制撤销权行使
的惯例。

示例：

A 是一个大型建筑项目合同的主承包人，A 向保险公司 B
办理了一份保单，承保在建过程中可能遭遇的损失。该保单
还明确承保该合同涉及的所有分包商的利益，并且所有分包
商均被告知该保单将保障其利益。其中一个分包商 C 没有自
行投保，但是也没有将此事告知 A 或 B。如果没有任何明确
的相反规定，C 的这种信赖使 A 和 B 签订的保险合同具有不
可撤销性。

ARTICLE 5.2.6
(Renunciation)

The beneficiary may renounce a right conferred on it.

COMMENT

The scheme of this Section assumes that, absent contrary provision, the contract between promisor and promisee creates rights in the beneficiary at once, without any need for acceptance by the beneficiary.

Although the third party will usually welcome the benefit which the parties have conferred upon it, it cannot be forced to accept it. It follows that the third party may expressly or impliedly renounce the benefit.

However, once the beneficiary has done something that amounts to acceptance, it should not normally be entitled to renounce.

Illustration

On the facts given in the Illustration to Article 5.2.5, C, a subcontractor, may not wish to take advantage of the insurance taken out by the main contractor because it already has relevant insurance in place (and it knows that there will be difficulties if there are two insurances covering the same risk). C is entitled to renounce.

第5.2.6条

（放弃权利）

受益人可以放弃为其设定的权利。

注释：

这部分规定是假设在没有相反规定的情况下，允诺人和受诺人之间的合同自动为受益人创设权利，无须受益人同意。

虽然第三方通常愿意接受合同当事人为其设定的权利，但也不能强迫其接受该权利。因此，第三方可以通过明示或默示的方式放弃权利。

然而，一旦受益人作出构成接受的行为，通常无权再放弃该权利。

示例：

按照第5.2.5条示例所给的事实，分包商C可能不希望采用主承包人办理的保险，因为他自己已经办理了适当的相关保险（且他知道对同一风险办理两份保险时可能会有一定的困难）。所以C有权主张主承包人为其办理的保险。

SECTION 3: CONDITIONS

ARTICLE 5.3.1
(Types of condition)

A contract or a contractual obligation may be made conditional upon the occurrence of a future uncertain event, so that the contract or the contractual obligation only takes effect if the event occurs (suspensive condition) or comes to an end if the event occurs (resolutive condition).

COMMENT

1. Scope of this Section

Parties to a contract may make their contract or one or several obligations arising under it dependent on the occurrence or non-occurrence of a future uncertain event. A provision to this effect is called a condition.

Conditions governed by the Principles include both those that determine whether a contract exists and those that determine obligations within a contract. Accordingly, application of the Principles may in some circumstances impose duties even in the absence of a contract (see, e.g., Articles 5.3.3 and 5.3.4).

A condition may refer to a range of events, including natural events or acts of a third person.

This Section only deals with conditions that originate in an agreement between the parties.

Conditions imposed by law are not covered by this Section unless they are incorporated into the contract by the parties. Thus, a public permission requirement imposed by law is outside the scope of this Section but may be governed by Article 6.1.14. However, if the parties introduce a provision making the contract, or their contractual obligations arising under it, dependent upon a public permission being granted, then that provision is a condition.

第三节　条件

第5.3.1条

（条件的类型）

一个合同或某项合同义务可以未来某一不确定事件的发生作为条件，从而该合同或该合同义务只有在该事件发生时才生效（先决条件），或者在该事件发生时失效（解除条件）。

注释：

1. 本节调整范围

合同当事人可以约定他们之间的合同或其项下的一项或多项义务取决于未来某个不确定事件的发生或不发生。具有这种效力的条款称为条件。

通则调整的条件包括两种类型：决定合同是否存在的条件以及确定合同义务的条件。因此，在某些情况下即使不存在合同，通则的适用也可能会施加一定的义务（参见第5.3.3条和第5.3.4条）。

条件可指多种事件，包括自然事件或者第三人的行为。

本节仅涉及产生于当事人之间协议的条件。

法律规定的条件不属本节调整的范围，除非当事人将其并入合同之中。因此，法律规定的公共许可要求不属于本节调整范围，但可能受第6.1.14条的管辖。然而如果当事人约定一项条款，规定合同或其项下的合同义务取决于一项公共许可的取得，则该条款属于一项条件。

2. Notion of condition

The word "condition" may have a number of meanings. For instance, in some jurisdictions condition means a major term of the contract. That is not the sense in which the term "condition" is used in this Section.

Some contracts may provide that the performance by one party is dependent upon the performance of the other party. These provisions are not conditions, they merely specify the obligations of both parties under their contract.

Illustration

1.   In a share purchase and sale agreement concluded between seller A incorporated in country X, and purchaser B incorporated in country Y, B's obligation to pay the agreed price is subject to A's having "performed all of its obligations hereunder to be performed on or before a certain date". This performance is not a condition, but a contractual obligation and as such is not an uncertain event.

The parties may also fix a specific date at which the contract, or one or several of the obligations arising under it, is to take effect or is to come to an end. In many jurisdictions these provisions are referred to as "terms". They are not conditions under this Section. The same holds true when the parties include a provision in their contract that makes the contract or one or several of the obligations arising under the contract dependent upon the occurrence of a future event that is bound to happen.

Illustrations

2.   A contract of sale is concluded on 2 October, with the delivery of the goods to be made on 10 October. The obligation to deliver is not conditional because it is not subject to a future uncertain event.

3.   Architect A, who intends to renovate her offices, borrows money from a bank and the loan agreement provides that title to a particular property A owns will pass to the bank on A's death. This is not a condition since A's death is certain to occur.

The parties may in their contract provide for a time by which the condition has to occur.

2. 条件的概念

"条件"一词可以有多种含义。例如在某些法域，条件是指合同的主要条款。这不是本节使用的"条件"术语一词的含义。

某些合同可能规定一方当事人的履行取决于另一方当事人的履行。该等条款不属于条件，它们仅仅规定了双方当事人在合同项下的义务。

示例：

　　1. 在 X 国设立的卖方 A 公司和在 Y 国设立的买方 B 公司，订立了一份股份买卖协议，B 支付约定价款的义务是以 A "已在某一日期或之前履行了约定的合同项下的全部义务"为前提。这种履行不属于条件，而属于合同义务，其本身不是一个不确定事件。

当事人还可能约定一个具体日期，合同或其项下一项或多项义务将于该日期产生效力或终止效力。在许多法域，这种规定被称为"条款"。在本节范围内，它们不属于条件。同样，如果合同当事人在合同中订立一个条款，规定合同或其项下一项或多项义务取决于一个必然的未来事件的发生，也不属于本节之条件。

示例：

　　2. 一份销售合同于 10 月 2 日订立，约定于 10 月 10 日交付货物。交付义务不是有条件的，因为它不取决于一项未来不确定的事件。

　　3. 建筑商 A 拟翻新办公室，向某银行贷款。贷款协议规定在 A 死亡时其拥有的某项财产的所有权将转让给该银行。这不是一项条件，因为 A 死亡是必然会发生的事件。

当事人可以在合同中约定条件成就的期限。

Illustration

> 4.   A share purchase agreement is concluded between A and B. It
> will take effect if all necessary authorisations are received by 30
> January. The agreement is conditional and it includes a date by
> which the condition has to occur if the parties' obligations are to
> come into effect.

If the contract does not state a specific time by which the condition
must occur, in appropriate circumstances the time may be implied on the
basis of an interpretation of the intentions of the parties under Chapter 4.

3. Suspensive and resolutive conditions

A contract or contractual obligation can be made to depend upon the
occurrence of a future uncertain event, so that it takes effect only if the
event occurs. Under the Principles this is a suspensive condition. In some
jurisdictions it is known as "condition precedent".

Illustration

> 5.   A merger contract is concluded between A and B subject to A's
> having received the necessary antitrust clearance for the transaction
> from the relevant authorities before a specific date.

A contract or a contractual obligation can be made to come to an end
upon the occurrence of a future uncertain event. Under the Principles this
is a resolutive condition. In some jurisdictions it is known as "condition
subsequent".

Illustration

> 6.   A contract appointing B as a fund manager to manage the
> investments of a company provides that the agreement is to come to
> an end if B loses its licence to conduct the fund management
> business.

Instead of agreeing on a resolutive condition, the parties to a contract
may agree that one or both of them may, under certain circumstances,
have the right to terminate the contract.

4. Condition entirely dependent on the will of the obligor

Sometimes the contract or contractual obligation is made dependent
upon an event which is entirely in the discretion of the obligor. In this
case the question is of whether the obligor really wants to be bound.
This is a question of interpretation. If it appears that there is no intention
to be bound, there is no contract, nor is there any contractual obligation.

示例：

> 4. A 和 B 订立了一份股份购买协议，约定如果 1 月 30 日之前取得所有必要的授权，该合同生效。该协议是有条件的，它包括一个当事人拟使义务产生效力、条件必须成就的日期。

如果合同未规定条件必须成就的具体期限，在适当情况下，可依第四章的规定，以对当事人意图的解释为基础通过默示方式得出一个期限。

3. 生效条件和解除条件

当事人可以约定合同或合同义务取决于某个未来不确定事件的发生，从而只有该事件发生时方才生效。在通则中，这被称为生效条件。在某些法域里，生效条件也称为"先决条件"。

示例：

> 5. A 和 B 订立一项合并合同，条件是在某具体日期之前，A 取得相关部门对该交易反托拉斯必要审查的通过。

当事人可以约定合同或合同义务于某个未来不确定事件发生时终止。在通则里，这被称为解除条件。在某些法域，解除条件也被称为"后决条件"。

示例：

> 6. 某个合同指定 B 作为基金经理，管理某公司的投资，并规定若 B 丧失从事基金管理业务的许可证，协议将终止。

作为约定解除条件的替代，当事人可以约定一方或双方当事人在某些情况下，具有终止合同的权利。

4. 完全取决于债务人意志的条件

有时当事人约定，合同或合同义务取决于某个完全由债务人自由决定的事件。这种情况下所要考察的问题是，债务人是否真的希望受到约束。这是一个解释问题。如果情况显示他没有受约束的意愿，即不存在合同或任何合同义务。

Illustration

> 7.   A document drawn up between A and B contains a list of provisions. One of them states that a contract of sale will come into being if A decides to sell certain goods. A is under no obligation, not even a conditional one, in view of the fact that it is within A's unfettered discretion to decide whether or not A wants to sell the goods. The fact that A may be under a pre-contractual obligation not to act in bad faith is irrelevant in this case.

In some cases there is a conditional obligation in spite of the fact that one party has a choice whether or not to conclude the contract. This holds true when the freedom of choice is in actual fact dependent upon external factors.

Illustration

> 8.   An international merger agreement provides for the merger within a certain period of time of two subsidiaries of a parent company, subject to approval by the Board of Directors of one of the companies. Under the applicable law the approval cannot be unreasonably withheld. There is a conditional obligation since the condition is not entirely dependent on the will of one of the parties.

5. Closing

Parties to complex and high-value business transactions that involve prolonged negotiations frequently provide for a so-called "closing" procedure, i.e. the formal acknowledgement ("closing") at a certain point in time ("closing date") that on or before that date all the stipulated conditions ("conditions precedent") have been satisfied. Normally, but not necessarily, on the "closing date" the parties will sign a document which confirms that no "condition precedent" survives or, if some conditions have not been satisfied, that they have been waived.

Despite the terminology used by the parties, not all the events referred to as "conditions precedent" are "conditions" as defined by this Article. In actual practice, there are mixed provisions. Thus, for instance, events such as the receipt of all necessary antitrust clearances, the admittance to trading on a stock exchange, the granting of an export licence, and the obtaining of a bank loan, may be true suspensive conditions because they are events that are not certain to occur. Other terms such as the accuracy of one party's representations or warranties, the commitment to perform or abstain from some specific acts, and the submission of a tax certificate that evidences that no taxes are due by the party concerned, are in fact obligations that the parties have agreed to fulfil before the formal conclusion ("completion") of the transaction.

示例：

> 7. A 和 B 起草的一份文件包含一系列条款。其中某个条款规定，如果 A 决定出售某些货物，将存在一项销售合同。鉴于 A 是否希望出售货物完全取决于其自由裁量权，A 不承担任何义务，即便是一个有条件的义务。A 可能承担的不恶意行事的前合同义务的事实，与本案也是不相关的。

有时，即使一方拥有是否订立合同的选择权，但仍可能存在一个有条件的合同。选择自由取决于外部因素的事实，就属这种情况。

示例：

> 8. 一项国际合并协议规定，某一母公司的两家子公司在某一时间内合并，前提条件是得到其中一家子公司董事会的批准。根据适用的法律，董事会不得不合理地拒绝批准。此时存在一个有条件的义务，因为该条件并非完全取决于一方当事人的意志。

5. 交割

复杂、大额的商业交易，涉及长期的谈判，当事人往往规定一个所谓的"交割"程序，即在某一时点（"交割日"）正式确认（"交割"）所有约定之条件（"先决条件"）均已在该日期或该日之前成就。通常但也不必然，在交割日当事人各方将签署一份文件，确认不存在未得满足的先决条件，或者若某些条件未成就，其已被放弃。

尽管当事人使用了这一术语，但并非所有被称为"先决条件"的事件都属于本条规定的"条件"。在商业实践中，存在一些混合条款。因此，由于下述条款不属于是确定会发生的事件，可能才是真正的生效条件：取得所有必须的反托拉斯审查、获准在证券交易所上市交易、获得出口许可证，以及取得银行贷款。而其他的一些条款，诸如，一方当事人陈述或保证的准确性、承诺履行或不从事某些具体行为，以及提交税收证书证明相关当事人未拖欠任何税款，事实上都属于当事人同意在正式达成交易（"交易完成"）之前应履行的义务，不属于不

These are not events that are uncertain to occur and, therefore, these provisions are not conditions under the Principles.

Also, with respect to the effects of a "closing", there is no clear-cut rule as to whether or not a term is a condition. In practice it is difficult to derive a logical answer from the clauses themselves. In particular, clauses named "conditions precedent" often mix up real conditions and specific matters that still need to be agreed upon or real obligations that the parties must fulfil in the course of the negotiations (see Article 2.1.13).

Illustration

> 9.   A Share Capital Increase Agreement negotiated between issuer A and lead manager B under the heading "Conditions precedent" provides as follows:
> "The obligation of the Lead Manager at the closing date to subscribe for the shares is subject to the realisation of the following conditions precedent on or prior to the closing date:
> > a.   Accuracy of representations and warranties;
> > b.   Performance of undertakings: the Issuer has performed all of those of its obligations hereunder to be performed on or before the closing date;
> > c.   Admittance to trading on stock exchange;
> > d.   Delivery of any and all closing documents: the Lead Manager shall have received the following documents on or before the closing date [...].
> If any one of the above conditions has not been satisfied at the time it should have been satisfied pursuant to this Section, the obligations of the Lead Manager may be terminated by the Lead Manager."

In this Illustration, the contract consists of a mixture of legal obligations and suspensive conditions: item (c) is a suspensive condition, as it is outside the control of the parties; items (a) and (b) embody contractual obligations; and item (d) embodies a contractual obligation as regards the documents a party is under an obligation to procure but a suspensive condition as regards other documents.

确定是否会发生的事件，因此，它们不属于《通则》规定的条件。

另外，关于"交割"的效果，并不存在确定一个条款是否属于条件的明确规则。事实上，很难从条款本身得到一个逻辑的答案。特别是，被冠以"先决条件"的条款，经常是真正条件与有待进一步同意之事项或当事人须在谈判过程中履行的真实义务的混合（参见第2.1.13条）。

示例：

9. 发行人 A 和牵头经理人 B 订立一份股本增加协议，在"先决条件"的标题下，协议规定：

"牵头经理人承担在交割日认购股份的义务，取决于在交割日或该日之前如下先决条件已经成就：

a. 陈述和保证准确；

b. 履行了保证：发行人在交割日或该日之前，已经履行了其在本协议项下应该履行的所有义务；

c. 获准在股票交易所交易；

d. 交付所有交割文件；牵头经理人应该在交割日或该日之前收到下列文件［……］。

如果上述任何一项条件在根据本条应该成就的时间尚未成就，牵头经理人可以终止自己的义务。"

在本示例中，合同包括了法律义务和生效条件的混合：(c)项是生效条件，因为它不受当事人的控制；（a）项和（b）项包含的是合同义务；（d）项就一方有义务取得的文件而言，属于一项合同义务，但就其他文件而言，则属一项先决条件。

ARTICLE 5.3.2
(Effect of conditions)

Unless the parties otherwise agree :
(a) the relevant contract or contractual obligation takes effect upon fulfilment of a suspensive condition;
(b) the relevant contract or contractual obligation comes to an end upon fulfilment of a resolutive condition.

COMMENT

1. A general default rule

Under the Principles, unless the parties otherwise agree, the fulfilment of a condition has prospective effect only. It does not operate retroactively.

Parties are encouraged to express whether a condition operates retroactively or prospectively.

2. No retroactive effect

In the case of a suspensive condition, the contract or contractual obligation automatically becomes effective from the moment the future uncertain event occurs.

Illustration

1. The facts are the same as in Illustration 5 to Article 5.3.1. The contract takes effect if and when the necessary antitrust clearance is obtained.

In the case of a resolutive condition, the contract or contractual obligation comes to an end from the moment the future uncertain event occurs.

Illustration

2. The facts are the same as in Illustration 6 to Article 5.3.1. The contract comes to an end if and when B loses its licence.

第5.3.2条

（条件的效果）

除非当事人另有约定，否则：

（a）相关合同或合同义务自先决条件成就时，生效；

（b）相关合同或合同义务自解除条件成就时，终止。

注释：

1. 一般默认规则

在《通则》范围内，除非当事人另有约定，条件的成就仅具朝前效力，而不具溯及力。

当事人定明某一条件具有溯及力还是朝前效力，应受到鼓励。

2. 不具有溯及力

对于生效条件，合同或合同义务于未来不确定事件发生之时，自动生效。

示例：

　　1. 事实同第5.3.1条示例5。合同于获得必要的反垄断审查通过时，生效。

对于解除条件，合同或合同义务于未来不确定事件发生时，终止。

示例：

　　2. 事实同第5.3.1条示例6。合同于B丧失许可证时，终止。

ARTICLE 5.3.3
(Interference with conditions)

(1) If fulfilment of a condition is prevented by a party, contrary to the duty of good faith and fair dealing or the duty of co-operation, that party may not rely on the non-fulfilment of the condition.

(2) If fulfilment of a condition is brought about by a party, contrary to the duty of good faith and fair dealing or the duty of co-operation, that party may not rely on the fulfilment of the condition.

COMMENT

This Article on interference with conditions is a specific application of the general rules on good faith and fair dealing (see Article 1.7), inconsistent behaviour (see Article 1.8) and co-operation between the parties (see Article 5.1.3).

Under this Article, the party is not under an obligation to use all reasonable efforts to bring about the fulfilment of the condition. This Article merely states that the party who, contrary to the duties of good faith and fair dealing or co-operation, prevents the condition from being fulfilled may not rely on the non-fulfilment of the condition. If, on the contrary, the party brings about the fulfilment of a condition contrary to the duties of good faith and fair dealing or co-operation, that party may not rely on the fulfilment of the condition.

Whether or not a party is under an obligation to use all reasonable efforts to bring about the fulfilment of a condition is a matter of interpretation. In commercial practice, the parties themselves may expressly provide for the observance of the principle of good faith as regards all the events upon which completion of the transaction is conditional or go beyond this minimum standard and impose a duty to use "their best efforts to bring about the fulfilment of the conditions as soon as practicable". These clauses may also be imposed on one party only (see Article 5.1.4).

The available remedies (right to performance or damages) are to be determined in accordance with the contractual provisions and the general rules on these remedies, as well as with the particular circumstances of the case.

第5.3.3条

（对条件的干扰）

（1）如果一方当事人违反诚实信用和公平交易义务，或合作义务，阻止条件的成就，则该方当事人不得依赖条件的未成就。

（2）如果一方当事人违反诚实信用和公平交易义务，或合作义务，促成条件的成就，则该方当事人不得依赖条件的成就。

注释：

本条关于干扰条件成就的规定，是对几个一般规则的具体适用，即诚实信用和公平交易规则（参见第1.7条）、不一致行为规则（参见第1.8条）和当事人之间合作规则（参见第5.1.3条）。

根据本条的规定，当事人不承担尽一切合理努力促使条件成就的义务。本条只是陈明如果一方当事人违反诚实信用和公平交易义务，或合作义务，阻止条件成就，则该方当事人不得依赖该条件的未成就。相反，如果一方当事人违反诚实信用和公平交易义务，或合作义务，促成条件成就，则该方当事人也不得依赖该条件的成就。

当事人是否具有尽一切合理努力促使一项条件成就的义务，属于解释问题。在商业实践中，当事人自己可明示规定，对涉及交易完成之条件的所有事件，均应遵守诚实信用原则；或者高于这一最低标准，规定一项"尽最大努力尽快促使条件成就"的义务。这些条款也可以只适用于一方当事人（参见第5.1.4条）。

存在的救济（履行权或者损害赔偿）应按照合同的规定和相关损害赔偿的一般规则，以及案件的具体情况而决定。

Four factual situations can be distinguished to illustrate the operation of this Article.

(a)   Where the fulfilment of a suspensive condition is prevented by a party contrary to the duty of good faith and fair dealing or the duty of cooperation, that party may not rely on the non-fulfilment of the condition.

Illustration

> 1.   The licensing of software by B to A is agreed by the parties to be dependent upon the professional approval of the software by an independent computer engineer, C, who is nominated by B. B regrets the bargain and bribes C not to approve the software. Because of the bribe, C states that it does not approve the software. B is not allowed to rely on the non-fulfilment of the condition, i.e. B cannot refuse to perform the obligation under the contract when asked by A to do so.

(b)   Where the fulfilment of a resolutive condition is prevented by a party contrary to the duty of good faith and fair dealing or the duty of cooperation, that party may not rely on the non-fulfilment of the condition.

Illustration

> 2.   A hires earth-moving equipment from B for the time necessary for A to purchase its own equipment. As a commercial favour to A, the rate of hire is below the market rate. B's obligation to make the earth-moving equipment available is subject to the resolutive condition that it comes to an end if A acquires its own earth-moving equipment. A turns down very attractive offers in order to continue benefiting from the favourable rate of hire. A may not rely on the non-fulfilment of the condition.

(c)   Where the fulfilment of a suspensive condition is brought about by a party contrary to the duty of good faith and fair dealing or the duty of cooperation, that party may not rely on the fulfilment of the condition.

Illustration

> 3.   The facts are the same as in Illustration 1, except that B bribes C to give its approval of the software despite C's professional misgivings about the software. B is not allowed to rely on the fulfilment of the condition, i.e. B cannot ask A to perform the contract.

为阐明本条的运用，可以区分四种情况。

（a）如果一方当事人违反诚实信用和公平交易义务，或合作义务，阻止生效条件的成就，则该方当事人不可依赖该条件的未成就。

示例：

　　1. A 和 B 约定 B 向 A 许可软件，前提条件是得到 B 指定的独立软件工程师 C 对于该软件的专业批准。B 想反悔交易，于是贿赂 C 不批准该软件。由于收受贿金 C 声称不批准该软件。B 不得依赖该条件的未成就，即在 A 提出履行时 B 不得拒绝履行合同项下的义务。

（b）如果一方当事人违反诚实信用和公平交易义务或合作义务，阻止解除条件的成就，则该方当事人不得依赖条件的未成就。

示例：

　　2. A 租用 B 的挖土设备，以供 A 在自己购买该等设备之前的期间内使用。作为 B 给予 A 一项商业优惠，租用费率低于市场价格。B 提供该挖土设备的义务受制约于如下解除条件，即在 A 购买自己的挖土设备时终止。为了继续享受优惠的租用价格，A 拒绝了一些非常有吸引力的设备出售要约。A 不得依赖条件的未成就。

（c）如果一方当事人违反诚实信用和公平交易义务或合作义务，促成生效条件成就，则该方当事人不得依赖条件的成就。

示例：

　　3. 事实同示例1，但是 B 贿赂 C 批准该软件，尽管 C 对于该软件的专业评价不好。B 不得依赖该条件的成就，即 B 不得要求 A 履行合同。

(d)   Where the fulfilment of a resolutive condition is brought about by a party contrary to the duty of good faith and fair dealing or the duty of cooperation, that party may not rely on the fulfilment of the condition.

Illustration

> 4.   A appoints B as its agent for the promotion and sale of A's products. The agreement is to come to an end if the gross amount of sales made by B fails to reach EUR 1,000,000 by 31 December the second year. A, who has found another party willing to act as agent on terms more favourable to A than B, withholds supplies to B with the result that by the above date B's gross sales fall well short of EUR 1,000,000. A may not rely on this to treat the agreement with B as having come to an end.

ARTICLE 5.3.4
(Duty to preserve rights)

Pending fulfilment of a condition, a party may not, contrary to the duty to act in accordance with good faith and fair dealing, act so as to prejudice the other party's rights in case of fulfilment of the condition.

COMMENT

This Article only relates to the acts performed during the period that precedes the time when the condition is fulfilled. It does not concern acts which amount to an interference with conditions. These acts are dealt with by Article 5.3.3.

The situation in which fulfilment of the condition is pending is specific and deserves special treatment in application of the general principle of good faith and fair dealing (see Article 1.7). Indeed, a person who would benefit from the fulfilment of a condition has a conditional right which deserves protection (particularly in the case of a suspensive condition). During the period pending fulfilment of the condition one party's actions may detrimentally affect the other party's position. This Article assumes that it is generally better to prevent such actions than to cure their effects.

(d) 如果一方当事人违反诚实信用和公平交易义务或合作义务，促成解除条件成就，则该方当事人不得依赖条件的成就。

示例：

4. A 指定 B 作为促销和销售产品的代理人。协议规定，如果在第二年 12 月 31 日前 B 的毛销售额不足 100 万欧元，协议终止。A 发现另一人愿意以较 B 更加优惠的条件担任代理人，于是停止向 B 供货，结果导致 B 在上述日期毛销售额远低于 100 万欧元。A 不得依赖该事实终止与 B 之间的协议。

第5.3.4条

（权利保护之义务）

条件成就之前，当事人不得违反依诚实信用和公平交易行事的义务行事，以损害另一方当事人于条件成就时可享有的权利。

注释：

本条仅适用于在条件成就之前发生的行为，不适用于干扰条件的行为，后者由第5.3.3条调整。

条件成就前的情况属于一种特殊情况，有必要在适用诚实信用和公平交易一般原则（参见第1.7条）时作特殊处理。事实上，将从条件（特别是对于生效条件）成就中获益的人拥有得到保护的有条件权利。在条件成就前的期间内，一方当事人的行为可能对另一方当事人的处境带来不利影响。本条认为阻止该等行为通常要好于救济其效果。

This Article is also important as a reminder to the parties to consider this issue and even state expressly what measures the person who would benefit from the fulfilment of the condition might take in order to preserve its rights. In commercial practice parties may draft a specific provision (sometimes known as "covenant of ordinary course of business") that produces effects between the date of signature and the "closing date" and restricts the parties' right to dispose of assets only to those transactions that fall within the ordinary course of business.

Illustration

> A share purchase agreement entered into between the seller A and the purchaser B provides that the transaction will be completed only if, at the closing date, all the conditions have been met, including B's having obtained the necessary credit from its banks. A is bound to restrict its activity to ordinary business management and B is under a duty of confidentiality as to any information concerning the company that it has received in the course of negotiations.

ARTICLE 5.3.5
(Restitution in case of fulfilment of a resolutive condition)

(1) On fulfilment of a resolutive condition, the rules on restitution set out in Articles 7.3.6 and 7.3.7 apply with appropriate adaptations.

(2) If the parties have agreed that the resolutive condition is to operate retroactively, the rules on restitution set out in Article 3.2.15 apply with appropriate adaptations.

COMMENT

When a contract subject to a resolutive condition comes to an end as a result of the fulfilment of the resolutive condition, the parties will often have performed, fully or in part, their obligations under the contract. The question then arises whether and, if so, under which rules, the parties have to make restitution of what they have received.

Under the Principles, the fulfilment of a resolutive condition normally has prospective effects only. For this reason restitution will

本条的价值还在于它提醒当事人对此事予以关注，最好对如下情况作出明确规定，即将从条件成就中获益的当事人为保全其权利可采取何种措施。在商业实践中，当事人可能起草一项具体规定（有时称为"正常商业过程承诺"），对签字日和"交割日"之间的交易加以约束，即将当事人处理资产的权利限制于属正常商业过程的交易。

示例：

卖方A和买方B订立一份股份购买协议。协议规定，只有在交割日所有条件（包括B取得银行贷款）均得成就时，交易才可完成。A有义务将自己的活动限制在正常商业管理的范围内，而B对于在谈判过程中获得的任何涉及A公司的信息均承担保密义务。

第5.3.5条

（解除条件成就时的恢复原状）

（1）解除条件成就时，适用经适当调整的第7.3.6条和第7.3.7条有关恢复原状的规定。

（2）如果当事人约定解除条件具有追溯力，适用经适当调整的第3.2.15条有关恢复原状的规定。

注释：

受制于解除条件的合同因该解除条件的成就而终止时，当事人通常已经部分或全部履行了自己在合同项下的义务。此时就会产生一个问题，即当事人是否必须返还其已经收到的履行，如果是，应适用什么样的规则。

在《通则》项下，解除条件的成就通常仅具有前瞻性效力。因此返还

have to follow the regime set out in Articles 7.3.6 and 7.3.7 on restitution following the termination of a contract, which also operates only prospectively. The specificity of this restitution regime vis-à-vis the restitution regime set out in Article 3.2.15 is that for contracts to be performed over a period of time, restitution cannot be claimed for the period prior to the moment when the contract came to an end.

However, under the Principles parties are free to determine that a resolutive condition is to operate retroactively. Under these circumstances it appears to be appropriate to apply the restitution regime set out in Article 3.2.15 (restitution following avoidance), since avoidance also operates retroactively. There is no special rule for restitution in the case of contracts performed over a period of time.

必须按照第7.3.6条和第7.3.7条有关合同终止后返还的制度处理，后两条也仅具有前瞻性效力。这一机制相对于第3.2.15条规定的返还机制的特殊性在于，对于一段期间内履行的合同，不得就合同终止前的期间请求返还。

然而，在通则项下当事人可以自由决定解除条件具有追溯力。在这种情况下，比较合适的做法似乎是适用第3.2.15条规定的返还机制（宣告合同无效后的返还），因为宣告合同无效也具有追溯力。对于一定期间内履行的合同，不存在特殊的返还规则。

CHAPTER 6

PERFORMANCE

SECTION 1: PERFORMANCE IN GENERAL

ARTICLE 6.1.1
(Time of performance)

A party must perform its obligations:
(a) if a time is fixed by or determinable from the contract, at that time;
(b) if a period of time is fixed by or determinable from the contract, at any time within that period unless circumstances indicate that the other party is to choose a time;
(c) in any other case, within a reasonable time after the conclusion of the contract.

COMMENT

With a view to determining when a contractual obligation is to be performed, this Article, which is inspired by Article 33 CISG, distinguishes three situations. The first is where the contract stipulates the precise time for performance or makes it determinable. If the contract does not specify a precise moment but a period of time for performing, any time during that period chosen by the performing party will be acceptable unless circumstances indicate that the other party is to choose the time. Finally, in all other cases, performance is due within a reasonable time.

Illustrations

1.   A offers to advise B in the latter's plans to buy computer equipment and software and it is agreed that A's experts will visit B "in May". It is in principle for A to announce when precisely in

第六章

履 行

第一节 履行的一般规定

第 6.1.1 条

（履行时间）

当事人必须在下列时间履行其合同义务：

（a）如果合同规定了时间，或者依合同可确定时间，则为此时间；

（b）如果合同规定了或依合同可确定一段时间，则为此段期间内的任何时间，除非情况表明履行时间应由另一方当事人选择；

（c）在其他任何情况下，则在合同订立后的一段合理时间之内。

注释：

为了确定履行某项合同义务的时间，本条借鉴《联合国国际货物销售合同公约》（CISG）第 33 条的规定，区分了三种情况：第一种情况是合同规定了明确的履行时间或者根据合同可以确定一个明确的时间；如果合同没有规定一个确切的履行时间而是规定了一段履行时间，则履行合同一方当事人可在这段时间内的任何时间履行，除非情况表明该时间应由另一方当事人选择；最后，在其他任何情况下，履行应该在一段合理时间内完成。

示例：

1. A 将为 B 购买计算机设备和软件提供咨询服务，双方约定 A 的专家将在"5 月份"访问 B。原则上，应由 A 宣布 5

May that visit will take place. The circumstances may however leave the option to B, as would be the case if the contract expressly left to B the choice of the precise dates, or where, for example, it was understood that some of B's staff who are often absent on business trips must be present when A's experts arrive (see Article 6.1.1(b)).

2.   A, a building contractor, encounters unusual difficulties when excavating a site and needs special equipment to continue the work which it does not have. A immediately telephones B, another contractor, who has the necessary equipment and agrees to lend it to A. Nothing however is said as to when the equipment should be delivered to A. Performance is then to take place "within a reasonable time" in the circumstances. Since the work has been interrupted because of the above-mentioned difficulties, A urgently needs to receive the equipment and in such a case "within a reasonable time" probably means that performance is due almost immediately (see Article 6.1.1(c)).

ARTICLE 6.1.2
(Performance at one time or in instalments)

In cases under Article 6.1.1(b) or (c), a party must perform its obligations at one time if that performance can be rendered at one time and the circumstances do not indicate otherwise.

COMMENT

A party's performance is of necessity sometimes rendered at one time (e.g. delivery of a single object), or, alternatively, must take place over a period of time (e.g. construction). There are however also cases where it can be rendered either at one time or in instalments (e.g. delivery of quantities of goods). This Article addresses the latter situation, in circumstances where there is no contractual provision as to how such performance should be rendered, or where it is not determinable from the contract. The principle stated is that performance is due at one time, unless the circumstances indicate otherwise.

Illustrations

1.   A promises to deliver 100 tons of coal to B "in March". It would be materially possible and perhaps convenient for A to deliver the 100 tons in instalments, for instance 25 tons each week

月份的什么具体时间访问 B。然而，情况可能表明应由 B 选择具体履行时间。例如，合同明确规定由 B 选择访问的确切日期；或者 B 的某些员工在 A 的专家访问时必须在场，而这些员工又经常出差不在（参见第6.1.1 条(b)项）。

2. 建筑承包商 A 在挖掘某工地时遇到了不同寻常的困难，需要特殊的设备才能继续其挖掘工作，而 A 没有这样的设备。A 立即致电拥有该设备的另一个承包商 B，B 同意将其设备借给 A 使用。然而双方没有规定交付设备的时间。在该情况下履行应该在"一段合理时间之内"完成。由于挖掘工作因上述困难而中断，A 迫切需要这样的设备，所以本例中，"一段合理时间之内"很可能意味着履行应该立即完成（参见第6.1.1 条(c)项）。

第6.1.2条

（一次或分期履行）

在属于第6.1.1 条(b)项或(c)项的情况下，如果合同义务能一次完成履行，并且情况未有相反的表示，则当事人必须一次履行其全部合同义务。

注释：

一方当事人履行合同义务有时必须一次完成（比如交付一个单一的物品），有时则必须在一段时间内完成（比如建筑）。然而还有一些情况下，履行既可以一次完成，也可以分期完成（比如交付一定数量的货物）。本条要调整的就是这后一种情形：合同没有规定如何完成该履行，或者根据合同不能确定怎样履行。本条确立的原则是，除非情况有相反的表示，履行应该一次完成。

示例：

1. A 承诺在"3月份"向 B 交付100吨煤炭。对 A 而言，它很可能也便于分期交付这100吨煤，比如在3月份每星期

of the month. In principle, however, according to Article 6.1.2, A must deliver the 100 tons at one time.

2.   The facts are the same as in Illustration 1, except that B needs the coal gradually, to meet the needs of its operations. B also has limited storage facilities and could not cope adequately with a consignment of 100 tons at any one time. A knows of B's specific needs. Here the circumstances suggest that A should deliver in instalments during the month of March.

ARTICLE 6.1.3
(Partial performance)

(1) The obligee may reject an offer to perform in part at the time performance is due, whether or not such offer is coupled with an assurance as to the balance of the performance, unless the obligee has no legitimate interest in so doing.

(2) Additional expenses caused to the obligee by partial performance are to be borne by the obligor without prejudice to any other remedy.

COMMENT

1. Partial performance distinguished from performance at one time or in instalments

The situation covered by this Article should be distinguished from that of Article 6.1.2.

Article 6.1.2 attempts to solve a preliminary question which concerns only certain special cases. If a party's performance can be rendered at one time or in instalments and if the contract does not make it clear or determinable how that party is to perform, it must in principle perform at one time.

This Article has a more general scope. It provides that at the time performance is due the obligee may in principle reject an offer of partial performance. This applies at maturity, irrespective of whether what is due then is a global performance or an instalment of a wider obligation (which, in some cases, has been previously determined on the basis of Article 6.1.2).

交付25吨。然而原则上，根据《通则》第6.1.2条之规定，A必须一次性交付这100吨煤。

2. 事实和示例1相同，不同之处在于，B的作业需求决定了其对煤的需求是分批次的。另外B的储存设施有限，在任何时候都不可能一次性地接收100吨煤。A知道B的特殊需要。因此，本例的情况表明A应该在3月份分期交付这100吨煤。

第6.1.3条

（部分履行）

（1）履行期限到来时，债权人可拒绝任何部分履行的请求，无论该请求是否附有对未履行部分的担保，除非债权人这样做无合法利益。

（2）部分履行给债权人带来的额外费用应由债务人承担，并且不得损害债权人的其他救济权利。

注释:

1. 部分履行不同于一次履行或分期履行

本条规定的情形不同于第6.1.2条规定的情形。

第6.1.2条要解决的是一个只涉及某些特殊案件的先决问题。如果一方当事人既可以一次完成履行又可以分期履行，而合同对履行方式又没有明确规定，并且根据合同也无法确定时，则原则上按照《通则》规定必须一次完成履行。

本条的适用范围更加广泛。它规定，在履行期限到来时，债权人原则上可以拒绝债务人部分履行的请求。这适用于履行期届满之时，无论到期的履行是整个一次履行还是分期履行中的一期（在某些情况下，这一问题已经根据第6.1.2条预先确定了）。

Illustration

> 1. A owes USD 1,000,000 to a bank and it has been agreed that A will pay back USD 100,000 on the first day of each month, starting in January. On 1 April A offers to reimburse only USD 50,000, and the balance two weeks later. In principle, the bank is entitled to refuse A's proposal.

2. Obligee entitled in principle to reject partial performance

When performance is due at maturity (be it the whole performance or an instalment), that which is due must be performed completely. In principle, the obligee may reject an offer of partial performance, whether or not it is coupled with an assurance as to the balance of the performance, since it is entitled to receive the whole of what was stipulated. Subject to what will be said below, partial performance normally constitutes a breach of contract. A party who does not obtain full performance at maturity may resort to the available remedies. As a rule, the obligee has a legitimate interest in requiring full performance of what was promised at the time that performance is due.

The obligee may of course also refrain from rejecting the offer to perform in part, while reserving its rights as to the breach, or may accept it without any reservation, in which case partial performance can no longer be treated as a non-performance.

Illustration

> 2. A wishes to open a branch office in country X and rents the necessary office space in a building under construction, due to be finished in time for the move on 1 September. On that date, only four of the ten offices are made available to A, with an assurance that the remaining six will be ready in one month. In principle, A may refuse to move into those four offices.

3. Obligee's right to reject partial performance conditional on its legitimate interest in so doing

There may be situations where the obligee's legitimate interest in receiving full performance is not apparent and where temporary acceptance of partial performance will not cause any significant harm to the obligee. If the party tendering partial performance proves this to be the case, the obligee cannot then refuse such partial performance (subject to paragraph (2)), and there is no non-performance in such cases. This may be seen as a consequence of the general principle of good faith and fair dealing enunciated in Article 1.7.

示例：

　　1. A 欠银行 100 万美元，双方约定从 1 月份开始 A 每月第一天向银行归还 10 万美元。4 月 1 日，A 向银行提示只归还 5 万美元，剩余部分将在随后的两个星期内归还。银行原则上有权拒绝 A 的请求。

2. 债权人原则上有权拒绝部分履行

当某一履行（不论是全部履行还是分期履行）期限届满时，到期的部分必须全部履行。原则上，债权人可以拒绝接受部分履行的提示，不论对未履行部分是否提供了担保，因为债权人有权接受合同规定的全部履行。除下述限制之外，部分履行通常构成违反合同。当事人在履行期限届满时如果未得到全部履行，可以采用任何可以采用的救济手段。原则上，债权人在履行期届满时对于要求全部履行享有合法利益。

当然，债权人也可以不拒绝接受部分履行的请求，但同时保留主张对方违约的权利；或者也可以无保留地接受部分履行的提示，此时，部分履行不能再被当作未履行对待。

示例：

　　2. A 希望在 X 国开一个办事处，在一座正在建造中的楼房租赁了必要的办公场地。该楼房计划于 A 9 月 1 日入驻前按时完工。但在 9 月 1 日，A 所租赁的十间办公室中只有四间可供使用，并且出租方保证其余六间将在一个月内完工。原则上，A 可以拒绝搬进已完工的四间办公室。

3. 债权人拒绝接受履行的权利须以其对此拥有合法利益为条件

在某些情况下，债权人接受全部履行的合法利益并不明显，并且暂时接受部分履行也不会对其造成任何明显的损害。如果请求部分履行的一方当事人能够证明这一点，那么债权人就不能拒绝这样的部分履行（需满足第（2）款），因此也不构成不履行。这可以被视为适用第 1.7 条所阐述的诚实信用和公平交易原则的结果。

Illustration

> 3.   An airline promises to transport 10 automobiles from Italy to Brazil in one single consignment due to be delivered on a definite date. When performance is due, some circumstances make it difficult, although not impossible, for the airline to find sufficient space in a single aircraft. The airline suggests making two successive deliveries within a week. It is established that this will cause no inconvenience to the purchaser of the cars, which will not actually be used before the following month. In such a case the obligee has no legitimate interest in refusing partial performance.

4. Additional expenses entailed by partial performance to be borne by obligor

If partial performance is accepted, it may entail additional expenses for the obligee. In all cases, such expenses are to be borne by the other party. If partial performance amounts to a non-performance (as it usually does), these expenses will be part of the damages, without prejudice to any other available remedy. If partial performance does not amount to a non-performance (the obligee has been shown not to have any legitimate interest in rejecting the offer of partial performance, or has found the offer to be acceptable without reservation), it will only be entitled to those expenses.

Illustration

> 4.   The facts are the same as in Illustration 3. If the purchaser has to meet additional expenses on account of having to make double arrangements for picking up the cars at the airport, those extra costs will be borne by the airline.

ARTICLE 6.1.4
(Order of performance)

(1)   To the extent that the performances of the parties can be rendered simultaneously, the parties are bound to render them simultaneously unless the circumstances indicate otherwise.

(2)   To the extent that the performance of only one party requires a period of time, that party is bound to render its performance first, unless the circumstances indicate otherwise.

示例:

　　3. 一家航空公司承诺在某一确定日期一次性地将 10 辆汽车从意大利运往巴西。履行期限到来时，某些情况使得该航空公司很难(尽管不是不可能)在一次航班中找到足够的舱位。航空公司建议在一个星期内连续两次将这些汽车运走。证据表明，这样做并不会对汽车购买人造成不方便，因为在下个月之前并不需要实际使用这些汽车。在这种情况下，债权人拒绝部分履行没有合法利益。

4. 部分履行导致的额外费用应当由债务人承担

　　债权人接受部分履行，可能会遭致额外费用。在任何情况下，这些额外费用都应当由债务人承担。如果部分履行构成不履行(通常情况下都如此)，则这些额外费用构成损害赔偿的一部分，并且不影响债权人采用任何其他救济手段的权利。如果部分履行不构成不履行（即如果证据表明债权人对于拒绝部分履行的请求没有任何合法利益，或者债权人认为可以无保留地接受部分履行请求），那么债权人只能请求这些额外费用。

示例:

　　4. 事实和示例 3 一样。如果汽车购买人因必须分两次到机场提货而遭受额外费用，这些额外费用应当由航空公司承担。

第6.1.4 条

(履行顺序)

　　(1) 在当事人各方能够同时履行的限度内，当事人各方应同时履行其合同义务，除非情况有相反的表示。

　　(2) 在仅有一方当事人需要在一段时间内履行的限度内，该方当事人应先行履行其义务，除非情况有相反的表示。

COMMENT

In bilateral contracts, where each of the parties has an obligation towards the other, the basic but complex question arises of which party is to perform first. If the parties have not made any specific arrangements, then in practice much will depend on usages and it must also be recalled that there are often several obligations on each side which may have to be performed at different times.

This Article states two broad principles, while recognising that in both cases the circumstances may indicate otherwise. In effect, the main purpose of this Article is to draw the parties' attention to the problem of order of performance, and to encourage them, where necessary, to draft appropriate contractual provisions.

A distinction is drawn between cases where the parties' performances can be rendered simultaneously and those where the performance of only one party requires a period of time.

1. Simultaneous performance to be made when possible

In the first situation, the rule is that the parties are bound to perform simultaneously (paragraph (1)). A seller is entitled to payment on delivery but circumstances may indicate otherwise, for example any exception originating from the terms of the contract or from usages which may allow a party to perform some time after the other.

Illustration

> 1. A and B agree to barter a certain quantity of oil against a certain quantity of cotton. Unless circumstances indicate otherwise, the commodities should be exchanged simultaneously.

2. Exception where performance requires a period of time

If the performance of only one party's obligation by its very nature requires a period of time, for example in construction and most service contracts, the rule established in paragraph (2) is that that party is bound to render its performance first. Circumstances may frequently however indicate the contrary. Thus, insurance premiums are normally paid in advance, as also are rent and freight charges. In construction contracts, payments are usually made in agreed instalments throughout the duration of the work.

注释：

在双务合同中，双方当事人互负义务，所以就产生了一个基本的但却是复杂的问题，即应该由哪方当事人先行履行。如果双方当事人没有对此作出明确的规定，则实践中履行顺序主要依据惯例而定。同时还应指出，每方当事人经常同时承担几项需要在不同时间履行的合同义务。

本条规定了两个宽泛的原则，并承认这两种情况下，具体情况都可能另有其他表示。事实上，本条的主要目的是引起合同当事人对履行顺序的注意，并且鼓励他们在必要时拟定合适的合同条款对此问题作出规定。

本条区分了两种情况：双方当事人能够同时履行的情况和仅一方当事人需要在一段时间内履行的情况。

1. 通常，双方当事人应当同时履行合同义务

第一种情况下适用的规则是，双方当事人应当同时履行合同义务（第(1)款）。卖方有权在交货时获得付款，但情况也可能另有表示，例如根据合同条款或惯例产生的例外情况，可能允许一方当事人在另一方当事人履行合同义务后的一段时间内才履行其义务。

示例：

> 1. A 和 B 约定一项易货贸易，以一定数量的石油交换一定数量的棉花。除非情况有相反的表示，两种货物应当同时交付。

2. 履行需要一段时间时的例外情况

如果只有一方当事人因其合同义务的性质而需要一段时间来履行其义务，例如建筑合同和大多数服务合同，第(2)款确立的规则是该方当事人应当先履行。然而情况经常可能有相反的表示，比如保险费通常先行支付，租金和运费同样如此。在建筑合同中，价款通常是在整个建筑过程中按约定分期支付。

Illustration

2.   A promises to write a legal opinion to assist B in an arbitration. If no arrangement is made as to when A should be paid for the services, A must prepare the opinion before asking to be paid.

3. Relation of order of performance to withholding of performance

This Article sets out the rules which will condition the application of Article 7.1.3 concerning the withholding of performance.

ARTICLE 6.1.5
(Earlier performance)

(1) The obligee may reject an earlier performance unless it has no legitimate interest in so doing.

(2) Acceptance by a party of an earlier performance does not affect the time for the performance of its own obligations if that time has been fixed irrespective of the performance of the other party's obligations.

(3) Additional expenses caused to the obligee by earlier performance are to be borne by the obligor, without prejudice to any other remedy.

COMMENT

1. Obligee in principle entitled to reject earlier performance

When performance is due at a certain moment (to be determined in accordance with Article 6.1.1), it must take place at that time and in principle the obligee may reject an earlier performance. Usually, the time set for performance is geared to the obligee's activities, and earlier performance may cause it inconvenience. The obligee has therefore a legitimate interest in refusing it. Earlier performance, in principle, constitutes non-performance of the contract.

示例：

　　2. A 允诺为 B 出具一份仲裁案件的法律意见书。如果双方没有就 A 应当在什么时候获得报酬作出规定，那么 A 应当在索取报酬前起草完法律意见书。

3. 履行顺序和中止履行的关系

适用第 7.1.3 条关于中止履行的规定时，需以本条确立的规则为前提条件。

第 6.1.5 条

（提前履行）

　　（1）债权人可拒绝提前履行，除非债权人这样做无合法利益。
　　（2）一方当事人接受提前履行并不影响其履行自己义务的时间，如果其履行的时间已经确定而且与另一方当事人义务的履行不相联系。
　　（3）提前履行给债权人造成的额外费用应由债务人承担，且不损害债权人的其他救济权利。

注释：

1. 原则上债权人有权拒绝提前履行

如果履行期限在某个时刻届满（根据第 6.1.1 条确定），则必须在该时间点履行，并且债权人原则上可以拒绝接受提前履行。通常情况下，履行时间都是根据债权人经营活动的需要在合同中加以约定的，提前履行可能会给债权人造成不便。因此，债权人享有拒绝接受提前履行的合法利益。原则上，提前履行构成不履行合同。

The obligee may of course also abstain from rejecting an earlier performance while reserving its rights as to the non-performance. It may also accept such performance without reservation, in which case earlier performance can no longer be treated as non-performance.

Illustration

> 1. A agrees to carry out the annual maintenance of all lifts in B's office building on 15 October. A's employees arrive on 14 October, a day on which important meetings, with many visitors, are taking place in the building. B is entitled to refuse such earlier performance which would cause it obvious inconvenience.

2. Obligee's right to reject earlier performance conditional on its legitimate interest in so doing

Situations may arise in which the obligee's legitimate interest in timely performance is not apparent and when its accepting earlier performance will not cause it any significant harm. If the party offering earlier performance proves this to be the case, the other party cannot reject earlier performance.

Illustration

> 2. The facts are the same as in Illustration 1, except that neither 14 nor 15 October has any special significance. A can probably prove that B has no legitimate interest in refusing the earlier performance.

3. Effect of acceptance by obligee on its own performance of earlier performance of the other party's obligations

If one party accepts earlier performance by the other, the question arises of whether this affects the time for performance of its own obligations. Paragraph (2) deals with cases where obligations are due at a certain time which is not linked to the performance of the other party's obligations; that time for performance remains unchanged.

This provision does not however deal with the converse case where the performances are linked in time. Several situations may then arise. This circumstance may in itself establish the obligee's legitimate interest in rejecting earlier performance. If earlier performance is thus rejected, the obligee's time of performance is unaffected. If earlier performance is accepted with all due reservations as to the non-performance involved, the obligee may also reserve its rights as to its

当然，债权人也可以不拒绝提前履行，但同时保留主张对方不履行的权利；债权人也可以无保留地接受提前履行，在这种情况下，提前履行不再被当作不履行对待。

示例：

1. A 同意在 10 月 15 日对 B 办公楼里所有的电梯进行年检。A 的雇员在 10 月 14 日到达 B 处，而当天该办公楼正在举行有许多客人参加的重要会议。在这种情况下，B 有权拒绝 A 的提前履行，因为这会对其造成明显的不便。

2. 债权人拒绝提前履行的权利须以其对此拥有合法利益为条件

在某些情况下，债权人对于按时履行的合法利益并不明显，并且债权人接受提前履行也不会对其造成任何明显的损害。如果请求提前履行的一方当事人能够证明存在这一点，则另一方当事人不能拒绝提前履行。

示例：

2. 事实和示例 1 一样，不同之处在于 10 月 14 日和 15 日都没有重大事情。A 能够证明 B 对于拒绝提前履行不存在合法利益。

3. 债权人接受债务人的提前履行，对其履行自身合同义务的影响

如果一方当事人接受另一方当事人的提前履行，会产生这样一个问题：即这样做是否影响该方当事人履行自身合同义务的时间。第(2)款规定针对的情况是，该方当事人的合同义务在某个确定的时间到期，并且该时间与另一方当事人履行合同义务之间并没有联系，这种情况下，该方当事人的履行时间保持不变。

然而，本条的规定并不涉及相反的情况，即双方的履行时间相互联系。此时可能产生以下几种情形。这种情况本身可能就证明了债权人对于拒绝提前履行具有合法利益。如果因而拒绝提前履行，则债权人的履行时间不受影响。如果接受提前履行，并对不履行问题作出了适当的保留，则债权人也可以保留自己按约定时间履行义务的权利。

time for performance. If earlier performance is acceptable to the obligee it may at the same time decide whether or not to accept the consequences as regards its own obligations.

Illustrations

3.   B undertakes to deliver goods to A on 15 May and A to pay the price on 30 June. B wishes to deliver the goods on 10 May and A has no legitimate interest in refusing such earlier performance. This will however have no effect on the time agreed for payment of the price, which was determined irrespective of the date of delivery.

4.   B undertakes to deliver goods to A on 15 May and A to pay the price "on delivery". If B tenders the goods on 10 May, A, depending on the circumstances, may reject such earlier performance, claiming that it is not in a position to pay at that date, take delivery of the goods subject to observing the original deadline for payment of the price, or decide to accept the goods and pay for them immediately.

4. Additional expenses entailed by earlier performance to be borne by the performing party

If earlier performance is accepted, it may entail additional expenses for the obligee. In all cases, such expenses are to be borne by the other party. If earlier performance amounts to non-performance (the normal case), those expenses will be part of the damages, without prejudice to any other remedy available. If earlier performance does not amount to non-performance (the obligee has been shown not to have any legitimate interest in rejecting the offer of earlier performance, or has found that offer to be acceptable without reservation), the obligee will only be entitled to those expenses.

Illustration

5.   A has no legitimate interest in refusing delivery of goods on 10 May instead of 15 May, but some additional storage fees are payable for those five extra days. Those costs will be borne by B.

如果提前履行对债权人来说是可以接受的，他可能同时要决定是否接受对于自身义务的影响。

示例：

3. B 承诺于 5 月 15 日向 A 交付货物，而 A 承诺于 6 月 30 日向 B 支付货款。B 希望于 5 月 10 日交付货物，A 对于拒绝 B 提前履行没有合法利益。但是 A 支付货款的时间不因此受到影响，因为该时间已经确定并且与 B 的交货日期不存在联系。

4. B 承诺于 5 月 15 日向 A 交付货物，A 承诺于"货到"时付款。如果 B 于 5 月 10 日交付货物，A 可以视情况拒绝接受该提前履行，并声称自己在 5 月 10 日无法做好付款的准备，也可以接受货物但坚持按原定的最后期限支付货款，或者也可以接受货物并立即支付货款。

4. 因提前履行而产生的额外费用应当由提前履行方承担

债权人接受提前履行，可能会招致额外费用。在任何情况下，这些额外费用都应当由另一方（债务人）承担。如果提前履行构成不履行（通常情况下都如此），则这些额外费用构成损害赔偿的一部分，并且不影响债权人采用任何其他救济手段的权利。如果提前履行不构成不履行（即如果证据表明债权人没有任何合法利益拒绝提前履行的请求，或者债权人认为可以无保留地接受提前履行提示），那么债权人只能请求这些额外费用。

示例：

5. A 对于拒绝 B 于 5 月 10 日交货没有合法利益，但是 A 将为提前 5 天交货而支付额外的储存费用。这些费用应由 B 承担。

ARTICLE 6.1.6
(Place of performance)

(1) If the place of performance is neither fixed by, nor determinable from, the contract, a party is to perform:

(a) a monetary obligation, at the obligee's place of business;

(b) any other obligation, at its own place of business.

(2) A party must bear any increase in the expenses incidental to performance which is caused by a change in its place of business subsequent to the conclusion of the contract.

COMMENT

1. Place of performance fixed by, or determined from, the contract when possible

The place where an obligation is to be performed is often determined by an express term of the contract or is determinable from it. It is obvious, for instance, that an obligation to build must be performed on the construction site, and that an obligation to transport goods must be performed in accordance with the agreed route.

2. Need for suppletive rules

Rules are however needed to cover cases in which the contract is silent on the matter and circumstances do not indicate where performance should take place. Paragraph (1) provides two solutions.

The general rule is that a party is to perform its obligations at its own place of business. The second rule is specific to monetary obligations where the converse solution applies, namely that the obligor is to perform its obligations at the obligee's place of business (subject to the application of Article 6.1.8 concerning payments by funds transfers).

These solutions may not be the most satisfactory in all cases, but they do reflect the need for rules where the parties have not made any other arrangement or where the circumstances do not indicate otherwise.

第6.1.6条

（履行地）

（1）如果合同既未规定履行地，依据合同也无法确定履行地，则应在下述地点履行：

（a）金钱债务，在债权人的营业地；

（b）任何其他义务，在债务人自己的营业地。

（2）当事人应承担合同订立后因其营业地改变而给履行增加的费用。

注释：

1. 通常，履行地应当由合同规定，或者可以根据合同确定

履行义务的地点通常由合同条款明确规定，或者可以根据合同条款确定。例如，很明显，建筑义务必须在建筑工地履行，运输货物的义务必须按约定的路线履行。

2. 必要的补充规则

然而，如果合同对履行地没有规定，而且个案情况也未指示应在何地履行时，就需要调整此类案件补充规则。第(1)款提供了两种解决方法。

一般规则是当事人应在自己的营业地履行其合同义务。第二个规则专门针对金钱债务，采用相反的方法，即债务人应当在债权人的营业地履行其义务(适用第6.1.8条转账支付的除外)。

虽然这些解决方法并不是在所有情况下都很令人满意，但是在合同当事人对履行地未作规定并且具体情况也没有其他表示时，本条的确可起到补充的作用。

Illustrations

> 1. A wishes some of its engineers to learn the language of country X, where they will be employed for some time. It agrees with B, a language school, for a series of intensive lessons. If nothing else is stipulated, the lessons are to take place at B's place of business (see Article 6.1.6(1)(b)).
>
> 2. The facts are the same as in Illustration 1. The language school sends its bill to A. The cost of the lessons must, in principle, be paid at B's place of business (see Article 6.1.6(1)(a)).

3. Consequences of change in a party's place of business subsequent to conclusion of contract

In view of the importance of the parties' respective places of business for the application of paragraph (1), it is necessary to cater for the situation where a party changes its location after the conclusion of the contract, a move which may involve additional expense for the performing party. The rule established in paragraph (2) is that each party must bear any such increase of expenses occasioned by a change in its place of business.

It is moreover possible that a party's move may entail other inconvenience for the other party. The obligation to act in good faith (Article 1.7) and the duty to cooperate (Article 5.1.3) will often impose on the moving party an obligation to inform the other party in due time so as to enable the latter to make such arrangements as may be necessary.

Illustrations

> 3. A enters into a technical assistance agreement with B, under the terms of which A undertakes to train ten of B's engineers for a period of two months on A's premises. The engineers are to be accommodated at a local hotel which offers very reasonable rates on account of A's location in a rural area. After the agreement has been concluded, but before B's engineers arrive, A notifies B that it has moved to the capital city where hotel rates are much higher. Irrespective of whether the initial costs of accommodation were to be paid by A or by B, the additional costs will be borne by A.
>
> 4. Each year on 3 May, A must pay royalties to B at B's place of business. B moves to another country, to which it takes some time (e.g. two months) for a payment to arrive. A formerly gave its bank the transfer order on or about 15 April, but from now on the order must be given towards the end of March at the latest if A

示例：

　　1. A希望它的一些工程师学习X国的语言，因为这些工程师将在X国工作一段时间。A和一所语言学校B约定由B提供一系列强化课程。如果没有其他规定，这些课程应当在B的营业地举行(参见第6.1.6条第(1)款(b)项)。

　　2. 事实和示例1一样。语言学校将账单寄送给A。原则上，讲课费应当在B的营业地支付(参见第6.1.6条第(1)款(a)项)。

3. 合同订立后一方当事人变更营业地之后果

鉴于合同当事人各自的营业地对于适用本条第(1)款所具有的重要性，有必要解决合同订立后一方当事人变更营业地的问题，因为该变更可能给履行方造成额外费用。本条第(2)款确立的规则是，各方当事人都应当承担因其变更营业地而增加的任何费用。

此外，一方当事人变更营业地还可能会给另一方当事人带来其他不便。所以根据第1.7条的诚实信用行事的义务和第5.1.3条的合作义务，变更营业地的一方当事人应当及时通知另一方当事人，以便后者能够作出必要的安排。

示例：

　　3. A和B签订了一份技术支持合同，约定由A在其营业地为B的10位工程师提供为期两个月的培训。这些工程师将住在A所在地的一个当地宾馆，因为A的所在地是乡村地区，所以该宾馆收费合理。在合同订立后、B的工程师到达之前，A通知B其营业地已搬至首都，那里的宾馆费用要高出很多。不管最初的住宿费是由A承担还是由B承担，额外的住宿费将由A承担。

　　4. 每年5月3日A应当在B的营业地向B支付特许费，后来B搬到另一个国家，付款到达该国需要一段时间（比如两个月）。以前A在4月15日前后向其银行发出转账指示，但是现在为了避免支付迟延，A必须最晚在3月底前向银行

wishes to avoid late payment. B is under a duty to inform A of its new place of business in sufficient time to permit A to make the necessary arrangements for payment and B will bear the additional costs.

ARTICLE 6.1.7

(Payment by cheque or other instrument)

(1) Payment may be made in any form used in the ordinary course of business at the place for payment.

(2) However, an obligee who accepts, either by virtue of paragraph (1) or voluntarily, a cheque, any other order to pay or a promise to pay, is presumed to do so only on condition that it will be honoured.

COMMENT

Discharge of monetary obligations is frequently made by cheques or similar instruments, or by transfers between financial institutions. The problems involved have however very seldom been the subject of codification, one notable exception being the *UNCITRAL Model Law on International Credit Transfers*. Without attempting to provide a detailed regulation, which would not be compatible with the very rapid evolution of techniques in this field, Articles 6.1.7 and 6.1.8 establish some basic principles which should be of assistance in regard to international payments.

1. General rule regarding form of payment

Paragraph (1) allows for payment to be made in any form that is usual at the place for payment. Subject to the reservation contained in paragraph (2), the obligor may for instance pay in cash, by cheque, banker's draft, a bill of exchange, credit card, or in any other form such as the newly developing electronic means of payment, provided it chooses a mode that is usual at the place for payment, i.e. normally at the obligee's place of business. In principle, the obligee should be satisfied to receive payment in a form that is customary at its place of business.

发出指示。B 应当将其新的营业地及时通知 A，以便 A 有充分的时间作出必要的支付安排，而且 B 应当承担由此产生的额外费用。

第6.1.7条

（以支票或其他票据支付）

（1）付款可以采用付款地正常商业做法中使用的任何支付方式做出。

（2）但是，如果债权人根据第（1）款的规定或者自愿接受支票、其他付款命令或付款承诺，则均应推定该接受是以这些票据能够获得支付为条件。

注释：

金钱债务通常通过支票或类似的票据，或者通过金融机构之间的转账得以清偿。然而，其中涉及的问题却很少被加以编纂，联合国国际贸易法委员会制定的《国际信贷转账示范法》是一个著名的例外。本《通则》第6.1.7条和第6.1.8条只规定了一些在国际支付方面有用的基本原则，并没有试图对此问题作详细的规定，因为这种努力显然与该领域技术的飞速发展不相适应。

1. 关于支付方式的一般规则

第(1)款允许以付款地使用的任何正常支付方式支付。在遵循第(2)款规定的保留前提下，债务人可以采用现金、支票、银行汇票、汇票、信用卡或者其他任何形式，比如新近发展的电子支付方式进行付款，只要其选择的支付方式是付款地通常使用的方式，而付款地通常也就是债权人的营业地。原则上，债权人应当接受以其营业地惯常使用的支付方式所作的付款。

Illustration

1. A, an importer in Luxembourg, receives a bill for goods bought from B, a firm in Central America, and sends a eurocheque in payment. B may reject this mode of payment if the banks in its country are not familiar with eurocheques.

2. Presumption that payment will be honoured a condition for acceptance

Paragraph (2) states the generally recognised principle according to which the obligee's acceptance of an instrument that has to be honoured by a financial institution or another person (a third person or the obligor itself) is given only on condition that the instrument will actually be honoured.

The presumption can sometimes be overturned by usages. There are for instance countries where delivery of instruments such as certified cheques, banker's drafts and cashier's cheques is considered as being equivalent to payment by the obligor, with the consequence that the risk of the bank's insolvency is transferred to the obligee. In such countries, the rule in Article 6.1.7(2) would apply only to so-called personal cheques.

Illustration

2. A, a contractor, must pay B, a sub-contractor, for work completed by the latter on a building site. A is experiencing a cash-flow crisis as its client C is late in paying the first instalment due. C has however given A a set of promissory notes up to the amount of its debt. A offers to pay B by assigning a sufficient number of promissory notes. If B accepts them (in this case it probably does not have to do so as this is not a usual form of payment), the effectiveness of the payment by A to B is conditional on C's honouring the promissory notes at maturity.

ARTICLE 6.1.8
(Payment by funds transfer)

(1) Unless the obligee has indicated a particular account, payment may be made by a transfer to any of the financial institutions in which the obligee has made it known that it has an account.

示例:

> 1. 一家位于卢森堡的进口商 A 收到一家位于中美洲的公司 B 的货款账单后,发出一张欧洲支票进行付款。如果 B 所在国的银行对这种欧洲支票不熟悉,则 B 可以拒绝接受该支付方式。

2. 推定获得支付是接受票据付款的条件

第(2)款阐述了一个被广泛接受的原则,也即,如果债权人接受的票据必须由金融机构或其他人(第三人或债务人自己)支付,那么债权人仅以该票据能够实际得到支付为条件接收该票据。

有时惯例能够推翻上述推定。例如,在有些国家,交付保付支票、银行汇票和现金支票这样的支付工具即被视为债务人付款,银行破产的风险随之转由债权人承担。在这些国家,第 6.1.7 条第(2)款的规则只适用于所谓的个人支票。

示例:

> 2. 承包商 A 必须支付分包商 B 已完成的建筑工程工作。A 由于其客户 C 未能按时向其支付到期的第一期工程款而陷入流动资金短缺的危机,但是 C 已经将金额与其债务相等的一些本票交给了 A,A 提出转让足够数量的本票给 B 以清偿债务。如果 B 接受这些本票(在本案中,B 可以以这种支付方式不是一种正常的支付方式为理由不予接受),那么 A 对 B 的付款以 C 在本票到期时进行支付为生效条件。

第 6.1.8 条

(转账支付)

(1) 除非债权人已指定特定账户,付款可以通过将款项转至债权人告知的其设有账户的任何金融机构来完成。

(2) In case of payment by a transfer the obligation of the obligor is discharged when the transfer to the obligee's financial institution becomes effective.

COMMENT

1. Admissibility of funds transfers

Although the principle enunciated in Article 6.1.6 that payment of a monetary obligation should be made at the obligee's place of business still stands, paragraph (1) of this Article provides that it can also be made to one of the financial institutions in which the obligee has made it known that it keeps an account. If however the obligee has indicated a particular account, payment should then be made to that account. Naturally, the obligee can also make it known that it does not wish payment to be made by transfer.

Illustration

> 1. A, a shipyard established in country X, repairs a ship belonging to B, a company from country Y, and the bill is sent on a letter-head that mentions a bank account in country X and another in country Y. Unless A states that payment has to be made to the account in country X, or by a means other than a bank transfer, B is entitled to make payment to the account in country Y.

2. Time at which the obligor's obligation is discharged by a funds transfer

Paragraph (2) of this Article deals with the difficult question of determining when a payment by funds transfer is to be considered as completed, i.e. when the obligor's obligation is discharged. This matter is of importance, for example when deciding whether a payment was made in time, or in the event of one of the banks not forwarding the funds it has received. The choice of a satisfactory solution has been the centre of considerable controversy in many countries and international fora. Various possible times have been suggested, such as that of the debiting of the account of the transferor, the crediting to the account of the transferee bank, the notice of credit to that account, the decision of the transferee bank to accept a credit transfer, the entry of credit to the transferee's account, the notice of credit to the transferee, etc. The matter is further complicated by the changes in the procedures for the transfer of funds entailed by new

(2) 若采用转账支付，债务人的义务在款项
有效转至债权人的金融机构时解除。

注释：

1. 允许转账支付

尽管第 6.1.6 条规定的原则依然有效，即金钱债务应当在债权人
营业地支付，但本条第(1)款规定，付款义务也可以通过向债权人已告
知其设有账户的金融机构支付得以解除。但是，如果债权人已指定了
某一账户，那么付款应当向该特定账户作出。自然，债权人也有权向
债务人明确表示他不希望后者通过转账方式付款。

示例：

1. 位于 X 国的造船厂 A 为一家 Y 国公司 B 修理一艘船
舶，发送账单所用的抬头提到了一个 X 国账户和一个 Y 国
账户。在这种情况下，除非 A 声明必须向 X 国账户付款，
或者采用银行转账以外的方式付款，那么 B 有权向 Y 国账
户付款。

2. 采用转账支付时，债务人义务解除的时间

本条第(2)款处理的难题是如何确定转账支付视为完成的时间，也
即债务人的义务何时解除。这一点有时非常重要，例如，确定付款是
否及时时，或者其中一家银行未转交其收到的资金时。选择一个令人
满意的解决办法在很多国家和国际研讨会一直是重大的争论焦点。各
方提出了各种各样可能的时间，比如借记转账人账户的时间，贷记受
让银行账户的时间，通知贷记受让银行账户的时间，受让银行决定接
受信贷转账的时间，登录贷记受让人账户的时间，通知贷记受让人
的时间，等等。新的电子转账机制使得转账程序发生改变，从而也使

electronic transfer mechanisms,while bank practices may also differ from one case to another.

This uncertainty makes it extremely difficult to establish a definite rule providing when payment by a transfer is completed. Paragraph (2) of this Article nevertheless serves a useful purpose in that it states the basic principle which will permit the finding of a more precise rule in each case. Such a payment will be effective when the transfer to the obligee's financial institution becomes effective, a solution founded on the notion that the institution acts as the obligee's agent. This means that the payment will not be effective simply because an order has been given to the transferor's financial institution, and the transferor's account has been debited. However, payment is effective before the transferee is notified or credited with it by its financial institution, although the precise moment at which payment to the obligee's financial institution can be considered as being effective will depend on banking practices in the case concerned.

Illustration

> 2.   A, a licensee, gives its bank, C, a transfer order for USD 5,000, royalties due to B, a licensor, who has an account with bank D. C debits A's account, but fails to forward the funds to D and becomes bankrupt. A has not effectively paid B.

ARTICLE 6.1.9

(Currency of payment)

(1) If a monetary obligation is expressed in a currency other than that of the place for payment, it may be paid by the obligor in the currency of the place for payment unless

(a) that currency is not freely convertible; or

(b) the parties have agreed that payment should be made only in the currency in which the monetary obligation is expressed.

(2) If it is impossible for the obligor to make payment in the currency in which the monetary obligation is expressed, the obligee may require payment in the currency of the place for payment, even in the case referred to in paragraph (1)(b).

得这个问题变得更加复杂。与此同时，银行业务实践也可能互不相同。

这种不确定性使得制定一个确切的规则以确定转账支付完成时间变得极其困难。尽管如此，本条第(2)款还是有实用价值的，因为它阐述了一个基本原则，有助于在个案中寻找一个更精确的规则。该付款将于向债权人的金融机构进行的转账生效时生效。这一规则的理论基础是，该金融机构是债权人的代理人。这意味着仅仅给转账人的金融机构发出命令并且借记转账人的账户，还不能使付款生效。然而，在受让人得到其金融机构的通知或被贷记账户之前付款即已生效，尽管对债权人金融机构的付款被视为生效的准确时间取决于个案中银行业务实践。

示例：

2. 被许可方 A 向其银行 C 发出指令，要求将 5,000 美元的使用费转账给许可方 B 在银行 D 中的账户。C 借记了 A 的账户，却未将这笔资金转入 D，C 随后破产。本例中，A 向 B 的付款没有生效。

第6.1.9条

（支付货币）

（1）如果金钱债务不以付款地货币以外的货币表示，债务人可以用付款地之货币支付，除非

（a）该货币不能自由兑换；或者

（b）当事人约定只能以表示金钱债务的货币进行支付。

（2）如果债务人无法以表示金钱债务的货币支付，债权人可要求以付款地之货币支付，即便属于第(1)款(b)项规定的情况亦可如此要求。

(3) Payment in the currency of the place for payment is to be made according to the applicable rate of exchange prevailing there when payment is due.

(4) However, if the obligor has not paid at the time when payment is due, the obligee may require payment according to the applicable rate of exchange prevailing either when payment is due or at the time of actual payment.

COMMENT

Monetary obligations are usually expressed in a certain currency (currency of account), and payment must normally be made in the same currency. However, when the currency of the place for payment is different from the currency of account, paragraphs (1) and (2) of this Article provide for those cases where the obligor may or must make payment in the former currency.

1. Monetary obligation expressed in currency different from that of place for payment

As a general rule, the obligor is given the alternative of paying in the currency of the place for payment, which may have definite practical advantages and, if that currency is freely convertible, this should cause no difficulty to the obligee.

If, however, the currency of the place for payment is not freely convertible, the rule does not apply. Parties may also exclude the application of the rule by agreeing that payment is to be made only in the currency in which the monetary obligation is expressed (*effectivo* clause). If it has an interest in the payment actually being made in the currency of account, the obligee should specify this in the contract.

Illustrations

1. A company from country X receives an order for machinery from a buyer from country Y, the price being expressed in US dollars. According to Article 6.1.6, payment of that monetary obligation must in principle be made at the obligee's place of business, i.e. country X. If the company from country Y finds it more convenient, it may pay the price in euro which is the currency of X (see Article 6.1.9(1)).

2. The same company from country X frequently needs to buy from suppliers in country Z certain parts to be included in the machines, and has stipulated that the buyer from country Y should

　　（3）以付款地的货币支付时，应按照付款义务到期时付款地适用的通行汇率进行支付。

　　（4）但是，如果债务人在付款到期时未履行付款义务，则债权人可要求债务人按照付款义务到期时或实际付款时所适用的通行汇率进行支付。

注释：

　　金钱债务通常以某种货币（记账货币）表示，正常情况下也应该以同种货币支付。然而，当付款地的货币与记账货币不同时，本条第（1）款和第（2）款对于债务人可以或必须以前种货币进行支付的情况作了规定。

1. 表示金钱债务的货币不同于付款地的货币

　　一般地，债务人可以选择以付款地的货币进行付款，这样做也许在实践上确实存在好处，并且如果该货币是可以自由兑换的，应该不会对债权人造成困难。

　　但是，如果付款地的货币不能自由兑换，那么本规则不适用。合同当事人也可以约定付款只能以记账货币进行"特约条款"（effectivo clause），从而排除本规则的适用。如果以记账货币进行实际支付对债权人有利，债权人应当在合同中对此作出明确规定。

　　示例：

　　　　1. X 国的 A 公司收到 Y 国买方一份购买机器的订单，记账货币为美元。依据第 6.1.6 条的规定，金钱债务原则上应当在债权人营业地也就是 X 国履行。因此，如果该 Y 国公司发现用 X 国的货币欧元进行支付更方便，则它可以用欧元支付（参见第 6.1.9 条第（1）款）。

　　　　2. 同一 X 国公司，经常需要从 Z 国供应商购买用于制造机器的零部件，并规定 Y 国买方只能以美元付款。在这种情

pay only in US dollars. In this case, payment may only be made in dollars (see Article 6.1.9(1)(b)).

3.   The same company from country X has a plant in country W, where the machines will be assembled. The contract provides that the buyer from country Y has to pay the price to the firm's subsidiary in country W. Since the currency of country W is not convertible, payment may only be made in dollars (see Article 6.1.9(1)(a)).

2. Impossibility for obligor to make payment in currency in which obligation is expressed

In some instances, the obligor may find it impossible to make payment in the currency in which the obligation was expressed. This may be the result of the application of exchange regulations or other mandatory rules, or due to any other cause preventing the obligor from obtaining that currency in sufficient quantity. Paragraph (2) gives the obligee the option of requiring payment in the currency of the place for payment, even if the contract contains an *effectivo* clause. This is an additional option open to the obligee who may find it acceptable or even advantageous in the circumstances. It does not preclude the exercise of any available remedy in the event of the obligor's inability to pay in the currency of account amounting to a non-performance of the contract (e.g. damages).

Illustration

4.   A, a Swiss bank, lends USD 1,000,000 to B, to be reimbursed in Geneva. At maturity, B is unable to find the necessary US dollars. A, which knows that B has deposits in Swiss francs with another local bank, may require payment in Swiss francs, even though the loan agreement stipulated that reimbursement was to be made only in US dollars (see Article 6.1.9(2)).

3. Determination of applicable rate of exchange

Paragraphs (3) and (4) deal with the problem of the determination of the rate of exchange to be chosen when payment is made in the currency of the place for payment rather than in a different currency stipulated in the contract. This may occur when the obligor avails itself of paragraph (1), or the obligee the provisions of paragraph (2).

况下，付款只能以美元为之（参见第 6.1.9 条第（1）款（b）
项）。

3. 同一 X 国公司在 W 国设有一个工厂来组装这些机器。
合同规定 Y 国买方必须向该公司在 W 国的子公司付款，由于
W 国的货币不能自由兑换，所以付款只能以美元作出（参见第
6.1.9 条第（1）款（a）项）。

2. 债务人无法以记账货币进行支付

在某些情况下，由于外汇管理法规或其他一些强制性规则的适用，
或者由于导致债务人不能获得足够记账货币的其他原因，债务人可能
发现用记账货币支付是不可能的。第（2）款授予债权人要求以付款地货
币支付的权利，即便合同包含特约条款也不例外。该条款赋予债权人
一个额外的选择，在具体情况下其可能发现这样做是可接受的甚至是
有利的。如果债务人不能以记账货币支付构成不履行合同，本款规定
并不排除债权人行使其请求任何可用救济手段的权利（比如损
害赔偿）。

示例：

4. 一家瑞士银行 A 借给 B 100 万美元，应在瑞士日内瓦
偿还。借款到期时，B 未能备齐必要的美元。A 知道 B 在另
一家当地银行存有瑞士法郎，其可以要求 B 以瑞士法郎还
款，即便贷款协议规定只能以美元还款（参见第 6.1.9 条第
（2）款）。

3. 确定适用的汇率

第（3）款和第（4）款所要处理的是当以付款地货币而非合同规定的
货币付款时，应使用何种汇率的问题。这个问题在债务人援引第（1）款
的规定，或者债权人援引第（2）款的规定时可能产生。

Two widely accepted solutions are offered. In normal cases, the rate of exchange is that prevailing when payment is due. If, however, the obligor is in default, the obligee is given an option between the rate of exchange prevailing when payment was due or the rate at the time of actual payment.

The double reference to the "applicable" rate is justified by the fact that there may be different rates of exchange depending on the nature of the operation.

Illustration

> 5.   The facts are the same as in Illustration 4. A chooses to be reimbursed in Swiss francs (CHF) and payment, which was due on 10 April, actually takes place on 15 September. The rate of exchange on 10 April was 2 Swiss francs to 1 US dollar. By 15 September it has become CHF 2,15 to USD 1. A is entitled to apply the latter rate. If the US dollar had depreciated rather than increased in value, A would have chosen the rate applicable on 10 April.

ARTICLE 6.1.10
(Currency not expressed)

Where a monetary obligation is not expressed in a particular currency, payment must be made in the currency of the place where payment is to be made.

COMMENT

Determining the currency of payment gives rise to a special problem if the contract does not state the currency in which a monetary obligation is due. Although such cases may be infrequent, they do exist; a contract may for example state that the price will be the "current price", or that it will be determined by a third person, or that some expenses or costs will be reimbursed by one party to the other, without specifying in which currency those sums are due. The rule laid down in Article 6.1.10 is that in such situations payment must be made in the currency of the place where payment is to be made.

Article 6.1.10 is not concerned with the currency in which damages are to be assessed, a matter dealt with in Article 7.4.12 in the context of non-performance.

本条提供了两种被广为接受的解决办法。在正常情况下，汇率以付款到期时的通行汇率为准。但是，如果债务人迟延履行付款义务，那么债权人有权在付款到期时的汇率和实际付款时的汇率两者中进行选择。

本条第(3)款和第(4)款中两次提到"适用的"汇率，原因在于，根据业务类型的不同可能存在不同的汇率。

示例：

> 5. 事实和示例 4 相同。A 选择以瑞士法郎获得偿还，偿还日期应该是 4 月 10 日，而实际偿还的日期则是 9 月 15 日。4 月 10 日瑞士法郎对美元的汇率是 2∶1，而 9 月 15 日则变为 2.15∶1，在这种情况下，A 有权选择后者作为还款汇率。但如果美元贬值而不是升值，A 可能选择 4 月 10 日的汇率作为还款汇率。

第 6.1.10 条

（未定明货币）

如果金钱债务未以某一特定货币表示，则付款必须以付款地之货币进行支付。

注释：

如果合同没有规定表示金钱债务的货币，确定付款货币时就会遇到一个特殊的问题。尽管这样的情况并不常见，但确实存在。比如合同可能规定价格为"时价"，或者规定价格由第三人确定，或者规定一方当事人应补偿另一方当事人发生的某些费用或成本，而没有规定这些款项到期时的支付货币。第 6.1.10 条确立的规则是，在这种情况下，付款应当以付款地的货币为之。

第 6.1.10 条不涉及计算损害赔偿金的货币，该问题在不履行的情况下由第 7.4.12 条予以规定。

Illustration

> A, a Japanese client, instructs its broker, B, to buy shares on the Shanghai stock exchange. If B pays for them in Chinese Yuan Renminbi (CNY), should A be billed in Yuan Renminbi or in Japanese Yen? If A is to pay B in Japan, it will pay in Yen.

ARTICLE 6.1.11
(Costs of performance)

Each party shall bear the costs of performance of its obligations.

COMMENT

The performance of obligations often entails costs, which may be of different kinds: transportation costs in delivering goods, bank commission in making a monetary transfer, fees to be paid when applying for a permission, etc. In principle, such costs are to be borne by the performing party.

Other arrangements may of course be made by the parties and there is nothing to prevent the performing party from including those costs in advance in the price it quotes. The rule set out in Article 6.1.11 applies in the absence of such arrangements.

The provision states who shall bear the costs, not who shall pay them. Usually, it will be the same party, but there may be different situations, for example where tax regulations place the burden of payment on a specific party. In such cases, if the person who has to pay is different from the person who must bear the costs under Article 6.1.11, the latter must reimburse the former.

Illustration

> A, a consultant, agrees to send five experts to perform an audit of B's company. Nothing is said concerning the experts' travel expenses, and A does not take those costs into account when determining its fees. A may not add the travel expenses to the bill.

示例：

　　日本客户 A 向其经纪人 B 发出指令，要求 B 购买在上海股票交易所上市的股票。如果 B 以人民币买进这些股票，那么它向 A 发出账单时应当使用人民币还是日元？如果 A 在日本向 B 付款，则 A 应当以日元支付。

第 6.1.11 条

（履行费用）

**　　每一方当事人应承担为履行其义务时所发生的费用。**

注释：

　　履行合同义务经常会产生各种费用：交付货物时的运费，转账时的银行手续费，申请许可证时所支付的费用，等等。原则上，这些费用应当由履行方承担。

　　然而，合同当事人亦可作出其他安排，履行方也可以自由地将这些费用事先计入其报价中。第 6.1.11 条确立的规则只在合同当事人未作安排时适用。

　　本条规定的是由谁承担这些费用，而不是由谁支付这些费用。通常情况下，承担费用的主体和支付费用的主体是一致的，但也可能存在不同的情况。比如税法规定某一特定方承担缴税的义务，在这种情况下，如果缴税当事人和依第 6.1.11 条应该承担这些费用的当事人不一致，那么后者必须偿还前者。

示例：

　　顾问机构 A 同意派五位专家到 B 的公司进行审计工作，双方对专家的差旅费未作任何规定，并且 A 在确定咨询费时也没有将这些差旅费考虑在内。A 不能把这些差旅费记入账单。

ARTICLE 6.1.12
(Imputation of payments)

(1) An obligor owing several monetary obligations to the same obligee may specify at the time of payment the debt to which it intends the payment to be applied. However, the payment discharges first any expenses, then interest due and finally the principal.

(2) If the obligor makes no such specification, the obligee may, within a reasonable time after payment, declare to the obligor the obligation to which it imputes the payment, provided that the obligation is due and undisputed.

(3) In the absence of imputation under paragraphs (1) or (2), payment is imputed to that obligation which satisfies one of the following criteria in the order indicated:

(a) an obligation which is due or which is the first to fall due;

(b) the obligation for which the obligee has least security;

(c) the obligation which is the most burdensome for the obligor;

(d) the obligation which has arisen first.

If none of the preceding criteria applies, payment is imputed to all the obligations proportionally.

COMMENT

Articles 6.1.12 and 6.1.13 deal with the problem of imputation of payments. If an obligor owes several monetary obligations at the same time to the same obligee and makes a payment the amount of which is not sufficient to discharge all those debts, the question arises of the debts to which that payment applies.

Article 6.1.12 offers the obligor the possibility of imputing its payment to a particular debt, provided that any expenses and interest due are discharged before the principal. In the absence of any imputation by the obligor, this provision enables the obligee to impute the payment received, although not to a disputed debt. Paragraph (3) lays down criteria which will govern in the absence of any imputation by either party.

第 6.1.12 条

（抵充支付）

（1）债务人如果对同一债权人负有多项金钱债务，可在付款时指明该款项用于其拟清偿的债务。但是，该款项应首先清偿费用，其次为应付利息，最后为本金。

（2）如果债务人未予指明，则债权人可在获得支付后的合理时间内向债务人声明该款项用于所抵充的债务，但该项债务必须是到期的，且不存在争议。

（3）如果未根据第（1）款或第（2）款的规定抵充债务，则依次清偿符合下列标准之债务：

（a）到期的债务，或者首先到期的债务；

（b）债权人享有担保最少的债务；

（c）属债务人负担最重的债务；

（d）最先发生的债务。

若以上标准均不适用，则按比例用于抵充各项债务。

注释：

第 6.1.12 条和第 6.1.13 条所要解决的是抵充支付这一经典问题。如果一个债务人对同一个债权人同时负有几项金钱债务，并且其所提供的款项不足以清偿所有债务，这时就产生了这样一个问题，即该款项用于偿还哪一项债务。

第 6.1.12 条的规定借鉴了一些被广泛承认的原则。依本条规定债务人可指定该款项用于清偿某一笔债务，前提条件是在用以清偿本金前，应首先用以清偿所有费用和到期的利息。当债务人没有指定时，本条规定授权债权人对其收到的款项加以指定，但有争议的债务除外。在双方当事人均未作指定时，适用第（3）款所确立的标准。

Illustration

> A receives under separate contracts three loans, each of USD
> 100,000, from bank B payment of which is due on 31 December. B
> receives USD 100,000 from A on 2 January with the imprecise
> message: "Reimbursement of the loan". B pays little attention to the
> matter and at first does not react, but three months later sues A for
> payment of the remaining USD 200,000 and the parties disagree as
> to which of the loans had been reimbursed by the January payment.
> B had similar security in each case, but the interest rates were not the
> same: 8% on the first loan, 8,50% on the second and 9% on the third.
> The January payment will be imputed to the third loan.

ARTICLE 6.1.13
(Imputation of non-monetary obligations)

**Article 6.1.12 applies with appropriate
adaptations to the imputation of performance of
non-monetary obligations.**

COMMENT

The problem of imputation of payments normally concerns monetary
obligations, but similar difficulties may sometimes occur in relation to
obligations of a different nature. Article 6.1.13 provides that the rules
governing monetary obligations will apply, with appropriate adaptations
also to these cases.

Illustration

> A is performing construction work on several sites in an African
> country and, through five separate and successive contracts with B,
> purchases different quantities of cement, all to be delivered in
> Antwerp on the same date and to be loaded on the same ship. The
> contracts are similar, except that the third and fifth contracts stipulate
> very high liquidated damages in the event of late delivery. On
> account of certain difficulties, B can only deliver part of what it was
> supposed to. Upon delivery B is entitled to specify that the quantities
> delivered are to be imputed to the third and fifth contracts.

示例：

　　A 依据三份独立的合同从银行 B 获得金额分别为 10 万美元的三项贷款，这些贷款均在 12 月 31 日到期。B 于 1 月 2 日从 A 处收到 10 万美元的还款以及不确切的信息："偿还贷款"。B 对此未加留意，因而起初并没有作出反应。但在三个月之后，因 A 没有偿还剩下的 20 万美元，B 对 A 提起诉讼。双方当事人对 1 月份付款偿还的是哪笔贷款发生了争议。B 对三笔贷款都享有同样的担保，但适用的利率不同：第一笔贷款的利率是 8%，第二笔和第三笔分别是 8.5% 和 9%。因此 1 月份的还款应用于清偿第三笔贷款。

第 6.1.13 条

（抵充非金钱债务）

**　　本章第 6.1.12 条的规定经适当修改后适用于对非金钱债务履行的抵充。**

注释：

　　抵充支付的问题通常涉及的是金钱债务，但是在履行非金钱债务时也可能发生类似的问题。第 6.1.13 条规定有关金钱债务的规则经适当修改，也可以适用于非金钱债务的抵充。

示例：

　　A 正在一个非洲国家的几个施工点同时开展建筑施工，A 先后跟 B 签订了五份独立的购买不同数量水泥的合同，所有的水泥将在同一天运到安特卫普并装上同一艘船。除了第三份合同和第五份合同规定了较高的迟延交货违约金外，这些合同都很相似。因为遭遇了某些困难，B 只能交付部分货物。交货时，B 有权指定其所交付的货物用于履行第三份和第五份合同。

ARTICLE 6.1.14
(Application for public permission)

Where the law of a State requires a public permission affecting the validity of the contract or its performance and neither that law nor the circumstances indicate otherwise

(a) if only one party has its place of business in that State, that party shall take the measures necessary to obtain the permission;

(b) in any other case the party whose performance requires permission shall take the necessary measures.

COMMENT

If the validity or the performance of a contract is subject to compliance with public permission requirements, several issues arise as to who has the burden of filing the application (see Article 6.1.14), the time for filing (see Article 6.1.15), the legal consequences of failure to obtain an administrative decision in due time (see Article 6.1.16) and the rejection of the application (see Article 6.1.17).

1. Scope of the permission requirement

The Principles do not deal with the relevance of public permission requirements. What kind of public permission is required, if any, is to be determined under the applicable law, including the rules of private international law.

Courts tend to give effect only to the public permission requirements of the *lex fori*, and sometimes to those prescribed by the *lex contractus*. Arbitral tribunals may enjoy wider discretion than courts in deciding which public permissions are relevant to the contract.

Under the relevant conflict of laws rules public permission requirements of the law of other jurisdictions connected with the contract may also come into play (see Article 9(3) of *EC Regulation No. 593/2008 (Rome I)*; Article 11(2) of the *1994 Inter-American Convention on the Law Applicable to International Contracts*). Long-arm statutes in some jurisdictions too may impose public permission requirements on licensees or subsidiaries of companies located abroad. This Article assumes that the requirements prescribed by the applicable law are to be observed.

第6.1.14条

（申请公共许可）

若一国法律所要求的公共许可影响到合同的效力或其履行，并且该法律或有关情况均无相反表示：

（a）如果只有一方当事人的营业地在该国，则该方当事人应采取为获得该许可所需的必要措施；

（b）在任何其他情况下，履行须经许可的一方当事人应当采取该等必要措施。

注释：

如果合同的效力或履行必须遵守公共许可的要求，就会产生一系列问题：比如谁负责申请该许可（参见第6.1.14条），申请许可的时间（参见第6.1.15条），不能按期取得行政部门决定的法律后果（参见第6.1.16条）以及申请被拒绝的法律后果（参见第6.1.17条）。

1. 许可要求的范围

本《通则》并不涉及公共许可要求的相关性问题。是否需要公共许可以及要求何种公共许可，由适用法（包括国际私法规则）决定。

法院倾向于只赋予法院地法所规定的公共许可要求以效力，有时也赋予由缔约地法所规定的公共许可要求以效力。在决定哪些公共许可与合同有关时，仲裁庭可能享有比法院更大的自由裁量权。

根据有关的冲突法规则，与合同有关的其他法域的法律所规定的公共许可要求也可能有效（参见欧共体第593/2008号条例（罗马第一条例）第9条第(3)款；以及1994年《国际合同适用法律美洲公约》第11条第(2)款）。一些法域的长臂法也可能对位于国外的被许可方或子公司施加公共许可的要求。本条假定适用法所规定的公共许可要求应得到遵守。

a. *Broad notion of "public permission"*

The term "public permission" is to be given a broad interpretation. It includes all permission requirements established pursuant to a concern of a public nature, such as health, safety, or particular trade policies. It is irrelevant whether a required licence or permit is to be granted by a governmental or by a non-governmental institution to which Governments have delegated public authority for a specific purpose. Thus, the authorisation of payments by a private bank pursuant to foreign exchange regulations is in the nature of a "public permission" for the purposes of this Article.

b. *Timing of public permission*

The provisions on public permissions refer primarily to those required by the applicable law or by a regulation in force at the time of the conclusion of the contract. However, these provisions may also apply to public permissions that may be introduced after the conclusion of the contract.

c. *Public permission may affect the contract in whole or in part*

The provisions on public permissions apply both to those requirements affecting the contract as a whole and to those merely affecting individual terms of the contract. However, where the legal consequences of failing to obtain a public permission differ according to whether such permission affects the contract in whole or in part, different rules are established (see Articles 6.1.16 (2) and 6.1.17).

d. *Public permission may affect the validity or performance of a contract*

The absence of the required permission may affect the validity of a contract or render its performance impossible. Notwithstanding differences in the legal consequences of failing to obtain a required public permission, the problems raised in connection with the application for, or the obtaining of, a public permission are the same. As to the further consequences, Article 6.1.17(2) provides that the rules on non-performance apply to a situation where the refusal of a permission makes the performance of a contract impossible in whole or in part.

2. Duty to inform of the existence of a public permission requirement

There is as a rule no duty to provide information concerning the requirement to obtain a public permission. However, the existence of

a. 广义的"公共许可"

对于"公共许可"应作广义的解释。它包括所有出于公共性质的考虑而设定的许可要求，比如健康、安全或者特定的贸易政策。所要求的特许或许可是由政府机构批准，还是由政府为特定目的而委托非政府机构批准，在所不问。因此，私人银行根据外汇管理法规所作的付款授权即属于本条意义上的"公共许可"。

b. 公共许可的时间

有关公共许可的规定主要是指合同订立时现行有效的适用法律或法规所要求的那些规定。然而，这些规定也可以适用于合同订立后出台的公共许可要求。

c. 公共许可可能对合同的全部或部分产生影响

本处有关公共许可的规定，既可以适用于影响合同整体的许可要求，也可以适用于仅影响合同个别条款的许可要求。然而，未能取得公共许可时根据该许可影响的是合同整体还是部分条款，法律后果可能会有所不同，这种情况下，《通则》分别制订了不同的规则（参见第 6.1.16 条第（2）款和第 6.1.17 条）。

d. 公共许可可能对合同的效力或履行产生影响

未取得所要求的许可，可能会影响合同的效力，或者使得合同的履行成为不可能。尽管未取得所要求的许可在法律后果上有所不同，但是两种情况下所产生的与公共许可的申请或取得有关的问题却是一样的。对于进一步的后果，第 6.1.17 条第（2）款规定，拒绝许可导致合同的全部或部分履行不可能时，适用关于不履行的规则。

2. 存在公共许可要求的告知义务

原则上，当事人没有义务提供关于要求取得公共许可的信息。然而,当公共许可要求是基于非一般所知的规则时，负责取得该公共许

such a requirement must be disclosed by the party upon whom rests the burden of obtaining a public permission when such permission is required under rules which are not generally accessible. Thus, the overriding principle of good faith and fair dealing (see Article 1.7) may require the party whose place of business is located in the State requiring a public permission to inform the other party of the existence of that requirement. Failure to do so may lead a court to disregard the permission requirement altogether or to conclude that the party who failed to communicate the existence of the requirement implicitly guaranteed that it would be obtained.

3. Which party is bound to take measures to obtain a public permission

a. *Party with place of business in State requiring public permission*

The rule set out in sub-paragraph (a) of this Article which places the burden to apply on the party who has its place of business in the State which requires the relevant public permission reflects current international trade practices. It is that party who is in the best position to apply promptly for a public permission, since it is probably more familiar with the application requirements and procedures.

If a party needs further information from the other to file an application (e.g. information relating to the final destination of the goods, or information as to the purpose or subject matter of the contract), the other party must furnish such information pursuant to the duty of co-operation (see Article 5.1.3). Should that party not furnish such information it may not rely on the obligation of the first party. This duty to cooperate with the other party applies even if the contract stipulates that one of the parties bears the burden of applying for a public permission. Thus, if the parties have incorporated in their contract the term "ex works", which imposes far-reaching obligations on the buyer, the seller is nevertheless bound "to render the buyer, at the latter's request, risk and expense, every assistance in obtaining [...] any export licence or other official authorisation necessary for the export of the goods" (INCOTERMS 2000, A 2, see also B 2).

b. *Party whose performance requires public permission*

Sub-paragraph (b) of this Article contemplates those cases where none of the parties has a place of business in the State requiring the permission. It also envisions a contract which is truly international notwithstanding the fact that both parties have their places of business in that State. In either case, the party whose performance requires the

可的一方当事人应当披露存在这样的许可要求。因此，根据诚实信用和公平交易原则（参见第 1.7 条），营业地位于要求公共许可的国家的一方当事人，可能需要告知另一方当事人存在公共许可的要求。若前者未尽通知义务，则可能导致法院完全不考虑该许可要求，或者认定未告知存在许可要求的一方当事人默示保证其能够取得该公共许可。

3. 哪方当事人应当采取措施取得公共许可

a. 营业地位于要求公共许可的国家的一方当事人

依据本条(a)项的规则，营业地位于要求取得相关公共许可的国家的一方当事人，承担取得许可之义务，这反映了目前的国际贸易实践。该方当事人所处的位置使得其能够及时申请取得公共许可，因为他可能更熟悉申请的要求和程序。

如果一方当事人为申请许可之目的需要另一方当事人提供更多的信息（比如关于货物最终目的地的信息，或者关于合同目的或合同标的的信息），则另一方当事人必须依据第 5.1.3 条规定的合作义务提供该等信息。如果该另一方当事人没有提供所要求的信息，则其不能依赖第一方当事人所承担义务。即便合同规定了应由某方负责申请公共许可，与对方当事人合作的义务仍然适用。因此，如果双方当事人在合同中采用的贸易术语是"工厂交货"，尽管买方在该术语下承担极大的义务，然而"应买方要求并由买方承担风险和费用，卖方应当向买方提供一切帮助以取得出口许可证或出口货物所必须的其他官方批准"（参见《国际贸易术语解释通则 2000》A2 和 B2）。

b. 履行须经公共许可的当事人

本条(b)项考虑了合同当事人的营业地均不在要求公共许可的国家的情形，同时还考虑到尽管合同当事人的营业地均在要求公共许可的国家，但当事人所签订的合同实际上是国际合同的情形。在这两种

public permission is bound to take the necessary measures to obtain such a permission.

Illustration

> 1.   A, a contractor whose place of business is located in country X, sells a plant on a turn-key basis to B, whose place of business is located in country Y. Acceptance is to take place after performance tests in country Y. On the one hand, A has to apply for all public permissions required in country X, as well as for permissions in third countries (transit, sub-deliveries). On the other, B has to apply for import licences, as well as for all other permissions relating to the site, the use of local services, and the technology imported into country Y. A is also bound to furnish the information and documentation needed by B to obtain import licences and other permissions related to B's performance. A is not responsible for applying for public permissions in country Y, unless this is agreed in the contract or is required, explicitly or implicitly, by the applicable law or the circumstances of the case (e.g. the applicable law may require certain technical permits in country Y to be applied for by the licensor).

c. *Suppletory nature of provisions on public permissions*

The purpose of this Article is to determine the party who must apply for a public permission in those cases where it is not clear who is to bear that burden. It is a suppletory rule to be applied when neither the contract, nor the law requiring the permission or the circumstances specify which party is under an obligation to apply for the required public permission.

Illustration

> 2.   The law of country X subordinates the granting of an export licence for computers to a sworn declaration indicating the country where the computers will ultimately be sent. However, neither the contract nor the law of country X indicates which party bears the burden of applying for a licence. Since it is reasonable to suppose that only the buyer knows what it plans to do with the computers, the policy behind the rule imposing the permission requirement leads to the conclusion that it is the buyer who has to file the application.

情形下，履行需要公共许可的一方当事人，应当采取必要措施以取得这样的许可。

示例：

　　　　1. 营业地位于 X 国的承包商 A，按"交钥匙合同"向营业地位于 Y 国的 B 出售一个工厂。B 将在 Y 国进行测试后验收。一方面，A 必须申请 X 国所要求的一切公共许可，以及第三国要求的许可（过境运输，转交货）；另一方面，B 必须申请进口许可证，以及关于场地、本地服务的使用、向 Y 国引进技术等方面的所有其他许可。A 还应当向 B 提供其为取得进口许可证和与 B 履行有关的其他许可所需要的信息和文件。A 不负责申请 Y 国的公共许可，除非合同规定如此，或适用法或具体情况明示或默示地要求如此（比如适用法可能要求许可方在 Y 国申请某些技术许可证）。

c. 对公共许可规定的补充

　　本条的目的是在合同没有明确规定应当由何方当事人申请公共许可时，确定应当由谁承担申请义务。当合同没有约定，并且根据要求申请许可证的法律或有关情况也无法确定应当由何方当事人申请公共许可时，本条作为补充规则予以适用。

示例：

　　　　2. X 国法律规定，只有在经宣誓的声明中指明计算机最终目的国时，才能授予计算机出口许可证。然而，不论是合同还是 X 国的法律，都没有表明应当由哪一方承担申请许可证的义务。因为可以合理假设，只有买方才知道他将如何处理这些计算机，所以根据该许可要求规则的背后的政策，我们可以得出的结论是：应当由买方申请许可证。

4. Nature of obligation to take the "necessary measures"

The party who has to apply for the permission must take the "necessary measures" to obtain such permission, but is not responsible for the outcome of the application. That party is bound to exhaust available local remedies to obtain the permission, provided that they have a good chance of success and that resorting to local remedies appears reasonable in view of the circumstances of the case (e.g. the value of the transaction, time constraints).

Which measures have to be taken depends on the relevant regulations and the procedural mechanisms available in the State where the permission is to be granted. The obligation is in the nature of an obligation of best efforts (see Article 5.1.4(2)).

Illustration

3.　A, a principal whose place of business is in country X, enters into a contract with B, a self-employed agent, whose place of business is in country Y. B, who has no authority to conclude contracts, is to represent A in countries Y and Z. Among other duties, B must exhibit A's goods at a fair which is to take place in country Z. B must apply for all permissions which are required to undertake these professional activities in countries Y and Z. B's duty to take "necessary measures" includes that of applying for public permissions required to import A's goods temporarily into countries Y and Z, as well as any other public permission that would enable B to participate in the fair. However, unless otherwise agreed, B is not required to apply for public permissions required for goods imported through B by customers located in countries Y and Z.

ARTICLE 6.1.15
(Procedure in applying for permission)

(1) The party required to take the measures necessary to obtain the permission shall do so without undue delay and shall bear any expenses incurred.

(2) That party shall whenever appropriate give the other party notice of the grant or refusal of such permission without undue delay.

4. 采取"必要措施"之义务的性质

负责申请许可的当事人应当采取取得该等许可所需的"必要措施"，但对申请的结果不负责任。该方当事人应当用尽当地可使用的救济手段以求取得许可，只要采用这些手段有较大的成功机会，并且根据具体情况（比如交易价值、时间限制）诉诸于当地救济是合理的。

应当采取何种措施，取决于在授予许可的国家所可以采用的相关规章和程序机制。该义务在本质上是一项要求尽最大努力的义务（参见第 5. 1. 4 条第（2）款）。

示例：

> 3. 营业地位于 X 国的本人 A 与营业地位于 Y 国的独立代理人 B 签订了一份合同，约定 B 在 Y 国和 Z 国代理 A 开展活动，但 B 没有缔结合同的权限。合同规定 B 的义务之一是，必须在 Z 国举办的交易会上展出 A 的货物。B 必须申请在 Y 国和 Z 国开展这些专业活动所必需的一切许可。B 所承担的采取"必要措施"的义务包括申请将 A 的货物临时进口到 Y 国和 Z 国所需要的公共许可，以及申请为使 B 能够参加交易会所需的任何其他公共许可。然而，除非另有约定，对于位于 Y 国和 Z 国的消费者通过 B 进口货物所需的公共许可，B 并不负有申请义务。

第 6. 1. 15 条

（申请许可的程序）

（1）有义务为取得许可而采取必要措施的当事人，应毫不迟延地采取该等措施，并承担由此产生的一切费用。

（2）该方当事人应在任何适当的时候，毫不迟延地向另一方当事人发出该许可已获批准或遭到拒绝的通知。

COMMENT

1. Time for filing an application

The party under an obligation to obtain a public permission must take action immediately after the conclusion of the contract and pursue this action as necessary under the circumstances.

2. Expenses

According to Article 6.1.11, each party shall bear the costs of performance of its obligations. This rule has been restated in paragraph (1) of this Article for the sake of clarity.

3. Duty to give prompt notice of the grant or refusal of the permission

The parties to the contract need to know as soon as possible whether the permission can be obtained. Accordingly, paragraph (2) of this Article provides that the party required to take the necessary measures must inform the other of the outcome of the application. This duty of information extends to other relevant facts, such as for example the timing and outcome of the application, whether a refusal is subject to appeal and whether an appeal is to be lodged.

4. Duty to give notice "whenever appropriate"

The "appropriateness" of giving notice of the grant or refusal refers to the need to give notice and the manner of providing it. The necessity of giving notice obviously exists where such notice is required by law, but may also be inferred from the mere fact that a permission requirement is referred to in the contract.

The "appropriateness" of the duty to give notice is also related to the relevance of the information to be provided. Accordingly, the applying party is not bound to inform the other party of the outcome of that application in cases where the latter party obtains the information from the granting authority, or where applications for permissions are regularly granted. The fact that the permission is, contrary to normal practice, refused in a given case makes the obligation to inform more compelling.

This Article does not establish particular requirements concerning the formalities relating to the communication (see Article 1.10).

注释:

1. 提交申请的时间

承担取得公共许可义务的一方当事人应当在合同订立后立即开始申请，并且采取具体情况下所需的措施推动该申请的进展。

2. 费用

依据第6.1.11条的规定，当事人应各自承担履行各自义务时发生的各种费用。为了明确合同当事人的义务，本条第(1)款重申了该规则。

3. 及时通知许可申请获得批准或者遭到拒绝的义务

合同当事人需要尽快知道许可申请能否得到批准。因此，本条第(2)款规定，承担申请义务的一方当事人应当将申请结果通知另一方当事人。该通知义务还延伸适用于其他一些相关事实，比如申请的时间和结果，拒绝决定是否可以上诉以及是否打算提起上诉。

4. 在"任何适当的时候"发出通知的义务

发出批准或拒绝通知的"适当性"所指向的是发出通知的必要性和发出通知的方式。如果法律要求发出该等通知，则发出通知的必要性显然存在；即便法律没有规定，如果合同提及了许可要求，那么单从这一事实也可以推断发出通知是必要的。

发出通知义务的"适当性"还与所提供信息的相关性有关。因此，如果申请方的对方当事人从批准机构获知了申请结果，或者许可申请通常都会得到批准，那么申请方当事人就没有义务将申请结果通知该对方当事人。如果与通常的做法相反，许可申请在特定的情况下遭到拒绝，那么通知义务就变得更为迫切。

本条对通知的形式未做具体要求(参见第1.10条)。

5. Consequences of the failure to inform

Failure to provide information regarding the grant or refusal of the permission amounts to non-performance. Accordingly, the general consequences of non-performance, as set forth in Chapter 7, apply. The duty to give notice of the grant of the public permission is a contractual obligation arising at the time the contract comes into existence. The duty to give notice of the refusal of the permission is part of the duty to take the "necessary measures" to obtain the permission under Article 6.1.14 (see Comment 4).

Illustrations

1.   A, whose place of business is in country X, and B, a contractor, enter into a contract for the construction of a plant in country X. The parties agree that B is not bound to begin the construction and A's advance payments are not due until the grant of a permission by the authorities of country X.

A applies for and obtains the permission but fails to inform B that the permission has been granted. Two months later, B learns through inquiries with the authorities of country X that the permission has been granted and begins work on the construction of the plant.

Although the parties had agreed that their performances were due as of the time of the granting of the permission, A's failure to inform B that the permission has been granted precludes A from relying on B's failure to perform as of that date (see Article 7.1.2). Thus, the contractual period begins to run for B as from when it learns of the granting of the permission.

Moreover, B may also claim damages if it is able to establish, for example, damage resulting from failure to use its production capacity, additional costs arising from storing raw materials during that two-month period, etc. (see Article 7.4.1 *et seq.*). A, who from the very beginning had notice of the grant of the permission, must observe the original date of its performance, as provided for in the contract. If A fails to make an advance payment due four weeks after the granting of the permission, A must pay interest as from that date.

5. 未尽通知义务的后果

未将许可得到批准或遭到拒绝的信息通知另一方，构成合同的不履行，因此，适用第七章关于不履行的一般后果的规定。通知许可申请获得批准的义务，是一项合同成立之时产生的合同义务。通知许可申请遭到拒绝的义务，是第 6.1.14 条规定的采取取得许可所需的"必要措施"义务的一部分（参见注释4）。

示例：

　　　1. 营业地位于 X 国的 A 与承包商 B 签订了一份关于在 X 国修建一个工厂的合同。双方约定，在取得 X 国有关当局的许可之后，B 的建筑义务和 A 的支付预付款义务才开始履行。

　　　A 对该许可证提出了申请并获得了批准，但 A 却未将这一事实通知 B。两个月以后，B 从 X 国的有关当局了解到该许可申请已经获得批准，于是开始修建工厂。

　　　尽管双方约定双方均应在取得许可之时开始履行各自的合同义务，但是由于 A 未尽其通知义务，所以 A 不能主张 B 在未取得许可之时开始履行合同义务（参见第 7.1.2 条）。因此，对 B 来说，合同期限应当从其了解到许可申请获得批准时算起。

　　　此外，如果 B 能够证明其因生产能力闲置而遭受了损失，或者在此两个月期间因储存原材料而支付了额外的仓储费，等等，那么 B 还可以要求损害赔偿（参见第 7.4.1 条及以下条文）。而 A 因为在一开始就获悉许可获得批准，所以应当按照合同规定的日期履行合同义务。如果 A 在取得许可后的四个星期内未支付预付款，那么 A 应当从该日起支付利息。

2.   The facts are the same as in Illustration 1, except that the proper authority simultaneously informs A and B that the permission has been granted. B may not avail itself of A's failure to inform in order to postpone its performance, nor is it entitled to damages for A's failure to inform.

ARTICLE 6.1.16
(Permission neither granted nor refused)

(1) If, notwithstanding the fact that the party responsible has taken all measures required, permission is neither granted nor refused within an agreed period or, where no period has been agreed, within a reasonable time from the conclusion of the contract, either party is entitled to terminate the contract.

(2) Where the permission affects some terms only, paragraph (1) does not apply if, having regard to the circumstances, it is reasonable to uphold the remaining contract even if the permission is refused.

COMMENT

Whereas Articles 6.1.14 and 6.1.15 are concerned with the duties of the contracting parties, Articles 6.1.16 and 6.1.17 deal with the legal consequences in cases respectively where there has been no decision on the application within a given period or where the public permission has been refused.

1. No decision taken as regards the permission

Paragraph (1) of this Article deals with the "nothing happens" situation, that is to say a situation where permission has neither been granted nor refused within the agreed period or, where no period has been agreed, within a reasonable time from the conclusion of the contract. The reasons for the absence of a pronouncement may vary, for example the slow pace of processing the application, a pending appeal, etc. In any event there is no longer any reason to keep the parties waiting and either party is entitled to terminate the contract.

2. 事实和示例 1 相同，不同之处在于有关当局将许可申请获得批准的消息同时通知了 A 和 B 。在这种情况下，B 不能因为 A 未尽通知义务而推迟其履行，也不能因此向 A 主张损害赔偿。

第6.1.16条

（未获批准又未拒绝之许可）

（1） 尽管负有义务的当事人采取了所有必要的措施，但在约定的期间之内，或若无此约定，在合同订立后的合理时间之内，许可既未获得批准又未遭到拒绝，则任何一方当事人均有权终止该合同。

（2） 当许可仅影响合同的某些条款时，如果考虑到具体情况，即便许可遭到拒绝，维持合同的其余部分仍是合理的，则不适用上述第（1）款的规定。

注释：

第6.1.14 条和第 6.1.15 条涉及的是合同当事人的义务，而第 6.1.16 条和第 6.1.17 条则分别处理下述情况下的法律后果：一定时间内主管机关未对申请作出决定，或者公共许可申请被拒绝。

1. 未对许可申请作出决定

本条第（1）款涉及的是"杳无音信"时的情形，也就是说，在约定的期间内或者（如果没有约定期间）在合同订立后的一段合理时间内，申请既没有被批准也没有被拒绝。出现这种情形的原因是多方面的，比如处理申请的速度缓慢，存在还未判决的上诉，等等。无论如何，此时已没有理由要求合同当事人继续等待，因此任何一方当事人均有权终止合同。

2. Termination of the contract

Remedies other than termination may be appropriate depending on the legal role played by the permission in the creation of the contractual obligations. This is in particular the case where the granting of the public permission is a condition for the validity of the contract, since in the absence of the permission either party may simply disregard the contract. The reason why this Article provides also in these cases for the termination of the contract is that the parties are, with a view to obtaining the permission, under a number of obligations which cannot be allowed to exist indefinitely.

The entitlement of the party responsible for obtaining the permission to terminate the contract under this Article is conditional on that party's having taken "the necessary measures" to that effect.

Illustration

> 1.   A, situated in country X, sells rifles to B for resale by B in the hunting season starting in four months. The validity of the sale is subject to a public permission to be granted by the authorities of country X. No period is agreed for obtaining that permission. Notwithstanding the fact that A takes all the necessary measures to obtain the permission, after three months no decision has yet been taken on A's application. Either party may terminate the contract.

The termination envisaged under this Article has no consequences for the expenses so far incurred by the parties for the purpose of obtaining the permission. The expenses will be borne by the party who has assumed the risk of not obtaining the permission.

3. Permission affecting individual terms only

Where the permission affects some terms only of the contract, paragraph (2) of this Article excludes the right of termination in cases where, even if the permission had been refused, it would according to Article 6.1.17(1) nevertheless be reasonable to uphold the contract.

Illustration

> 2.   A, situated in country X, enters into a contract with B, which contains a penalty clause for delay the validity of which is subject to a public permission to be granted by the authorities of country X. Notwithstanding the fact that A takes all the necessary measures to obtain the permission, time continues to pass without any decision being taken. It would be reasonable in the circumstances to uphold the contract. Even if the permission were to have been refused, neither party may terminate the contract.

2. 合同的终止

根据许可在创设合同义务过程中所起的法律作用的不同,终止合同之外的其他救济措施可能更加合适。当获得公共许可是合同生效的前提条件时尤其如此,因为在没有获得许可时,双方当事人均可以完全不顾合同的存在。本条之所以仍然对此种情况作了终止合同的规定,原因在于,为取得许可双方当事人承担了一系列义务,当事人不能毫无期限地承担这些义务。

承担取得许可义务的一方当事人要享有本条规定的终止合同的权利,必须满足这样一个条件,即该方当事人已经采取了取得许可所需的"必要措施"。

示例:

> 1. 位于 X 国的 A 向 B 出售一批步枪,B 将在四个月后的狩猎季节将这批步枪转售。该买卖合同的效力取决于能否取得 X 国有关当局的公共许可。双方没有约定取得该许可的期限。尽管 A 采取了一切必要措施申请许可,但三个月之后,有关当局对其申请仍未作出任何决定。在这种情况下,双方都可以终止合同。

本条规定的终止合同,不影响当事人为取得许可而产生的费用。该等费用应当由对不能取得许可承担风险的一方当事人承担。

3. 许可只对合同的个别条款产生影响

如果许可影响的仅仅是合同部分条款的效力,并且即便许可已经被拒绝,根据第 6.1.17 条第(1)款维持合同的效力仍然是合理的,那么依据本条第(2)款,当事人就不享有终止合同的权利。

示例:

> 2. A 位于 X 国,与 B 订立的合同中包含一个迟延履行罚金条款,该条款的效力取决于 X 国有关当局对公共许可的批准。尽管 A 为取得许可采取了一切必要的措施,但随着时间的推移,有关当局对该许可申请迟迟未作出任何决定。在此案的情况下,维持合同的效力是合理的。即便许可申请被拒绝,任何一方当事人都不得终止合同。

ARTICLE 6.1.17
(Permission refused)

(1) The refusal of a permission affecting the validity of the contract renders the contract void. If the refusal affects the validity of some terms only, only such terms are void if, having regard to the circumstances, it is reasonable to uphold the remaining contract.

(2) Where the refusal of a permission renders the performance of the contract impossible in whole or in part, the rules on non-performance apply.

COMMENT

1. Application for permission rejected

This Article contemplates the situation where the application for a permission is expressly refused. The nature of the obligation imposed on the responsible party with respect to the application for the permission is such that a refusal under this Article is one which is not subject to an appeal which has a reasonable prospect of success (see Comment 4 on Article 6.1.14). Moreover, means of recourse against the refusal need not be exhausted whenever a final decision on the permission would be taken only after the time at which the contract could meaningfully be performed.

2. Legal consequences of a refusal of permission

The consequences of a refusal to grant the permission vary depending on whether the permission affects the validity of the contract or its performance.

a. *Refusal of permission affecting validity of the contract*

Where the permission affects the validity of the whole contract, a refusal renders the whole contract void, i.e. the contract is considered as never having come into being.

第6.1.17条

(拒绝许可)

(1) 当一项许可影响到合同的效力时,则拒绝该许可导致合同无效。但如果拒绝许可只影响到合同部分条款的效力,考虑到具体情况,维持合同的其余部分是合理的,则仅该受影响部分的条款无效。

(2) 当拒绝许可导致合同的全部或部分履行不可能时,适用有关不履行的规定。

注释:

1. 许可申请被拒绝

本条考虑的是许可申请被明确拒绝的情形。承担申请许可义务的一方当事人所承担的义务的性质决定了,对本条项下的拒绝决定提起的上诉成功几率不大(参见第6.1.14条的注释4)。而且,如果最终决定只有在合同有可能得到有意义的履行之后才能作出,则无须用尽关于拒绝许可的救济措施。

2. 拒绝许可的法律后果

拒绝许可的后果,取决于相关许可影响的是合同的效力还是合同的履行。

a. 拒绝许可影响合同的效力

如果许可影响的是整个合同的效力,那么拒绝许可将使得整个合同无效,也即视为合同从未成立。

Illustration

> 1.   A, situated in country X, enters into a contract with B, the validity of which is subject to a public permission to be granted by the authorities of country X. Notwithstanding the fact that A takes all the necessary measures to obtain the permission, A's application is refused. The contract is considered never to have come into existence.

Where, on the other hand, a refusal affects the validity of some terms only of the contract, only such terms are void, while the remaining part of the contract may be upheld provided that such a result is reasonable in the circumstances.

Illustration

> 2.   A, situated in country X, enters into a contract with B, which contains a penalty clause for delay the validity of which is subject to a public permission to be granted by the authorities of country X. Notwithstanding the fact that A takes all the necessary measures to obtain the permission, A's application is refused. If it is reasonable in the circumstances, the contract will be upheld without the penalty clause.

b. *Refusal rendering performance of the contract impossible*

If the refusal of the permission renders the performance impossible in whole or in part, paragraph (2) of this Article refers to the rules on non-performance embodied in Chapter 7.

Illustration

> 3.   Under a contract entered into with B, A owes B USD 100,000. The transfer of the sum from country X, where A is situated, to B's bank account in country Y is subject to a permission by the Central Bank of country X. Notwithstanding the fact that A takes all the necessary measures to obtain the permission, A's application is refused. The refusal of the permission renders it impossible for A to pay B. The consequences of A's non-performance are determined in accordance with the provisions of Chapter 7.

The refusal of the permission may render the performance of a party impossible only in the State imposing the permission requirement, while it may be possible for that party to perform the same obligation elsewhere. In such cases the general principle of good faith and fair dealing (see Article 1.7) will prevent that party from relying on the refusal of the permission as an excuse for non-performance.

示例：

　　1. A 位于 X 国，与 B 订立了一份合同，该合同的效力取决于 X 国有关当局对某项公共许可的批准。尽管 A 为取得许可采取了一切必要的措施，但其申请仍然遭到拒绝。该合同视为从未成立。

另一方面，如果拒绝许可影响的只是合同部分条款的效力，并且根据具体情况，维持合同其余条款的效力是合理的，那么，只有受影响的这部分合同条款归于无效，而其余条款依然有效。

示例：

　　2. A 位于 X 国，与 B 订立的合同中包含一项迟延罚金条款，该条款的效力取决于 X 国有关当局对某项公共许可的批准。尽管 A 为取得该许可采取了一切必要措施，但其申请仍然遭到拒绝。根据此案的具体情况，该合同除迟延罚金条款外将被认定为有效，只要这样做是合理的。

b. 拒绝许可使得合同的履行成为不可能

如果拒绝许可使得合同的履行变为完全不可能或部分不可能，本条第(2)款规定应适用第七章关于不履行的规定。

示例：

　　3. 根据 A 与 B 签订的一份合同，A 欠 B 10 万美元。A 位于 X 国。将这笔款项从 X 国转账到 B 所在国的银行账户，必须获得 X 国中央银行的许可。尽管 A 为取得该许可采取了一切必要的措施，但 A 的申请仍然遭到拒绝。对该许可的拒绝使得 A 无法向 B 偿付。A 不履行合同的后果根据第七章的有关规定予以决定。

拒绝许可可能仅导致一方当事人在要求取得该许可的国家不能履行其义务，但在其他地方履行却依然可能。在这种情况下，根据诚实信用和公平交易的一般原则（参见第1.7条），该方当事人不能以许可被拒绝作为其不履行合同义务的借口。

Illustration

4.   The facts are the same as in Illustration 3, except that A has sufficient funds to pay B in country Z, where no such permission requirement exists. A may not rely on the refusal of the permission by the authorities of country X as an excuse for not paying B.

示例：

　　4. 事实和示例 3 相同，不同之处在于，A 在 Z 国有足够的资金偿付 B，而 Z 国不要求取得公共许可。A 不能以 X 国有关当局拒绝许可为借口而不偿付 B。

SECTION 2: HARDSHIP

ARTICLE 6.2.1
(Contract to be observed)

Where the performance of a contract becomes more onerous for one of the parties, that party is nevertheless bound to perform its obligations subject to the following provisions on hardship.

COMMENT

1. Binding character of the contract the general rule

The purpose of this Article is to make it clear that as a consequence of the general principle of the binding character of the contract (see Article 1.3) performance must be rendered as long as it is possible and regardless of the burden it may impose on the performing party. In other words, even if a party experiences heavy losses instead of the expected profits or the performance has become meaningless for that party the terms of the contract must nevertheless be respected.

Illustration

A, a forwarding agent, enters into a two-year shipping contract with B, a carrier. Under the contract B is bound to ship certain goods from country X to country Y at a fixed rate, on a monthly basis throughout the two-year period. Two years later, alleging a substantial increase in the price of fuel in the aftermath of a political crisis in the region, B requests a five per cent increase in the rate. B is not entitled to such an increase because B bears the risk of its performance becoming more onerous.

2. Change in circumstances relevant only in exceptional cases

The principle of the binding character of the contract is not however an absolute one. When supervening circumstances are such that they lead to a fundamental alteration of the equilibrium of the contract, they create an exceptional situation referred to in the Principles as "hardship" and dealt with in the following Articles of this Section.

第二节　艰难情形

第6.2.1条

（合同必须遵守）

如果合同一方当事人履行合同的负担加重，该方当事人仍应履行其义务，但需受到下列有关艰难情形规定的限制。

注释：

1. 合同具有约束性是一般规则

本条旨在阐明，根据合同约束性的一般规则（参见第1.3条），只要有可能，合同义务就应当得到履行，而不管履行方可能因此承担什么样的负担。换句话说，即使一方当事人不仅不会因履行合同获益，反而会遭受重大损失，或者对该方当事人来说，履行合同已变得毫无意义，合同条款仍然应当得到尊重。

示例：

货运代理人 A 与承运人 B 签订了一份为期两年的海上运输合同。依据该合同，B 应在这两年内每月以固定的费率将特定货物从 X 国运往 Y 国。两年后，B 声称，该地区的政治危机导致燃料价格大幅度上涨，因此要求将运费标准提高 5%。B 无权要求提价，因为它承担了履行负担加重的风险。

2. 情况改变只在例外情况下是相关的

然而，合同具有约束性原则并不是绝对的。如果随后发生的情况导致合同均衡发生了根本改变，即构成一种例外情形，《通则》称之为"艰难情形"。本节以下条款对其作了具体规定。

The phenomenon of hardship has been acknowledged by various legal systems under the guise of other concepts such as frustration of purpose, *Wegfall der Geschäftsgrundlage*, *imprévision*, *eccessiva onerosità sopravvenuta*, etc. The term "hardship" was chosen because it is widely known in international trade practice as confirmed by the inclusion in many international contracts of so-called "hardship clauses".

ARTICLE 6.2.2
(Definition of hardship)

There is hardship where the occurrence of events fundamentally alters the equilibrium of the contract either because the cost of a party's performance has increased or because the value of the performance a party receives has diminished, and

(a) the events occur or become known to the disadvantaged party after the conclusion of the contract;

(b) the events could not reasonably have been taken into account by the disadvantaged party at the time of the conclusion of the contract;

(c) the events are beyond the control of the disadvantaged party; and

(d) the risk of the events was not assumed by the disadvantaged party.

COMMENT

1. Hardship defined

This Article defines hardship as a situation where the occurrence of events fundamentally alters the equilibrium of the contract, provided that those events meet the requirements which are laid down in sub-paragraphs (a) to (d).

2. Fundamental alteration of equilibrium of the contract

Since the general principle is that a change in circumstances does not affect the obligation to perform (see Article 6.2.1), it follows that

很多法律制度都以不同形式承认艰难情形现象的存在，如合同目的落空、合同基础消失、意外事件等。《通则》之所以选择"艰难情形"这一术语，是因为它在国际贸易实践中广为所知，并且许多国际合同都包含有所谓的"艰难情形条款"。

第6.2.2条

（艰难情形的定义）

所谓艰难情形，是指发生的事件致使一方当事人的履约成本增加，或者所获履约的价值减少，因而根本改变了合同的均衡，并且

（a）该事件在合同订立之后发生或为受到不利影响的当事人所知悉；

（b）受到不利影响的当事人在订立合同时不能合理地预见到该事件；

（c）该事件不能为受到不利影响的当事人所控制；而且

（d）该事件的风险不由受到不利影响的当事人承担。

注释：

1. 艰难情形的定义

本条将艰难情形定义为，某些事件的发生从根本上改变了合同均衡的情形，但这些事件须满足(a)项至(d)项所规定的要求。

2. 对合同均衡的根本改变

因为一般原则是情况的改变不影响履行合同的义务（参见第6.2.1条），

hardship may not be invoked unless the alteration of the equilibrium of the contract is fundamental. Whether an alteration is "fundamental" in a given case will of course depend upon the circumstances.

Illustration

1. In September 1989 A, a dealer in electronic goods situated in the former German Democratic Republic, purchases stocks from B, situated in country X, also a former socialist country. The goods are to be delivered by B in December 1990. In November 1990, A informs B that the goods are no longer of any use to it, claiming that after the unification of the German Democratic Republic and the Federal Republic of Germany and the opening of the former German Democratic Republic to the international market there is no longer any market for such goods imported from country X. Unless the circumstances indicate otherwise, A is entitled to invoke hardship.

a. *Increase in cost of performance*

In practice a fundamental alteration in the equilibrium of the contract may manifest itself in two different but related ways. The first is characterised by a substantial increase in the cost for one party of performing its obligation. This party will normally be the one who is to perform the non-monetary obligation. The substantial increase in the cost may, for instance, be due to a dramatic rise in the price of the raw materials necessary for the production of the goods or the rendering of the services, or to the introduction of new safety regulations requiring far more expensive production procedures.

b. *Decrease in value of the performance received by one party*

The second manifestation of hardship is characterised by a substantial decrease in the value of the performance received by one party, including cases where the performance no longer has any value at all for the receiving party. The performance may relate either to a monetary or a non-monetary obligation. The substantial decrease in the value or the total loss of any value of the performance may be due either to drastic changes in market conditions (e.g. the effect of a dramatic increase in inflation on a contractually agreed price) or the frustration of the purpose for which the performance was required (e.g. the effect of a prohibition to build on a plot of land acquired for building purposes or the effect of an export embargo on goods acquired with a view to their subsequent export).

Naturally the decrease in value of the performance must be capable of objective measurement: a mere change in the personal opinion of the receiving party as to the value of the performance is of no relevance. As

由此，除非合同均衡的改变是根本性的，否则不得援引艰难情形。对合同均衡的改变是否是"根本性的"，当然取决于特定案件的具体情况。

示例：

1. 位于前德意志民主共和国的电子产品经销商 A，于 1989 年 9 月向位于另一前社会主义国家 X 国的 B 购买货物。B 应当在 1990 年 12 月交付这些货物。1990 年 11 月，A 通知 B，说这些货物对他来说已经毫无用处了，因为德意志民主共和国和德意志联邦共和国统一及前德意志民主共和国对世界开放后，从 X 国进口的这些货物不再有任何市场了。除非情况另有表示，A 有权援引艰难情形。

a. 履约成本增加

在实践中，合同均衡的根本改变可以通过两种不同的但却相关的方式表现出来。第一种方式的特征是，一方当事人的履约成本大幅度增加。该方当事人通常是履行非金钱性债务的一方。履约成本大幅度增加的原因可能是，例如，生产货物或提供服务所必需的原材料价格大幅度上升，或者新出台的安全法规致使生产程序的成本增加。

b. 一方当事人所获得的履约价值减少

艰难情形的第二种表现方式的特征是，一方当事人从对方履约中获得的价值大幅度减少，包括履约对接受方来说已经变得毫无价值。履行既可以涉及金钱债务，也可以涉及非金钱债务。履约价值的大幅度减少或完全丧失可能是因为市场行情的急剧变化导致的（比如严重的通货膨胀对合同约定价格产生的影响），也可能是因为履行合同的目的落空（比如建筑禁令对为建筑房屋所购土地的影响，或者出口禁令对为出口所购货物的影响）。

当然，履约价值的减少必须能够加以客观地计算，仅仅是接受方关于履约价值的个人看法所发生的改变是不够的。至于履行目的落空，

to the frustration of the purpose of the performance, this can only be taken into account when the purpose in question was known or at least ought to have been known to both parties.

3. Additional requirements for hardship to arise

a. *Events occur or become known after conclusion of the contract*

According to sub-paragraph (a) of this Article, the events causing hardship must take place or become known to the disadvantaged party after the conclusion of the contract. If that party had known of those events when entering into the contract, it would have been able to take them into account at that time. In such a case that party may not subsequently rely on hardship.

b. *Events could not reasonably have been taken into account by disadvantaged party*

Even if the change in circumstances occurs after the conclusion of the contract, sub-paragraph (b) of this Article makes it clear that such circumstances cannot cause hardship if they could reasonably have been taken into account by the disadvantaged party at the time the contract was concluded.

Illustration

2.   A agrees to supply B with crude oil from country X at a fixed price for the next five years, notwithstanding the acute political tensions in the region. Two years after the conclusion of the contract, a war erupts between contending factions in neighbouring countries. The war results in a world energy crisis and oil prices increase drastically. A is not entitled to invoke hardship because such a rise in the price of crude oil was not unforeseeable.

Sometimes the change in circumstances is gradual, but the final result of those gradual changes may constitute a case of hardship. If the change began before the contract was concluded, hardship will not arise unless the pace of change increases dramatically during the life of the contract.

Illustration

3.   In a sales contract between A and B the price is expressed in the currency of country X, a currency the value of which was already depreciating slowly against other major currencies before the conclusion of the contract. One month thereafter a political crisis in country X leads to a massive devaluation of its currency of the order

只有在双方当事人都知道或者至少都应当知道该目的时，才能予以考虑。

3. 构成艰难情形的其他要求

a. 该事件于合同成立后发生或者为当事人所知悉

根据本条(a)项的规定，导致艰难情形的事件应当在合同成立之后发生，或者为处于不利地位的当事人所知悉。如果该当事人在订立合同时就知道该等事件，那么其应当能够在当时将这些事件纳入考虑。在此情况下，该方当事人不能嗣后援引艰难情形。

b. 受到不利影响的当事人不能合理预见该事件

即使情况的改变发生在合同订立之后，本条(b)项也明确规定，如果受到不利影响的当事人在订立合同时能够合理地考虑这些事件，那么该等情况改变就不能导致艰难情形。

示例：

　　2. 尽管 A 知道相关地区的政治局势非常紧张，仍同意在今后五年里以固定价格从 X 国向 B 提供原油。合同订立两年后，相互敌对的邻国派系间爆发了战争，该战争导致了世界能源危机，石油价格急剧上涨。A 无权援引艰难情形，因为该等原油价格上涨是可以预见的。

有时情况的改变是渐进的，但是这些情况改变的最终结果却可能构成艰难情形。如果在合同订立之前这些改变就已经开始，那么除非改变速度在合同有效期内急剧加快，否则不构成艰难情形。

示例：

　　3. A 和 B 之间的一份销售合同以 X 国的货币表示价款，该货币对其他主要货币的价值在合同订立之前已经在慢慢贬值。一个月之后 X 国发生政治危机，导致该国货币贬值80%

of 80%. Unless the circumstances indicate otherwise, this constitutes a case of hardship, since such a dramatic acceleration of the loss of value of the currency of country X was not foreseeable.

c. *Events beyond the control of disadvantaged party*

Under sub-paragraph (c) of this Article a case of hardship can only arise if the events causing the hardship are beyond the control of the disadvantaged party.

d. *Risks must not have been assumed by disadvantaged party*

Under sub-paragraph (d) there can be no hardship if the disadvantaged party had assumed the risk of the change in circumstances. The word "assumption" makes it clear that the risks need not have been taken over expressly, but that this may follow from the very nature of the contract. A party who enters into a speculative transaction is deemed to accept a certain degree of risk, even though it may not have been fully aware of that risk at the time it entered into the contract.

Illustration

4.   A, an insurance company specialised in the insurance of shipping risks, requests an additional premium from those of its customers who have contracts which include the risks of war and civil insurrection, so as to meet the substantially greater risk to which it is exposed following upon the simultaneous outbreak of war and civil insurrection in three countries in the same region. A is not entitled to such an adaptation of the contract, since by the war and civil insurrection clauses insurance companies assume these risks even if three countries are affected at the same time.

4. Hardship relevant only to performance not yet rendered

By its very nature hardship can only become of relevance with respect to performances still to be rendered: once a party has performed, it is no longer entitled to invoke a substantial increase in the costs of its performance or a substantial decrease in the value of the performance it receives as a consequence of a change in circumstances which occurs after such performance.

If the fundamental alteration in the equilibrium of the contract occurs at a time when performance has been only partially rendered, hardship can be of relevance only to the parts of the performance still to be rendered.

左右。除非情况另有表示,这将构成艰难情形,因为 X 国货币如此剧烈地加速贬值是无法预见的。

c. 该事件不能为受到不利影响的当事人所控制

依据本条(c)项之规定,只有导致艰难情形的事件是受到不利影响的当事人所无法控制的,才构成艰难情形。

d. 该事件的风险不由受到不利影响的当事人承担

依据本条(d)项之规定,如果受到不利影响的当事人已经承担了情况改变的风险,那么他就不能援引艰难情形。"承担"(assumption)一词表明,明示地承担风险并不是必须的,而是可以根据合同性质本身推断出来。签订投机性交易合同的当事人应当被视作承担了一定程度的风险,即使他在订立合同时并没有完全意识到该等风险。

示例:

> 4. 精于海运保险业务的保险公司 A,要求与其签订含有战争险和内乱险条款的保险合同的投保人支付额外的保险费,因为该地区三个国家同时爆发战争和内乱致其承保的风险水平大幅提高。A 无权对合同作出如此修改,因为根据该战争和内乱险条款,保险公司承担了该等风险,即使三个国家同时受到影响。

4. 艰难情形只与尚待履行的部分有关

究其本质,艰难情形就其本质来讲,只与尚未完成的履行有关:一方当事人一旦完成了履行,就不能再主张履行完成之后发生的情况改变导致自己的履约成本大幅增加或其所得到的履约价值大幅减少。

如果合同均衡的根本改变发生时只履行了部分义务,那么艰难情形只能与尚待履行的部分有关。

Illustration

> 5.   A enters into a contract with B, a waste disposal company in country X, for the purpose of arranging the storage of its waste. The contract provides for a four-year term and a fixed price per ton of waste. Two years after the conclusion of the contract, the environmental movement in country X gains ground and the Government of country X prescribes prices for storing waste which are ten times higher than before. B may successfully invoke hardship only with respect to the two remaining years of the life of the contract.

5. Hardship normally relevant to long-term contracts

Although this Article does not expressly exclude the possibility of hardship being invoked in respect of other kinds of contract, hardship will normally be of relevance to long-term contracts, i.e. those where the performance of at least one party extends over a certain period of time.

6. Hardship and force majeure

In view of the definitions of hardship in this Article and force majeure in Article 7.1.7, under the Principles there may be factual situations which can at the same time be considered as cases of hardship and of force majeure. If this is the case, it is for the party affected by these events to decide which remedy to pursue. If it invokes force majeure, it is with a view to its non-performance being excused. If, on the other hand, a party invokes hardship, this is in the first instance for the purpose of renegotiating the terms of the contract so as to allow the contract to be kept alive although on revised terms.

7. Hardship and contract practice

The definition of hardship in this Article is necessarily of a rather general character. International commercial contracts often contain much more precise and elaborate provisions in this regard. The parties may therefore find it appropriate to adapt the content of this Article so as to take account of the particular features of the specific transaction.

示例：

　　5. A与X国的废品处理公司B签订了一份合同，约定B为A提供废品储存服务。该合同为期四年，每吨废品的储存费是固定的。合同签订两年后，由于X国的环保运动取得了进展，X国政府提高了储存废品的价格，比以前的价格高出十倍。B仅能就剩余两年的履行成功主张艰难情形。

5. 艰难情形通常与长期合同有关

尽管本条并未明确排除就其他合同援引艰难情形的可能性，但艰难情形通常都与长期合同有关，即那种至少一方当事人需在一定期间内持续履行的合同。

6. 艰难情形与不可抗力

根据本条对艰难情形和第7.1.7条对不可抗力所作的定义，实践中可能会出现同时被视为艰难情形和不可抗力的事实情况。如果出现这种情形，应当由受到影响的一方当事人决定采取何种救济措施。如果该当事人援引不可抗力，那么其目的是为不履行合同免责；而如果该当事人援引的是艰难情形，其目的首先是要对合同条款作重新谈判，以便使合同按修改后的条款继续有效。

7. 艰难情形与合同实践

本条对于艰难情形的定义不免比较抽象。国际商事合同对此经常有更加精确和详细的规定。因此合同当事人可能会发现，根据特定交易的具体情况对本条的规定加以修改是适当的。

ARTICLE 6.2.3
(Effects of hardship)

(1) In case of hardship the disadvantaged party is entitled to request renegotiations. The request shall be made without undue delay and shall indicate the grounds on which it is based.

(2) The request for renegotiation does not in itself entitle the disadvantaged party to withhold performance.

(3) Upon failure to reach agreement within a reasonable time either party may resort to the court.

(4) If the court finds hardship it may, if reasonable,

(a) terminate the contract at a date and on terms to be fixed, or

(b) adapt the contract with a view to restoring its equilibrium.

COMMENT

1. Disadvantaged party entitled to request renegotiations

Since hardship consists in a fundamental alteration of the equilibrium of the contract, paragraph (1) of this Article in the first instance entitles the disadvantaged party to request the other party to enter into renegotiation of the original terms of the contract with a view to adapting them to the changed circumstances.

Illustration

1. A, a construction company situated in country X, enters into a lump sum contract with B, a governmental agency, for the erection of a plant in country Y. Most of the sophisticated machinery has to be imported from abroad. Due to an unexpected devaluation of the currency of country Y, which is the currency of payment, the cost of the machinery increases dramatically. A is entitled to request B to renegotiate the original contract price so as to adapt it to the changed circumstances.

第6.2.3条

（艰难情形的后果）

（1）出现艰难情形时，受到不利影响的当事人有权要求重新谈判。但该要求应毫不迟延地提出，而且应说明提出该要求的理由。

（2）重新谈判的要求本身并不使受到不利影响的当事人有权暂停履行。

（3）如在合理时间内不能达成协议，任何一方当事人均可诉诸法院。

（4）如果法院认定存在艰难情形，只要合理，法院可以：

（a）按其确定的日期和条件终止合同，或者

（b）为恢复合同的均衡而调整合同。

注释：

1. 受到不利影响的当事人有权要求重新谈判

因为艰难情形构成合同均衡的根本性改变，所以本条第(1)款的规定首先赋予受到不利影响的一方当事人要求另一方当事人对原合同条款进行重新谈判的权利，以使其适应改变后的情况。

示例：

1. 位于 X 国的建筑公司 A 与一政府机构 B 签订了一份在 Y 国修建一座工厂的合同，合同价款为一次总付。建筑所需的大部分精密机器必须从国外进口。由于作为支付货币的 Y 国货币发生了不可预见的贬值，导致购买上述机器的成本激增。A 有权要求 B 对原来的合同价款重新谈判，以使其适应改变后的情况。

A request for renegotiations is not admissible where the contract itself already incorporates a clause providing for the automatic adaptation of the contract (e.g. a clause providing for automatic indexation of the price if certain events occur).

Illustration

> 2.   The facts are the same as in Illustration 1, except that the contract contains a price indexation clause relating to variations in the cost of materials and labour. A is not entitled to request a renegotiation of the price.

However, even in such a case renegotiation on account of hardship would not be precluded if the adaptation clause incorporated in the contract did not contemplate the events giving rise to hardship.

Illustration

> 3.   The facts are the same as in Illustration 2, except that the substantial increase in A's costs is due to the adoption of new safety regulations in country Y. A is entitled to request B to renegotiate the original contract price so as to adapt it to the changed circumstances.

2. Request for renegotiations without undue delay

The request for renegotiations must be made as quickly as possible after the time at which hardship is alleged to have occurred (paragraph (1)). The precise time for requesting renegotiations will depend upon the circumstances of the case: it may, for instance, be longer when the change in circumstances takes place gradually (see Comment 3(b) on Article 6.2.2).

The disadvantaged party does not lose its right to request renegotiations simply because it fails to act without undue delay. The delay in making the request may however affect the finding as to whether hardship actually existed and, if so, its consequences for the contract.

3. Grounds for request for renegotiations

Paragraph (1) of this Article also imposes on the disadvantaged party a duty to indicate the grounds on which the request for renegotiations is based, so as to permit the other party better to assess whether or not the request for renegotiations is justified. An incomplete request is to be considered as not being raised in time, unless the grounds of the alleged hardship are so obvious that they need not be spelt out in the request.

但如果合同本身已经包含有自动调整合同的条款（比如合同条款规定某些事件发生时自动的价格指数调整机制），则不允许要求重新谈判。

示例：

　　2. 事实和示例1一样，不同之处在于，合同包含有一个原材料和劳动力成本变化联动的价格指数调整条款。那么，A就没有权利要求对价格进行重新谈判。

然而，即使合同中包含有自动调整条款，但如果该条款没有考虑到引起艰难情形的事件，亦不应该排除以此艰难情形为由要求重新谈判的权利。

示例：

　　3. 事实和示例2一样，不同之处在于，导致A的履行成本激增的原因是Y国通过了新的安全法规。A有权要求B对原来的合同价格进行重新谈判，以使其适应改变后的情况。

2. 重新谈判的要求应当毫不迟延地提出

重新谈判的要求应当在声称的艰难情形发生后尽快提出（第(1)款）。要求重新谈判的确切时间取决于具体情况：比如，如果情况的改变是逐渐的，则提出要求的时间可以长一些（参见第6.2.2条注释3(b)）。

受到不利影响的一方当事人并不会仅仅因为没有毫不迟延地提出重新谈判的要求而丧失该权利，但是迟延提出重新谈判的要求可能会影响到对于艰难情形是否存在的认定及（如果存在）其对合同的影响。

3. 要求重新谈判的理由

本条第(1)款要求受到不利影响的一方当事人在要求重新谈判时必须指明理由，以便另一方当事人能更好地评估该重新谈判的要求是否正当。不完整的要求应当视作未及时提出要求，除非所称的艰难情形的理由非常明显，无须在要求中明确指出。

Failure to set forth the grounds on which the request for renegotiations is based may have similar effects to those resulting from undue delay in making the request (see Comment 2 on this Article).

4. Request for renegotiations and withholding of performance

Paragraph (2) of this Article provides that the request for renegotiations does not of itself entitle the disadvantaged party to withhold performance. The reason for this lies in the exceptional character of hardship and in the risk of possible abuses of the remedy. Withholding performance may be justified only in extraordinary circumstances.

Illustration

4.   A enters into a contract with B for the construction of a plant. The plant is to be built in country X, which adopts new safety regulations after the conclusion of the contract. The new regulations require additional apparatus and thereby fundamentally alter the equilibrium of the contract making A's performance substantially more onerous. A is entitled to request renegotiations and may withhold performance in view of the time it needs to implement the new safety regulations, but it may also withhold the delivery of the additional apparatus, for as long as the corresponding price adaptation is not agreed.

5. Renegotiations in good faith

Although nothing is said in this Article to that effect, both the request for renegotiations by the disadvantaged party and the conduct of both parties during the renegotiation process are subject to the general principle of good faith and fair dealing (see Article 1.7) and to the duty of co-operation (see Article 5.1.3). Thus the disadvantaged party must honestly believe that a case of hardship actually exists and not request renegotiations as a purely tactical manoeuvre. Similarly, once the request has been made, both parties must conduct the renegotiations in a constructive manner, in particular by refraining from any form of obstruction and by providing all the necessary information.

6. Resort to the court upon failure to reach an agreement

If the parties fail to reach agreement on the adaptation of the contract to the changed circumstances within a reasonable time, paragraph (3) of this Article authorises either party to resort to the court. Such a situation may arise either because the non-disadvantaged party completely ignored the request for renegotiations or because the renegotiations,

未指出要求重新谈判的理由，其后果与迟延提出要求的后果相似（参见本条注释2）。

4. 要求重新谈判和暂停履行

本条第(2)款规定，要求重新谈判本身并不赋予受到不利影响的一方当事人暂停履行的权利。之所以这样规定，是因为艰难情形所具有的例外性以及该救济可能被滥用的风险。只有在极端情况下暂停履行才是正当的。

示例：

> 4. A和B签订了一份在X国修建工厂的合同。合同签订后，X国通过了新的安全法规，新法规要求使用额外的设备，从而导致合同均衡发生根本性改变，大幅加重了A的履约负担。A有权要求重新谈判，并可以在执行新法规所需的时间内中止履行；但是，在对相应的价格调整未达成一致意见之前，A还可以暂停交付该额外的设备。

5. 善意地重新谈判

不论是受到不利影响的一方当事人提出重新谈判要求的行为，还是双方当事人重新谈判过程中的行为，都应当遵守诚实信用和公平交易原则（参见第1.7条）和合作义务（参见第5.1.3条），尽管本条对此未作规定。因此，受到不利影响的一方当事人必须诚实地认为艰难情形确实存在，不得将重新谈判纯粹作为一种策略手段。同样地，一旦提出要求，双方当事人就应当以积极的态度进行谈判，特别是，不得制造任何障碍，并提供一切必要信息。

6. 若重新谈判未达成协议，则可诉诸法院

如果双方当事人依改变后的情况在合理的时间内对修改合同未达成一致意见，本条第(3)款规定任何一方当事人均可诉诸法院。出现这种情况的原因既可能是未受到不利影响的一方当事人完全不理睬重新谈判的要求，也可能是尽管双方当事人都善意地进行谈判，但还是

although conducted by both parties in good faith, did not have a positive outcome.

How long a party must wait before resorting to the court will depend on the complexity of the issues to be settled and the particular circumstances of the case.

7. Court measures in case of hardship

According to paragraph (4) of this Article a court which finds that a hardship situation exists may react in a number of different ways.

A first possibility is for it to terminate the contract. However, since termination in this case does not depend on non-performance by one of the parties, its effects on the performances already rendered might be different from those provided for by the rules governing termination in general (see Articles 7.3.1. *et seq.*). Accordingly, paragraph (4)(a) provides that termination shall take place "at a date and on terms to be fixed" by the court.

Another possibility would be for a court to adapt the contract with a view to restoring its equilibrium (paragraph (4)(b)). In so doing the court will seek to make a fair distribution of the losses between the parties. This may or may not, depending on the nature of the hardship, involve a price adaptation. However, if it does, the adaptation will not necessarily reflect in full the loss entailed by the change in circumstances, since the court will, for instance, have to consider the extent to which one of the parties has taken a risk and the extent to which the party entitled to receive a performance may still benefit from that performance.

Paragraph (4) of this Article expressly states that the court may terminate or adapt the contract only when this is reasonable. The circumstances may even be such that neither termination nor adaptation is appropriate and in consequence the only reasonable solution will be for the court either to direct the parties to resume negotiations with a view to reaching agreement on the adaptation of the contract, or to confirm the terms of the contract as they stand.

Illustration

> 5.   A, an exporter, undertakes to supply B, an importer in country X, with beer for three years. Two years after the conclusion of the contract new legislation is introduced in country X prohibiting the sale and consumption of alcoholic drinks. B immediately invokes hardship and requests A to renegotiate the contract. A recognises that hardship has occurred, but refuses to accept the modifications of the contract proposed by B. After one month of fruitless discussions B resorts to the court.

未能取得一个积极的结果。

一方当事人应等待多长时间才能诉诸法院，取决于待解决问题的复杂程度以及个案的具体情况。

7. 存在艰难情形时法院可采取的措施

根据本条第(4)款，法院如果认定存在艰难情形，可能采取多种不同的措施。

第一种可能是终止合同。然而，由于在这种情况下终止合同的根据不是一方当事人不履行合同义务，所以此种终止对已履行部分的效果，可能不同于调整一般性合同终止的规则所规定的效果（参见第7.3.1条及以下条款）。因此，第(4)款(a)项规定，应当按法院"确定的日期和条件"终止合同。

另一种可能是法院对合同的规定加以调整以恢复合同均衡（第(4)款(b)项）。在这种情况下，法院将极力在双方当事人之间公平地分配损失。是否涉及对价格的调整，取决于艰难情形的性质。但是，如果涉及对价格的调整，调整也未必完全反映因情况的变化所导致的损失，因为法院在调整价格时，必须考虑多种因素，如一方当事人承担风险的程度，以及有权接受履行的一方当事人仍然有权从该履行中获得利益的程度。

本条第(4)款明确规定只有在这样做合理的时候，法院才可以终止或修改合同。甚至情况可能表明，不论是终止合同还是修改合同都不合适。从而，法院唯一可采用的合理的解决办法是，要么命令合同当事人继续谈判以对合同的修改达成一致意见，要么维持合同现有条款。

示例：

5. 出口商 A 许诺在三年内向 X 国的进口商 B 供应啤酒。合同订立两年后，X 国通过了新的法规，禁止销售和消费含酒精的饮料。B 立即援引艰难情形并要求 A 对合同重新谈判。A 承认发生了艰难情形，但却拒绝接受 B 提出的修改合同的建议，在经过一个月毫无结果的协商后，B 诉诸法院。

If B has the possibility to sell the beer in a neighbouring country, although at a substantially lower price, the court may decide to uphold the contract but to reduce the agreed price.

If on the contrary B has no such possibility, it may be reasonable for the court to terminate the contract, at the same time however requiring B to pay A for the last consignment still en route.

如果 B 有可能在邻国销售这些啤酒，尽管价格将大幅度下降，那么法院可判决维持合同，并调低原约定的价格。

相反，如果 B 不具有这样的可能性，那么法院终止合同就是合理的，但同时应当要求 B 向 A 支付仍在运输途中的最后一批货物的价款。

CHAPTER 7

NON-PERFORMANCE

SECTION 1: NON-PERFORMANCE IN GENERAL

ARTICLE 7.1.1
(Non-performance defined)

Non-performance is failure by a party to perform any of its obligations under the contract, including defective performance or late performance.

COMMENT

This Article defines "non-performance" for the purpose of the Principles. Particular attention should be drawn to two features of the definition.

The first is that "non-performance" is defined so as to include all forms of defective performance as well as complete failure to perform. Thus, it is non-performance for a builder to erect a building which is partly in accordance with the contract and partly defective or to complete the building late.

The second feature is that for the purposes of the Principles the concept of "non-performance" includes both non-excused and excused non-performance.

Non-performance may be excused by reason of the conduct of the other party to the contract (see Articles 7.1.2 (*Interference by the other party*) and 7.1.3 (*Withholding performance*) and Comments) or because of unexpected external events (see Article 7.1.7 (*Force majeure*) and Comment)). A party is not entitled to claim damages or specific performance for an excused non-performance of the other party but a party who has not received performance will as a rule be entitled to terminate the contract whether or not the non-performance is excused (see Article 7.3.1 *et seq.* and Comment).

第七章

不履行

第一节　不履行的一般规定

第7.1.1条

（不履行的定义）

**不履行是指一方当事人未履行其合同项下的
任何一项义务，包括瑕疵履行和迟延履行。**

注释：

本条是为《通则》之目的对"不履行"下的定义，对此定义有两点
需要特别注意：

首先，"不履行"的定义除包括完全不履行外，还包括各种形式的
瑕疵履行。因此，对于建筑商来说，不履行既可以是指其修建的建筑
物部分符合合同规定而部分有瑕疵的情形，或者也可以是指迟延完成
该建筑义务的情形。

其次，依据《通则》之目的，"不履行"概念的第二个特点是，不
履行既包括不可免责的不履行，也包括可以免责的不履行。

不履行可以因为合同另一方当事人的行为（参见第7.1.2条（另一
方当事人的干预）和第7.1.3条（暂停履行）以及注释），或者不可预见
的外来事件（参见第7.1.7条（不可抗力）及注释）而获得免责。对于
另一方可以免责的不履行，一方当事人无权要求损害赔偿或实际履行，
但原则上，没有得到履行的一方当事人有权终止合同，不论该不履行是
否可以免责（参见第7.3.1条及以下相关条款的规定和注释）。

There is no general provision dealing with cumulation of remedies. The assumption underlying the Principles is that all remedies which are not logically inconsistent may be cumulated. So, in general, a party who successfully insists on performance will not be entitled to damages but there is no reason why a party may not terminate a contract for non-excused non-performance and simultaneously claim damages (see Articles 7.2.5 (*Change of remedy*), 7.3.5 (*Effects of termination in general*) and 7.4.1 (*Right to damages*)).

ARTICLE 7.1.2

(Interference by the other party)

A party may not rely on the non-performance of the other party to the extent that such non-performance was caused by the first party's act or omission or by another event for which the first party bears the risk.

COMMENT

1. Non-performance caused by act or omission of the party alleging non-performance

This Article can be regarded as providing two excuses for non-performance. However conceptually, it goes further than this. When the Article applies, the relevant conduct does not become excused non-performance but loses the quality of non-performance altogether. It follows, for instance, that the other party will not be able to terminate for non-performance.

Two distinct situations are contemplated. In the first, one party is unable to perform either wholly or in part because the other party has done something which makes performance in whole or in part impossible.

Illustration

> 1. A agrees to perform building work on B's land beginning on 1 February. If B locks the gate to the land and does not allow A entry, B cannot complain that A has failed to begin work. B's conduct will often amount to non-excused non-performance either because of an express provision entitling A to access the land or because B's conduct infringes the obligations of good faith and co-operation.

《通则》没有关于累积救济的一般规定。但《通则》一般性地假定所有在逻辑上不矛盾的救济手段均可累积。所以，一般情况下，坚持要求并获得履行的一方当事人无权要求损害赔偿，但是对于不可免责的不履行，如果不允许一方当事人终止合同并同时要求损害赔偿，则是不合理的（参见第7.2.5条（变更救济）、第7.3.5条（终止合同的一般效果）以及第7.4.1条（请求损害赔偿的权利））。

第7.1.2条

（另一方当事人的干预）

如果一方当事人的作为或不作为，或者由其承担风险的其他事件，导致了另一方当事人的不履行，则在此限度内，该方当事人不得依赖另一方当事人的不履行。

注释：

1. 主张不履行一方的作为或不作为导致的不履行

本条可被看做是为不履行提供了两个免责理由，但从概念上说，并不止于此。当适用本条时，相关行为并不是变成可免责的不履行，而是完全失去了不履行的性质。因此，另一方当事人不能以不履行为由终止合同。

本条考虑了两种不同的情况。第一种情况是，一方当事人不能履行其合同义务，完全或部分是因为另一方当事人的作为导致该履行变得完全不可能或部分不可能。

示例：

1. A同意于2月1日在B的土地上开始履行建筑义务，如果B锁上通往该地块的大门而不允许A进入，则B就不能主张A未开始工作。B的行为常常因以下两种理由之一构成不可免责的不履行：合同明确规定A有权进入该土地，或B的行为违反了诚实信用原则和合作义务。但不能工作的结果

This result does not however depend on B's non-performance being non-excused. The result will be the same where B's non-performance is excused, for instance because access to the land is barred by strikers.

The Principles contemplate the possibility that one party's interference result only in a partial impediment to performance by the other party. In such cases it will be necessary to decide the extent to which non-performance was caused by the first party's interference and that to which it was caused by other factors.

2. Non-performance caused by event for which party alleging non-performance bears the risk

Another possibility is that non-performance may result from an event the risk of which is expressly or impliedly allocated by the contract to the party alleging non-performance.

Illustration

2. A, a builder, concludes a construction contract to be performed on the premises of B, who already has many buildings on those premises which are the subject of an insurance policy covering any damage to the buildings. If the parties agree that the risk of accidental damage is to fall on B as the person insured, there would normally be no reason to reject the parties' allocation of risk since risks of this kind are normally covered by insurance. Even therefore if a fire were to be caused by A's negligence, the risk may be allocated to B, although it would clearly need more explicit language to carry this result than would be the case if the fire which destroyed the building were the fault of neither party.

ARTICLE 7.1.3
(Withholding performance)

(1) Where the parties are to perform simultaneously, either party may withhold performance until the other party tenders its performance.

(2) Where the parties are to perform consecutively, the party that is to perform later may withhold its performance until the first party has performed.

并不取决于 B 的不履行不可以免责。即使 B 的不履行是可以免责的，比如因为罢工者阻挡了进入该土地的大门，B 仍不能主张 A 未开始工作。

《通则》考虑到存在如下可能情况，即一方当事人的干预只是部分地阻碍了另一方当事人履行，在这种情况下，有必要确定该一方当事人的干预和其他因素在导致不履行过程中各自发挥作用的程度。

2. 由主张不履行一方承担风险的事项所导致的不履行

另一种情况是，不履行是由某一事件导致的，而合同明示或默示地将该事件的风险分配给由主张不履行一方来承担。

示例：

2. 建筑商 A 与 B 签订了一份在 B 的地基上履行的建筑合同，该地基上已有许多建筑物，而这些建筑物已投保了涵盖任何损害的全险。如果双方约定意外损害风险应当由作为被保险人的 B 承担，则一般没有理由否定双方对风险的这种分配，因为这类风险通常处于承保范围之内。因此，即使是由于 A 的疏忽导致了火灾，该风险也可分配给 B 承担。尽管这种情况下，相对于导致建筑物灭失的火灾非任何一方过错之情况下，要达到这一结果需要使用更加清晰明确的语言作出规定。

第 7.1.3 条

（暂停履行）

（1）当事人各方应同时履行合同义务的，任何一方当事人可在另一方当事人提供履行前暂停履行。

（2）当事人各方应相继履行合同义务的，后履行的一方当事人可在应先履行的一方当事人完成履行之前暂停履行。

COMMENT

This Article must be read together with Article 6.1.4 (*Order of performance*). This Article is concerned with remedies and corresponds in effect to the civil law concept of *exceptio non adimpleti contractus*.

Illustration

> A agrees to sell B a thousand tons of white wheat, payment to be made by confirmed letter of credit opened on a bank from country X. A is not obliged to ship the goods unless and until B opens the letter of credit in conformity with its contractual obligations.

The text does not explicitly address the question which arises where one party performs in part but does not perform completely. In such a case the party entitled to receive performance may be entitled to withhold performance but only where in normal circumstances this is consonant with good faith and fair dealing (see Article 1.7).

ARTICLE 7.1.4
(Cure by non-performing party)

(1) The non-performing party may, at its own expense, cure any non-performance, provided that

(a) without undue delay, it gives notice indicating the proposed manner and timing of the cure;

(b) cure is appropriate in the circumstances;

(c) the aggrieved party has no legitimate interest in refusing cure; and

(d) cure is effected promptly.

(2) The right to cure is not precluded by notice of termination.

(3) Upon effective notice of cure, rights of the aggrieved party that are inconsistent with the non-performing party's performance are suspended until the time for cure has expired.

(4) The aggrieved party may withhold performance pending cure.

注释:

本条应当与第 6.1.4 条(履行顺序)结合起来解释。本条涉及的是救济手段,这实际上与大陆法系关于不履行合同的例外的概念是一致的。

示例:

A 同意向 B 出售 1,000 吨白面,付款以一家 X 国银行开出的保兑信用证用欧元支付。A 在 B 开出符合合同要求的信用证之前,没有义务起运货物。

本条没有对一方当事人只是部分履行而未完全履行的情形作出明确的规定,在这种情况下,有权接受履行的一方当事人将有权暂停履行,但正常情况下必须符合诚实信用和公平交易原则(参见第 1.7 条)。

第 7.1.4 条

(不履行方的补救)

(1) 不履行一方当事人可自己承担费用对其不履行进行补救,但须符合下述条件:

(a) 该方当事人毫不迟延地通知另一方当事人其拟进行补救的方式和时间;

(b) 该补救在具体情况下是适当的;

(c) 受损害方拒绝补救并无合法利益;并且

(d) 补救立即进行。

(2) 补救的权利并不因终止合同的通知被排除。

(3) 在收到有效的补救通知后,受损害方所享有的与不履行方的履行行为不一致的权利应予中止,直至补救期限届满。

(4) 受损害方在补救期间有权暂停履行。

(5) Notwithstanding cure, the aggrieved party retains the right to claim damages for delay as well as for any harm caused or not prevented by the cure.

COMMENT

1. General principle

Paragraph (1) of this Article provides that, if certain conditions are met, the non-performing party may cure by correcting the non-performance. In effect, by meeting these conditions, the non-performing party is able to extend the time for performance for a brief period beyond that stipulated in the contract, unless timely performance is required by the agreement or the circumstances. This Article thus favours the preservation of the contract. It also reflects the policy of minimising economic waste, as incorporated in Article 7.4.8 (*Mitigation of harm*), and the basic principle of good faith stated in Article 1.7. This Article is related to the cure provisions contained in Articles 37 and 48 CISG and in some domestic laws governing contracts and sales. Even many of those legal systems that do not have a rule permitting cure would normally take a reasonable offer of cure into account in assessing damages.

2. Notice of cure

Cure may be effected only after the non-performing party gives notice of cure. The notice must be reasonable with regard to its timing and content as well as to the manner in which it is communicated. Notice of cure must be given without undue delay after the non-performing party learns of the non-performance. To the extent information is then available, the notice must indicate how cure is to be effected and when. Notice must also be communicated to the aggrieved party in a manner that is reasonable in the circumstances.

Notice of cure is considered to be "effective" when the requirements of paragraph (1)(a) - (c) have been met.

3. Appropriateness of cure

Whether cure is appropriate in the circumstances depends on whether it is reasonable, given the nature of the contract, to permit the non-performing party to make another attempt at performance. As indicated in paragraph (2), cure is not precluded merely because the failure to perform amounts to a fundamental non-performance. The factors to be

　　（5）尽管进行了补救，受损害方仍保留对迟
延以及因补救所造成的、或补救未能阻止的损害，
要求损害赔偿的权利。

注释：

1. 一般原则

　　本条第(1)款规定，如果满足特定条件，不履行方可以通过改正其不履行而进行补救。事实上，如果满足了这些条件，除非合同或具体情况要求及时履行，不履行方能够短暂地延长合同规定的履行时间。因此，该条有利于维持合同的存在。本条也反映了第7.4.8条（损害的减轻）所体现的减少经济浪费的方针和第1.7条规定的诚实信用的基本原则。本条的规定与《联合国国际货物销售合同公约》第37条和第48条以及一些规范合同和买卖的国内法对补救所作的规定是相关联的。甚至许多没有补救规则的法律体系在确定损害赔偿时也通常会考虑合理的补救措施。

2. 补救通知

　　补救只有在不履行方作出补救通知后才可实施。作出补救通知的时间、内容以及通信方式必须是合理的。补救通知应当在不履行方得知存在不履行后毫不迟延的作出。在当时所获信息允许的限度内，通知应当表明将如何进行补救，以及何时进行补救。通知还应当以具体情况下合理的方式传达给受损害方。

　　当第(1)款(a)项至(c)项的要求均得到满足时，补救通知被视为"有效"。

3. 补救适当

　　鉴于合同的具体性质，在具体情况下补救是否适当取决于允许不履行方作出再次履行的尝试是否合理。正如本条第(2)款表明，仅因为不履行构成根本不履行这一事实，并不能排除补救。确定补救的适

considered in determining the appropriateness of cure include whether the proposed cure promises to be successful in resolving the problem and whether the necessary or probable delay in effecting cure would be unreasonable or would itself constitute a fundamental non-performance. However, the right to cure is not defeated by the fact that the aggrieved party subsequently changes its position. If the non-performing party gives effective notice of cure, the aggrieved party's right to change position is suspended. Nonetheless, the situation may be different if the aggrieved party has changed position before receiving notice of cure.

4. The aggrieved party's interest

The non-performing party may not cure if the aggrieved party can demonstrate a legitimate interest in refusing cure. However, if notice of cure is properly given and if cure is appropriate in the circumstances, it is presumed that the non-performing party should be permitted to cure. A legitimate interest may arise, for example, if it is likely that, when attempting cure, the non-performing party will cause damage to person or property. On the other hand, a legitimate interest is not present if, on the basis of the non-performance, the aggrieved party has simply decided that it does not wish to continue contractual relations.

Illustration

> 1.   A agrees to construct a road on B's property. When the road is complete, B discovers that the road grade is steeper than the contract permits. B also discovers that, during construction, A's trucks caused damage to B's timber. A gives notice of cure to regrade the road. Even if cure would otherwise be appropriate in the circumstances, B's desire to prevent further damage to the timber may provide a legitimate interest for refusing cure.

5. Timing of cure

Cure must be effected promptly after notice of cure is given. Time is of the essence in the exercise of the right to cure. The non-performing party is not permitted to lock the aggrieved party into an extended waiting period. The lack of inconvenience on the part of the aggrieved party does not justify the non-performing party in delaying cure.

6. Proper forms of cure

Cure may include repair and replacement as well as any other activities that remedy the non-performance and give to the aggrieved party all that it is entitled to expect under the contract. Repairs constitute cure only when they leave no evidence of the prior non-performance

当性时应考虑的因素包括：拟进行的补救是否保证能成功解决问题，以及实施补救必然或可能导致的迟延是否不合理，或者其本身是否构成根本不履行。然而补救的权利不因受损害方随后改变立场而丧失。如果不履行方作了有效的补救通知，受损害方改变立场的权利则被中止。但是，如果受损害方在收到补救通知之前改变立场，情况就不同了。

4. 受损害方的利益

如果受损害方能够证明其对拒绝补救有合法利益，则不履行方不得予以补救。然而，如果已适当地发出补救通知，并且根据具体情况该补救是适当的，则应推定允许不履行方进行补救。有时，受损害方对于拒绝补救具有合法利益，例如，当试图补救时，不履行方可能会对人身或财产造成损害。另一方面，基于不履行，如果受损害方仅仅因为该不履行而不希望继续保持合同关系，则拒绝补救的合法利益就不存在。

示例：

　　1. A 同意在 B 的地产上修建一条道路。当道路修好后，B 发现路的坡度比合同规定的陡，B 还发现在建筑过程中，A 的卡车毁坏了他的树木。A 向 B 发出补救道路坡度的通知。即使根据情况采取补救措施本来是适当的，但 B 不希望对其树木造成进一步的损害的想法能成为拒绝该补救的一种合法利益。

5. 补救时间

补救应当在发出补救通知后及时实施。在行使补救权利时，时间因素是至关重要的。不履行方不能使受损害方陷入持久的等待。迟延补救没有给受损害方造成不便利，并不成为不履行方延迟补救的理由。

6. 补救的适当形式

补救可以包括修理、替换以及其他任何纠正不履行以及赋予受损害方依合同有权期待得到的一切利益的行为。修理只有在完全弥补了

and do not threaten the value or the quality of the product as a whole. It is left to the courts to determine the number of times the non-performing party may attempt a cure.

Illustration

> 2.   A agrees to install an assembly line for high temperature enamel painting in B's factory. The motors are installed with insufficient lubricant and as a result "lock up" after a few hours of operation. A replaces the motors in a timely fashion, but refuses to examine and test the rest of the equipment to ensure that other parts of the line have not been damaged. A has not effectively cured.

7. Suspension of other remedies

When the non-performing party has given effective notice of cure, the aggrieved party may, in accordance with paragraph (4), withhold its own performance but, pursuant to paragraph (3), may not exercise any remedies inconsistent with the non-performing party's right to cure until it becomes clear that a timely and proper cure has not been or will not be effected. Inconsistent remedies include giving notice of termination, entering into replacement transactions and seeking damages or restitution.

8. Effect of a notice of termination

If the aggrieved party has rightfully terminated the contract pursuant to Articles 7.3.1(1) and 7.3.2(1), the effects of termination (see Articles 7.3.5, 7.3.6 and 7.3.7) are also suspended by an effective notice of cure. If the non-performance is cured, the notice of termination is inoperative. On the other hand, termination takes effect if the time for cure has expired and any fundamental non-performance has not been cured.

9. Right of aggrieved party to damages

Under paragraph (5) of this Article, even a non-performing party who successfully cures is liable for any harm that, before cure, was occasioned by the non-performance, as well as for any additional harm caused by the cure itself or by the delay or for any harm which the cure does not prevent. The principle of full compensation for damage suffered, as provided in Article 7.4.2, is fundamental to the Principles.

先前的不履行并且不影响产品整体的价值或质量的情况下才构成补救。不履行方可以尝试补救的次数由法院决定。

示例：

2. A 同意在 B 的工厂里安装一条高温瓷漆绘画生产线。因为发动机在安装时没有足够的润滑剂，结果在运转了数小时后就停机了。A 及时更换了发动机，但却拒绝检查和测试该生产线的其他部分，以确保生产线的其他部件没有遭到损坏。因此，A 没有提供有效的补救。

7. 其他救济措施的中止

当不履行方发出有效的补救通知后，受损害方可以根据第(4)款的规定停止履行其本身的义务，但是根据第(3)款的规定，除非情况表明对方未实施或将不会实施及时的和适当的补救，他不得实施任何与不履行方的补救权利不一致的救济措施。不一致的救济手段包括发出终止合同的通知、达成替代交易以及要求损害赔偿或恢复原状。

8. 终止合同通知的效力

如果受损害方根据第7.3.1条第(1)款和第7.3.2条第(1)款的规定合法地终止了合同，终止合同的效力（参见第7.3.5条、第7.3.6条和第7.3.7条）也因有效的补救通知而中止。如果不履行得到补救，终止合同的通知就不再有效。另一方面，如果补救期限已过，并且任何根本的不履行都没有得到补救，则终止合同的通知生效。

9. 受损害方要求损害赔偿的权利

根据本条第(5)款，即使不履行方已成功补救，仍然要对补救之前不履行导致的任何损害，以及补救本身或迟延履行导致的任何额外损害，或者补救未能阻止的任何损害承担责任。第7.4.2条规定的对所遭受的损害进行全面赔偿是本《通则》的一项基本原则。

10. The aggrieved party's obligations

The decision to invoke this Article rests on the non-performing party. Once the aggrieved party receives effective notice of cure, it must permit cure and, as provided in Article 5.1.3, cooperate with the non-performing party. For example, the aggrieved party must permit any inspection that is reasonably necessary for the non-performing party to effect cure. If the aggrieved party refuses to permit cure when required to do so, any notice of termination is ineffective. Moreover, the aggrieved party may not seek remedies for any non-performance that could have been cured.

Illustration

> 3. A agrees to construct a shed on B's property in order to protect B's machinery from the weather. The roof is constructed in a defective manner. During a storm, water leaks into the shed and B's machinery is damaged. B gives notice of termination. A gives timely notice of cure. B does not wish to deal further with A and refuses the cure. If cure is appropriate in the circumstances and the other conditions for cure are met, B cannot invoke remedies for the faulty construction but can recover for damage caused to the machinery before the cure was to be effected. If cure is inappropriate in the circumstances, or if the proposed cure would not have solved the problem, the contract is terminated by B's notice.

ARTICLE 7.1.5
(Additional period for performance)

(1) In a case of non-performance the aggrieved party may by notice to the other party allow an additional period of time for performance.

(2) During the additional period the aggrieved party may withhold performance of its own reciprocal obligations and may claim damages but may not resort to any other remedy. If it receives notice from the other party that the latter will not perform within that period, or if upon expiry of that period due performance has not been made, the aggrieved party may resort to any of the remedies that may be available under this Chapter.

10. 受损害方的义务

援引本条的决定权在于不履行方。受损害方一旦收到有效的补救通知，就应当允许补救，并应按照第5.1.3条的规定配合不履行方进行补救。比如，受损害方应允许任何对不履行方实施补救来说是合理而必要的检验。在应当进行补救时，如果受损害方拒绝补救，则任何终止合同的通知都将无效。而且，受损害方不得对任何能够得到补救的不履行寻求其他救济。

示例：

> 3. 为保护B的机器不受风吹日晒雨淋，A同意在B的地产上修建一工棚。但因棚顶建筑不合格，在一场暴风雨中，雨水流进了工棚，B的机器被毁。B向A发出终止合同的通知。A及时发出补救通知，但B不愿意再和A继续做交易，因此拒绝补救。如果当时情况下，补救是适当的并且也满足了补救的其他条件，B不能因为A的瑕疵履行而援引其他救济手段，但可对实施补救前机器遭受的损害请求赔偿。如果在当时情况下补救是不适当的，或者采取的补救措施不能解决问题，合同因B的通知而终止。

第7.1.5条

（履行的额外期间）

（1）当出现不履行情况时，受损害方可通知另一方当事人，允许其有一段额外期间履行义务。

（2）在此额外期间内，受损害方可暂停履行其对应的义务，并且可要求损害赔偿，但不得采取任何其他的救济手段。如果受损害方收到另一方当事人在此额外期间内将不会履行的通知，或者，在此额外期间届满时，该另一方当事人仍未完成对其应做的履行，则受损害方可采取本章所规定的任何救济手段。

(3) Where in a case of delay in performance which is not fundamental the aggrieved
party has given notice allowing an additional
period of time of reasonable length, it may
terminate the contract at the end of that period. If
the additional period allowed is not of reasonable
length it shall be extended to a reasonable length.
The aggrieved party may in its notice provide
that if the other party fails to perform within the
period allowed by the notice the contract shall
automatically terminate.

(4) Paragraph (3) does not apply where
the obligation which has not been performed is
only a minor part of the contractual obligation of
the non-performing party.

COMMENT

This Article deals with the situation where one party performs late
and the other party is willing to give extra time for performance. It is
inspired by the German concept of *Nachfrist* although similar results are
obtained by different conceptual means in other legal systems.

1. Special characteristics of late performance

The Article recognises that late performance is significantly different
from other forms of defective performance. Late performance can never
be remedied since once the date for performance has passed it will not
occur again, but nevertheless in many cases the party who is entitled to
performance will much prefer even a late performance to no
performance at all. Secondly, at the moment when a party fails to
perform on time it is often unclear how late performance will in fact be.
The commercial interest of the party receiving performance may often
therefore be that a reasonably speedy completion, although late, will be
perfectly acceptable but that a long delayed completion will not. The
procedure enables that party to give the performing party a second
chance without prejudicing its other remedies.

（3）如延迟履行不属根本不履行，而且受损害方已发出通知，给予不履行方一段合理的额外期间履行其义务，则受损害方在该段期间届满时可终止合同。如果所允许的额外期间的长度不合理，则应延长至合理的长度。受损害方可在其通知中规定，如果另一方当事人在此额外期间内仍不履行其义务，合同应自动终止。

（4）如果未履行的义务只是不履行方合同义务中的一项轻微义务，则本条第(3)款不适用。

注释：

本条调整的情形是一方当事人迟延履行，而另一方当事人愿意给予其一段额外的履行时间。这是受德语"宽限期"概念启发而制定的，尽管其他法律制度中不同的概念也能获得相似的结果。

1. 迟延履行的特性

本条承认迟延履行和其他瑕疵履行是明显不同的。迟延履行是不可以补救的，因为约定的履行日期一过就不会再重现。不过尽管如此，在很多情况下，有权获得履行的一方当事人还是愿意获得迟延履行，而不是根本不履行。其次，在一方当事人不能按时履行时，往往很难弄清履行的迟延程度究竟如何。因此，接受履行的一方当事人的商业利益通常是合理快速地完成履行，尽管有所迟延，也是可以接受的；但如果延误太长，则是不可接受的。这个程序使得一方当事人在不损害自己请求其他救济的情况下，给予履行方第二次履行的机会。

2. Effects of granting extension of time for performance

The party who grants the extension of time cannot terminate or seek specific performance during the extension time. The right to recover damages arising from late performance is not affected.

The position at the end of the period of extension depends on whether the late performance was already fundamental at the time when the extension was granted. In this situation, if the contract is not completely performed during the extension, the right to terminate for fundamental non-performance simply springs into life again as soon as the extension period expires. On the other hand, if the late performance was not yet fundamental, termination would only be possible at the end of the period of extension if the extension was reasonable in length.

Illustrations

1.   A agrees to construct a special bullet-proof body for B's Mercedes. The contract provides that the body is to be finished by 1 February so that the car can be shipped to B's country of residence. On 31 January the car is needed but not yet quite finished. A assures B that it will be able to complete the work if given another week and B agrees to a week's extension of time. If the car is finished within the week B must accept it but may recover any damages, for example extra shipping charges. If the work is not finished within the week, B may refuse to accept delivery and terminate the contract.

2.   A, a company in country X, concludes a contract with B, a company in country Y, to build 100 km. of motorway in the latter country. The contract provides that the motorway will be finished within two years from the start of the work. After two years, A has in fact built 85 km. and it is clear that it will take at least three more months to finish the motorway. B gives A notice to complete within a further month. B is not entitled to terminate at the end of the month because the additional period of time is not reasonable; it shall be extended to the reasonable period of three months.

2. 准予延长履行时间的效果

准予延长履行时间的一方当事人在延长期内不能终止合同或要求实际履行。但就迟延履行请求损害赔偿的权利不受影响。

延长期结束时的情况取决于在准予延长时延迟履行是否已是根本性的。如果是根本性的迟延履行，并且在延长期内合同没有得到完全履行，在延长期届满时，对根本性不履行的终止合同的权利自然恢复。另一方面，如果迟延履行不是根本性的，如果延长期是合理的，则只有延长期结束时才可能终止合同。

示例：

1. A 同意为 B 的奔驰汽车制造一种特殊的防弹体。合同规定该防弹体必须在 2 月 1 日前完成，以便汽车能够装船运往 B 的住所地。1 月 31 日，该汽车就应当就绪，但此时防弹体却还未完全装好。A 向 B 保证若再多给一个星期就能完成工作，B 同意了 A 的要求。在这种情况下，如果 A 在一个星期内完成了工作，则 B 必须接受，但他可以要求损害赔偿，比如因迟延而导致的额外的运费；如果 A 在一个星期内没有完成工作，则 B 可以拒绝接受交货并终止合同。

2. X 国的 A 公司与 Y 国的 B 公司签订了一份合同，约定 A 在 Y 国为 B 修建一条 100 公里的汽车高速公路。合同规定该高速路必须在开始工作后的两年内完成。两年过后，A 事实上只完成了 85 公里，并且很明显至少还需要三个月才能全部完成。B 通知 A 将给予一个月的宽限期，在一个月结束后 B 没有权利终止合同，因为一个月的宽限期是不合理的，该期间应当延长至三个月的合理期间。

A clause which limits or excludes one party's liability for non-performance or which permits one party to render performance substantially different from what the other party reasonably expected may not be invoked if it would be grossly unfair to do so, having regard to the purpose of the contract.

COMMENT

1. The need for a special rule on exemption clauses

The Principles contain no general rule permitting a court to strike down abusive or unconscionable contract terms. Apart from the principle of good faith and fair dealing (see Article 1.7) which may exceptionally be invoked in this respect, there is only one provision permitting the avoidance at any time of the contract as a whole as well as of any of its individual terms when they unjustifiably give one party an excessive advantage (see Article 3.2.7).

The reason for the inclusion of a specific provision on exemption clauses is that they are particularly common in international contract practice and tend to give rise to much controversy between the parties.

Ultimately, this Article has opted in favour of a rule which gives the court a broad discretionary power based on the principle of fairness. Terms regulating the consequences of non-performance are in principle valid but the court may ignore clauses which are grossly unfair.

2. "Exemption clauses" defined

For the purpose of this Article exemption clauses are in the first instance those terms which directly limit or exclude the non-performing party's liability in the event of non-performance. Such clauses may be expressed in different ways (e.g. fixed sum, ceiling, percentage of the performance in question, deposit retained).

Exemption clauses are further considered to be those which permit a party to render a performance substantially different from what the other party reasonably expected. In practice clauses of this kind are in particular those the purpose or effect of which is to allow the performing party unilaterally to alter the character of the performance

第 7.1.6 条

（免责条款）

若一项条款限制或排除一方当事人对不履行合同义务的责任，或者允许一方当事人的履行可与另一方当事人的合理期待有实质差异，则在考虑到合同的目的的情况下，如援引该条款明显不公平，则不得援引该条款。

注释：

1. 免责条款的特殊规则的必要性

本《通则》未规定允许法院否决滥用性和显失公平的合同条款的一般规则。关于这个问题，除可以例外地援引诚实信用和公平交易原则（参见第 1.7 条）外，只有一个条款（第 3.2.7 条），即当合同或合同的个别条款不合理地给予一方当事人过分利益时，允许在任何时间宣布整个合同或合同部分条款无效。

本《通则》对免责条款作出专门规定的原因是，免责条款在国际合同实践中相当普遍，并容易引起合同当事人之间的争议。

最后，本条选择了规定一项规则，赋予法院在公平原则的基础上行使更广泛的自由裁量权，即：调整不履行后果的合同条款原则上是有效的，但法院可以不考虑明显不公平的条款。

2. 对"免责条款"的界定

为本条的目的，免责条款首先是指那些直接限制或排除不履行方在不履行情况下的责任的条款。这种条款可以用不同方式表达（比如固定的金额、最高限额、有关履行的比例、扣留保证金）。

免责条款还指那些允许一方当事人提供的履行与另一方当事人的合理期待有实质差异的条款。实践中这类条款尤其表现为其目的或作用在于允许履行方单方面改变约定的履行的性质以至于变更合同的条

promised in such a way as to transform the contract. Such clauses are to be distinguished from those which are limited to defining the performance undertaken by the party in question.

Illustrations

1. A tour operator offers at a high price a tour providing for accommodation in specifically designated luxury hotels. A term of the contract provides that the operator may alter the accommodation if the circumstances so require. If the operator puts up its clients in second class hotels, it will be liable to them notwithstanding the contractual term since the clients expected to be accommodated in hotels of a category similar to that which had been promised.

2. A hotelkeeper exhibits a notice to the effect that the hotel is responsible for cars left in the garage but not for objects contained in the cars. This term is not an exemption clause for the purpose of this Article since its purpose is merely that of defining the scope of the hotelkeeper's obligation.

3. Exemption clauses to be distinguished from forfeiture clauses

Exemption clauses are to be distinguished from forfeiture clauses which permit a party to withdraw from a contract on payment of an indemnity. In practice, however, there may be forfeiture clauses which are in reality intended by the parties to operate as disguised exemption clauses.

4. Exemption clauses and agreed payment for non-performance

A contract term providing that a party who does not perform is to pay a specified sum to the aggrieved party for such non-performance (see Article 7.4.13) may also have the effect of limiting the compensation due to the aggrieved party. In such cases the non-performing party may not be entitled to rely on the term in question if the conditions laid down in this Article are satisfied.

Illustration

3. A enters into a contract with B for the building of a factory. The contract contains a penalty clause providing for payment of Australian dollars (AUD) 10,000 for each week of delay. The work is not completed within the agreed period because A deliberately suspends the work for another project which was more lucrative for it and in respect of which the penalty for delay was higher. The actual harm suffered by B as a result of the delay amounts to AUD

款。这些条款应与其效果仅限于对有关当事人承担的履行义务加以界定的条款相区别。

示例：

1. 一个旅游经营人提供一种在特别指定的头等豪华宾馆里住宿的高价旅游服务。合同的一项条款规定如果情况需要，该经营人可以改变住宿地。如果该经营人把客人安排在一个次等的宾馆住宿，尽管存在上述合同条款，其仍要对顾客们承担责任，因为顾客们希望住在与允诺的住宿条件相似的饭店里。

2. 某一饭店的管理者发布一通知，说明饭店只对停在车库里的汽车承担责任，对汽车里的物品不负责任。因为该通知的目的只是界定饭店管理者的责任范围，该规定并不是本条意义上的免责条款。

3. 免责条款区别于没收条款

免责条款与允许一方当事人支付赔偿金后退出合同的条款，即没收条款是有区别的。然而，在实践中也可能出现这种情况，即双方当事人的真实意图是将没收条款以免责条款的形式呈现。

4. 免责条款与对不履行的约定支付

规定不履行方应就该不履行向受损害方支付确定数额款项（参见第7.4.13条）的合同条款，也可能具有限制受损害方获得赔偿的效果。在这种情况下，如果本条规定的条件得到满足时，则不履行方无权依赖该合同条款。

示例：

3. A与B签订了一份建造工厂的合同，合同包含一罚金条款，规定每延误一星期支付10,000澳元。工厂在约定的时间内没有建成，因为A为建筑另一个利润更大且迟延罚金更高的工程而故意暂停了该工厂的建造。B因迟延遭受的实际损失是每星期20,000澳元。在这种情况下，A无权依赖合

20,000 per week. A is not entitled to rely on the penalty clause and B may recover full compensation of the actual harm sustained, as the enforcement of that clause would in the circumstances be grossly unfair in view of A's deliberate non-performance.

5. Cases where exemption clauses may not be relied upon

Following the approach adopted in most national legal systems, this Article starts out from the assumption that in application of the doctrine of freedom of contract (see Article 1.1) exemption clauses are in principle valid. A party may not however invoke such a clause if it would be grossly unfair to do so.

This will above all be the case where the term is inherently unfair and its application would lead to an evident imbalance between the performances of the parties. Moreover, there may be circumstances in which even a term that is not in itself manifestly unfair may not be relied upon: for instance, where the non-performance is the result of grossly negligent conduct or where the aggrieved party could not have obviated the consequences of the limitation or exclusion of liability by taking out appropriate insurance.

In all cases regard must be had to the purpose of the contract and in particular to what a party could legitimately have expected from the performance of the contract.

Illustrations

4.   A, an accountant, undertakes to prepare B's accounts. The contract contains a term excluding any liability of A for the consequences arising from any inaccuracy whatsoever in A's performance of the contract. As a result of a serious mistake by A, B pays 100% more taxes than were due. A may not rely on the exemption clause which is inherently unfair.

5.   A, a warehouse operator, enters into a contract with B for the surveillance of its premises. The contract contains a term limiting B's liability. Thefts occur in the terminal resulting in loss exceeding the amount of the limitation. Although the term, agreed upon by two professional parties, is not inherently unfair, it may not be relied upon by B if the thefts were committed by B's servants in the course of their employment.

同约定的罚金条款，B 可以要求 A 全额赔偿其所遭受的实际损失，因为考虑到 A 的故意不履行行为，在这种情况下执行罚金条款将明显不公平。

5. 不得依赖免责条款的情形

根据大多数国内法律制度所采用的做法，本条首先假定适用合同自由原则（参见第 1.1 条），免责条款在原则上是有效的。但是，如果援引免责条款明显不公平，则一方当事人就不能援引。

首先一种情况是，免责条款本身就是不公平的，并且其适用会导致双方当事人之间的履行明显失衡。其次，在有些情况下，即使免责条款本身并不存在明显的不公平，也不得依赖该条款：比如，不履行是严重疏忽所导致，或者受损害方通过适当的保险仍不能消除因限制或排除责任而产生的后果。

在所有情况下都应当考虑合同的目的，尤其应考虑一方当事人从履行合同中所能合法期待的利益。

示例：

> 4. 会计师 A 承担为 B 整理账目的义务。合同中有一条规定，A 对履行合同中的任何不准确所导致的后果均不承担责任。由于 A 的一个严重错误，B 多支付了 100% 的税款。A 不得依赖这条本身就不公平的免责条款。

> 5. 货栈经营者 A 与 B 签订了一份看管场地的合同。合同中包含一个限制 B 责任的条款。后来发生了盗窃行为，造成的损失超过了 B 的责任限额。尽管专业的双方约定的免责条款本身并不是不公平的，但如果盗窃行为是由 B 的雇员在履行职务过程中实施的，B 亦不得依赖该免责条款。

6. Consequence of inability to rely on exemption clauses

If a party is not entitled to rely on an exemption clause, its liability is unaffected and the aggrieved party may obtain full compensation for the non-performance. Contrary to the rule laid down with respect to agreed payment for non-performance in Article 7.4.13, the court has no power to modify the exemption clause.

ARTICLE 7.1.7

(Force majeure)

(1) Non-performance by a party is excused if that party proves that the non-performance was due to an impediment beyond its control and that it could not reasonably be expected to have taken the impediment into account at the time of the conclusion of the contract or to have avoided or overcome it or its consequences.

(2) When the impediment is only temporary, the excuse shall have effect for such period as is reasonable having regard to the effect of the impediment on the performance of the contract.

(3) The party who fails to perform must give notice to the other party of the impediment and its effect on its ability to perform. If the notice is not received by the other party within a reasonable time after the party who fails to perform knew or ought to have known of the impediment, it is liable for damages resulting from such non-receipt.

(4) Nothing in this Article prevents a party from exercising a right to terminate the contract or to withhold performance or request interest on money due.

COMMENT

1. The notion of force majeure

This Article covers the ground covered in common law systems by the doctrines of frustration and impossibility of performance and in civil law systems by doctrines such as force majeure, *Unmöglichkeit,*

6. 不能依赖免责条款的后果

如果一方当事人无权依赖免责条款，他所承担的责任不受影响，受损害方可以就不履行导致的损失获得全部赔偿。与第 7.4.13 条规定的关于对不履行的约定付款的规则相反，法院没有权力修改免责条款。

第 7.1.7 条

（不可抗力）

（1）若不履行的一方当事人证明，其不履行是由于非他所能控制的障碍所致，而且在合同订立之时该方当事人无法合理地预见该障碍，或者不能合理地避免或克服该障碍或其后果，则不履行方应予免责。

（2）若障碍只是暂时的，则在考虑到该障碍对合同履行影响的情况下，免责只在一段合理的期间内具有效力。

（3）未能履行义务的一方当事人必须将障碍及其对履约能力的影响通知另一方当事人。若另一方当事人在未履行方知道或应当知道该障碍后的一段合理时间内没有收到该通知，则未履行方应对另一方当事人因未收到该通知而导致的损害，负赔偿责任。

（4）本条并不妨碍一方当事人行使终止合同、暂停履行或对到期应付款项要求支付利息的权利。

注释：

1. 不可抗力的概念

本条涵盖了普通法系的目的落空、履行不可能以及大陆法系的不可抗力、履行不能等原则所涵盖的事由，但它和这些概念中的任何一

etc. but it is identical with none of these doctrines. The term "force majeure" was chosen because it is widely known in international trade practice, as confirmed by the inclusion in many international contracts of so-called "force majeure" clauses.

Illustration

1. A, a manufacturer in country X, sells a nuclear power station to B, a utility company in country Y. Under the terms of the contract A undertakes to supply all the power station's requirements of uranium for ten years at a price fixed for that period, expressed in US dollars and payable in New York. The following separate events occur:

(1) After five years the currency of country Y collapses to 1% of its value against the dollar at the time of the contract. B is not discharged from liability as the parties have allocated this risk by the payment provisions.

(2) After five years the Government of country Y imposes foreign exchange controls which prevent B paying in any currency other than that of country Y. B is excused from paying in US dollars. A is entitled to terminate the contract to supply uranium.

(3) After five years the world uranium market is cornered by a group of speculators. The price of uranium on the world market rises to ten times the contract figure. A is not excused from delivering uranium as this is a risk which was foreseeable at the time of making the contract.

2. Effects of force majeure on the rights and duties of the parties

The Article does not restrict the rights of the party who has not received performance to terminate if the non-performance is fundamental. What it does do, where it applies, is to excuse the non-performing party from liability in damages.

In some cases the impediment will prevent any performance at all but in many others it will simply delay performance and the effect of the Article will be to give extra time for performance. It should be noted that in this event the extra time may be greater (or less) than the length of the interruption because the crucial question will be what is the effect of the interruption on the progress of the contract.

Illustration

2. A contracts to lay a natural gas pipeline across country X. Climatic conditions are such that it is normally impossible to work between 1 November and 31 March. The contract is timed to finish on 31 October but the start of work is delayed for a month by a civil war in a neighbouring country which makes it impossible to bring in all the piping on time. If the consequence is reasonably to prevent

个都不完全相同。之所以选择"不可抗力"这个术语，是因为该术语在国际贸易实践中得到了广泛的认可，许多国际合同中都包含有一条所谓的"不可抗力"条款即证明了这一点。

示例：

1. X 国的制造商 A 将一座核电站卖给 Y 国的公共事业公司 B。根据合同规定，A 应当在今后的十年内以固定价格提供核电站所需的铀，计价货币为美元，付款地为纽约。随之发生了下列相互独立的事件：

（1）五年后，Y 国货币与美元的比价跌至订立合同时的 1%。在这种情况下，B 不能免责，因为根据付款规定当事人已对承担这种风险的责任进行了分配。

（2）五年后，Y 国实施外汇管制，B 只能以 Y 国货币进行付款。在这种情况下，B 可以免除用美元进行付款的义务，而 A 有权终止合同，不再向 B 供应铀。

（3）五年后，世界铀市场被一个投机集团所垄断，因此，世界市场铀的价格比订立合同时上涨了十倍。在这种情况下，A 不能免除供应铀的义务，因为该风险在订立合同时是可以预见的。

2. 不可抗力对合同当事人权利义务的影响

如果不履行是根本性的，本条并不限制没有得到履行的一方当事人终止合同的权利。本条规定的目的是，在适用本条时，免除不履行方的损害赔偿责任。

在有些情况下，不可抗力的障碍会从根本上阻止履行；但在许多其他情况下，它会迟延履行，本条的效果只是提供一段额外的履行时间。值得注意的是，在这种情况下给予的额外时间可能比中断的时间长（或短），因为此时关键的问题在于中断对于合同履行进程的影响如何。

示例：

2. A 承担铺设一条经过 X 国的天然气管道的义务。根据天气情况，在 11 月 1 日到 3 月 31 日之间通常无法开展工作。合同约定的完工时间是 10 月 31 日，但因为邻国发生内战，开工延迟了一个月，使得将所有管道运往 Y 国成为不可能。

the completion of the work until its resumption in the following spring, A may be entitled to an extension of five months even though the delay was itself of one month only.

3. Force majeure and hardship

This Article must be read together with Chapter 6, Section 2 of the Principles dealing with hardship (see Comment 6 on Article 6.2.2).

4. Force majeure and contract practice

The definition of force majeure in paragraph (1) of this Article is necessarily of a rather general character. International commercial contracts often contain much more precise and elaborate provisions in this regard. The parties may therefore find it appropriate to adapt the content of this Article so as to take account of the particular features of the specific transaction.

如果这种结果合理地阻碍了工程按时完工，直到来年春天才
能复工。在这种情况下，尽管只迟延开工一个月，A 也有权
将完工期限延长五个月。

3. 不可抗力和艰难情形

本条应当与《通则》第六章第二节关于艰难情形的规定结合起来解
释（参见第 6. 2. 2 条的注释 6）。

4. 不可抗力和合同实践

本条第(1)款对不可抗力的定义不免相当抽象。国际商事合同往往
对不可抗力做了更加精确和详细的规定。因此合同当事人可能会发现，
根据特定交易的特殊情况对本条的规定加以修改是适当的。

SECTION 2: RIGHT TO PERFORMANCE

ARTICLE 7.2.1
(Performance of monetary obligation)

Where a party who is obliged to pay money does not do so, the other party may require payment.

COMMENT

This Article reflects the generally accepted principle that payment of money which is due under a contractual obligation can always be demanded and, if the demand is not met, enforced by legal action before a court. The term "require" is used in this Article to cover both the demand addressed to the other party and the enforcement, whenever necessary, of such a demand by a court.

The Article applies irrespective of the currency in which payment is due or may be made. In other words, the right of the obligee to require payment extends also to cases of payment in a foreign currency. For the determination of the currency in which a monetary obligation is due or payment may be made, see Articles 6.1.9, 6.1.10 and 7.4.12.

Exceptionally, the right to require payment of the price of the goods or services to be delivered or rendered may be excluded. This is in particular the case where a usage requires a seller to resell goods which are neither accepted nor paid for by the buyer. For the applicability of usages, see Article 1.9.

ARTICLE 7.2.2
(Performance of non-monetary obligation)

Where a party who owes an obligation other than one to pay money does not perform, the other party may require performance, unless

    (a) performance is impossible in law or in fact;

    (b) performance or, where relevant, enforcement is unreasonably burdensome or expensive;

第二节　要求履行的权利

第7.2.1条

（金钱债务的履行）

如果有义务付款的一方当事人未履行其付款义务，则另一方当事人可以要求付款。

注释：

本条反映了一项被普遍接受的原则：合同项下应支付的款项总是能够被要求履行的，如果此要求没有得到满足，可向法院提起诉讼要求强制履行。本条中的"要求"一词既指一方当事人向另一方当事人提出的要求，又指必要时法院对这一要求作出的强制执行。

本条的适用与表示支付义务或者支付款项所用的货币的种类如何无关。换句话说，债权人要求付款的权利也延伸至以外国货币支付的情况。关于金钱债务以何种货币表示或支付，参见第6.1.9条、第6.1.10条和第7.4.12条的规定。

要求对交付的货物或提供的服务支付价款的权利在例外情况下可以被排除。这种例外尤其见于惯例要求卖方重新出卖买方既不接受又不为此付款的货物的情况。惯例的适用参见第1.9条。

第7.2.2条

（非金钱债务的履行）

如果一方当事人未履行其应履行的非金钱支付的义务，则另一方当事人可要求履行，除非：

（a）履行在法律上或事实上不可能；

（b）履行或相关的执行带来不合理的负担或费用；

(c) the party entitled to performance may reasonably obtain performance from another source;

(d) performance is of an exclusively personal character; or

(e) the party entitled to performance does not require performance within a reasonable time after it has, or ought to have, become aware of the non-performance.

COMMENT

1. Right to require performance of non-monetary obligations

In accordance with the general principle of the binding character of the contract (see Article 1.3), each party should as a rule be entitled to require performance by the other party not only of monetary, but also of non-monetary obligations, assumed by that party. While this is not controversial in civil law countries, common law systems allow enforcement of non-monetary obligations only in special circumstances.

Following the basic approach of CISG (Article 46) this Article adopts the principle of specific performance, subject to certain qualifications.

The principle is particularly important with respect to contracts other than sales contracts. Unlike the obligation to deliver something, contractual obligations to do something or to abstain from doing something can often be performed only by the other contracting party itself. In such cases the only way of obtaining performance from a party who is unwilling to perform is by enforcement.

2. Remedy not discretionary

While CISG provides that "a court is not bound to enter a judgement for specific performance unless the court would do so under its own law in respect of similar contracts of sale not governed by [the] Convention" (Article 28), under the Principles specific performance is not a discretionary remedy, i.e. a court must order performance, unless one of the exceptions laid down in this Article applies.

3. Exceptions to the right to require performance

a. *Impossibility*

A performance which is impossible in law or in fact, cannot be required (sub-paragraph (a)). However, impossibility does not nullify a （c）有权要求履行的一方当事人可以合理地从其他渠道获得履行；

　　（d）履行完全属于人身性质；或者

　　（e）有权要求履行的一方当事人在已经知道或应当知道该不履行后的一段合理时间内未要求履行。

注释：

1. 要求履行非金钱债务的权利

　　根据合同具有约束力的一般原则（参见第 1.3 条），原则上，各方当事人不仅有权要求另一方当事人履行其承担的金钱债务，而且有权要求其履行非金钱债务。这在大陆法系国家是没有争议的，但普通法系国家则只在特殊情况下才允许对非金钱债务强制执行。

　　沿用《联合国国际货物销售合同公约》（第 46 条）的基本原则，本条采用了受一定限制的实际履行原则。

　　该原则对货物销售合同以外的其他合同尤其重要。与交付某种物品的合同义务不同，做某事或不做某事的合同义务往往只能由另一方合同当事人自己来履行。在这种情况下，从不愿履行义务的一方当事人获得履行的唯一途径是强制执行。

2. 非自由裁量性的救济

　　《联合国国际货物销售合同公约》规定"法院没有义务作出要求实际履行的判决，除非法院依照其本身的法律对不属于本公约范围内的类似的销售合同愿意这样做"（第 28 条），但根据本《通则》，实际履行不是一种自由裁量性的救济，即法院必须裁定实际履行，除非存在本条规定的例外情形。

3. 要求履行权的例外情况

　　a. 不可能

　　在法律上或在事实上不可能的履行不能被要求实际履行（本条（a）项）。但是，履行不可能并不使合同无效，受损害方可以采用其他救济

contract: other remedies may be available to the aggrieved party (see Articles 3.1.3 and 7.1.7(4)).

The refusal of a public permission which is required under the applicable domestic law and which affects the validity of the contract renders the contract void (see Article 6.1.17(1)), with the consequence that the problem of enforceability of the performance cannot arise. When, however, the refusal merely renders the performance impossible without affecting the validity of the contract (see Article 6.1.17(2)), sub-paragraph (a) of this Article applies and performance cannot be required.

b. *Unreasonable burden*

In exceptional cases, particularly when there has been a drastic change of circumstances after the conclusion of a contract, performance, although still possible, may have become so onerous that it would run counter to the general principle of good faith and fair dealing (see Article 1.7) to require it.

Illustration

1. An oil tanker has sunk in coastal waters in a heavy storm. Although it would be possible to lift the ship from the bottom of the sea, the shipper may not require performance of the contract of carriage if this would involve the shipowner in expense vastly exceeding the value of the oil (see Article 7.2.2(b)).

The words "where relevant, enforcement" take account of the fact that in common law systems it is the courts and not the obligees who supervise the execution of orders for specific performance. As a consequence, in certain cases, especially those involving performances extended in time, courts in those countries refuse specific performance if supervision would impose undue burdens upon courts.

As to other possible consequences arising from drastic changes of circumstances amounting to a case of hardship, see Articles 6.2.1 *et seq.*

c. *Replacement transaction*

Many goods and services are of a standard kind, i.e. the same goods or services are offered by many suppliers. If a contract for such staple goods or standard services is not performed, most customers will not wish to waste time and effort extracting the contractual performance from the other party. Instead, they will go into the market, obtain substitute goods or services and claim damages for non-performance. In view of this economic reality sub-paragraph (c) excludes specific performance whenever the party entitled to performance may reasonably

手段（参见第3.1.3条和第7.1.7条第(4)款）。

如果所适用的国内法要求的并且影响合同效力的公共许可遭到拒绝，会导致合同无效（参见第6.1.17条第(1)款），其结果是不会产生强制履行的问题。然而，如果拒绝许可仅使得履行变得不可能，而没有影响到合同的效力（参见第6.1.17条第(2)款），则将适用本条(a)项的规定，不能要求实际履行。

b. 不合理的负担

在例外情况下，尤其是合同订立后情况发生了重大变化，尽管履行仍然可能，但却会使履行方的负担过重，以致要求实际履行将违背诚实信用和公平交易的一般原则（参见第1.7条）。

示例：

1. 一艘油轮在一场暴风雨中沉入海中，尽管将该油轮从海底打捞起来是可能的，但是如果油轮所有人因此支出的费用大大超过了所运石油的价值，托运人不能要求其实际履行运输合同（参见第7.2.2条(b)项）。

"相关的执行"一词考虑到这样的情况，即在普通法系中，由法院而非债权人监督实际履行命令的执行情况。因此，在某些情况下，尤其是在那些涉及漫长履行时间的情况下，如果监督会给法院造成过分的负担，这些国家的法院将拒绝实际履行。

至于构成艰难情形的情况剧烈变化所可能导致的其他后果，参见第6.2.1条的有关规定。

c. 替代交易

许多货物和服务都属于标准类型，也就是说，同样的货物和服务有许多供应商提供。如果有关这类常用货物或标准服务的合同没有得到履行，大多数客户都不愿意浪费时间和精力去要求另一方当事人履行合同，而更愿到市场上去获得替代货物或服务，并对另一方当事人的不履行要求损害赔偿。出于这种经济现实的考虑，当有权获得履行的一方当事人可以通过另一渠道合理地得到履行时，本条(c)项排除了

obtain performance from another source. That party may terminate the contract and conclude a replacement transaction (see Article 7.4.5).

The word "reasonably" indicates that the mere fact that the same performance can be obtained from another source is not in itself sufficient, since the aggrieved party could not in certain circumstances reasonably be expected to have recourse to an alternative supplier.

Illustration

2. A, situated in a developing country where foreign exchange is scarce, buys a machine of a standard type from B, a manufacturer situated in country X, a developed country. In compliance with the contract, A pays the price of USD 100,000 before delivery. B does not deliver. Although A could obtain the machine from another source in country X, it would be unreasonable, in view of the scarcity and high price of foreign exchange in its home country, to require A to take this course. A is therefore entitled to require delivery of the machine from B.

d. Performance of an exclusively personal character

Where performance has an exclusively personal character, enforcement would interfere with the personal freedom of the obligor. Moreover, enforcement of performance often impairs its quality. The supervision of a very personal performance may also give rise to insuperable practical difficulties, as is shown by the experience of countries which have saddled their courts with this kind of responsibility. For all these reasons, sub-paragraph (d) excludes enforcement of performance of an exclusively personal character.

The precise scope of this exception depends essentially upon the meaning of the phrase "exclusively personal character". The modern tendency is to confine this concept to performances of a unique character. The exception does not apply to obligations undertaken by a company. Nor are ordinary activities of a lawyer, a surgeon or an engineer covered by the phrase for they can be performed by other persons with the same training and experience. A performance is of an exclusively personal character if it is not delegable and requires individual skills of an artistic or scientific nature or if it involves a confidential and personal relationship.

实际履行。该方当事人可以终止合同并达成替代交易（参见第7.4.5条）。

"合理地"一词表明，能够从其他渠道获得相同履行的事实本身是不充分的，因为在某些情况下，期望受损害方求助于某个替代供应者，是不合理的。

示例：

> 2. A是位于一个外汇短缺的发展中国家的公司，它向位于X国的制造商B购买了一台标准型号的机器。根据合同，在交货前A向B支付了100,000美元，而B没有交货。尽管A可以从X国的其他销售商获得该机器，但鉴于A所在国外汇短缺和需要高价兑换，要求A从其他销售商获得机器是不合理的。在这种情况下，A有权要求B交付机器。

d. 完全属人身性质的履行

如果履行具有一种完全的人身性质，强制执行将妨碍债务人的人身自由。另外，强制执行往往会损害履行的质量。正如使法院承担此类责任的那些国家的实践所显示的那样，对具有完全人身性质的履行的监督也会带来难以克服的实际困难。基于这些原因，本条(d)项排除了对完全属人身性质履行的强制执行。

这种例外的确切范围本质上取决于"完全属于人身性质"一词的含义。现在的趋势是将该概念限定于具有独特性质的履行。这种例外不适用于公司承担的义务，也不涉及律师、医生或工程师的一般行为，因为这些行为可以由获得同样培训和具有相同经验的其他人履行。如果一种履行是不可委托的，并且需要艺术性或科学性的个人技能，或者涉及到保密性和私人性的关系，就属于具有完全人身性质的履行。

Illustrations

> 3. An undertaking by a firm of architects to design a row of ten buildings can be specifically enforced as the firm can delegate the task to one of the partners or employ an outside architect to perform it.
>
> 4. By contrast, an undertaking by a world-famous architect to design a new city hall embodying the idea of a city of the 21st century cannot be enforced because it is highly unique and calls for the exercise of very special skills.

The performance of obligations to abstain from doing something does not fall under sub-paragraph (d).

e. *Request within reasonable time*

Performance of a contract often requires special preparation and efforts by the obligor. If the time for performance has passed but the obligee has failed to demand performance within a reasonable time, the obligor may be entitled to assume that the obligee will not insist upon performance. If the obligee were to be allowed to leave the obligor in a state of uncertainty as to whether performance will be required, the risk might arise of the obligee's speculating unfairly, to the detriment of the obligor, upon a favourable development of the market.

For these reasons sub-paragraph (e) excludes the right to performance if it is not required within a reasonable time after the obligee has become, or ought to have become, aware of the non-performance.

For a similar rule concerning the loss of the right to terminate the contract, see Article 7.3.2(2).

ARTICLE 7.2.3
(Repair and replacement of defective performance)

The right to performance includes in appropriate cases the right to require repair, replacement, or other cure of defective performance. The provisions of Articles 7.2.1 and 7.2.2 apply accordingly.

示例：

　　3. 一个建筑师行承担的一项设计10座建筑的义务是明显能够得到强制执行的，因为它可以将该义务委托给自己的一个合作伙伴，或者雇用外部建筑师完成该设计。

　　4. 相反，由一个世界著名建筑师承担的一项体现21世纪城市构想的新市政厅的设计则不能得到强制执行，因为它具有较高的独特性，并要求该建筑师发挥非常特殊的技能。

不作为义务的履行不适用本条(d)项的规定。

e. 在合理的时间内要求履行

履行合同义务经常需要债务人进行特定的准备和努力。如果履行期限已过，并且债权人未在合理的时间内要求履行，债务人有权推定债权人不再坚持履行。如果允许债权人把债务人置于一种对是否要求履行的不确定状态之中，从有益于市场发展的角度看，债权人这种投机性的行为将会不公平地产生不利于债务人的风险。

基于这些原因，如果债权人在已经知道或应当知道不履行后的一段合理时间内未要求履行，本条（e）款就排除其要求履行的权利。

对丁丧失终止合同的权利，也有相似的规定，参见第7.3.2条第(2)款。

第7.2.3条

（对瑕疵履行的修补和替换）

要求履行的权利，在适当的情况下，包括对瑕疵履行要求修补、替换或做其他补救的权利。这里也适用第7.2.1条和第7.2.2条的规定。

COMMENT

1. Right to performance in case of defective performance

This Article applies the general principles of Articles 7.2.1 and 7.2.2 to a special, yet very frequent, case of non-performance, i.e. defective performance. For the sake of clarity the Article specifies that the right to require performance includes the right of the party who has received a defective performance to require cure of the defect.

2. Cure of defective performance

Under the Principles cure denotes the right both of the non-performing party to correct its performance (see Article 7.1.4) and of the aggrieved party to require such correction by the non-performing party. This Article deals with the latter right.

The Article expressly mentions two specific examples of cure, namely repair and replacement. Repairing defective goods (or making good an insufficient service) is the most common case and replacement of a defective performance is also frequent. The right to require repair or replacement may also exist with respect to the payment of money, for instance in case of an insufficient payment or of a payment in the wrong currency or to an account different from that agreed upon by the parties.

Apart from repair and replacement there are other forms of cure, such as the removal of the rights of third persons over goods or the obtaining of a necessary public permission.

3. Restrictions

The right to require cure of a defective performance is subject to the same limitations as the right to performance in general.

Most of the exceptions to the right to require performance that are set out in Article 7.2.2 are easily applicable to the various forms of cure of a defective performance. Only the application of sub-paragraph (b) calls for specific comment. In many cases involving small, insignificant defects, both replacement and repair may involve "unreasonable effort or expense" and are therefore excluded.

Illustration

> A new car is sold which has a small painting defect which decreases the value of the car by 0.01 % of the purchase price. Repainting would cost 0.5% of the purchase price. A claim for repair is excluded but the buyer is entitled to require a reduction in the purchase price.

注释：

1. 在瑕疵履行情况下要求履行的权利

本条将第7.2.1条和第7.2.2条的一般原则适用于一种特殊的但却是经常发生的不履行情形，也就是瑕疵履行。为了清楚起见，本条详细规定了要求履行的权利包括得到瑕疵履行的一方当事人要求补救瑕疵的权利。

2. 瑕疵履行的补救

根据本《通则》，补救包含两层含义：既可以是指不履行方改正其履行的权利（参见第7.1.4条），也可以是指受损害方要求不履行方改正其履行的权利，本条涉及的是后一种权利。

本条明确提到了两种具体的补救方式，即修补和替换。修补瑕疵货物（或改善不足服务）是最普遍的方式，替换瑕疵履行也时常发生。就付款而言，也存在要求修补或替换的权利，例如，在付款不足、以错误的货币付款或者向非双方约定的账户付款等情况下。

除了修补和替换外，还有其他形式的补救，比如排除第三人对货物的权利或者获得必要的公共许可。

3. 限制

通常，对瑕疵履行要求补救的权利同样也要受到要求履行的权利所受到的限制。

第7.2.2条列举的要求履行的权利的例外，多数都能比较容易地适用于瑕疵履行的各种补救形式。只有该条(b)项的适用需要在此特别注释。在许多情况下，履行瑕疵都是细微的、无关紧要的，而修理和替换又可能涉及"不合理的负担或花费"，因此在此情况下，将排除修理和替换。

示例：

　　　出售一辆新车的喷漆有一点小瑕疵，并因此导致其购买价格降低0.01%，重新喷漆将花费购买价格的0.5%。在这种情况下，修补的要求将被排除，但买方有权要求降低购买价格。

ARTICLE 7.2.4
(Judicial penalty)

(1) Where the court orders a party to perform, it may also direct that this party pay a penalty if it does not comply with the order.

(2) The penalty shall be paid to the aggrieved party unless mandatory provisions of the law of the forum provide otherwise. Payment of the penalty to the aggrieved party does not exclude any claim for damages.

COMMENT

1. Judicially imposed penalty

Experience in some legal systems has shown that the threat of a judicially imposed penalty for disobedience is a most effective means of ensuring compliance with judgments ordering the performance of contractual obligations. Other systems, on the contrary, do not provide for such sanctions because they are considered to constitute an inadmissible encroachment upon personal freedom.

This Article takes a middle course by providing for monetary but not for other forms of penalty, applicable to all kinds of orders for performance including those for payment of money.

2. Imposition of penalty at discretion of the court

The use of the word "may" in paragraph (1) of this Article makes it clear that the imposition of a penalty is a matter of discretion for the court. Its exercise depends upon the kind of obligation to be performed. In the case of money judgments, a penalty should be imposed only in exceptional situations, especially where speedy payment is essential for the aggrieved party. The same is true for obligations to deliver goods. Obligations to pay money or to deliver goods can normally be easily enforced by ordinary means of execution. By contrast, in the case of obligations to do or to abstain from doing something, which moreover cannot easily be performed by a third person, enforcement by means of judicial penalties is often the most appropriate solution.

3. Beneficiary

Legal systems differ as to the question of whether judicial penalties should be paid to the aggrieved party, to the State, or to both. Some

第 7.2.4 条

（法院判决的罚金）

（1） 法院判决一方当事人履行义务时，亦可做出若该方当事人不执行该判决须支付罚金的指令。

（2） 罚金应支付给受损害方，除非法院地的强制性规则另有规定。向受损害方支付罚金并不排除其要求损害赔偿的任何权利。

注释：

1. 司法惩罚

一些法律制度的实践表明，威胁对不遵守判决的行为处以司法惩罚，对于确保遵从命令履行合同义务的判决是一种极为有效的手段。相反，其他法律制度没有规定此类惩罚手段，因为这些制裁被认为构成了对人身自由所不能容许的侵犯。

本条采取了折中的做法，只规定了罚金而未规定其他形式的惩罚手段，其可适用于所有类型的履行命令，包括付款命令。

2. 依法院的自由裁量权判处罚金

本条第(1)款中"可以"一词的运用表明，是否判处罚金是法院的一种自由裁量权，其运用取决于所要履行的义务的类型。对于有关金钱债务的判决，只有在例外情况下特别是当迅速付款对受损害方很重要时，才可以判处罚金。对交付货物的义务同样如此。付款或交付货物的义务通常能通过普通的执行手段较容易地得到执行。相反，对于作为或不作为的义务，由于很难由第三人代为履行，则通过法院判处罚金强制执行通常是最适当的解决办法。

3. 受益人

法院判处的罚金应给予受损害方还是给予国家，或者两者都给予，

systems regard payment to the aggrieved party as constituting an unjustified windfall benefit which is contrary to public policy.

While rejecting this latter view and indicating the aggrieved party as the beneficiary of the penalty, the first sentence of paragraph (2) of this Article expressly mentions the possibility of mandatory provisions of the law of the forum not permitting such a solution and indicating other possible beneficiaries of judicial penalties.

4. Judicial penalties distinguished from damages and from agreed payment for non-performance

The second sentence of paragraph (2) makes it clear that a judicial penalty paid to the aggrieved party does not affect its claim for damages. Payment of the penalty is regarded as compensating the aggrieved party for those disadvantages which cannot be taken into account under the ordinary rules for the recovery of damages. Moreover, since payment of damages will usually occur substantially later than payment of a judicial penalty, courts may to some degree be able, in measuring the damages, to take the payment of the penalty into account.

Judicial penalties are moreover to be distinguished from agreed payments for non-performance which are dealt with in Article 7.4.13, although the latter fulfil a function similar to that of the former. If the court considers that the contractual stipulation of the payment of a sum in case of non-performance already provides a sufficient incentive for performance, it may refuse to impose a judicial penalty.

5. Form and procedure

A judicial penalty may be imposed in the form of a lump sum payment or of a payment by instalments.

The procedure relating to the imposition of a judicial penalty is governed by the *lex fori*.

6. Penalties imposed by arbitrators

Since according to Article 1.11 "court" includes an arbitral tribunal, the question arises of whether arbitrators might also be allowed to impose a penalty.

While a majority of legal systems seems to deny such a power to arbitrators, some modern legislation and recent court practice have recognised it. This solution, which is in keeping with the increasingly important role of arbitration as an alternative means of dispute

对此各种法律制度的规定有所不同。一些法律制度认为将罚金判给受损害方将构成不当得利，这是违背公共政策的。

在否定这种观点并且指明受损害方是罚金的受益者的同时，本条第(2)款第一句明确指出存在如下可能，即法院所在地法的强制性法规不允许这种解决办法，并指明以其他人作为司法罚金的受益人。

4. 法院判处的罚金区别于损害赔偿和对不履行的约定付款

本条第(2)款第二句表明向受损害方支付法院判处的罚金并不影响其要求损害赔偿的权利。支付罚金被认为是对受损害方所遭受的、按照损害赔偿的一般赔偿规则无法计算的损失的补偿。而且，由于损害赔偿金的支付通常总是大大晚于司法罚金的支付，所以法院在计算损害赔偿金的数额时，在一定程度上可能会考虑罚金的支付情况。

另外，司法罚金和第7.4.13条所规定的对不履行的约定付款也是有区别的，尽管后者的作用和前者相似。如果法院认为合同中有关对不履行的约定付款的规定已经为履行提供了充分的保障，它可以不判处罚金。

5. 形式和程序

司法罚金可以采取一次付款或者分期付款的形式。
法院判处罚金的程序由法院地法管辖。

6. 仲裁员裁决的罚金

根据第1.11条的规定，"法院"包括仲裁庭，因此就产生了仲裁员是否也能裁决罚金的问题。

尽管大多数法律制度似乎否定仲裁员有这种权力，但一些现代立法和近来的审判实践已经认可了这种权力。特别在国际商事活动中，伴随着仲裁作为替代性争议解决手段的重要性日益上升，本《通则》

resolution, especially in international commerce, is endorsed by the Principles. Since the execution of a penalty imposed by arbitrators can only be effected by, or with the assistance of, a court, appropriate supervision is available to prevent any possible abuse of the arbitrators' power.

7. Recognition and enforcement of decisions imposing penalties

Attention must be drawn to the problems of recognition and enforcement, in countries other than the forum State, of judicial decisions and of arbitral awards imposing penalties. Special rules on this matter are sometimes to be found in national law and to some extent in international treaties.

ARTICLE 7.2.5

(Change of remedy)

(1) An aggrieved party who has required performance of a non-monetary obligation and who has not received performance within a period fixed or otherwise within a reasonable period of time may invoke any other remedy.

(2) Where the decision of a court for performance of a non-monetary obligation cannot be enforced, the aggrieved party may invoke any other remedy.

COMMENT

1. Aggrieved party entitled to change of remedy

This Article addresses a problem which is peculiar to the right to require performance. The aggrieved party may abandon the remedy of requiring performance of a non-monetary obligation and opt instead for another remedy or remedies.

This choice is permitted on account of the difficulties usually involved in the enforcement of non-monetary obligations. Even if the aggrieved party first decides to invoke its right to require performance, it would not be fair to confine that party to this single option. The non-performing party may subsequently become unable to perform, or its inability may only become evident during the proceedings.

也认可了这种解决办法。因为由仲裁员裁决的罚金只能由法院或在法院的协助下执行，这样对仲裁员可能滥用这种权力就有了适当的监督。

7. 处以罚金的判决或裁定的承认和执行

处以罚金的法院判决和仲裁裁决在法院地以外的承认和执行问题，应该引起重视。关于这个问题的特殊规则有时在国内法中能够找到，并且一定程度上会出现在国际条约中。

第7.2.5条

（变更救济）

（1）　如果要求履行非金钱债务的受损害方，在规定的期限内或若无此规定在一段合理的时间内，未获得履行，则该方当事人可诉诸任何其他的救济手段。
（2）　当对责令履行非金钱债务的法院判决不能得到执行时，受损害方可诉诸任何其他的救济手段。

注释：

1. 受损害方有权变更救济

本条论述的是一个对要求履行的权利来说所特有的问题：受损害方可以放弃对非金钱债务要求实际履行，转而要求另一种或几种其他救济。

由于强制执行非金钱债务往往存在困难，因此允许这种选择。即使受损害方最初选择了行使要求履行的权利，将其限定于这个单一的选择也是不公平的。因为，不履行方随后可能变成不能履行，或者在履行过程中其履行不能才显现出来。

2. Voluntary change of remedy

Two situations must be addressed.

In the first case, the aggrieved party has required performance but changes its mind before execution of a judgment in its favour, perhaps because it has discovered the non-performing party's inability to perform. The aggrieved party now wishes to invoke one or more other remedies. Such a voluntary change of remedy can only be admitted if the interests of the non-performing party are duly protected. It may have prepared for performance, invested effort and incurred expense. For this reason paragraph (1) of this Article makes it clear that the aggrieved party is entitled to invoke another remedy only if it has not received performance within a fixed period or otherwise within a reasonable period of time.

How much additional time must be made available to the non-performing party for performance depends upon the difficulty which the performance involves. The non-performing party has the right to perform provided it does so before the expiry of the additional period.

For similar conditions which restrict the right of termination in case of delay in performance, see Article 7.3.2(2).

3. Unenforceable decision

Paragraph (2) addresses the second and less difficult case in which the aggrieved party has attempted without success to enforce a judicial decision or arbitral award directing the non-performing party to perform. In this situation it is obvious that the aggrieved party may immediately pursue other remedies.

4. Time limits

In the event of a subsequent change of remedy the time limit provided for a notice of termination under Article 7.3.2(2) must, of course, be extended accordingly. The reasonable time for giving notice begins to run, in the case of a voluntary change of remedy, after the aggrieved party has or ought to have become aware of the non-performance at the expiry of the additional period of time available to the non-performing party to perform; and in the case of paragraph (2) of this Article, it will begin to run after the aggrieved party has or ought to have become aware of the unenforceability of the decision or award requiring performance.

2. 自愿变更救济

有两种情形必须加以说明:

第一种情况是,受损害方已要求实际履行,但在对其有利的判决被执行之前改变了想法,这可能是因为他发现不履行方没有能力履行。这时受损害方希望采用一种或多种其他救济手段。只有在不履行方的利益得到充分保护的情况下,这种自愿变更救济才被许可。不履行方可能已经为履行作了准备,付出了努力并发生了费用。因此,本条第(1)款明确指出,受损害方只有在规定的时间或合理的时间内没有得到履行时,才有权寻求另一种救济。

不履行方履行义务需要的额外时间的长短,取决于履行的难度。不履行方在额外期间届满前都有权履行义务。

在迟延履行情况下,终止合同权利受到类似条件的限制,参见第7.3.2条第(2)款。

3. 不能强制执行的决定

本条第(2)款论述了第二种不太困难的情形,即受损害方试图执行责令不履行方履行的司法判决或仲裁裁决,但未获成功。在这种情况下,受损害方显然可以立即寻求其他救济。

4. 时限

如果发生事后变更救济的情况,则第7.3.2条第(2)款规定的作出终止合同通知的时限应当相应地延长。在发生自愿变更救济的情况下,发出通知的合理时间应当从受损害方知道或者应当知道供不履行方履行的额外履行时间届满时其仍未履行后,开始起算;对于本条第(2)款规定的情况,上述时间应当从受损害方知道或者应当知道要求履行的法院判决或仲裁裁决不能强制执行后开始起算。

SECTION 3: TERMINATION

ARTICLE 7.3.1
(Right to terminate the contract)

(1) A party may terminate the contract where the failure of the other party to perform an obligation under the contract amounts to a fundamental non-performance.

(2) In determining whether a failure to perform an obligation amounts to a fundamental non-performance regard shall be had, in particular, to whether

(a) the non-performance substantially deprives the aggrieved party of what it was entitled to expect under the contract unless the other party did not foresee and could not reasonably have foreseen such result;

(b) strict compliance with the obligation which has not been performed is of essence under the contract;

(c) the non-performance is intentional or reckless;

(d) the non-performance gives the aggrieved party reason to believe that it cannot rely on the other party's future performance;

(e) the non-performing party will suffer disproportionate loss as a result of the preparation or performance if the contract is terminated.

(3) In the case of delay the aggrieved party may also terminate the contract if the other party fails to perform before the time allowed it under Article 7.1.5 has expired.

COMMENT

1. Termination even if non-performance is excused

The rules set out in this Section are intended to apply both to cases where the non-performing party is liable for the non-performance and to those where the non-performance is excused so that the aggrieved party

第三节　合同的终止

第7.3.1条

（终止合同的权利）

（1）合同一方当事人可终止合同，如果另一方当事人未履行其合同项下的某项义务构成对合同的根本不履行。

（2）在确定不履行某项义务是否构成根本不履行时，应特别考虑到是否存在以下情况：

（a）不履行实质上剥夺了受损害方根据合同有权期待的利益，除非另一方当事人并未预见而且也不可能合理地预见到此结果；

（b）对该项未履行义务的严格遵守是合同的实质性约定；

（c）不履行是有意所致还是疏忽所致；

（d）不履行使受损害方有理由相信，不能信赖另一方当事人的未来履行；

（e）若合同被终止，不履行方将因已做的准备或履行而蒙受不相称的损失。

（3）在迟延履行的情况下，如果另一方当事人未在第7.1.5条允许的额外期间届满前履行合同，受损害方亦可终止合同。

注释：

1. 即使不履行是可免责的也可以终止合同

本节列举的规则意欲适用于两种情况：其一，不履行方对不履行负有责任；其二，不履行被免责致使受损害方既不能对不履行主张实

can claim neither specific performance nor damages for non-performance.

Illustration

> 1.   A, a company located in country X, buys wine from B in country Y. The Government of country X subsequently imposes an embargo upon the import of agricultural products from country Y. Although the impediment cannot be attributed to A, B may terminate the contract.

2. Right to terminate the contract dependent on fundamental non-performance

Whether in a case of non-performance by one party the other party should have the right to terminate the contract depends upon the weighing of a number of considerations. On the one hand, performance may be so late or so defective that the aggrieved party cannot use it for its intended purpose, or the behaviour of the non-performing party may in other respects be such that the aggrieved party should be permitted to terminate the contract.

On the other hand, termination will often cause serious detriment to the non-performing party whose expenses in preparing and tendering performance may not be recovered.

For these reasons paragraph (1) of this Article provides that an aggrieved party may terminate the contract only if the non-performance of the other party is "fundamental", i.e. material and not merely of minor importance. See also Articles 7.3.3. and 7.3.4.

3. Circumstances of significance in determining whether non-performance is fundamental

Paragraph (2) of this Article lists a number of circumstances which are relevant to the determination of whether, in a given case, failure to perform an obligation amounts to fundamental non-performance.

a. *Non-performance substantially depriving the other party of its expectations*

The first factor referred to in paragraph (2)(a) is that the non-performance is so fundamental that the aggrieved party is substantially deprived of what it was entitled to expect at the time of the conclusion of the contract.

际履行也不能要求损害赔偿。

示例：

> 1. 位于 X 国的 A 公司向 Y 国的 B 购买酒。X 国政府后来发布禁令禁止从 Y 国进口农产品。尽管该障碍不能归咎于 A，B 也可以终止合同。

2. 终止合同的权利取决于是否构成根本不履行

在一方当事人不履行的情况下，另一方当事人是否有权终止合同取决于对许多因素的权衡。一方面，履行太迟或瑕疵太严重以至于受损害方无法据此实现其预想的目的，或者不履行方的行为可能在其他方面存在问题，从而应当允许受损害方终止合同。

另一方面，终止合同经常会给不履行方造成严重的损失，因为其为准备履行和提供履行所支出的费用可能得不到补偿。

基于这些原因，本条第(1)款规定，只有在不履行方的不履行是"根本性的"，即是实质性的而不仅仅是微不足道的情况下，受损害方才能终止合同。参见第 7.3.3 条和第 7.3.4 条。

3. 确定不履行是否是根本性的重要情况

本条第(2)款列举了许多关于在特定情况下确定不履行某项合同义务是否构成根本不履行的相关情形。

a. 不履行实质上剥夺了另一方当事人的期待

第(2)款(a)项提到的第一个因素是不履行是根本性的，以至于在实质上剥夺了受损害方在订立合同时有权期待的利益。

Illustration

> 2.   On 1 May A contracts to deliver standard software before 15 May to B who has requested speedy delivery. If A tenders delivery on 15 June, B may refuse delivery and terminate the contract.

The aggrieved party cannot terminate the contract if the non-performing party can show that it did not foresee, and could not reasonably have foreseen, that the non-performance was fundamental for the other party.

Illustration

> 3.   A undertakes to remove waste from B's site within thirty days without specifying the exact date of commencement. B fails to inform A that B has hired excavators at high cost to begin work on the site on 2 January. B cannot terminate its contract with A on the ground that A had not cleared the site on 2 January.

b. *Strict performance of contract of essence*

Paragraph (2)(b) looks not at the actual gravity of the non-performance but at the nature of the contractual obligation for which strict performance might be of essence. Such obligations of strict performance are not uncommon in commercial contracts. For example, in contracts for the sale of commodities the time of delivery is normally considered to be of the essence, and in a documentary credit transaction the documents tendered must conform strictly to the terms of the credit.

c. *Intentional non-performance*

Paragraph (2)(c) deals with the situation where the non-performance is intentional or reckless. It may, however, be contrary to good faith (see Article 1.7) to terminate a contract if the non-performance, even though committed intentionally, is insignificant.

d. *No reliance on future performance*

Under paragraph (2)(d) the fact that non-performance gives the aggrieved party reason to believe that it cannot rely on the other party's future performance is of significance. If a party is to make its performance in instalments, and it is clear that a defect found in one of the earlier performances will be repeated in all performances, the aggrieved party may terminate the contract even if the defects in the early instalment would not of themselves justify termination.

Sometimes an intentional breach may show that a party cannot be trusted.

示例：

　　2. 5 月 1 日 A 与 B 签订合同，规定 5 月 15 日之前 A 应向 B 交付标准软件，B 要求快速交付。如果 A 在 6 月 15 日才交付，B 可以拒绝接受交付并终止合同。

如果不履行方能证明他没有预见到也不可能合理预见到不履行对受损害方来说是根本性的，则受损害方不能终止合同。

示例：

　　3. A 负责在 30 天内为 B 的工地清理完废物，但并没有明确具体的开始时间。B 没有通知 A 他已经以高价雇佣了挖掘工人于 1 月 2 日开始在工地施工。B 不能以 A 没有于 1 月 2 日前完成清理工作为由而终止合同。

b. 严格履行合同至关重要

第(2)款(b)项不是着眼于不履行的实际危害性，而是着眼于合同义务的性质是否决定了严格履行至关重要。这类应该严格履行的义务在商事合同中并非罕见。比如，在销售合同中，交付时间通常被认为至关重要，在跟单信用证交易中，提交的单据也必须严格与信用证条款相符。

c. 故意不履行

第(2)款(c)项涉及的情形是不履行是故意的或是疏忽的。然而，如果不履行是微不足道的，则即便是故意为之，终止合同仍可能违背诚实信用原则（参见第 1.7 条）。

d. 不能依赖未来履行

根据第(2)款(d)项的规定，不履行使受损害方有理由相信他不能依赖另一方当事人的未来履行，这一事实很重要。如果一方当事人分期履行义务，并且在某一先期履行中出现的瑕疵很明显地要在整个履行中重复，尽管先期履行中的瑕疵本身并不构成终止合同的法律依据，受损害方仍可以终止合同。

有时，故意违反合同可能表明一方当事人不值得信赖。

Illustration

> 4.   A, the agent of B, who is entitled to reimbursement for expenses, submits false vouchers to B. Although the amounts claimed are insignificant, B may treat A's behaviour as a fundamental non-performance and terminate the agency contract.

e. *Disproportionate loss*

Paragraph (2)(e) deals with situations in which a party who fails to perform has relied on the contract and has prepared or tendered performance. In these cases regard is to be had to the extent to which that party suffers disproportionate loss if the non-performance is treated as fundamental. Non-performance is less likely to be treated as fundamental if it occurs late, after the preparation of performance, than if it occurs early before such preparation. Whether a performance tendered or rendered can be of any benefit to the non-performing party if it is refused or has to be returned to that party is also of relevance.

Illustration

> 5.   On 1 May A undertakes to deliver software which is to be produced specifically for B. It is agreed that delivery shall be made before 31 December. A tenders delivery on 31 January, at which time B still needs the software, which A cannot sell to other users. B may claim damages from A, but cannot terminate the contract.

4. Termination after *Nachfrist*

Paragraph (3) makes reference to Article 7.1.5, paragraph (3) of which provides that the aggrieved party may use the *Nachfrist* procedure to terminate a contract which may not otherwise be terminated in case of delay (see Comment 2 on Article 7.1.5).

ARTICLE 7.3.2
(Notice of termination)

(1) The right of a party to terminate the contract is exercised by notice to the other party.

示例：

　　4. A作为B的代理人，有权要求B偿付费用，但向B提交了虚假的单据。尽管要求偿付的数额不大，B仍可以认为A的行为是一种根本不履行，并终止代理合同。

e. 不相称的损失

第(2)款(e)项涉及的是未履行义务的一方当事人已经信赖合同、并已准备履行或已提供履行的情形。在这些情况下，如果不履行被认为是根本性的，有必要考虑该方当事人承受不相称损失的程度。在准备履行之后发生的不履行，比准备履行之前发生的不履行，更不大可能被视为根本性的不履行。如果提示的或提供的履行遭拒绝或必须返还给不履行方，这种履行是否对该方当事人具有任何利益，也是相关的考虑。

示例：

　　5. A于5月1日与B订立合同，约定A向B交付专为其制造的软件，约定的交付时间为12月31日之前。A在次年1月31日才交付，此时B仍然需要该软件，并且A不能将该软件出售给其他用户。B可以要求损害赔偿，但不能终止合同。

4. 宽限期之后的终止合同

第(3)款涉及第7.1.5条，该条第(3)款规定受损害方可以运用宽限期程序终止在迟延情况下也许不能被终止的合同（参见第7.1.5条注释2）。

第7.3.2条

（终止通知）

(1) 一方当事人终止合同的权利应通过向另一方当事人发出通知来行使。

(2) If performance has been offered late or otherwise does not conform to the contract the aggrieved party will lose its right to terminate the contract unless it gives notice to the other party within a reasonable time after it has or ought to have become aware of the offer or of the non-conforming performance.

COMMENT

1. The requirement of notice

Paragraph (1) of this Article reaffirms the principle that the right of a party to terminate the contract is exercised by notice to the other party. The notice requirement will permit the non-performing party to avoid any loss due to uncertainty as to whether the aggrieved party will accept the performance. At the same time it prevents the aggrieved party from speculating on a rise or fall in the value of the performance to the detriment of the non-performing party.

2. Performance overdue

When performance is due but has not been made, the aggrieved party's course of action will depend upon its wishes and knowledge.

It may be the case that the aggrieved party does not know whether the other party intends to perform, and either no longer wants the performance or is undecided. In this case the aggrieved party may wait and see whether performance is ultimately tendered and make up its mind if and when this happens (paragraph (2)). Alternatively, it may still want the other party to perform, in which case it must seek performance within a reasonable time after it has or ought to have become aware of the non-performance (see Article 7.2.2(e)).

This Article does not deal with the situation where the non-performing party asks the aggrieved party whether it will accept late performance. Nor does it deal with the situation where the aggrieved party learns from another source that the non-performing party intends nevertheless to perform the contract. In such cases good faith and fair dealing (see Article 1.7) may require that the aggrieved party inform the other party if it does not wish to accept the late performance. If it does not do so, it may be held liable in damages.

　　（2）若属迟延履行或其他形式的履行与合同不符，受损害方将丧失终止合同的权利，除非他在已经知道或理应知道迟延履行或不符履行后一段合理时间内通知另一方当事人。

注释：

1. 通知要求

　　本条第（1）款重申了如下原则，即一方当事人通过向另一方当事人发出通知来行使终止合同的权利。通知要求有助于不履行方避免因在受损害方是否接受履行方面存在的不确定性而遭受损失。同时它也有助于防止受损害方视履行的价值的增减进行投机而有损于不履行方。

2. 过期履行

　　如果履行到期但却未得到履行，受损害方采取何种行动将取决于他的愿望和知悉状况。

　　一种情况可能是，受损害方不知道另一方当事人是否打算履行，并且他自己可能不再想要履行或者还没有决定。在这种情况下，受损害方可以等待，看另一方当事人最终是否提供履行，如提供则在提供履行时做出决定（参见第（2）款）。另一种情况是，受损害方仍然希望另一方当事人履行义务，在这种情况下，他必须在知道或者应当知道发生不履行后一段合理时间内要求履行（参见第7.2.2条(e)项）。

　　本条不涉及不履行方询问受损害方是否接受迟延履行的情况，也不涉及受损害方从另一渠道得知不履行方仍然打算履行合同的情况。在这两种情况下，根据诚实信用和公平交易原则（参见第1.7条），如果受损害方不希望接受迟延履行，应当通知另一方当事人，如果没有通知，则受损害方可能要承担损害赔偿责任。

3. "Reasonable time"

An aggrieved party who intends to terminate the contract must give notice to the other party within a reasonable time after it becomes or ought to have become aware of the non-performance (paragraph (2)).

What is "reasonable" depends upon the circumstances. In situations where the aggrieved party may easily obtain a substitute performance and may thus speculate on a rise or fall in the price, notice must be given without delay. When it must make enquiries as to whether it can obtain substitute performance from other sources the reasonable period of time will be longer.

4. Notice must be received

The notice to be given by the aggrieved party becomes effective when the non-performing party receives it (see Article 1.10).

ARTICLE **7.3.3**

(Anticipatory non-performance)

Where prior to the date for performance by one of the parties it is clear that there will be a fundamental non-performance by that party, the other party may terminate the contract.

COMMENT

This Article establishes the principle that a non-performance which is to be expected is to be equated with a non-performance which occurred at the time when performance fell due. It is a requirement that it be clear that there will be non-performance; a suspicion, even a well-founded one, is not sufficient. Furthermore, it is necessary that the non-performance be fundamental and that the party who is to receive performance give notice of termination.

An example of anticipatory non-performance is the case where one party declares that it will not perform the contract; however, the circumstances also may indicate that there will be a fundamental non-performance.

3. "合理时间"

打算终止合同的受损害方必须在知道或应该知道不履行后一段合理时间内通知另一方当事人（第(2)款）。

何为"合理"，取决于具体情况。如果受损害方可以轻易地获得替代履行，并且可能因此对价格的升降进行投机，则应当毫不迟延地做出通知。如果受损害方必须对是否能从其他渠道获得替代履行进行调查，则合理时间应当长一些。

4. 通知必须收到

受损害方发出的通知在不履行方收到时生效（参见第 1.10 条）。

第 7.3.3 条

（预期不履行）

　　如果在一方当事人履行合同日期之前，情况表明该方当事人将根本不履行其合同义务，则另一方当事人可终止合同。

注释：

本条确立了一项原则，即预期的不履行与履行到期后实际发生的不履行是相同的。但一个必要条件是：将会发生不履行是很明显的。怀疑，即使是一种有理由的怀疑，也是不充分的。另外，不履行必须是根本性的，并且应得到履行的当事人必须发出终止合同的通知。

预期不履行的一个例子是一方当事人宣布他将不履行合同义务。不过，具体情况也可以表明将会出现根本不履行。

Illustration

A promises to deliver oil to B by M/S Paul at the terminal in country X on 3 February. On 25 January M/S Paul is still 2,000 kilometres from the terminal. At the speed it is making it will not arrive on 3 February, but at the earliest on 8 February. As time is of the essence, a substantial delay is to be expected, and B may terminate the contract before 3 February.

ARTICLE 7.3.4
(Adequate assurance of due performance)

A party who reasonably believes that there will be a fundamental non-performance by the other party may demand adequate assurance of due performance and may meanwhile withhold its own performance. Where this assurance is not provided within a reasonable time the party demanding it may terminate the contract.

COMMENT

1. Reasonable expectation of fundamental non-performance

This Article protects the interest of a party who has reason to believe that the other will be unable or unwilling to perform the contract at the due date but who cannot invoke Article 7.3.3 since there is still a possibility that the other party will or can perform. In the absence of the rule laid down in this Article the former party would often be in a dilemma. If it were to wait until the due date of performance, and this did not take place, it might incur loss. If, on the other hand, it were to terminate the contract, and it then became apparent that the contract would have been performed by the other party, its action will amount to non-performance of the contract, and it will be liable in damages.

2. Right to withhold performance pending adequate assurance of performance

Consequently this Article enables a party who reasonably believes that there will be a fundamental non-performance by the other party to demand an assurance of performance from the other party and in the

示例：

　　A 承诺通过一艘油船（M/S Paul）于 2 月 3 日在 X 国某终点将石油交付给 B。1 月 25 日该油船还在距该终点 2,000 公里的地方，并且根据目前的速度，该油船在 2 月 3 日不能到达，最早也得 2 月 8 日到达。因为在该合同中时间是至关重要的，可以预料到这种实质的延误，B 可以在 2 月 3 日前终止合同。

第7.3.4条

（如约履行的充分保证）

　　一方当事人如果有理由相信另一方当事人将根本不履行，可要求其对适当履行提供充分保证，并可同时暂停履行其自己的合同义务。若另一方当事人未在合理时间内提供此保证，则要求提供保证的一方当事人可终止合同。

注释：

1. 合理地预料到根本不履行

　　若一方当事人有理由相信另一方当事人在履行到期时将不能或不愿履行其合同义务，但由于仍然存在该另一方当事人到时能够或愿意履行的可能性，他并不能援引第7.3.3条，本条将保护这种当事人的利益。如果没有本条规定的规则，该方当事人往往会陷于一种两难境地。如果等到履行到期之日，但却没得到履行，他将遭受损失。另一方面，如果他终止合同，而情况却显示另一方当事人本来会履行合同，他的行为将构成对合同的不履行，而且他要承担损害赔偿的责任。

2. 得到履行的充分保证前暂停履行的权利

　　因此，本条使合理确信另一方当事人将发生根本不履行的一方当

meantime to withhold its own performance. What constitutes an adequate assurance will depend upon the circumstances. In some cases the other party's declaration that it will perform will suffice, while in others a request for security or for a guarantee from a third person may be justified.

Illustration

> A, a boatbuilder with only one berth, promises to build a yacht for B to be delivered on 1 May, and no later. Soon afterwards, B learns from C that A has promised to build a yacht for C during the same period. B is entitled to ask A for an adequate assurance that the yacht will be delivered on time and A will then have to give B a satisfactory explanation of how it intends to perform its contract with B.

3. Termination of the contract

If adequate assurance of due performance is not given the other party may terminate the contract.

ARTICLE 7.3.5
(Effects of termination in general)

(1) Termination of the contract releases both parties from their obligation to effect and to receive future performance.

(2) Termination does not preclude a claim for damages for non-performance.

(3) Termination does not affect any provision in the contract for the settlement of disputes or any other term of the contract which is to operate even after termination.

COMMENT

1. Termination extinguishes future obligations

Paragraph (1) of this Article states the general rule that termination has effects for the future in that it releases both parties from their duty to effect and to receive future performance.

事人能够要求前者提供履约保证，并且同时暂停履行自己的义务。何为充分的保证取决于具体情况。在有些情况下，另一方当事人宣布他将履行就是充分的，而在其他情况下，要求提供担保或者由第三人提供保证也许是正当的。

示例：

> 只有一个船台的造船商 A 承诺为 B 建造一艘快艇，最迟于 5 月 1 日交货。之后不久，B 从 C 处得知 A 也承诺在同样的时间里为 C 建造一艘快艇。在这种情况下，B 有权要求 A 对按时交付快艇提供充分的保证，A 必须就打算怎样履行与 B 之间的合同向 B 作出满意的解释。

3. 终止合同

如果没有提供如约履行的充分保证，另一方当事人可以终止合同。

第 7.3.5 条

（终止合同的一般效果）

（1）合同终止解除双方当事人履行和接受未来履行的义务。

（2）终止并不排除对不履行要求损害赔偿的权利。

（3）终止并不影响合同中关于解决争议的任何规定，或者即便在合同终止后仍应执行的其他合同条款。

注释：

1. 合同终止解除未来的义务

本条第（1）款规定了终止合同影响未来的一般规则，即它解除了双方当事人履行和接受未来履行的义务。

2. Claim for damages not affected

The fact that, by virtue of termination, the contract is brought to an end, does not deprive the aggrieved party of its right to claim damages for non-performance in accordance with the rules laid down in Section 4 of this Chapter.

Illustration

> 1.   A sells B specified production machinery. After B has begun to operate the machinery serious defects in it lead to a shutdown of B's assembly plant. B declares the contract terminated but may still claim damages (see Article 7.3.5(2)).

3. Contract provisions not affected by termination

Notwithstanding the general rule laid down in paragraph (1), there may be provisions in the contract which survive its termination. This is the case in particular with provisions relating to dispute settlement but there may be others which by their very nature are intended to operate even after termination.

Illustration

> 2.   The facts are the same as in Illustration 1, except that A discloses to B confidential information which is necessary for the production and which B agrees not to divulge for as long as it does not become public knowledge. The contract further contains a clause referring disputes to the courts of A's country. Even after termination of the contract by B, B remains under a duty not to divulge the confidential information, and any dispute relating to the contract and its effects are to be settled by the courts of A's country (see Article 7.3.5(3)).

ARTICLE 7.3.6

*(Restitution with respect to contracts
to be performed at one time)*

(1) On termination of a contract to be performed at one time either party may claim restitution of whatever it has supplied under the contract, provided that such party concurrently makes restitution of whatever it has received under the contract.

2. 要求损害赔偿不受影响

通过终止合同使合同终结的事实，并不剥夺受损害方根据本章第四节规定的规则对不履行主张损害赔偿的权利。

示例：

1. A 向 B 出售特定的生产机器。在 B 开始操作该机器后，由于机器本身存在的严重缺陷导致 B 的装配厂停工。B 宣布终止合同，但仍可以主张损害赔偿（参见第 7.3.5 条第(2)款）。

3. 不受合同终止影响的合同规定

尽管存在第(1)款规定的一般规则，但合同的有些规定在合同终止后仍然有效。这特别是指与争端解决有关的条款，但也有其他情况，即由于这些条款的特殊性质，即使合同终止后，其仍要执行。

示例：

2. 事实和示例 1 相同，不同之处在于 A 向 B 透露了生产所必需的保密信息，并且 B 同意在该信息不为公众所知前不得予以泄露。该合同还包含一个将争端提交 A 国法院管辖的条款。即使 B 终止合同后，B 仍然承担不得泄露保密信息的义务，并且与合同及其效力有关的任何争议都将由 A 国法院处理（参见第 7.3.5 条第(3)款）。

第 7.3.6 条

（一次性履行合同的恢复原状）

（1）一次性履行合同终止时，合同任何一方当事人均可主张返还其依据合同所提供的一切，但该方当事人亦应同时返还其依据合同所收到的一切。

(2) If restitution in kind is not possible or appropriate, an allowance has to be made in money whenever reasonable.

(3) The recipient of the performance does not have to make an allowance in money if the impossibility to make restitution in kind is attributable to the other party.

(4) Compensation may be claimed for expenses reasonably required to preserve or maintain the performance received.

COMMENT

1. Contracts to be performed at one time

This Article refers only to contracts to be performed at one time. A different regime applies to contracts under which the characteristic performance is to be made over a period of time (see Article 7.3.7). The most common example of a contract to be performed at one time is an ordinary contract of sale where the entire object of the sale has to be transferred at one particular moment. This Article however refers also to, e.g. construction contracts in which the contractor is under an obligation to produce the entire work to be accepted by the customer at one particular time. A turnkey contract provides an important example.

Under a commercial contract one party will usually have to pay money for the performance received. That obligation is not the one that is characteristic of the contract. Thus, a contract of sale where the purchase price has to be paid in instalments, will fall under this Article provided that the seller's performance is to be made at one time.

2. Right of parties to restitution on termination

Paragraph (1) of this Article gives each party a right to claim the return of whatever the party has supplied under the contract provided that that party concurrently makes restitution of whatever it has received.

Illustration

1. In the process of a takeover of a company, controlling shareholder A agrees to sell and transfer to B shares for GBP 1,000,000. B only pays GBP 600,000 after the shares have been transferred and A therefore terminates the contract. A can claim back the shares. At the same time, A has to return the GBP 600,000 received from B.

（2）如果返还实物不可能或不适当，只要合理，应做折价补偿。

（3）如果不能进行实物返还之原因归咎于对方当事人，则收到履行的当事人无需折价补偿。

（4）对于为保存或维护收到的履行而合理发生的费用，可请求赔偿。

注释：

1. 一次性履行合同

本条仅涉及一次性履行合同。其标志性履行需要持续一段时期的合同，适用不同的规则（参见第 7.3.7 条）。最常见的一次性履行合同的例子就是普通的买卖合同，其交易标的须在某一时间点转移。然而，本条也适用于其他合同，例如建筑合同，承包商有义务完成全部工程并在某一时间点转交客户接受。交钥匙合同就是一个重要的例子。

在商业合同中，一方当事人通常必须为收到的履行付款。但该义务不是决定合同性质的义务。因此，以分期付款方式支付购买价款的买卖合同，只要卖方的履行是一次性完成的，仍应该受本条调整。

2. 合同终止时当事人之恢复原状的权利

本条第(1)款赋予每一方当事人可请求返还其在合同项下所提供的一切的权利，但他须同时返还自己收到的一切。

示例：

1. 在某起公司收购过程中，公司控股股东 A 同意以 100 万英镑的价格向 B 出售股票。B 在股票转让之后只支付了 60 万英镑。之后，A 终止了合同。A 可以请求返还股票，与此同时 A 必须返还从 B 处收到的 60 万英镑。

This rule also applies when the aggrieved party has made a bad bargain. If, in the case mentioned in Illustration 1, the real market value of the shares is GBP 1,200,000, A may still require the return of the shares.

This Article also applies to the situation where the aggrieved party has supplied money in exchange for property, services, or other performances which the party has not received or which are defective.

Illustration

> 2. Art dealer A sells a Constable painting to art dealer B for EUR 600,000. B only pays EUR 200,000 for the painting, and A therefore terminates the contract. Subsequently it turns out that the painting is not a Constable but a copy. On termination of the contract, B can reclaim the purchase price and must return the painting to A.

As regards the costs involved in making restitution, Article 6.1.11 applies.

3. Restitution in kind not possible or appropriate

Restitution must normally be made in kind. There are, however, instances where instead of restitution in kind, an allowance in money has to be made. This is the case first of all where restitution in kind is not possible. The allowance will normally amount to the value of the performance received.

Illustrations

> 3. Company A, which has contracted to excavate company B's site, leaves it after only part of the work has been done. B, which then terminates the contract, will have to pay A a sum in compensation for the work done, measured by the value that work has for B. At the same time B will have a claim against A for whatever damages B may have suffered as a result of A's breach of contract (see Article 7.3.5 (2)).

> 4. Company A charters a ship for a company cruise for its employees which is to take them up the Australian Coral Reef. Half-way the cruise ship breaks down and cannot continue the cruise. A terminates the contract with B, the owner of the business organising the cruise, and decides to fly its employees home. If A had already paid the price A can now claim it back. At the same time, A owes B an allowance amounting to the value of the cruise so far. In addition, A can claim damages for the loss suffered as a result of B's non-performance (see Article 7.3.5 (2)).

An allowance is further envisaged by paragraph (2) of this Article whenever restitution in kind would not be appropriate. This is so in

即便受害方最初做了一笔糟糕的交易,本规则仍然适用。如果,在示例1中,股票的真实市场价值是120万英镑,A仍然可以请求返还这些股票。

本条也可以适用于如下情况：受害方为购买财产、服务或其他履行,已支付了价金,但他却未收到该等财产、服务或其他履行,或者所收之履行存在瑕疵。

示例：

2. 艺术品交易商A以60万欧元的价格向艺术品交易商B出售一幅康斯特勃尔油画。B只支付了20万欧元,A于是终止合同。后来,发现该油画不是康斯特勃尔的真品,而是一副赝品。在终止合同后,B可以请求返还购买价款,但必须将该油画返还给A。

对于在返还过程中发生的费用,适用第6.1.11条的规定。

3. 实物返还不可能或不适当

返还通常必须是对实物的返还。然而,在某些情况下,只能以折价返还的方式代替实物的返还。第一种情况是,实物返还不可能。此时折价的金额通常等于所收到之履行的价值。

示例：

3. A公司约定为B公司挖掘工地,但在完成部分工作后撤离。于是B终止合同,但B必须就已完成工作部分向A付款。付款金额等于该部分工作对于B具有的价值。与此同时,B有权请求A赔偿因A违约给B造成的所有损害(参见第7.3.5条第(2)款)。

4. A公司租用一艘船为公司员工举办一次海上旅行,目的地是澳大利亚的大堡礁。完成一半行程时船出了故障,不能继续前行。A与组织这次旅游的公司老板B终止合同,并决定安排员工乘飞机返回。如果A已经支付了此次旅行的价款,其可以请求返还。与此同时,A应向组织此次海上旅游的公司B支付已提供旅游行程所具有的价值。此外A尚可就B的未履行部分给其造成的损失请求损害赔偿 (参见第7.3.5条第(2)款)。

本条第(2)款面对的是另一种折价补偿的情况,即实物返还不适

particular when returning the performance in kind would cause unreasonable effort or expense. The standard, in that respect, is the same as under Article 7.2.2(b).

Illustration

> 5.   A, an artist, sells 200 silver-plated rings to dealer B. B fails to pay for the rings and A thereupon terminates the contract. It turns out that B has, in the meantime, attempted to ship the rings to his business premises. However, the boat on which they had been stored has sunk. Although it would be possible, at great expense, to rescue the rings from the wrecked ship, this cannot be expected of B. B has to pay a reasonable sum to A, measured by the value of the rings.

The purpose of specifying that an allowance has to be made in money "whenever reasonable" is to make it clear that an allowance only has to be made if, and to the extent that, the performance has conferred a benefit on its recipient. That is not the case, for example, where the defect which gives the recipient of the performance a right to terminate has only become apparent in the course of processing the object of that performance.

Illustration

> 6.   Company A hires company B to develop a specialised software to improve its existing internal communication system. Once B has developed and installed the software, the software does not perform the functions it was intended to. A can terminate the contract and re-claim the price paid, but since the installed system has no value for A, it would not be reasonable to expect A to pay B an allowance for the installed software.

4. The allocation of risk

The rule contained in paragraph (2) implies an allocation of risk: it imposes a liability on the recipient of the performance to make good the value of that performance if it is unable to make restitution in kind. The rule in paragraph (2) applies even if the recipient was responsible for the deterioration or destruction of what it had received. Such allocation of the risk of deterioration or destruction is justified, in particular, because the risk should lie with the person in control of the performance. On the contrary, there is no liability to make good the value where the deterioration or destruction is attributable to the other party: either because it was due to the other party's fault, or because it was due to a defect inherent in the performance. Hence the rule in paragraph (3).

当。返还已履行的实物会造成不合理的努力或不合理的费用开支，就属这种情况。此时，适用的标准与第7.2.2条(b)项的规定相同。

示例：

> 5. 艺术家A向交易商B出售200只镀银戒指。B未支付价款，A因此终止了合同。与此同时，B已经将该批戒指装上了运往其营业场所的船只。然而，装戒指的船只不幸沉没。此时，尽管以巨大成本从失事船只中打捞戒指是可能的，但不能期望B这样做。但B必须向A支付一个合理的、反映该批戒指价值的金额。

该条规定"只要合理"需做折价补偿的目的是明确，只有在履行授予接收方一种利益，而且在此限度内时，才需要折价补偿。但是，如果履行标的物的缺陷在加工过程中才显现出来，而且该缺陷赋予了履行接收方终止合同的权利，这就不属于折价补偿的情况。

示例：

> 6. A公司聘请B公司开发一套专业软件，以提升现有内部通信系统。当B完成开发并安装软件之后，发现该软件并不具有约定的功能，A可终止合同并请求返还已支付的价款。但由于已安装的系统对A没有任何价值，此时期望A对B就已安装的软件折价补偿是不合理的。

4. 风险分配

第(2)款规定的规则默示着这样一种风险分配：收到履行的一方当事人，如果不能返还实物，则有责任补偿该履行所具有的价值。即便接收方对其收到的东西的贬值或损坏应承担负责，第(2)款的规则亦应适用。如此分配贬值或损坏之风险是有道理的，特别是风险应该由控制履行(标的物)的一方承担。相反，如果贬值或损坏归责于另一方当事人，无论是因为该另一方当事人之过错，还是因为其履行存在内在缺陷，则不存在补偿履行价值的责任。于是就有了第(3)款之规则。

Illustration

> 7. Manufacturer A sells and delivers a luxury car to company B. The car has defective brakes. Due to this defect it crashes into another car and is totally destroyed. Since the car was unfit to be used for its intended purpose, B can terminate the contract and reclaim the purchase price. B does not have to make an allowance for not being able to return the car.

The recipient's liability to make good the value of the performance received is not excluded in cases where the deterioration or destruction would also have occurred had the performance not been rendered.

Illustration

> 8. Manufacturer A sells and delivers a car to company B. After delivery has taken place, the car is totally destroyed by a hurricane flooding the properties of both A and B. B terminates the contract because of a defect attaching to the car. B can reclaim the purchase price but, at the same time, has to make an allowance for the value of the car prior to its destruction.

The question of the recipient's liability to pay the value of the performance only arises in cases where the deterioration or destruction occurs before termination of the contract. If what has been performed deteriorates or is destroyed after termination of the contract, the normal rules on non-performance apply, as after termination the recipient of the performance is under a duty to return what the recipient has received. Any non-performance of that duty gives the other party a right to claim damages according to Article 7.4.1, unless the non-performance is excused under Article 7.1.7.

Illustration

> 9. Company A sells and delivers to company B a limousine with a leaking roof. Since the limousine is unfit to be used for its intended purpose, B can terminate the contract. As a result, B can reclaim the purchase price but is under a duty to return the limousine. Before B can return the car it is totally destroyed by a thunderstorm. A cannot claim damages because B is excused under Article 7.1.7.

5. Compensation for expenses

The recipient of a performance may have incurred expenses for the preservation or maintenance of the object of the performance. It is reasonable to allow the recipient to claim compensation for these expenses where the contract has been terminated and where, therefore, the parties have to return what they have received.

示例：

> 7. 生产商 A 向 B 公司出售并交付一辆豪华轿车。该车存在刹车缺陷。该缺陷导致它与另一辆车相撞并完全被毁。由于该车不符合原定用途，B 可以终止合同并请求返还购买价款。B 无须因为不能返还车辆而折价补偿。

如果即便不交付履行，也会发生贬值或损坏，接收方并不能因此被免除补偿所收到履行之价值的义务。

示例：

> 8. 生产商 A 向 B 公司出售并交付一辆轿车。随后该车在飓风中被毁，该飓风同时破坏了 A 和 B 的场地。B 以该车存在缺陷为由终止了合同。B 可以请求返还购车价款，但同时必须折价补偿该车被毁之前所具有的价值。

接收方补偿履行价值的义务问题，只有在合同终止之前发生贬值或损坏时，才会发生。如果履行的贬值或损坏发生在合同终止之后，应适用关于不履行的一般规则，因为合同终止后，收到履行的当事方有义务退还收到的一切。如果不履行该义务，另一方当事人有权根据第 7.4.1 条请求损害赔偿，除非根据 7.1.7 条该不履行可以免责。

示例：

> 9. A 公司向 B 公司交付一辆顶篷漏水的豪华轿车。由于该轿车不符约定的使用目的，B 可终止该合同，索回购车价款，但有义务返还该轿车。然而，在 B 可以返还轿车之前，该车遭雷暴袭击完全毁损。A 不能请求损害赔偿，因为依第 7.1.7 条 B 可以免责。

5. 补偿费用

收到履行方为保存或维护履行标的可能会发生费用。在合同已被终止并且双方当事人因此返还各自所收到东西的情况下，允许收到履行方请求补偿该等费用是合理的。

Illustration

> 10. Company A has sold and delivered a race horse to company B. Some time later it becomes apparent that the horse is not, as A had promised, a descendant of a particular stallion. B terminates the contract. B can claim compensation for the costs incurred in feeding and caring for the horse.

This rule applies only to reasonable expenses. What is reasonable depends on the circumstances of the case. In Illustration 10 it would matter whether the horse had been sold as a race horse or as an ordinary farm horse.

Compensation cannot be claimed for other expenses linked to the performance received, even if they are reasonable.

Illustration

> 11. Company A has sold and delivered a software package to company B. B then discovers that the software is lacking a certain functionality it was supposed to have. B therefore asks software expert C to check whether that functionality can still be implemented. Since that turns out not to be possible, B terminates the contract. B cannot recover the fee paid to C as expenses under paragraph (4) from A.

6. Benefits

The Principles do not take a position concerning benefits that have been derived from the performance, or interest that has been earned. In commercial practice it will often be difficult to establish the value of the benefits received by the parties as a result of the performance. Furthermore, often both parties will have received such benefits.

7. Rights of third persons not affected

In common with other Articles of the Principles, this Article deals with the relationship between the parties and not with any rights on the goods concerned that third persons may have acquired. Whether, for instance, an obligee of the buyer, the buyer's receivers in bankruptcy, or a purchaser in good faith may oppose the restitution of goods sold is to be determined by the applicable law.

示例：

> 10. A 公司向 B 公司出售并交付一匹赛马。一段时间后，B 发现该马匹并非属 A 许诺的那种牡马的后代，B 终止合同。B 可以请求补偿为饲养和看护马匹所发生的费用。

该规则仅适用于合理费用。何谓合理取决于个案具体情况。在示例 10 中，该马匹是作为赛马还是普通耕作用马匹出售，至关重要。

对与收到履行相关的其他费用，即便该费用是合理的，亦不能请求补偿。

示例：

> 11. A 公司向 B 公司出售并交付一套软件包。之后，B 发现该软件包不具有原应具有的某些功能。于是，B 请求软件专家 C 检查是否可以实施该功能，结果发现不可能，B 终止了合同。B 不得根据第(4)款的规定请求 A 补偿其向 C 支付的费用。

6. 利益

对于从履行中取得的利益，或者从履行中所取得的利息，《通则》未作规定。商业实践中通常难以认定当事人因履行而取得利益之价值。另外，通常双方均取得了该种利益。

7. 第三方的权利不受影响

跟《通则》其他条款一样，本条仅处理当事人之间的关系，而不处理第三方可能取得相关货物的任何权利。例如，买方的债权人、买方的破产管理人，或者善意购买人是否能够反对返还所售货物，应该依据适用法律决定。

ARTICLE 7.3.7
(Restitution with respect to contracts
to be performed over a period of time)

(1) On termination of a contract to be performed over a period of time restitution can only be claimed for the period after termination has taken effect, provided the contract is divisible.

(2) As far as restitution has to be made, the provisions of Article 7.3.6 apply.

COMMENT

1. Contracts to be performed over a period of time

Contracts to be performed over a period of time are at least as commercially important as contracts to be performed at one time, such as contracts of sale where the object of the sale has to be transferred at one particular moment. These contracts include leases (e.g. equipment leases), contracts involving distributorship, out-sourcing, franchising, licensing and commercial agency, as well as service contracts in general. This Article also covers contracts of sale where the goods have to be delivered in instalments. Performances under such contracts can have been made over a long period of time before the contract is terminated, and it may thus be inconvenient to unravel these performances. Furthermore, termination is a remedy with prospective effect only. Restitution can, therefore, only be claimed in respect of the period after termination.

Illustration

1. A contracts to service company B's computer hardware and software for a period of five years. After three years of regular service A is obliged by illness to discontinue the services and the contract is terminated. B, who has paid A for the fourth year, can claim restitution of the advance payment for that year but not for the money paid for the three years of regular service.

Since contracts are terminated only for the future, any outstanding payments for past performances can still be claimed. This Article does not prevent a claim for damages being brought.

第 7.3.7 条

（一段期间内履行合同之恢复原状）

（1）一段期间内履行之合同终止时，只可就终止生效后的期间，主张恢复原状，而且要以合同可分割为条件。

（2）就所涉及的返还而言，应适用第 7.3.6 条之各项规定。

注释：

1. 一段期间内履行的合同

一段期间内履行的合同与一次性履行的合同，例如，销售标的须在某一时间点转移的买卖合同，至少在商业上具有同样的重要性。该等合同包括租赁（如设备租赁合约），涉及分销、外包、特许经营、许可和商业代理的合同，以及大多数服务合同。本条还调整须以分期交付的买卖合同。在该等合同下，履行在合同终止前要进行很长的时间，因此要分割这些履行会是不方便的。另外，合同终止只是具有朝前效力的救济方式，即只能就终止后的期间请求返还。

示例：

1. A 约定为 B 公司电脑的软件和硬件提供维护服务，为期五年。在提供三年正常的维护服务后，A 因疾病无法继续提供服务，因此终止了合同。B 已经支付了前四年的服务费，其可请求返还第四年预付的服务费，但不得请求返还为前三年正常服务支付的价款。

由于合同终止仅指向未来，因此，对过去履行所欠的任何款项仍可请求支付。本条不阻止提起损害赔偿之请求。

Illustrations

> 2.   Company A leases equipment to company B for three years at a rental of EUR 10,000 a month. B pays punctually for the first two months but then fails to make any further payments despite repeated requests by A. After a lapse of five months A terminates the lease. A is entitled to retain the EUR 20,000 already received (see Article 7.3.7 (1)) and to recover the EUR 50,000 accrued due (on the basis of the contract of lease which is terminated only for the future), together with whatever damages for breach it has sustained (see Article 7.3.5 (2)).

> 3.   A, a hospital, engages B to carry out cleaning services for the hospital, the contract to run for three years. After a year B informs A that it cannot continue with the cleaning services unless the price is doubled. A refuses to agree and B ceases to provide the service. On terminating the contract A can recover damages for any additional expense it incurs in hiring another cleaning firm (see Article 7.4.1 in conjunction with Article 7.3.5 (2)), while B is entitled to retain the payments it has received for services already provided (see Article 7.3.7 (1)).

The rule that restitution can only be claimed for the period after termination has taken effect does not apply if the contract is indivisible.

Illustration

> 4.   A undertakes to paint ten pictures depicting one and the same historical event for B's festival hall. After delivering and having been paid for five paintings, A abandons the work. In view of the fact that the decoration of the hall is supposed to consist of ten paintings to be painted by the same painter and showing different aspects of one historical event, B can claim the return of the advances paid to A and must return the five paintings to A.

2. Restitution

This Article is a special rule which, for contracts to be performed over a period of time, excludes restitution for performances made in the past. To the extent that there is restitution under this Article, it is governed by the provisions under Article 7.3.6.

示例：

> 2. A 公司向 B 公司出租一台设备，为期三年，月租金为 1 万欧元。B 在前两个月，按时支付了租金，但之后虽经 A 多次催促，B 一直再未支付任何租金。在 B 拖欠五个月租金后，A 终止了租约。A 有权保留已经收到的 2 万欧元（参见第 7.3.7 条(1)款），并有权求偿已发生的 5 万欧元（因依据租约，终止仅针对未来），以及因 B 违约给 A 招致的损害赔偿（参见第 7.3.5 条(2)款）。

> 3. 医院 A 聘请 B 提供医院保洁服务，为期三年。履行一年后，B 通知 A，除非价格翻倍否则不能继续提供服务。A 未同意，B 停止服务。在终止合同时，A 可以就其因聘请另一家保洁公司发生的任何额外费用向 B 请求损害赔偿（参见第 7.4.1 条，并结合第 7.3.5 条第(2)款），而 B 有权持有就已提供的服务所收到之价款（参见第 7.3.7 条第(1)款）。

如果合同是不可分割的，则只可就合同终止生效后的期间主张恢复原状的规则不适用。

示例：

> 4. A 承诺为 B 的礼堂作画 10 幅，这 10 幅画描述同一个历史事件。在 A 交付了 5 幅画并收到画款后，A 放弃了工作。鉴于该礼堂的装饰计划使用同一个画家所作的 10 幅描述同一历史事件各个不同方面的画作，故 B 可请求返还已预支 A 的预款项，但 B 须将收到的 5 幅画返还给 A。

2. 返还

本条是一个特殊规则，对于需在一定期间内履行的合同，它排除了就过去已做的履行进行返还。在本条项下允许返还的限度内，返还应受第 7.3.6 条的管辖。

SECTION 4: DAMAGES

ARTICLE 7.4.1
(Right to damages)

Any non-performance gives the aggrieved party a right to damages either exclusively or in conjunction with any other remedies except where the non-performance is excused under these Principles.

COMMENT

1. Right to damages in general

This Article establishes the principle of a general right to damages in the event of non-performance, except where the non-performance is excused under the Principles, as in the case of force majeure (see Article 7.1.7) or of an exemption clause (see Article 7.1.6). Hardship (see Article 6.2.1 *et seq.*) does not in principle give rise to a right to damages.

The Article recalls that the right to damages, like other remedies, arises from the sole fact of non-performance. It is enough for the aggrieved party simply to prove the non-performance, i.e. that it has not received what it was promised. In particular, it is not necessary in addition to prove that the non-performance was due to the fault of the non-performing party. The degree of difficulty in proving the non-performance will depend upon the content of the obligation and in particular on whether the obligation is one of best efforts or one to achieve a specific result (see Article 5.1.4).

The right to damages exists in the event of failure to perform any of the obligations which arise from the contract. Thus, it is not necessary to draw a distinction between principal and accessory obligations.

2. Damages may be combined with other remedies

This Article also states that the aggrieved party may request damages either as an exclusive remedy (for example, damages for delay in the case of late performance or for defective performance accepted by the aggrieved party; damages in the event of impossibility of performance for which the non-performing party is liable), or in conjunction

第四节　损害赔偿

第7.4.1条

（请求损害赔偿的权利）

任何不履行均使受损害方取得损害赔偿之请求权，该权利既可以单独行使，也可以和任何其他救济手段一并行使，但该不履行根据本通则属可以免责的情况除外。

注释：

1. 损害赔偿请求权的一般规定

本条确立了不履行情况下损害赔偿请求权的一般原则，除非根据《通则》不履行可以免责，如不可抗力（参见第7.1.7条）或免责条款（参见第7.1.6条）等情形。艰难情形（参见第6.2.1条及其以下有关条款）原则上不产生损害赔偿请求权。

本条重申，像其他救济手段一样，损害赔偿请求权产生于不履行这一事实本身。受损害方只要能证明不履行，即他没有得到被承诺的履行就足够了。尤其没有必要再去证明不履行是由不履行方的过错导致的。证明不履行的困难程度取决于义务的内容，特别是该义务是属于尽最大努力的义务，还是获得特定结果的义务（参见第5.1.4条）。

损害赔偿请求权存在于未能履行产生自合同的任何义务的情形。因此没有必要区分主义务和从义务。

2. 损害赔偿可与其他救济手段相结合

本条还阐明，受损害方既可以把要求损害赔偿作为唯一的救济手段（比如，对迟延履行的延误或对受损害方接受的瑕疵履行要求损害赔偿;对不履行方应承担责任的履行不可能要求损害赔偿），也可以和

with other remedies. Thus, in the case of termination of the contract, damages may be requested to compensate the loss arising from such termination, or again, in the case of specific performance, to compensate for the delay with which the aggrieved party receives performance and for any expenses which might have been incurred. Damages may also be accompanied by other remedies (cure, publication in newspapers of, for example, an admission of error, etc.).

3. Damages and pre-contractual liability

The right to damages may arise not only in the context of non-performance of the contract, but also during the pre-contractual period (see, for instance, Article 2.1.15 in case of negotiations in bad faith, Article 2.1.16 in the event of breach of the duty of confidentiality, or Article 3.2.16 in the case of mistake, fraud, threat or gross disparity). The rules governing damages for non-performance as laid down in this Section may be applied by analogy to those situations.

ARTICLE 7.4.2

(Full compensation)

(1) The aggrieved party is entitled to full compensation for harm sustained as a result of the non-performance. Such harm includes both any loss which it suffered and any gain of which it was deprived, taking into account any gain to the aggrieved party resulting from its avoidance of cost or harm.

(2) Such harm may be non-pecuniary and includes, for instance, physical suffering or emotional distress.

COMMENT

1. Aggrieved party entitled to full compensation

Paragraph (1) of this Article establishes the principle of the aggrieved party's entitlement to full compensation for the harm it has sustained as a result of the non-performance of the contract. It further affirms the need for a causal link between the non-performance and the harm (see also Comment 3 on Article 7.4.3). Non-performance must be a source neither of gain nor of loss for the aggrieved party.

其他救济手段相结合。因此，在终止合同的同时，可以要求损害赔偿金用来补偿因合同终止而产生的损失，或者在请求实际履行的同时，可以要求损害赔偿用来补偿受损害方接受的迟延履行所发生的迟延以及其可能发生的任何费用。损害赔偿也可以附带其他救济手段（比如补救、在报纸上公开承认错误等）。

3. 损害赔偿和前合同义务

损害赔偿请求权并不仅产生于合同的不履行过程中，也产生于合同订立前的阶段（比如，参见第 2.1.15 条针对恶意谈判、第 2.1.16 条针对违反保密义务，或第 3.2.16 条针对错误、欺诈、胁迫或重大失衡所规定的损害赔偿）。本节规定的针对不履行的损害赔偿的规则类推适用于这些情况。

第 7.4.2 条

（完全赔偿）

（1）受损害方对由于不履行而遭受的损害有权得到完全赔偿。该损害既包括该方当事人遭受的任何损失，也包括其被剥夺的任何收益，但应当考虑到受损害方因避免发生的成本或损害而得到的任何收益。

（2）此损害可以是非金钱性质的，并且包括例如肉体或精神上的痛苦。

注释：

1. 受损害方有权得到完全赔偿

本条第(1)款确立的原则是受损害方对由合同的不履行导致其遭受的损害有权得到完全赔偿。它进一步肯定了在不履行和损害之间必须存在因果关系（还可以参见第 7.4.3 条的注释 3）。对受损害方来说，不履行必须既不对其产生收益，也不使其遭受损失。

The solution to be found in some legal systems which allows the court to reduce the amount of damages having regard to the circumstances has not been followed, since in international situations it could risk creating a considerable degree of uncertainty and its application might moreover vary from one court to another.

2. Damages cover loss suffered, including loss of profit

In specifying the harm for which damages are recoverable, paragraph (1) of this Article, following the rule laid down in Article 74 CISG, states that the aggrieved party is entitled to compensation in respect not only of loss which it has suffered, but also of any gain of which it has been deprived as a consequence of the non-performance.

The notion of loss suffered must be understood in a wide sense. It may cover a reduction in the aggrieved party's assets or an increase in its liabilities which occurs when an obligee, not having been paid by its obligor, must borrow money to meet its commitments. The loss of profit or, as it is sometimes called, consequential loss, is the benefit which would normally have accrued to the aggrieved party if the contract had been properly performed. The benefit will often be uncertain so that it will frequently take the form of the loss of a chance (see Article 7.4.3(2)).

Illustrations

 1. A national library sends a rare manuscript by special courier abroad for an exhibition. The manuscript is irreparably damaged during transport. Its loss in value is estimated at EUR 100,000 and it is this sum which is due by the courier.

 2. A, who has not been paid by B under the terms of their contract, must borrow money from its bank at a high rate of interest. B must compensate A for the interest due by the latter to its bank.

 3. A, a construction company, hires a crane from company B. The boom of the crane, which has been poorly maintained, breaks and in falling crushes the architect's car and results in an interruption of work on the site for eight days, for which A must pay a penalty for delay of EUR 50,000 to the owner. B must reimburse A for the expenses incurred as a consequence of the interruption of the work, the amount of the penalty and the cost of repairing the architect's car which A has had to pay.

 4. A, a singer, cancels an engagement with B, an impresario. A must pay damages to B in respect not only of the expenses incurred by B in preparing the concert, but also of the loss of profit resulting from the cancellation of the concert.

一些法律制度允许法院根据具体情况减少损害赔偿金额，《通则》没有采取这种解决方法，因为在国际合同情况下，这种方法会导致相当程度的不确定性风险，并且其适用也可能因法院的不同而相异。

2. 损害赔偿弥补所遭受的损失，包括利益的损失

在确定可求偿的损害赔偿的损害种类时，本条第(1)款遵循《联合国国际货物销售合同公约》(CISG) 第 74 条的规定，规定受损害方不仅有权要求赔偿其实际遭受的损失，也有权要求赔偿因不履行而被剥夺的任何收益。

对所遭受的损失这个概念应当从广义上加以理解。它可以包括受损害方财产的减少，也包括债务的增加，例如，没有得到债务人支付的债权人必须借款履行其本身义务时。利润的损失，有时被称作结果性（间接）损失，是指合同如果被适当履行，受损害方在正常情况下可以获得的收益。这种收益经常是不确定的，因此，它经常以机会丧失的形式出现（参见第 7.4.3 条第(2)款）。

示例：

　　1. 一国家图书馆通过特殊信使把一份罕见的手稿送到国外展览，该手稿在运输途中遭到了无法修补的损害。估计的损失大约是 100,000 欧元，这笔数额应由信使负责赔偿。

　　2. 由于 B 没有按合同条款向 A 付款，A 因此必须以较高的利率向其银行借款，在这种情况下，B 必须补偿 A 向其银行应支付的利息。

　　3. 建筑公司 A 向公司 B 租用了一辆起重机。由于维护极差，该起重机底部断裂并下落，压碎了某建筑师的轿车，并因此导致工地停工 8 天，A 必须为此向工程所有人支付 50,000 欧元的迟延罚金。在这种情况下，B 必须偿还 A 因工程停工而支付的迟延罚金，以及 A 必须支付的修理工程师轿车的费用。

　　4. 歌手 A 取消了与演出主办者 B 的聘约。A 不仅应当赔偿 B 为准备该音乐会所支出的费用，而且还应赔偿 B 因取消音乐会所遭受的利润损失。

3. Damages must not enrich the aggrieved party

However, the aggrieved party must not be enriched by damages for non-performance. It is for this reason that paragraph (1) also provides that account must be taken of any gain resulting to the aggrieved party from the non-performance, whether that be in the form of expenses which it has not incurred (e.g. it does not have to pay the cost of a hotel room for an artist who fails to appear), or of a loss which it has avoided (e.g. in the event of non-performance of what would have been a losing bargain for it).

Illustration

> 5.   A rents out excavating machinery to B for two years at a monthly rental of EUR 10,000. The contract is terminated after six months for non-payment of the rentals. Six months later, A succeeds in renting out the same machinery at a monthly charge of EUR 11,000. The gain of EUR 12,000 realised by A as a result of the re-letting of the machinery for the remainder of the initial contract, that is to say one year, should be deducted from the damages due by B to A.

4. Damages in case of changes in the harm

In application of the principle of full compensation regard is to be had to any changes in the harm, including its expression in monetary terms, which may occur between the time of the non-performance and that of the judgment. The rule however is not without exceptions: for example, if the aggrieved party has itself already made good the harm at its own expense, the damages awarded will correspond to the amount of the sums disbursed.

5. Compensation of non-material harm

Paragraph (2) of this Article expressly provides for compensation also of non-pecuniary harm. This may be pain and suffering, loss of certain amenities of life, aesthetic prejudice, etc. as well as harm resulting from attacks on honour or reputation.

The rule might find application, in international commerce, in regard to contracts concluded by artists, outstanding sportsmen or women and consultants engaged by a company or by an organisation.

3. 受损害方不应从损害赔偿中不当得利

然而，受损害方不能因不履行损害赔偿而不当得利，为此第(1)款还规定必须考虑受损害方因不履行而获得的任何利益，不管这种利益表现为未发生的费用(比如，演出主办者不需为不能到场的艺术家支付宾馆住宿费)，还是表现为避免了某种损失(比如，发生不履行的是一笔对其而言的亏损交易)。

示例：

　　5. A 将挖掘机以月租 10,000 欧元的租金出租给 B 使用两年。六个月后，由于 B 未支付租金而导致合同终止。又过了六个月，A 成功的以 11,000 欧元的月租将同一台机器出租了。在这种情况下，A 在原合同剩余的一年时间里将该机器予以转租所多获得的 12,000 欧元的收益，应从 B 对 A 应支付的损害赔偿金中扣除。

4. 损害发生变化时的损害赔偿

适用完全赔偿原则时，应当考虑到在不履行和作出判决之间的这段时间可能发生的损害的任何变化，包括记账货币的变化。然而该规则并非没有例外，比如，如果受损害方已经自担费用弥补了损害，则所得到的损害赔偿应当与付出的数额一致。

5. 非物质损害的赔偿

本条第(2)款还明确规定对非金钱性损害的赔偿。这种损害可能是悲痛和痛苦、失去生活的某些快乐、丧失美感等，也指对名誉或荣誉进行攻击造成的损害。

这条规则可能适用于国际商事活动中的下列相关合同，比如与受雇于一个公司或一个组织的艺术家、杰出的男女运动员以及顾问所订立的合同。

In these cases also, the requirement of the certainty of harm must be satisfied (see Article 7.4.3), together with the other conditions for entitlement to damages.

Illustration

> 6. A, a young architect who is beginning to build up a certain reputation, signs a contract for the modernisation of a municipal fine arts museum. The appointment receives wide press coverage. The municipal authorities subsequently decide to engage the services of a more experienced architect and terminate the contract with A. A may obtain compensation not only for the material loss suffered but also for the harm to A's reputation and the loss of the chance of becoming better known which the commission would have provided.

The compensation of non-material harm may assume different forms and it is for the court to decide which of them, whether taken alone or together, best assures full compensation. The court may not only award damages but also order other forms of redress such as the publication of a notice in newspapers designated by it (e.g. in case of breach of a clause prohibiting competition or the reopening of a business, defamation etc.).

ARTICLE 7.4.3
(Certainty of harm)

(1) Compensation is due only for harm, including future harm, that is established with a reasonable degree of certainty.

(2) Compensation may be due for the loss of a chance in proportion to the probability of its occurrence.

(3) Where the amount of damages cannot be established with a sufficient degree of certainty, the assessment is at the discretion of the court.

在这些情况下，损害的确定性要求（参见第7.4.3条），也必须和享有损害赔偿请求权的其他条件一并得到满足。

示例：

6. 一个刚开始小有名气的年轻建筑师 A 订立了一份装饰市立艺术博物馆的合同。媒体对该委任做了大量报道。市政当局随后决定雇佣一个更有经验的建筑师来完成该任务，并终止了与 A 的合同。在这种情况下，A 不仅有权获得所遭受的物质损失的赔偿，还有权要求赔偿对其声誉所造成的损害以及因完成该任务而变得更知名的机会的丧失。

非物质损害的赔偿可以采用不同的形式，至于采取何种形式（无论是单独还是结合使用）能确保完全赔偿，将由法院决定。法院不仅可以判决损害赔偿，还可以命令采取其他形式的救济，如在其指定的报刊上发布通告（比如，对违反禁止竞争或重新开业条款的行为以及诽谤等都可以发布通告）。

第7.4.3条

（损害的确定性）

（1）赔偿仅适用于根据合理的确定性程度而证实的损害，包括未来损害。

（2）对机会损失的赔偿可根据机会发生的可能性程度按比例确定。

（3）凡不能以充分确定性程度来确定损害赔偿金额的，赔偿金额依法院的自由裁量权确定。

COMMENT

1. Occurrence of harm must be reasonably certain

This Article reaffirms the well-known requirement of certainty of harm, since it is not possible to require the non-performing party to compensate harm which may not have occurred or which may never occur.

Paragraph (1) permits the compensation also of future harm, i.e. harm which has not yet occurred, provided that it is sufficiently certain. Paragraph (2) in addition covers loss of a chance, obviously only in proportion to the probability of its occurrence: thus, the owner of a horse which arrives too late to run in a race as a result of delay in transport cannot recover the whole of the prize money, even though the horse was the favourite.

2. Determination of extent of harm

Certainty relates not only to the existence of the harm but also to its extent. There may be harm the existence of which cannot be disputed but which it is difficult to quantify. This will often be the case in respect of loss of a chance (there are not always "odds" as there are for a horse, for example for an engineering company preparing for the making of a bid) or of compensation for non-material harm (detriment to someone's reputation, pain and suffering, etc.).

Illustration

> A entrusts a file to B, an express delivery company, in response to an invitation to submit tenders for the construction of an airport. B undertakes to deliver the file before the closing date for tenders but delivers it after that date and A's application is refused. The amount of compensation will depend upon the degree of probability of A's tender having been accepted and calls for a comparison of it with the applications which were admitted for consideration. The compensation will therefore be calculated as a proportion of the profit which A might have made.

According to paragraph (3), where the amount of damages cannot be established with a sufficient degree of certainty then, rather than refuse any compensation or award nominal damages, the court is empowered to make an equitable quantification of the harm sustained.

注释：

1. 损害的发生必须具有合理确定性

本条重申了广为人知的损害确定性的要求，因为不可能要求不履行方对没有发生或将永远不会发生的损害进行赔偿。

第(1)款允许对未来损害，即尚未发生的损害，进行赔偿，只要它是充分确定的。第(2)款还涉及机会的损失，但明显仅按其发生的概率予以赔偿。因此，对由于运输延误未能参加比赛的马，其主人不能获得全部奖金作为赔偿，即使该马最有希望获胜。

2. 损害程度的确定

确定性不仅涉及损害的存在，还涉及它的程度。有的损害其存在无可争辩，但却难以量化。机会的丧失（并不是所有的事情都像赛马一样有一定的"概率"，例如，一家准备投标的工程公司）或者对非物质损害的赔偿（对某人名誉的损害、悲痛、痛苦，等等）就属于这种情况。

示例：

A将一份建设某机场的投标书委托快递公司B予以递交。B承诺将该投标书于投标结束日前递交到，但B于结束日后才送到，于是A的投标申请被拒绝了。损害赔偿的数额将取决于A的投标申请被接受的概率，因此要求将A的投标申请与被接受用参与评标的其他申请进行比较。因此，赔偿数额将根据A可能获得的相称的利润进行计算。

根据第(3)款，当损害赔偿数额不能以充分的确定性予以确立时，不是拒绝任何赔偿或只给予名义上的赔偿，而是授权法院对所受损害进行公平的估算。

3. Harm must be a direct consequence of non-performance as well as certain

There is a clear connection between the certainty and the direct nature of the harm. Although the latter requirement is not expressly dealt with by the Principles, it is implicit in Article 7.4.2(1) which refers to the harm sustained "as a result of the non-performance" and which therefore presupposes a sufficient causal link between the non-performance and the harm. Harm which is too indirect will usually also be uncertain as well as unforeseeable.

ARTICLE 7.4.4

(Foreseeability of harm)

The non-performing party is liable only for harm which it foresaw or could reasonably have foreseen at the time of the conclusion of the contract as being likely to result from its non-performance.

COMMENT

The principle of limitation of recoverable harm to that which is foreseeable corresponds to the solution adopted in Article 74 CISG. This limitation is related to the very nature of the contract: not all the benefits of which the aggrieved party is deprived fall within the scope of the contract and the non-performing party must not be saddled with compensation for harm which it could never have foreseen at the time of the conclusion of the contract and against the risk of which it could not have taken out insurance.

The requirement of foreseeability must be seen in conjunction with that of certainty of harm set out in Article 7.4.3.

The concept of foreseeability must be clarified since the solution contained in the Principles does not correspond to certain national systems which allow compensation even for harm which is unforeseeable when the non-performance is due to wilful misconduct or gross negligence. Since the present rule does not provide for such an exception, a narrow interpretation of the concept of foreseeability is called for. Foreseeability relates to the nature or type of the harm but not to its extent unless the extent is such as to transform the harm into one of a different kind. In any event, foreseeability is a flexible concept which leaves a wide measure of discretion to the judge.

3. 损害必须不但是确定的，而且是不履行的直接结果

损害的确定性和损害的直接性之间存在明确的联系。尽管本《通则》没有专门涉及后一要求，但第 7.4.2 条第(1)款暗含了这一要求，该款提及"因不履行而遭受的损害"，因此它预设了在不履行和损害之间存在充分的因果联系。过于间接的损害通常也是不确定的和无法预见的。

第 7.4.4 条

（损害的可预见性）

不履行方仅对在订立合同时他已经预见到的或应当合理预见到的、因其不履行可能产生的损害承担责任。

注释：

把可赔偿的损害限定于可预见的损害，这一原则和《联合国国际货物销售合同公约》第 74 条采取的解决办法是一致的。这种限制与合同本身的性质有关：并不是受损害方被剥夺的所有利益都属于合同范围之内，不履行方不需对其在订立合同时不能预见的、从而不可能对其风险进行投保的损害承担赔偿责任。

可预见性要求必须和第 7.4.3 条规定的损害的确定性联系起来。

可预见性的概念必须予以澄清，因为本《通则》包含的解决办法与某些国内法律制度不一致，这些国内法律制度甚至允许对归咎于故意不当行为或重大疏忽的不履行所产生的不可预见的损害承担赔偿责任。因为本条没有规定这样的例外，所以要求对可预见性概念作狭义解释。可预见性和损害的性质或类型有关，但和损害的程度无关，除非该程度足以改变损害类型。无论如何，可预见性是一个灵活的概念，它留给法官广泛的自由裁量权。

What was foreseeable is to be determined by reference to the time of the conclusion of the contract and to the non-performing party itself (including its servants or agents), and the test is what a normally diligent person could reasonably have foreseen as the consequences of non-performance in the ordinary course of things and the particular circumstances of the contract, such as the information supplied by the parties or their previous transactions.

Illustrations

1.   A cleaning company orders a machine which is delivered five months late. The manufacturer is obliged to compensate the company for lost profit caused by the delay in delivery as it could have foreseen that the machine was intended for immediate use. On the other hand the harm does not include the loss of a valuable Government contract that could have been concluded if the machine had been delivered on time since that kind of harm was not foreseeable.

2.   A, a bank, usually employs the services of a security company for the conveyance of bags containing coins to its branches. Without informing the security company, A sends a consignment of bags containing new coins for collectors worth fifty times the value of previous consignments. The bags are stolen in a hold-up. A can only recover compensation corresponding to the value of the normal consignments as this was the only kind of harm that could have been foreseen and the value of the items lost was such as to transform the harm into one of another kind.

Unlike certain international conventions, particularly in the field of transport, the Principles follow CISG in not making provision for full compensation of harm, albeit unforeseeable, in the event of intentional non-performance.

ARTICLE 7.4.5
*(Proof of harm in case of
replacement transaction)*

Where the aggrieved party has terminated the contract and has made a replacement transaction within a reasonable time and in a reasonable manner it may recover the difference between the contract price and the price of the replacement transaction as well as damages for any further harm.

确定何为可预见的基准是订立合同的时间和不履行方自身的情况（包括他的雇员或代理人），所用的标准是一个正常勤勉的人能够合理预见到的、按照事情正常进展过程以及合同的特定情况（比如合同当事人提供的信息或他们之前的交易行为）不履行将会导致的后果。

示例：

　　1. 一个清洁公司定购了一台机器，但该机器迟延交货五个月。制造商有义务赔偿因迟延交货而给清洁公司造成的利益损失，因为制造商预见到清洁公司打算立即使用该机器。但另一方面，损害不包括如果机器按时交付，清洁公司本来能和政府签订的一个有价值的合同的损失，因为这种损害是不可预见的。

　　2. 银行A经常雇佣一个保安公司的服务人员护送其装有硬币的钱袋到各分支机构。在没有通知保安公司的情况下，A送交了一批装有供收藏者购买的新硬币的袋子，这批硬币的价值是以前硬币价值的50倍。结果这些钱袋被抢劫了。在这种情况下，A只能要求与之前正常运送价值相符的赔偿，因为只有这种损害才是可预见的，实际损失的硬币价值如此之大，已经达到改变损害类型的程度。

不像有些国际公约，尤其是与运输领域国际公约的规定不同，本《通则》遵循《联合国国际货物销售合同公约》的规定，即没有规定对因故意不履行而产生的不可预见的损害进行完全赔偿。

第7.4.5条

（替代交易时损害的证明）

受损害方已终止合同并在合理时间内以合理方式进行了替代交易的，该方当事人可对合同价格与替代交易价格之间的差额以及任何进一步的损害要求赔偿。

COMMENT

1. Amount of harm presumed in case of replacement transaction

It seems advisable to establish, alongside the general rules applicable to the proof of the existence and of the amount of the harm, presumptions which may facilitate the task of the aggrieved party.

The first of these presumptions is provided by this Article which corresponds in substance to Article 75 CISG. It concerns the situation where the aggrieved party has made a replacement transaction, for instance because so required by the duty to mitigate harm or in conformity with usages. In such cases, the harm is considered to be the difference between the contract price and the price of the replacement transaction.

The presumption comes into play only if there is a replacement transaction and not where the aggrieved party has itself performed the obligation which lay upon the non-performing party (for example when a shipowner itself carries out the repairs to its vessel following the failure to do so of the shipyard which had been entrusted with the work).

Nor is there replacement, and the general rules will apply, when a company, after the termination of a contract, uses its equipment for the performance of another contract which it could have performed at the same time as the first ("lost volume").

The replacement transaction must be performed within a reasonable time and in a reasonable manner so as to avoid the non-performing party being prejudiced by hasty or malicious conduct.

2. Further damages recoverable for additional harm

The rule that the aggrieved party may recover the difference between the two contract prices establishes a minimum right of recovery. The aggrieved party may also obtain damages for additional harm which it may have sustained.

Illustration

> A, a shipyard, undertakes to accommodate a ship belonging to B, a shipowner, in dry dock for repairs costing USD 500,000 as from 1 July. B learns on 1 June that the dry dock will only be available as from 1 August. B terminates the contract and after lengthy and costly negotiations concludes with C, another shipyard, an identical contract at a price of USD 700,000. B is entitled to recover from A not only the difference in the price of USD 200,000 but also the expenses it has incurred and compensation for the longer period of unavailability of the ship.

注释：

1. 存在替代交易时损害数额的推定

根据适用于证明损害存在和损害数额的一般规则，确立某些有助于受损害方完成证明任务的推定，是可取的。

其中第一项推定与《联合国国际货物销售合同公约》第75条在本质上是相一致的。它所涉及的情况是，受损害方已经采取了替代交易，比如这是为减轻损害或符合惯例而必须为之的。在这种情况下，损害被认为是合同价格和替代交易价格之间的差额。

只有当进行了替代交易，而不是受损害方自身履行了应当由不履行方承担的义务（比如，已接受委托修理船只的修船厂没有进行修理，船主则自己修理了船只）时，才适用这一推定。

当一个公司在终止合同后，用其自身的设备去履行另一个本来可以和第一个合同同时履行的合同（"失去业务额"）时，此时也不存在替代交易，因此应适用一般规则。

替代交易必须在合理的时间以合理的方式履行，以避免因草率或恶意行为而使不履行方受到损害。

2. 对额外损害可以要求进一步赔偿

规定受损害方可以要求补偿两个合同之间的差额的规则，确立了补偿的最低权限。受损害方还可以对其遭受的额外损害获得赔偿。

示例：

> 修船厂A承诺为船舶所有人B的一艘船舶提供船坞，以便从7月1日开始在该船坞进行检修工作，费用是50万美元。B于6月1日得知该船坞只能在8月1日才可以使用，于是B终止了合同，并在经过漫长而付出重大代价的谈判后与另一个修船厂C签订了同样内容的合同，但合同价格为70万美元。在这种情况下，B不仅有权要求A补偿两个合同之间的价差20万美元，而且还有权要求A补偿其发生的各种费用以及船舶在更长一段时间内不能使用所遭受的损失。

ARTICLE 7.4.6
(Proof of harm by current price)

(1) Where the aggrieved party has terminated the contract and has not made a replacement transaction but there is a current price for the performance contracted for, it may recover the difference between the contract price and the price current at the time the contract is terminated as well as damages for any further harm.

(2) Current price is the price generally charged for goods delivered or services rendered in comparable circumstances at the place where the contract should have been performed or, if there is no current price at that place, the current price at such other place that appears reasonable to take as a reference.

COMMENT

1. Amount of harm presumed when no replacement transaction

The purpose of this Article, which corresponds in substance to Article 76 CISG, is to facilitate proof of harm where no replacement transaction has been made, but there exists a current price for the performance contracted for. In such cases the harm is presumed to be equal to the difference between the contract price and the price current at the time the contract was terminated.

2. Determination of "current price"

According to paragraph (2) "current price" is the price generally charged for the goods or services in question. The price will be determined in comparison with that which is charged for the same or similar goods or services. This will often, but not necessarily, be the price on an organised market. Evidence of the current price may be obtained from professional organisations, chambers of commerce etc.

For the purpose of this Article the place relevant for determining the current price is that where the contract should have been performed or, if there is no current price at that place, the place that appears reasonable to take as a reference.

第7.4.6条

（依时价证明损害）

（1）受损害方已终止合同但未进行替代交易的，如果对于合同约定的履行存在时价，则该方当事人可对合同价格与合同终止时的时价之间的差额以及任何进一步的损害要求赔偿。

（2）时价是指在合同应当履行的地点，对应交付之货物或应提供之服务在可比情况下通常所收取的价格，或者如果该地无时价，则为可合理参照的另一地的时价。

注释：

1. 不存在替代交易时损害数额的推定

本条的规定与《联合国国际货物销售合同公约》第76条在实质上是一致的，其目的是为了在不存在替代交易但合同约定的履行存在时价时，便于证明损害。在此类情况下，损害推定为合同价格和终止合同时的时价之间的差额。

2. "时价"的确定

根据第（2）款，"时价"是指所涉及的货物或服务通常收取的价格。该价格通过对相同或相似货物或服务所收取的价格进行比较后予以确定。这种价格常常是但并非必须是有组织的市场上的价格。有关时价的证明材料可以从专业组织、商业协会等机构获得。

为本条之目的，确定时价的相关地点是合同应当被履行的地方，或者如果该地方没有时价，则为其价格可供合理参照的地方。

3. Further damages recoverable for additional harm

The rule that the aggrieved party may recover the difference between the contract price and the current price at the time of termination establishes only a minimum right of recovery. The aggrieved party may also obtain damages for additional harm which it may have sustained as a consequence of termination.

ARTICLE 7.4.7

(Harm due in part to aggrieved party)

Where the harm is due in part to an act or omission of the aggrieved party or to another event for which that party bears the risk, the amount of damages shall be reduced to the extent that these factors have contributed to the harm, having regard to the conduct of each of the parties.

COMMENT

1. Contribution of the aggrieved party to the harm

In application of the general principle established by Article 7.1.2 which restricts the exercise of remedies where non-performance is in part due to the conduct of the aggrieved party, this Article limits the right to damages to the extent that the aggrieved party has in part contributed to the harm. It would indeed be unjust for such a party to obtain full compensation for harm for which it has itself been partly responsible.

2. Ways of contributing to the harm

The contribution of the aggrieved party to the harm may consist either in its own conduct or in an event for which it bears the risk. The conduct may take the form of an act (e.g. it gave a carrier a mistaken address) or an omission (e.g. it failed to give all the necessary instructions to the constructor of the defective machinery). Most frequently such acts or omissions will result in the aggrieved party failing to perform one or another of its own contractual obligations; they may however equally consist in tortious conduct or non-performance of

3. 对额外损害可要求进一步赔偿

规定受损害方可以对合同价格和终止合同时的时价之间的差额要求补偿的规则，只是确立了补偿的最低权利。此外，受损害方还可以对因终止合同所遭受的额外损害要求获得赔偿。

第7.4.7条

（部分归咎于受损害方的损害）

如果损害部分归咎于受损害方的作为或不作为，或是部分归咎于由该方当事人承担风险的其他事件，在考虑到各方当事人行为的基础上，损害的赔偿金额应扣除因上述因素所导致的损害部分。

注释：

1. 受损害方部分导致的损害

根据第7.1.2条，当不履行部分归咎于受损害方的行为时，救济手段的采用受到限制。适用这个一般原则，本条规定，受损害方因部分导致了损害，其要求损害赔偿的权利受到限制。因为允许一方当事人对自己负有部分责任的损害要求获得完全赔偿确实是不公平的。

2. 部分导致损害的方式

受损害方既可能因其自身的行为部分导致损害，也可能因由其承担风险的事件部分导致损害。行为的形式可以是作为（比如他给运输者一个错误的地址）或者不作为（比如未能对瑕疵机器的制造者给予所有必要的指导）。这种作为或不作为往往导致受损害方不能履行其这项或那项合同义务；然而，这些行为同样可能是侵权行为或对另一个

another contract. The external events for which the aggrieved party bears the risk may, among others, be acts or omissions of persons for whom it is responsible such as its servants or agents.

Illustrations

1.   A, a franchisee bound by an "exclusivity" clause contained in the contract with B, acquires stock from C because B has required immediate payment despite the fact that the franchise agreement provides for payment at 90 days. B claims payment of the penalty stipulated for breach of the exclusivity clause. B will obtain only part of the sum due thereunder as it was B who provoked A's non-performance.

2.   A, a passenger on a liner effecting a luxury cruise, is injured when a lift fails to stop at the floor requested. B, the shipowner, is held liable for the consequences of A's injury and seeks recourse against C, the company which had checked the lifts before the liner's departure. It is proved that the accident would have been avoided if the floor had been better lit. Since this was B's responsibility, B will not obtain full recovery from C.

3. Apportionment of contribution to the harm

The conduct of the aggrieved party or the external events as to which it bears the risk may have made it absolutely impossible for the non-performing party to perform. If the requirements of Article 7.1.7 (*Force majeure*) are satisfied, the non-performing party is totally exonerated from liability.

Otherwise, the exoneration will be partial, depending on the extent to which the aggrieved party contributed to the harm. The determination of each party's contribution to the harm may well prove to be difficult and will to a large degree depend upon the exercise of judicial discretion. In order to give some guidance to the court this Article provides that the court shall have regard to the respective behaviour of the parties. The more serious a party's failing, the greater will be its contribution to the harm.

Illustrations

3.   The facts are the same as in Illustration 1. Since it was B who was the first not to observe the terms of the contract, B is deemed to have caused A's failure to respect the exclusivity clause. B may only recover 25% of the amount stipulated in the penalty clause.

合同的不履行。受损害方承担风险的外部事件可以是其应对之负责的人(例如其雇员或代理人)的作为或不作为。

示例:

1. 特许经营 A 受其与 B 订立的合同中的一条"排他"条款的约束。尽管特许合同规定进货后 90 天内付款,B 却要求立即付款,A 因此从 C 处进货。B 以 A 违反该排他性条款为由主张罚金。在这种情况下,B 只能获得部分罚金,因为是他自己的行为导致了 A 的不履行。

2. 一豪华班轮的吊机没有按要求停落在船的甲板上,结果导致一乘客 A 被砸伤。船舶所有人 B 对 A 的受伤结果负有责任,并对班轮起航前对吊机进行检查的 C 公司拥有追偿权。然而事实证明如果甲板的照明好一些,则该事故可以避免。因为提供甲板照明是 B 的责任,所以 B 不能从 C 处获得完全赔偿。

3. 导致损害的责任划分

受损害方的行为或由其承担风险的外部事件可能会使不履行方的履行变得完全不可能。如果第 7.1.7 条(不可抗力)规定的条件得到满足,则不履行方将完全免除责任。

否则,将根据受损害方导致损害的程度,使不履行方获得部分免责。要确定各方当事人导致损害的程度可能非常困难,这将很大程度上取决于司法裁量权的运用。为了给法院一些指导,本条规定法院应当考虑合同当事人各自的行为。一方的过错越严重,则他对损害承担的责任就越大。

示例:

3. 事实和示例 1 相同。因为是 B 首先不遵守合同条款,视为 B 的行为致使 A 不能遵守"排他"条款。B 只能得到罚金条款规定的赔偿金额的25%。

4.   The facts are the same as in Illustration 2. Since the failings of B and C seem to be equivalent, B can only recover from C 50% of the compensation it had to pay A.

4. Contribution to harm and mitigation of harm

This Article must be read in conjunction with the following Article on mitigation of harm (see Article 7.4.8). While this Article is concerned with the conduct of the aggrieved party in regard to the cause of the initial harm, Article 7.4.8 relates to that party's conduct subsequent thereto.

ARTICLE 7.4.8

(Mitigation of harm)

(1) The non-performing party is not liable for harm suffered by the aggrieved party to the extent that the harm could have been reduced by the latter party's taking reasonable steps.

(2) The aggrieved party is entitled to recover any expenses reasonably incurred in attempting to reduce the harm.

COMMENT

1. Duty of aggrieved party to mitigate harm

The purpose of this Article is to avoid the aggrieved party passively sitting back and waiting to be compensated for harm which it could have avoided or reduced. Any harm which the aggrieved party could have avoided by taking reasonable steps will not be compensated.

Evidently, a party who has already suffered the consequences of non-performance of the contract cannot be required in addition to take time-consuming and costly measures. On the other hand, it would be unreasonable from the economic standpoint to permit an increase in harm which could have been reduced by the taking of reasonable steps.

The steps to be taken by the aggrieved party may be directed either to limiting the extent of the harm, above all when there is a risk of it lasting for a long time if such steps are not taken (often they will consist in a replacement transaction: see Article 7.4.5), or to avoiding any increase in the initial harm.

4. 事实和示例 2 相同。因为 B 和 C 的过失相当，所以 B 只能要求 C 补偿其向 A 支付的赔偿数额的 50%。

4. 部分导致损害和损害的减轻

本条必须和接下来的减轻损害的规定(参见第 7.4.8 条)结合起来理解。本条涉及的是受损害方的行为与原始损害的原因之间的关系，第 7.4.8 条涉及的是该方当事人在原始损害发生后的行为。

第 7.4.8 条

(损害的减轻)

(1) 不履行方对于受损害方所蒙受的本来可以通过其采取合理措施减少的那部分损害，不承担责任。

(2) 受损害方有权对因试图减少损害而发生的一切合理费用要求偿付。

注释：

1. 受损害方减轻损害的义务

本条的目的是为了避免受损害方消极坐等对本应可以防止或减轻的损害获得补偿。对于受损害方通过其采取合理措施本应能够防止的损害，他不能获得赔偿。

显然，对于已经遭受不履行合同后果的一方当事人来说，不能再额外地要求他采取费时费钱的措施。另一方面，从经济学的角度讲，对通过采取合理措施可以减轻的损害，放任增加其损害程度也是不合理的。

受损害方采取的措施，可以是限制损害的程度，或是避免原始损害的增加。前一种措施尤其适用于如果不采取这类措施(通常情况下他们构成替代交易：参见第 7.4.5 条)损害将持续很长时间的情况下。

Illustrations

> 1.   On 2 May, A requests B, a travel agency, to reserve a hotel room in city X for 1 June, at a cost of EUR 200. On 15 May, A learns that B has not made the reservation. A waits however until 25 May before making a new reservation and can only find a room costing EUR 300, whereas accommodation could have been secured for EUR 250 if A had taken action already on 15 May. A can recover only EUR 50 from B.

> 2.   A, a company which has been entrusted by B with the building of a factory, suddenly stops work when the project is nearing completion. B looks for another company to finish the building of the factory but takes no steps to protect the buildings on the site the condition of which deteriorates as a result of bad weather. B cannot recover compensation for such deterioration as it is attributable to its failure to take interim protective measures.

2. Reimbursement of expenses

The reduction in damages to the extent that the aggrieved party has failed to take the necessary steps to mitigate the harm must not however cause loss to that party. The aggrieved party may therefore recover from the non-performing party the expenses incurred by it in mitigating the harm, provided that those expenses were reasonable in the circumstances (paragraph (2)).

Illustrations

> 3.   The facts are the same as in Illustration 2, except that B has the necessary work carried out to ensure the interim protection of the buildings. The cost of such work will be added to the damages due by A for non-performance of the contract on condition that those costs were reasonable. If they were not, they will be reduced.

> 4.   The facts are the same as in Illustration 1, except that A takes a room costing EUR 500 in a luxury hotel. A may only recover the 50 euro difference in respect of the room which A could have obtained for EUR 250.

示例：

　　1. A 于 5 月 2 日要求旅行社 B 为其在 X 城预订一间 6 月 1 日的客房，价格为 200 欧元。5 月 15 日，A 得知 B 根本没有预订。然而 A 一直等到 5 月 25 日才重新预订房间，而当时只能找到 300 欧元标准的房间，然而如果 A 在 5 月 15 日就采取行动，则住宿费只要 250 欧元。在这种情况下，A 只能从 B 处获得 50 欧元的赔偿。

　　2. 公司 A 接受 B 的委托修建一个工厂，在工程接近完工时却突然停止了工作。B 寻找另一家公司来完成工厂的修建，但却没有采取任何措施保护工地上还未建好的建筑，从而使其状况因恶劣天气而恶化。在这种情况下，B 不能对这种恶化要求赔偿，因为这是由于其没有采取临时保护措施而导致的。

2. 费用的偿付

　　然而，因受损害方没有采取必要措施减轻损害而减少损害赔偿的金额，不得给该方当事人造成损失。因此，受损害方对为减轻损害所产生的费用可以要求不履行方补偿，只要那些费用根据当时情况是合理的(第(2)款)。

示例：

　　3. 事实和示例 2 一样，不同之处在于 B 采取了必要的措施对该建筑物进行临时保护。只要这些措施的费用合理，就应当计入 A 因不履行合同而应当承担的损害赔偿金中。如果这些费用不合理，则要从中减去。

　　4. 事实和示例 1 一样，不同之处在于 A 在一家豪华宾馆预订了一间价值 500 欧元的房间。A 只能获得他应能以 250 欧元预定到的房间的差额，即 50 欧元。

ARTICLE 7.4.9
(Interest for failure to pay money)

(1) If a party does not pay a sum of money when it falls due the aggrieved party is entitled to interest upon that sum from the time when payment is due to the time of payment whether or not the non-payment is excused.

(2) The rate of interest shall be the average bank short-term lending rate to prime borrowers prevailing for the currency of payment at the place for payment, or where no such rate exists at that place, then the same rate in the State of the currency of payment. In the absence of such a rate at either place the rate of interest shall be the appropriate rate fixed by the law of the State of the currency of payment.

(3) The aggrieved party is entitled to additional damages if the non-payment caused it a greater harm.

COMMENT

1. Lump sum compensation for failure to pay a sum of money

This Article reaffirms the widely accepted rule according to which the harm resulting from delay in the payment of a sum of money is subject to a special regime and is calculated by a lump sum corresponding to the interest accruing between the time when payment of the money was due and the time of actual payment.

Interest is payable whenever the delay in payment is attributable to the non-performing party, and this as from the time when payment was due, without any need for the aggrieved party to give notice of the default.

If the delay is the consequence of force majeure (e.g. the non-performing party is prevented from obtaining the sum due by reason of the introduction of new exchange control regulations), interest will still be due not as damages but as compensation for the enrichment of the debtor as a result of the non-payment as the debtor continues to receive interest on the sum which it is prevented from paying.

The harm is calculated as a lump sum. In other words, subject to paragraph (3) of this Article, the aggrieved party may not prove that it

第 7.4.9 条

（未付金钱债务的利息）

（1）如果一方当事人未支付一笔到期的金钱债务，受损害方有权就该笔债务要求支付自到期时起至支付时止的利息，而不管该不付款是否可被免责。

（2）利率应为付款地银行对优惠借款人借贷支付货币时适用的短期平均贷款通行利率。若该地无此利率，则为支付货币国家的此种利率。若上述两地均无此利率，则为支付货币国法律规定的适当利率。

（3）受损害方有权对不付款给其造成的更大的损害要求额外的损害赔偿。

注释：

1. 对未付款的一次总付赔偿

本条重申了一个被广泛接受的规则，即对于迟延支付一笔金钱债务造成的损害应予特殊处理，这种赔偿要按一次总付方法计算，其金额相当于该金钱债务应支付的时间和实际支付的时间之间发生的利息。

只要迟延付款应归责于不履行方，就可以要求支付从支付到期起的利息，无需受损害方发出违约通知。

如果迟延是由于不可抗力导致的（比如，因为实施新的外汇管制条例导致不履行方不能获得应付款项），仍应作为补偿而非作为损害赔偿支付利息，因为债务人就其不能支付的款项可以继续得到利息，不付款的结果是债务人的收益增加。

损害以一次总付的方式计算。换句话说，根据本条第（3）款，受损害

could have invested the sum due at a higher rate of interest or the non-performing party that the aggrieved party would have obtained interest at a rate lower than the average lending rate referred to in paragraph (2).

The parties may of course agree in advance on a different rate of interest (which would in effect subject it to Article 7.4.13).

2. Rate of interest

Paragraph (2) of this Article fixes in the first instance as the rate of interest the average bank short-term lending rate to prime borrowers. This solution seems to be that best suited to the needs of international trade and most appropriate to ensure an adequate compensation of the harm sustained. The rate in question is the rate at which the aggrieved party will normally borrow the money which it has not received from the non-performing party. That normal rate is the average bank short-term lending rate to prime borrowers prevailing at the place for payment for the currency of payment.

No such rate may however exist for the currency of payment at the place for payment. In such cases, reference is made in the first instance to the average prime rate in the State of the currency of payment. For instance, if a loan is made in pounds sterling payable in country X and there is no rate for loans in pounds on country X financial market, reference will be made to the rate in the United Kingdom.

In the absence of such a rate at either place, the rate of interest will be the "appropriate" rate fixed by the law of the State of the currency of payment. In most cases this will be the legal rate of interest and, as there may be more than one, that most appropriate for international transactions. If there is no legal rate of interest, the rate will be the most appropriate bank rate.

3. Additional damages recoverable

Interest is intended to compensate the harm normally sustained as a consequence of delay in payment of a sum of money. Such delay may however cause additional harm to the aggrieved party for which it may recover damages, always provided that it can prove the existence of such harm and that it meets the requirements of certainty and foreseeability (paragraph (3)).

方不得证明他本可以把这笔款项用作更高利率投资，而不履行方也不得证明受损害方本来只能获得低于依第(2)款提到的平均贷款利率计算所得到的利息。

当然，合同当事人可以事先约定一个不同的利率(该约定适用第7.4.13 条的规定)。

2. 利率

本条第(2)款首先将利率规定为对优惠借款人适用的平均银行短期贷款利率。这个解决办法似乎最符合国际贸易的需要并且最适宜确保遭受的损害得到充分补偿。在此涉及的利率是指受损害方要借贷不履行方没有支付的款项所通常支付的利率。通常的利率是付款地通行的对优惠借款人借贷支付货币所适用的银行短期平均贷款利率。

然而，支付地可能没有这种支付货币的利率。在这种情况下，首先应参照支付货币国家的平均优惠利率。比如，如果一项贷款应当在 X 国用英镑偿还，而在 X 国金融市场上没有英镑贷款利率，可以参照英国的利率。

在两地都无此利率时，应为支付货币国法律规定的"适当的"利率。在大多数情况下，它是指法定利率，并且因为法定利率可能不止一个，适用最适合国际交易的利率。如果没有法定利率，则利率应为最适当的银行利率。

3. 可得到的额外损害赔偿

利息旨在补偿因迟延支付金钱债务通常所遭受的损害。然而这种迟延还可能给受损害方造成额外损害，只要他能证明该损害存在以及满足了确定性和可预见性的要求，他就可以就此额外损害得到损害赔偿(第(3)款)。

Illustration

>A concludes a contract with B, a specialised finance company, for a loan which will permit the renovation of its factory in country X. The loan specifically mentions the use of the funds. The money lent is transferred three months later than agreed. During that period the cost of the renovation has increased by ten percent. A is entitled to recover this additional sum from B.

ARTICLE 7.4.10

(Interest on damages)

Unless otherwise agreed, interest on damages for non-performance of non-monetary obligations accrues as from the time of non-performance.

COMMENT

This Article determines the time from which interest on damages accrues in cases of non-performance of obligations other than monetary obligations. In such cases, at the time of non-performance the amount of damages will usually not yet have been assessed in monetary terms. The assessment will only be made after the occurrence of the harm, either by agreement between the parties or by the court.

This Article fixes as the starting point for the accrual of interest the date of the occurrence of the harm. This solution is that best suited to international trade where it is not the practice for businesspersons to leave their money idle. In effect, the aggrieved party's assets are diminished as from the occurrence of the harm whereas the non-performing party, for as long as the damages are not paid, continues to enjoy the benefit of the interest on the sum which it will have to pay. It is only natural that this gain passes to the aggrieved party.

However, when making the final assessment of the harm, regard is to be had to the fact that damages are awarded as from the date of the harm, so as to avoid double compensation, for instance when a currency depreciates in value.

This Article takes no stand on the question of compound interest, which in some national laws is subject to rules of public policy limiting compound interest with a view to protecting the non-performing party.

示例:

> A 和一家专业金融公司 B 签订了一份借贷合同, A 向 B 借款用于改造其在 X 国的工厂。贷款协议特别规定了资金的用途。但 B 支付该贷款的时间比约定时间晚了三个月, 在这期间, 改造工厂的费用上升了 10%。在这种情况下, A 有权从 B 那儿得到一笔额外赔偿。

第7.4.10条

(损害赔偿的利息)

除非另有约定, 对非金钱债务不履行的损害赔偿的利息自不履行之时起算。

注释:

本条确定了在不履行非金钱债务的情况下, 损害赔偿产生利息的起始时间。在这种情况下, 不履行合同之时损害赔偿的数额往往还不能以货币形式计算。只有在损害发生后, 才能依据双方约定或法院判决确定损害赔偿额。

本条确定以损害发生之日为利息产生的起点, 这种解决办法最适宜于国际贸易, 因为国际贸易中的商人通常不会把资金闲置。事实上, 受损害方的资产从损害发生时开始减少, 而不履行方只要没有支付损害赔偿金, 他就可以继续以其应该支付的款项获得利息。因此, 自然应该把这笔收益转给受损害方。

然而, 当确定最后的损害数额时, 为避免重复赔偿, 例如某种货币贬值, 必须考虑到损害赔偿的计算起点是损害发生之日。

本条没有讨论复利的问题。为了保护不履行方的利益, 一些国内法根据公共利益原则限制复利。

ARTICLE 7.4.11
(Manner of monetary redress)

(1) Damages are to be paid in a lump sum. However, they may be payable in instalments where the nature of the harm makes this appropriate.

(2) Damages to be paid in instalments may be indexed.

COMMENT

1. Lump sum or instalments

Although this Article does not impose a fixed rule as to the manner in which damages are to be paid, the payment of damages as a lump sum is in general considered to be the mode of payment best suited to international trade. There are however situations in which payment by instalments will be more appropriate, having regard to the nature of the harm, for instance when the harm is on-going.

Illustrations

1.   A, a consultant, is retained by B for the purpose of checking the safety of its factories. A is killed when travelling by helicopter to one of B's factories, for which accident B is held responsible. A leaves two children aged twelve and eight. So as to compensate for the loss of the maintenance of the family, a monthly allowance will be payable to the children until they reach the age of majority.

2.   A, a consultant in safety matters, is recruited by B for a three year period. The remuneration is fixed at 0.5% of the production. A is wrongfully dismissed after six months. It may be appropriate that B be ordered to pay A monthly a sum corresponding to the agreed salary until A has found new employment or, at the most, for thirty months.

2. Indexation

Paragraph (2) of this Article contemplates the possibility of indexation of damages to be paid in instalments so as to avoid the complex mechanism of a review of the original judgment in order to take account of inflation. Indexation may however be prohibited by the law of the forum.

第 7. 4. 11 条

（支付赔偿金的方式）

（1）损害赔偿应一次付清。但是，如果损害的性质适于分期支付，也可分期支付。
（2）分期支付损害赔偿金时，可以按指数调整。

注释：

1. 一次付清或分期支付

尽管本条对应该采取何种方式支付损害赔偿金没有强制规定一个固定的规则，但是一次总付的方式通常被认为是最符合国际贸易的支付方式。然而，考虑到损害的性质，比如损害仍在持续，在有些情况下采取分期支付的方式更为适当。

示例：

1. B 为了检查其工厂的安全而聘用了顾问 A。A 在乘坐直升机前往 B 的一个工厂途中丧生，B 对此事故负有责任。A 遗有两个孩子，分别 12 岁和 8 岁。为了补偿 A 家人丧失的抚养费，B 应当每月向这两个孩子支付赔偿金直到他们成人为止。

2. B 聘用 A 为安全事务顾问，为期三年，报酬为产量的 0.5%。六个月之后 A 被错误解聘。对此以下做法也许是适当的：责令 B 每月向 A 支付一笔相当于约定工资数额的款项，支付期间为直至 A 找到新工作，或者（最多）30 个月。

2. 指数

为避免为考虑通货膨胀而需对原判决进行重估的复杂程序，本条第（2）款考虑了在分期支付损害赔偿金的情况下设定调整指数的可能性。然而，指数调整可能会被法院地法所禁止。

Illustration

3. The facts are the same as in Illustration 1. The monthly allowance may be adjusted in accordance with the cost of living index applicable where the children live.

ARTICLE 7.4.12
(Currency in which to assess damages)

Damages are to be assessed either in the currency in which the monetary obligation was expressed or in the currency in which the harm was suffered, whichever is more appropriate.

COMMENT

The harm resulting from the non-performance of an international contract may occur in different places and the question therefore arises of the currency in which it is to be assessed. This question is dealt with by this Article and should be kept distinct from that of the currency of payment of the damages addressed in Article 6.1.9.

The Article offers a choice between the currency in which the monetary obligation was expressed and that in which the harm was suffered, whichever is more appropriate in the circumstances.

While the first alternative calls for no particular comment, the second takes account of the fact that the aggrieved party may have incurred expenses in a particular currency to repair damage which it has sustained. In such a case it should be entitled to claim damages in that currency even if it is not the currency of the contract. Another currency which may be considered the most appropriate is that in which the profit would have been made.

The choice is left to the aggrieved party, provided that the principle of full compensation is respected.

Finally, it may be noted that in the absence of any indication to the contrary, a party is entitled to interest and to liquidated damages and penalties in the same currency as that in which the main obligation is expressed.

示例：

3. 事实和示例 1 相同，每月的津贴应根据当地儿童生活所适用的生活成本指数加以调整。

第7.4.12条

（计算损害赔偿金的货币）

损害赔偿金既可以用表示金钱债务的货币计算，也可以用损害发生时所使用的货币计算，以两者中最为适当的货币为准。

注释：

不履行国际合同导致的损害可能发生在不同的地方，这样就产生了以哪种货币计算损害赔偿金的问题。本条涉及的就是这个问题，它应该区别于第6.1.9条所述的损害赔偿金的支付货币。

本条规定可在以下两种货币间选择适用，以具体情况下最合适者为准：表示金钱债务的货币和表示所遭受损害的货币。

第一种选择即表示金钱债务的货币并不需要特别的解释。第二种选择考虑到了如下情况，即受损害方为补救他所遭受的损害以某种货币支出了花费。在这种情况下，他有权要求以这种货币来赔偿，尽管并非是合同规定的货币。此外，另一种可能被认为最适当的货币是将会从中得到利润的货币。

只要遵守完全赔偿的原则，受损害方有权选择。

最后，值得注意的是，在没有任何相反表示的情况下，一方当事人有权要求以表示主要债务的货币获得利息、损害赔偿金和罚金。

ARTICLE 7.4.13
(Agreed payment for non-performance)

(1) Where the contract provides that a party who does not perform is to pay a specified sum to the aggrieved party for such non-performance, the aggrieved party is entitled to that sum irrespective of its actual harm.

(2) However, notwithstanding any agreement to the contrary the specified sum may be reduced to a reasonable amount where it is grossly excessive in relation to the harm resulting from the non-performance and to the other circumstances.

COMMENT

1. Agreed payment for non-performance defined

This Article gives an intentionally broad definition of agreements to pay a specified sum in case of non-performance, whether such agreements be intended to facilitate the recovery of damages (liquidated damages according to the common law) or to operate as a deterrent against non-performance (penalty clauses proper), or both.

2. Agreed payment for non-performance in principle valid

National laws vary considerably with respect to the validity of the type of clauses in question, ranging from their acceptance in the civil law countries, with or without the possibility of judicial review of particularly onerous clauses, to the outright rejection in common law systems of clauses intended specifically to operate as a deterrent against non-performance, i.e. penalty clauses.

In view of their frequency in international contract practice, paragraph (1) of this Article in principle acknowledges the validity of any clauses providing that a party who does not perform is to pay a specified sum to the aggrieved party for such non-performance, with the consequence that the latter is entitled to the agreed sum irrespective of the harm actually suffered by it. The non-performing party may not allege that the aggrieved party sustained less harm or none at all.

第7.4.13条

（对不履行的约定付款）

（1） 如果合同规定不履行方应就不履行向受损害方支付一笔约定的金额，则受损害方不管其实际损害如何，均有权获得该笔金额。

（2） 但是，如果约定金额相对于该不履行所导致的损害以及相对于其他情况严重过高，则可将该约定金额减少至一个合理的数目，而不管是否有任何与此相反的约定。

注释：

1. 对不履行的约定付款的定义

本条对于在不履行情况下支付一笔特定金额的约定有意作了广义上的界定，而不管这类约定是为了便于求偿损害赔偿金（普通法的约定违约金），还是为了阻吓不履行（真正的罚金），或者二者兼具。

2. 对不履行的约定付款在原则上有效

关于此类条款的有效性，各国法律的规定存在很大不同。大陆法系国家承认该等条款，同时允许或不允许对负担特别沉重的条款作司法审查，普通法系国家对于旨在阻吓不履行的条款（即罚金条款）则明确反对。

鉴于国际商事合同实践中经常存在对不履行的约定付款条款，本条第(1)款原则上承认任何规定不履行方对于其不履行要向受损害方支付一笔特定金额的条款的有效性，其结果是受损害方有权获得该金额，而不管其实际损害如何。不履行方不能以受损害方遭受的损害较小或根本没有受到损害为由拒绝支付约定的金额。

Illustration

> 1.   A, a former international football player from country X, is recruited for three years to train the players of B, a football team from country Y, at a monthly salary of AUD 10,000. Provision is made for a severance allowance of AUD 200,000 in the event of unjustified dismissal. A is dismissed without any justification after six months. A is entitled to the agreed sum, even though A was immediately recruited by another team at double the salary received from B.

Normally, the non-performance must be one for which the non-performing party is liable, since it is difficult to conceive a clause providing for the payment of an agreed sum in case of non-performance operating in a force majeure situation. Exceptionally, however, such a clause may be intended by the parties also to cover non-performance for which the non-performing party is not liable.

In the case of partial non-performance, the amount may, unless otherwise agreed by the parties, be reduced in proportion.

3. Agreed sum may be reduced

In order to prevent the possibility of abuse to which such clauses may give rise, paragraph (2) of this Article permits the reduction of the agreed sum if it is grossly excessive "in relation to the harm resulting from the non-performance and to the other circumstances". The same paragraph makes it clear that the parties may under no circumstances exclude such a possibility of reduction.

The agreed sum may only be reduced, but not entirely disregarded as would be the case were the judge, notwithstanding the agreement of the parties, to award damages corresponding to the exact amount of the harm. It may not be increased, at least under this Article, where the agreed sum is lower than the harm actually sustained (see however Comment 4 on Article 7.1.6). It is moreover necessary that the amount agreed be "grossly excessive", i.e. that it would clearly appear to be so to any reasonable person. Regard should in particular be had to the relationship between the sum agreed and the harm actually sustained.

Illustration

> 2.   A enters into a contract with B for the purchase of machinery which provides for payment in five instalments of EUR 50,000 each. The contract contains a clause allowing immediate termination in the event of non-payment by A of one instalment, and authorises B to keep the sums already paid and to recover future instalments as damages. A fails to pay the third instalment. B keeps the EUR 100,000 already paid and claims, in addition to the return of the

示例：

  1. 前 X 国国际足球运动员 A 受聘于一个 Y 国足球队 B，为 B 训练球员，为期三年，月薪 1 万澳元。合同规定如果 A 被不公正解雇，B 要支付 20 万澳元的解雇赔偿金。六个月后，在没有任何合理理由的情况下 A 被解雇了。A 有权获得这笔约定的金额，尽管 A 立即又被另一支球队以双倍于 B 所支付的工资的报酬所聘用。

通常情况下，不履行必须是不履行方负有责任的不履行，因为很难想象当事人会规定一条对因不可抗力发生的不履行支付约定金额的条款。然而，例外情况下，双方也可能有意让该等条款适用于不履行方不应负责的不履行。

在部分不履行的情况下，除非双方另有约定，约定的付款数额可以按比例减少。

3. 约定的金额可以减少

为了防止滥用这类合同条款的可能性，如果约定金额相对于"不履行导致的损害或其他情况"而言过高，本条第(2)款允许减少该金额。该款明确规定无论如何双方都不能排除这种减少的可能性。

约定的金额只能减少，而不能完全弃之不顾，例如尽管当事人约定了支付金额，法官却判决支付与损害的确切数额相一致的损害赔偿金。如果约定的金额低于实际遭受的损害，至少根据本条，该金额不能增加（参见第 7.1.6 条注释 4）。另外，约定的金额必须"过高"，即它对于任何理性人来说都是显而易见的。尤其应当考虑约定的金额与实际遭受的损害之间的关系。

示例：

  2. A 和 B 签订了一份购买机器的合同，规定每次支付 50,000 欧元，分五次付清。合同有一个条款规定在 A 不支付任何一期分期款项时，将允许 B 立即终止合同，并且 B 有权占有已获得支付的款项，还有权求偿未来各期的分期付款抵作损害赔偿金。A 没有支付第三次分期付款，B 扣留了已支付的 10 万欧元，除要求返还机器外，还要求 A 支付未付的 3 次

machinery, the EUR 150,000 representing the three outstanding instalments. The court will reduce the amount since A's non-performance would result in a grossly excessive benefit for B.

4. Agreed payment for non-performance to be distinguished from forfeiture and other similar clauses

The type of clauses dealt with in this Article must be distinguished from forfeiture and other similar clauses which permit a party to withdraw from a contract either by paying a certain sum or by losing a deposit already made. On the other hand a clause according to which the aggrieved party may retain sums already paid as part of the price falls within the scope of this Article.

Illustrations

3.   A undertakes to sell real estate to B for EUR 450,000. B must exercise the option to purchase within three months and must pay a deposit of EUR 25,000, which A is entitled to retain if B does not exercise the option. Since this is not an agreed payment for non-performance it does not fall under this Article and the sum cannot be reduced thereunder even if grossly excessive in the circumstances.

4.   A enters into a contract with B for the lease of a machine. The contract provides that in the event of A's failure to pay one single rental the contract will be terminated and that the sums already paid will be retained by B as damages. The clause falls under this Article and the agreed amount may be subject to reduction.

分期付款共计 15 万欧元。因为 A 的不履行将会导致 B 得到大大超出实际损害的收益,法院将减少这笔约定的金额。

4. 对不履行的约定付款区别于没收条款或其他类似条款

本条所涉及的条款类型必须区别于允许一方当事人以支付一定金额或丧失定金的方式撤销合同的没收条款和其他类似条款。另一方面,如果一个条款规定受损害方可以保留已支付的金额作为价格的一部分,这种条款属于本条规范的条款类型。

示例:

3. A 答应以 45 万欧元的价格将其不动产出售给 B。B 必须在三个月内行使购买此不动产的选择权,而且要预付 2.5 万欧元的定金,若 B 没有行使购买选择权,A 有权保留该定金。这不是对不履行约定的付款,因此不属本条管辖的范围,并且即使该定金的数额根据情况过高,也不能据此予以减少。

4. A 和 B 签订了一份租赁机器的合同。合同规定如果 A 不能交付任何一笔租金,合同将终止,并且 B 可以将已支付的租金抵作损害赔偿金。在这种情况下,该条款属于本条管辖的范围,约定的金额在适当情况下可以减少。

CHAPTER 8

SET-OFF

ARTICLE 8.1
(Conditions of set-off)

(1) Where two parties owe each other money or other performances of the same kind, either of them ("the first party") may set off its obligation against that of its obligee ("the other party") if at the time of set-off,

(a) the first party is entitled to perform its obligation;

(b) the other party's obligation is ascertained as to its existence and amount and performance is due.

(2) If the obligations of both parties arise from the same contract, the first party may also set off its obligation against an obligation of the other party which is not ascertained as to its existence or to its amount.

COMMENT

1. Use of set-off

Under the Principles, when two parties owe each other an obligation arising from a contract or any cause of action, each party may set off its obligation against the obligation of the other party. By mutual deduction, both obligations are discharged up to the amount of the lesser obligation (see Article 8.5). Set-off avoids the need for each party to perform its obligation separately.

The obligor from whom payment is asked, and who sets off its own obligation, is called "the first party". The obligee who first asks its obligor for payment and against whom the right of set-off is exercised, is called "the other party".

第八章

抵　销

第 8.1 条

（抵销的条件）

（1）当双方当事人互负金钱或其他同类履行时，任何一方（"第一方当事人"）可以将自己的债务与其债权人（"另一方当事人"）的债务抵销，如果抵销发生时满足以下条件：

（a）第一方当事人有权履行其债务；

（b）另一方当事人债务的存在和数量已确定，且履行到期。

（2）如果双方当事人的债务基于同一合同产生，第一方当事人可将自己的债务与另一方当事人的债务抵销，即使另一方当事人债务的存在或数量尚未确定。

注释：

1. 抵销的用法

根据《通则》，当双方当事人互负因合同或其他诉因引起的债务时，任何一方当事人可将自身的债务与另一方当事人的债务抵销。通过相互扣减，双方债务以数额较小者为限得以解除（参见第 8.5 条）。抵销避免了双方分别履行债务的必要。

被要求为清偿且主张抵销其债务的债务人，被称为"第一方当事人"。首先要求其债务人为清偿并且其债务人要求对其行使抵销权的债权人，被称为"另一方当事人"。

Illustrations

> 1.   A, a sea carrier, has carried goods belonging to B from country X to country Y. A asks B for EUR 10,000 as payment for the carriage. B, who had previously become an obligee of A for an amount of EUR 10,000 as compensation for harm to other goods carried, may set off its own obligation to pay A EUR 10,000 against A's obligation to pay it EUR 10,000. If it does so, neither A nor B will remain the other's obligor.
>
> 2.   A sells B a plot of land for the price of AUD 100,000. Subsequently B, who is a contractor, builds a house for A. The price of the construction is AUD 200,000. When A asks for the payment of the land, B may set off the price of the construction. The obligation of B to pay A AUD 100,000 is totally discharged, but A remains B's obligor for AUD 100,000.

For a party to be allowed to set off its own obligation against the obligation of the other party the conditions laid down in this Article must be satisfied.

2. Obligation owed to each other

A first condition is that each party is the obligor and the obligee of the other (paragraph (1), opening sentence). To be noted is that the parties must be so in the same capacity. Thus, set-off is not possible if the first party has an obligation to the other party in its own name but is the obligee of the other party in another capacity, for example as a trustee or as the absolute owner of a company.

Illustration

> 3.   Company A sells company B machinery for 600,000 Japanese Yen (JPY). B, which is in business with company C, a subsidiary of A, sells C products for JPY 500,000. When A asks B to pay the sales price of the machinery, B cannot set off its obligation for the sale of the products to C, even if the capital of C is totally subscribed by A, as C is an independent entity. A and B are not obligor and obligee of each other.

The condition that the obligations must be owed to each other may give rise to a problem where the other party has assigned the obligation owed to it by the first party to a third party. The first party may nonetheless set off its obligation against the other party's obligation if the right of set-off existed against the assignor's obligation before the assignment was notified to the obligor (see Article 9.1.13).

示例:

 1. 海上承运人 A 将 B 的货物从 X 国运往 Y 国，A 要求 B 支付 10,000 欧元运费。因为 A 对其先前承运的货物造成损害，向 B 承担支付 10,000 欧元损害赔偿的债务。B 可要求将其对 A 承担的 10,000 欧元的债务与 A 对 B 承担的 5,000 欧元的债务抵销。如此，A 和 B 都不再是对方的债务人。

 2. A 以 100,000 澳元向 B 出售一块土地，之后，承包商 B 为 A 建造一栋房屋，造价为 200,000 澳元。当 A 要求 B 支付土地价款时，B 可要求以造价抵销。B 对 A 承担的 100,000 澳元债务完全解除，但是 A 对 B 仍负有 100,000 澳元的债务。只有在满足本条规定的条件时，一方当事人才可以将自身的债务与另一方当事人的债务抵销。

2. 互负债务

抵销需要满足的第一个条件是，任何一方当事人都同时既是另一方当事人的债务人又是其债权人(第(1)款开首语)。要注意的是当事人双方必须以同种身份互负债务。因此，如果一方当事人以自己的名义对另一方当事人负有债务，但又以其他身份对另一方当事人享有债权，比如其作为受托人或一个公司的绝对所有人，则抵销不可能发生。

示例:

 3. A 公司以 600,000 日元的价格向 B 公司出售设备，B 公司与 A 公司的子公司 C 公司有商业往来，B 公司以 500,000 日元向 C 公司出售产品。即使 C 的资本完全归属于 A，由于 C 为一个独立实体，当 A 要求 B 向其支付价款时，B 不能以向 C 公司出售产品产生的债权来抵销债务。A 和 B 不是互负债务的债权人和债务人。

另一方当事人将第一方当事人对其承担的债务转让给第三方时，双方当事人必须互负债务这一条件可能会受到影响。但如果在转让通知到达受让人之前，针对转让债务的抵销权存在，那么第一方当事人仍可将自身的债务与另一方当事人承担的债务抵销(参见第 9.1.13 条)。

3. Obligations of the same kind

Both obligations must be of the same kind (paragraph (1), opening sentence). In some legal systems obligations have to be "fungible". A monetary obligation may be set off only against a monetary obligation. A delivery of grain may be set off only against a delivery of grain of the same kind.

The concept of "obligations of the same kind" is broader than that of "fungible obligations". Performances of non-monetary obligations may be of the same kind while at the same time not being fungible. Two obligations to deliver wine of the same vineyard but not of the same year may be obligations of the same kind, but would not be fungible. Cash and securities are not performances of the same kind in the sense of this Article. Nevertheless, as is the case with different foreign currencies, set-off may be exercised if the securities are easily convertible and if there is no agreement to the effect that only the payment of specified cash or securities is possible. Whether or not obligations are of the same kind may depend on commercial practices or special trade rules.

A personal obligation cannot be of the same kind as another type of obligation. Set-off is thus not available if one of the obligations is of a personal nature.

Illustrations

4. A, a crude oil producer, contracts to deliver 1,500 tonnes of crude oil by pipe-line every month to B in country X. B, in turn, must each week transfer 1,000 tonnes of crude oil by road. The crude oil produced by A and the crude oil delivered by B do not have the same origin and are not totally similar, but as their use could be identical, the two obligations relating to the crude oil can be said to be of the same kind, and if A and B are obligor and obligee for the delivery of some quantity of crude oil, set-off will be available.

5. A holds 100 ordinary shares of the company C. Shareholder B of the same company holds 120 redeemable preferred shares. They are obligee and obligor of each other, and in an earlier contract it was provided that payment would be possible by means of shares of equal value. Since the shares held by A and the shares held by B are not of the same kind, set-off cannot be exercised.

4. First party's obligation performable

The first party must have the right to perform its obligation (paragraph (1)(a)). It cannot impose on the other party a performance which either has not yet been ascertained, or is not yet due.

3. 同类债务

双方当事人的债务必须是同类的(第(1)款开首语)。在一些法律体系中，债务必须是"可替代的"。金钱性债务只能与金钱性债务相抵销，交付谷物的债务只能与交付同一种类谷物的债务相抵销。

"同类债务"的概念比"可替代的债务"概念外延更广泛。非金钱性债务的履行可以是同类的但却是不可替代的。交付产自同一葡萄园不同年份的酒的债务，可以是同类的债务，但却不是可替代的。现金和有价证券不是本条规定的同类履行。但是，正如涉及不同外汇的抵销，如果证券容易兑现，且没有约定只能使用规定的现金或证券进行支付，抵销可以发生。是否属于同类债务要根据商业实践或特殊的交易规则来判断。

人身性质的债务和其他类型的债务不是同类债务。因此，如果债务之一是人身性质的债务，则抵销不能发生。

示例：

> 4. 合同规定原油生产商 A 每月通过管道向位于 X 国的 B 交付 1,500 吨原油。而 B 每周必须通过陆路交付 1,000 吨原油。A 生产的原油和 B 交付的原油来源不同且不完全相似，但是因为它们的用途完全相同，两项有关原油的债务可被认为同类。如果 A 和 B 相互是交付一定数量原油的债权人和债务人，抵销将是可能的。

> 5. A 拥有 C 公司普通股 100 股。B 也是该公司的股东，他拥有可回购的优先股 120 股。他们是相互的债权人和债务人，且他们之间早先的一个合同规定可以同类股票清偿。因为 A 持有的股票和 B 持有的股票不是同类，所以抵销不能发生。

4. 第一方当事人的债务是可履行的

第一方当事人必须有权履行其债务(第(1)款(a)项)。但第一方当事人不能强迫另一方当事人履行其尚未确定，或尚未到期之债务。

Illustrations

6. A has sold ten trucks to B for USD 1,000,000. B must pay for the trucks before 30 September. B wishes to set off an obligation it has towards A arising from a loan to A, repayment of which is due on 30 November. Before this date B may not set off its obligation towards A, as it cannot pay A before 30 November. B's obligation to A is not yet due.

7. A owes B EUR 200,000 for the repayment of a loan. The repayment must take place on 30 January. B is obliged to pay A for a claim for damages of EUR 140,000, under a judgment handed down on 25 January. A asks B to pay on 9 February. B, whose obligation can be performed, is allowed to set off its obligation against A's obligation.

8. A has sold B 10,000 bottles of wine, the price of which must be paid at the latest on 30 October. B is also A's obligee and A's obligation is already due. B may set off its own obligation against A's obligation on 10 October even if the latest date B's obligation should be paid is 30 October, because A is bound to accept a payment before such date.

5. Other party's obligation ascertained

Set-off may be exercised only when the other party's obligation is ascertained both as to its existence and as to its amount (paragraph (1)(b)).

The existence of an obligation is ascertained when the obligation itself cannot be contested, for example, when it is based on a valid and executed contract or a final judgment or award which is not subject to review.

Conversely, an obligation to pay damages is not ascertained when the obligation may be contested by the other party.

Even if the existence of the other party's obligation is not contested, it is not possible to exercise set-off if the obligation is not ascertained as to its amount. If the existence of the harm is not disputed, but the amount of the compensation has not been fixed, set-off will not be available.

Illustrations

9. A judgment requires A to pay B 200,000 Chinese Yuan Renminbi (CNY), for breach of contract. B is in turn A's obligor for the repayment of a loan of CNY 240,000, repayment of which is already due. A asks B to pay the CNY 240,000. B may set off its obligation against A's obligation arising from the judgment.

示例：

6. A 以 1,000,000 美元的价格向 B 出售 10 辆卡车，B 须在 9 月 30 日前支付车款。B 希望对 A 的贷款债权进行抵销，贷款的还款到期日是 11 月 30 日。在此日期之前，B 不可以用其对 A 的债权与此债务抵销，因为 B 不能要求 A 在 11 月 30 日之前向 B 还贷，A 对 B 的债务尚未到期①。

7. A 欠 B 贷款 200,000 欧元，还贷时间是 1 月 30 日。1 月 25 日，依 A 提出的损害赔偿请求，法院判决 B 有义务向 A 支付 14,000 欧元的损害赔偿金。2 月 9 日，A 要求 B 支付。B 的债务是可履行的，应允许 B 将其债务与 A 的债务相抵销。

8. A 向 B 出售 10,000 瓶葡萄酒，货款最迟必须在 10 月 30 日支付。B 也是 A 的债权人，并且 A 的债务已到期。B 可以在 10 月 10 日将其债务与 A 的债务进行抵销，即使 B 清偿其债务的最后期限是 10 月 30 日，因为 A 有义务接受在该日期前的支付。

5. 另一方当事人的债务已确定

只有在另一方当事人债务的存在和金额都已确定的情况下，才可实施抵销（第(1)款(b)项）。

对债务本身无可争辩时，比如，基于有效并已履行的合同，或不受审查的终局判决或仲裁裁决之债务，即视债务的存在已被确定。

相反，当另一方当事人对支付损害赔偿的债务提出争辩时，支付损害赔偿的债务就属未确定。

即使对另一方当事人债务的存在未做争辩，如果该债务的金额没有确定，抵销也不能实施。如果对损害的存在没有争议，但是赔偿数额尚未确定，抵销也不复存在。

示例：

9. 判决裁定 A 因违反合同须向 B 支付 200,000 元人民币。同时 B 负有向 A 偿还 240,000 元人民币贷款的债务，该债务已经到期。A 要求 B 支付 240,000 人民币。B 可将其承担的债务与 A 在判决项下承担引起的债务相抵销。

---

① 译者注：示例 6 意在表明债权人即便对债务人在另外的交易中对债务人负有债务，但若履行该债务的期限未到，该债务人也不能以其债务与债权人欠他的债务进行抵消，即示例前所讲的"不能强迫另一方当事人履行其尚未确定，或尚未到期之债务"。英文示例 6 的文字未讲清楚，经与工作组主席 Bonell 沟通，他同意译者对示例的改进。中文示例 6 已据此改进，但英文仍维持原文。此处读者应以中文为准。

10.   A sells B a yacht for EUR 300,000. A is liable to B for tort. The harm is not contested, but the amount of damages has not yet been fixed. A will not be permitted to set off its own obligation, as A's obligation has not been ascertained.

The Principles do not deal with the impact of insolvency proceedings on the right to exercise set-off, which is therefore to be determined by the applicable law. Most domestic laws grant the first party the right to exercise set-off even after the other party has become involved in insolvency proceedings, thereby derogating from the principle of the equality of the creditors in insolvency proceedings.

6. Other party's obligation due

The other party's obligation must furthermore be due (paragraph (1)(b)). An obligation is due when the obligee has the right to request performance by the obligor, and the obligor has no available defence against that request. A defence will, for example, be available if the time of payment has not yet arrived. As a natural or moral obligation is not enforceable, the first party may not set off its obligations against such an obligation owed by the other party. The enforceability or non-enforceability of an obligation may depend on the otherwise applicable law. Consequently, in some cases the possibility to exercise the right of set-off may depend on the otherwise applicable law.

Illustration

11.   By a final judgment of 10 April, A was ordered to pay B USD 20,000 for the sale of cotton. A, who is B's obligee for the repayment of a loan of USD 12,000 which was enforceable as from 10 January, may set off its own obligation against B's obligation. B, whose obligation is ascertained and due cannot contest the set-off exercised by A.

Since the expiration of the limitation periods prevents the enforcement of the obligation but does not extinguish the right itself, the first party who is not allowed to enforce the time-barred obligation may nonetheless set off that time-barred obligation (see Article 10.10).

7. Set-off of obligations arising from the same contract

Set-off is a convenient means of discharging obligations at once and at the same time. Therefore, if the two obligations arise from the same contract, the conditions of set-off are modified.

If the obligations of the two parties arise from the same contract, the first party is allowed to set off its own obligation against an obligation of the other party even where that other party's obligation is not

10. A 以 10,000 欧元的价格向 B 出售一艘游艇。A 因侵权对 B 负有债务。损害不存在异议，但是损害赔偿的数额尚未确定。因为 A 的债务没有确定，B 不能抵销其债务。

《通则》不涉及破产程序对抵销权的影响，这一问题因此受适用法的调整。即使涉及另一方当事人的破产程序已经开始，大部分国内法仍赋予第一方当事人抵销的权利，从而违背了破产程序中债权人平等的原则。

6. 另一方当事人债务已到期

另一方当事人债务必须到期（第（1）款(b)项）。债务到期是指债权人有权要求债务人履行债务且债务人对履行请求提不出任何抗辩。例如，履行期限未到就是债务人可以主张的抗辩。因为自然或道德债务没有强制执行力，第一方当事人不可将其债务与另一方当事人这样的债务抵销。债务是否具有强制执行力要依据其他适用法确定。因此，在有些情况下，能否行使抵销权取决于其他适用法。

示例：

11. 根据 4 月 10 日的终局判决，A 应向 B 支付 20,000 美元的棉花货款。B 向 A 偿还 12,000 美元贷款的债务于 1 月 10 日到期。A 可要求以自身的债务与 B 的债务抵销。B 的债务是确定的且已到期，因此他不能抗辩 A 的抵销请求。

虽然时效期间届满阻止对债务的强制执行，但权利本身并未消灭。因丧失时效而不被允许强制执行债务的第一方当事人，仍然可以抵销该丧失时效的债务（参见第10.10条）。

7. 基于同一合同产生的债务的抵销

抵销是一种在同一时间一次性解除两个债务的便捷作法。因此，如果两个债务基于同一合同产生，抵销的前提条件则有所不同。

如果双方的债务基于同一合同产生，即使另一方当事人债务的存在或数额尚未确定，第一方当事人依然有权以其自身债务与另一方当

ascertained as to its existence or to its amount (paragraph (2)). Thus, for instance, an obligation to pay damages may be ascertained as to its existence but not as to its amount. If the minimum amount payable cannot be contested, the first party may set off its own obligation up to that minimum amount, even if the total amount of the other party's obligation is unknown.

Even though one of the obligations is contested, the right to set-off can be exercised because all the relevant obligations capable of being set off arise from the same contract and can therefore be easily identified. This could be useful to parties in a business relationship to facilitate quick settlements of claims. Judicial intervention may however be necessary to determine whether the conditions of set-off are in fact satisfied. In international commerce, the obligations of the two parties may frequently arise from the same contract.

> Illustrations

> 12. A carries turkeys for B from country X to country Y. The carriage charge is 35,000 Russian Roubles (RUB). During the carriage one hundred turkeys die due to the fault of the carrier which it acknowledges. A asks B for the payment of the carriage. B may set off the obligation to pay for the harm caused by the loss of the turkeys against A's obligation. Although the amount of the damages is not ascertained, it would be easy to estimate the damages and determine if the conditions for set off are satisfied as the two obligations arise from the same contract.

> 13. A, a carrier, accepts to carry a piano for pianist B from country X to country Y. A provision of the contract expressly provides that delay penalties are to be paid if the piano is not delivered at the concert hall five days before the date of the concert. The piano is delivered at the place of destination only two days before the date of the concert. A asks for the payment of the carriage. B may set off its claim for the agreed delay penalties against A's claim even if A contests the amount of the penalties owed for the delay.

8. Set-off by agreement

Even if the conditions of this Article are not met, the parties may achieve the effects of set-off by agreement. Likewise, parties may agree that their mutual obligations are set off automatically either at a specific date or periodically. Also, more than two parties may agree that their respective obligations shall be discharged, for example by netting.

事人债务抵销(第(2)款)。因此,比如一项支付损害赔偿的债务,可能其存在已经确定但数额尚未确定。如果双方当事人对于最低赔偿数额没有异议,即使赔偿总额尚未确定,第一方当事人依然能够以该最低赔偿数额为限进行抵销。

即使债务之一存有异议,抵销权仍可以行使,因为所有能够抵销的相关债务均基于同一合同产生,债务的确定相对容易。这有利于有商业往来的当事人之间简单、便捷地清偿各种债权债务。但在确认抵销条件事实上是否满足时,可能需要司法介入。在国际商事交易中,双方的债务可能经常基于同一合同产生。

示例:

> 12. A将B的一批火鸡从X国运输到Y国,运费是35,000俄罗斯卢布。该承运人承认由于其过失,100只火鸡在运输途中死亡。A要求B支付运费。B可以要求以火鸡短少造成的损失赔偿来抵销运费(A的债务)。虽然损害赔偿的数额尚未确定,但是由于债务是基于同一合同产生的,很容易计算损害赔偿的金额并决定债务抵销的各个条件是否已经得到满足。

> 13. 承运人A承诺将钢琴家B的一架钢琴从X国运往Y国。合同明确规定,如果钢琴不能在音乐会开幕前五天运到音乐厅,A将支付延误罚金。钢琴在音乐会开幕前两天才运到目的地。A要求B支付运费,B可以请求A支付约定的延误罚金的债权与A的债权抵销,即使A对于延误罚金的具体金额持有异议。

8. 约定抵销

即使本条规定的条件没有得到满足,双方也可以约定方式取得抵销的效果。同样,双方也可以约定在一个特定的日期或者定期自动抵销互负的债务。另外,两个以上的当事人也可通过约定彼此解除债务,如通过相互抵销。

ARTICLE 8.2
(Foreign currency set-off)

Where the obligations are to pay money in different currencies, the right of set-off may be exercised, provided that both currencies are freely convertible and the parties have not agreed that the first party shall pay only in a specified currency.

COMMENT

1. Convertible currencies

Payments in different currencies are not performances of the same kind as required by Article 8.1. However, if the payments are to be made in currencies that are both convertible, set-off may nevertheless be exercised. According to Article 6.1.9, if there is no agreement to the contrary, payment may be made by the obligor in the currency of the place for payment, if this currency is convertible. On the contrary, since the relative value of a currency that is not freely convertible cannot be readily ascertained for the purpose of set-off, set-off cannot be used to impose payment in such a currency on the other party.

Illustration

> 1. A, a wine producer in country X, sells 5,000 bottles of wine for USD 200,000 to B, a cork producer. B sells 100,000 corks to A for the price of 100,000 livros, which is the currency of the country where corks are produced and which is not convertible. A asks B for payment of the USD 200,000. B may not set off the 100,000 livros against the USD 200,000.

2. Currency specified by contract

If a contract expressly requires a party to pay in a specified currency, and if the other party has to perform its own obligation in a currency different from that currency, it will not be able to set off its own obligation against the other party's obligation.

第8.2条

（外汇抵销）

当以不同货币支付金钱债务时，亦可行使抵销权，但要以该两种货币均为可自由兑换的货币，而且当事人没有约定第一方当事人必须以特定货币支付为条件。

注释：

1. 可兑换的货币

以不同货币支付金钱不属于第8.1条规定的同类履行。但是，如果用以支付的货币都是可自由兑换的，也可以发生抵销。根据第6.1.9条的规定，如果没有相反的规定，债务人可以用支付地货币支付，只要该货币是可自由兑换。相反，由于不能自由兑换的货币，为抵销之目的，其相对价值不易确定，就不能行使抵销，因为这样做实际上是强迫对方当事人以该种货币履行债务。

示例：

1. X国酒制造商A以200,000美元的价格向软木塞制造商B出售5,000瓶酒。B以100,000里夫（livros）的价格向A出售100,000个软木塞，里夫是软木塞产地的货币，不能自由兑换。A要求B支付200,000美元货款，B不能以该100,000里夫与该200,000美元抵销。

2. 合同约定的货币

如果合同明确要求一方当事人以某一特定货币支付，而该方当事人只能以另一种货币履行其债务，则该方当事人不能以自己的债务抵销对方当事人的债务。

Illustration

> 2.   A sells B products for USD 100,000. The sales contract expressly provides that the price is to be paid by the buyer in US dollars. B, an Asian carrier, is A's obligee for an unpaid invoice for carriage charges which must be paid in Korean Won. A requires payment of the USD 100,000. B, who contractually is obliged to pay the price of the products in US dollars, is not allowed to set off its obligation against the obligation of A to pay the carriage charges.

ARTICLE 8.3
(Set-off by notice)

The right of set-off is exercised by notice to the other party.

COMMENT

The right of set-off is exercised by notice to the other party. It does not operate automatically or by declaration of the court. The first party must inform the other party that it will discharge its own obligation by set-off. Notice must not be conditional.

To be effective, notice must be sent after the conditions for set-off are fulfilled.

Notice may be given by any means appropriate to the circumstances and is effective when it reaches the person to whom it is given (see Article 1.10).

ARTICLE 8.4
(Content of notice)

(1) The notice must specify the obligations to which it relates.

(2) If the notice does not specify the obligation against which set-off is exercised, the other party may, within a reasonable time, declare to the first party the obligation to which set-off relates. If no such declaration is made, the set-off will relate to all the obligations proportionally.

示例：

2. A 向 B 出售价值 100,000 美元的产品。买卖合同明确规定，买方需以美元支付货款。亚洲承运人 B 是 A 未付运费的债权人，该运费必须以韩币支付。A 要求 B 支付该 100,000 美元。依合同规定，B 应该以美元支付货款，因此他不能将其债务与 A 支付运费的债务抵销。

第8.3条

（抵销通知）

抵销权以向另一方当事人发出通知来行使。

注释：

抵销权以向另一方当事人发出通知来行使。抵销的效力不会自动产生，也不以法院的宣告为要件。第一方当事人必须通知另一方当事人通过抵销解除自身债务的意图。通知不得附带任何条件。

有效的通知只能在抵销条件成就之后发出。

通知可采用相关情况下合适的方式发出，并在到达被通知人时生效（参见第1.10条）。

第8.4条

（通知的内容）

（1）通知必须指明拟抵销的债务。

（2）如果通知没有指明拟抵销的债务，另一方当事人可在合理的时间内向第一方当事人声明有关抵销的债务。如果未作出该声明，则抵销将按比例适用于所有债务。

COMMENT

According to paragraph (1), the notice must specify the obligations of both parties that are to be set off. The other party, receiving the notice, must know the grounds for set-off and the amount of set-off.

1. Declaration by the other party

If the first party has two or more obligations against the other party, and if the first party has not specified the obligations it wants to be paid by set-off, the other party may freely choose which of the first party's obligations it wants to be discharged (paragraph (2), first part).

Illustration

> 1.   A regularly sells B cloth. On 30 December B asks A for the payment of USD 50,000 that A owes it. At that date B owes A the payment of the price relating to three different sales contracts, i.e. USD 40,000, USD 35,000 and USD 45,000 respectively. If A wants to set off B's obligation, it has to indicate in the notice which of the three obligations owed by B it wants to set off. If A does not indicate in the notice which obligation owed by B it wants to set off, B may in a reasonable time indicate to A that its obligation of USD 45,000 will be totally discharged by set off and that the obligation of USD 35,000 will be discharged up to USD 5,000. After set-off has been applied, B remains the obligor of A for USD 70,000.

2. Absence of declaration

If the notice does not specify the obligations that the first party wants to set off, and if the other party does not make any declaration as to which obligation set-off relates within a reasonable time, all the obligations of the other party will be discharged by set-off proportionally, up to the value of the first party's obligation (paragraph (2), second part).

Illustration

> 2.   The facts are the same as in Illustration 1, except that B does not declare to which obligation set-off relates. In the absence of such a declaration, set-off will discharge the obligation of USD 40,000 of the first contract up to USD 16,670; the obligation of USD 35,000 of the second contract up to USD 14,580 and the obligation of USD 45,000 of the third contract up to USD 18,750.

注释:

根据第(1)款, 通知必须指明双方当事人用以抵销的债务。另一方在接到通知时, 必须能够知道抵销的原因和抵销的金额。

1. 另一方当事人的声明

如果另一方当事人向第一方当事人承担两项或两项以上债务, 且该第一方当事人没有指明通过抵销清偿哪一项债务, 另一方当事人可以自由选择通过抵销解除其向第一方当事人承担的哪一项债务 (第(2)款前半部分)。

示例:

> 1. A 经常向 B 出售布匹。12 月 30 日, B 要求 A 支付 50,000美元的欠款。同一天, B 应该向 A 支付依三个买卖合同产生的价款, 金额分别是 40,000 美元、35,000 美元和 45,000美元。如果 A 希望抵销欠 B 的债务, 他必须在通知中指明希望以抵销方式清偿 B 承担的哪一项债务。如果 A 在通知中没有指明他希望抵销 B 承担的哪项债务, B 可以在合理的时间内向 A 声明以抵销方式全部解除 45,000 美元的那项债务并解除 35,000 美元那项债务中的 5,000 美元。抵销之后, B 仍然欠 A 70,000 美元。

2. 没有声明

如果第一方当事人在通知中没有指明希望用以抵销的债务, 且另一方当事人也没有在合理的时间内做出抵销何项债务的任何声明, 另一方当事人的所有各项债务将以第一方当事人的债务金额为限按比例得到解除 (第(2)款后半部分)。

示例:

> 2. 案件事实和示例 1 相同, 不同之处在于 B 没有声明抵销哪一项债务。在没有声明的情况下, 抵销将解除第一笔合同款项 (40,000 美元) 中的 16,670 美元, 第二笔合同款项 (即 35,000 美元) 中的 14,580 美元和第三笔合同款项 (即 45,000 美元) 中的 18,750 美元。

ARTICLE 8.5
(Effect of set-off)

(1) Set-off discharges the obligations.

(2) If obligations differ in amount, set-off discharges the obligations up to the amount of the lesser obligation.

(3) Set-off takes effect as from the time of notice.

COMMENT

1. Discharge by set-off

If the conditions of set-off specified in Article 8.1 are satisfied, the obligations of both parties are discharged to the extent of the set-off, as if two reciprocal payments had been made.

Illustration

> 1. A owes USD 100,000 to B and B owes USD 100,000 to A. B asks for the payment of its obligation. A by notice declares to B that it sets off its own obligation. After set-off takes effect, the two obligations are discharged.

If the two obligations differ in their amount, set-off will discharge the obligations, but only up to the amount of the lesser obligation.

Illustration

> 2. B owes USD 100,000 to A, who in turn owes B USD 70,000. A asks for the payment of the USD 100,000 it is owed, B declares that it wants to set off A's obligation of USD 70,000. If the conditions for set-off are met, A is no longer the obligor of B, as its obligation has been entirely discharged, but A is still the obligee of B for USD 30,000, corresponding to the part of the obligation not paid by set-off.

2. Set-off effective at the time of notice

The obligations are discharged at the time of notice if at that time the conditions required for set-off are fulfilled. Set-off does not operate retroactively. It has prospective effect only.

The date of effectiveness of set-off is consistent with the necessity to declare set-off by notice, and in practice the date when set-off is effective will be easy to know.

第8.5条

（抵销的效力）

（1）抵销解除相关债务。

（2）如果债务的金额不等，则抵销以金额较小者为限解除相关债务。

（3）抵销自通知之时起生效。

注释：

1. 以抵销方式解除债务

如果满足第8.1条规定的条件，双方当事人的债务在抵销的限度内得以解除，其效力相当于相互单独支付。

示例：

1. A欠B 100,000美元，B欠A 100,000美元。B要求支付债务。A通知B抵销其债务。抵销生效后，两项债务均得以解除。

如果两项债务金额不等，抵销也产生解除双方债务的效果，但是抵销仅以金额较小者的数额为限。

示例：

2. B欠A 100,000美元，A欠B 70,000美元。A要求B支付该100,000美元的欠款，B声称他希望以此抵销A所欠的70,000美元债务。如果抵销的条件全部成就，A不再是B的债务人，因为他的债务已全部解除；但是A仍然是B的债权人，尚有30,000美元的债务没有得到清偿。

2. 抵销自通知时生效

如果通知时抵销的条件已经成就，债务在通知时得以解除。抵销的效力不溯及继往，只针对未来。

抵销的生效日期与需要以通知宣告抵销这种必要性相一致，事实上很容易确定抵销的生效日期。

The situation has to be evaluated as if both obligations were paid at the time of notice. Two consequences derive from this rule. Firstly, interest on the obligations runs until the time of notice. A party who may and wants to set off its obligation, must declare set-off as soon as possible if it wishes to stop the accrual of interest. Secondly, if an undue payment has been made after set-off has been declared, restitution will take place, as the payment has no legal grounds. If the payment had been made before the notice, it is an effective payment and restitution cannot be required.

Illustration

> 3. A owes B USD 100,000 dollars for goods sold by B. A's obligation is ascertained and payment is due on 20 November. By a judgement dated 30 November, B is ordered to pay A USD 80,000 in damages. The obligation to pay USD 80,000 is due and ascertained at the date of the judgement, i.e. on 30 November. Set-off is exercised by A by notice on 10 December. The set-off will take place at the time of notice as all the conditions required have been satisfied before this date. The two obligations are discharged up to the amount of the lesser obligation. A will remain the obligee of B for USD 20,000. After 10 December, interest no longer accrues, except on the amount of USD 20,000.

At the time when the conditions for set-off are satisfied and notice has been given, not only are the principal obligations discharged but also related rights, e.g. rights securing an obligation, are discharged accordingly.

Illustration

> 4. A, a banker, had lent architect B EUR 100,000 and has obtained a personal security for the payment from B's wife. B is the obligee of A for EUR 120,000, which is money that B holds on its account in A's bank. A asks B for the payment of the EUR 100,000. B declares set-off by notice on 12 December. The conditions required for A's obligation and B's obligation were fulfilled on 10 December. At the date of notice on 12 December, A's and B's obligations are discharged, as is the personal security given by B's wife.

评估抵销的效力时，遵照双方债务在通知之时得以实际支付时所具有的效力。这一规则产生两种法律效果。首先，债务的利息于通知之时停止计算。欲行使抵销权的当事人必须尽快主张抵销，这样才可以阻止利息的计算。第二，主张抵销之后如果又发生了不必要的支付，接受方需返还利益，因为该支付行为没有法律上的依据。如果支付发生在通知之前，则是一个有效的支付，不得要求返还利益。

示例：

3. A 欠 B 100,000 美元货款。A 的债务已经确定且在 11 月 20 日到期。11 月 30 日作出的一项判决命令 B 向 A 支付 80,000 美元的损害赔偿。B 支付该 80,000 美元的债务于判决作出之日（即 11 月 30 日）到期并得以确定。A 于 12 月 10 日通知行使抵销权。抵销在通知时生效，因为该日之前抵销的各个条件都已成就。两项债务以金额较小者为限得以解除。B 仍然是 A 的债权人，债权金额是 20,000 美元。12 月 10 日以后，除了剩余的 20,000 美元，债务停止计息。

抵销条件成就且通知到达之时，除了主债务得以解除之外，从权利也一并解除，例如，为债务提供担保的权利。

示例：

4. 银行家 A 借给建筑师 B 100,000 欧元，并获得 B 的妻子对该债务提供的个人担保。B 也是 A 的债权人，债权金额为 120,000 欧元，这是 B 在 A 银行开立的账户上拥有的存款。A 要求 B 支付 100,000 欧元。B 于 12 月 12 日以通知主张抵销权。双方债务抵销的条件在 12 月 10 日都已成就。12 月 12 日通知时，A 和 B 的债务被解除，B 妻子提供的个人担保也被解除。

CHAPTER 9

ASSIGNMENT OF RIGHTS, TRANSFER OF OBLIGATIONS, ASSIGNMENT OF CONTRACTS

SECTION 1: ASSIGNMENT OF RIGHTS

ARTICLE 9.1.1
(Definitions)

"Assignment of a right" means the transfer by agreement from one person (the "assignor") to another person (the "assignee"), including transfer by way of security, of the assignor's right to payment of a monetary sum or other performance from a third person ("the obligor").

COMMENT

In many circumstances an obligee entitled to the payment of a monetary sum or to another performance from an obligor may find it useful to assign its right to another person. For instance, an assignment to a bank is a common way to finance the credit granted to a customer. The Articles of the present Section cover the assignment of rights as defined in this Article.

1. Transfer by agreement

Only transfers by agreement are concerned, as opposed to situations in which the applicable law may provide for legal transfers of certain rights (such as, in certain jurisdictions, the transfer of a seller's rights against an insurer to the purchaser of an insured building, or the automatic transfer of rights in the case of the merger of companies (see Article 9.1.2(b)).

The definition equally does not cover unilateral transfers, which in certain jurisdictions may take place without the assignee's participation.

第九章

权利的转让、
债务的转移、合同的转让

第一节　权利的转让

第9.1.1条

（定义）

"权利的转让"是指一人（"让与人"），将其请求第三人（"债务人"）金钱支付或其他履行的权利，以协议方式转让给另一人（"受让人"），包括以担保为目的的转让。

注释：

有权请求债务人支付金钱或者为其他履行的债权人，很多时候可能发现把其拥有的权利转让给另一人对己有益。例如，将权利转让给银行是一种常用的向客户提供信贷的融资手段。本条定义的权利转让受本节各规则的调整。

1. 以协议方式转让

本条仅涉及协议方式的转让，而某些适用法可能规定了某些权利的法定转让（比如，在某些法域，被保险建筑物卖方可对保险人主张的权利向买方的转让，或者在公司合并情况下权利的自动转让）（参见第9.1.2条(b)项）。

本定义同样不包括单方面的转让，即在某些法域，在无受让人参与情况下发生的转让。

2. Right to payment of a monetary sum or to other performance

On the other hand, the definition is not restricted to the assignment of rights to the payment of a monetary sum. It also covers rights to other kinds of performance, such as the rendering of a service. Nor are the assignable rights limited to rights of a contractual nature. Claims deriving from non-contractual claims or based on a judgment, for instance, can be governed by the present Section, subject to Article 1.4. Future rights may also be transferred under the conditions of Article 9.1.5.

3. Notion of "transfer"

The "transfer" of the right means that it leaves the assignor's assets to become part of those of the assignee. The definition also covers transfers for security purposes.

4. Third party rights

Transfers from the assets of the assignor to those of the assignee remain subject to third party rights. Different third persons can be affected by the assignment of a right between an assignor and an assignee, such as, first and foremost, the obligor, but also the assignor's creditors and successive assignees. Third party rights are covered in part by other provisions of this Section (see Articles 9.1.10 and 9.1.11 concerning the obligor and successive assignees). They may in some instances be governed by mandatory rules of the otherwise applicable law (e.g. the law of bankruptcy).

ARTICLE 9.1.2
(Exclusions)

This Section does not apply to transfers made under the special rules governing the transfers:

(a) of instruments such as negotiable instruments, documents of title or financial instruments, or

(b) of rights in the course of transferring a business.

2. 请求支付金钱或者为其他履行的权利

另一方面，该定义不局限于请求支付金钱的权利转让，还包括请求为其他履行的权利的转让，比如提供服务。可转让的权利也不局限于合同性质的权利。例如，基于非合同性质的请求权或者法院判决而产生的请求，在不违背第 1.4 条规定的前提下可以受本节调整。根据第 9.1.5 条的规定，未来权利也可以转让。

3. "转让"的含义

权利的"转让"是指让与人的资产转让为受让人资产的一部分。这一概念包含以担保为目的的转让。

4. 第三方权利

让与人财产转让给受让人须受第三方权利的制约。让与人和受让人之间的权利转让可能会影响到多个第三方，比如，最重要是债务人，还有让与人的债权人和连续受让人。本节其他条款部分规定了第三方权利（参见第 9.1.10 条和 9.1.11 条，它们涉及债务人和连续受让人）。某些情况下他们受其他适用法的强制性规则调整（如破产法）。

第 9.1.2 条

（排除适用）

本节不适用于由特殊规则调整的下列转让：
（a）票据转让，例如流通票据、权利凭证或金融票据，或者
（b）一项商业转让过程中发生的权利转让。

COMMENT

Some types of assignment of rights are normally subject to very specific rules under the applicable law, and are therefore not governed by this Section.

1. Transfer of instruments governed by special rules

The transfer of certain types of instrument governed by special rules are outside the scope of this Section. This applies for instance to negotiable instruments, such as bills of exchange, that are usually transferred by endorsement or delivery of the document, and which are subject to further distinct rules, e.g. concerning defences that would have been available to the transferor. This exclusion also applies to documents of title, such as bills of lading or warehouse receipts, and financial instruments such as stocks and bonds. The transfer of such instruments are all normally subject to specific rules.

This does not exclude the possibility that such rights, in certain jurisdictions, could also be transferred by a normal assignment, which would then be subject to this Section.

2. Transfer of a business

Another exclusion is assignment made in the course of transferring a business under special rules governing such transfers, as may happen in the case of the merger of companies. The applicable law often provides for mechanisms that cause all rights and obligations, under certain conditions, to be transferred in their entirety by operation of law.

Article 9.1.2(b) does not prevent this Section from applying when certain rights pertaining to the transferred business are assigned individually. On the contrary, the mere transfer of shares in a company may fall under Article 9.1.2(a) and therefore not be covered by this Section.

Illustrations

1. Company A is transferred to company B. If the otherwise applicable law provides that all rights pertaining to the former company are automatically transferred to the latter, the Principles do not apply.

2. The initial facts are the same as in Illustration 1, but B is not interested in taking over a specific claim against customer X, and prefers that right to be assigned to company C. This particular transfer is subject to the Principles.

注释：

某些类型的权利转让，适用法中通常都有非常具体的规定，因此不受本节调整。

1. 受特殊规则调整的票据转让

受特殊规则调整的某些类型票据的转让不受本节调整。比如流通票据(如汇票)，通常以背书或交付方式转让，并受其他不同规则的调整，如涉及转让方可主张的抗辩的规则。这一例外也适用于权利凭证(如提单或者仓单) 以及金融票据(如股票和债券)。这类票据的转移一般都受具体规则的调整。

本条并不排除，像某些国家规定的那样，这些权利可以通过普通方式转让的可能性，此时这种转让受本节的调整。

2. 商业的转让

另一种例外是，在依照调整商业转让的特殊规则进行的商业转让过程中所发生的权利转让，例如公司合并过程中所发生的转让。适用法往往规定，在满足一定条件时，所有权利义务按照规定的机制整体转让。

与被转让商业相关的某些权利单独转让时，第 9.1.2 条(b)项并不妨碍本节的适用。而仅仅转让公司股票则因为属于第 9.1.2 条(a)项的范围而不受本节调整。

示例：

1. A 公司被转让给 B 公司。如果适用法规定原公司相关的所有权利都自动转移给后者，则不适用《通则》。

2. 初步事实与示例 1 相同，但是 B 公司无意接管对 X 客户的某一项请求权，而是希望将该权利转让给 C 公司。该特定转让交易受《通则》调整。

ARTICLE 9.1.3
(Assignability of non-monetary rights)

A right to non-monetary performance may be assigned only if the assignment does not render the obligation significantly more burdensome.

COMMENT

The assignment of a right does not in principle affect the obligor's rights and obligations. However, to a certain extent the fact that performance is now due to another obligee can modify the conditions under which the obligation is to be performed. The place of performance may be different. The change of obligee may in itself render the obligation more burdensome.

Article 9.1.8 entitles the obligor to be compensated by the assignor or the assignee for any additional costs caused by the assignment. That provision should be sufficient to take care of the problem in the case of the assignment of monetary obligations. However, when the assigned right concerns a non-monetary performance, the remedy may not always be sufficient. This Article excludes the possibility of assigning such rights when the transfer would render the obligation significantly more burdensome for the obligor.

Illustrations

1.   Company X has undertaken to provide the security service aimed at preventing theft in warehouses used by company A for the storage of wood. The premises are sold to company B, which intends to apply them to the same use. Nothing in this provision prevents A from assigning to B its right to the security services provided by X.

2.   The initial facts are the same as in Illustration 1, but B intends to use the warehouses for the storage of electronic equipment. A's right to the security services provided by X may not be assigned to B: such services would become significantly more burdensome since the security risks are obviously much higher with electronic equipment than with the storage of wood.

第9.1.3条

（非金钱权利的转让）

一项请求非金钱履行的权利，只有转让不导致明显加重履行负担时，方可转让。

注释：

权利的转让原则上不会影响债务人的权利和义务。但是，权利转让后债务人改向另一个债权人履行债务，这在一定程度上会改变债务的履行条件。履行的地点可能有所不同。单是债权人的变化就可能加重了债务履行的困难。

第9.1.8条赋予债务人一项获得补偿的权利，即要求让与人或受让人补偿转让给其带来的额外成本。这一规定很好地解决了金钱性权利转让所带来的此类问题。但是，如果被转让的权利涉及非金钱性的履行，这种救济就未必充分。如果会明显加重债务人的履行负担，则本条就排除该种权利转让。

示例：

1. X 公司承诺向 A 公司提供保安服务，防止 A 存放木材的仓库失窃。该场地出售给了 B 公司，B 公司打算将该仓库用于同样目的。本条规定不妨碍 A 将其享有的由 X 公司提供保安服务的权利转让给 B 公司。

2. 初步事实与示例1同样，但是 B 计划以该仓库存放电子设备。A 享有的由 X 公司提供保安服务的权利不能转让给 B：这样的转让明显加重了提供服务的困难，因为存放电子设备的安全风险比存放木材高得多。

ARTICLE 9.1.4
(Partial assignment)

(1) A right to the payment of a monetary sum may be assigned partially.

(2) A right to other performance may be assigned partially only if it is divisible, and the assignment does not render the obligation significantly more burdensome.

COMMENT

1. Economic interest

The partial assignment of a right may serve different economic purposes. A contractor may for instance want to assign part of its right to payment from a customer to a financing institution and keep the rest for itself. Or it may want to assign the other part to a supplier of raw materials.

Permitting partial assignment may however affect the principle that the assignment should not worsen the obligor's situation. If the right is split, the obligor will have to perform in several parts, which could entail extra costs.

2. Monetary and non-monetary rights

The obligor's burden of having to make two or several monetary payments instead of one is not in itself deemed to be excessive, and partial assignments of monetary rights are therefore permitted in principle (paragraph (1)).

Another rule prevails for the assignment of non-monetary rights, where the validity of the partial assignment is made dependent on two cumulative conditions: the divisibility of the performance due and the degree of additional burden the partial assignment may place on the obligor. Article 9.1.3 already excludes the possibility to assign non-monetary rights in their entirety if the assignment would render the obligation significantly more burdensome. Paragraph (2) applies the same rule to the partial assignment of such rights.

In any event, additional costs borne by the obligor as a result of having to perform in several parts must be compensated under Article 9.1.8.

第9.1.4条

（部分转让）

（1）请求金钱支付的权利可以部分转让。

（2）请求其他履行的权利，只有当该履行是可分割的，并且转让不导致明显加重履行负担时，才可以部分转让。

注释：

1. 经济意义

权利的部分转让可能服务于多种经济目的。比如，一个承包商可能希望将请求某一客户支付金钱的权利的一部分转让给一家金融机构，并保有余下部分；或者他想将另一部分债权转让给原料供应商。

不过，允许部分转让可能会削弱如下原则：权利转让不能减损债务人的利益。因为如果权利被分割，债务人将被迫分别履行多项义务，因而招致额外成本。

2. 金钱性和非金钱性权利

债务人支付金钱的义务，由一次性支付变为两次或多次分别支付，这本身并不被认为有什么不当，因此《通则》允许金钱性权利的部分转让（第(1)款）。

非金钱性权利的转让则适用另一条规则。该种权利的部分转让需要同时满足以下两个条件：债务履行的可分割性以及部分转让可能加重债务人负担的程度。第9.1.3条已经排除了在可能明显加重履行负担时整体转让非金钱性权利的可能性。对这种权利的部分转让，本条第(2)款规定了同样规则。

无论何种情况，债务人因多次分别履行债务而产生的额外成本，都必须依照第9.1.8条的规定得到补偿。

Illustrations

1.   Buyer X is due to pay a price of USD 1,000,000 to seller A on 31 October. A urgently needs USD 600,000 and assigns a corresponding part of its right to bank B. Notice of the partial assignment is given to X. On 31 October, both A and B claim payment of their respective parts. X must pay A USD 400,000 and B USD 600,000.

2.   Metal company X is to deliver 1,000 tons of steel to carmaker A on 31 October. Due to a decrease in sales, A estimates that it will not need that much steel at that time, and assigns the right to delivery of up to 300 tons to carmaker B. Notice of the partial assignment is given to X. On 31 October both A and B claim delivery of their respective quantities. X must deliver 700 tons to A and 300 tons to B.

3.   Tax consultant X has promised to spend 30 days in examining the accounts of company A in order to determine the proper policy to be followed in the light of new tax regulations. A subsequently regrets this arrangement, in consideration of the level of the fees to be paid. It proposes to assign 15 of the days to company B. X can argue against such a partial assignment on the grounds that performance of tasks of that nature is not divisible. It can also argue that the accounts of B are of a significantly more complex nature than those of A.

ARTICLE 9.1.5
(Future rights)

A future right is deemed to be transferred at the time of the agreement, provided the right, when it comes into existence, can be identified as the right to which the assignment relates.

COMMENT

1. Economic interest

For the purposes of this Section, a future right is a right that will or might come into existence in the future (as opposed to a present right to a performance due in the future). Examples of future rights are rights that a bank may have against a customer who might be granted a credit line in the future, or that a company may have against another

示例：

1. 买方 X 应在 10 月 31 日向卖方 A 支付 100 万美元的货款。A 急需 60 万美元并将该权利的相应部分转让给银行 B，并向 X 发出了部分转让的通知。10 月 31 日，A 和 B 请求各自的支付请求权利。X 必须向 A 支付 40 万美元，向 B 支付 60 万美元。

2. 金属公司 X 应于 10 月 31 日向汽车制造商 A 交付 1,000 吨钢材。由于销售的下滑，A 预计届时不需要这么多钢材，就将请求运输 300 吨钢材的权利转让给汽车制造商 B，并向 X 发出部分转让的通知。10 月 31 日，A 和 B 都请求交付各自部分的钢材。X 必须向 A 交付 700 吨钢材，向 B 交付 300 吨。

3. 税务顾问 X 承诺用 30 天的时间检查 A 公司的账户，并据此确定在新的税收制度下采取何种公司政策。考虑到需要支付的费用金额，A 后来对这一安排感到后悔。它提议将其中 15 天转让给 B 公司。X 能够以此种性质的任务履行不可分割为理由提出抗辩。X 还能够以 B 账户比 A 账户明显复杂提出抗辩。

第 9.1.5 条

（未来权利）

未来权利视为在转让协议达成时转让，但以在该项权利出现时能够确定其为被转让的权利为条件。

注释：

1. 经济意义

本节所指的未来权利是指在未来会或者可能会出现的权利（而不是请求履行将来到期的债务的现实权利）。例如，对于将来可能被授予信用额度的客户,银行可能拥有的权利;或者一公司基于将来可能达

company on the basis of a contract which might be concluded in the future. The assignment of such future rights can be highly significant economically.

2. Determinability

According to this Article a future right can be assigned on condition that it can be determined as the right to which the assignment relates when it comes into existence. The reason for this is the need to avoid the difficulties that might be caused by a transfer of future rights that are described in vague and too broad general terms.

3. Retroactive effect

This Article also provides that the assignment of future rights is effective with retroactivity between the assignor and the assignee. When the right comes into existence, the transfer is considered to have taken place at the time of the assignment agreement.

As regards third parties, it will be recalled that their rights may in some instances be governed by mandatory rules of the otherwise applicable law (e.g. the law of bankruptcy). However, third party rights are partly covered by other provisions of this Section, including the consequences of notices specified in Articles 9.1.10 and 9.1.11.

Illustration

> In order to finance new investments, company A assigns the royalties to be earned from future licences of a certain technology to lending institution B. Six months later, A licenses that technology to company X. The royalties due are considered to have been assigned to B from the date of the assignment agreement, provided the royalties can be related to this agreement.

ARTICLE 9.1.6
(Rights assigned without individual specification)

A number of rights may be assigned without individual specification, provided such rights can be identified as rights to which the assignment relates at the time of the assignment or when they come into existence.

成的合同而对另一公司可能拥有的权利。此类未来权利的转让具有经济上的重大意义。

2. 未来权利是可确定的

根据本条，未来权利可以转让的前提条件是，该权利产生时能够被确定为是作为转让对象的权利。如果描述未来权利的转让条款过于模糊和宽泛就会给转让带来困难，规定前述条件的目的就在于避免这种困难。

3. 溯及力

本条还规定，未来权利的转让在让与人和受让人之间具有溯及继往的效力。权利产生时，转让被认为于转让协议订立时已经发生。

至于第三方当事人，他们的权利有时可能受相关适用法强制性规则的调整（如破产法）。但是，本节其他条款对第三方权利亦作了部分规定，包括第9.1.10条和第9.1.11条对于通知效力所作的规定。

示例：

> 出于为新投资筹措资金的需要，A公司将其未来许可某项技术应得的使用费转让给借贷机构B。六个月后，A将该技术许可给X公司。应得的使用费视为于转让协议订立时就已经转让给了B，只要该使用费能够被确定是转让协议所指向的使用费。

第9.1.6条

（未逐一指明的权利的转让）

数项权利可同时转让，而无需逐一指明，但以在这些权利转让时或出现时能够确定其为被转让的权利为条件。

COMMENT

Rights are often assigned as a bundle or in bulk. A company may for instance assign all its receivables to a factoring company. In practice it would be excessively burdensome to require individual specification of each assigned right, but the global identification of the rights assigned as a bundle must be such as to permit the recognition of each right concerned as part of the assignment.

In the case of existing rights, such recognition must be possible at the time of the assignment. If future rights are included in the bundle, in accordance with Article 9.1.5 identification must be possible when the rights come into existence.

Illustration

> Retailer A assigns all its receivables to factor B. There are thousands of existing and/or future rights. The assignment does not require the specification of each single claim. Later, B gives notice of the assignment to the obligor of a specific receivable. B must be able to demonstrate the inclusion of that receivable in the bundle either at the time of the assignment, or, in the case of a right which did not exist yet at that time, when the right came into existence.

ARTICLE 9.1.7
*(Agreement between assignor
and assignee sufficient)*

(1) A right is assigned by mere agreement between the assignor and the assignee, without notice to the obligor.

(2) The consent of the obligor is not required unless the obligation in the circumstances is of an essentially personal character.

COMMENT

In the definition of Article 9.1.1 the assignment of a right is described as a "transfer by agreement". Articles 9.1.7 to 9.1.15 govern the respective legal positions of assignor, assignee and obligor.

注释：

数项权利经常捆绑转让或整体转让。比如，一个公司可能将其所有的应收账款转让给一家保理公司。逐一指明每一项被转让的权利在实践中将非常困难。不过，总体指明整体转让的权利时，通过该种指明必须能够确定每项相关权利就是该转让的一部分。

对于现存权利，该种确定必须是转让之时就是可能的。如果整体转让中包括未来权利，根据第 9.1.5 条，必须于权利产生时有可能作出该种确定。

示例：

零售商 A 将其全部应收账款转让给保理商 B，其中包括数以千计的现存权利和/或未来权利。该转让不要求指明每一项单独的权利。之后，B 向某一项具体的应收账款的债务人发出转让通知。B 必须能够证明该项具体权利于如下时间就是该转让的一部分：转让之时，或者（如果转让时该权利尚不存在）该权利产生之时。

第 9.1.7 条

（让与人和受让人协议即可转让）

（1）一项权利仅凭让与人和受让人之间的协议即可转让，而无需通知债务人。

（2）转让无需债务人同意，除非依据具体情况债务实质上具有人身性质。

注释：

在第 9.1.1 条定义中，权利的转让被描述为"以协议方式转让"。第 9.1.7 条至第 9.1.15 条分别调整让与人、受让人和债务人的各自法律地位。

1. Mere agreement between assignor and assignee

According to paragraph (1) of this Article, the assignment of a right is effective, i.e. the right is transferred from the assignor's assets to the assignee's assets, by mere agreement between these two parties. The provision is an application to the assignment of a right of the general principle laid down in Article 1.2 according to which nothing in the Principles requires a contract to be concluded in a particular form. Yet it does not affect the possible application of mandatory rules of the otherwise applicable law according to Article 1.4: thus, for instance, an assignment for security purposes may be subject to special requirements as to form.

As already stated in Comment 4 on Article 9.1.1, the rule laid down in paragraph (1) remains subject to third party rights, which are partly covered by other provisions of this Section (see Articles 9.1.10 and 9.1.11 concerning the obligor and successive assignees), and may in some instances be governed by mandatory rules of the otherwise applicable law (e.g. the law of bankruptcy) according to Article 1.4. However, it should be stressed that notice to the obligor as provided for by Article 9.1.10 is not a condition for the effectiveness of the transfer of the right(s) between the assignor and the assignee.

2. Consent of the obligor in principle not required

Paragraph (2) states explicitly what is already implied in paragraph (1), i.e. that the obligor's consent is not required for the assignment to be effective between the assignor and the assignee.

3. Exception: obligation of an essentially personal character

An exception is made for the case in which the right to be assigned relates to an obligation of an essentially personal character, i.e. a right that has been granted by the obligor specifically to the person of the obligee. This characteristic prevents the right from being assigned without the consent of the obligor, since it would be inappropriate to oblige the obligor to perform in favour of another person.

Illustrations

1. Company X promises to sponsor activities organised by organisation A, engaged in the defence of human rights. A wishes to assign the right to organisation B, active in the protection of the environment. The assignment can only take place with X's agreement.

1. 仅凭让与人和受让人之间的协议

根据本条第(1)款，权利转让仅凭双方之间的协议而生效，也即双方只要协商一致，即发生权利转让，让与人的资产转移为受让人的资产。本规定是第 1.2 条基本原则在权利转让背景下的具体适用，根据该原则，《通则》不要求合同以某一特定形式订立。但是，这不影响第 1.4 条规定的其他适用法下强制性规则的适用：例如，为担保目的的转让可能需要满足形式方面的特殊要求。

如第 9.1.1 条注释 4 所述，该条第(1)款规定的规则受第三方权利的制约，本节其他条款对第三方权利作了部分规定（参见第 9.1.10 条和第 9.1.11 条涉及债务人和连续受让人）；另外，根据第 1.4 条，第三方权利有时受其他适用法的强制性规则调整（如破产法）。但是必须强调，第 9.1.10 条之通知债务人的规定，并不是让与人和受让人之间权利转让生效的前提条件。

2. 原则上转让无需债务人同意

第(2)款明确陈述了第(1)款已有暗示的内容，也即，债务人同意并不是让与人和受让人之间权利转让生效的前提条件。

3. 例外：债务实质上具有人身性质

被转让的权利有时涉及一项实质上具有人身性质的债务，也即，债务人将接受履行的权利给予了特定的债权人本人。对于这种情形，本条规定了一项例外。由于这种性质，不经债务人同意该权利不得转让，因为强制债务人向另一个人履行债务是不恰当的。

示例：

　　1. X 公司承诺赞助 A 机构组织的维护人权的活动。A 希望将这一权利转让给热衷环保事业的 B 机构。该转让必须征得 X 的同意。

2.   A famous soprano has made a contract with agent A to sing in concerts organised by A. A sells its claims against the soprano to agent B. This transfer will require the soprano's consent, if the circumstances reveal that she was willing to sing only for A.

4. Effect of other provisions

The possibility to assign a right without the obligor's consent may be affected by the presence of a non-assignment clause in the contract between the assignor and the obligor (see Article 9.1.9), although such a clause does not in itself necessarily imply the essentially personal character of the obligation.

This Article does not address the issue of the necessity to give notice of the assignment to the obligor in order to avoid that the obligor pay the assignor after the assignment has taken place. On these issues, see Articles 9.1.10 and 9.1.11.

ARTICLE 9.1.8
(Obligor's additional costs)

**The obligor has a right to be compensated
by the assignor or the assignee for any additional
costs caused by the assignment.**

COMMENT

1. Compensation for additional costs

The assignment of a right does not necessarily affect the obligor's rights and obligations. However, should the obligor bear additional costs due to the fact that performance has to be rendered to the assignee instead of the original obligee, this Article entitles the obligor to require due compensation.

Illustration

1.   Company X is obliged to reimburse a loan of EUR 1,000,000 to company A. Both companies are located in country M. A assigns its right to company B, located in country N. X has a right to be compensated for the additional costs involved in what has now become an international transfer.

2. 一著名女高音与经纪人 A 签订合同，许诺在 A 举办的音乐会上演唱。A 将请求该女高音演唱的权利转让给经纪人 B。如果情况表明她只希望为 A 演唱，该转让需要女高音的同意。

4. 其他条款的效力

无需债务人同意转让权利的原则，可能受到让与人和债务人之间合同中约定的非转让条款（参见第9.1.9条）的影响，虽然条款本身并不一定涉及实质上具有人身性质的债务。

本条不涉及为如下目的向债务人发出通知的问题，即避免债务人于转让发生后仍向让与人履行债务。这一问题参见第9.1.10条和第9.1.11条。

第9.1.8条

（债务人的额外成本）

因权利转让产生的任何额外成本，债务人有权要求让与人或受让人给予补偿。

注释：

1. 额外成本的补偿

权利的转让并不必然影响债务人的权利和义务。但是，如果由于债务人须向受让人而非原债权人履行债务而产生了额外成本，债务人有权根据本条要求获得适当的补偿。

示例：

1. X 公司应偿还 A 公司 100 万欧元的贷款，两公司都位于 M 国。A 将此权利转让给位于 X 国的 B 公司，付款义务变成了一项国际支付，由此造成的额外成本，X 有权要求获得补偿。

The rule laid down in this Article is in conformity with Article 6.1.6, which provides a similar solution if a party to the contract changes its place of business after the conclusion of the contract.

2. Compensation by the assignor or the assignee

The obligor may claim compensation for additional costs either from the assignor or from the assignee. In the case of a monetary obligation, the obligor will often be in a position to set off its right to compensation against the obligation it owes to the assignee.

3. Partial assignment

Additional costs may arise in particular in the case of partial assignment (see Article 9.1.4). This Article applies accordingly.

Illustration

> 2. In Illustration 2 to Article 9.1.4, A has assigned to B part of its right to receive a delivery of steel from X. Instead of having to deliver 1,000 tons to A, X became obliged to deliver 700 tons to A and 300 tons to B. X is entitled to be compensated for the additional costs resulting from having to deliver in two parts.

4. Obligation becoming significantly more burdensome

In two cases compensation for additional costs is not considered to be a sufficient remedy. Firstly, under Article 9.1.3 the assignment of a right to a non-monetary performance is not allowed when it would render the obligation significantly more burdensome. Secondly, under Article 9.1.4 the partial assignment of a right to a non-monetary performance is also not allowed in similar circumstances.

ARTICLE 9.1.9
(Non-assignment clauses)

(1) The assignment of a right to the payment of a monetary sum is effective notwithstanding an agreement between the assignor and the obligor limiting or prohibiting such an assignment. However, the assignor may be liable to the obligor for breach of contract.

本条规定的规则与第6.1.6条一致。如果一方当事人在合同订立后变换营业所，第6.1.6条规定了类似的处理办法。

2. 要求让与人或受让人给予补偿

债务人可以要求让与人或受让人补偿由此造成的额外成本。如果是金钱性质的债务，债务人通常有权以其获得补偿的权利抵销向受让人承担的债务。

3. 部分转让

部分转让情形下更容易发生额外成本（参见第9.1.4条）。本条同样适用。

示例：

> 2. 第9.1.4条示例2中，A 将请求 X 交付钢材的部分权利转让给 B。X 因此必须向 A 交付700吨钢材，向 B 交付300吨钢材，而不再是向 A 交付1,000吨。对于因为分两部分交付而产生的额外成本，X 有权要求获得补偿。

4. 履行负担明显加重的债务

以下两种情况下，补偿额外成本不构成充分的救济。首先，依据第9.1.3条，如果转让会明显加重履行负担，则不得转让请求非金钱性履行的权利。其次，依据第9.1.4条，在类似情况下，也不得部分转让请求非金钱性履行的权利。

第9.1.9条

（非转让条款）

（1）尽管让与人和债务人之间存在限制或禁止转让的协议，请求金钱支付权利的转让仍然具有效力。但是，让与人可能因此向债务人承担违约责任。

(2) The assignment of a right to other performance is ineffective if it is contrary to an agreement between the assignor and the obligor limiting or prohibiting the assignment. Nevertheless, the assignment is effective if the assignee, at the time of the assignment, neither knew nor ought to have known of the agreement. The assignor may then be liable to the obligor for breach of contract.

COMMENT

1. Balance of interests

According to Article 9.1.7(2) the consent of the obligor is not required for the assignment to be effective between the assignor and the assignee unless the obligation is of an essentially personal character. However, in practice it is frequent for the contract between the original obligee/assignor and the obligor to contain a clause limiting or prohibiting the assignment of the original obligee/assignor's rights as the obligor may not wish to change obligee. Should the original obligee/assignor subsequently assign such rights in spite of the non-assignment clause, the conflicting interests of the obligor and of the assignee must be weighed. The obligor suffers a violation of its contractual rights, but the assignee must equally be protected. At a more general level, it is also important to favour the assignment of rights as an efficient means of financing.

In this respect this Article makes a distinction between the assignment of monetary rights and the assignment of rights to other performances.

2. Monetary rights

In the case of the assignment of monetary rights, paragraph (1) gives preference to the needs of credit. The assignee of a monetary right is protected against non-assignment clauses and the assignment is fully effective. However, as the assignor acts contrary to its contractual duties, it is liable in damages to the obligor for non-performance of the contract under Chapter 7, Section 4.

Illustrations

1.   Contractor A is entitled to the payment of USD 100,000 from its customer X after a certain stage of construction work has been completed. The contract contains a clause prohibiting A from

（2）请求其他履行的权利的转让，如果违反让与人与债务人之间限制或禁止转让的协议，则转让无效。但是，如果受让人在转让发生时既不知道也不应知道该协议，则转让有效。但让与人可能因此向债务人承担违约责任。

注释：

1. 利益的平衡

根据第 9.1.7 条第（2）款，权利转让在让与人和受让人之间发生效力无需经债务人事先同意，除非相关债务本质上具有人身性质。但实践中，原始债权人/让与人和债务人之间的合同往往包含一个限制或禁止原始债权人/让与人转让其权利的条款，因为债务人可能不希望变更债权人。如果原始债权人/让与人后来不顾该非转让条款转让了权利，则有必要对债务人和受让人之间相互冲突的利益加以平衡。债务人的合同权利被侵犯，而受让人同样应该得到保护。从更一般的角度看，权利转让是一种有效的融资手段，保护这种融资功能也非常重要。

在这方面，针对金钱性权利的转让和请求为其他履行的权利的转让，本条作了区别对待。

2. 金钱性权利

对于金钱性权利的转让，第（1）款更侧重于满足信贷需要的功能。金钱性权利受让人不受非转让条款的约束，权利转让完全有效。但是，由于让与人违反了其承担的合同义务，依据第七章第四节须向债务人承担不履行合同的损害赔偿责任。

示例：

1. 完成某一阶段的建筑工程后，承包商 A 有权从客户 X 获得10万美元的支付。合同包含一个禁止A转让该权利的条

assigning the right. A nevertheless assigns the right to bank B. B can rely on the assignment despite the clause, and can claim payment when it is due. X is however entitled to sue A for acting in breach of the clause. X could for instance claim damages if it demonstrates that it has suffered some prejudice.

2.   Company X is to reimburse EUR 500,000 to company A at a date when it can set off this obligation partially with a claim of EUR 200,000 it has against A. The contract between X and A contains a non-assignment clause. Disregarding that clause, A assigns its right to reimbursement to company B. X may claim damages against A for the costs it incurs in having to engage in a separate procedure to recover the sum of EUR 200,000.

3. Non-monetary rights

The assignment of rights to non-monetary performances does not have the same relationship to credit, thus justifying another solution which is to be found in paragraph (2). In order to achieve a fair balance between the conflicting interests of the three parties concerned, the rule is that non-assignment clauses are given effect vis-à-vis the assignee with the result that the assignment is ineffective. The solution is however reversed if it can be established that, at the time of the assignment, the assignee did not know and ought not to have known of the non-assignment clause. In such a case, the assignment is effective, but the assignor may be liable in damages to the obligor for non-performance of the contract under Chapter 7, Section 4.

Illustration

3.   Company X has agreed to communicate to company A all improvements it will develop to a technical process over a period of time. Their contract stipulates that A's rights towards X may not be assigned. A does not need the technology for itself any longer and attempts to assign its rights to company B. Such an assignment is ineffective. X does not become B's obligor. In such a case, B has a claim against A under Article 9.1.15(b).

款，但A却将这一权利转让给了银行B。尽管有此条款的限制，B获得的权利仍然有效，并可在债务到期时请求支付。但是X有权以违约为由起诉A。如果能够证明受到了某种损害，X可以请求获得损害赔偿。

2. X公司应偿还A公司50万欧元，与此同时，它可以以A对其承担的20万欧元的债务主张部分抵销。尽管X和A之间的协议包含一个禁止转让的条款，A仍然将其请求偿还的权利转让给了B。X被迫通过专门手续收取自己的20万欧元，它可以就此引起的成本要求A给予补偿。

3. 非金钱性权利

请求为非金钱性履行的权利，其转让与信贷需求之间就不具有同样的联系，因此第(2)款规定的另一种规则也有其合理性。为了在转让所涉三方相互冲突的利益之间寻求一种合理的平衡，依据该规则，非转让条款对受让人有效，进而权利转让无效。但是如果能够证明，受让人于转让之时既不知道也不应知道该非转让条款，该规则的效果就发生了逆转。此时，权利转让有效，但是依据第七章第四节让与人须向债务人承担不履行合同的损害赔偿责任。

示例：

3. X公司与A公司约定，一定时期内，前者向后者通报其就一项技术流程所作的各项改进。合同还规定，A所拥有的该项权利不得转让。A自己不再需要该项技术，希望将此权利转让给B公司。该转让无效，X不因此成为B的债务人。这种情况下，B可以根据第9.1.15条(b)项要求A给予赔偿。

ARTICLE **9.1.10**
(Notice to the obligor)

(1) Until the obligor receives a notice of the assignment from either the assignor or the assignee, it is discharged by paying the assignor.
(2) After the obligor receives such a notice, it is discharged only by paying the assignee.

COMMENT

1. Effect of notice on the obligor

Whereas the assignment is effective between the assignor and the assignee as a result of their agreement (see Article 9.1.7), the obligor will be discharged by paying the assignor until it receives notice of the assignment. If the obligor pays the assignor, the assignee can recover that payment from the assignor (see Article 9.1.15(f)). Only after the obligor receives a notice of assignment does the assignment become effective towards the obligor. The obligor can then be discharged only by paying the assignee.

Illustrations

1. Seller A assigns its right to payment from buyer X to bank B. Neither A nor B gives notice to X. When payment is due, X pays A. This payment is fully valid and X is discharged. It will be up to B to recover it from A under Article 9.1.15(f).

2. Seller A assigns to bank B its right to payment from buyer X. B immediately gives notice of the assignment to X. When payment is due, X still pays A. X is not discharged and B is entitled to oblige X to pay a second time.

Before the obligor receives a notice of the assignment, it is discharged when it pays the assignor irrespective of whether it knew, or ought to have known, of the assignment. The purpose is to place the burden of informing the obligor of the assignment on the parties to the assignment agreement, i.e. the assignor and the assignee. This solution is considered to be justified in the context of international commercial contracts. However, it does not necessarily exclude that in certain circumstances the obligor will be liable for damages if it acted in bad faith when it paid the assignor.

第 9.1.10 条

（通知债务人）

（1）在收到让与人或受让人发出的转让通知以前，债务人可通过向让与人清偿来解除债务。

（2）在收到该通知后，债务人只有通过向受让人清偿才能解除债务。

注释：

1. 通知债务人的效力

尽管权利转让在让与人和受让人之间仅凭协议生效（参见第 9.1.7 条），债务人在收到转让通知以前通过向让与人清偿即可解除债务。如果债务人向让与人清偿，受让人可以要求让与人返还该清偿（参见第 9.1.15 条（f）项）。只有在债务人收到转让通知后，转让才对债务人生效。此后，债务人只能通过向受让人清偿才能解除债务。

示例：

　1. 卖方 A 将其请求买方 X 付款的权利转让给银行 B，A 或 B 都没有通知 X。债务到期时 X 向 A 支付货款。该支付有效，并且 X 的债务得以解除。B 必须根据第 9.1.15 条（f）项自己向 A 追讨该款项。

　2. 卖方 A 将其请求买方 X 支付货款的权利转让给银行 B，B 即刻向 X 发出了转让通知。债务到期时，X 仍然向 A 支付。X 的债务没有解除，B 有权要求 X 第二次支付。

在债务人收到转让通知以前，他向让与人清偿之后债务即得以解除，不论他是否知道或者应该知道转让的发生。该条款的目的是将通知债务人的负担加之于转让协议的当事人，也即让与人和受让人。对于国际商业合同而言，这一规定是合理的。但是，如果债务人在向让与人清偿时存有恶意，并不排除某些情况下需要承担损害赔偿责任。

Parties sometimes resort to so-called "silent assignments", where the assignor and the assignee agree not to inform the obligor of the assignment. This arrangement is valid between parties, but since the obligor receives no notice, it will be discharged by paying the assignor, as provided in Article 9.1.10(1).

2. Meaning of "notice"

"Notice" is to be understood in the broad sense of Article 1.10. Although this Article does not specify the content of the notice, the latter should indicate not only the fact of the assignment, but also the identity of the assignee, the specifications of the right transferred (subject to Article 9.1.6) and, in the case of partial assignment, the extent of the assignment.

3. Who should give notice

Article 9.1.10(1) leaves the question of who should give notice open, i.e. whether it should be the assignor or the assignee. In practice, it is probable that in most cases the assignee will take the initiative, as it has a major interest in avoiding that the obligor will perform in favour of the assignor notwithstanding the assignment. But notice given by the assignor has the same effect. When notice is given by the assignee, the obligor may request adequate proof of the assignment (see Article 9.1.12).

4. When must notice be given

This Article does not explicitly require notice to be given only after the assignment agreement has been concluded. In some cases the contract between a future assignor and the obligor will provide that the rights arising from it will be assigned to a financial institution. Whether this can be considered to be adequate notice having the consequences provided for in this Article is a matter of interpretation, and may possibly depend on the definiteness of the clause regarding the identity of the future assignee.

5. Revocation of notice

Notice given to the obligor can be revoked in certain circumstances, e.g. if the assignment agreement itself becomes invalid, or if an assignment made for security purposes is no longer necessary. This will not affect payments made before the revocation to the person who was the assignee at the time, but if the obligor pays that person after the revocation it would no longer be discharged.

有时当事人会使用所谓的"沉默转让"，也即，让与人和受让人约定不将转让事实通知给债务人。这一安排在当事人之间有效，但是因为债务人未收到通知，根据第 9.1.10 条第(1)款，债务人向让与人清偿后其债务便得到解除。

2. "通知"的含义

"通知"应该按照第 1.10 条所说的宽泛含义加以理解。虽然本条对于通知的内容未加明确规定，但其中不但应该指明转让的事实，还要指明受让人的身份、指明被转让的权利(根据第 9.1.6 条)，对于部分转让还要指明转让的范围。

3. 发出通知的主体

第 9.1.10 条第(1)款对于发出通知的主体没有作出规定，也即，由让与人还是受让人发出通知。事实上，大多数都是受让人发出通知，因为他对此具有重大利益，以避免债务人在转让发生后仍向让与人履行债务。但是让与人发出的通知具有同等效力。如果是受让人发出通知，债务人可以要求其提供充分的转让证明（参见第 9.1.12 条）。

4. 必须在何时发出通知

本条并没有明确要求，只能在转让合同订立后才可发出通知。有时，未来让与人和债务人之间的合同规定，源自该合同的权利将被转让给一个金融机构。这种规定是否能被视为具有本条规定效力的充分通知，是一个解释问题，而且可能还取决于涉及未来受让人身份的条款的明确程度。

5. 通知的撤销

向债务人发出的通知某些情况下可以撤销，比如，转让协议本身失去效力，或者以担保为目的的转让失去了原有的必要性。撤销之前向当时的受让人所为的清偿，不受本规则的影响；但是如果支付发生在撤销之后，债务并没有因此解除。

ARTICLE 9.1.11
(Successive assignments)

If the same right has been assigned by the same assignor to two or more successive assignees, the obligor is discharged by paying according to the order in which the notices were received.

COMMENT

1. Priority of first notice

This Article deals with the case where the same assignor assigns the same right to different assignees. Normally this should not happen, although in practice it may occur, whether the assignor does so consciously or inadvertently. Preference is then given to the assignee who was the first to give notice. The other assignees can only claim against the assignor under Article 9.1.15(c) below.

Illustration

> On 5 February seller A assigns its right to payment from buyer X to bank B, and then on 20 February to bank C. C notifies the assignment on 21 February, and B does so only on 25 February. X is discharged by paying C, even though the right was assigned to C after it had been assigned to B.

Unlike the solution prevailing under certain jurisdictions, this Article does not take into consideration the actual or constructive knowledge the obligor may have of the assignment(s) in the absence of notice. This approach is motivated by the wish to encourage the giving of notice, thus ensuring a degree of certainty that is especially advisable in the context of international contracts.

2. No notice given

If no notice is given by any of the successive assignees the obligor will be discharged by paying the assignor (see Article 9.1.10(1)).

3. Notice without adequate proof

Notice by an assignee without there being adequate proof that the assignment has been made, may be ineffective under Article 9.1.12.

第 9. 1. 11 条

（连续转让）

如果同一让与人将同一权利连续转让给两个
或两个以上受让人，则债务人按照收到通知的时
间顺序清偿后，其债务得以解除。

注释：

1. 最先通知的优先权

本条规定所要调整的是，同一让与人将同一权利转让给不同受让人
的情况。虽然一般来说这种情况不应该发生，但出于让与人的有意或疏
忽，实践中却可能出现。所以本条赋予第一个发出通知的受让人获得权
利的优先权。其他受让人只能依据第9.1.15条(c)项向让与人索赔。

示例：

卖方 A 于 2 月 5 日将请求买方 X 支付货款的权利转让给银行
B,又于 2 月 20 日将该权利转让给银行 C。C 于 2 月 21 日就此转
让事项作了通知,而 B 迟至 2 月 25 日才发出转让通知。即便该权
利在转让给 B 之后才转让给 C,X 向 C 支付之后便解除了债务。

与某些法域采用的原则不同，本条并不考虑假设没有收到通知债
务人是否实际知道或推定知道转让发生的事实。这种方式旨在鼓励发
出通知，从而确保一定程度的确定性。确定性在国际合同中尤其重要。

2. 未给予通知

如果没有任何一个连续受让人向债务人发出通知，债务人通过清
偿让与人来解除债务（参见第9.1.10条第(1)款）。

3. 没有充分证据的通知

受让人发出通知时，如果缺少证明转让的充分证据，该通知依据
第9.1.12条可能无效。

ARTICLE 9.1.12
(Adequate proof of assignment)

(1) If notice of the assignment is given by the assignee, the obligor may request the assignee to provide within a reasonable time adequate proof that the assignment has been made.

(2) Until adequate proof is provided, the obligor may withhold payment.

(3) Unless adequate proof is provided, notice is not effective.

(4) Adequate proof includes, but is not limited to, any writing emanating from the assignor and indicating that the assignment has taken place.

COMMENT

Since receiving the notice of assignment has the important effects provided for in Articles 9.1.10 and 9.1.11, this Article intends to protect the obligor against the risk of receiving a fraudulent notice from a fake "assignee" by requiring adequate proof that the assignment has actually been made. Until adequate proof is provided, the obligor may withhold payment to the alleged assignee. If adequate proof is provided, notice is effective from the date it was provided.

Illustration

On 1 December purchaser X has to pay USD 200,000 to contractor A as an instalment of the sum due for the construction of a plant. In October A assigns the right to bank B. Either A or B may give notice of the assignment to X. If B takes the initiative and writes to X that it has become the assignee of the sum, X may require B to provide adequate proof. Without prejudice to other types of evidence, B will probably produce the assignment agreement or any other writing from A confirming that the right has been assigned. Until such adequate proof is provided, X may withhold payment.

第9.1.12条

（转让的充分证据）

（1）当转让通知由受让人发出，债务人可以要求受让人在合理时间内提供转让已发生的充分证据。

（2）在提供充分证据之前，债务人可以暂停清偿。

（3）在提供充分证据之前，通知不产生效力。

（4）充分证据包括但不限于，让与人做出的并能够表明转让已做出的任何书面文件。

注释：

由于收到转让通知具有第9.1.10条和9.1.11条所规定的重要后果，本条赋予债务人要求提供证明转让实际发生的充分证据的权利，防范收到假冒"受让人"发出的虚假通知，以此保护债务人。在声称的受让人提供充分证据之前，债务人可暂停向其清偿。如果提供了充分的证据，通知自该证据提供之日起生效。

示例：

买方 X 需于12月1日向承包商 A 支付200,000美元，作为工厂造价的其中一期付款。A 于10月份将此权利转让给银行 B。A 或 B 都可以向 X 发出转让通知。如果 B 首先通知并致函 X 告知其已经成为该款项的受让人，则 X 可以要求 B 提供充分的证据。除了可以提供其他类型的证据外，B 可以提供转让协议或者源自 A 的任何其他能够确认权利转让的书面材料。在收到充分证据之前，X 可以暂停支付。

ARTICLE 9.1.13
(Defences and rights of set-off)

(1) The obligor may assert against the assignee all defences that the obligor could assert against the assignor.

(2) The obligor may exercise against the assignee any right of set-off available to the obligor against the assignor up to the time notice of assignment was received.

COMMENT

1. Assertion of defences

A right can in principle be assigned without the obligor's consent (see Article 9.1.7(2)). This solution rests on the assumption that the assignment will not adversely affect the obligor's legal situation.

It can happen that the obligor would have been able to withhold or refuse payment to the original obligee on the basis of a defence such as the defective performance of that obligee's obligations vis-à-vis the obligor. To determine whether such defences can be asserted also against the assignee, the respective interests of the parties have to be weighed: the obligor's situation should not deteriorate as a result of the assignment, while the assignee has an interest in the integrity of the right it has acquired.

According to paragraph (1) of this Article, the obligor may assert against the assignee all the defences that it would have been able to assert if the claim had been made by the assignor. In this case, however, the assignee will have a claim against the assignor under Article 9.1.15(d).

Illustration

1.   Software company A promises customer X to install a new accounting application before the end of the year. The main payment is to take place one month after completion. A immediately assigns the right to bank B. When the payment is due, B wants to claim it from X, but the latter explains that the new software is not working properly and that the accounting department is in chaos. X refuses to pay until this catastrophic situation has been remedied. X is justified in asserting this defence against B, which can then claim against A under Article 9.1.15(d).

The same solution applies to defences of a procedural nature.

第9.1.13条

（抗辩权和抵销权）

（1）债务人得以其对抗让与人的所有抗辩权，对抗受让人。

（2）债务人在收到转让通知时，可向受让人主张其可向让与人主张的任何抵销权。

注释：

1. 主张抗辩

一项权利原则上可以不经债务人同意而转让（参见第9.1.7条第（2）款）。该规定的理论前提是，债权转让不会对债务人的法律地位造成负面影响。

有时候，债务人可以根据某种抗辩暂停或者拒绝向原债权人清偿，例如，债权人向债务人提供的履行有瑕疵。要确定这样的抗辩是否也可以用于对抗受让人，必须对各方当事人各自的利益加以平衡：债务人的地位不应该因该转让而减损，而受让人有受让完整权利的利益。

根据本条第（1）款的规定，债务人可以以其对抗让与人的所有抗辩，对抗受让人。但是这种情形下，受让人可根据第9.1.15条（d）项向让与人提出请求。

示例：

1. 软件公司A允诺年底以前为客户X安装一个新的会计应用软件；主体款项在安装完成后一个月内支付。A当即将此权利转让给银行B。债务到期时，B要求X支付，但是X解释说新的软件不能正常工作，其会计部门一片混乱。X拒绝在问题得到解决以前支付。X有权向B提出该抗辩，B有权根据第9.1.15条（d）项向A提出请求。

同样的原则也适用于程序性抗辩。

Illustration

> 2.   Company X sells a gas turbine to contractor A, to be incorporated into a plant built for customer B. When the work has been completed, A assigns the guarantee of satisfactory performance to B. When the turbine does not work properly, B sues X before a court at its place of business. X will successfully invoke the arbitration clause included in its contract with A.

2. Set-off

According to paragraph (2), the obligor may exercise against the assignee any right of set-off provided that the right of set-off was available to the obligor under Article 8.1 before the notice of the assignment was given.

This solution is in accord with the principle that the obligor's situation should not deteriorate as a result of the assignment. The assignee's interests are protected by the claim it may then have against the assignor under Article 9.1.15(e).

Illustration

> 3.   Company A assigns to company B the right to the payment of EUR 100,000 that it has against company X. X however has a claim of EUR 60,000 against A. The two claims have not yet been set off by notice given under Article 8.3 of the Principles, but the required conditions for set-off were satisfied before the assignment was notified. X may still exercise its right of set-off by giving notice to the assignee. B can then only claim EUR 40,000 from X. B can recover the difference from A which had undertaken under Article 9.1.15(e) that the obligor would not give notice of set-off as regards the assigned right.

ARTICLE 9.1.14
(Rights related to the right assigned)

The assignment of a right transfers to the assignee:

(a) all the assignor's rights to payment or other performance under the contract in respect of the right assigned, and

(b) all rights securing performance of the right assigned.

示例：

　　2. X 公司向承包商 A 出售一个燃气涡轮，该涡轮将被用于 A 为客户 B 建造的一个工厂。工厂完工后，A 将 X 提供的该涡轮表现令人满意这一保证转让给了 B。当燃气涡轮运作不正常时，B 向其营业地法院对 X 提起诉讼。X 能够成功援引他与 A 之间的合同中包含的仲裁条款。

2. 抵销

根据第(2)款，债务人可以向受让人行使抵销权，但前提条件是，在收到转让通知之前他就有权依第 8.1 条主张这些抵销权。

该规定与债务人地位不因权利转让而受损的原则相一致。保护受让人利益的方法是，他可以转而根据第 9.1.15 条(e)项向让与人提出请求。

示例：

　　3. A 公司有权请求 X 公司支付 100,000 欧元，它将该权利转让给 B 公司。而 X 对 A 享有 60,000 欧元的债权。两项债务尚未凭第 8.3 条规定的通知相抵销，但在收到转让通知前抵销条件都已成就。X 仍可通过向受让人发出通知行使抵销权。B 只能要求 X 支付 40,000 欧元。B 可以要求 A 支付差额部分，因为 A 违反了第 9.1.15 条(e)项规定的保证，即债务人将不会就被转让的权利发出抵销通知。

第 9.1.14 条

（与被转让权利相关的权利）

一项权利的转让导致向受让人转移：

（a）让与人依合同所享有的全部请求金钱支付或者其他履行的权利，以及

（b）担保被转让之权利得以履行的所有权利。

COMMENT

1. Scope of the assignment

This provision is inspired by the same principle as Article 9.1.13. The assignment transfers the assignor's right as it is, not only with the defences the obligor may be able to assert, but also with all the rights to payment or to other performances under the contract in respect of the right assigned, and all rights securing performance of the right assigned.

Illustrations

1.   Bank A is entitled to receive reimbursement of a loan of EUR 1,000,000 made to customer X, bearing interest at a rate of 3%. A assigns its right to reimbursement of the principal to bank B. The assignment also operates as a transfer of the right to interest and of the underlying security.

2.   The initial facts are the same as in Illustration 1, but the loan contract entitles A to claim early repayment if X fails to pay the interest due. This right is also transferred to B.

3.   The initial facts are the same as in Illustration 1, but X has deposited some shares as security to the benefit of A. This benefit is transferred to B, subject to the possible application of mandatory requirements of the otherwise applicable law under Article 1.4.

2. Partial assignment

When a right is partially assigned, if the rights covered by Article 9.1.14 are divisible they will be transferred in proportion. If they are not, parties should decide whether they are transferred to the assignee or whether they will remain with the assignor.

3. Contractual deviations

The rule laid down in paragraph (1) may however be modified by an agreement between the assignor and the assignee, who may stipulate, for instance, a separate assignment of interest.

4. Assignor's co-operation

It follows from the general duty to co-operate laid down in Article 5.1.3 that the assignor is obliged to take all the steps necessary to permit the assignee to enjoy the benefit of accessory rights and securities.

注释：

1. 转让的范围

本条的理论基础与第9.1.13条相同，采用同一原则。债权转让的结果是按照转让时让与人的权利状况转移权利，不但包括债务人可主张的各种抗辩，还包括合同项下与被转让权利相关的请求债务人支付金钱或者履行其他义务的所有权利，以及用以保证被转让之权利能够履行的所有权利。

示例：

1. 银行A有权请求客户X偿还100万欧元的贷款本金，该笔贷款的利率是3%。A将请求该本金的权利转让给银行B。该转让也使请求利息的权利及基础担保权利发生了转移。

2. 初步事实和示例1相同，但是贷款合同规定如果X不能支付到期利息，A有权要求提前偿还。这一权利也转移给了B。

3. 初步事实和例1相同，但X在A银行存入一些股票，作为A的权益的担保。这一权益也转移给了B，但这并不排除可能要根据第1.4条适用其他适用法的强制性规定。

2. 部分转让

发生部分权利转让时，若受第9.1.4条调整的权利具有可分割性，这些权利按比例转移。如果不可分割，当事人必须确定这些权利是转移给了受让人还是仍归让与人所有。

3. 约定偏离

不过，第(1)款规定的规则可以依让与人和受让人之间的合同加以修改，比如他们可以单独规定利息的转让。

4. 让与人的合作

第5.1.3条规定了当事人之间相互合作的基本义务。根据这一义务，让与人有义务采取一切必要的措施，保证受让人享有各项从权利和担保权益。

ARTICLE 9.1.15
(Undertakings of the assignor)

The assignor undertakes towards the assignee, except as otherwise disclosed to the assignee, that:

(a) the assigned right exists at the time of the assignment, unless the right is a future right;

(b) the assignor is entitled to assign the right;

(c) the right has not been previously assigned to another assignee, and it is free from any right or claim from a third party;

(d) the obligor does not have any defences;

(e) neither the obligor nor the assignor has given notice of set-off concerning the assigned right and will not give any such notice;

(f) the assignor will reimburse the assignee for any payment received from the obligor before notice of the assignment was given.

COMMENT

When assigning a right by agreement to the assignee, the assignor assumes several undertakings.

1. Existence of the right

The assigned right should exist at the time of the assignment. This would, for instance, not be the case if the payment had already been made or if the right to a payment had previously been avoided.

Illustration

1. Company A assigns a bundle of rights to factor B. When required to pay by B, customer X demonstrates that the amount due had been paid to A before the assignment. B has a claim against A, since at the time of the assignment the right no longer existed.

If, as permitted by Article 9.1.5, a future right is assigned, no such undertaking exists.

第 9.1.15 条

（让与人的担保）

除非已向受让人作了另外披露，让与人对受让人承担下述担保义务：

（a）被转让之权利在转让发生时已经存在，但未来权利除外；

（b）让与人有权转让该权利；

（c）该权利此前没有转让给其他受让人，并且不会有第三方提出权利或请求；

（d）债务人不拥有任何抗辩权；

（e）债务人和让与人针对被转让权利均未发出抵销通知，而且今后也不会发出此类通知；

（f）让与人应将在转让通知发出前从债务人收到的任何清偿，退还给受让人。

注释：

以协议方式向受让人转让权利时，让与人承担了多项担保义务。

1. 权利存在

被转让之权利必须在转让发生时已经存在。举例而言，如果债务已经清偿或者请求清偿的权利已被宣告无效，权利就是不存在的。

示例：

1. A 公司向保理商 B 整体转让一批权利。当 B 要求客户 X 支付时，X 证明其已在转让前向 A 作了清偿。B 获得对 A 的请求权，因为转让发生时权利已经不复存在。

若按照第9.1.5 条转让未来权利时，则不存在这样的担保。

Illustration

> 2.   Company A assigns to bank B the royalties from a technology licence that is to be granted in the near future to company X. The licence never materialises. B has no claim against A.

2. Assignor entitled to assign the right

The assignor is entitled to assign the right. This is, for instance, not the case if there is a legal or contractual prohibition to assign the right.

Illustration

> 3.   Company X has agreed to communicate to company A all the improvements to a technical process that it will develop over a period of time. Their contract stipulates that A's rights towards X cannot be assigned. A no longer needs the technology itself, and attempts to assign its rights to company B. This illustration was already given above, under Article 9.1.9, to give an example of an ineffective assignment. In this case, B has a claim against A under Article 9.1.15(b). It will be recalled that the solution would be reversed, should B demonstrate that it neither knew nor ought to have known of the non-assignment clause.

3. No previous assignment, no third party rights or claims

If the assignor has already assigned a right to another assignee, it is generally not entitled to make a second assignment of that same right and this prohibition could be considered as already covered by the undertaking under sub-paragraph (b). The practical importance of this hypothesis is such that a separate and explicit provision is justified. It will however be recalled that under Article 9.1.11 the second assignee may prevail over the first one if it gives earlier notice to the obligee.

However, a previous assignment may have been made merely for security purposes. In this case, the right is still assignable, with proper disclosure to the second assignee.

4. No defence from the obligor

According to Article 9.1.13(1), the obligor may assert against the assignee all the defences that the obligor would have been able to assert against the assignor. In such a case, the assignee has a claim against the assignor on the basis of this undertaking.

示例：

> 2. A 公司打算近期内向 X 公司授予一项技术许可，并将由此产生的使用费转让给银行 B。如果许可交易落空，则 B 对 A 无请求权。

2. 让与人有权转让该权利

让与人有权转让该权利。如果法律禁止或者合同禁止转让该权利，让与人就无权转让。

示例：

> 3. X 公司与 A 公司约定，一定时期内，前者向后者通报其就一项技术流程所作的各项改进。合同还规定，A 所拥有的该项权利不得转让。A 自己不再需要该项技术，希望将此权利转让给 B 公司（本案已在作为一个无效转让的例证有所介绍）。本案中，根据第 9.1.15 条(b)项 B 取得对 A 的请求权。第 9.1.9 条已经述及，如果 B 可以证明他既不知道也无理由知道该非转让条款，则适用相反的规则。

3. 事先没有转让，不会有第三方提出权利或请求

如果让与人已经将某一项权利转让给了另一个受让人，通常就无权将同一权利作第二次转让。可以认为本条(b)项所规定的担保义务已经包含了这一禁止规则。这种情况具有重大的现实意义，因此有必要作此单独和明示的规定。请注意，根据第 9.1.11 条的规定，如果第二受让人率先通知了债务人，他就取得了相对第一受让人的优先权。

但是，原先的转让可能仅仅用于担保目的。若如此，权利仍然可以转让，但须对第二受让人作适当的事前披露。

4. 债务人不拥有任何抗辩权

根据第 9.1.13 条第(1)款，债务人可用来对抗让与人的所有抗辩权，亦可对抗受让人。在这种情况下，则受让人依此担保取得针对让与人的请求权。

Illustration

> 4. Bank B is the assignee of contractor A's right to payment of a certain sum from customer X. When payment is due, X refuses to pay arguing that A did not perform its obligations properly. Such defence can be successfully set up against B under Article 9.1.13(1). B would then have a claim against A.

5. No notice of set-off

The right of set-off may be exercised by the obligor against the assignee if it was available to the obligor before the notice of assignment was received (see Article 9.1.13(2)). The assignor undertakes vis-à-vis the assignee that neither the assignor nor the obligor has already given notice of set-off affecting the assigned right. The assignor also undertakes that such notice will not be given in the future. If, for instance, the obligor were to give such a notice to the assignee after the assignment, as permitted by Article 9.1.13(2), the assignee would have a claim against the assignor under Article 9.1.15(e).

6. Reimbursement of payment by the obligor

Article 9.1.10(1) provides that until it receives the notice of assignment the obligor is discharged by paying the assignor. This is the correct solution to protect the obligor, but the assignor and the assignee have agreed between themselves on the transfer of the right. The assignor therefore undertakes that it will reimburse the assignee for any payment it received from the obligor before the notice of assignment was given.

Illustration

> 5. Seller A assigns to bank B its right to payment from buyer X. Neither A nor B gives notice to X. When payment is due, X pays A. As already explained in the Comment on Article 9.1.10, this payment is fully valid and B is discharged. However, Article 9.1.15(f) enables B to recover the sum paid from A.

7. No undertaking concerning the obligor's performance or solvency

Parties to the assignment may certainly provide for an undertaking by the assignor concerning the obligor's present or future solvency, or, more generally, the obligor's performance of its obligations. However, without such an agreement, there is no such undertaking under this Article.

示例：

　　4. 银行 B 是承包商 A 对客户 X 请求某笔款项权利的受让人。债务到期时，X 拒绝支付，辩称 A 没有适当履行其债务。按照9.1.13条第(1)款的规定，此抗辩可有效对抗 B。B 转而取得对 A 的请求权。

5. 不存在抵销通知

债务人在收到转让通知时可向让与人主张的任何抵销权，都可以向受让人主张（参见第9.1.13条第(2)款）。让与人向受让人保证，债务人和让与人未做出过针对被转让权利的抵销通知。转让人还保证，他们今后也不会发出此类通知。如果债务人根据第9.1.13条第(2)款，在权利转让以后发出了此类通知，受让人可以根据第9.1.15条(e)项向让与人提出请求。

6. 退还债务人清偿

第9.1.10条第(1)款规定，在收到转让通知以前，债务人可以通过向让与人清偿而解除债务。

这是一个保护债务人的适当方法。但让与人和受让人之间已经以协议方式完成了权利的转移。因此，让与人保证，让与人应将在转让通知做出前从债务人收到的任何清偿，退还给受让人。

示例：

　　5. 卖方 A 将自己享有的请求买方 X 支付货款的权利转让给 B 银行。A 或 B 都没有向 X 发出转让通知。债务到期时，X 向 A 支付货款。如第9.1.10条注释所述，该清偿行为完全有效，B 的债务得到解除。但是，根据第9.1.15条(f)项，B 有权要求 A 退还支付。

7. 对债务人是否履行或偿付能力不承担担保义务

权利转让的当事人当然可以约定，让与人承担保证债务人目前或者将来具有偿付能力的义务，或者，更常见的是担保债务人将会履行债务。但如果当事人没有如此约定，则本条项下并没有这样的担保义务。

Illustration

> 6.   Company B is the assignee of company A's right to payment of a certain sum from customer X. When payment is due, B finds out that X has become insolvent. B has to bear the consequences. The solution would be the same if B discovered that X was already insolvent at the time of the assignment.

In case of breach of one of the assignor's undertakings, the remedies provided for in Chapter 7 become available. The assignee may for instance claim damages from the assignor or terminate the agreement if the conditions of Article 7.3.1 *et seq.* are fulfilled.

8. Effect of disclosure on undertaking

Some of the assignor's undertakings may be affected by disclosures made at the time of the transfer. The assignor may for instance advise the assignee of the existence of a claim by a third party, in which case the assignee may accept the transfer of the right at its own risk, with no undertaking on that matter on the part of the assignor.

示例:

> 6. A 公司对 X 客户享有请求支付一定金额的权利,B 公司是这一权利的受让人。债务到期时,B 发现 X 丧失了清偿能力,B 须承担这一后果。如果 B 发现 X 在转让时即已无清偿能力,结果相同。

如果让与人违背某项担保义务,便得以适用第七章规定的救济措施。比如受让人可向让与人请求损害赔偿,或者在第 7.3.1 条及其以下各条规定的条件成就时终止合同。

8. 披露对于担保义务的影响

让与人的某些担保义务,可能受转让时所作的披露的影响。比如,让与人可以告知受让人存在第三方权利主张,这种情况下,受让人接受权利就要自担风险,让与人对此事项不承担担保义务。

SECTION 2: TRANSFER OF OBLIGATIONS

ARTICLE 9.2.1
(Modes of transfer)

An obligation to pay money or render other performance may be transferred from one person (the "original obligor") to another person (the "new obligor") either

    (a) by an agreement between the original obligor and the new obligor subject to Article 9.2.3, or

    (b) by an agreement between the obligee and the new obligor, by which the new obligor assumes the obligation.

COMMENT

As is the case with the assignment of rights covered by Section 1 of this Chapter, also the transfer of obligations may serve useful economic purposes. For instance, if company A can claim payment from its customer B, but itself owes a similar amount to its supplier X, it may be practical to arrange for the customer to become the supplier's obligor.

Such a transfer of an obligation may occur in two different ways.

1. Transfer by agreement between the original obligor and the new obligor

In practice, the more frequent of the two ways indicated in this Article to transfer an obligation is by agreement between the original obligor and the new obligor, with the obligee's consent as required by Article 9.2.3.

Illustration

    1.   Company A owes its supplier X EUR 50,000, and customer B owes the same sum to A. A and B agree that the latter will take over the former's obligation towards X. The obligation is transferred if X agrees to the transaction.

2. Transfer by agreement between the obligee and the new obligor

Another possibility is an agreement between the obligee and the new obligor, by which the new obligor accepts to take over the obligation.

第二节 债务的转移

第9.2.1条

(转移的模式)

支付金钱或者为其他履行的债务,可以通过以下方式之一由一人("原债务人")转移到另一人("新债务人"):

(a) 原债务人和新债务人之间达成协议,但要受到第9.2.3条的约束,或

(b) 债权人和新债务人之间达成的由新债务人承担债务的协议。

注释:

同本章第一节调整的权利转让一样,债务转移同样服务于一定的经济目的。例如,如果 A 公司有权请求 B 客户支付货款,他自己又欠供货人 X 等量的金钱,就可以安排客户清偿供货人。

这样的债务转移可通过两种不同的方式实现。

1. 通过原债务人和新债务人之间协议的转移

事实上,本条所指的两种债务转移方式中,较为常用的方式是通过原债务人和新债务人之间的协议转移,但需按照第9.2.3条的要求征得债权人的同意。

示例:

1. A 公司欠供货商 X 50,000 欧元,客户 B 欠 A 同样金额的价款。A 和 B 约定由后者承担前者对 X 承担的债务。如果 X 同意该交易,就发生了债务的转移。

2. 通过债权人和新债务人之间的协议转移

债务转移的另一种途径是,债权人和新债务人达成协议,新债务人据此同意承担债务。

Illustration

> 2.   The products of company X are sold by distributor A on a certain market. The contract between the parties is close to termination. Distributor B enters into negotiations with X, proposing to take over the distributorship. In order to gain X's acceptance, B promises that it will assume a debt of EUR 50,000 still owed by A to X, and X accepts. B has become X's obligor.

3.   Obligee's consent necessary

In both cases, the obligee must give its consent to the transfer. This is obvious when the transfer occurs by agreement between the obligee and the new obligor. If it occurs by an agreement between the original obligor and the new obligor, the requirement is stated in Article 9.2.3. Consent may be given in advance under Article 9.2.4.

Without the obligee's consent, the obligor may agree with another person that the latter will perform the obligation under Article 9.2.6.

4.   Transfer by agreement only

Only transfers by agreement are governed by this Section, as opposed to situations where the applicable law may provide for legal transfers (such as, under certain jurisdictions, the automatic transfer of obligations in the case of the merger of companies – see Article 9.2.2).

5.   Obligations in respect of payment of money or other performance

This Section is not restricted to the transfer of obligations in respect of payment of money. It covers also the transfer of obligations relating to other kinds of performance, such as the rendering of a service. Nor are transferable obligations limited to obligations of a contractual nature. Obligations deriving from tort law or based on a judgment, for instance, can be governed by this Section, subject to Article 1.4.

6.   What is meant by "transfer"

The "transfer" of an obligation means that it leaves the original obligor's assets to enter those of the new obligor.

However, in some cases although the new obligor becomes bound towards the obligee, the original obligor is not discharged (see Article 9.2.5).

示例：

> 2. 在某一市场，X 公司的产品售给分销商 A。双方之间的合同临近终止。分销商 B 与 X 谈判，希望获得该分销权。为取得 X 的同意，B 许诺偿还 A 欠 X 的 50,000 欧元，X 接受。B 成为 X 的债务人。

3. 需征得债权人同意

前述两种方式的债务转移，都需要债权人的同意。如果债务转移是通过债权人和新债务人之间的协议实现的，则同意是显而易见的。如果债务转移是通过原债务人和新债务人之间的协议实现的，第 9.2.3 条对于同意的要求作了规定。根据第 9.2.4 条，同意也可以是预先作出的。

在没有债权人同意的情况下，债务人和另一人可以根据第 9.2.6 条达成协议，约定由后者履行债务。

4. 只调整协议转移

本节只调整依协议发生的债务转移，而不涉及其他适用法规定的法定转移（比如，在某些法域，公司合并时债务自动转移，参见第 9.2.2 条）。

5. 支付金钱之债或者为其他履行的债务

本节不限于支付金钱之债的转移，还涉及其他债务的转移，比如提供服务。可转移的债务也并不限于合同性的债务。例如，在不违反第 1.4 条的前提下，由依侵权行为法产生的债务或基于判决产生的债务也可以受本节调整。

6. "转移" 的含义

债务的 "转移" 是指，该债务从原债务人的资产负债表转移到新债务人的资产负债表。

但在有些情况下，虽然新债务人开始向债权人承担债务，但原债务人的债务并没有解除（参见第 9.2.5 条）。

ARTICLE 9.2.2

(Exclusion)

This Section does not apply to transfers of obligations made under the special rules governing transfers of obligations in the course of transferring a business.

COMMENT

The Articles contained in this Section do not apply to transfers of obligations made in the course of transferring a business under any special rules governing such transfers, as may happen in the case of the merger of companies. The applicable law often provides for mechanisms that cause all rights and obligations to be transferred under certain conditions in their entirety by operation of law.

Article 9.2.2 does not prevent this Section from applying when certain obligations pertaining to the transferred business are transferred individually.

Illustrations

1. Company A is transferred to company B. If the otherwise applicable law provides that all obligations pertaining to the former company are automatically transferred to the latter, the Principles do not apply.

2. The facts are the same as in Illustration 1, but B has reasons to prefer not to become the obligor of company X, one of A's suppliers. A can transfer the obligations concerned to company C, with the consent of X. This particular transfer is subject to the Principles.

ARTICLE 9.2.3

(Requirement of obligee's consent to transfer)

The transfer of an obligation by an agreement between the original obligor and the new obligor requires the consent of the obligee.

第9.2.2条

（排除适用）

本节不适用于在一项商业转让过程中，依管辖债务转移的特殊规则所做的债务转移。

注释：

商业转让过程中的债务转移若有特殊规则调整，则依此等规则所做的债务转移不适用本节规定的规则，例如公司合并过程中所发生的转移。适用法往往规定，在满足一定条件时，所有权利义务按照规定的机制自动概括转移。

与被转移商业相关的某些债务单独转移时，第9.2.2条并不妨碍本节的适用。

示例：

1. A公司被转移到B公司。如果其他适用法规定原公司相关的所有债务都自动转移给后者，则不适用《通则》。

2. 初步事实与示例1相同，但是B公司有理由不对A的一家供应商X公司承担债务。A可以在征得X同意的前提下将该相关债务转移给C公司。该笔特定转移受《通则》调整。

第9.2.3条

（须债权人同意转移）

原债务人和新债务人以协议方式转移债务，须经债权人同意。

COMMENT

1. Agreement between the original and the new obligor

As stated in Article 9.2.1(a), the transfer of an obligation may occur by an agreement between the original obligor and the person who will become the new obligor.

2. Obligee's consent required

This agreement, however, does not suffice to transfer the obligation. It is also necessary for the obligee to give its consent.

This is different from the corresponding rule on the assignment of rights, where the operation is in principle effective without the consent of the obligor (see Article 9.1.7). The assignment of a right does not affect the obligor's situation, except that the obligor will have to deliver performance to another person. On the contrary, a change of obligor may considerably affect the obligee's position, as the new obligor may be less reliable than the original one. The change may therefore not be imposed on the obligee, who must consent to it.

Illustration

> Company A owes USD 150,000 to company X, located in Asia, for services rendered. Due to a reorganisation of the group, A's activities in Asia are taken over by affiliate company B. A and B agree that B will take over A's debt towards X. The obligation is transferred only if X gives its consent.

3. Original obligor not necessarily discharged

With the obligee's consent, the new obligor becomes bound by the obligation. It does not necessarily follow that the original obligor is discharged (see Article 9.2.5).

4. Lack of consent by the obligee

If the obligee refuses to consent to the transfer, or if its consent is not solicited, an arrangement for a third party performance is possible under Article 9.2.6.

注释：

1. 原债务人和新债务人之间的协议

如第9.2.1条(a)项所述，债务转移可以依原债务人和新债务人之间的转移协议而发生。

2. 必须经债权人同意

债务转移仅凭前述协议尚不能发生，还需要债权人的同意。

这与权利转让的相应规则不同，权利转让原则上无需债务人的同意（参见第9.1.7条）。除债务人须向另一人履行债务外，权利转让不会影响债务人的地位。相反，债务人的变化可能会严重影响债权人的地位，因为新债务人可能没有原债务人那么值得信赖。因此，不能将这种变化强加到债权人身上，债务转移必须经过他的同意。

示例：

> A公司应向位于亚洲的X公司支付150,000美元的服务费。根据集团的重组计划，A在亚洲的活动交由其关联公司B接管。A和B约定B将承担A欠X的债务，该债务只有在X同意时才发生转移。

3. 原债务人的债务不一定解除

经债权人同意，新债务人承担该债务。但这并不必然解除原债务人的债务（参见第9.2.5条）。

4. 缺少债权人的同意

如果债权人拒绝同意债务的转移，或者根本就没有征求他的同意，可以根据第9.2.6条安排第三方履行。

ARTICLE 9.2.4
(Advance consent of obligee)

(1) The obligee may give its consent in advance.

(2) If the obligee has given its consent in advance, the transfer of the obligation becomes effective when a notice of the transfer is given to the obligee or when the obligee acknowledges it.

COMMENT

1. Advance consent by the obligee

Paragraph (1) of this Article provides that the obligee's consent, required under Article 9.2.3, may be given in advance.

Illustration

> 1. Licensor X enters into a transfer of technology agreement with licensee A. For a period of ten years, A will have to pay royalties to X. When the contract is concluded, A envisages that at some time in the future it will prefer the royalties to be paid by its affiliate, company B. X may agree in advance in the contract to the obligation to pay the royalties being transferred by A to B.

2. When the transfer is effective as to the obligee

According to paragraph (2), if the obligee has given its consent in advance, the transfer of the obligation becomes effective when it is notified to the obligee or when the obligee acknowledges it. This means that it is sufficient for either the original or the new obligor to notify the obligee of the transfer when it occurs. Notification is not needed if it appears that the obligee has acknowledged the transfer, to which it had given its consent in advance. "Acknowledgement" means giving an overt sign of having become aware of the transfer.

Illustrations

> 2. The facts are the same as in Illustration 1, but there comes a time when A actually agrees with B that from then on the latter will take over the obligation to pay the royalties. This decision becomes effective when notice is given to X.

第9.2.4条

（债权人的预先同意）

（1）债权人可以预先同意。

（2）债权人预先同意的，债务转移自转移通知到达债权人时，或者债权人认可该债务转移时，产生效力。

注释：

1. 债权人的预先同意

本条第(1)款规定，第9.2.3条规定的债权人同意可以预先作出。

示例：

> 1. 许可人 X 与被许可人 A 之间达成一项技术转让合同，据此，A 须在10年内向 X 支付使用费。合同订立时，A 遇见到自己可能在将来某时希望由其附属公司 B 支付使用费。X 可以在合同中预先同意 A 将支付使用费的债务转移给 B。

2. 转移针对债权人生效的时间

根据第(2)款，如果债权人作了预先同意，通知到达债权人时或债权人认可时，债务转移即产生效力。也就是说，在转移发生时，原债务人或新债务人之一向债权人作出通知就足够了。如果债权人就此转移作出了预先同意，并且情况表明债权人认可了该转移，就无需通知。"认可"是指公开表明自己已获悉该转移事项。

示例：

> 2. 事实和示例1相同，但 A 在某时确实与 B 约定此后由 B 承担支付使用费的债务，这一决定在 X 收到通知时生效。

3.   The facts are the same as in Illustration 1. No notice is given, but the first time B pays the yearly royalties, X writes to B to acknowledge receipt of the payment and to confirm that from then on it will expect B to pay the royalties. The transfer is effective with this acknowledgement.

ARTICLE **9.2.5**

(Discharge of original obligor)

(1) The obligee may discharge the original obligor.

(2) The obligee may also retain the original obligor as an obligor in case the new obligor does not perform properly.

(3) Otherwise the original obligor and the new obligor are jointly and severally liable.

COMMENT

1. Extent of original obligor's discharge

The obligee's consent, whether given under Article 9.2.1(b) or under Article 9.2.3, has the effect of binding the new obligor to the obligation. What still remains to be determined is whether the original obligor is discharged. It is primarily up to the obligee to choose among different options. Only in the case of Article 9.2.1(b) will the choice depend also on the original obligor.

2. Obligee's choice: full discharge

The obligee may first of all fully discharge the original obligor.

Illustration

1.   Supplier X accepts that its obligor company A transfer its obligation to pay the price to customer B. Fully confident that the new obligor is solvent and reliable, X discharges A. Should B fail to perform, the loss will be on X who will have no recourse against A.

3. 事实和示例 1 相同。在没有给予通知的情况下，B 第
一次支付年度使用费时，X 书面致意 B 表示收到支付且确认
此后将期待由 B 交纳使用费。转让自该确认时起生效。

第9.2.5条

（原债务人债务的解除）

（1） 债权人可以解除原债务人的债务。

（2） 债权人亦可保留原债务人在新债务人履
行不适当时，继续作为债务人，。

（3） 其余情况下，原债务人和新债务人承担
连带责任。

注释：

1. 原债务人得以解除债务的程度

债权人的同意，无论是依据第9.2.1 条（b）项还是依据第9.2.3 条
给出的，其效力都是使新债务人承担清偿债务的义务。剩下的问题是，
原债务人是否解除了债务。这主要取决于债权人选择。只有在第9.2.1
条（b）项的情况下，这种选择同时也依赖于原债务人。

2. 债权人的选择之一：完全解除

首先，债权人可以完全解除原债务人的债务。

示例：

1. 供应商 X 接受债务人 A 公司将其支付货款的债务转移
给 B 客户。X 充分相信新债务人的偿付能力和可靠性，因此
解除了 A 的债务。如果 B 不能履行，X 将承担该损失，而不
能向 A 追索。

3. Obligee's choice: original obligor retained as a subsidiary obligor

Another possibility is for the obligee to accept the transfer of the obligation from the original obligor to the new obligor on condition that it retain a claim against the original obligor.

There are two options.

The first option is that the original obligor is retained as an obligor in the event that the new obligor does not perform properly. In this case the obligee must claim performance first from the new obligor, but if the new obligor does not perform properly the obligee may call upon the original obligor.

Illustration

> 2. Supplier X accepts that its obligor company A transfer its obligation to pay the price to customer B, but this time stipulates that A will remain bound if B does not perform properly. X no longer has a direct claim against A, and must first request performance from B. However, should B fail to perform, X will have a claim against A.

4. Obligee's choice: original obligor and new obligor jointly and severally liable

The second option, the one most favourable to the obligee, is to consider the original obligor and the new obligor jointly and severally liable. This means that when performance is due, the obligee can exercise its claim against either the original or the new obligor (see Articles 11.1.3 *et seq.*). Should the obligee obtain performance from the original obligor, the latter would then have a claim against the new obligor (see Articles 11.1.10 *et seq.*).

Illustration

> 3. Supplier X accepts that its obligor company A transfer its obligation to pay the price to customer B, but stipulates that A and B will remain jointly and severally liable. In this case X may request performance from either A or B. Should B perform properly, both A and B would be fully discharged. Should A have to render performance to X, it would then have right of recourse against B.

3. 债权人的选择之二：保留原债务人作为次级债务人

另一种可能是，对原债务人保留请求权的前提下，债权人接受原债务人将债务转移给新债务人。

这时，债权人有两种选择。

第一种选择是，如果新债务人没有适当履行债务，原债务人的债务不能解除。如果作出了这种选择，债权人必须首先请求新债务人履行债务，但如果新债务人没有适当履行，债权人可以要求原债务人履行。

示例：

> 2. 供应商X公司同意其债务人A公司将付款的债务转让给客户B，但规定如果B没有适当履行A仍须承担义务。X对A不再享有直接的请求权，而必须首先要求B履行。但是，如果B没有履行，债权人可以对A提出请求。

4. 债权人的选择之三：原债务人和新债务人承担连带责任

第二种选择，也是对债权人最为有利的选择，是由原债务人与新债务人承担连带责任。这意味着，履行期限届满时债权人可以直接请求原债务人或新债务人履行（参见第11.1.3条及以下有关条款）。如果债权人获得了原债务人的履行，后者取得对新债务人的请求权（参见第11.1.10条及以下有关条款）。

示例：

> 3. 供应商X公司同意其债务人A公司将付款的债务转让给客户B，但规定A和B承担连带责任。这种情况下，X既可以请求A也可以请求B履行。如果B适当地履行了债务，A和B都完全解除了债务。如果A向X履行了债务，则A有权向B追索。

5. Default rule

The language of this Article makes it clear that the last-mentioned option is the default rule. In other words, if the obligee has neither indicated that it intends to discharge the original obligor, nor indicated that it intends to keep the original obligor as a subsidiary obligor, the original obligor and the new obligor are jointly and severally liable.

Illustration

4.   Supplier X accepts that its obligor company A transfer its obligation to pay the price to customer B, but says nothing about the liability of A. Also in this case X may request performance from either A or B. Should B perform properly, both the original and the new obligor would be fully discharged. Should A have to render performance to X, it would then have right of recourse against B.

6. Original obligor refusing to be discharged

When the obligation is assumed by means of an agreement between the obligee and the new obligor, as provided in Article 9.2.1(b), and the agreement provides that the original obligor is discharged, the agreement amounts to a contract in favour of a third party. Under Article 5.2.6 such a benefit cannot be imposed on the beneficiary, who may have reasons not to accept it. The original obligor may thus refuse to be discharged by the agreement between the obligee and the new obligor.

If such a refusal occurs, the new obligor is bound to the obligee, but the original obligor and the new obligor are jointly and severally liable, in accordance with the default rule of Article 9.2.5(3).

Illustration

5.   The facts are the same as in Illustration 1, except that the obligation is assumed by an agreement between X and B, and that X discharges A. If A is no longer interested in a business relationship with B, it may accept to be discharged. On the other hand, if A wants to keep the possibilities it has of benefiting from a renewal of its contract with X, it might wish to keep the relationship and may therefore refuse to be discharged.

5. 默认规则

从本条的文字上可以看出，上述最后一种选择是默认规则。换言之，如果债权人既没有表明他希望解除原债务人的债务，也没有表示希望保留原债务人作为次级债务人，则原债务人和新债务人承担连带责任。

示例：

> 4. 供应商 X 公司同意其债务人 A 公司将付款的债务转让给客户 B，但没有就 A 的债务作任何规定。这种情形下，X 也既可以请求 A 也可以请求 B 履行。如果 B 适当地履行了债务，A 和 B 都完全解除了债务。如果 A 被迫向 X 履行了债务，则 A 有权向 B 追索。

6. 原债务人拒绝解除债务

如果债权人和新债务人依第 9.2.1 条(b)项以协议方式约定由新债务人承担债务，并且规定解除原债务人的债务，该协议构成一个第三方受益合同。按照第 5.2.6 条的规定，这种受益不能强加给受益人，后者有理由不接受这种受益。因此原债务人可以拒绝接受依债权人和新债务人之间的协议解除债务。

如果出现这种拒绝解除的情况，新债务人对债权人承担债务，但是原债务人和新债务人根据第 9.2.5 条(3)款默认规则承担连带责任。

示例：

> 5. 事实和示例 1 相同，区别在于 B 依据他和 X 之间的协议承担债务，并且 X 解除了 A 的债务。如果 A 对于与 B 的商业关系失去了兴趣，他将接受解除自己的债务。但是，如果 A 希望能够通过与 X 续订合同继续受益，可能会保持这种关系并拒绝解除债务。

ARTICLE **9.2.6**
(Third party performance)

(1) Without the obligee's consent, the obligor may contract with another person that this person will perform the obligation in place of the obligor, unless the obligation in the circumstances has an essentially personal character.

(2) The obligee retains its claim against the obligor.

COMMENT

1. Agreement on performance by another party

Obligations can be transferred either by an agreement between the original obligor and the new obligor, with the obligee's consent (see Article 9.2.1(a)), or by an agreement between the obligee and the new obligor (see Article 9.2.1(b)).

There may be situations in which the consent of the obligee is lacking, either because it has not been solicited, or because it has been refused. In such cases the obligor may agree with another person that this person will perform the obligation in its place. When performance becomes due, the other person will render it to the obligee.

While an obligee may refuse to accept a new obligor before performance is due, in principle it may not refuse to accept the performance itself when it is offered by another party.

Illustration

> 1. Companies A and B have entered into a co-operation agreement for their activities on a certain market. At a certain point they decide to redistribute some of their tasks. Thus, B will take over all operations concerning telecommunications which were previously A's responsibility. On the following 30 October A would have been bound to pay company X, a local operator, a sum of USD 100,000. The two partners agree that B will pay that amount when it is due. On 30 October X may not refuse such a payment made by B.

2. Obligation of an essentially personal character

Third party performances may not be refused by the obligee in all the cases in which they would be equally satisfactory as performances rendered by the obligor. The situation is different when the performance due is of an essentially personal character, linked to the

第 9.2.6 条

（第三方履行）

（1）在没有债权人同意的情况下，债务人可以与另一个人约定由该人替代该债务人履行债务，但债务本质上具有人身性质的除外。

（2）债权人保留对债务人的请求权。

注释：

1. 由另一人替代履行的协议

债务可以经债权人的同意、依原债务人与新债务人之间的协议而转移（参见第 9.2.1 条（a）项），或者依债权人与新债务人之间的协议而转移（参见第 9.2.1 条（b）项）。

有时会出现债权人同意缺失的情形，如没有征求债权人的同意或者债权人拒不同意。这种情况下，债务人可以与另一人约定由后者替代其履行债务。债务到期时，该人向债权人履行债务。

虽然债权人可以在债务到期前拒绝接受新的债务人，但原则上不能拒绝接受另一个人履行债务。

示例：

1. A 公司和 B 公司签订了一份在某市场进行业务合作的协议。此后，他们决定重新分配某些业务。据此，B 接手 A 原来负责的所有电信相关的工作。A 原本须在临近的 10 月 30 日向一个本地运营者 X 公司支付 100,000 美元。两位合作者约定该债务到期时由 B 支付。10 月 30 日，X 不能拒绝 B 支付的款项。

2. 本质上具有人身性质的债务

如果第三方履行能够达到与债务人亲自履行同样的效果，债权人就不能拒绝第三方履行。但如果债务本质上具有人身性质，即与债务

obligor's specific qualifications. The obligee may then insist on receiving performance by the obligor itself.

Illustration

> 2.   In Illustration 1, B also takes over operations for the maintenance of some sophisticated technological equipment developed by A and sold to company Y. The partners agree that the next yearly maintenance will be carried out by B. When B's technicians arrive at Y's premises, Y may refuse their intervention, invoking the fact that due to the highly technical nature of the verifications involved, they are entitled to receive performance from the specialised staff of A.

ARTICLE 9.2.7
(Defences and rights of set-off)

(1) The new obligor may assert against the obligee all defences which the original obligor could assert against the obligee.

(2) The new obligor may not exercise against the obligee any right of set-off available to the original obligor against the obligee.

COMMENT

1. Assertion of defences

The obligation transferred to the new obligor is the very same obligation that used to bind the original obligor (and, in some cases, still binds it - see Article 9.2.5).

Whenever the original obligor would have been able to withhold or refuse payment to the obligee on the basis of a defence, such as the defective performance of the obligee's own obligations, the new obligor may rely on the same defence against the obligee.

Illustration

> 1.   Company A owes company X EUR 200,000, due to be paid at the end of the year, as payment for facilities management services. With X's consent A transfers this obligation to company B. X renders A extremely defective services which would have given A a valid defence for refusing payment. When payment is due, B may assert the same defence against X.

人的具体资格紧密相连，情况就有所不同。债权人可以坚持只接受债务人本人履行债务。

示例：

2. 在示例1，B同时还接手了维护Y公司某些精密技术设备的债务，这些设备是A开发的并卖给了Y公司。两位合作者约定下一年度的维护工作由B承担。B的技术员到达Y的厂房时，Y可以拒绝他们参与，因为相关认证工作技术性很强，他们有权只接受A公司专业人员的履行。

第9.2.7条

（抗辩权和抵销权）

（1）新债务人可援用原债务人对抗债权人的所有抗辩，对抗债权人。
（2）新债务人不可向债权人主张原债务人可以向债权人主张的抵销权。

注释：

1. 主张抗辩

转移给新债务人的债务就是原债务人原来所承担的债务（并且，某些情形下，原债务人仍然承担该债务。参见第9.2.5条）。

原债务人可以根据某种抗辩暂停或者拒绝向债权人清偿，例如，债权人自己的履行就有瑕疵。新债务人可以向债权人主张同样的抗辩。

示例：

1. A公司应向X公司支付设备管理服务费200,000欧元，该债务于年底到期。经X同意，A将该债务转移给B公司。X向A提供的服务存在严重缺陷，A因此获得了拒绝支付的正当抗辩。支付债务到期时，B可以向X主张同样的抗辩。

2. Defences of a procedural nature

The same solution applies to defences of a procedural nature.

Illustration

> 2.   The facts are the same as in Illustration 1, except that X sues B before a court at its place of business. B can successfully invoke the arbitration clause included in the contract between A and X.

3. Set-off

The right of set-off relating to an obligation owed by the obligee to the original obligor may however not be exercised by the new obligor. The reciprocity requirement is not fulfilled between the obligee and the new obligor. The original obligor may still exercise its right of set-off if it has not been discharged.

ARTICLE 9.2.8
(Rights related to the obligation transferred)

(1) The obligee may assert against the new obligor all its rights to payment or other performance under the contract in respect of the obligation transferred.

(2) If the original obligor is discharged under Article 9.2.5(1), a security granted by any person other than the new obligor for the performance of the obligation is discharged, unless that other person agrees that it should continue to be available to the obligee.

(3) Discharge of the original obligor also extends to any security of the original obligor given to the obligee for the performance of the obligation, unless the security is over an asset which is transferred as part of a transaction between the original obligor and the new obligor.

2. 程序性的抗辩

同样的原则适用于程序性抗辩。

示例：

    2. 事实和示例1相同，区别在于 X 在其营业地法院对 B 提起诉讼。B 能够成功援引 A 与 X 之间的合同中包含的仲裁条款。

3. 抵销

但是，因债权人对原债务人承担的债务而产生的抵销权，新债务人不能行使。债权人和新债务人之间没有满足相互性要求。如果原债务人的债务没有解除，则原债务人仍然可以行使其抵销权。

第9.2.8条

（与被转移债务相关的权利）

（1） 债权人可以在被转移债务的范围内，对新债务人主张其合同项下享有的全部请求金钱支付或者其他履行的权利。

（2） 原债务人根据第**9.2.5**条第**（1）**款解除债务的，除新债务人以外的任何其他人对于债务履行提供的担保，随之解除，但是该其他人同意该担保对债权人继续有效的除外。

（3） 原债务人之债务的解除，还包括原债务人向债权人提供的保证债务履行的任何担保的解除，但是设立担保的资产已作为原债务人和新债务人之间交易的一部分而转移的除外。

COMMENT

1. Scope of the transfer

The rules laid down in this Article are inspired by the same principle as Article 9.2.7. The obligation is transferred to the new obligor as it is, not only with the defences the original obligor was able to assert, but also with all the rights to payment or to other performances under the contract that the obligee had in respect of the obligation transferred.

The following illustrations provide examples of such rights.

Illustrations

> 1.   Company A must reimburse bank X for a loan of EUR 1,000,000 bearing an interest rate of 3%. A transfers its obligation to reimburse the principal to company B. The transfer also includes the obligation to pay the 3% interest.
>
> 2.   The facts are the same as in Illustration 1, except that the loan contract entitles X to claim premature reimbursement if A fails to pay the interest due. X can assert also this right against B.

2. Contractual deviations

Party autonomy permits deviations from the rules laid down in this Article, such as a separate transfer of the obligation to pay interest.

3. Securities in assignment of rights and transfer of obligations compared

In the case of the assignment of a right, all rights securing performance are automatically transferred to the assignee (see Article 9.1.14(b)). This solution is justified by the fact that the assignment of a right does not alter the obligor's situation, i.e. securities can continue to serve their purposes in unchanged circumstances.

The transfer of an obligation to a new obligor on the contrary modifies the context in which the security has been granted. If the original obligor is discharged, and if the security were to be transferred with the obligation, the risk of breach or insolvency to be covered would be that of another person, thus completely altering the object of the security.

注释：

1. 转移的范围

本条的理论基础与第 9.2.7 条相同，采用同一原则。债务按照转移时的现时状况发生转移，不但包括原债务人可主张的各种抗辩，还包括合同项下与被转移的债务相关的金钱支付或者履行其他义务的所有权利。

以下是这些权利的例证。

示例：

1. A 公司须偿还 X 银行 100 万欧元贷款本金，该笔贷款的利率是 3% 。A 将偿还该笔本金的债务转移给 B 公司。这一转移也使支付 3% 利息的债务发生了转移。

2. 事实和示例 1 相同，区别在于贷款合同规定如果 A 没有偿还到期利息，X 可以请求 A 提前偿还。X 也可以向 B 主张该权利。

2. 约定偏离

当事人自治原则允许当事人修改本条规定的规则，比如支付利息之债的单独转让。

3. 权利转让和债务转移制度下的担保问题之比较

对于权利转让，用以担保债务履行的所有各项权利自动转移给受让人（参见第 9.1.14 条(b)项）。这一规定的合理之处在于，权利转让不会改变债务人的地位，因而担保可以在未变的情势下继续有效。

而债务一旦转移到一个新债务人，要求担保的情势则发生了改变。如果原债务人解除了债务，而担保随着债务的转移而发生转移，担保所要保证的违约或丧失清偿能力的风险也将变成另一人的风险，因此完全改变了担保的对象。

4. Suretyship

If the original obligor's obligation was covered by a suretyship granted by another person, this suretyship can survive if the original obligor remains bound. If, on the other hand, the original obligor is discharged, the suretyship cannot be transferred to cover the new obligor, unless the person who granted the suretyship agrees that it should continue to be available to the obligee.

Illustration

> 3.   Company A owes USD 1,000,000 to company X. Bank S has agreed to guarantee due performance of this obligation. With X's agreement, A transfers the obligation to company B, and X accepts to discharge A. S does not guarantee B's obligation, unless it agrees to continue to provide the security.

A special case occurs when the suretyship was granted by the person who was itself to become the new obligor. In such a case, the security necessarily disappears, since a person cannot provide a security for its own obligation.

5. Securities over assets

The original obligor may have given one of its assets as security. In this case, if the obligation is transferred and the original obligor is discharged, the security ceases to cover the obligation now binding the new obligor.

Illustration

> 4.   Bank X has granted a loan of EUR 100,000 to company A, secured by a deposit of shares by the obligor. With X's agreement, A transfers the obligation to pay back the loan to company B, and X accepts to discharge A. The shares cease to serve as security.

The solution is different if the asset given as security is transferred as part of a transaction between the original and the new obligor.

Illustration

> 5.   The facts are the same as in Illustration 4, but the transfer of the obligation between A and B occurs as part of a broader operation in which ownership of the shares is also transferred to B. In such a situation, the shares will continue to serve as security for B's obligation to reimburse the loan.

4. 保证关系

如果为原债务人的债务提供担保的是新债务人之外的其他人，并且原债务人没有被解除债务，则该担保可以继续有效。相反，如果原债务人解除了债务，这种保证不能转而用以担保新债务人，除非提供担保的人同意该担保对债权人继续有效。

示例：

> 3. A 公司欠 X 公司 100 万美元，S 银行保证该债务能够按期履行。经 X 同意，A 将该债务转移给 B 公司，并且 X 同意解除 A 的债务。除非 S 同意继续提供该项保证，S 不再为 B 的债务提供担保。

可能也有一种特殊情况出现，即保证人与新债务人归于一人。这种情况下，担保必然失效，因为一人不能为自己的债务提供担保。

5. 财产担保

原债务人可能以自己的某项资产作为担保物。这种情况下，如果债务发生转移且原债务人解除了债务，该资产对于转而约束新债务人的该债务不再提供担保。

示例：

> 4. X 银行向 A 公司提供 10 万欧元的贷款，以该债务人在该银行存入的股票作为担保物。经 X 同意，A 将偿还贷款的债务转移给 B 公司，并且 X 解除了 A 的债务。相关股票不再是担保物。

如果担保财产的转移只是原债务人和新债务人之间一项交易的一部分，则适用不同的规定。

示例：

> 5. 事实和示例 4 相同，但是 A、B 之间的债务转移是一笔大型交易的一部分，相关股票的所有权据此交易也转移给了 B。这种情形下，相关股票继续是保证 B 偿还贷款的担保物。

SECTION 3: ASSIGNMENT OF CONTRACTS

ARTICLE 9.3.1
(Definitions)

"Assignment of a contract" means the transfer by agreement from one person (the "assignor") to another person (the "assignee") of the assignor's rights and obligations arising out of a contract with another person (the "other party").

COMMENT

Rights and obligations can be transferred separately, under the respective rules of Sections 1 and 2 of this Chapter. In some cases, however, a contract is assigned as a whole. More precisely, a person transfers to another person all the rights and obligations deriving from its being a party to a contract. A contractor, for instance, may wish to let another contractor replace it as one of the parties in a construction contract. The Articles of this Section cover the assignment of contracts as defined in this Article.

Only transfers by agreement are concerned, as opposed to various situations where the applicable law may provide for legal transfers (such as, under certain jurisdictions, the automatic transfer of contracts in the case of the merger of companies - see Article 9.3.2).

ARTICLE 9.3.2
(Exclusion)

This Section does not apply to the assignment of contracts made under the special rules governing transfers of contracts in the course of transferring a business.

COMMENT

The assignment of contracts may be subject to special rules of the applicable law when it is made in the course of the transfer of a

第三节 合同的转让

第9.3.1条

(定义)

"合同的转让"是指一人("让与人")将其在与另一人("另一方当事人")订立的合同项下的权利与义务,以协议方式转移给另一人("受让人")。

注释:

权利和债务可以分别根据本章第一、二节规定的规则单独转移。但是,某些情况下,一项合同作为一个整体被概括转让。准确地说,一人将其作为合同当事人而享有的所有权利和承担的所有债务都转让给另一人。例如,一个承包商可能希望另一个承包商取代自己成为某一建筑合同的一方当事人。本节的规则调整本条所定义的合同转让。

本条仅适用于依协议发生的合同转让,而不涉及适用法已经有所规定的各种法定转移(如,在一些法域,公司合并过程中发生的合同自动转移。参见第9.3.2条)。

第9.3.2条

(排除适用)

本节不适用于由特殊规则调整的商业转让过程中的合同转让。

注释:

商业转让过程中发生的合同转让,可能受适用法的特殊规则调整。

business. Such special rules often provide for mechanisms that cause all contracts of the business to be transferred, under certain conditions, by operation of law.

This Article does not prevent the present Section from applying when certain contracts pertaining to the transferred business are assigned individually.

Illustrations

1.   Company A is transferred to company B. If the otherwise applicable law provides that all contracts to which the former company was a party are automatically transferred to the latter, the Principles do not apply.

2.   The facts are the same as in Illustration 1, but B is not interested in taking over a particular contract with company X, and prefers that contract to be assigned to company C. This particular transfer is subject to the Principles.

ARTICLE 9.3.3

(Requirement of consent of the other party)

The assignment of a contract requires the consent of the other party.

COMMENT

1. Agreement between assignor and assignee

The first requirement for the assignment of a contract is that the assignor and the assignee agree on the operation.

2. Other party's consent required

This agreement does not however suffice to transfer the contract. It is also necessary for the other party to give its consent.

If it were only for the assignment of the rights involved, such a consent would in principle not be needed (see Article 9.1.7). However, the assignment of a contract also involves a transfer of obligations, which cannot be effective without the obligee's consent (see Article 9.2.3). The assignment of a contract can thus only occur with the other party's consent.

这些特殊规则往往规定，在满足一定条件时，该业务涉及的所有合同按照规定的机制自动概括转移。

与被转移商业相关的某些合同单独转让时，本条并不妨碍本节的适用。

示例：

1. A 公司被转移到 B 公司。如果其他适用法规定原公司订立的所有合同都自动转移给后者，则不适用《通则》。

2. 事实和示例 1 相同，但是 B 无意接手 A 与 X 公司之间的一项合同，并希望将该合同转让给 C 公司。该笔特定转让受《通则》调整。

第9.3.3条

（须另一方当事人同意）

一项合同的转让须经另一方当事人的同意。

注释：

1. 让与人和受让人之间的协议

合同转让需要满足的第一个要件是，让与人和受让人就该转让达成协议。

2. 必须经另一方当事人同意

合同转让仅凭前述协议尚不能发生，还需要合同另一方的同意。

如果只涉及权利的转让，原则上不需要上述同意（参见第9.1.7条）。但是，合同转让还涉及债务的转移，不经债权人同意的债务转移不能产生效力（参见第9.2.3条）。因此，合同转让只有在另一方同意时才能有效。

Illustration

> Office space is let by owner X to company A. The contract expires only six years from the date of the contract. Due to the development of its business, A wants to move to larger premises. Company B would be interested in taking over the lease. The contract can be assigned by an agreement between A and B, but the operation also requires X's consent.

3. Assignor not necessarily discharged of its obligations

With the other party's consent, the assignee becomes bound by the assignor's obligations under the assigned contract. It does not necessarily follow that the assignor is discharged (see Article 9.3.5).

ARTICLE 9.3.4
(Advance consent of the other party)

(1) The other party may give its consent in advance.

(2) If the other party has given its consent in advance, the assignment of the contract becomes effective when a notice of the assignment is given to the other party or when the other party acknowledges it.

COMMENT

1. Advance consent by the other party

Paragraph (1) of this Article provides that the other party's consent, required under Article 9.3.3, may be given in advance.

This rule, concerning the assignment of contracts, corresponds to the rule in Article 9.2.4 according to which the obligee, who must consent to the transfer of the obligation may give its consent in advance. Similarly, the other party, who must consent to the assignment of the contract, may also give its consent in advance.

Illustration

> 1. Company X enters into an agreement with agency A, providing that the latter will be responsible for advertising X's products in country M for the next five years. A, however, is

示例：

业主 X 将办公室出租给 A 公司，该租赁合同自成立之日起六年后到期。由于业务发展的需要，A 欲迁入一个更大的场所。B 公司乐于接手该租赁。该租赁合同可以通过 A 和 B 之间的协议实现转让，但是需经 X 同意。

3. 让与人的债务不一定解除

经另一方同意，受让人承担让与人根据被转让合同承担的债务。但这并不必然解除让与人的债务（参见第9.3.5条）。

第9.3.4条

（另一方当事人的预先同意）

（1）另一方当事人可预先同意。
（2）另一方当事人预先同意的，合同转让自转让通知到达该另一方当事人时，或者当该另一方当事人认可该合同转让时，产生效力。

注释：

1. 另一方的预先同意

本条第(1)款规定，第9.3.3条规定的另一方当事人的同意可以预先作出。

本条规定的涉及合同转让的规则，与第9.2.4条相一致；后者规定，债权人对于债务转移的同意可以预先作出。同样，合同转让必须经另一方当事人同意，而他也可以预先同意合同转让。

示例：

1. X 公司和代理商 A 之间的合同规定，此后五年，A 负责 X 在 M 国的产品广告事宜。但是，当时 A 已经考虑到它要

already considering ceasing its activities in country M in the not too distant future, and obtains X's advance consent to the subsequent assignment of the contract to agency B, located in country M's capital. This advance consent is effective under Article 9.3.4.

2. When the assignment of the contract is effective vis-à-vis the other party

According to paragraph (2), if the other party has given its consent in advance, the assignment of the contract becomes effective when it is notified to the other party or when the other party acknowledges it. This means that it is sufficient for either the assignor or the assignee to notify the assignment when it occurs. Notification is not needed if it appears that the obligee has acknowledged the transfer, to which it had given its consent in advance. "Acknowledgement" means giving an overt sign of having become aware of the transfer.

Illustrations

2.   The facts are the same as in Illustration 1. When A actually assigns its contract to B, the assignment becomes effective vis-à-vis the other party when either A or B notifies it to X.

3.   The facts are the same as in Illustration 1. No notice is given, but B sends X a proposal for a new advertising campaign. X understands that the assignment has taken place and sends its comments on the proposal to B. The assignment of the contract is effective with this acknowledgement.

ARTICLE 9.3.5
(Discharge of the assignor)

(1) The other party may discharge the assignor.

(2) The other party may also retain the assignor as an obligor in case the assignee does not perform properly.

(3) Otherwise the assignor and the assignee are jointly and severally liable.

在不久的将来停止在 M 国的业务活动，并征得 X 预先同意接受将该合同转让给位于 M 国首都的代理商 B。根据第 9.3.4 条的规定，该预先同意有效。

2. 合同转让针对另一方生效的时间

根据第(2)款，如果另一方作了预先同意，转让通知到达另一方当事人时或另一方当事人认可时，合同转让即为生效。也就是说，在转让发生时，让与人或受让人之一向另一方当事人作出通知就足够了。如果债权人就此转让作出了预先同意，并且情况表明债权人认可了该转让，就无需通知。"认可"是指公开表明自己已获悉该转让事项。

示例：

2. 事实和示例 1 相同。A 确实将合同转让给 B 时，该合同的转让自 A 或 B 通知 X 时对 X 生效。

3. 事实和示例 1 相同。在没有给予通知的情况下，B 向 X 发出一个发起新的广告活动的建议。X 据此知道发生了合同转让，并向 B 发出了对于该提议的评价。合同转让由此认可而生效。

第9.3.5条

（让与人债务的解除）

（1）另一方当事人可解除让与人的债务。

（2）另一方当事人亦可保留让与人在受让人履行不适当时，继续作为债务人。

（3）其余情况下，让与人和受让人承担连带责任。

COMMENT

1. Extent of assignor's discharge

This Article, concerning the assignment of contracts, corresponds to Article 9.2.5. To the extent that the assignment of a contract causes obligations to be transferred from the assignor to the assignee, the other party, as an obligee, may decide the effect that the acceptance of the assignee as a new obligor will have on the assignor's obligations. This Article gives the other party several choices and provides for a default rule.

2. Other party's choice: full discharge

The other party may first of all fully discharge the assignor.

Illustration

> 1.   By contract with company X, company A has undertaken to dispose of the waste produced by an industrial process. At a certain point, X accepts that the contract is assigned by A to company B. Fully confident that B is solvent and reliable, X discharges A. Should B fail to perform properly, X will have no recourse against A.

3. Other party's choice: assignor retained as a subsidiary obligor

Another possibility is for the other party to accept the assignment of the contract on condition that it retain a claim against the assignor.

There are two options.

The first option is that the assignor is retained as an obligor in the event that the assignee does not perform properly. In this case the other party must necessarily claim performance first from the assignee, but if the assignee does not perform properly, the other party may call upon the assignor.

Illustration

> 2.   The facts are the same as in Illustration 1, except that X, when consenting to the assignment, has stipulated that A will remain bound if B does not perform properly. X no longer has a direct claim against A, and must first request performance from B. However, should B fail to perform, then X would have a claim against A.

注释：

1. 让与人债务解除的程度

本条规定的涉及合同转让的规则，与第9.2.5条相对应。单就合同转让导致债务从让与人转移到受让人而言，另一方当事人作为债权人可以决定受让人被接纳为新债务人将对让与人的债务产生何种影响。该条为另一方当事人提供了几个可供选择的选项，并规定一个默认规则。

2. 另一方当事人的选择之一：完全解除

首先，另一方可以完全解除受让人的债务。

示例：

> 1. A公司和X公司约定，前者承诺处理后者某一工业流程产生的废料。后来，X同意A将该合同转让给B。X充分相信B的偿付能力和可靠性，因此解除了A的债务。如果B没有适当履行，X将承担该损失，而不能向A追索。

3. 另一方当事人的选择之二：保留让与人作为次级债务人

另一种可能是，另一方当事人在保留针对让与人请求权的前提下接受合同转让。

这时，另一方当事人有两种选择。

第一种选择是，如果受让人没有适当履行债务，让与人不能解除债务。如果作出了这种选择，另一方当事人必须首先请求受让人履行债务，但如果受让人没有适当履行，另一方当事人可以要求让与人履行。

示例：

> 2. 事实和示例1相同，区别在于X在同意转让时规定，如果B没有适当履行A仍须承担义务。X对A不再享有直接的请求权，而必须首先要求B履行。但是，如果B没有履行，债权人可以对A提出请求。

4. Other party's choice: assignor retained as jointly and severally liable with the assignee

The second option, the one most favourable to the other party, is to consider the assignor and the assignee jointly and severally liable. This means that when performance is due, the other party can exercise its claim against either the assignor or the assignee (see Articles 11.1.3 *et seq.*). Should the other party obtain performance from the assignor, the latter would then have a claim against the assignee (see Articles 11.1.10 *et seq.*).

Illustration

> 3.   Company X accepts that company A assign the contract to company B, but stipulates that A and B will remain jointly and severally liable. In this case X may require performance from either A or B. Should B perform properly, both A and B would be fully discharged. Should A have to render performance to X, it would then have a right of recourse against B.

5. Default rule

The language of this Article makes it clear that the last-mentioned option is the default rule. In other words, if the other party has neither indicated that it intends to discharge the assignor, nor indicated that it intends to keep the assignor as a subsidiary obligor, the assignor and the assignee are jointly and severally liable.

Illustration

> 4.   Company X accepts that company A assign the contract to company B, but says nothing about the liability of A. Also in this case X may request performance from either A or B. Should B perform properly, both A and B would be fully discharged. Should A have to render performance to X, it would then have a right of recourse against B.

6. Differentiated options possible

A party to a contract is often subject to a whole set of obligations. When the contract is assigned, the other party may choose to exercise different options with regard to the different obligations. The other party may for instance accept to discharge the assignor for a certain obligation, but to retain it either as a subsidiary obligor or to consider it jointly and severally liable with the assignee with respect to other obligations.

4. 另一方当事人的选择之三：让与人和受让人承担连带债务

第二种选择，也是对另一方最为有利的选择，是由让与人和受让人承担连带责任。这意味着，履行期限届满时另一方可以直接请求让与人或受让人履行（参见第11.1.3条及以下有关条款）。如果另一方获得了让与人的履行，后者取得对受让人的请求权（参见第11.1.10条及以下有关条款）。

示例：

　　3. X公司同意A公司将合同转让给B公司，但是规定A和B承担连带责任。这种情况下，X既可以请求A也可以请求B履行。如果B适当地履行了债务，A和B都完全解除了债务。如果A向X履行了债务，则A有权向B追索。

5. 默认规则

本条用词清楚地表明，上述最后一种选择是默认规则。换言之，如果另一方当事人既没有表明他希望解除让与人的债务，也没有表示希望保留让与人作为次级债务人，则让与人和受让人承担连带责任。

示例：

　　4. X公司同意A公司将合同转让给B公司，但没有就A的责任作任何规定。这种情形下，X同样既可以请求A也可以请求B履行。如果B适当地履行了债务，A和B都完全解除了债务。如果A被迫向X履行了债务，则A有权向B追索。

6. 有可能区别对待不同的债务

合同的一方当事人往往同时承担一系列合同义务。一项合同被转让时，针对不同的合同义务，另一方可以做出不同的选择。例如，另一方就其中某项债务可能完全解除让与人的债务，但是就其余债务却可能保留让与人作为次级债务人或者视其与受让人承担连带责任。

Illustration

5.　Company A has entered into a know-how licence contract with company X. In return for the transferred technology, A has undertaken to pay royalties and to co-operate with X in the development of a new product. When X later on accepts that A assign the contract to company B, X discharges A from the obligation to participate in the joint research, for which it will deal with the assignee only, but retains A as a subsidiary or a jointly and severally liable with B for the payment of royalties.

ARTICLE 9.3.6
(Defences and rights of set-off)

(1)　To the extent that the assignment of a contract involves an assignment of rights, Article 9.1.13 applies accordingly.

(2)　To the extent that the assignment of a contract involves a transfer of obligations, Article 9.2.7 applies accordingly.

COMMENT

The assignment of a contract entails both an assignment of the original rights and a transfer of the original obligations from the assignor to the assignee. The transaction should not adversely affect the other party's situation as an obligor and it should put the assignee in the same situation as the assignor in its capacity as obligor.

As a consequence, the provisions concerning defences in Sections 1 and 2 of this Chapter apply accordingly. When the assignee exercises its rights, the other party may assert all the defences it could have asserted as obligor if the claim had been made by the assignor (see Article 9.1.13). When the other party exercises its rights, the assignee may assert all the defences that the assignor could have asserted as obligor if the claim had been made against it (see Article 9.2.7).

Illustrations

1.　Company X has out-sourced its risk management department to consultant A. With X's consent, the contract is assigned to consultant B. Due to A's incompetence, X was not properly insured for a loss it subsequently suffered. Pending indemnification, X may suspend paying B the agreed fees.

示例：

5.A公司和X公司签订一个专有技术许可合同。作为获得转让技术的对价，A承诺支付使用费并且就某项新产品的开发与A进行合作。X后来同意A将该合同转让给B公司，X解除A参加联合研发的义务，这一义务由受让人单独承担；但对于支付使用费的义务，A是一个次级债务人或者与B承担连带责任。

第9.3.6条

（抗辩权和抵销权）

（1）在合同转让涉及权利转让的范围内，适用第9.1.13条的规定。

（2）在合同转让涉及债务转移的范围内，适用第9.2.7条的规定。

注释：

合同转让的结果是，原有各项权利和原有各项债务同时由让与人转移到受让人。该项交易不得对作为债务人的另一方产生不利的影响，同时，作为债务人，受让人和让与人也应该处于同样的地位。

因此，本章第一、二节中有关抗辩的相应规定同样得以适用。当受让人行使其权利时，另一方可以主张所有下述抗辩，即，如果行使该权利的是让与人，另一方能够以债务人身份主张的抗辩（参见第9.1.13条）。当另一方行使其权利时，受让人可以主张所有下述抗辩，即，如果该权利主张是针对让与人的，让与人作为债务人可以主张的抗辩（参见第9.2.7条）。

示例：

1.X公司将其风险管理部门外包给顾问A。经X同意，该合同转让给了顾问B。由于A能力不济，X后来遭受的一笔损失被认定为不在承保范围之内。获得补偿之前，X可以暂时停止向B支付约定的服务费。

2. Airline A has a contract with catering company X. A transfers the operation of its flights to certain destinations to airline B. With X's consent, the catering contract is assigned by A to B. Litigation later arises, and X sues B before a court at its place of business. As a procedural defence B may successfully invoke that the assigned contract includes an arbitration clause.

ARTICLE 9.3.7

(Rights transferred with the contract)

(1) To the extent that the assignment of a contract involves an assignment of rights, Article 9.1.14 applies accordingly.

(2) To the extent that the assignment of a contract involves a transfer of obligations, Article 9.2.8 applies accordingly.

COMMENT

The assignment of a contract entails both an assignment of the original rights and a transfer of the original obligations from the assignor to the assignee. In parallel to what has been said about defences under Article 9.3.6, the operation should not adversely affect the other party's situation as an obligee and it should place the assignee in the same situation as the assignor in its capacity as obligee.

As a consequence, the provisions of Sections 1 and 2 of this Chapter concerning rights related to the claim assigned and to the obligation transferred will apply accordingly.

When the assignee acts against the other party, it may assert all the rights to payment or other performances under the contract assigned with respect to the rights assigned, as well as all rights securing such performance (see Article 9.1.14). When the other party exercises its rights, it may assert all its rights to payment or other performances under the contract with respect to the obligation transferred against the assignee (see Article 9.2.8(1)). Securities granted for the performance of the assignor's obligations are maintained or discharged in accordance with Article 9.2.8(2) and (3).

2. A 航空公司和 X 餐饮公司订立了一项合同。A 将其经营的飞往某地的航班业务转让给 B 航空公司。经 X 同意，A 将餐饮合同转让给 B。随后发生诉讼，X 在其营业地法院对 B 提起诉讼。作为程序性的抗辩理由，B 能够成功援引被转让的合同中包含的仲裁条款。

第9.3.7条

（随合同转让的权利）

　　（1）在合同转让涉及权利转让的范围内，适用第 9.1.4 条的规定。
　　（2）在合同转让涉及债务转移的范围内，适用第 9.2.8 条的规定。

注释：

　　合同转让的结果是，原有各项权利和原有各项债务同时由让与人转移到受让人。与第 9.3.6 条项下的抗辩制度一样，该项交易不得对作为债权人的另一方产生不利的影响，同时，作为债务人，受让人和让与人在能力上也应该处于同样的地位。

　　因此，本章第一、二节中涉及被转让权利和被转移债务相关权利的相应规定同样得以适用。

　　受让人可以针对另一方主张下述权利，也即，合同项下与被转让权利相关的让与人请求所有金钱支付或者其他履行的权利，以及担保被转让的权利得以履行的所有权利（参见第 9.1.14 条）。另一方行使其权利时，他可以针对受让人主张以下权利：合同项下与被转移之债务相关的请求金钱支付或者其他履行的所有各项权利（参见第 9.2.8 条第(1)款）。用以保证让与人履行债务的各项担保，依据第 9.2.8 条第(2)款和第(3)款的规定维持或者解除。

Illustrations

1. A service contract provides that late payment of the yearly fees due by customer X to supplier A will bear interest at the rate of 10%. With X's consent, A assigns the contract to supplier B. When X fails to pay the yearly fees on time, B is entitled to claim such interest (see Article 9.1.14(a)).

2. The facts are the same as in Illustration 1, but X has also provided A with a bank guarantee covering payment of the fees. B may call upon that guarantee should X fail to pay the fees (see Article 9.1.14(b)).

3. Company X has ordered the construction and installation of industrial equipment from company A. Performance levels have been agreed between the parties, and the contract provides for liquidated damages should actual performance be insufficient. With X's consent, A assigns the contract to company B. The assignee delivers equipment that does not meet the required performance levels. X may avail itself of the liquidated damages against B (see Article 9.2.8(1)).

4. The facts are the same as in Illustration 3, but A has provided X with a bank guarantee covering satisfactory performance. The bank guarantee will not apply to B's obligations resulting from the assignment, unless the bank accepts to continue to offer its guarantee in respect of the assignee's obligations (see Article 9.2.8(2)).

示例：

　　1. 一项服务合同规定，客户 X 应向供应商 A 支付的到期年费，支付迟延者须承担利率为 10% 的利息。经 X 同意，A 将该合同转让给了供应商 B。若 X 未能准时交付年费，B 有权主张利息（参见第9.1.14条(a)项）。

　　2. 事实和示例 1 相同，但 X 向 A 提供一个银行担保，保证年费得到支付。若 X 不交纳年费，B 可以请求该担保（参见第9.1.4条(b)项）。

　　3. X 公司向 A 公司定制了一批工业设备。双方约定了履行的标准，以及实际履行达不到标准时须支付的违约金。经 X 同意，A 将该合同转让给 B 公司。受让人交付的设备不符合约定的履行标准，X 有权请求 B 支付违约金（参见第9.2.8条第(1)款）。

　　4. 事实和示例 3 相同，但 A 向 X 提供一个银行担保，保证 A 将提供满意的履行。除非银行接受继续对受让人承担的债务提供保证，银行担保并不适用于 B 公司因转让而承担的债务（参见第9.2.8条第(2)款）。

CHAPTER 10

LIMITATION PERIODS

ARTICLE 10.1
(Scope of the Chapter)

(1) The exercise of rights governed by the Principles is barred by the expiration of a period of time, referred to as "limitation period", according to the rules of this Chapter.

(2) This Chapter does not govern the time within which one party is required under the Principles, as a condition for the acquisition or exercise of its right, to give notice to the other party or to perform any act other than the institution of legal proceedings.

COMMENT

1. Notion of limitation period

All legal systems recognise the influence of passage of time on rights. There are two basic systems. Under one system, the passage of time extinguishes rights and actions. Under the other system, the passage of time operates only as a defence against an action in court. Under the Principles a lapse of time does not extinguish rights, but operates only as a defence (see Article 10.9).

This Article refers in general to "rights governed by the Principles" to indicate that not only the right to require performance or the right to another remedy for non-performance can be barred, but also the exercise of rights which directly affect a contract, such as the right of termination or a right of price reduction contractually agreed upon.

第十章

时效期间

第 10.1 条

（本章范围）

（1）根据本章的规则，受通则调整的权利行使因一段时间期间，即"时效期间"的届满，而被禁止。

（2）本章并不调整依据本通则的规定，要求一方当事人作为取得或行使其权利的条件而须通知另一方当事人，或须履行司法程序之外的任何行为的时间期间。

注释：

1. 时效期间的概念

任何法律体系都承认时间流逝对于权利的影响。这些法律体系可分为两个基本类型。在一种体系下，时间流逝导致权利和诉讼权利的消灭。在另一种体系下，时间流逝只是对抗司法诉讼的一个抗辩理由。根据《通则》，时间流逝并不消灭权利，而只是一个抗辩理由（见第10.9 条）。

本条使用"受《通则》管辖的权利"这一总体概念。这表明受阻的权利，不仅包括要求履行的权利或者在不履行情况下获得救济的权利，而且包括能够直接影响合同的那些权利的行使，例如终止合同的权利或协议约定的要求减价的权利。

Illustrations

> 1.   A sells a tanker to B. Upon delivery the ship turns out not to be in conformity with the specifications contained in the contract, but it is only three and a half years later that B brings an action against A for the cure of the defects. A may raise the defence of B's claim being time-barred under Article 10.2.
>
> 2.   The facts are the same as in Illustration 1, except that the contract between A and B contains a clause allowing B a price reduction of up to 30% in case of missing equipment or spare parts. B's right to a price reduction is also barred.

2. Notice requirements and other prerequisites for enforcing rights

Under the Principles rights can be lost if the party entitled to acquire or exercise a right fails to give notice or to perform an act within a reasonable period of time, without undue delay, or within another fixed period of time (see Articles 2.1.1 – 2.1.22 (communications in the context of formation of contracts), Article 3.15 (avoidance of contract for defects of intent), Article 6.2.3 (request for re-negotiation), Article 7.2.2(e) (request for performance), Article 7.3.2(2) (termination of the contract for non-performance)). Although they serve a function similar to limitation periods, these special time-limits and their effects are not affected by the limitation periods provided for in this Chapter as they are designed to meet special needs. As they are generally much shorter than the limitation periods provided for in this Chapter, they take effect regardless of the latter. In the exceptional case that in the circumstances a "reasonable period of time" is longer than the applicable limitation period, the former will prevail.

Illustration

> 3.   The facts are the same as in Illustration 1, except that B sets A an additional period of time of 60 days for the cure of the defects. A fails to cure the defects, but it is only two months after the expiry of the additional period fixed that B sends A a notice of termination under Article 7.3.2. Although B's claim is not time-barred under Article 10.2, it has lost the right to terminate the contract because it has not given notice of termination within a reasonable time as required by Article 7.3.2(2).

示例：

　　1. A 出售一艘油轮给 B。实际交付的油轮不符合合同规定的标准，但是三年半以后 B 才对 A 提起诉讼，要求弥补这些瑕疵。A 可以根据第 10.2 条提出时效期间抗辩，提出 B 主张权利的时效期间已过。

　　2. 事实同示例 1，区别在于 A 与 B 的合同中包含一个减价条款，规定如有设备或零部件遗失，B 可以获得不超过 30% 的减价。B 要求减价的权利也受到阻碍。

2. 行使权利的通知要求和其他要件

根据《通则》，如果有权取得或行使某项权利的当事人未能在合理期间内、未能在无过分延迟的情况下、或者未能在其他固定的期间发出通知或履行某种行为，将导致这些权利的丧失。（见第 2.1.1 条至第 2.1.22 条（合同订立过程中的沟通），第 3.2.12 条（因意思瑕疵而宣告合同无效）[①]，第 6.2.3 条（重新谈判的请求），第 7.2.2 条(e)项（请求履行），第 7.3.2 条(2)款（因不履行而终止合同））尽管它们的功能与时效期间相似，但这些特殊时限及其效力并不受本章规定的时效期间的影响，因为它们旨在用于特殊目的。由于这些特殊时限通常比本章规定的时效期间要短，它们的效力通常不受后者的影响。例外情况下，"合理期间"比适用的时效期间要长，此时则适用前者。

示例：

　　3. 事实同示例 1，不同之处在于 B 为 A 弥补瑕疵提供了 60 天的额外时间。A 没有弥补这些瑕疵，该额外期限届满两个月后 B 才根据第 7.3.2 条向 A 发出终止合同的通知。尽管根据第 10.2 条 B 的请求权并未罹于时效，但它丧失了终止合同的权利，因为它未能在第 7.3.2 条(2)款要求的合理时间内发出终止通知。

---

　　① 英文原文为"3.15 条"，仍沿用了通则 2004 版条文编号，实际上 2010 版已将该条调整为"第 3.2.12 条"，故中文版采用了正确条文号。

3. Mandatory rules of domestic law

In cases in which the parties' reference to the Principles is considered to be only an agreement to incorporate them in the contract, mandatory rules on limitation periods of national, international or supranational origin relating to the length, suspension, and renewal of the limitation periods as well as to the right of the parties to modify them, prevail over the rules laid down in this Chapter (see Comment 2 on Article 1.4). Yet even in cases in which the Principles are applied as the law governing the contract, domestic mandatory rules on limitation periods prevail over the rules laid down in this chapter, provided that they claim application whatever the law governing the contract (see Comment 3 on Article 1.4).

Illustration

> 4.   Seller A in country X sells and delivers component parts to car manufacturer B in country Y. Some of the parts are defective and the same year of delivery the defects cause accidents for which B has to pay damages. Four years later, B asks A to be indemnified for its costs. A refuses to pay. The contract provides for arbitration in country Z with the UNIDROIT Principles as the applicable law. In an arbitration commenced by B, A raises the defence of the expiration of the three-year limitation period provided for in Article 10.2. B responds that under the law of country X the claim for damages for defective goods is time-barred only after 5 years, and that this rule claims to apply irrespective of the law governing the contract. The rule of the law of country X prevails.

ARTICLE 10.2
(Limitation periods)

(1) The general limitation period is three years beginning on the day after the day the obligee knows or ought to know the facts as a result of which the obligee's right can be exercised.

(2) In any event, the maximum limitation period is ten years beginning on the day after the day the right can be exercised.

3. 国内法的强制性规则

在当事人引用通则仅仅被认为是约定将通则并入合同之中的情况下，有关时效期间的长短、中止、重新起算，以及当事人对它们的修改权利，相关的国内法、国际法，或超国家法中的强制性时效期间规则，优于本章规则（参见第 1.4 条注释 2）。然而，即便如果通则被作为管辖合同的法律得以适用，有关时效期间的国内强制性规则亦优先于本章规定的规则，条件是该强制性规则规定无论管辖合同的法律是什么自己均应得以适用（参见第 1.4 条注释 3）。

示例：

4. 位于 X 国的卖方 A 向位于 Y 国的制造商 B 出售并交付零部件。某些部件存在瑕疵，在交付的同一年该瑕疵导致了意外事故的发生，B 必须对此支付损害赔偿。四年后，B 要求 A 补偿自己为此支付的成本。A 拒绝支付。双方合同规定争议应在 Z 国提交仲裁，并以《通则》为仲裁适用法。B 将此争议提交仲裁，A 根据第 10.2 条提出三年期间届满的抗辩理由。B 反驳道，根据 X 国的法律，对于货物瑕疵造成的损害赔偿五年后才会丧失时效，该法还规定不论合同的适用法如何规定都应该适用这一规定。X 国的法律规定应优先适用。

第 10.2 条

（时效期间）

（1）一般时效期间为三年，自债权人知道或应该知道导致其权利能够行使的事实之日的次日起计算。

（2）任何情况下最长时效期间为十年，自权利能够行使之日的次日起计算。

COMMENT

1. No common solution

Although periods of limitation of rights and claims are common to all legal systems, they differ in length. They range from six months or one year for claims for breach of warranties, to up to 15, 20 or even 30 years for other claims. At international level the *1974 United Nations Convention on the Limitation Period in the International Sale of Goods* (as amended in 1980) ("UN Limitation Convention") provides uniform rules but is restricted to the international sale of goods.

2. Relevant factors

The stated length of a limitation period does not always in itself determine the time after which the exercise of rights is barred. That time may be affected by the prerequisites for the starting of the period and by circumstances affecting its running (see Articles 10.4 to 10.9). It may also be affected by the agreement of the parties (see Article 10.3). Party autonomy with regard to limitation periods is of great practical importance, as periods that are either too long or too short may be tolerable if the parties may modify them freely according to their needs.

3. Balance between interests of obligee and obligor

The Principles strike a balance between the conflicting interests of the obligee and the obligor of a dormant claim. An obligee should have a reasonable chance to pursue its right, and should therefore not be prevented from pursuing its right by the lapse of time before the right becomes due and can be enforced. Furthermore, the obligee should know or at least have a chance to know its right and the identity of the obligor. On the other hand, the obligee should be able to close its files after some time regardless of the obligor's knowledge, and consequently a maximum period should be established. Contrary to the UN Limitation Convention which has only one absolute limitation period of four years which begins on the date of accrual of the claim (see Articles 8 and 9(1)), the Principles provide for a two-tier system.

4. Basic structure of the limitation regime

The two-tier system adopts the policy that the obligee should not be barred before it has had a real possibility to pursue its right as a result of having actual or constructive knowledge of the right. Paragraph (1) therefore provides for a rather short three-year limitation period starting the day after the obligee knows or ought to know the facts on which its

注释：

1. 不存在普遍的解决方式

尽管所有法律体系都有关于权利和请求权的时效期间的规定，但各个法律体系下期间的长短却不同，如违反保证的请求权为 6 个月或 1 年，而其他请求权可能长达 15 年、20 年甚至 30 年。在国际层面上，1974 年《联合国国际货物销售时效公约》（经 1980 年修订）（以下简称"《联合国时效公约》"）规定了一套统一规则，但是其适用范围限于国际货物销售。

2. 相关因素

权利行使受阻的时间并不完全取决于本条所述时效期间的长度。受阻时间可能受到期间起算要件和影响期间计算的情况的影响（见第 10.4 条至第 10.9 条），它也可能受到当事人之间的约定的影响（见第 10.3 条）。在时效期间问题上，当事人自治具有非常重要的现实意义，因为如果当事人可以根据实际需要自由修改期间，规则中规定过长或过短的时效期间都可以接受。

3. 债权人和债务人之间利益的平衡

对于潜伏性的请求权，《通则》在债权人和债务人相互冲突的利益之间维持了一种平衡。债权人应有行使自己权利的合理机会，因此在权利到期并因而能够行使之前，不应该以时间流逝为理由阻碍其行使权利。另外，在行使权利受阻以前，债权人应当知道或至少有机会知道其权利以及债务人的身份。另一方面，债务人应该能在一定时间之后了结此事，无论债权人是否知道或有机会知道，因此应该规定一个最长时效期间。① 与《联合国时效公约》仅规定一个单一的时效期间不同，《通则》规定了双层体系；前者规定，时效期间为四年，自请求权产生之日起计算（见第 8 条和第 9 条(1)款）。

4. 时效制度的基本框架

双层体系采纳这样一种政策，即债权人在真正有可能行使其权利之前不应该受到阻碍，这种可能性产生于债权人实际知道或推定知道

---

① 译者注：英文中"obligee"和"obligor"位置放颠倒了，中译文已更正。

right is based and this right can be exercised. Paragraph (2) provides for a ten-year maximum limitation period, commencing at the time when the right can be exercised, regardless of the obligee's actual or constructive knowledge.

5. Right can be exercised

The obligee has a real possibility to exercise its right only if it has become due and can be enforced. Paragraph (2) therefore provides that the maximum limitation period starts only at such date.

6. Knowledge of the facts as distinguished from knowledge of the law

The general three-year limitation period starts the day after the day "the obligee knows or ought to know the facts as a result of which the obligee's right can be exercised". "Facts" within the meaning of this provision are the facts on which the right is based, such as the formation of a contract, the delivery of goods, the undertaking of services, and non-performance. The facts indicating that a right or claim has fallen due must be known or at least knowable by the obligee before the general limitation period starts. The identity of the obligor may also be in doubt, e.g. in cases of agency, the transfer of debts or entire contracts, the winding-up of companies, or unclear third-party beneficiary contracts. In these cases, the obligee must know or have reason to know whom to sue before it can be blamed for not having pursued the right or claim. Actual or constructive knowledge of "facts", however, does not mean that the obligee must know the legal implications of the facts. If, despite full knowledge of the facts, the obligee is mistaken about its rights, the three-year limitation period may nevertheless start to run.

Illustrations

1. A designs and builds a bridge under a contract with county B. A's engineers make a mistake in calculating the strength of some steel girders. Four years later, the bridge collapses due to a combination of the weight of some heavy trucks and a storm. B's claims for damages are not barred, because the general limitation period started only at the time of the collapse, when B was in a position to discover A's breach.

2. The facts are the same as in Illustration 1, except that the bridge collapses eleven years after its construction. B's claims are barred under the maximum limitation period under Article 10.2(2). Parties to such a contract are well advised to adjust the maximum period while remaining within the limits of Article 10.3.

该项权利。因此第(1)款规定了一个较短的时效期间,即三年,自债权人知道或应该知道其权利所基于的事实以及该权利能够行使的第二日开始计算。第(2)款规定了 10 年的最长时效期间,自权利能够行使时开始计算,而无需考虑债权人是否已经实际知道或推定知道。

5. 权利能够行使

只有在权利到期并且能够强制执行时,债权人才真正有可能行使其权利。因此,第(2)款规定,最长时效期间只有在这样的日期到来时才开始计算。

6. 知道事实不同于知道法律

"三年"的一般时效期间自"知道或应该知道导致其权利能够行使的事实之日的次日起计算"。该条意义上的"事实"是指产生权利的基础事实,例如订立合同、交付货物、提供服务和不履行。表明权利或请求权到期的事实,必须已经为债权人所知或者至少有可能知道,只有这样,一般时效期间才能开始计算。而且,债务人的身份有时可能不很清楚,例如下列情形下就会产生这种情况:代理、债务转移或整个合同的转让、公司清算,或不明确的第三方受益人合同。这些情况下,债权人因没有行使权利或请求权而承担不利后果之前,必须已经知道或者有理由知道应该起诉谁。但是,实际或推定知道"事实"并不意味着债权人必须知道这些事实所具有的法律意义。如果债权人虽然充分知晓了事实,但却对自己的权利产生了误解,三年的时效期间仍然起算。

示例:

1. A 根据与 B 县的合同,设计并建造了一座桥梁。A 的工程师在计算某些钢轨的强度时出了错误。四年后,桥梁因同时遭受重型卡车的重压和暴风雨袭击而坍塌。B 要求损害赔偿的请求权并未受阻,原因是一般时效期间从坍塌时起才开始计算,因为直到那时 B 才有可能发现 A 违约。

2. 事实同示例 1,区别在于桥梁在建成后第 11 年坍塌。根据第 10.2 条第(2)款最长时效期间的规定,B 的请求权受到阻碍。这类合同的当事人最好在不违反第 10.3 条限制的前提下修改最长时效期间。

3.   A sends B a notice under Article 7.3.2 terminating a sales contract between A and B because B refuses to take delivery of goods tendered by A. Thirty-seven months after receipt of the note of termination, B demands the return of an advance on the purchase price paid prior to the termination, asserting that, due to an error in its bookkeeping, it had overlooked its payment of the advance with the consequence that it had only recently become aware of the claim for restitution it had under Article 7.3.6(1). B's claim for restitution is barred by the three-year limitation period, as B ought to have known of its payment when the contract was terminated and the claim to repay the advance arose.

4.   The facts are the same as in Illustration 1, except that B asserts that it had not realised the legal effects of a notice of termination. B's claim for restitution is nevertheless barred. An error of law with regard to the legal effects of a notice of termination cannot absolve the obligee since "ought to know" includes seeking legal advice if the party is uncertain about the legal effects of the circumstances.

7. Day of commencement

Since, in the absence of an agreement to the contrary, the obligor can normally perform its obligation in the course of the whole day of the debt's maturity, the limitation period does not start on that same day but only on the following day.

Illustration

5.   A is obliged to pay a sum of money on 24 November. If A does not pay by that date, the limitation period starts on 25 November.

8. Right must be exercisable

An obligation may exist even if performance cannot as yet be required (see, e.g., Article 6.1.1(a)). While a creditor's claim to the repayment of a loan is founded on the contract and may therefore arise at the time of the conclusion of the contract or of the payment of the loan to the debtor, the repayment claim will usually fall due much later. Furthermore, a right may not be enforceable if the obligor has a defence.

Illustrations

6.   A loan agreement obliges the borrower to repay the loan on 15 November. The lender grants the borrower an extension of the date of repayment until 15 December. The limitation period starts on 16 December.

3. A 根据第 7.3.2 条通知 B 终止双方之间的销售合同，理由是 B 拒绝接受 A 提示交付的货物。在收到终止通知 37 个月后，B 要求返还合同终止前预付的部分购买价款。B 声称，由于其记账错误，他忽视了这笔预付款，结果最近才发现第 7.3.6 条第(1)款项下请求返还的权利。B 的返还请求权受到三年时效期间的阻碍，因为合同终止时便产生了返还预付款的请求权，B 当时就应该已经知道了这笔支付。

4. 事实同示例 3[①]，区别在于 B 主张他并未意识到终止通知的法律效力。虽然如此，B 的返还请求权仍然受到阻碍。在终止通知的效力问题上产生法律错误，这并不能成为债权人免受时效阻碍的借口，因为"应该知道"包括当事人对于某些情况的法律效力没有把握时应该寻求法律意见。

7. 起算日期

如果没有相反约定，债务人通常能够在债务到期之日任何时刻履行其义务，因此，时效期间不是从该天起算，而是从第二天起算。

示例：

5. A 有义务在 11 月 24 日支付一笔款项。如果 A 没有在该日支付，时效期间自 11 月 25 日起算。

8. 权利必须是能够行使的

即便债权人还不能要求债务人履行，该项债务也可能已经存在（参见，例如第 6.1.1 条(a)项）。虽然债权人要求偿还贷款的请求权基于合同而产生，并可能于该合同订立或将该款项交付债务人之时产生，但是，要求偿还的请求权通常在很久之后才到期。另外，债务人如果有可以主张的抗辩，权利也可能无法强制执行。

示例：

6. 贷款协议规定借款人应该在 11 月 15 日偿还贷款。贷款人将借款人还款的日期延至 12 月 15 日，时效期间自 12 月 16 日起算。

---

① 译者注：原文为"例 1"，依据上下文应为"例 3"。

7.   A contracts to build a fertiliser plant for B. The price is to be paid in three instalments, the last instalment being due four weeks after completion of the work as certified by an engineering firm. After certification there are still malfunctionings of the plant. B is entitled to withhold performance of the last instalment under Articles 7.1.3(2) and 7.1.4(4). The limitation period for the claim for payment does not begin until the right to withhold payment is extinguished by cure of the malfunctionings.

9. Maximum period

Under paragraph (2) the obligee is in any event, i.e. irrespective of whether it knew or ought to have known the facts giving rise to its right, prevented from exercising the right ten years after it could have exercised it. The objectives of this maximum period of ten years are the restoration of peace and the prevention of speculative litigation where evidence has faded.

Illustration

8.   B borrows money from A and orders its accountant to repay the loan when repayment falls due in January. Fifteen years later, a dispute arises over whether the loan was repaid fully or only in part as A claims. A's asserted claim is barred by Article 10.2(2), because the maximum limitation period has expired.

10. Ancillary claims

This Article applies to all rights, including so-called "ancillary claims".

Illustrations

9.   In a loan agreement, the borrower agrees to pay an interest of 0.7% per month if there is default in repayment. Thirty-five months after repayment is due, the borrower repays the principal. The lender need not sue for all successive monthly instalments of interest at once, but can wait up to thirty-six months for each instalment before it is barred.

10.   Under the contract of builder A with owner B, A agrees to complete construction by 1 October and to pay EUR 50,000 for every month of delay up to a maximum amount of EUR 2,500,000. Completion is delayed for 40 months. Claims for damages for non-performance or delay are barred 36 months after 2 October. The claim for the penalty for each month of delay is barred 36 months after it arises.

7. A 与 B 缔结合同，规定 A 为 B 建造一座化肥厂。工程款分三期支付，最后一期在竣工并经工程公司认证后四个星期内付款。认证后，该工厂仍然带有一些故障。B 有权根据第 7.1.3 条第 (2) 款和第 7.1.4 条第 (4) 款停止支付最后一期工程款。付款请求权的时效期间，直至停止支付的权利因故障排除而消灭时才开始计算。

9. 最长期间

根据第 (2) 款，债权人无论是否已知或应知产生其权利的事实，自他能够行使之日起十年后就不能再行使该权利。10 年最长期间的目的是要恢复平静，并防止在证据灭失后提起投机性的诉讼。

示例：

8. B 向 A 借钱，并令其会计在 1 月份还款义务到期时偿还贷款。15 年后，双方发生如下争议：贷款已经足额偿还？还是如 A 所称仅偿还了一部分？ A 主张的请求权受到第 10.2 条第 (2) 款的阻碍，因为最长时效期间已经期满。

10. 附带请求权

本条适用于所有权利，其中包括所谓的"附带请求权"。

示例：

9. 贷款协议约定，如果拖欠偿还贷款，借款人每月支付 0.7% 的利息。还款到期 35 个月后，借款人才归还本金。贷款人无需立即通过起诉请求各月的利息，相反，每期利息他都可以最长等待 36 个月，在受阻前起诉。

10. 建筑商 A 和业主 B 之间的合同约定 A 须在 10 月 1 日完工，每延误一个月要支付 5 万欧元，最高不超过 250 万欧元。A 延误了 40 个月。因不履行或延误而要求损害赔偿的请求权，自 10 月 2 日起 36 个月后受阻。要求每个月的延迟罚金的请求权，自该权利产生时起 36 个月后受阻。

11. "年"的含义

本条没有给"年"下一个定义，因为国际上提及"年"时通常被

11. "Year"

This Article does not provide a definition of "year", because at international level a reference to "year" is usually understood as being a reference to the Gregorian calendar (see Article 1(3)(h) of the UN Limitation Convention). In any event, calendars deviating from the Gregorian calendar will in most cases have the same number of days per year, with the consequence that they do not influence the length of limitation periods. A different meaning of "year" can be agreed upon by the parties under Article 1.5. Such an agreement may be explicit or derived from an interpretation of the contract.

ARTICLE 10.3
(Modification of limitation periods by the parties)

(1) The parties may modify the limitation periods.

(2) However they may not

(a) shorten the general limitation period to less than one year;

(b) shorten the maximum limitation period to less than four years;

(c) extend the maximum limitation period to more than fifteen years.

COMMENT

1. Basic decision: modifications possible

In some legal systems the power of the parties to modify limitation periods and their effects is restricted out of concern for the weaker parties and, in particular, consumers. A distinction is sometimes made between very short limitation periods, which can be prolonged, and other limitation periods, which cannot be modified or can only be shortened. Since the Principles apply to international contracts between businesspersons who are normally experienced and knowledgeable persons who do not need to be protected, they permit the parties to adapt the limitation periods applicable to the rights arising out of their contracts to their needs in a given case. Restrictions to the parties' autonomy in this respect may, however, follow from the mandatory rules of the otherwise applicable law (see Article 1.4).

理解为是指公历（见《联合国时效公约》第 1 条第（3）款（h）项）。无论如何，与公历不同的其他历法，每年包含的天数通常并无不同，因而并不影响时效期间的长度。各方可以根据第 1.5 条就"年"约定不同的含义。该种约定既可以是明示的，也可以是通过对合同的解释得来的。

<h2 style="text-align:center">第 10.3 条</h2>

（当事人对时效期间的修改）

（1） 当事人可以修改时效期间。

（2） 但是他们不得：

（a） 将一般时效期间缩短至不足一年；

（b） 将最长时效期间缩短至不足四年；

（c） 将最长时效期间延长至超过十五年。

注释：

1. 基本原则：可以修改

在某些法律体系下，出于保护弱势当事人（特别是消费者）的考虑，当事人修改时效期间的权力及这些修改的效力受到法律的限制。有时则会区分非常短的时效期间和其他时效期间，前者可以延长，而后者不能修改或只能缩短。因为《通则》适用于商人之间的国际合同，而他们通常都是富有经验和知识的人，不需要法律的特别保护，所以《通则》允许当事人根据具体情况下的特殊需要，修改其合同产生的权利所适用的时效期间。但是，当事人在这方面的自治，可能受到其他法律下强行性规则的限制（参见第 1.4 条）。

2. Limits of modifications

The possibility nevertheless remains that a party with superior bargaining power or better information may take advantage of the other party by either unduly shortening or lengthening the limitation period. This Article therefore limits the power to shorten the general limitation period by stating that it may not be shortened to less than one year starting from the moment of actual or constructive knowledge, and to shorten the maximum period by stating that it may not be shortened to less than four years. The maximum limitation period and, necessarily, the general period cannot exceed fifteen years.

Illustrations

1.   The facts are the same as in Illustration 2 to Article 10.2, except that in their contract the parties provide that the maximum limitation period for all claims based on hidden defects is fifteen years. B's claim for damages is not yet barred.

2.   The facts are the same as in Illustration 2 to Article 10.2, except that in their contract the parties provide that the maximum limitation period for all claims based on hidden defects is twenty-five years and the bridge collapsed after sixteen years. B's claim for damages is barred, because the maximum limitation period can be extended to only fifteen years.

3.   The facts are the same as in Illustration 2 to Article 10.2, except that in their contract the parties provide that the general limitation period in case of harm resulting from the non-conformity of the bridge starts only upon the submission of a written report of experts of an independent engineering firm. After the collapse of the bridge, it is uncertain what the causes were, and it takes two years for the engineering firm to submit its report. The general limitation period begins to run only from the day after the day on which the report was submitted.

3. Time of modification

A modification can be agreed upon before or after the commencement of a limitation period. A modification agreed upon before or after the commencement of a limitation period differs from an agreement concluded after the limitation period has expired. Such an agreement, although too late to modify the applicable limitation period, may have legal consequences either as a waiver of the defence that the limitation period has expired or as a new promise by the obligor.

2. 对修改的限制

尽管如此，仍然存在如下可能，即交易地位优越或者掌握更多信息的一方，可能通过不适当地缩短或延长时效期间而不适当地从另一方获得好处。因此，本条限制了缩短一般时效期间和最长时效期间的权力；对于前者，规定不得短于一年，自实际知道或推定知道之时起算；对于后者，规定不得短于四年。最长时效期间不得超过 15 年，一般时效期间自然也不能超过 15 年。

示例：

  1. 事实同第 10.2 条之示例 2，不同之处在于，当事人在合同中约定，产生于潜在瑕疵的请求权的最长时效期间是 15 年。B 要求损害赔偿的请求权尚未受阻。

  2. 事实同第 10.2 条之示例 2，不同之处在于，当事人在合同中约定，产生于潜在瑕疵的请求权的最长时效期间是 25 年，桥梁在 16 年后坍塌。B 要求损害赔偿的请求权受到阻碍，因为最长时效期间最多可以延长至 15 年。

  3. 事实同第 10.2 条之示例 2，不同之处在于，当事人在合同中约定，因桥梁不符合要求造成的损害的一般时效期间，只有在独立工程公司的专家出具书面报告时起算。桥梁坍塌后，坍塌原因不明，工程公司花费两年时间才出具其报告。一般时效期间自报告出具之日的次日起算。

3. 修改的时间

修改可以在时效期间起算之前或之后通过约定完成。这类修改不同于时效期间届满后约定的修改。后一类约定，尽管由于太迟而不具有修改适用的时效期间的效力，但仍然可以通过以下其中一种方式获得法律效力：作为一种弃权，即放弃时效期间届满这一抗辩；或者作为债务人做出的一项新的允诺。

ARTICLE 10.4
(New limitation period by acknowledgement)

(1) **Where the obligor before the expiration of the general limitation period acknowledges the right of the obligee, a new general limitation period begins on the day after the day of the acknowledgement.**

(2) **The maximum limitation period does not begin to run again, but may be exceeded by the beginning of a new general limitation period under Article 10.2(1).**

COMMENT

1. Acknowledgement of rights

Most legal systems permit the running of the limitation period to be altered by acts of the parties or other circumstances. Sometimes acts of the parties or other circumstances "interrupt" the running of the limitation period, with the effect that a new limitation period starts. Sometimes acts or other circumstances cause a "suspension" of the running of the limitation period, with the effect that the period of suspension is not counted in computing the limitation period. According to this Article the acknowledgement of a right by the obligor causes an interruption of the limitation period (see also Article 20 of the UN Limitation Convention,).

2. Commencement of a new general limitation period

The new limitation period that starts following acknowledgement of the right of the obligee is the general limitation period, because by virtue of such an acknowledgement the obligee will necessarily possess the knowledge required for commencement of the limitation period under Article 10.2(1). There is therefore no need to protect the obligee by granting it a new maximum limitation period.

第 10.4 条

（认可导致时效期间重新计算）

（1）债务人在一般时效期间届满前认可债权人权利的，自认可之日的次日起，一般时效期间重新开始计算。

（2）最长时效期间不得重新开始计算，但可因第 10.2 条第 (1) 款一般时效期间的重新开始而超期。

注释：

1. 认可权利

多数法律体系下，当事人的行为或其他情况会改变时效期间的计算。有时，当事人的行为或其他情况造成时效期间的"中断"，其效果是时效期间重新计算。有时，当事人行为或其他情况造成时效期间的"中止"，其效果是中止的时间不计算在内。根据本条规定，债务人认可权利造成时效期间的中断（也见《联合国时效公约》第 20 条）。

2. 一般时效期间的重新起算

认可债权人的权利后重新开始计算的时效期间是一般时效期间，因为此类认可必然使得债权人满足了第 10.2 条第 (1) 款项下时效期间起算所要求的知悉要件。因此没有必要通过赋予债权人一个新的最长时效期间来保护他。

Illustration

> 1.   A defectively performs a construction contract with B and B informs A of the non-conformities in October without receiving any response from A. Two years later B again approaches A, threatening to bring an action for damages. This time A responds and acknowledges the non-conformity of its performance and promises to cure the non-conformity. On the following day a new general limitation period starts to run for B's right to damages.

The commencement of a new general limitation period following acknowledgement can take place either during the general limitation period under Article 10.2(1), or during the maximum limitation period under Article 10.2(2). While the maximum limitation period will not in itself begin again, the new general limitation period may exceed the maximum period by up to three years if the obligor acknowledges the right of the obligee after more than seven years but before the maximum period has already expired.

Illustration

> 2.   B discovers defects in the construction work of A only nine years after completion of the work. The defects could not have been discovered earlier. B threatens to initiate legal action, and A acknowledges the defects. A new general limitation period begins to run on acknowledgement, so that altogether the limitation period amounts to twelve years.

3. Novation and other acts creating a new obligation

Acknowledgement does not create a new obligation, it merely interrupts the running of the limitation period. Accessory rights are therefore not extinguished. Consequently, if the limitation period has already ended, a mere acknowledgement under this Article does not retroactively remove or invalidate the limitation defence.

Illustration

> 3.   The facts are the same as in Illustration 2, except that B knows or ought to know of A's defective construction at the time of completion. B approaches A only 7 years later, and A acknowledges the defective performance. B's claim is nevertheless already barred under Article 10.2(1) and is not revived by A's acknowledgement.

示例：

1. A 在履行与 B 的建筑合同过程中存有瑕疵，B 在 10 月份就此履行瑕疵告知 A，但没有收到 A 的任何回应。两年后，B 再次联系 A，声称将提起损害赔偿之诉。A 这次做出回应，认可其履行与合同不符，并承诺弥补瑕疵。B 要求损害赔偿的请求权，适用一个新的一般时效期间，该时效期间从次日开始起算。

经债务人认可产生的新的时效期间，可以在第 10.2 条第(1)款规定的一般时效期间内起算，也可能在第 10.2 条第(2)款规定的最长时效期间内起算。虽然最长时效期间本身不能重新起算，但新的一般时效期间最多可以超越最长时效期间三年，例如债务人在七年以后但是最长时效期间届满以前认可了债权人的权利。

示例：

2. B 在工程完成九年后发现 A 在施工过程中存在瑕疵。瑕疵不可能在之前发现。B 声称要提起诉讼，A 认可了该瑕疵。认可之后，新的一般时效期间开始起算。因而，时效期间合计达到 12 年。

3. 债务更新和其他创设新债务的行为

认可并不能创设一项新的债务，它仅仅中断了时效期间的计算。因而附带权利并未消灭。所以，如果时效期间已经届满，仅凭本条予以认可并不能溯及地消除时效期间已过的抗辩或使该抗辩归于无效。

示例：

3. 事实同示例 2，不同之处在于，工程完成时 B 知道或应该知道 A 的履行过程存在瑕疵。B 在七年后才联系 A，A 认可履行存在瑕疵。即便如此，根据第 10.2 条第(1)款 B 的请求权已经受到阻碍，A 的认可并不能使其重新生效。

If the parties want to undo the effects of a completed limitation period, they can create a new obligation by a "novation" or an unilateral act on the part of the obligor, or the obligor can waive the defence of the expiration of a limitation period. The parties can also prolong the duration of the obligee's right beyond the end of the maximum limitation period under Article 10.2(2).

Illustrations

> 4.   The facts are the same as in Illustration 3, except that A, in order to maintain a profitable business relation, not only acknowledges the defective performance, but promises to cure the defects regardless of any question of A's liability. This agreement creates a new obligation for A, which is barred only three years later.
>
> 5.   Nine years after completion B discovers defects in A's construction work which could not have been discovered earlier. On notice to A, A responds that it will investigate the causes of the defects and will therefore not invoke the limitation period until six months after the experts investigating the defects submit their report. The report is submitted twelve months later, confirming B's notice of defects. When B asks A to cure the defects, A argues that the maximum period of Article 10.2(2) has expired with the consequence that no claim for damages can be made by B. A's argument is incorrect if B abstained from initiating judicial proceedings on account of A's waiver.

4. Interruption of limitation periods modified by the parties

To the extent that the parties have modified the general limitation period under Article 10.2(1), acknowledgement and the commencement of a new limitation period affect the general period as modified. If, for example, the parties have shortened the general limitation period to one year, acknowledgement causes a new one-year period to run.

Illustration

> 6.   A and B have agreed to shorten the limitation period for claims arising from the non-conformity of A's performance to two years. After nine and a half years B discovers defects in A's performance, and A acknowledges its obligation to cure. B has another two years to pursue its claim before it is barred under Article 10.2(1).

如果当事人想要消除时效期间届满的影响，他们可以通过"债务更新"或者债务人的单方面行为创设一项新的债务，或者债务人放弃时效期间届满的抗辩。当事人也能够延长债权人权利的有效期，使其超越第10.2条第(2)款项下的最长时效期间。

示例：

　4. 事实同示例3，不同之处在于，为了维持与B之间利润丰厚的商业关系，A不仅认可瑕疵履行，而且允诺不管自己是否有责任都将修复瑕疵。这一协议为A创设了一项新的义务，直到三年后才会受到阻碍。

　5. 完工九年后B发现A的施工存在瑕疵，这些瑕疵是之前所不能发现的。A收到通知后作出回应说，他将调查瑕疵出现的原因，并在调查瑕疵专家出具报告6个月后才会援引时效期间的抗辩。报告在12个月后出具，确认了B的瑕疵通知。当B要求A修复瑕疵时，A声称第10.2条第(2)款项下的最长时效期间已经届满，因此B不能提出损害赔偿请求权。如果B是因为A的弃权而放弃启动司法程序，A的主张不能成立。

4. 经当事人修改的时效期间之中断

如果当事人修改了第10.2条第(1)款项下的一般时效期间，则认可以及新时效期间的起算适用于经修改的一般时效期间。例如，如果当事人将一般时效期间缩短至一年，则认可导致的新时效期间也为一年。

示例：

　6. 对于由A的履行不符产生的请求权，A和B约定将时效期间缩短至两年。九年半以后，B发现A的履行存在瑕疵，并且A认可了自己的修复义务。在受到第10.2条第(1)款阻碍之前，B还有两年时间寻求其主张。

Since the obligor can acknowledge more than once, the limited effect of an acknowledgement that causes only the general limitation period to start again can be overcome by a subsequent acknowledgement.

Illustration

7.   A delivers non-conforming goods to B in November. B suffers loss resulting from the non-conformity because its customers complain and return the goods. Since two years later the total amount of loss is not yet clear, B pressures A to acknowledge its liability and in December of that year A complies with B's request. Two years later, there are still uncertainties regarding the exact extent of B's obligations towards its customers, some of whom have sued for compensation for consequential damages allegedly caused by the goods. B therefore turns to A again, who acknowledges its obligation to compensate B should the claims of B's customers be well-founded. B has three more years before its claims against A are barred.

ARTICLE 10.5
(Suspension by judicial proceedings)

(1) The running of the limitation period is suspended

(a) when the obligee performs any act, by commencing judicial proceedings or in judicial proceedings already instituted, that is recognised by the law of the court as asserting the obligee's right against the obligor;

(b) in the case of the obligor's insolvency when the obligee has asserted its rights in the insolvency proceedings; or

(c) in the case of proceedings for dissolution of the entity which is the obligor when the obligee has asserted its rights in the dissolution proceedings.

(2) Suspension lasts until a final decision has been issued or until the proceedings have been otherwise terminated.

认可只能使一般时效期间重新计算。因为债务人可以进行多次认可，所以认可的这种有限效力能够通过连续认可得以克服。

示例：

　　7. A 在 11 月向 B 交付了与合同不符的货物，B 因其顾客投诉和退货遭受了损失。两年后损失总额尚不清楚，B 迫使 A 认可其责任，A 在该年 12 月按照 B 的请求给予认可。两年后，B 对其顾客应该承担的责任的确切范围仍不确定，因为有些顾客就货物造成的附带损失起诉要求获得赔偿。B 因此再次要求 A 认可，A 认可如果 B 的顾客的请求权证据确凿他将对 B 承担的义务。B 对 A 的请求权在未来三年内不会受阻碍。

第 10.5 条

（因司法程序而中止）

　　（1）时效期间在以下情况下中止计算：

　　（a）通过启动司法程序或者在已经启动的司法程序中，债权人采取被法院认可的债权人向债务人主张其权利的任何行为；

　　（b）在债务人破产的情况下，债权人在破产程序中主张其权利；

　　（c）在债务人实体进入解散程序的情况下，债权人在解散程序中主张其权利。

　　（2）时效中止持续至终局判决做出之时或持续至其他方式的程序终止之时。

COMMENT

1. Judicial proceedings

In all legal systems judicial proceedings affect the running of a limitation period in either of two manners. Judicial proceedings can cause an interruption of the limitation period, so that a new limitation period begins when the judicial proceedings end. Alternatively, judicial proceedings can cause only a suspension, so that a period that has already lapsed before the judicial proceedings began will be deducted from the applicable period, the remaining period starting at the end of the judicial procedure. This Article adopts the latter solution (see also Article 13 of the UN Limitation Convention).

2. Commencement of proceedings

The requirements for the commencement of judicial proceedings are determined by the law of procedure of the court where the proceedings are instituted. The law of procedure of the forum also determines whether the raising of counterclaims amounts to the instituting of judicial proceedings in regard to these claims: where the counterclaims raised as a defence are treated as if they were brought in separate proceedings, raising them has the same effect on the limitation period as if they had been filed independently.

Illustrations

1. A purchases from B a truck that turns out to be defective. A notifies B of the defects but, because of other pending contracts between A and B, A does not press the matter for 24 months. When the negotiations between A and B on the other contracts break down, B turns down a request by A to cure the defects, asserting that the defects were caused by A's mishandling of the truck. A files a law suit against B by depositing it with the clerk of the competent court. Under the procedural law applicable in that court, this is sufficient to initiate litigation with respect to A's claims. The running of the limitation period is suspended, until a final decision is handed down. This includes not only a decision of the court of first instance, but also, if appeal is allowed, that of a higher court on any available appeal. If the parties reach a settlement or the plaintiff withdraws its complaint, this ends the litigation if it is so regarded under the applicable domestic procedural law.

注释：

1. 司法程序

在所有法律体系下，司法程序都以两种方式之一影响着时效期间的计算。司法程序可以导致时效期间的中断，因此时效期间在司法程序结束后重新计算。或者，司法程序只导致时效期间的中止，因此司法程序开始之前已经过去的期间将从适用期间中筛选出来，余下的期间自司法程序结束后开始起算。本条采纳的是第二种方式（另见《联合国时效公约》第 13 条）。

2. 启动程序

司法程序的启动要件由受理程序的法院适用的程序法决定。法院地程序法也决定了提起反请求是否构成就反请求涉及的诉讼请求启动了司法程序：如果作为抗辩提出的反请求被视为等同于在单独程序中提出，那么，提起反请求对于时效期间的影响就如同单独提起诉讼请求时的影响。

示例：

1. A 向 B 购买了一辆卡车，后来发现该车存在瑕疵。A 告知 B 这一瑕疵情况，但是因为 A 和 B 正在就其他合同进行谈判，A 在 24 个月内并未就此向 B 施压。A 和 B 就其他合同的谈判破裂后，B 拒绝了 A 要求修复瑕疵的请求，B 声称瑕疵是由 A 错误操作造成的。A 向适格法院的书记官提交诉状，从而对 B 提起诉讼。根据该法院适用的程序法，这一步骤足以启动 A 行使其请求权的诉讼。时效期间的计算中止，直至作出终局判决之时。这里所指的判决不仅包括初审法院的判决，也包括更高一级法院在上诉审中做出的判决（如果允许上诉的话）。适用的国内程序法如有规定，当事人和解或者原告撤诉也将结束诉讼。

2.   B initiates litigation for the purchase price of goods by filing a complaint as required by the procedural law of the country of the competent court. A raises claims under an asserted guarantee either as counterclaims or by way of set-off. The limitation period for A's warranty claims is suspended until there is a final decision on the counterclaims or a settlement or withdrawal of A's counterclaims.

3. Termination

"Termination" by a final decision or otherwise is to be determined by the rules of procedure of the forum. These rules decide when a decision is final and therefore brings the litigation on the litigated subject-matter to an end. These rules also have to decide whether and when the litigation comes to an end without a final decision on the merits, e.g. by the withdrawal of a complaint or by a settlement of the parties.

4. Suspension by insolvency or dissolution proceedings

For the purpose of this Article, insolvency and dissolution proceedings are regarded as judicial proceedings (Article 10.5(1)(b) and (c)). The dates of the commencement and ending of these proceedings are determined by the law governing the proceedings.

ARTICLE 10.6
(Suspension by arbitral proceedings)

(1)   The running of the limitation period is suspended when the obligee performs any act, by commencing arbitral proceedings or in arbitral proceedings already instituted, that is recognised by the law of the arbitral tribunal as asserting the obligee's right against the obligor. In the absence of regulations for arbitral proceedings or provisions determining the exact date of the commencement of arbitral proceedings, the proceedings are deemed to commence on the date on which a request that the right in dispute should be adjudicated reaches the obligor.

(2) Suspension   lasts   until   a   binding decision has been issued or until the proceedings have been otherwise terminated.

2. B 按照适格法院所在国程序法的要求提交诉状，提起索要货物价款的诉讼。A 以反请求或抵销的方式提出一项有关担保义务的诉讼请求。该担保请求的时效期间自此中止，直至就反请求做出终局判决或双方和解或 A 撤回反请求之时。

3. 终止程序

以终局判决或其他方式"终止程序"的判断标准，由法院地的程序法决定。这些规则决定了一项判决何时构成终局判决，以此结束针对系争标的提起的诉讼。这些规则还决定了，在没有针对案件实体做出终局判决的情况下（例如通过撤诉或当事人和解），诉讼是否结束以及何时结束。

4. 破产或解散程序引起的中止

为本条之目的，破产和解散程序视为司法程序（第 10.5 条(1)款(b)项和(c)项）。这些程序的开始和结束日期，由调整这些程序的适用法确定。

第 10.6 条

（因仲裁程序而中止）

（1）通过启动仲裁程序或者在已经启动的仲裁程序中，自债权人采取被仲裁庭法则所认可的债权人向债务人主张其权利的行为之时起，时效期间中止计算。如果仲裁程序的规定或条款没有对启动仲裁程序的确切日期做出规定，则仲裁程序启动之日应为要求审理争议之权利的请求送达债务人之日。

（2）时效中止持续至有约束力的裁决做出之时或持续至其他方式程序终止之时。

COMMENT

1. Arbitral proceedings

Arbitration has the same effect as judicial proceedings. The commencement of arbitral proceedings therefore has the same suspensive effect as judicial proceedings. In general, the date of commencement is determined by the applicable arbitration rules and the starting point of suspension is also determined by these rules. For cases in which the rules on arbitration do not exactly determine the date of commencement of the proceedings, the second sentence of paragraph (1) of this Article provides a default rule.

Illustration

A cancels a distributorship contract with B, claiming that B has defaulted payments due for A's delivery of goods to B. B counterclaims damages for lost profits, but B changes its law firm and allows almost 30 months to pass from the termination of the agreement. The agreement contains an arbitration clause, providing that all disputes and claims "shall be settled under the Rules of Conciliation and Arbitration of the International Chamber of Commerce", and B submits a request for arbitration under those rules. The rules provide that the date of receipt of the request is to be regarded "for all purposes" as the date of the commencement of the arbitral proceedings. The running of the limitation period is suspended until a final award is handed down or the case is otherwise disposed of.

2. Termination of arbitration

While the most frequent cases of termination will, as in judicial proceedings, be those that end with a decision on the merits of the case, arbitration can also end otherwise, e.g. by the withdrawal of an application, by a settlement or by an order or injunction of the competent court. The applicable rules on arbitration and civil procedure have to determine whether or not such events terminate the arbitration and thereby also the suspension.

注释：

1. 仲裁程序

仲裁与司法程序具有相同的效力。因此仲裁程序的开始与司法程序一样具有中止时效的效力。通常，仲裁程序的启动日期根据适用的仲裁规则确定，并且中止起始时间也要根据这些规则确定。如果仲裁规则针对程序开始日期没有作出明确规定，本条第(1)款第二句话提供了一个默认的规则。

示例：

> A 声称 B 拖欠其货物价款而取消了其与 B 之间的分销合同。B 就遭受的利润损失提起反请求。后来 B 更换了律师事务所，自合同终止 30 个月后才重新追诉。合同中包含一个仲裁条款，规定所有争议和请求"都应该根据《国际商会调解和仲裁规则》加以解决"，B 根据该《规则》提交了仲裁请求。《规则》规定，收到请求的日期"为各种目的"应视为仲裁程序开始的日期。时效期间中止计算，直至作出终局裁决或以其他方式结束案件之时。

2. 终止仲裁程序

与司法程序一样，最常见的仲裁终止方式是就案件实体做出裁决，但是仲裁程序也可能以其他方式结束，例如撤回仲裁申请书、和解或适格法院的命令或禁令。适用的仲裁规则和民事程序规则需要确定此类事由是否终止了仲裁程序，并因此结束了时效期间的中止。

ARTICLE 10.7
(Alternative dispute resolution)

The provisions of Articles 10.5 and 10.6 apply with appropriate modifications to other proceedings whereby the parties request a third person to assist them in their attempt to reach an amicable settlement of their dispute.

COMMENT

1. Alternative dispute resolution

Before resorting to judicial proceedings or arbitration, parties may start negotiations or agree on conciliation or other forms of alternative dispute resolution.

Under the Principles negotiations do not automatically suspend the limitation period. Parties who want the limitation period to be suspended should come to an express agreement to this effect.

By contrast, this Article provides that conciliation and other forms of alternative dispute resolution cause a suspension of the limitation period. The definition of "alternative dispute resolution" as proceedings whereby the parties request a third person to assist them in their attempt to reach an amicable settlement of their dispute, is inspired by Article 1(3) of the *2002 UNCITRAL Model Law on International Commercial Conciliation.*

2. Absence of statutory regulations

As only few countries have enacted statutes on alternative dispute resolution and rules for such proceedings are relatively rare, this Article refers to the provisions on judicial and arbitral proceedings, which have to be applied with "appropriate modifications". This means that, in the absence of an applicable legal regulation, the commencement of proceedings of alternative dispute resolution is governed by the default provision in the second sentence of Article 10.6(1), the proceedings starting on the date on which one party's request to have such proceedings reaches the other party. Since the end of a dispute resolution procedure will very often be uncertain, the reference to Articles 10.5 and 10.6, and in particular to the phrase "until the proceedings have been otherwise terminated" in their paragraphs (2), is also to be applied with appropriate modifications. Thus, a unilateral termination of the dispute resolution procedure by one of the parties

第 10.7 条

（替代性争议解决）

第 10.5 条和第 10.6 条的规定经适当修改，
适用于下述程序：当事人各方请求第三方协助其
友好解决争议的程序。

注释：

1. 替代性争议解决

诉诸司法程序或仲裁程序之前，当事人往往首先采用协商程序，
或就调解或其他替代性争议解决达成协议。

根据《通则》，协商并不自动中止时效期间的计算。想要中止时效
期间的当事人应当就此达成明示的协议。

相比之下，本条规定，调解或其他替代性争议解决机制则导致时
效期间的中止。借鉴 2002 年《联合国国际贸易法委员会国际商事调解
示范法》第 1 条第(3)款之规定，"替代性争议解决"被定义为当事人
请求第三方协助他们通过友好的方式解决他们之间争议的程序。

2. 缺乏法定规则

因为仅有少数几个国家就替代性争议解决制定了法律，针对此类
程序的规则相对较少，本条规定参照有关司法和仲裁程序的规定，此
类规定必须"经适当修改"才能适用。这意味着，在缺乏可适用的法
律规则时，替代性争议解决机制的启动时间受第 10.6 条第(1)款第二
句话默认规定的调整，即一方当事人要求此类程序的请求到达另一方
当事人之日启动。因为争议解决程序的结束时间往往非常难以确定，
参照第 10.5 条和第 10.6 条时，特别是参照其中第(2)款"至有约束力
的裁决做出之时或以其他方式程序终止之时"的短语时，经适当修
改后也可以适用。因此，一方当事人单方面终止争议解决程序，将足

will suffice to terminate the suspension. A unilateral termination that is made in bad faith is subject to Article 1.7.

Illustration

> The parties, a hospital and a supplier of hospital equipment, agree to submit disputes over prices to a board of mediation. Under the applicable rules a review by this board starts on the date on which one party submits a complaint to the other party, who then has to invite the board to review the case under the applicable rules. The mediation ends either when the board decides on the claim, or there is a settlement between the parties, or the claimant's request is withdrawn.

ARTICLE 10.8
(Suspension in case of force majeure,
death or incapacity)

(1) Where the obligee has been prevented by an impediment that is beyond its control and that it could neither avoid nor overcome, from causing a limitation period to cease to run under the preceding Articles, the general limitation period is suspended so as not to expire before one year after the relevant impediment has ceased to exist.

(2) Where the impediment consists of the incapacity or death of the obligee or obligor, suspension ceases when a representative for the incapacitated or deceased party or its estate has been appointed or a successor has inherited the respective party's position. The additional one-year period under paragraph (1) applies accordingly.

COMMENT

1. Effects of impediments

Most legal systems take into account impediments that prevent the obligee from pursuing its rights in court, as does the UN Limitation Convention (see Articles 15 and 21). It is a basic policy concept that

以结束时效期间的中止。以恶意方式单方面终止程序受第 1.7 条调整。

示例：

当事双方是一家医院和一家医疗设备供应商，他们同意将其间关于价格的争议提交一个调停委员会解决。根据适用的规则，该委员会的审查自一方向另一方送达申诉书之日开始，该方随后必须邀请委员会根据适用的规则审查案件。调停于该委员会就该请求做出决定，或当事人之间达成和解，或请求方撤回请求时结束。

第 10.8 条

（因不可抗力、死亡或无行为能力而中止）

（1）如果债权人因其无法控制、无法避免，也无法克服的障碍，不能根据前述条款阻止时效期间的计算，则一般时效期间中止计算，以使其不会在相关障碍消失之后一年内届满。

（2）如果债权人或债务人的无行为能力或死亡构成上述障碍，时效期间的中止持续至无行为能力人，或死者或其遗产指定了代理人，或者继承人继承了前述相关人的地位之时。第 (1) 款规定的一年额外期间同样适用于本款。

注释：

1. 障碍的影响

大多数法律体系都对阻止债权人通过法庭行使其权利的障碍事由作了规定，例如《联合国时效公约》（见第 15 条和第 21 条）。一个基

the obligee must have the possibility to pursue its rights before it can be deprived of them as a result of the lapse of time. Practical examples of impediments include war and natural disasters that prevent the obligee from reaching a competent court. Other cases of force majeure may also prevent the pursuance of a right and at least cause the suspension of the limitation period. The impediment must be beyond the obligee's control. Imprisonment, therefore, would suspend the limitation period only where it could not have been avoided, such as in the case of a prisoner of war, but the imprisonment of a criminal would not. Only the general limitation period is suspended, however. If the maximum period has elapsed before the obligee could pursue this right, the obligee is subject to the defence of the expiration of the maximum limitation period.

Illustration

1. A's lawyer plans to file a complaint against B, an engineering firm, for alleged professional malpractice by B's employees. The limitation period will expire on 1 December, and A's lawyer has completed the complaint on 25 November, intending to file it by express mail or in person with the clerk of the competent court. On 24 November, terrorists attack A's country with biological weapons of mass destruction, causing all traffic, mail service, and other social services to completely cease, thus preventing the timely filing of A's complaint. The limitation period ceases to run and will not expire until one year after some means of communication has been restored in A's country. If, however, the disruption of all means of communication in A's country lasts ten years, A's right is barred by the maximum limitation period.

2. Additional period of deliberation

Since impediments beyond the control of the obligee may occur and cease to exist towards the end of the limitation period, it is possible that after the ceasing of the impediment only a very short time or no time at all might be left for the obligee to decide what to do. This Article therefore provides for an additional one-year period of time from the date on which the impediment ceases to exist with a view to enabling the obligee to decide what course of action to take.

3. Incapacity and death

Incapacity and death of the obligee or of the obligor are but special examples of impediments to an effective pursuance of the obligee's right. Paragraph (2) provides for the same solution as in the case of general impediments.

本的政策性概念是，债权人在因为时间流逝而被剥夺权利之前，必须有机会行使自己的权利。障碍的实际例子包括，发生阻止债权人向适格法院提起诉讼的战争和自然灾害。其他不可抗力事件也可能阻止对权利的行使，至少造成时效期间的中止。障碍必须是债权人无法控制的。因此，只有在不可避免时，例如战犯，监禁才会造成中止时效期间的效果，但对于刑事罪犯的监禁则不具有这种效果。不过，以上障碍事由只能对一般（而非最长）时效期间产生中止效力。如果最长期间在债权人能够行使其权利之前已经届满，债权人将受到最长时效期间届满的抗辩。

示例：

　　　　1. A 的律师计划对工程公司 B 提起诉讼，要求 B 应该对其雇员的职业过失负责。时效期间将在 12 月 1 日届满，A 的律师已经在 11 月 25 日起草完了起诉书，打算通过快递或亲自交给适格法庭的书记员来提起诉讼。11 月 24 日，恐怖分子用大规模杀伤性武器袭击了 A 的国家，造成所有铁路、邮政和其他社会服务陷入全面瘫痪，因此阻止了 A 及时提起诉讼。时效期间停止计算，并且直到 A 国某些通信渠道恢复一年后才届满。但是，如果 A 国所有通信渠道持续瘫痪了 10 年，A 的权利受到最长时效期间的阻碍。

2. 额外的考虑时间

债权人无法控制的障碍可能在时效期间临近结束时发生并消失，因此，障碍停止后债权人可能必须在非常短暂的时间或者根本没有时间决定如何做。因此本条规定了一年的额外期间，自障碍消失之日起计算，以使债权人能够决定采取什么措施。

3. 丧失行为能力和死亡

债权人或债务人丧失行为能力和死亡，只不过是阻碍债权人有效行使权利的障碍的特例。第(2)款规定了与一般性障碍情况下相同的解决办法。

Illustration

2.   A lends B money which is due to be repaid on 1 January. A does not seek repayment for a long time and dies thirty-five months after the date for repayment. The law of succession applicable to A's estate requires that an administrator appointed by the court administer the estate and collect outstanding debts. Since the docket of the competent court is overcrowded, it takes two and a half years for an administrator to be appointed. The administrator has one month left of the three-year general limitation period plus an additional one-year period to pursue the deceased party's claim against B before the limitation period expires.

ARTICLE 10.9

(Effects of expiration of limitation period)

(1) The expiration of the limitation period does not extinguish the right.

(2) For the expiration of the limitation period to have effect, the obligor must assert it as a defence.

(3) A right may still be relied on as a defence even though the expiration of the limitation period for that right has been asserted.

COMMENT

1. No extinction of the right

The expiration of the limitation period does not extinguish the obligor's right, but only bars its enforcement.

2. Expiration of the limitation period must be raised as a defence

The effects of the expiration of the limitation period do not occur automatically. They only occur if the obligor raises the expiration as a defence. The obligor can do so in any proceedings in accordance with the applicable law, and also outside of proceedings by invoking the expiration of the limitation period. The existence of the defence can also be the subject of a declaratory judgement.

示例：

　　2. A 借给 B 一笔钱，B 还款日期为 1 月 1 日。A 在很长时间内未催促还款，并在还款之日到期 35 个月后死亡。适用于 A 遗产的继承法要求法院任命一名遗产管理人，由其负责管理遗产并且追收尚未收回债务。因为适格法院的日程表过于拥挤，两年半以后法院才任命了遗产管理人。在时效期间届满前，遗产管理人有 13 个月的时间来行使死者对 B 的请求权，即三年一般时效期间的最后一个月加上一年的额外期间。

第 10.9 条

（时效期间届满的效力）

　　（1）时效期间届满不消灭权利。
　　（2）经债务人作为抗辩提出，时效期间届满方产生效力。
　　（3）即使对一项权利已提出时效期间届满的主张，仍可依赖该权利作为抗辩。

注释：

1. 不消灭权利

时效期间的届满并不消灭债权人①的权利，仅仅阻碍该权利的强制执行。

2. 时效期间届满必须作为抗辩事由提出

时效期间届满的效力并不自动产生，仅在债务人作为抗辩提出届满事由时才产生。债务人可以在任何程序中根据适用法提出，也可以在程序之外援引时效期间届满。法院可以以宣告性判决对该抗辩是否存在作出裁定。

---

　　① 　译者注：英文为 "obligor"，依据上下文应为 "obligee"。

Illustration

> 1.   A purchases goods from B. Part of the purchase price is due on 1 April and is not paid. Thirty-eight months later, B files a complaint against A. A does not invoke the expiration of the limitation period, nor does it appear in court, and B moves for a default-judgment. Judgment will be for B, since A did not raise the expiration of the limitation period as a defence.

3. Use of a time-barred right as a defence

Since under the Principles the expiration of a limitation period does not extinguish the right, but only gives a defence that must be asserted by the obligor (paragraphs (1) and (2)), it follows that the obligee's right still exists, although a claim for its performance may be barred by the obligor's assertion of the expiration of the limitation period. It can, therefore, be used as a defence, e.g. as grounds for the retention of performance by the obligee (paragraph (3)).

Illustration

> 2.   A leases a printing press to B for ten years. Under the contract A is obliged to maintain the press in working condition and to undertake repairs, unless a defect is caused by B's negligence in operating the machine. The machine breaks down, but A refuses to do the necessary repairs. B, after futile requests and negotiations with A, has the repairs done by another company and asks A to pay the necessary costs. A does not react, and B does not pursue the matter. Five years later, at the end of the lease, B again requests payment of the costs of the repairs. A refuses to pay and invokes Article 10.2(1), requesting the return of the printing press. B is entitled to damages for breach of contract and to withhold delivery of the press.

ARTICLE 10.10

(Right of set-off)

The obligee may exercise the right of set-off until the obligor has asserted the expiration of the limitation period.

COMMENT

As the obligee's right continues to exist, it can be used for set-off if the prerequisites of set-off under Article 8.1 are met.

示例：

> 1. A 从 B 处购买货物。部分货款于 4 月 1 日到期，且未支付。38 个月后，B 对 A 提起诉讼。A 未援引时效期间届满的抗辩，也没有到案；B 提出缺席判决的动议。法院将作出对 B 有利的判决，因为 A 未提出时效期间届满的抗辩。

3. 以时效届满的权利作为抗辩

根据《通则》的规定，时效期间届满并不消灭权利，而只是提供了一个必须由债务人提出主张才阻碍权利行使的抗辩事由（本条第(1)款款和第(2)款），因此，债权人的权利仍然存在，虽然行使该权利将受到债务人提出的时效期间届满抗辩的阻碍。因此，该权利能够作为一个抗辩事由使用，例如债权人可以此为理由扣留债务人已经作出的履行（第(3)款）。

示例：

> 2. A 出租给 B 一台印刷机，租期 10 年。根据合同，A 有义务维持印刷机处于良好使用状态并且承担修理事宜，除非故障是由 B 操作机器过程中的疏忽造成的。机器出现故障后，A 拒绝进行必要的修理。请求和协商没有结果，于是 B 请另一家公司进行维修，并要求 A 偿还必要的费用。A 未做出回应，而 B 也没有追诉这一事项。五年之后，临近租期结束时，B 再次要求支付维修成本。A 拒绝支付并援引第 10.2 条第(1)款，请求归还印刷机。B 有权以 A 违约为由获得损害赔偿，并且扣留印刷机。

第 10.10 条

（抵销权）

债权人可以行使抵销权，除非债务人主张时效期间已届满。

注释：

因为债权人的权利仍然存在，如果第 8.1 条项下抵销的前提条件都得到满足，该权利可以用于抵销。

Illustration

> 1. The facts are the same as in Illustration 2 to Article 10.9, except that A not only asks for the return of the press, but also for the payment of the unpaid rent. B is entitled to set off its counterclaim for damages against this monetary claim despite the expiration of the limitation period.

Although the expiration of the limitation period does not in itself extinguish the right of the obligee, the situation changes when the obligor invokes the time bar as a defence by asserting it against the obligee. By so doing, the obligor makes the limitation period effective, with the consequence that the right can no longer be enforced. Since set-off may be considered the self-enforcement of a right, it is not available after the defence of the expiration of the limitation period has been invoked.

Illustration

> 2. The facts are the same as in Illustration 1, except that B requests the payment of damages and threatens to sue four years after having had the repairs done. A objects, asserting that the machine broke down due to B's fault. Since this is hard to prove, A in a letter to B also invokes the time bar under Article 10.2(1). B can no longer set off its claim for damages.

ARTICLE **10.11**

(Restitution)

Where there has been performance in order to discharge an obligation, there is no right of restitution merely because the limitation period has expired.

COMMENT

1. Time-barred claim as valid basis for performance

Another consequence of the fact that under the Principles the expiration of the limitation period does not extinguish the right of the obligee but can only be asserted as a defence, is that if the obligor performs despite its defence, the obligation it performs remains effective as a legal basis for the obligee's retaining the performance. Mere expiration of a limitation period cannot be used as grounds for an action to reclaim the performance under restitutionary or unjust enrichment principles.

示例：

1. 事实同第 10.9 条示例 2，区别在于 A 不仅要求归还印刷机，还要求支付未付的租金。尽管时效期间届满，B 仍然有权以要求损害赔偿的反请求抵销该货币请求。

尽管时效期间届满本身并不消灭债权人的权利，但如果债务人援引了时效期间作为对抗债权人的抗辩，情况就发生变化。时效期间届满因此产生效力，从而使得该权利不能再强制执行。因为抵销可以视为权利的自行执行，所以提出时效期间届满的抗辩后就不能使用了。

示例：

2. 事实同示例 1，区别在于，修理完工四年后 B 请求支付损害赔偿，并威胁提起诉讼。A 反对，主张机器因为 B 的疏忽而损坏。由于这一点很难证明，A 在致 B 的一封信中还援引了第 10.2 条第（1）款项下的时效障碍。B 此后不能再以其损害赔偿请求权主张抵销。

第 10.11 条

（恢复原状）

若为解除一项债务已做了履行，则无权仅凭时效期间届满要求恢复原状。

注释：

1. 罹于时效的请求权可以作为有效的履行依据

根据《通则》，时效期间届满并不消灭债权人的权利，而只能作为抗辩事由。这一事实的另一个后果是，如果债务人不顾该抗辩仍然履行了债务，其履行是有效的，可以作为债权人扣留该履行的法律依据。债务人并不能仅以时效期间届满为依据，根据返还原则或不当得利原则提起要求归还履行的诉讼。

2. Restitutionary claims based on other grounds

Despite the lapse of the limitation period, a restitutionary claim can be based on grounds other than performance, e.g. where a payor claims to have paid a non-existing debt due to a mistake.

Illustrations

1.   Bank B lends money to borrower A, who does not repay on the date required by the loan agreement. A's debt is overlooked and forgotten because of a book-keeping error on the part of B. Four years later, B discovers its error and sends A a notice claiming repayment. A complies with this request, but later learns from a lawyer that it could have refused repayment on account of the expiration of the limitation period. A cannot reclaim the payment as unjust enrichment from B.

2.   The facts are the same as in Illustration 1, except that A has in fact repaid the loan, but both sides are unaware of this. Four years later, B erroneously requests payment from A, and A complies. A can recover the second payment because A has already paid a debt which has thus been extinguished by full performance.

2. 基于其他理由的返还请求权

尽管时效期间届满，仍然可以根据履行之外的其他理由主张返还请求权，例如付款人主张自己因错误清偿了不存在的债务。

示例：

　　1. B 银行借给借款人 A 一笔钱，A 未按贷款合同规定按期偿还。由于簿记错误，B 忽视和遗忘了 A 的债务。四年后，B 发现了错误并就此事通知 A，要求还款。A 按照这一请求偿还了贷款。但后来他从一律师处了解到，由于时效期间届满可以拒绝偿还。A 不能以不当得利为由要求 B 归还还款。

　　2. 事实同示例 1，区别在于，A 事实上已经归还了贷款，但是双方不知道这一事实。四年后，B 错误地要求 A 还款，A 按照这一请求偿还了贷款。A 可以收回第二次付款，因为 A 支付后债务已经因充分履行而消灭。

CHAPTER 11

PLURALITY OF OBLIGORS AND OF OBLIGEES

SECTION 1: PLURALITY OF OBLIGORS

ARTICLE 11.1.1
(Definitions)

When several obligors are bound by the same obligation towards an obligee:

(a) the obligations are joint and several when each obligor is bound for the whole obligation;

(b) the obligations are separate when each obligor is bound only for its share.

COMMENT

This Chapter deals with situations where an obligation binds several obligors or gives rights to several obligees.

Section 1 concerns the plurality of obligors.

1. Several obligors

There are frequent cases when an obligation binds several obligors.

Illustrations

1.   Companies A, B and C decide to join efforts to penetrate a new market abroad. They need financing and they obtain a loan together from bank X. A, B and C are co-obligors of the obligation to reimburse the loan.

2.   Contractors A and B are awarded a contract for the construction of a bridge based on a submission they have filed together. A and B are co-obligors of the obligation to build the bridge.

第十一章

多个债务人与多个债权人

第一节　多个债务人

第11.1.1条

（定义）

当多个债务人对某个债权人承担同一债务时：

（a）如每一个债务人对全部债务均负有清偿义务，则该债务为连带债务；

（b）如每一个债务人仅对其份额内债务负有清偿义务，则该债务为可分债务。

注释：

本章规则处理的是一项债务约束多个债务人或者一项债务赋予多个债权人权利之情况。

第一节规范的是多个债务人之情况。

1. 多个债务人

一项债务约束多个债务人是一种普遍存在的情况。

示例：

1. A、B 和 C 三家公司决定共同努力打入国外一个新市场，它们需要融资并因此一同向 X 银行贷款。A、B 和 C 是偿还该笔贷款的共同债务人。

2. 承包商 A 和 B 凭借他们共同提交的申请文件，得到一份建设一座桥梁的合同。A 和 B 是履行建设这座桥梁的共同债务人。

> 3. A large industrial plant has to be insured against fire and other hazards. The risk is too large for the capacity of any single insurer. Several insurers co-insure the risk. These insurers are co-obligors of the obligation to cover the risk.

> 4. Bank X grants a loan to company A but requires a guarantee. Parent company B agrees to bind itself together with A for the reimbursement of the loan. A and B are co-obligors of the obligation to reimburse the loan.

2. The same obligation

This Section only applies if the different obligors are bound by the same obligation.

It also frequently happens that several obligors are involved in the same operation, but with distinct obligations. They are not co-obligors under the Articles of this Section.

Illustration

> 5. A new aeroplane is being built. Many sub-contractors are involved in the various elements. For instance, sub-contractor A is in charge of profiling the wings and sub-contractor B of studying the electronic equipment. Their respective obligations are different. They are not "co-obligors".

The "same obligation" usually, but not necessarily, arises from a single contract. In Illustrations 1 and 2, there will normally be a single loan contract, or a single construction contract binding the different obligors. However, in the case of co-insurance (Illustration 3), it is frequent that each insurer, even though undertaking to cover the same risk, has its own distinct contract with the insured. The guarantee offered in Illustration 4 will often be granted in a distinct contract. Other examples of obligations undertaken by a different contract are cases in which obligations are transferred by agreement (see Article 9.2.1 *et seq.*).

However, the obligations concerned must be contractual, irrespective of whether they arise from a single contract or out of several contracts. Tortious obligations of multiple tortfeasors are not governed by this Chapter, since the Principles govern international commercial contracts. Contractual damage claims may fall under this Chapter.

3. 一座大型工业工厂必须针对火险和其他风险投保。该笔风险金额巨大，超出任何一个保险人的个人承保能力。几家保险人共同承保这笔风险。这些保险人是承保该风险的共同债务人。

4. X 银行向 A 公司发放一笔贷款，但要求一位保证人提供担保。母公司 B 同意与 A 共同承担还贷义务。A 和 B 是履行还贷义务的共同债务人。

2. 同一债务

本节仅适用于不同债务人受同一笔债务约束的情况。

实践中还经常出现几个债务人同时参与一项业务之中，但承担不同债务的情况。这时他们不属于本节调整的共同债务人。

示例：

5. 在一架新型飞机的制造中，多家分包商参与不同组成部分的制造工作。例如，分包商 A 负责机翼，分包商 B 负责研究电子设备。他们由于各自承担的债务不同，因此不属于"共同债务人"。

"同一债务"通常但不必然产生自同一合同。在示例 1 和示例 2 中，通常只有一份贷款合同或者一份建筑合同，约束不同的债务人。然而，在共同承保的情况下（示例 3），通常每一家保险人都与被保险人签订一份单独的合同，尽管他们承保同一项风险。示例 4 中的保证也往往通过一项单独合同提供。通过单独合同来承担义务，常见的例子还有协议转让债务的情况（参见第 9.2.1 条及其以下相关条款）。

但是，涉及的债务必须是基于合同之债，无论它们产生自同一份合同还是几份合同。多个侵权人导致的侵权之债不属于本章的管辖范围，因为通则管辖的是国际商事合同。合同损害赔偿请求权属本章调整之范围。

3. Two main types of obligation

Article 11.1.1 defines the two main types of obligation which exist in practice when several obligors are bound by the same obligation towards an obligee.

The first is where each obligor is bound for the whole obligation, which means that the obligee may require performance from any one of them (see Article 11.1.3), subject to contributory claims between the obligors at a later stage (see Article 11.1.10).

The second is where each obligor is bound only for its share, which entitles the obligee to claim only that much from each of the obligors.

In the former situation, which is the default rule (see Article 11.1.2), obligations are called "joint and several". In the latter situation, obligations are called "separate".

Whether co-obligors are jointly and severally, or separately bound is determined in accordance with Article 11.1.2 (see Illustrations 1 to 4).

4. Other possible situations

The two main types of obligation illustrated above are the most common, but this Section does not intend to cover all possible arrangements.

Other situations which can occur are those of so-called "joint" or "communal" obligations, in which the obligors are bound to render performance together and the obligee may claim performance only from all of them together. A typical example is that of a group of musicians having undertaken to perform a string quartet. Situations of this type are of less practical importance.

ARTICLE 11.1.2

(Presumption of joint and several obligations)

> **When several obligors are bound by the same obligation towards an obligee, they are presumed to be jointly and severally bound, unless the circumstances indicate otherwise.**

3. 债务的两个主要类型

第 11.1.1 条定义了在几个债务人就同一债务向同一债权人承担清偿义务时，实践中存在的两个主要债务类型。

第一种是每一债务人就全部债务承担责任，即指债权人可以向任何一位债务人请求清偿全部债务（第 11.1.3 条），但要以之后债务人相互之间可以提起分担请求为条件（第 11.1.10 条）。

第二种是每一债务人仅就自己的债务份额承担清偿义务，即指债权人只能向每一债务人请求其份额之内的债务。

前一种情况是默认规则（第 11.1.2 条），称为"连带"债务。后一种情况称为"可分"债务。

共同债务人承担的是连带债务，还是可分债务，应根据第 11.1.2 条确定（参见示例 1 至 4）。

4. 其他可能的情况

上文列举的两大主要债务类型是最常见的类型，但本节无意涵盖所有可能的安排。

可能出现的其他情况是所谓的"共同"或"共有"之债务，指债务人有义务共同进行清偿债务，而且债权人也只能同时向所有债务人请求清偿债务。典型的例子是一组音乐家承诺演出一场弦乐四重奏。这些类型的情况实践意义较小。

第 11.1.2 条

（推定连带债务）

多个债务人对同一债权人承担同一债务的，推定该多个债务人承担连带清偿义务，除非情况有相反的表示。

COMMENT

1. Default rule

In commercial practice the normal case is that several obligors that have undertaken the same obligation are jointly and severally bound towards the obligee. This justifies the default rule expressed in Article 11.1.2.

Illustration

> 1.   Companies A, B and C have together obtained a loan from bank X (as in Illustration 1 under Article 11.1.1). The loan contract fails to indicate how each of the parties is bound. They are presumed to be joint and several obligors, i.e. towards the bank each of them is bound for the whole amount of the loan.

2. Circumstances indicating otherwise

The presumption of joint and several obligations is rebutted when the circumstances indicate otherwise. This will often be the result of an explicit contractual provision to the contrary.

Illustration

> 2.   Insurers A, B and C have agreed to co-insure an industrial plant (as in Illustration 3 under Article 11.1.1). The scheme provides that each co-insurer is only bound for a percentage of the risk.

Other circumstances can also discard the presumption that plural obligors are jointly and severally bound.

Illustration

> 3.   The facts are the same as in Illustration 2, but insurers A, B and C have omitted to stipulate that they are not jointly and severally bound. However, the very purpose of co-insurance is to cover large risks without putting any insurer beyond the limits of its own capacity. This may be considered as a circumstance indicating that A, B and C are only bound for their respective shares.

3. Suretyship and joint and several obligations

A different situation is that of suretyship, an accessory agreement by which a person binds itself for another already bound, in case the main obligor defaults. The surety is not bound as a principal, but will only have to perform if the main obligor fails to do so. Principal and surety are bound separately – and in a successive order.

注释：

1. 默认规则

商业实践中，正常的情况是承担同一项债务的多个债务人对债权人承担连带债务。正因为如此，第 11.1.2 条规定了连带债务的默认规则。

示例：

> 1. A、B 和 C 三家公司从 X 银行取得一笔贷款（如第 11.1.1 条示例 1 所述情况）。贷款合同并未规定每个公司应如何承担责任。他们被推定为连带债务人，即每一债务人应向银行承担偿还全部贷款的义务。

2. 情况有相反表示

如果情况有相反表示，连带债务的推定将被推翻。常见的情况是合同有明确的相反规定。

示例：

> 2. A、B 和 C 三家保险人约定承保一座工业工厂（如第 11.1.1 条示例 2 所述情况）。承保计划规定每一共同保险人仅对风险的一定百分比承担责任。

其他情况也可构成放弃多个债务人承担连带债务责任的推定。

示例：

> 3. 事实同示例 2，但 A、B 和 C 三家保险人因疏忽未规定他们不承担连带债务之责任。然而，共同承保巨额风险的目的正是为了避免每一保险人超出自己的承保能力。这可被认为 A、B 和 C 三家保险公司仅对各自份额内承担责任的情况。

3. 保证协议和连带债务

保证协议指另外一种情况，它是一项附属协议，约定在主债务人违约时，某人为已受约束的主债务人而自己代为承担清偿之责任。保证人不是作为主债务人承担清偿义务，而是仅在主债务人不履行时才承担责任。主债务人和保证人分别承担清偿义务，并按先后顺序承担。

Illustration

> 4. Company A wants to borrow EUR 1,000,000 from bank X. The loan is granted on the condition that parent company B will act as surety for reimbursement of the loan. A is X's main obligor. B will be required to pay only if and when A defaults.

It may happen that the technique of joint and several obligations is used as a mechanism by which the economic benefit of suretyship may be obtained. The obligee requests the company willing to guarantee the initial obligor's obligation to intervene next to the latter as a joint and several obligor, instead of entering into a separate agreement of suretyship. The obligee's advantage is that in such a case, it can require payment directly from the intervening company. This does not necessarily deprive the intervening company of the special rights provided to a surety under the law of suretyship.

Illustration

> 5. The facts are the same as in Illustration 4, but X requires B to bind itself as a joint and several obligor, next to A, for reimbursement of the loan. X may then require reimbursement directly from B as well as from A.

This particular use of the technique of joint and several obligations has some specific consequences: see Comment 3 to Article 11.1.9, concerning apportionment among joint and several obligors. The law of suretyship may, of course, provide additional consequences.

ARTICLE 11.1.3
(Obligee's rights against joint and several obligors)

When obligors are jointly and severally bound, the obligee may require performance from any one of them, until full performance has been received.

示例：

　　4. A 公司计划向 X 银行借款 100 万欧元。银行贷款发放的条件是 A 的母公司 B 须为偿还贷款作保证人。此时 A 是 X 的主债务人，B 仅在 A 违约时，才负清偿责任。

连带债务的方式有时会作为一种机制加以运用，以从中取得保证的经济利益。债权人要求愿意为主债务人的债务提供保证的公司，仅次于主债务人作为连带债务人介入，而无须订立一项单独的保证协议。这种情况对债权人的好处是，它可以直接要求该介入公司履行清偿义务。当然，这并不必然剥夺介入公司在担保法项下的保证人所具有的特殊权利。

示例：

　　5. 事实同示例 4，但 X 要求 B 就贷款的偿还作为 A 之后的连带债务人承担责任。此时，X 可以直接要求 B，以及 A 偿还贷款。

这种使用连带债务的方式会产生一些特定后果：参见第 11.1.9 条注释 3 有关连带债务人之间责任分配的规定。当然担保法还可能规定其他后果。

第 11.1.3 条

（债权人对连带债务人之权利）

**　　多个债务人承担连带清偿义务的，债权人可要求其中任何一个债务人清偿，直至取得全部清偿。**

COMMENT

The main effect of joint and several obligations from the obligors' point of view has already been stated in the definition given in Article 11.1.1, namely that each obligor is bound for the whole obligation.

Article 11.1.3 states the main effect for the obligee: it may require performance from each obligor, until full performance has been received.

Illustrations

> 1. Farmers A, B and C have bought a tractor together, for shared use in their respective fields. They are jointly and severally bound to pay the price of USD 45,000. Seller X may require payment of the whole sum from A, B or C. X's claim is extinguished when it has received full performance, from one or more of its obligors.
>
> 2. The facts are the same as in Illustration 1. A pays only USD 30,000 (in spite of being bound for USD 45,000). X, while still retaining a claim against A for the unpaid part, may claim that amount of USD 15,000 from B or C. If X, at this stage, only receives USD 10,000 from B (though B was still bound for USD 15,000), X may still claim USD 5,000 from C, as well as from A and B.

ARTICLE 11.1.4
(Availability of defences and rights of set-off)

A joint and several obligor against whom a claim is made by the obligee may assert all the defences and rights of set-off that are personal to it or that are common to all the co-obligors, but may not assert defences or rights of set-off that are personal to one or several of the other co-obligors.

COMMENT

This Article deals with the possibilities for a joint and several obligor to assert different defences and rights of set-off. It distinguishes between, on one side, defences and rights of set-off that are personal to one of the obligors or common to all of them, and, on the other side, defences and rights of set-off which are personal to one or several of the other co-obligors.

注释：

连带债务对于债务人的主要效果，已由第 11.1.1 条的定义作出了规定，即每一债务人对全部债务要承担清偿义务。

第 11.1.3 条则规定了对债权人的主要效果，即债权人可向每一个债务人要求清偿，直至取得全部清偿。

示例：

1. A、B 和 C 三个农场共同购买一辆拖拉机，用于各自田地的耕作。三家对于 4.5 万美元的拖拉机价款负连带清偿义务。卖方 X 可以要求 A、B 或者 C 支付全部价款。但当 X 从其中一家或多家债务人获得全部清偿后，则其债权消灭。

2. 事实同示例 1，A 只支付了 3 万美元（尽管有义务支付 4.5 万美元）。尽管 X 仍然对 A 就剩余价款享有请求权，但可以向 B 或者 C 请求支付 1.5 万美元。如果此时 X 仅从 B 处得到 1 万美元（尽管 B 此时有义务支付 1.5 万美元），X 仍然可以向 C，以及 A 和 B 请求支付 5000 美元。

第 11.1.4 条

（存在的抗辩权与抵销权）

一个连带债务人当被债权人要求清偿时，可以主张属于其自身的抗辩权和抵销权，或者属于所有共同债务人共有的抗辩权和抵销权，但不得主张那些仅属于其他共同债务人中一个或几个债务人自身的抗辩权或抵销权。

注释：

本条规范的情况是连带债务人可以主张不同抗辩权和抵销权的可能性。本条区分两种情况：一种是一个债务人自有的或者所有债务人共有的抗辩权和抵销权；另一种是其他共同债务人中一个或几个共同债务人自有的抗辩权和抵销权。

Illustrations

1.   Together, companies A, B and C have purchased machinery from manufacturer X, to be used in their respective plants for a common project. Part of the purchase price has to be paid at a future date, the outstanding amount being jointly and severally due. A has obtained a separate undertaking from X that the machinery would meet a certain performance level. If X requires A to pay the outstanding amount of the price, A may assert the fact that the machinery does not meet the guaranteed level of performance. On the other hand, if X claims payment from B and C, the latter may not assert that the level of performance is insufficient, since the defence is personal to A.

2.   Companies A and B jointly and severally have undertaken to purchase a certain quantity of steel from seller X. Government authorities in the buyers' country declare an embargo on all trade with the seller's country, which renders performance of the contract unlawful. This is a common defence which each of the co-obligors may assert against X.

3.   Bank X has lent EUR 2,000,000 to joint and several obligors A and B. As a result of the selling of shares belonging to A on the stock market, X becomes A's obligor for an amount of EUR 500,000. A may exercise its right of set-off against X, with the effects provided for in Article 11.1.5. On the contrary, B may not assert this right, which is personal to A.

ARTICLE 11.1.5

(Effect of performance or set-off)

Performance or set-off by a joint and several obligor or set-off by the obligee against one joint and several obligor discharges the other obligors in relation to the obligee to the extent of the performance or set-off.

COMMENT

1. Performance by a joint and several obligor

If one of the co-obligors has already fully or partially performed the obligation, the other obligors may successfully assert this as a defence should the obligee still attempt to claim performance from the other co-obligors.

示例：

1. A、B 和 C 三家公司向生产商 X 购买一套机器，为一个共同项目而用于各自工厂。在未来某个日期必须支付部分购买价款。该部分欠款属连带债务。A 从 X 获得一项单独保证，即 X 保证该机器要满足某些特定功能。如果 X 要求 A 支付该笔剩余价款，A 可以主张该机器未满足保证的功能而拒付。但是如果 X 请求 B 和 C 支付该笔欠款，后两者不得主张机器功能不达标，因为该抗辩是专属于 A 的抗辩。

2. A 公司和 B 公司连带承诺向卖方 X 购买一定数量的钢材。买方所在国的政府宣布对与卖方所在国之间的所有贸易实施禁运，禁运导致合同的履行为非法。这是每一共同债务人均可向 X 主张的共有抗辩。

3. X 银行向连带债务人 A 和 B 贷款 200 万欧元。X 由于在股市出售了 A 拥有的股票，收入 50 万欧元，成为欠 A50 万欧元的债务人。A 可以向 X 主张抵销权，并取得第 11.1.5 条规定的各项效果。但 B 不得主张该抵销权，因为该抵销权是 A 自有的。

第 11.1.5 条

（清偿或抵销之效力）

一个连带债务人的清偿或抵销，或者债权人对一个连带债务人进行了抵销，则应以该清偿或抵销为限，解除其他债务人对该债权人所负的清偿义务。

注释：

1. 一个连带债务人的清偿

一个连带债务人履行了部分或全部清偿债务之后，若债权人仍然试图要求其他共同债务人清偿，则其他债务人可以成功地以此作为抗辩。

Illustrations

> 1. Companies A, B and C are jointly bound to reimburse a loan of EUR 100,000. Upon lender X's request, A fully reimburses the loan. B and C can avail themselves of A's performance if X still claims reimbursement of the loan from them.
>
> 2. The facts are the same as in Illustration 1, but A only reimburses EUR 30,000. B and C are still jointly and severally bound for EUR 70,000 (see Article 11.1.3), but they may invoke A's partial payment if X still claims the full amount from them.

2. Set-off

The rule laid down in this Article with respect to performance by one of the co-obligors also applies, with appropriate adaptations, in the case of set-off between the obligee and one of the obligors. Rights of set-off have already been mentioned in Article 11.1.4, where the issue is to determine which of the co-obligors could assert rights of set-off. Article 11.1.5 deals with the subsequent issue of the effects of set-off, once it has been exercised. On the rules governing set-off itself, see Articles 8.1 to 8.5.

Illustration

> 3. The facts are the same as in the preceding illustrations: A, B and C are jointly bound to reimburse a loan of EUR 100,000 to X. However, on the basis of a different transaction A has become X's obligee for an amount of EUR 60,000. If A exercises its right of set-off against X by serving appropriate notice (as provided in Article 8.3), it will have the same effect as partial performance by A of its joint and several obligation, thus discharging B and C for the corresponding amount.

The same rule applies if the right of set-off has been exercised by the obligee against one of the joint and several obligors.

Illustration

> 4. The facts are the same as in Illustration 3, but it is X who takes the initiative to give the set-off notice to A. The effects are identical. A is discharged for the amount of set-off (EUR 60,000), and the other co-obligors B and C are also discharged for the same amount.

示例：

> 1. A、B 和 C 三家公司共同承担偿还 10 万欧元贷款的义务。经放贷人 X 请求，A 全部偿还了贷款。如果 X 还向 B 和 C 请求偿还贷款，B 和 C 可以成功地援引 A 的清偿作为抗辩。

> 2. 事实同示例 1，但 A 只偿还了 3 万欧元。B 和 C 仍负有连带清偿 7 万欧元的义务（参见第 11.1.3 条），但如果 A 仍然请求他们偿还全部贷款，B 和 C 可以援引 A 的部分清偿作为抗辩。

2. 抵销

本条规定的有关一个共同债务人清偿的规则，经适当调整，也适用于债权人与其中一个债务人进行抵销的情况。第 11.1.4 条已提及抵销权，处理的是共同债务人中的哪一个人可以主张抵销权。第 11.1.5 条规范的是一旦行使了抵销权，抵销效果的后续问题。有关调整抵销权的规则，参见第 8.1 条至第 8.5 条。

示例：

> 3. 事实同示例 1 和 2，A、B 和 C 共同承担向 X 负归还 10 万欧元贷款的义务。但是，基于另外一笔交易，A 是 X 的债权人，债权金额为 6 万欧元。如果 A（依第 8.3 条规定）发出了适当的通知，对 X 行使了抵销权，则该抵销与 A 部分清偿连带债务具有同样的效果，即解除了 B 和 C 相应金额的清偿义务。

同样的规则也适用于债权人针对某一共同债务人行使抵销权的情况。

示例：

> 4. 事实同示例 3，但此处是由 X 向 A 发出抵销通知。效果相同。A 被解除了抵销金额（6 万欧元）的义务，其他共同债务人 B 和 C 也被解除了清偿该等金额的义务。

ARTICLE 11.1.6
(Effect of release or settlement)

(1) Release of one joint and several obligor, or settlement with one joint and several obligor, discharges all the other obligors for the share of the released or settling obligor, unless the circumstances indicate otherwise.

(2) When the other obligors are discharged for the share of the released obligor, they no longer have a contributory claim against the released obligor under Article 11.1.10.

COMMENT

1. Release of one joint and several obligor

If the obligee releases one of its joint and several obligors with no further qualifications, Article 11.1.6 provides as the default rule that the release affects only the share of the released obligor, as determined by Article 11.1.9. As a consequence, the other obligors are discharged for the share of the released obligor only, and remain bound for the difference.

Illustration

1.   Bank X lends EUR 300,000 to companies A, B and C. The obligors are jointly and severally bound; their respective contributory shares are equal, i.e. EUR 100,000 each. X releases A, with no further qualification. The consequence for B and C is that they are released for the amount of A's share of EUR 100,000. B and C remain jointly and severally bound towards X for an amount of EUR 200,000.

2. Settlement with one joint and several obligor

Sometimes the obligee receives payment from one of the co-obligors of an amount less than that obligor's share as determined by Article 1.9, as part of a separate settlement with that obligor, pursuant to which the payment received is accepted as discharging all of the settling obligor's share. Consequently, the other obligors' joint and several obligations are reduced not only by the amount paid, but by the full initial amount of the settling obligor's share.

第11.1.6条

（免除或和解之效力）

（1）对一个连带债务人的债务免除，或与一个连带债务人达成和解，则解除所有其他债务人对该被免除或和解之债务人的债务份额，除非情况有相反的表示。

（2）如果解除了其他债务人对某个债务人的被免除了的债务份额，则该其他债务人对该被免除了债务的债务人不再享有第11.1.10条规定的分担请求权。

注释：

1. 免除一个连带债务人的债务

如果债权人不做任何限制地免除了多个连带债务人中一个债务人的债务，则第11.1.6条作为默认规则，规定了该免除仅影响到依第11.1.9条确定的被免除之债务人的债务份额。其结果是，其他债务人仅就该债务人被免除了的债务份额，被解除债务，对差额部分要继续承担清偿义务。

示例：

1. X银行向A、B和C三家公司贷款30万欧元。三个债务人负连带清偿义务，他们各自分担的份额相等，即10万欧元。X不做任何限制地解除了A的清偿义务。该行为对于B和C的后果是，他们被免除了清偿A承担的10万欧元份额的义务。但B和C要继续就剩余20万欧元向X承担连带清偿义务。

2. 与一个连带债务人达成和解

有时债权人以收到某一债务人支付一定金额为条件与债务人达成单独部分和解，但金额少于依第11.1.9条①确定的该人债务份额，并且根据和解方案该支付作为解除和解之债务人全部债务份额的条件被接受。其结果是，其他债务人承担的连带清偿义务减少的金额不是实际支付的金额，而是达成和解之债务人债务份额的原始金额。

---

① 译者注：英文版为"1.9"，经核对条文应为"11.1.9"，已与本章报告员比利时Marcel Fontaine教授确认。

Illustration

> 2. Investors A, B and C are jointly and severally bound to pay seller X USD 3,000,000 for an acquisition of shares. A and X come to a settlement of different disputes between themselves. One of the terms of the settlement is that A will be discharged of its obligations towards X under the share purchase agreement by paying an amount of USD 600,000, i.e. USD 400,000 less than A's contributory share towards the other co-obligors. Under these circumstances, X may not claim the whole remaining USD 2,400,000 against B and C. Their joint and several obligations are reduced by the full initial amount of A's share, i.e. USD 1,000,000. They are still jointly and severally bound for USD 2,000,000 only.

3. Circumstances indicating otherwise

There can be circumstances where the other obligors are discharged for another amount other than that of the released or settling obligor's share.

For instance, the obligee may release one of its obligors only for part of the latter's share, as determined by Article 11.1.9. The other obligors will be discharged only for the amount of that released part. All obligors will remain jointly and severally bound for the reduced total amount.

Illustration

> 3. The facts are the same as in Illustration 1, except that X releases A for an amount of EUR 60,000. The consequence for B and C is that they are released for the same amount of EUR 60,000. A, B and C remain jointly and severally bound towards X for an amount of EUR 240,000.

On the other hand, the obligee may also intend to fully release all of its obligors. If the obligee expresses its intention so to do, Article 11.1.6 does not apply.

As to settlement, it will frequently not be separate, but concern all joint and several obligors. The consequences for the different obligors' obligations will in these cases be determined by the terms of the settlement agreed by all parties, and the contributory claims will be adjusted accordingly.

4. No more contributory claim

If the obligee has released one of the co-obligors, or settled with it, and the other co-obligors have been discharged of the released obligor's share, the other co-obligors have no more contributory claim against the released obligor.

示例：

> 2. 投资者 A、B 和 C 因购买股票而向卖方 X 承担偿付 300 万美元的连带清偿义务。A 和 X 之间因其他争议达成和解，和解条件规定 A 通过支付 60 万美元（比 A 与其他共同债务人承担的分担份额少 40 万美元）被解除其在股份购买协议项下对 X 承担的债务。在此种情况下，X 不得向 B 和 C 请求支付全部剩余的 240 万美元。B 和 C 的连带债务应按 A 的全部原始金额 100 万美元得以减少，仅继续对 200 万美元承担连带清偿义务。

3. 情况另有其他表示

在有些情况下，其他债务人被解除的是另外一笔金额，而不是被免除债务或达成和解之债务人的债务份额。

例如，债权人仅解除了依第 11.1.9 条决定的其中一个债务人之债务的部分份额。此时，其他债务人仅被解除了该解除金额部分的债务。所有债务人应继续对减少后的总金额承担连带清偿义务。

示例：

> 3. 事实同示例 1，但 X 对 A 免除了 6 万欧元的债务。此举对于 B 和 C 的效果是他们被免除了相同的 6 万欧元的债务。A、B 和 C 继续对 X 应承担清偿 24 万欧元的连带债务。

另一方面，债权人也可能有意全部免除所有债务人的债务。如果债权人明示表达了这样做的意图，则不适用第 11.1.6 条的规定。

关于和解，通常不是分开和解，而是涉及与所有连带债务人进行和解。在这种情况下，对于不同债务人债务的效果由所有当事人同意的和解条款决定，分担请求权也将因此作相应调整。

4. 不再享有分担请求权

如果债权人免除了共同债务人中一个债务人的债务，或者与之达成和解，并且其他共同债务人被解除了清偿被免除之债务人的债务份额，则其他共同债务人对该被免除之债务人不再享有分担请求权。

Illustrations

4.   The facts are the same as in Illustration 1: A is released by X, while B and C remain jointly and severally bound for an amount of EUR 200,000. If B pays X EUR 200,000, B has a contributory claim of EUR 100,000 against C, but no claim against A.

5.   The facts are the same as in Illustration 2: B and C continue to be jointly and severally bound for an amount of USD 2,000,000. If B pays USD 2,000,000 to X, B has a contributory claim of USD 1,000,000 against C; but B has no claim against A, even though A has paid X only USD 600,000 as agreed in their separate settlement.

ARTICLE 11.1.7
*(Effect of expiration or suspension
of limitation period)*

(1) Expiration of the limitation period of the obligee's rights against one joint and several obligor does not affect:

(a) the obligations to the obligee of the other joint and several obligors; or

(b) the rights of recourse between the joint and several obligors under Article 11.1.10.

(2) If the obligee initiates proceedings under Articles 10.5, 10.6 or 10.7 against one joint and several obligor, the running of the limitation period is also suspended against the other joint and several obligors.

COMMENT

1. Expiration of the limitation period against one obligor

The obligee's rights against one (or several) of the joint and several obligors may become time-barred. This does not prevent the obligee from exercising its claim against the other co-obligors whose obligations are not yet affected by the expiration of a period of limitation.

示例：

　　4. 事实同示例1，A 被 X 免除了债务，B 和 C 继续对 20 万欧元承担连带清偿义务。如果 B 向 X 清偿了 20 万欧元，B 对 C 则享有 10 万欧元的分担请求权，但对 A 不享有该等请求权。

　　5. 事实同示例2，B 和 C 继续对 200 万美元承担连带清偿义务。如果 B 向 X 清偿 200 万美元，B 对 C 则享有 100 万美元的分担请求权，但 B 对 A 不享有该等请求权，尽管根据 A 和 X 之间的另外和解协议，A 只向 X 支付了 60 万美元。

第 11.1.7 条

（时效期间届满或中止的后果）

　　（1）债权人对一个连带债务人所享权利的时效届满，并不影响：

　　（a）其他连带债务人对该债权人所承担的债务；或者

　　（b）第 11.1.10 条规定的连带债务人之间的追索权。

　　（2）如果债权人对一个连带债务人启动第 10.5 条、第 10.6 条或第 10.7 条项下的程序，则时效期间对其他连带债务人也中止计算。

注释：

1. 针对一个债务人时效期间的届满

　　如果债权人针对一个（或几个）连带债务人享有的权利已丧失时效，但对其他连带债务人的债务却未受时效届满的影响，此时并不阻止债权人针对这些其他连带债务人行使请求权。

Illustration

> 1.   Companies A and B are jointly and severally bound to pay consultant X fees of USD 500,000 on 1 January. A and B refuse to pay, arguing that the services rendered by X were unsatisfactory. The parties enter into lengthy discussions. Two years later, in the course of the year B comes to acknowledge X's rights, but A continues to challenge them. In March the following year X finally sues both clients for payment. More than three years after the date when X's fees were due (see Article 10.2), X's claim against A is time-barred. The situation is different for B, who acknowledged the right of the obligee before the expiration of the limitation period, thus triggering the running of a new period (see Article 10.4). X can still claim USD 500,000 from B.

Co-obligors who have paid the obligee under such circumstances can exercise their rights of recourse in accordance with Article 11.1.10, even against the co-obligor who could avail itself of the expiration of a period of limitation against the obligee, in accordance with Article 10.9. These rights of recourse are subject to their own limitation periods.

Illustration

> 2.   In the case described in Illustration 1, B, after paying USD 500,000 to X, can claim contribution from A under Article 11.1.10.

2. Suspension of the limitation period against one obligor

Initiation by the obligee of legal or arbitral proceedings or an ADR procedure against one of the joint and several obligors suspends the running of the limitation period against that obligor under Articles 10.5, 10.6 or 10.7. Article 11.1.7(2) extends the effect of the suspension to the other co-obligors.

Illustration

> 3.   Co-buyers A and B are jointly and severally bound to pay seller X a sum of GBP 800,000, which was due on 31 December. In spite of several reminders, A and B are still in default close to the end of the three-year limitation period. On 20 December three years later X initiates legal proceedings against A. The limitation period is suspended not only against A, but also against B.

示例：

　　1. A 公司和 B 公司对 X 顾问连带承担支付 50 万美元咨询费的义务，于 1 月 1 日到期。A 和 B 拒绝付款，理由是 X 提供的服务不令人满意。双方当事人进行了长时间的谈判。两年后，在第三年期间 B 承认了 X 的权利，但 A 继续质疑该权利。在下一年的 3 月 X 最终向两个客户提起了支付服务费的诉讼。由于此时离 X 的咨询费到期日（参见第 10.2 条）已超过 3 年时间，X 针对 A 的请求权已丧失时效。但 B 的情况不同，因为它在时效期间届满前承认了债权人的权利，从而导致一个新的时效期间的起算（参见第 10.4 条）。X 仍能向 B 请求 50 万美元。

在该等情况下，向债权人进行了清偿的共同债务人，可以根据第 11.1.10 条的规定行使追索权，甚至可以针对依据第 10.9 条主张时效期间届满来对抗债权人的共同债务人，行使该权利。这些追索权受其自身时效期间的约束。

示例：

　　2. 在示例 1 描述的案件中，B 向 X 支付了 50 万美元之后，可以根据第 11.1.10 条之规定，向 A 请求分担份额。

2. 针对一个债务人的时效期间中止

债权人针对一个连带债务人启动法律或仲裁程序，或者替代争端解决程序，根据第 10.5 条、第 10.6 条或第 10.7 条之规定，针对该债务人的时效期间计算中止。第 11.1.7 条第(2)款将该中止效力延伸适用于其他共同债务人。

示例：

　　3. 共同购买方 A 和 B 对卖方 X 连带承担支付 80 万英镑的责任，该债务于 12 月 31 日到期。虽经多次提醒，在三年时效期间接近届满时 A 和 B 仍未支付。三年后的 12 月 20 日 X 对 A 启动法律程序。时效期间不仅针对 A 中止，对 B 也同时中止。

The rule in Article 11.1.7(2), which creates effects towards all co-obligors, adopts an approach different from that in the rule in Article 11.1.7(1), which provides for individual effects. Indeed, different effects are concerned: those of expiration of the limitation period and those of initiating legal proceedings. The solution adopted in paragraph (2) saves the expenses involved in initiating proceedings against all obligors. The obligee should however keep in mind the rule in Article 11.1.8 concerning effect of judgments.

ARTICLE 11.1.8

(Effect of judgment)

(1) A decision by a court as to the liability to the obligee of one joint and several obligor does not affect:

(a) the obligations to the obligee of the other joint and several obligors; or

(b) the rights of recourse between the joint and several obligors under Article 11.1.10.

(2) However, the other joint and several obligors may rely on such a decision, except if it was based on grounds personal to the obligor concerned. In such a case, the rights of recourse between the joint and several obligors under Article 11.1.10 are affected accordingly.

COMMENT

1. No effect on the other obligors' obligations

If the obligee commences judicial or arbitral proceedings against only one (or some) of the joint and several obligors, any decision by the court will not in principle affect the obligations of the co-obligors who were not called to court. Whatever the decision, the other obligors will still be bound in the original terms.

Illustrations

1. Bank C has loaned EUR 1,000,000 to joint and several borrowers A and B. A is sued for reimbursement by X and the court orders A to pay X EUR 1,000,000. This decision in itself

第11.1.7条第(1)款是对个别效果做出了规定，第11.1.7条第(2)款则采取了不同的方法，是对所有共同债务人效果做出了规定。事实上，两款规定涉及的是不同的效果：时效期间届满的效果，和启动法律程序的效果。第(2)款采用的解决方案节省了因为需要对所有债务人提起诉讼而发生的费用。但债权人应铭记有关判决效力的第11.1.8条的规则。

第11.1.8条

（判决之效力）

（1） 法院就一个连带债务人对债权人之责任所做出的判决，不影响：

（a） 其他连带债务人对该债权人所承担的债务；或者

（b） 依据第11.1.10条规定的连带债务人之间的追索权。

（2） 但是，除非该判决是基于相关债务人自身之原因做出，否则其他连带债务人可以依赖该判决。在此情况下，第11.1.10条规定的连带债务人之间的追索权将据此受到影响。

注释：

1. 对其他债务人之债务不发生效力

如果债权人仅针对连带债务人中一个(或几个)启动法律或仲裁程序，法庭做出的任何决定原则上均不影响未到庭的共同债务人之债务。无论做出何种决定，其他债务人仍将继续按原始条件承担清偿义务。

示例：

1. X银行向连带借款人A和B发放100万欧元贷款①。X起诉A偿还贷款，法院命令A向X支付100万欧元。该判决

---

① 译者注：英文版本是"C银行"，实际应为"X银行"，属原文笔误，故调整，已与本章报告员比利时的Marcel Fontaine教授确认。

does not affect B's obligation; B is still bound to pay EUR 1,000,000 to X. Naturally, if the judgment is enforced and A pays X EUR 1,000,000, B' obligation towards X will be extinguished under Article 11.1.5 and B will be subject to A's contributory recourse under Article 11.1.10.

2.   Company A and company B have jointly and severally undertaken to provide transportation for company X's deliveries to its clients. Performance is defective and X sues A. The court orders A to pay damages. B is not bound by that finding of defective performance, and its obligations are not increased by the amount of the damages.

2. No effect on the rights of recourse

A court decision rendered against one joint and several obligor furthermore has no effect on the rights of recourse between the joint and several obligors under Article 11.1.10.

Illustration

3.   The facts are the same as in Illustration 2. A pays X the damages ordered by the court. A may not claim to recover part of the damages from B.

3. Right of the other joint and several obligors to avail themselves of the decision

The principle stated in paragraph (1) of this Article does not have to be enforced when the other co-obligors find it in their interest to rely on the decision. For such cases, paragraph (2) grants the other joint and several obligors the right to rely on it. However, the rule does not apply when the decision was based on grounds personal to the obligor concerned.

Illustrations

4.   Art collectors A and B have joined in purchasing a painting at an auction and they are jointly and severally bound to pay the price of GBP 800,000. The price is not paid and the auction house sues A. The court accepts some of A's arguments concerning the quality of the painting, which appears to have been restored, and reduces the price to GBP 600,000. B may rely on that decision to benefit from the same reduction of its obligations towards the auction house.

5.   The facts are the same as in Illustration 4, except that A's refusal to pay the auction house is grounded on a claim that the painting is a fake. This is confirmed by an expert opinion ordered

本身并不影响 B 的债务；B 仍然对 X 承担偿还 100 万欧元的义务。当然，如果该判决已得到执行，并且 A 向 X 支付了 100 万欧元，则根据第 11.1.5 条的规定，B 对 X 承担的债务归于消灭。但 B 要受到 A 根据第 11.1.10 条的规定行使追索分担份额的约束。

　　2. A 公司和 B 公司连带承担为 X 公司向客户运送货物的义务。因存在履行瑕疵，X 起诉 A。法院命令 A 支付损害赔偿。B 不受该履行瑕疵认定的约束，其债务金额也不因该损害赔偿的金额而增加。

2. 不影响追索权

另外，法院针对一个连带债务人做出的判决，对第 11.1.10 条规定的连带债务人之间的追索权也不具任何影响。

示例：

　　3. 事实同示例 2。A 向 X 支付了法院判决的损害赔偿金。但 A 不得要求 B 部分分担该损害赔偿金。

3. 其他连带债务人有权依赖该判决

如果其他共同债务人认为依赖该判决符合自己的利益，则本条第(1)款规定的原则就不得予以实施。在这种情况下，第(2)款赋予了其他连带债务人之依赖该判决的权利。然而，如果判决是基于相关债务人自身之理由，则不适用该规则。

示例：

　　4. 艺术品收藏家 A 和 B 在一次拍卖会上共同购得一幅画作，他们负有支付 80 万英镑价款的连带债务。因他们未付价款，拍卖行起诉 A。法院接受了 A 有关画作质量问题的抗辩，即该油画被修复过，法院将油画价格下调至 60 万英镑。B 可以依赖该判决，就自己向拍卖行承担的义务，享有同样价格降低的好处。

　　5. 事实同示例 4，但 A 拒绝支付拍卖行价款的理由是该画作是赝品。该理由得到法院指定的专家证人的确认。合同

by the court. Accordingly, the contract is avoided. B may also rely on that decision to be discharged of its obligations towards the auction house.

6.   The facts are the same as in Illustration 4, except that A had separately obtained from the auction house a certificate stating that the painting had been shown at some major exhibitions. This turns out to be untrue, and a court orders the auction house to pay damages to A. B may not rely on that decision, since it is based on grounds personal to A.

4. Rights of recourse affected accordingly

If a joint and several obligor avails itself of a court decision rendered against its co-obligor, the right of recourse of the co-obligor will be affected accordingly.

Illustration

7.   The facts are the same as in Illustration 4. A's obligation towards the auction house has been reduced to GBP 600,000. If A, after having paid this amount to the auction house, initiates a contributory recourse against B, the latter may avail itself of the court decision to have its contributory share reduced accordingly.

ARTICLE 11.1.9
(Apportionment among joint and several obligors)

> **As among themselves, joint and several obligors are bound in equal shares, unless the circumstances indicate otherwise.**

COMMENT

Articles 11.1.9 to 11.1.13 of this Section deal with contributory claims. An obligor who has performed the obligation in favour of the obligee has a claim against the other joint and several obligors to recuperate their respective shares.

The first issue is to determine these respective shares. As a default rule, Article 11.1.9 states that these shares are equal.

因此被宣告无效。B 同样可以依赖该判决，解除其对拍卖行承担的义务。

> 6. 事实同示例 4，但 A 单独从拍卖行取得一份证书，证明该画作曾在某些大型展览上展出过。事实证明并非如此。法院命令拍卖行向 A 支付损害赔偿，B 不得依赖该判决，因为它是基于 A 自有的理由做出的。

4. 追索权因此受到影响

如果一个连带债务人依赖法院就另一共同债务人所做出的判决，则该共同债务人的追索权因此应受到影响。

示例：

> 7. 事实同示例 4。A 向拍卖行承担的义务金额被减少至 60 万英镑。如果 A 向拍卖行支付该金额之后，对 B 提出份额追索，则 B 可依赖法院之判决，相应减少自己的分担份额。

第 11.1.9 条

（连带债务人之责任分摊）

连带债务人之间对债务承担均等份额，除非情况有相反的表示。

注释：

本节第 11.1.9 条至第 11.1.13 条处理的是分担请求权。一个已向债权人清偿了债务的债务人，有权请求其他连带债务人补交其各自的份额。

第一个问题是确定各自的份额。作为默认规则，第 11.1.9 条规定这些份额是均等的。

Illustration

> 1.   Companies A and B have borrowed EUR 10,000,000 from
> Bank X to finance the acquisition of stock in another company. In
> principle, A's and B's shares in the final allocation will be EUR
> 5,000,000 each.

However, circumstances can indicate otherwise, i.e. that the shares
are unequal. This will often result from the contractual arrangements
between the co-obligors.

Illustration

> 2.   The facts are the same as in Illustration 1, except that A and B
> have agreed that their respective participations in the acquisition
> would be 75% and 25%. There is a presumption that these
> percentages will also govern the final allocation.

The circumstances may indicate that some obligors are ultimately to
bear the whole amount of the obligation. This is the case when a party
agrees to be bound as joint and several obligor not because of its own
interest in the operation, but to serve as guarantor for the other ("main")
obligor (see Comment 3 on Article 11.1.2).

Illustration

> 3.   Company A applies for a loan of EUR 10,000,000 from bank
> X. The loan is granted on the condition that company B intervene as
> joint and several obligor. As between the two companies, it is
> understood that B only serves as a guarantor. The circumstances
> indicate that the shares in the final allocation should be 100 % for A
> and 0 % for B.

ARTICLE 11.1.10
(Extent of contributory claim)

**A joint and several obligor who has
performed more than its share may claim the
excess from any of the other obligors to the extent
of each obligor's unperformed share.**

示例：

　　1. A 和 B 公司为融资购买另一家公司的股票，向 X 银行借款 1,000 万欧元。原则上，A 和 B 最终分摊的份额每一方分别是 500 万欧元。

然而情况可以有相反的表示，即份额可以是不均等的。这往往是共同债务人之间协议安排的结果。

示例：

　　2. 事实同示例1，但 A 和 B 约定其各自参与购买的比例分别是 75% 和 25%。据此推定该百分比将约束最终的份额比例。

情况可能表明最终某些债务人将承担全部债务。例如，一方当事人之所以同意作为连带债务人受约束，不是因为在该经营中的自身利益，而是因为要担任其他("主")债务人的担保人（参见第 11.1.2 条注释 3）。

示例：

　　3. A 公司申请向 X 银行申请贷款 1,000 万欧元。X 发放贷款的前提条件是，B 公司作为连带债务人参与交易。在 A、B 两公司之间，B 只是作为担保人。该情况表明，在最终份额分摊中 A 的比例为 100%，B 为 0%。

第 11.1.10 条

（分担请求之限度）

一个连带债务人如超出自身份额清偿了债务，则有权向其他任何债务人在其各自未清偿之份额内，请求超额清偿的部分。

COMMENT

After a joint and several obligor has paid more than its share to the obligee, it has contributory claims against the other obligors to recover the excess, on the basis of the respective shares.

Illustrations

1.   Companies A and B have borrowed EUR 10,000,000 from bank X to finance the acquisition of stock in another company. A's and B's shares are in principle equal. If A has reimbursed the full amount to X, it can claim contribution from B for the amount in excess of A's own share of 50 %, i.e. EUR 5,000,000.

2.   The facts are the same as in Illustration 1, except that A and B have agreed that their respective participations in the acquisition would be 75% and 25%. If A has ultimately to bear 75% of the reimbursement, A can only recuperate the excess, i.e. B's share of EUR 2,500,000.

3.   Company A applies for a loan of EUR 10,000,000 from bank X. The loan is granted on the condition that company B intervene as a joint and several obligor. As between the two companies, it is understood that B only serves as a guarantor. A's share is 100 %. If B has repaid the loan to X, B can claim full reimbursement from A.

The rule in Article 11.1.10 can also apply in more complex circumstances.

Illustration

4.   Investors A, B and C have joined efforts to buy an office building. The total price amounts to USD 1,000,000 but the respective agreed shares are 50%, 30% and 20%. The seller is entitled to request payment of USD 1,000,000 from any of the obligors but it can only recover USD 650,000 from A; the seller then recovers the remaining USD 350,000 from B. A has paid USD 150,000 in excess of its share of USD 500,000; B has paid USD 50,000 in excess of its share of USD 300,000. C's share, on the other hand, is totally unpaid. A and B will respectively have contributory claims of USD 150,000 and USD 50,000 against C.

Articles 11.1.6(2), 11.1.7(1)(b) and 11.1.8(b) provide for particular rules on the availability of contributory claims under the circumstances respectively governed by these provisions.

注释:

一个连带债务人超过自己的份额向债权人清偿债务之后,享有对其他债务人以其各自份额为基础,追偿超付部分的分担请求权。

示例:

1. A 公司和 B 公司为融资购买另一家公司的股票,向 X 银行借款 1,000 万欧元。A 和 B 的份额原则上是均等的。如果 A 向 X 全部偿还了贷款,A 可就超出自己 50%,即 500 万欧元份额的部分,请求 B 分担。

2. 事实同示例 1,但 A 和 B 约定参与购买的比例分别是 75% 和 25%。如果 A 最终承担还贷是 75%,A 只能就超过自己份额的部分,即 B 的 250 万欧元份额,要求 B 归还。

3. A 公司申请向 X 银行贷款 1,000 万欧元。X 发放贷款的前提条件是,B 公司作为连带债务人参与交易。此时应理解,在 A、B 两公司之间,B 只是作为担保人。A 的份额是 100%。如果 B 向 X 银行偿还了贷款,B 可要求 A 偿还全部还贷金额。

第 11.1.10 条规定的规则还可以适用于更加复杂的情况。

示例:

4. A、B 和 C 三位投资者共同购买一座写字楼。总金额为 100 万美元,但三人约定各自份额分别为 50%、30% 和 20%。卖方有权请求任何一个债务人清偿 100 万美元,但他仅从 A 处获得了 65 万美元;然后卖方从 B 处获得了剩余的 35 万美元。A 超过自己的份额 50 万美元多支付了 15 万美元;B 超过自己的份额 30 万美元多支付了 5 万美元。C 完全没有支付自己的份额。A 和 B 分别对 C 具有 15 万美元和 5 万美元的份额分担请求权。

第 11.1.6 条第(2)款、第 11.1.7 条第(1)款(b)项和第 11.1.8 条(b)项对各自管辖情况下分担请求权的运用,分别作了具体规定。

ARTICLE 11.1.11
(Rights of the obligee)

(1) A joint and several obligor to whom Article 11.1.10 applies may also exercise the rights of the obligee, including all rights securing their performance, to recover the excess from all or any of the other obligors to the extent of each obligor's unperformed share.

(2) An obligee who has not received full performance retains its rights against the co-obligors to the extent of the unperformed part, with precedence over co-obligors exercising contributory claims.

COMMENT

1. Subrogation in the obligee's rights

A joint and several obligor who has paid more than its share to the obligee has a contributory claim against the other obligors under Article 11.1.10. Article 11.1.11(1) gives the co-obligor who has such a contributory claim the possibility of benefiting from the rights of the obligee, including all rights securing their performance. This possibility is of particular value to the joint and several obligor when the rights of the obligee are secured, because the contributory right under Article 11.1.10 is not secured.

Illustration

1. Bank X has lent EUR 500,000 to companies A and B as joint and several obligors, secured by a mortgage on A's premises. B reimburses the full amount of the loan. Under Article 11.1.10, B has an unsecured claim against A for contribution in the amount of EUR 250,000. B may also exercise X's rights against A up to the amount of EUR 250,000, including enforcement of the mortgage on A's premises.

2. Obligee's rights reserved and preferred

By providing that an obligee who has not received full performance retains its rights against the joint and several obligors, and by giving those retained rights of the obligee precedence over the rights of the performing obligor, the rule in Article 11.1.11(2) assures that the

第11.1.11条

（债权人之权利）

（1）一个行使第**11.1.10**条规定的连带债务人，为向所有或任何其他债务人求偿其超出份额清偿之部分，在每个债务人未清偿份额的限度内，亦可行使债权人的权利，包括确保其他债务人履行清偿的各项权利。

（2）未获得全部清偿的债权人，以共同债务人未清偿部分为限，优于行使分担请求权的共同债务人，对共同债务人保有各项权利。

注释：

1. 债权人权利的代位求偿

超过自己份额对债权人履行清偿的连带债务人，根据第11.1.10条之规定，对其他债务人享有分担请求权。第11.1.11条第（1）款赋予拥有分担请求权的共同债务人，享有从债权人的权利，包括保证债务履行的所有权利中，获得好处的可能性。这种可能性在债权人的权利具有担保的情况下，对连带债务人尤其具有价值，因为第11.1.10条规定的分担权是没有担保的。

示例：

1. X 银行向 A 公司和 B 公司贷款 50 万欧元，A 和 B 是连带债务人，并以 A 的场地作为抵押担保。B 偿还了全部贷款。根据第11.1.10条之规定，B 对 A 享有无担保的分担请求权，金额为 25 万欧元。B 此时尚可行使 X 对 A 的权利，包括执行对 A 场地的抵押权，要求 A 偿还完 25 万欧元的份额。

2. 债权人的权利的保留及优先

通过规定对未得到全额清偿的债权人对连带债务人的保留权利，并规定该等被保留的债权人之权利对已履行清偿之债务人的权利具有优先权，第11.1.11条第（2）款的规定则在于确保：第11.1.11条第（1）款规定的赋予连带债务人之好处不会对债权人的保留权利造成不利

benefit given to the joint and several obligor in Article 11.1.11(1) does not detrimentally affect the remaining rights of the obligee. This precedence may be effectuated by deferring enforcement of the claim of the performing joint and several obligor under Article 11.1.11(1) until full performance is received by the obligee.

Illustration

> 2.   The facts are the same as in Illustration 1, except that B has reimbursed only EUR 400,000 of the loan, and the remaining EUR 100,000 remain unpaid. B has a contributory claim against A for the amount in excess of its own share, i.e. EUR 150,000 (EUR 400,000 - EUR 250,000). B also has the right to exercise X's rights against A up to that amount, including enforcement of the mortgage on A's premises. However, as X's rights with respect to the remaining EUR 100,000 have precedence over the rights of B, enforcement of B's rights against A may not occur until after X has received repayment of the remaining EUR 100,000.

The rule on precedence is subject to the possible application of mandatory rules providing otherwise in insolvency proceedings.

ARTICLE 11.1.12
(Defences in contributory claims)

A joint and several obligor against whom a claim is made by the co-obligor who has performed the obligation:

(a)   may raise any common defences and rights of set-off that were available to be asserted by the co-obligor against the obligee;

(b)   may assert defences which are personal to itself ;

(c)   may not assert defences and rights of set-off which are personal to one or several of the other co-obligors.

COMMENT

This provision deals with the defences and rights of set-off that may be asserted between co-obligors when contributory claims are exercised.

影响。该等优先权可以通过以下方式实行：将清偿连带债务人按第 11.1.11 条第(1)款行使的请求权，推迟至债权人获得全部清偿之后行使。

示例：

　　2. 事实同示例 1，但 B 仅偿还了 40 万欧元的贷款，剩余 10 万欧元未偿还。B 就超过自己份额清偿部分的 15 万欧元（40 万欧元 ~ 25 万欧元），对 A 享有分担请求权。B 在金额内还有权行使 X 对 A 的权利，包括执行对 A 场地的抵押权。然而，X 就剩余 10 万欧元所享有的权利，优先于 B 的权利。在 X 取得剩余 10 万欧元之前，B 对 A 不得执行追索权。

关于优先权的规则，可能会受到适用有关破产程序另外规定的强制性规则的制约。

第 11.1.12 条

（对分担请求权之抗辩）

　　如果一个已清偿债务的共同债务人对一个连带债务人提出请求，则该连带债务人：

　　（a）可提出共同债务人对该债权人可主张的任何共有的抗辩权和抵销权；

　　（b）可主张属于其自身的抗辩权；

　　（c）不可主张属于其他共同债务人中一个或几个自身的抗辩权和抵销权。

注释：

　　本条规范的是在行使分担请求权时，共同债务人相互之间可以主张的抗辩权和抵销权。

1. Common defences and rights of set-off

Pursuant to Article 11.1.4, the co-obligor that is asked to perform by the obligee may assert all defences and rights of set-off common to all the co-obligors. If that co-obligor has failed to raise such a defence or right of set-off which would have extinguished or reduced the obligation, any other joint and several obligor against which the former obligor exercises a contributory claim may assert that defence or right of set-off.

Illustration

> 1.   Joint and several obligors A and B have purchased a know-how licence together. Licensor X has undertaken that the technology was fit for both licencees. If this appeared not to be the case, each obligor could invoke this common defence against X. If A fails to do so when required to pay the fees by X, B may refuse to pay its contributory share to A.

2. Personal defences

A co-obligor may also assert a defence personal to itself against a contributory claim.

Illustration

> 2.   Companies A, B and C are jointly and severally bound to pay the price of products to be purchased from seller X. A, however, was induced to enter the contract by fraud within the meaning of Article 3.8. B pays the full price to X. A may assert the fraud it had been subjected to as a personal defence against B's contributory claim.

Under Article 11.1.12, rights of set-off are not subject to the same rule as defences, as they usually are in the Principles. The reason for this is that the rights of set-off cannot be treated in the same manner as defences when it comes to the asserting of a personal right of set-off against the obligee to counter a contributory claim. In actual fact, under Article 11.1.5, performance by the other co-obligor has discharged the first obligor from its obligations towards the obligee, with the consequence that the right of set-off does not exist any more. The first obligor will have to pay its contributory share to the other obligor, while remaining in a position to exercise its distinct claim against the obligee.

1. 共有的抗辩权和抵销权

根据第 11.1.4 条的规定，被债权人请求履行的共同债务人可以主张对所有共同债务人共有的所有抗辩权和抵销权。如果该共同债务人没有主张原本可以消灭债务或减少债务的是项抗辩权或抵销权，任何其他连带债务人均可对前一债务人行使的分担请求权，主张抗辩权或抵销权。

示例：

> 1. 连带债务人 A 和 B 共同购买了一项专有技术许可。许可方 X 承诺该技术同时符合两个被许可方的需要。如果结果并非如此，此时，任一债务人均可对 X 主张该共有抗辩权。如果在 X 要求 A 支付许可费时，A 没有主张该抗辩权（而对 X 履行了支付），B 可以拒绝向 A 支付其应分担的份额。

2. 自有抗辩权

一个共同债务人也可以对分担请求权主张属于其自有的抗辩权。

示例：

> 2. A、B 和 C 三家公司就从卖方 X 购买的货物承担支付货款的连带义务。然而，A 是在受到第 3.8 条规定的欺诈情况下被引诱订立了合同。B 向 X 全额支付了货款。A 可主张以其受到的欺诈作为自有抗辩权来对抗 B 的分担请求权。

与通则的一贯做法不同，在第 11.1.12 条项下，抵销权不受作为抗辩权的同样规则的制约。原因在于，当主张以自有抵销权来对抗债权人的分担请求权时，该抵销权不能按抗辩权同样的方式来对待。事实上，在第 11.1.5 条项下，其他共同债务人的清偿已经解除了第一方债务人对债权人承担的债务，从而导致了抵销权丧失的结果。第一方债务人将必须对其他债务人支付其分担份额，并同时有权对债权人行使独立的请求权。

3.   Bank X has lent EUR 3,000,000 to joint and several obligors A and B. As a result of the selling of shares belonging to A on the stock market, X then becomes A's obligor for an amount of EUR 500,000, thus giving A a right of set-off for that amount. X claims reimbursement of EUR 3,000,000 from B, which pays the full amount. If B then claims contribution from A, the latter may not assert its own right of set-off against B. Such a right does not exist any more since payment to X by B has also discharged A towards X. A will have to pay its contributory share to B and will be able to exercise its own claim of EUR 500,000 against X.

3. Defences and rights of set-off personal to other co-obligors

A co-obligor may not assert a defence or right of set-off which is personal to one or several of the other co-obligors.

Illustrations

4.   The facts are the same as in Illustration 2. If B claims contribution against C, the latter may not invoke the fraud to which A was subject, since this defence is personal to A.

5.   The facts are the same as in Illustration 3. If B claims contribution from C, the latter may not assert A's right of set-off, since this right is personal to another obligor.

ARTICLE 11.1.13
(Inability to recover)

If a joint and several obligor who has performed more than that obligor's share is unable, despite all reasonable efforts, to recover contribution from another joint and several obligor, the share of the others, including the one who has performed, is increased proportionally.

COMMENT

1. Proportional sharing of the loss

A co-obligor exercising a contributory claim against another co-obligor may be unable to recover because the latter is insolvent or has

示例：

3. X 银行向连带债务人 A、B 和 C 贷款 300 万欧元①。由于在股市出售 A 拥有的股票，X 成为 A 的债务人，需向 A 支付 50 万欧元，从而赋予 A 有 50 万欧元的抵销权。X 向 B 请求还贷 300 万欧元，B 全额支付。如果随后 B 向 A 请求份额分担，A 不得对 B 主张其自己的抵销权。该权利已不复存在，因为 B 向 X 清偿时同时也解除了 A 对 X 的债务。A 必须向 B 支付其分担份额，并可对 X 行使其自己 50 万欧元的请求权。

3. 其他共同债务人自有的抗辩权和抵销权

一个共同债务人不得主张属于其他共同债务人中一个或多个的自有抗辩或抵销权。

示例：

4. 事实同示例 2。如果 B 向 C 主张分担请求权，C 不得援用 A 遭到的欺诈为由拒绝支付，因为该欺诈属 A 自有抗辩权。

5. 事实同示例 3。如果 B 向 C 主张分担请求权，后者不得主张 A 的抵销权，因为该权利是另一债务人自有的，另外，A 的抵销权已不复存在，因为 B 向 X 清偿时同时也解除了 A 对 X 的债务。②

第 11.1.13 条

（补救不能）

如果一个连带债务人超过自己的债务份额清偿了债务，且虽经一切合理努力，仍不能从另一个连带债务人处补救其超出部分，则包括已履行清偿的债务人在内的所有其他债务人之份额，均应按比例增加。

注释：

1. 按比例分担损失

一个共同债务人对另一个共同债务人行使分担请求权，有可能无

---

① 译者注：英文原文并无连带债务人 C，但若无 C，就无法与下面示例 5 项对应。经与报告员 Marcel Fontaine 教授协调，在此示例中加上 C。

② 译者注：最后一句"另外，A 的抵销权已不复存在，因为 B 向 X 清偿时同时也解除了 A 对 X 的债务"，是经与本章报告员 Marcel Fontaine 协调后加上的，目前英文文本并无此句话。

disappeared or its assets are out of reach. In this case the burden of the loss is spread among the other co-obligors.

Illustration

> 1.   Companies A, B and C borrow EUR 6,000,000 from bank X, their contributory shares being equal. After reimbursing the loan, A claims EUR 2,000,000 from B and EUR 2,000,000 from C. B turns out to be insolvent. The loss of EUR 2,000,000 has to be borne proportionally by the other co-obligors, including the one who has performed. Since their shares are identical, both A and C will bear an equal part of the loss, i.e. EUR 1,000,000 each. Consequently, A can recover EUR 3,000,000 from C.

2. All reasonable efforts

Before invoking this Article in order to claim increased contributions from the other co-obligors, the obligor who has performed must exert all reasonable efforts to recover from the defaulting co-obligor in the light of Article 5.1.4(2).

Illustration

> 2.   The facts are the same as in Illustration 1. A does not question B's assertion that it is unable to pay because of financial difficulties and immediately asks for an increased contribution from C. However, in order to avail itself of Article 11.1.13, A must demonstrate that it has exerted all reasonable efforts to recover from B, such as reminders, injunctions, attachments or legal proceedings, as may be appropriate.

法追偿成功，因为后者可能破产、失踪，或其资产消失。在这种情况下，该损失的负担应由所有其他共同债务人共同分摊。

示例：

  1. A、B 和 C 三家公司向 X 银行借款 600 万欧元，他们的分担比例均等。A 在偿还贷款之后，向 B 和 C 分别请求 200 万欧元的分担份额。但是 B 破产。该 200 万欧元的损失应该由其他共同债务人按比例分摊，包括已经进行了清偿的共同债务人。由于他们的份额均等，A 和 C 应该均摊该损失，即各自承担 100 万欧元。因此 A 可以请求 C 偿还 300 万欧元。

2. 尽一切合理努力

在援引本条向其他共同债务人请求增加分担金额之前，已履行了清偿义务的债务人必须按照第 5.1.4 条第（2）款的规定，尽一切合理努力对不履行共同债务人进行追偿。

示例：

  2. 事实同示例 1。A 对 B 所声称的财务困难、无力支付，未提出质疑，便立即请求 C 增加分担金额。然而，为援引第 11.1.13 条，A 必须证明自己已尽一切合理努力对 B 进行追偿，例如根据个案情况，其已采取了提醒、禁令、扣押，或者提起了诉讼。

SECTION 2: PLURALITY OF OBLIGEES

ARTICLE 11.2.1
(Definitions)

When several obligees can claim perform-ance of the same obligation from an obligor:

(a) the claims are separate when each obligee can only claim its share;

(b) the claims are joint and several when each obligee can claim the whole performance;

(c) the claims are joint when all obligees have to claim performance together.

COMMENT

1. Several obligees

Plurality of obligees occurs in different situations.

Illustration

1. Banks A, B and C join in a syndicated loan agreement to lend company X USD 12,000,000. The three banks are plural obligees with regard to claiming reimbursement from X.

Other instances of plurality of obligees occur, among others, with co-insurers, multiple buyers and/or sellers in share acquisition agreements and partners in consortium agreements in various sectors, such as the construction sector or the petroleum industry.

2. The same obligation

This Section applies when the different obligees can claim performance of the same obligation from the obligor. This is the case in Illustration 1 (reimbursement of the syndicated loan). Situations where different obligees of the same obligor have rights deriving from different obligations do not fall under the scope of this Section.

第二节　多个债权人

第 11.2.1 条

（定义）

当多个债权人均可向同一债务人主张清偿同一债务时：

（a）如每一个债权人只可主张其自身之份额，则该请求权为可分债权；

（b）如每一个债权人均可主张全部清偿，则该请求权为连带债权；

（c）如所有债权人必须共同请求清偿，则该请求权为共同债权。

注释：

1. 几个债权人

多个债权人可发生于不同情况。

示例：

1. A、B 和 C 三家银行参加一个辛迪加贷款协议，向 X 公司贷款 1,200 万美元。三家银行在向 X 要求还款上，属于多个债权人。

其他涉及多个债权人的情况，出其他事例外，包括共同保险人，在股份购买协议中的多个买方和/或卖方，以及各行业，例如，建筑行业或石油业中财团协议的合伙人。

2. 同一债务

本节适用于多个债权人可向债务人请求清偿同一债务的情况。示例 1 即属于这种情况（偿还辛迪加贷款）。多个债权人源于不同的债务对同一债务人所享有权利的情况，不属于本节调整的范围。

Illustration

> 2. Architect A and contractor B are both involved in the construction of a new industrial plant. Their respective claims against the client concern different obligations (payment of their respective types of services). The claims are not subject to the Articles in this Section, but to the respectively applicable law.

On the other hand, when different actors in a construction project join in a consortium and claim one payment for all their services, they are to be considered as plural obligees for that payment.

The "same obligation" usually derives from a single contract. In Illustration 1, the syndicated loan agreement is a single contract. It could however also happen, in the same situation, that each lender would choose to have its own contract with the borrower. Co-insurers joining to cover the same risk usually have distinct contractual relationships with the insured.

Illustration

> 3. Eight insurance companies agree to co-insure the liability risks of a pharmaceutical group. The co-insurance agreement provides that each co-insurer has a distinct contractual relationship with the insured, but the insured's obligations towards the co-insurers are the same (payment of the agreed premium, required prevention measures, loss notification, etc.). These co-insurers are plural obligees, subject as such to the Articles in this Section.

3. Three main types

Article 11.2.1 defines three main types of claims available in practice when several obligees can claim performance of the same obligation from an obligor.

The claims can be separate. Each obligee can then claim only its share.

Illustration

> 4. The facts are the same as in Illustration 1. If the claims of banks A, B and C against X totalling USD 12,000,000 are separate and if their shares are equal, each bank may only claim reimbursement of USD 4,000,000 from X.

The claims can be joint and several, which means that each obligee can claim full performance (see Article 11.2.2), subject to subsequent allocation between the different obligees (see Article 11.2.4).

示例：

> 2. 建筑师 A 和承包商 B 均参与了一个新工业工厂的建筑工作。他们各自对客户的请求权涉及不同的债务（其各自类型的服务价款）。这些请求权不受本节各条的调整，而分别受各自的适用法律调整。

另一方面，如果一个建筑项目的不同参与者加入一个联合体并就他们提供的所有服务请求一次性付款，不同参与者可被视为该款项的多个债权人。

"同一债务"通常源自于单一合同。在示例 1 中，辛迪加贷款协议即属于单一合同。但是，也可以出现在相同的情况下，每一个出借人会选择与借款人订立单独的合同。联合承保同一风险的共同保险人，通常与被保险人就建立单独的合同关系。

示例：

> 3. 八家保险公司同意对一家医药集团的责任风险进行联合承保。共同保险协议规定每一个共同保险人与被保险人建立单独的合同关系，但被保险人向所有共同保险人承担的责任示相同的（支付约定的保险金，采取规定的防范措施，通知损失等）。这些共同保险人属于多个债权人，因此，受本节各条规定的调整。

3. 三个主要类型

第 11.2.1 条规定了当多个债权人就同一个债务向一个债务人请求清偿时，实践中存在的请求权的三种主要类型。

这些请求权可以是可分的。此时每一债权人仅可请求其自己的债权份额。

示例：

> 4. 事实同示例 1。如果 A、B 和 C 三家银行针对 X 的 1,200 万美元的请求权是可分的，并且他们的债权份额是均等的，每家银行只能请求 X 偿还 400 万美元。

这些请求权可以是连带的，即每一债权人均可请求全额清偿（参见第 11.2.2 条），但要以随后在各个债权人之间进行分配（参见第 11.2.4 条）为条件。

Illustration

> 5.   Companies A and B are co-owners of a storage house, which they rent to transport company X. The contract provides that the co-owners' claims for the rent are joint and several. A and B may each claim payment of the full amount of the rent from X.

The claims are "joint" when all obligees have to claim together; consequently, the obligor may only perform in favour of all of them together. This situation is sometimes also referred to as "communal claims".

Illustration

> 6.   Companies A and B rent an office together, to share in a foreign capital. Due to the nature of their claim on occupation of the office, A and B are joint obligees. This would not prevent them from designating one of them as agent for dealings with the owner of the premises.

4. No presumption provided

In the case of plurality of obligors, Article 11.1.2 sets a presumption of joint and several obligations, because this corresponds to the most frequent commercial practice.

On the contrary, when it comes to determining to which of the three types defined in this Article claims by plural obligees belong, the Principles do not provide any presumption. The reason is that none of these types seems to be dominant in practice; choices vary considerably, mainly depending on the operation concerned.

Consequently, in situations where plural obligees are involved, parties are encouraged to choose the relevant type by an express stipulation.

Illustrations

> 7.   Banks A, B and C join in a syndicated loan agreement to offer financing to company X. The agreement provides that "All amounts due, and obligations owed, to each Bank are separate and independent obligations. Each Bank may separately enforce its rights under this agreement". This express provision makes the banks' claims separate.

> 8.   Art collectors A and B, co-owners of a painting by Rothko, sell it to a Museum for the price of USD 20,000,000. The contract stipulates that each seller can claim payment of the whole price. The claims are joint and several.

示例：

　　5. A 公司和 B 公司是一家仓库的共同所有人，它们把该仓库租给运输公司 X。租赁合同规定共同所有人对租金享有连带债权。A 或 B 每一家公司均可向 X 请求全额租金。

　　如果所有债权人必须一同请求支付，则属于"共同"请求权；此时，债务人只能向所有债权人共同清偿。这种情况有时也称为"公有请求权"。

示例：

　　6. A 公司和 B 公司在某外国首都共同租用一间办公室。鉴于它们对于占用办公室享有请求权之性质，A 和 B 是共同债权人。但这并不阻止他们指定其中之一作为代理人与业主进行交涉。

4. 未规定任何推定

　　在属于多个债务人的情况下，第 11.1.2 条规定了推定连带债务规则，因为这符合商业实践中最常见的情况。

　　相反，在决定多个债权人享有的请求权属于本条规定的三种类型中哪一种类型时，通则并未规定任何推定。原因在于其中任何一种类型在实践中都不具有支配地位；选择差别相当大，主要取决于相关操作。

　　因此，在涉及多个债权人时，通则鼓励当事人通过明确的约定来选择相关的类型。

示例：

　　7. A、B 和 C 三家银行参加一个辛迪加贷款协议，以向 X 公司提供融资。协议规定"对每一家银行的所有到期金额，以及对每家银行所欠债务，均属分别的、独立的债务。每家银行可以在本协议项下独立行使其权利"。该明示的规定表明三家银行的请求权是可分的。

　　8. 艺术品收藏家 A 和 B 是一幅罗斯科画作的共同所有人，他们以 2,000 万美元的价格将其出售给一家博物馆。合同规定每一个卖方均可向博物馆请求支付全部价款。该请求权为连带债权。

> 9. The facts are the same as in Illustration 8, except that the sales contract with the Museum provides that A and B's claims are separate. This means that each of them can only claim payment of the price for its own share of the claim, normally corresponding to its previous share of ownership.

Before making such a contractual choice, parties should pay attention to the advantages and disadvantages of each of the different types of plural claim.

In particular, joint and several claims have the advantage of avoiding the multiplication of law suits. This is an especially important concern in international trade. Any of the obligees may claim the whole performance. Joint and several claims also simplify the situation of the obligor, who will not have to divide performance between its different obligees. From the point of view of the plural obligees themselves, claims are normally easier if they are joint and several.

On the other hand, plural obligees have to be aware that if their claims are joint and several they lose exclusive control of their respective shares. Any other joint and several obligee may claim and collect the whole performance, with the risk that later allocation under Article 11.2.5 could create difficulties. This explains why separate claims seem to be more prevalent in certain sectors (see for instance Illustration 1).

If the parties have failed to make an explicit contractual choice, the type to which a plural claim should be assigned will be determined by interpretation of the contract in accordance with the provisions in Chapter 4. In many instances circumstances such as the nature or the purpose of the contract will be especially relevant (see Article 4.3 (d)).

Illustrations

> 10. Company A, located in country X, and company B, located in country Y, join in ordering a large quantity of cars from a manufacturer. The cars for country X are right-hand drive, those for country Y left-hand drive. When delivery is to be claimed, these circumstances indicate that A and B are separate obligees, each one being entitled to claim its type of car.

> 11. Tax consultant X has undertaken to give tax advice to companies A and B concerning the operations of a joint venture in which the latter are involved. Since the tax advice concerns the common venture of A and B and this advice is hardly divisible, A and B are to be considered as joint and several obligees when claiming performance from X.

9. 事实同示例 8，但与博物馆之间的销售合同规定，A 和 B 的请求权是可分的。这意味着每一方只能请求支付合同价款中属于其自己的请求份额，该份额通常等于先前其对画作所有权的份额。

在做这种合同选择之前，当事人应该注意到不同类型复数请求权的利弊之处。

具体来说，连带债权具有避免多重诉讼的好处。这是在国际贸易中非常重要的一项考虑因素。任何一个债权人均可以请求全部清偿。连带债权还可以简化债务人的处境，不必在不同的债权人之间分别进行清偿。从多个债权人的角度而言，如果他们是连带债权，请求通常更加容易。

另一方面，多个债权人又必须清楚，当债权属连带债权时，他们将失去对自己债权份额的独自控制权，因为任何其他连带债权人均可以请求并取得全部清偿，而依据第 11.2.5 条的规定进行的后续分配，可能会出现困难，带来风险。正因为如此，在某些行业中（例如示例 1）可分债权似乎更加流行。

如果当事人未做出明确的合同选择，一项复数债权应被定为何种类型，将根据第 4 章的规定，通过对合同的解释予以确定。许多情况下，诸如合同的性质或目的等情况，将会特别相关（参见第 4.3 条（d）项）。

示例：

10. 位于 X 国的 A 公司和位于 Y 国的 B 公司，共同向一家汽车制造商订购了一批汽车。X 国汽车是右座驾驶，而 Y 国是左座驾驶。在请求交付时，该等情况表明 A 和 B 是可分债权人，各自有权请求本国类型的汽车。

11. 税务顾问 X 承担对 A、B 两家公司就其间合营公司的运作提供税务咨询。由于税务咨询涉及 A 和 B 的共同项目，该咨询很难进行分割，在请求 X 履行时，A 和 B 将被视为连带债权人。

5. Possible designation of an agent

In practice, plural obligees often designate an agent with the authority to deal with the obligor on behalf of all of them, within agreed limits. This seems to be especially frequent, for practical reasons, when the claims are separate. However, in that case, each obligee intends to keep full control of its own rights, often reserving the possibility to revoke the agent's authority at any time.

Illustration

> 12. Banks A, B and C have joined in a syndicated loan agreement to lend USD 12,000,000 to company X. The claims are separate, USD 4,000,000 for each bank. However, A has been designated as agent of the consortium with authority to collect reimbursement of the full amount.

The initiative of designating an intermediary may come from an obligor who wants to exert some control over claims which could be separately brought by its numerous obligees.

Illustration

> 13. Under the terms of issue of a bearer bond trustees are appointed to represent the interests of bondholders. The issuer covenants to make payments to each bondholder in accordance with the terms of issue and gives the trustee a parallel payment covenant. Upon the issuer's default the trustee may at its discretion enforce payment and must do so if so required by a given percentage in value of bondholders. Individual bondholders are precluded from taking action on default by the issuer, unless the trustee for the bondholders has failed to fulfil its obligation under the trust deed to take enforcement action. Each bondholder is a separate obligee. The purpose of the trust is simply to monitor performance by the issuer and co-ordinate enforcement in order to avoid precipitate action by an individual bondholder.

ARTICLE 11.2.2
(Effects of joint and several claims)

Full performance of an obligation in favour of one of the joint and several obligees discharges the obligor towards the other obligees.

5. 指定代理人的可能性

实践中，多个债权人往往指定一个代理人，并授权其在约定权限内代表所有债权人与债务人进行交涉。在债权为可分债权时，出于实践方面的原因，这种情况尤为常见。然而，在这种情况下，每一债权人均有意保持自己对其权利的完全控制，往往保留随时可撤销代理权的可能性。

示例：

12. A、B 和 C 三家银行参加一项辛迪加贷款协议，以向 X 公司贷款 1,200 万美元。该债权为可分债权，每家银行的债权金额为 400 万美元。然而 A 被指定为该财团的代理人，有权收取全部贷款。

指定中间人的提议也可能是由债务人提出的，因为他希望对多个债权人分别提出的债权请求具有一定的控制权。

示例：

13. 根据一批无记名债券的发行条件，受托人被指定代表债券持有人的利益。发行人承诺根据发行条件向每一个债券持有人进行支付并给予受托人平行的支付承诺。当发行人违约时，受托人可以自行决定追索付款，而且，在代表一定金额比例的债券持有人就此提出要求时，受托人必须这样做。在发行人违约时，单个债券持有人被排除采取此项行动的权利，除非债券持有人的受托人没有履行其在受托协议项下采取追索行动的义务。每一个债券持有人是一个可分债权人。委托的目的仅仅是为了监督发行人的履行，协调履行情况，以避免单个债券持有人的轻率行动。

第 11.2.2 条

（连带债权之效力）

对其中一个连带债权人进行全部债务清偿，
即解除了该债务人对所有其他债权人的清偿义务。

COMMENT

1. Each obligee can claim full performance

The main effect of joint and several claims has already been stated in the definition of Article 11.2.1(2). When claims are joint and several each obligee is entitled to claim full performance from the obligor.

Illustration

> 1.   Co-owners A and B sell their hotel to buyer X for a price of EUR 5,000,000. Their shares of co-ownership are equal. The sales contract provides that the sellers' claims concerning payment of the price are joint and several. A may claim EUR 5,000,000 from X, subject to further allocation under Article 11.2.4.

2. Obligor's choice

This Article states two other major effects of joint and several claims.

First, if the obligor takes the initiative to spontaneously perform its obligation, it is entitled to render performance in favour of any of its obligees.

Illustration

> 2.   The facts are the same as in Illustration 1. X takes the initiative of paying the price before being invited to do so by either of its obligees. X may validly pay to A or to B.

3. Obligor's discharge

Another main effect of joint and several claims is that the obligor who has rendered full performance in favour of one of the obligees is discharged towards the other obligees.

Illustration

> 3.   The facts are the same as in Illustration 1. X has paid the whole price of EUR 5,000,000 to A. B, having difficulties to recover its share from A, requests payment of EUR 2,500,000 from X. Under Article 11.2.2(2), the claim will be rejected since full payment to A has discharged X towards the other obligee.

注释：

1. 每一债权人均可请求全额清偿

连带债权的主要效果在第 11.2.1 条第(2)款的定义中已做了说明。当债权为连带债权时，每一债权人均可向债务人请求全额清偿。

示例：

> 1. 某一酒店的共同所有人 A 和 B 以 500 万欧元的价格将酒店出售给买家 X。他们的所有权份额是均等的。销售合同规定卖方关于价款支付的请求权为连带债权。A 可以向 X 请求支付 500 万欧元，但应根据第 11.2.4 条的规定进一步进行分配。

2. 债务人的选择

本条规定了连带债权的另外两项主要效果。

首先，如果债务人自发地主动的履行债务，他有权向任何一个债权人进行清偿。

示例：

> 2. 事实同示例 1，X 在任何一个债权人提出请求付款前，主动支付价款。X 可以有效地向 A 或者 B 支付。

3. 债务人被解除债务

连带债权的另一项主要效果是，债务人在向任何一个债权人进行全额清偿之后，他即被解除了对其他债权人的债务。

示例：

> 3. 事实同示例 1，X 向 A 全额支付了 500 万欧元的价款。B 因难以向 A 追偿自己的债权份额，请求 X 支付 250 万欧元。根据第 11.2.2 条第(2)款的规定，该请求应被驳回，因为 X 对向 A 的全额清偿即解除了 X 对其他债权人的债务。

4. Practical aspects

The right given to each of the joint or several obligees to claim full performance may call for some coordination to avoid duplication of initiatives and unnecessary costs. Either the obligees have agreed in advance on which of them will claim performance, or at least the obligee envisaging to take the initiative should consult with its co-obligees.

On the other hand, when the obligor takes the initiative its choice of obligee to which it will perform may be affected by the fact that another obligee is already requesting performance. Some prior consulting may then be appropriate. Furthermore, an obligee who has received payment should immediately inform the others that performance has been rendered.

These solutions could usefully be agreed in advance by all parties involved. Otherwise the requirements of good faith and fair dealing are always applicable (Article 1.7).

ARTICLE 11.2.3
*(Availability of defences against
joint and several obligees)*

(1) The obligor may assert against any of the joint and several obligees all the defences and rights of set-off that are personal to its relationship to that obligee or that it can assert against all the co-obligees, but may not assert defences and rights of set-off that are personal to its relationship to one or several of the other co-obligees.

(2) The provisions of Articles 11.1.5, 11.1.6, 11.1.7 and 11.1.8 apply, with appropriate adaptations, to joint and several claims.

COMMENT

1. Availability of defences

The defences which may entitle the obligor to refuse to perform do not necessarily exist against all obligees. Some of the defences may be personal to the obligor's relationship with one obligee only. These defences can be asserted only against the obligee concerned.

4. 实践方面

赋予每一连带债权人请求全额清偿的权利，要求一定的协调，以避免请求重复和不必要的费用。一种办法是，债权人之间事先约定由谁负责请求清偿，或者至少打算率先请求清偿的债权人应与其他共同债权人进行协商。

另一方面，当债务人主动选择向一个债权人进行清偿时，其选择可能会受到另一个债权人已经提出了请求清偿的影响。因此，一定的事先协商是适当的。另外，某个债权人如已收到款项，应该将履行清偿的事实立即通知其他债权人。

这些解决办法，可以由所有相关各方事先有益地约定。否则，诚实信用和公平交易的要求总是适用的（参见第 1.7 条）。

第 11.2.3 条

（对连带债权人的抗辩权）

（1）债务人可对连带债权人中的任何人主张属于其自身的、在与该债权人关系中的抗辩权和抵销权，或者其可向所有债权人主张的抗辩权和抵销权，但不可主张属于其自身的、与其他共同债权人中一个或几个人关系中的抗辩权和抵销权。

（2）第 11.1.5 条、第 11.1.6 条、第 11.1.7 条和第 11.1.8 条经适当调整，可适用于连带债权。

注释：

1. 可供抗辩权

债务人据以拒绝清偿的抗辩，不一定对所有债权人都有效。其中一些抗辩可能只是债务人与其中一个债权人的关系中所自有的，这样的抗辩只能针对相关债权人主张。

Illustration

> 1. Grain producer X has agreed to supply a certain quantity of wheat seeds to companies A, B and C which are engaged in a common agricultural project in a developing country. The contract provides that A, B and C are joint and several obligees as concerns the deliveries. X discovers that the premises where it has to deliver the seeds are not equipped with appropriate facilities for convenient unloading, the availability of which only A has guaranteed. X may invoke this as a defence against A requiring delivery, but not against B and C which had not guaranteed that the premises for the delivery would be equipped with appropriate facilities.

The obligor may also assert defences that it has in common against all obligees.

Illustration

> 2. The facts are the same as in Illustration 1. X finds out that the agricultural project involves child labour by A, B and C in violation of applicable mandatory rules. This is a common defence that X may assert against any one of the obligees claiming delivery of the wheat seeds.

2. Effects of certain defences

Section 1 of this Chapter contains particular rules about the effects of certain types of defence (see Articles 11.1.5, 11.1.6, 11.1.7 and 11.1.8) available to joint and several obligors. Paragraph (3) of this Article provides that these rules apply, with appropriate adaptations, to joint and several claims.

a. *Performance and set-off (reference to Article 11.1.5)*

Article 11.1.5 provides that "*Performance or set-off by a joint and several obligor or set-off by the obligee against one joint and several obligor discharges the other obligors in relation to the obligee to the extent of the performance or set-off*". Similarly, performance received by (or set-off exercised by) one of the joint and several obligees discharges the obligor towards the other obligees to the extent of the performance or set-off.

Illustrations

> 3. Companies A, B and C have jointly and severally loaned EUR 300,000 to X. A receives full payment. If B or C still claims reimbursement, X may assert that it has fully performed to A.

示例：

  1. 谷物生产商 X 同意向 A、B 和 C 三家公司供应一定数量的小麦种子，三家公司在某一发展中国家从事一个共同农业项目。合同规定 A、B 和 C 就货物的交付属连带债权人。X 发现约定交付种子的场地没有适当设施，以便利卸货，但，只有 A 曾担保存在这种设施。X 只可以针对 A 援引该担保作为抗辩，要求交付，但不得以此对抗 B 和 C，因为他们没有担保卸货场地备有适当的设施。

债务人也可以主张其对所有债权人共同拥有的抗辩。

示例：

  2. 事实同示例 1，X 发现 A、B 和 C 的共同农业项目违反应适用的强制性规则，涉及使用童工。这是 X 可主张的一个面对任一要求交付小麦种子之债权人的共同抗辩。

2. 某些抗辩的效果

本章第一节就连带债务人可援引的某些类型抗辩之效果制定了具体规则（参见第 11.1.5 条、第 11.1.6 条、第 11.1.7 条和第 11.1.8 条）。本条第 3 款规定该等规则经适当调整后适用于连带债权。

a. 清偿和抵销（参考第 11.1.5 条）

第 11.1.5 条规定，"一个连带债务人的清偿或抵销，或者债权人对一个连带债务人进行了抵销，则应以该清偿或抵销为限，解除其他债务人对该债权人所负的清偿义务。"同样，若其中一个连带债权人收到清偿（或者行使抵销权），则应以该清偿或抵销为限，解除该债务人对其他债权人的债务。

示例：

  3. A、B 和 C 三家公司以连带方式向 X 放贷 30 万欧元。A 收到全额还贷。如果 B 或 C 继续请求还贷，X 可主张其已向 A 做了全额清偿。

4. The facts are the same as in Illustration 3, except that X can claim EUR 300,000 from A for the sale of office equipment. X exercises the right of set-off under Article 8.3. Its obligation under the loan agreement is extinguished not only vis-à-vis A but also vis-à-vis B and C.

b. *Release and settlement (reference to Article 11.1.6)*

Article 11.1.6 provides that *"Release of one joint and several obligor, or settlement with one joint and several obligor, discharges all the other obligors for the share of the released or settling obligor, unless the circumstances indicate otherwise"*. Similarly, release granted to the obligor by one of the obligees (or settlement with the obligor by one of the obligees) discharges the obligor towards the other obligees to the extent of the release or settlement.

Illustrations

5. Pamela, a famous race horse, has been sold by its co-owners A and B to buyer X. Concerning payment of the price, the contract provides that A and B are joint and several obligees. If A releases X from A's share of X's obligation, B's claim against X is reduced by the amount of A's share. A has no contributory recourse against B under Article 11.2.4 (see Article 11.1.6(2)).

6. The facts are the same as in Illustration 3, but A, whose share in the loan is EUR 100,000, settles with X, accepting a payment of EUR 60,000, i.e. an amount below its share. The joint and several claims of B and C against X are reduced by the full amount of A's share, i.e. by EUR 100,000, and both remain X's joint and several obligees for EUR 200,000. Settling obligee A has no recourse under Article 11.2.4 against B or C (see Article 11.1.6(2)).

As in Article 11.1.6, with appropriate adaptations, the reference to settlement concerns the special case where a separate settlement intervenes between the obligor and one of the joint and several obligees for the latter's share. In this case the issue to be solved is that of the consequences of such a settlement for the other obligees' claims.

In the more frequent situation where the settlement concerns all the joint and several claims, the consequences for the different obligees' claims are determined by the terms of the settlement agreed by all parties and the contributory claims are adjusted accordingly.

4. 事实同示例 3，但 X 有权向 A 主张 30 万欧元的办公设备销售款。X 根据第 8.3 条行使了抵销权。X 在贷款协议项下的义务不但针对 A 而且针对 B 和 C 均归消灭。

b. 债务免除与和解（参考第 11.1.6 条）

第 11.1.6 条规定，"（1）对一个连带债务人的债务免除，或与一个连带债务人达成和解，则解除所有其他债务人对该被免除或和解之债务人的债务份额，除非情况有相反的表示。"同样，若其中一个债权人免除了债务人之债务（或者一个债权人与债务人达成和解），则以债务免除或和解金额为限，解除债务人对其他债权人承担的债务。

示例：

5. 一匹著名赛马——帕米拉的共同所有人 A 和 B 将马出售给买主 X。合同关于价款的支付规定 A 和 B 是连带债权人。如果 A 对 X 免除了其享有的债权份额，B 对 X 的请求权以 A 的债权份额为限相应减少。根据第 11.2.4 条的规定，A 对 B 不享有分担追索权（参见第 11.1.6 条第（2）款）。

6. 事实同示例 3，A 在贷款中的份额是 10 万欧元，但按低于该份额，以接受 X 支付 6 万欧元为条件与 X 达成和解。此时，B 和 C 针对 X 享有的连带债权按照 A 的债权份额 10 万欧元全额减少，但他们仍是 X 的连带债权人，债权金额为 20 万欧元。达成和解的债权人 A 针对 B 或 C 不享有第 11.2.4 条规定的追索权（参见第 11.1.6 条第（2）款）。

与第 11.1.6 条的规定相似，经适当调整，关于和解的规定涉及如下特殊情况：债务人与连带债权人之一达成的一项单独和解涉及后者的债权份额问题。这种情况需要解决的是，该和解对于其他债权人的债权产生何种后果。

在较为常见的和解涉及全部连带债权的情况下，和解对不同债权人债权的后果应由所有各方同意的和解条件决定，而且对分担请求权应因此做出调整。

c. *Expiration of limitation periods (reference to Article 11.1.7)*

Article 11.1.7 provides that the expiration of the limitation period of the obligee's rights against one joint and several obligor affects neither (a) the obligations to the obligee of the other joint and several obligors, nor (b) the rights of recourse between the joint and several obligors under Article 11.1.10. Similarly, the expiration of the limitation period of one of the obligees' rights against the obligor affects neither (a) the obligor's obligations towards the other joint and several obligees, nor (b) the rights of recourse between the joint and several obligees under Article 11.2.4.

Illustration

> 7.   Obligor X has three joint and several obligees, A, B and C. A's claim against X is time-barred. This does not affect B and C's claims against X. If B or C receives performance from X, A can claim its share from the co-obligee having received payment.

Article 11.1.7 also provides that if the obligee initiates proceedings under Articles 10.5, 10.6 or 10.7 against one joint and several obligor, the running of the limitation period is suspended also against the other joint and several obligors. Similarly, if one of the obligees initiates proceedings against the obligor, the running of the limitation period is also suspended in favour of the other joint and several obligees.

d. *Effect of judgment (reference to Article 11.1.8)*

Article 11.1.8 provides that a decision by a court as to the liability to the obligee of one joint and several obligor affect neither (a) the obligations to the obligee of the other joint and several obligors, nor (b) the rights of recourse between the joint and several obligors under Article 11.1.10. Similarly, a decision by a court as to the obligor's liability towards one of the joint and several obligees affects neither (a) the obligor's obligations towards the other joint and several obligees, nor (b) the rights of recourse between the joint and several obligees under Article 11.2.4.

Illustration

> 8.   Obligor X has three joint and several obligees, A, B and C. A, acting alone, sues X for performance. The judgement grants A only part of its claim. Such judgment does not affect the obligations of X towards B or C, nor the recourses between the co-obligees under Article 11.2.4.

c. 时效期间届满（参考第 11.1.7 条）

第 11.1.7 条规定，债权人对一个连带债务人所享权利的时效期间届满，并不影响：(a)其他连带债务人对该债权人所承担的债务；(b)连带债务人之间依据第 11.1.10 条之规定所行使的追索权。同样，某一债权人针对债务人享有的权利的时效届满，也不影响：(a)债务人对其他连带债权人承担的债务；(b)连带债权人之间依据第 11.2.4 条之规定所行使的追索权。

示例：

> 7. 债务人 X 有三个连带债权人 A、B 和 C。A 对 X 享有的债权已丧失时效。但这并不影响 B 和 C 对 X 请求债权。如果 B 或 C 从 X 取得清偿，A 可以向取得清偿的共同债权人请求其债权份额。

第 11.1.7 条还规定，如果债权人对一个连带债务人启动第 10.5、10.6 或 10.7 规定的程序，则时效期间对其他连带债务人也中止计算。同样，如果其中一个债权人对债务人启动程序，时效期间的计算也有利于对其他连带债权人中止。

d. 判决的效力（参考第 11.1.8 条）

第 11.1.8 条规定，法院对一个连带债务人对债权人之责任所做出的判决，不影响：(a)其他连带债务人对该债权人所承担的债务；(b)连带债务人之间依据第 11.1.10 条之规定所行使的追索权。同样，法院针对债务人向其中一个连带债权人所负责任作出的判决，也不影响：(a)债务人对其他连带债权人承担的债务；(b)连带债权人之间依据第 11.2.4 条之规定所行使的追索权。

示例：

> 8. 债务人 X 有三个连带债权人 A、B 和 C。A 单独对 X 提起清偿之诉。法院判决 A 仅获得部分清偿。该判决不影响 X 对 B 或 C 所承担的债务，也不影响第 11.2.4 条规定的共同债权人之间的追索权。

However, Article 11.1.8(2) also provides that the other joint and several obligors may rely on such a decision, except if it were based on grounds personal to the obligor concerned. In this case, the rights of recourse between the joint and several obligors under Article 11.1.10 are affected accordingly. Similarly, the other joint and several obligees may rely on the decision if they find it in their interest, except if it was based on grounds personal to the obligee concerned.

Illustration

> 9.   The facts are the same as in Illustration 8. This time, however, the judgment gives full satisfaction to A, including the awarding of additional damages. The other obligees may avail themselves of this favourable decision.

ARTICLE 11.2.4
(Allocation between joint and several obligees)

(1)   As among themselves, joint and several obligees are entitled to equal shares, unless the circumstances indicate otherwise.

(2)   An obligee who has received more than its share must transfer the excess to the other obligees to the extent of their respective shares.

COMMENT

1. Presumption of equal shares

Joint and several obligees may each claim full performance of the whole obligation under Article 11.2.2. However, as among themselves, they are only entitled to their respective shares. These shares are presumed to be equal.

Illustration

> 1.   Co-owners A and B have sold their factory for SFR 10,000,000, and they are joint and several obligees for the payment of the price. However, once the buyer has paid SFR 10,000,000, each co-owner will be entitled to receive its share in the final allocation. In principle, the shares are considered to be equal. Each co-owner should receive SFR 5,000,000.

然而，第 11.1.8 条第（2）款还规定，其他连带债务人可以依赖该判决，除非该判决是基于相关债务人自有原因做出的。在此情况下，连带债务人之间按第 11.1.10 条的规定，所行使的追索权将据此受到影响。同样，其他连带债权人如果发现判决符合自己的利益，也可以依赖该判决，除非该判决是基于相关债权人自有原因做出的。

示例：

9. 事实同示例 8，但法院判决 A 获得全额清偿，包括额外的损害赔偿金。此时，其他债权人可以依赖这一有利判决。

第 11.2.4 条

（连带债权人间的分配）

（1）连带债权人之间，对债权有权享有均等份额，除非情况有相反的表示。

（2）一个债权人若收到之清偿超过其份额，必须将超过其份额之部分，以其他债权人各自份额为限，转移给其他债权人。

注释：

1. 推定份额均等

根据第 11.2.2 条的规定，连带债权人均可全额请求清偿全部债务。但是，在连带债权人之间，他们仅有权获得各自的债权份额并推定该等份额均等。

示例：

1. 共同所有人 A 和 B 以 1,000 万瑞士法郎的价格将其一座工厂出售，他们在收取价款上属于连带债权人。一旦买方支付了 1,000 万瑞士法郎，每一个共同所有人在最终分配时均有权取得自己的份额。原则上该等份额视为均等，即每一共同所有人应得到 500 万瑞士法郎。

However, the circumstances may indicate otherwise.

Illustration

> 2.   The facts are the same as in Illustration 1, except that the shares of co-ownership of the factory were not equal, but 75% for A and 25% for B. This will indicate that A should receive SFR 7,500,000 and B SFR 2,500,000.

2. Transfer of excess received

It will usually happen that the co-obligee claiming payment receives more than its share, as it is entitled to claim full performance under Article 11.2.2. When an obligee has received more than its share, it must transfer the excess to the other obligees to the extent of their respective shares.

Illustration

> 3.   The facts are the same as in Illustration 1. A has been paid the full price of the factory, i.e. SFR 10,000,000, and its share of co-ownership was 50%. A must transfer SFR 5,000,000 to B.

Whether the claim of the other obligees to the sums in excess is a property right or merely a personal claim against the obligee who received more than its share is outside the scope of the Principles.

然而，情况可能有相反表示。

示例：

　　2. 事实同示例 1，但 A 和 B 对工厂的共同所有份额上不是均等的，而是 A 占 75%，B 占 25%。这表明 A 应得到 750 万瑞士法郎，B 应得到 250 万瑞士法郎。

2. 转交多收取的清偿

通常会出现请求付款的共同债权人会收到超过自己债权份额的清偿，因为按照第 11.2.2 条的规定他有权请求全额清偿。如果一个债权人收到的款项超过了自己的份额，他必须以其他债权人各自的债权份额为限，将多收取的部分转交给其他债权人。

示例：

　　3. 事实同示例 1，A 全额收到工厂价款，即 1,000 万瑞士法郎。A 在共同所有权中的份额是 50%，故 A 必须将 500 万瑞士法郎转移给 B。

至于其他债权人对于超额收取部分的请求权，是属于超额收取债权人的财产权，还是仅仅属于超额收取债权人的自身请求权，这一问题不属通则的调整范围。

附 录

ANNEX

1. 国际统一私法协会简介①

张玉卿

协会的概况

国际统一私法协会（UNIDROIT—International Institute for the Unification of Private Law）（以下简称"协会"）是一个独立的政府间国际组织，总部设在意大利罗马，其宗旨是研究不同国家以及国家集团之间私法，特别是商业法律，致力于实体私法方面的统一和协调。协会最早作为国际联盟的一个附属机构成立于1926年，该机构随着国际联盟的解散在1940年基于多边协定（协会规约）重新建立。截至2011年年底，协会共有63个成员国，②涵盖了世界各不相同国家的法律、经济、政治制度以及文化背景。中国于1985年加入该组织，是其正式会员。

协会主要组成机构为秘书处、理事会和成员大会。秘书处是协会的执行机构，负责协会工作计划的日常实施。秘书处由协会主席提名并经理事会通过的秘书长领导。理事会由意大利政府指定的协会主席以及其他25位被选举的成员组成，主要职责是拟订协会的工作计划，批准协会各项活动，组织专家草拟统一法草案，决定召开外交会议和制定协会预算。成员大会是协会最高决策机构。由每个成员国各派一名代表组成。成员大会的职责是每年审批协会的财政预算，每三年批准一次工作计划，每五年选举理事会成员。协会的正式语言是英语、法语、德语、意大利语和西班牙语，工作语言为英语和法语。协会致

---

① 本文是根据作者最早于1985年发表在《中国国际法年刊》上的《国际统一私法协会》一文重新整理而成。限于篇幅，作者对原文进行了删节，同时又增加了其后的一些主要统一法项目及目前正在从事的课题。

② 截至2011年年底UNIDROIT成员国为：阿根廷、澳大利亚、奥地利、比利时、玻利维亚、巴西、保加利亚、加拿大、智利、中国、哥伦比亚、克罗地亚、古巴、塞浦路斯、捷克、丹麦、埃及、爱沙尼亚、芬兰、法国、德国、希腊、梵蒂冈、匈牙利、印度尼西亚、印度、伊朗、伊拉克、爱尔兰、以色列、意大利、日本、拉脱维亚、立陶宛、卢森堡、马耳他、墨西哥、荷兰、尼加拉瓜、尼日利亚、挪威、巴基斯坦、巴拉圭、波兰、葡萄牙、韩国、塞尔维亚、罗马尼亚、俄罗斯、圣马力诺、沙特阿拉伯、斯洛伐克、斯洛文尼亚、南非、西班牙、瑞典、瑞士、突尼斯、土耳其、英国、美国、乌拉圭、委内瑞拉。

力于为建立国际统一私法而准备统一法和公约草案，制定私法领域的统一规则、示范法及法律指南，积极参与其他组织在私法领域的统一法项目，推进法律和立法技术方面的统一。

协会对国际条约具有存管职能，近年对 2001《开普敦公约》、2001《航空器协定》、2007《卢森堡铁路议定书》、2009《日内瓦证券公约》等多个国际公约进行了存管。

协会还积极开展法律合作项目，与成员国、非成员国法律机构、法律界人士合作，推动统一法律的实施进程，例如向成员国提供信息，以实施或加入协会通过的法律文件。向优秀的律师和法学院教师学生提供研究奖学金，在协会进行学习研究。

协会出版物有：《统一法评论》(*Uniform Law Review*)，《国际组织法律活动摘要》(*Digest of Legal Activities of International Organization*)，以及年刊《统一私法协会公报和文件》(*UNIDROIT Proceedings and Papers*)，并创建网络统一法数据库 (*Uniform Law Data Bas UNILAW*)，收集与协会通过的法律文件相关的法律文本，法院判决以及仲裁裁决的案例。

自成立至今，协会已经完成了七十多项有关统一私法方面的研究、公约起草等工作，重点涉及有关货物买卖、商事合同信贷法、货物运输法、国际贸易代理、民事责任、程序法和旅游法等，其形式包括公约（12 件）、示范法（2 部）、统一规则（UNIDROIT 称"原则"，2套）、法律指南（1 部）等。

UNIDROIT 的主要成果

1. 2012 年《移动设备国际权益公约空间财产议定书草案》(Draft Protocol to the Convention on International Interests in Mobile Equipment on Matters specific to Space Assets)，是《移动设备国际权益公约》的配套统一法，拟于 2012 年 2 月 27 日至 3 月 9 日在德国柏林召开外交会议通过该公约议定书。

2. 2010 年《国际商事合同通则》，是在通则 1994 与 2004 版基础上又增加了恢复原状、条件、违法、多个债务人与多个债权人章节。

3. 2009 年《UNIDROIYT 中介化证券实体规则公约》(2009 UNIDROIT Convention on Substantive Rules for Intermediated Securities)

4. 2008 年《UNIDROIT 租赁示范法》

5. 2007 年《UNIDROIT 国际特许专营安排指南》(UNIDROIT Guide to International Master Franchise Arrangements)，第二版。

6. 2007 年《移动设备国际权益公约铁路车辆议定书》(Protocol to the Convention on International Interests in Mobile Equipment on Matters Specific to Railway Rolling Stock)(亦称卢森堡铁路议定书 2007 Luxembourg Rail Protocol),如同航空器议定书一样,是《移动设备国际权益公约》的配套法律文件,现草就初步文本,共 34 条。

7. 2004 年《UNIDROIT 国际商事合同通则 2004》,是在 1994 年版的的基础上增加了代理人权限、第三方权利、抵销、权利转让、债务转移、合同转让,以及时效期间等内容;

8. 2004 年《跨国民事诉讼程序原则》(Principles of Transnational Civil Procedure),为便于跨国商事纠纷审判采用统一的程序规则,协会工作组与美国法学研究所合作,起草该原则;

9. 2002 年《UNIDROIT 特许专营披露示范法》;

10. 2001 年《移动设备国际权益公约》(Convention on International Interests in Mobile Equipment),亦称《开普敦公约》,已有 26 个国家(含中国)在公约上签字,公约已于 2006 年 3 月 1 日生效;

11. 2001 年《移动设备国际权益公约航空器议定书》(开普敦)(Protocol to the Convention on International Interests in Mobile Equipment on Matters specific to Aircraft Equipment),目前已有 26 个国家(含中国)在公约上签字,4 个国家批准加入。公约已于 2006 年 3 月 1 日生效;

12. 1998 年《国际特许专营指南》(Guide to International Master Franchise Arrangements),第一版,有中文翻译;

13. 1995 年《关于被盗或非法出口文物的公约》(罗马)(UNIDROIT Convention on Stolen or Illegally Exported Cultural Objects),中国政府已经加入该公约;

14. 1994 年《UNIDROIT 国际商事合同通则》(UNIDROIT Principles of International Commercial Contracts),第一版;

15. 1988 年《UNIDROIT 国际保付代理公约》(渥太华)(UNIDROIT Convention on International Factoring);

16. 1988 年《UNIDROIT 国际融资租赁公约》(渥太华)(UNIDROIT Convention on International Financial Leasing);

17. 1983 年《国际货物销售代理公约》(日内瓦)(Convention on Agency in the International Sale of Goods);

18. 1973 年《国际遗嘱格式统一法公约》(华盛顿)(Convention providing a Uniform Law on the Form of an International Will);

19. 1970 年《国际旅游合同公约》(布鲁塞尔)(International Convention on the Travel Contract);

20. 1964 年《关于国际货物销售统一法公约》(海牙)(Convention relating to a Uniform Law on the International Sale of Goods);

21. 1964 年《关于国际货物销售合同成立统一法公约》(海牙)(Convention relating to a Uniform Law on the Formation of Contracts for the International Sale of Goods);

另外,以 UNIDROIT 的研究、起草为基础,其他国际组织通过的国际公约还有十来件,其中最知名的有:

1. 1980 年《联合国国际货物销售合同公约》(United Nations Convention on Contracts for the International Sale of Goods)(联合国国际贸易法委员会),该公约是对 1964 年《关于国际货物销售合同成立统一法公约》和《关于国际货物销售统一法公约》合并、修改、增添的结果。这两个海牙公约最初也是 UNIDROIT 起草的,后由海牙国际私法会议组织通过。

2. 1965 年内陆船舶运输注册公约(联合国/欧洲经济委员会)附件:关于内陆船舶运输对物权第一议定书;关于内陆船舶运输财产扣押与强制出售第二议定书 (联合国/欧洲经济委员会);

3. 1962 年《关于旅馆经营者对其住客财产的责任欧洲公约》(European Convention on the Liability of Hotel-keepers concerning the Property of their Guests)(欧洲理事会);

4. 1961 年《保护表演者、音像制品制作者和广播组织国际公约》(International Convention for the Protection of Performers, Producers of Phonograms and Broadcasting Organizations);

5. 1959 年《关于强制投保机动车民事责任欧洲公约》(European Convention on Compulsory Insurance against Civil Liability in respect of Motor Vehicles)(欧洲理事会);

6. 1958 年《关于承认和执行抚养未成年人义务之判决公约》(Convention on the Recognition and Enforcement of Decisions involving Obligations to Support Minor Children)(海牙国际私法会议通过);

7. 1956 年《关于国际公路货物运输合同公约》(Convention on the Contract for the International Carriage of Goods by Road, CMR)(联合国/欧洲经济委员会);

8. 1955 年《关于强制投保机动车民事责任比荷卢条约》(Benelux

Treaty on Compulsory Insurance against Civil Liability in respect of Motor Vehicles)（欧洲理事会）；

9. 1955 年《欧洲设立公约》（欧洲理事会）；

10. 1954 年《战时文化财产保护公约》（Convention for the Protection of Cultural Property in the Event of Armed Conflict）（联合国教科文组织（UNNESCO））；

协会正在开展的工作

1.《跨国与关联资本市场交易统一规则》（Transactions on Transnational and Connected Capital Markets），该项目拟制定一套统一的规范，以为全球证券市场提供法律的确定性以及经济上的有效性。

2. 提高新兴市场证券交易的原则与规则指南（Principles and rules capable of enhancing trading in securities in emerging markets），协会计划制定一部有助于推进新兴证券市场交易的原则和规则的立法指南，即中介化证券的持有和交易规则。作为第一步，这是为参加 2009 年《日内瓦证券公约》国家准备的指南文件，以利于这些国家能将公约条文纳入其国内法之中。

3. 统一违约轧差的相关法律研究计划

违约轧差（close-out netting）是金融机构为减少对手方破产而新兴的一种减少风险的手段，是金融市场上金融机构日常交易中降低信贷风险敞口的重要机制。违约轧差是合同一方违约时，另一方有权终止待履行的合同义务，对合同义务进行估价，得出一个净额。如果未破产方应向破产方支付，则未破产方支付。如果破产方应支付，则未破产方成为破产方的一般债权人。违约轧差与破产管理人挑选履行的权力相冲突。20 世纪 90 年代之后主要资本市场国家确立了违约轧差的法律地位。但近年来金融市场国际化的趋势要求违约轧差的法律具有更高的确定性。协会开始了统一违约轧差的原则和规则的研究工作，2011 年已召集了两次工作组研讨会，2012 年将召集第三次会议，然后拟制定相应的统一法。

4. 协会目前正与联合国教科文组织协商，准备拟定《文物财产保护示范法》（Proposal for a Model Law on the Protection of Cultural Property），目的之一是规范国家对文物财产的所有权。

5. 协会正考虑从私法方面在农业投资与生产方面开展规则制定工作，目前正就规则的范围、就农地投资、小农场主的农业商业化、资本流动和设备融资等举办研讨会，为制定统一规则进行准备。

6. 另外，协会正与相关领域进行磋商，探讨将《开普敦公约》的适用范围扩大到农业、采矿和建筑设备领域的可能性，以制定《〈开普敦公约〉有关农业、采矿和建筑设备的议定书草案》

7. 全球导航卫星系统服务的第三方责任问题，协会秘书处正进行非正式磋商，以确定此项目的可行性和范围，主要目的是考察是否能够制定一部文件，设定一个责任限制，以提高此类活动的可保性，包括责任分担，提供额外赔偿，以及确定管辖权的标准。该项目仍在探讨之中。

2. Table of correspondence of the articles of the 1994, 2004 and 2010 editions of the UNIDROIT Principles

[Note that (*) indicates that both the black letter rule and the comments have been, at least in part, amended with respect to the previous edition, while (**) indicates that only the comments have been amended with respect to the previous edition.]

2010 edition	2004 edition	1994 edition
Preamble	*Preamble* (*)	*Preamble*
1.1	1.1	1.1
1.2	1.2 (*)	1.2
1.3	1.3 (**)	1.3
1.4 (**)	1.4	1.4
1.5	1.5	1.5
1.6	1.6	1.6
1.7 (**)	1.7 (**)	1.7
1.8	1.8	–
1.9	1.9	1.8
1.10	1.10 (**)	1.9
1.11	1.11	1.10
1.12	1.12 (*)	2.8 (2)
2.1.1	2.1.1 (**)	2.1
2.1.2	2.1.2	2.2
2.1.3	2.1.3 ·	2.3
2.1.4	2.1.4	2.4
2.1.5	2.1.5	2.5
2.1.6	2.1.6	2.6
2.1.7	2.1.7 (**)	2.7
2.1.8	2.1.8 (*)	2.8 (1)
2.1.9	2.1.9	2.9
2.1.10	2.1.10	2.10
2.1.11	2.1.11	2.11
2.1.12	2.1.12	2.12
2.1.13	2.1.13	2.13
2.1.14	2.1.14	2.14

2010 edition	2004 edition	1994 edition
2.1.15	2.1.15 (**)	2.15
2.1.16	2.1.16	2.16
2.1.17	2.1.17	2.17
2.1.18	2.1.18 (*)	2.18
2.1.19	2.1.19	2.19
2.1.20	2.1.20	2.20
2.1.21	2.1.21	2.21
2.1.22	2.1.22	2.22
2.2.1	2.2.1	–
2.2.2	2.2.2	–
2.2.3	2.2.3	–
2.2.4	2.2.4	–
2.2.5	2.2.5	–
2.2.6	2.2.6	–
2.2.7	2.2.7	–
2.2.8	2.2.8	–
2.2.9	2.2.9	–
2.2.10	2.2.10	–
3.1.1 (*)	3.1	3.1
3.1.2	3.2	3.2
3.1.3	3.3	3.3
3.1.4 (*)	3.19	3.19
3.2.1	3.4	3.4
3.2.2	3.5	3.5
3.2.3	3.6	3.6
3.2.4	3.7	3.7
3.2.5	3.8	3.8
3.2.6	3.9	3.9
3.2.7	3.10	3.10
3.2.8	3.11	3.11
3.2.9	3.12	3.12
3.2.10	3.13	3.13
3.2.11	3.14	3.14
3.2.12	3.15	3.15
3.2.13	3.16	3.16

Table of Correspondence

2010 edition	2004 edition	1994 edition
3.2.14	3.17 (1)	3.17 (1)
3.2.15 (*)	3.17 (2)	3.17 (2)
3.2.16	3.18	3.18
3.2.17	3.20	3.20
3.3.1	–	–
3.3.2	–	–
4.1	4.1	4.1
4.2	4.2	4.2
4.3	4.3	4.3
4.4	4.4	4.4
4.5	4.5	4.5
4.6	4.6	4.6
4.7	4.7	4.7
4.8	4.8	4.8
5.1.1	5.1.1	5.1
5.1.2	5.1.2	5.2
5.1.3	5.1.3	5.3
5.1.4	5.1.4	5.4
5.1.5	5.1.5	5.5
5.1.6	5.1.6	5.6
5.1.7	5.1.7	5.7
5.1.8	5.1.8	5.8
5.1.9	5.1.9	–
5.2.1	5.2.1	–
5.2.2	5.2.2	–
5.2.3	5.2.3	–
5.2.4	5.2.4	–
5.2.5	5.2.5	–
5.2.6	5.2.6	–
5.3.1	–	–
5.3.2	–	–
5.3.3	–	–
5.3.4	–	–
5.3.5	–	–
6.1.1	6.1.1	6.1.1
6.1.2	6.1.2	6.1.2

Table of Correspondence

2010 edition	2004 edition	1994 edition
6.1.3	6.1.3	6.1.3
6.1.4	6.1.4	6.1.4
6.1.5	6.1.5	6.1.5
6.1.6	6.1.6	6.1.6
6.1.7	6.1.7	6.1.7
6.1.8	6.1.8	6.1.8
6.1.9	6.1.9	6.1.9
6.1.10	6.1.10	6.1.10
6.1.11	6.1.11	6.1.11
6.1.12	6.1.12	6.1.12
6.1.13	6.1.13	6.1.13
6.1.14	6.1.14	6.1.14
6.1.15	6.1.15	6.1.15
6.1.16	6.1.16	6.1.16
6.1.17	6.1.17	6.1.17
6.2.1	6.2.1	6.2.1
6.2.2	6.2.2 (**)	6.2.2
6.2.3	6.2.3	6.2.3
7.1.1	7.1.1	7.1.1
7.1.2	7.1.2	7.1.2
7.1.3	7.1.3	7.1.3
7.1.4	7.1.4	7.1.4
7.1.5	7.1.5	7.1.5
7.1.6	7.1.6	7.1.6
7.1.7	7.1.7	7.1.7
7.2.1	7.2.1	7.2.1
7.2.2	7.2.2	7.2.2
7.2.3	7.2.3	7.2.3
7.2.4	7.2.4	7.2.4
7.2.5	7.2.5	7.2.5
7.3.1	7.3.1	7.3.1
7.3.2	7.3.2	7.3.2
7.3.3	7.3.3	7.3.3
7.3.4	7.3.4	7.3.4
7.3.5	7.3.5	7.3.5

Table of Correspondence

2010 edition	2004 edition	1994 edition
7.3.6 (*)	7.3.6 (1)	7.3.6 (1)
7.3.7 (*)	7.3.6 (2)	7.3.6 (2)
7.4.1	7.4.1	7.4.1
7.4.2	7.4.2	7.4.2
7.4.3	7.4.3	7.4.3
7.4.4	7.4.4	7.4.4
7.4.5	7.4.5	7.4.5
7.4.6	7.4.6	7.4.6
7.4.7	7.4.7	7.4.7
7.4.8	7.4.8	7.4.8
7.4.9	7.4.9	7.4.9
7.4.10	7.4.10	7.4.10
7.4.11	7.4.11	7.4.11
7.4.12	7.4.12	7.4.12
7.4.13	7.4.13	7.4.13
8.1	8.1	–
8.2	8.2	–
8.3	8.3	–
8.4	8.4	–
8.5	8.5	–
9.1.1	9.1.1	–
9.1.2	9.1.2	–
9.1.3	9.1.3	–
9.1.4	9.1.4	–
9.1.5	9.1.5	–
9.1.6	9.1.6	–
9.1.7	9.1.7	–
9.1.8	9.1.8	–
9.1.9	9.1.9	–
9.1.10	9.1.10	–
9.1.11	9.1.11	–
9.1.12	9.1.12	–
9.1.13	9.1.13	–
9.1.14	9.1.14	–
9.1.15	9.1.15	–

2010 edition	2004 edition	1994 edition
9.2.1	9.2.1	–
9.2.2	9.2.2	–
9.2.3	9.2.3	–
9.2.4	9.2.4	–
9.2.5	9.2.5	–
9.2.6	9.2.6	–
9.2.7	9.2.7	–
9.2.8	9.2.8	–
9.3.1	9.3.1	–
9.3.2	9.3.2	–
9.3.3	9.3.3	–
9.3.4	9.3.4	–
9.3.5	9.3.5	–
9.3.6	9.3.6	–
9.3.7	9.3.7	–
10.1	10.1	–
10.2	10.2	–
10.3	10.3	–
10.4	10.4	–
10.5	10.5	–
10.6	10.6	–
10.7	10.7	–
10.8	10.8	–
10.9	10.9	–
10.10	10.10	–
10.11	10.11	–
11.1.1	–	–
11.1.2	–	–
11.1.3	–	–
11.1.4	–	–
11.1.5	–	–
11.1.6	–	–
11.1.7	–	–
11.1.8	–	–
11.1.9	–	–
11.1.10	–	–

Table of Correspondence

2010 edition	2004 edition	1994 edition
11.1.11	–	–
11.1.12	–	–
11.1.13	–	–
11.2.1	–	–
11.2.2	–	–
11.2.3	–	–
11.2.4	–	–

3. 理事会和工作组名单

THE UNIDROIT GOVERNING COUNCIL
(2009-2013)

Berardino LIBONATI † Alberto MAZZONI (since 2011)	President of UNIDROIT
Chief Michael Kaase AONDOAKKA	Nigeria
Hans-Georg BOLLWEG	Germany
Núria BOUZA VIDAL	Spain
Baiba BROKA	Latvia
Antonio Paulo CACHAPUZ DE MEDEIROS	Brazil
Sergio M. CARBONE	Italy
Sergiu DELEANU	Romania
Michael B. ELMER	Denmark
Henry D. GABRIEL	United States of America
Ian GOVEY	Australia
Attila HARMATHY	Hungary
Arthur S. HARTKAMP	Netherlands
Monique JAMETTI GREINER	Switzerland
Ricardo Luis LORENZETTI	Argentina
LYOU Byung-Hwa	Republic of Korea
MO John Shijian	People's Republic of China
Didier OPERTTI BADÁN	Uruguay
Kathryn SABO	Canada
Jorge SÁNCHEZ CORDERO DAVILA	Mexico
Rachel SANDBY-THOMAS	United Kingdom
Biswanath B. SEN	India
Stanislaw J. SOLTYSINSKI	Poland
Itsuro TERADA	Japan
Daniel TRICOT	France
Ioannis VOULGARIS	Greece

WORKING GROUP
FOR THE PREPARATION OF
THE UNIDROIT PRINCIPLES 2010

MEMBERS

Berhooz AKHLAGHI — Partner, International Law Office Dr. Berhooz Akhlaghi & Associates, Tehran

Guido ALPA — Professor of Law, University of Rome I "La Sapienza"

Michael Joachim BONELL — Professor of Law (*emeritus*), University of Rome I "La Sapienza"; Consultant, UNIDROIT; *Rapporteur on Chapter 3, Section 3 (2009-2010) and on the Revised Comments to Article 1.4; Chairman of the Working Group*

Paul-André CREPEAU — Professor of Law (*emeritus*), McGill University, Montreal

Samuel K. DATE-BAH — Justice, Supreme Court of Ghana

Bénédicte FAUVARQUE-COSSON — Professor of Law, Université Panthéon-Assas Paris II; *Rapporteur on Chapter 5, Section 3*

Paul FINN — Judge, Federal Court of Australia

Marcel FONTAINE — Professor of Law (*emeritus*), Centre de droit des Obligations, Université Catholique de Louvain, Louvain-la-Neuve; *Rapporteur on Chapter 11; Chairman of the Editorial Committee for the French language version*

Michael P. FURMSTON — Dean of Law and Professor of Law, Singapore Management University; *Rapporteur on Chapter 3, Section 3 (2006-2008)*

Henry D. GABRIEL — Professor of Law, Elon University Law School, Greensboro, N.C.; Member of the UNIDROIT Governing Council; *Chairman of the Editorial Committee*

Lauro GAMA Jr. — Professor of Law, Pontifical Catholic University of Rio de Janeiro (PUC-Rio); Partner, Binenbojm, Gama & Carvalho Britto Advogados, Rio de Janeiro (2008-2010)

Sir Roy GOODE — Professor of Law (*emeritus*), University of Oxford; Honorary Member of the UNIDROIT Governing Council

Arthur S. HARTKAMP — Professor of European Private Law, Radboud University Nijmegen; Member of the UNIDROIT Governing Council

Alexander S. KOMAROV — Professor of Law, Head of Private Law Department, Russian Academy of Foreign Trade, Moscow; Honorary Member of the UNIDROIT Governing Council

Ole LANDO — Professor of Law (*emeritus*), Copenhagen Business School

Takashi UCHIDA — Professor of Law, Faculty of Law, University of Tokyo; Senior Advisor on Legislative Reform, Civil Affairs Bureau, Ministry of Justice, Tokyo

João Baptista VILLELA — Professor of Law, Universidade Federal de Minas Gerais, Belo Horizonte (2006-2007)

Pierre WIDMER — Professor of Law (*emeritus*), Former Director of the Swiss Institute of Comparative Law, Lausanne; Honorary Member of the UNIDROIT Governing Council

ZHANG Yuqing — Professor of Law, Zhang Yuqing Law Firm, Beijing; Honorary Member of the UNIDROIT Governing Council

Reinhard ZIMMERMANN — Professor of Law, Director at the *Max-Planck-Institut für ausländisches und internationales Privatrecht*, Hamburg; *Rapporteur on Articles 3.2.14, 3.2.15, 7.3.6 and 7.3.7*

OBSERVERS

Ibrahim Hassan AL MULLA — General Manager, Emirates International Law Center, Dubai; Observer for the Emirates International Law Center

Eckart BRÖDERMANN — Partner, Brödermann & Jahn, Hamburg; Observer for the Space Law Committee, International Bar Association

Alejandro CARBALLO — Lawyer, Cuatrecasas Law Firm, Madrid; Observer for the American Society of International Law, Private International Law Group

Christine CHAPPUIS — Professor of Law, Faculty of Law, University of Geneva; Observer for the *Groupe de Travail Contrats Internationaux*

Chang-ho CHUNG — Judge, Gwang-ju District Court of Korea; Observer for the Government of the Republic of Korea

Neil B. COHEN — Jeffrey D. Forchelli Professor of Law, Brooklyn Law School, New York; Observer for the American Law Institute

François DESSEMONTET — Professor of Law, University of Lausanne; Observer for the Swiss Arbitration Association

Lauro GAMA Jr. — Professor of Law, Pontifical Catholic University of Rio de Janeiro (PUC-Rio); Partner, Binenbojm, Gama & Carvalho Britto Advogados, Rio de Janeiro; Observer for the Brazilian Branch of the International Law Association (2007)

Alejandro GARRO — Professor of Law, Columbia Law School, New York; Observer for the New York City Bar

Attila HARMATHY — Professor of Law (*emeritus*), Faculty of Law Eötvös Loránd University, Budapest; Member of the UNIDROIT Governing Council; Observer for the Arbitration Court of the Hungarian Chamber of Commerce and Industry

Emmanuel JOLIVET — General Counsel, ICC International Court of Arbitration; Observer for the ICC International Court of Arbitration

Timothy LEMAY — Principal Legal Officer and Head of the Legislative Branch, International Trade Law Division, United Nations Commission on International Trade Law (UNCITRAL); Observer for UNCITRAL (2010)

Pilar PERALES VISCASILLAS — Professor of Law, Universidad de La Rioja, Logroño; Observer for the National Law Center for Inter-American Free Trade

Marta PERTEGÁS — Secretary, Hague Conference on Private International Law; Observer for the Hague Conference on Private International Law

Hilmar RAESCHKE-KESSLER — Honorary Professor of Law, *Rechtsanwalt beim Bundesgerichtshof*, Karlsruhe; Observer for the German Arbitration Institution

Giorgio SCHIAVONI — Vice President of the Milan Chamber of National and International Arbitration; Observer for the Milan Chamber of National and International Arbitration

Jeremy SHARPE — Attorney-Adviser (International), U.S. Department of State, Washington; Observer for the Institute for

Transnational Arbitration of the Center for American and International Law

Matthew SILLET — Deputy Registrar, London Court of International Arbitration; Observer for the London Court of International Arbitration

Renaud SORIEUL — Director, International Trade Law Division, United Nations Office of Legal Affairs and Secretary of the United Nations Commission on International Trade Law (UNCITRAL); Observer for UNCITRAL (2006-2009)

Christian von BAR — Professor of Law, Director *Institut f. Europäische Rechtswissenschaft*, University of Osnabruck; Observer for the Study Group for a European Civil Code

WANG Wenjing — Director, Arbitration Research Institute, China International Economic and Trade Arbitration Commission; Observer for the China International Economic and Trade Arbitration Commission

Secretaries to the Working Group were Paula HOWARTH and Lena PETERS of the UNIDROIT Secretariat

WORKING GROUP
FOR THE PREPARATION OF
THE UNIDROIT PRINCIPLES 2004

MEMBERS

Luiz Olavo BAPTISTA — Professor of Law, University of São Paulo

Michael Joachim BONELL — Professor of Law, University of Rome I "La Sapienza"; Consultant, UNIDROIT; *Rapporteur on Chapter 2 Section 2 and on paragraphs 4 and 6 of the Preamble; CHAIRMAN OF THE WORKING GROUP*

Paul-André CREPEAU — Professor of Law (*emeritus*), Quebec Research Center for Private and Comparative Law, McGill University, Montreal

Samuel K. DATE-BAH — Justice, Supreme Court of Ghana

Adolfo DI MAJO — Professor of Law, University of Rome III

Aktham EL KHOLY — Attorney at Law (Supreme Court), Cairo

E. Allan FARNSWORTH — McCormack Professor of Law, Columbia University in the City of New York School of Law; *Chairman of the Editorial Committee; Rapporteur on the Model Clause*

Paul FINN — Judge, Federal Court of Australia; *Rapporteur on Article 1.8*

Marcel FONTAINE — Professor of Law (*emeritus*), Centre de droit des Obligations, Université Catholique de Louvain, Louvain-la-Neuve; *Rapporteur on Chapter 9*

Michael P. FURMSTON — Professor of Law (*emeritus*), University of Bristol; *Rapporteur on Chapter 5, Section 2*

Arthur S. HARTKAMP — Procureur-Général at the Supreme Court of The Netherlands; Professor of Law, University of Amsterdam; Member of the UNIDROIT Governing Council; *Rapporteur on Article 5.1.9*

HUANG Danhan — Attorney, Professor of Law, Vice-President of the Chinese International Private Law Society, Beijing

Camille JAUFFRET-SPINOSI — Professor of Law, University of Paris II; *Rapporteur on Chapter 8*

Alexander S. KOMAROV — Head of Private Law Chair, Russian Academy of Foreign Trade; President of International Commercial Arbitration Court at the Chamber of Commerce and Industry of the Russian Federation

Ole LANDO — Professor of Law (*emeritus*), Copenhagen School of Economics and Business Administration; Chairman of the Commission on European Contract Law (1980-2001)

Peter SCHLECHTRIEM — Professor of Law (*emeritus*), University of Freiburg; *Rapporteur on Chapter 10*

Takashi UCHIDA — Professor of Law, University of Tokyo

OBSERVERS

François DESSEMONTET — Professor of Law, University of Lausanne; Observer for the Swiss Arbitration Association

Horacio GRIGERA NAÓN — Secretary-General of the ICC International Court of Arbitration; Observer for the ICC International Court of Arbitration (1998-2001)

Gerold HERRMANN — Secretary of the United Nations Commission on International Trade Law (UNCITRAL); Observer for UNCITRAL (1998-2000)

Giorgio SCHIAVONI — Vice President of the Milan Chamber of National and International Arbitration; Observer for the Milan Chamber of National and International Arbitration

Jernej SEKOLEC — Secretary of the United Nations Commission on International Trade Law (UNCITRAL); Observer for UNCITRAL (2001-2003)

Anne Marie WHITESELL — Secretary-General of the ICC International Court of Arbitration; Observer for the ICC International Court of Arbitration (2002-2003)

Secretaries to the Working Group were Paula HOWARTH and Lena PETERS of the UNIDROIT Secretariat

THE UNIDROIT GOVERNING COUNCIL
(1994-1998)

Riccardo MONACO	President of UNIDROIT
Ömer I. AKIPEK	Turkey
Antonio BOGGIANO	Argentina
Isabel de MAGALHÃES COLLAÇO	Portugal
Charles R.M. DLAMINI	South Africa
E. Allan FARNSWORTH	United States of America
Luigi FERRARI BRAVO	Italy
Royston M. GOODE	United Kingdom
Yasuo HAMASAKI	Japan
Arthur S. HARTKAMP	Netherlands
Tsvetana KAMENOVA	Bulgaria
Roland LOEWE	Austria
LYOU Byung-Hwa	Republic of Korea
Ferenc MÁDL	Hungary
Vicente MAROTTA RANGEL	Brazil
Jörg PIRRUNG	Germany
Jean-Pierre PLANTARD	France
Jacques PUTZEYS	Belgium
Alan D. ROSE	Australia
Jorge SÁNCHEZ CORDERO DAVILA	Mexico
Biswanath B. SEN	India
Leif SEVÓN	Finland
Anne-Marie TRAHAN	Canada
Ioannis VOULGARIS	Greece
Pierre WIDMER	Switzerland
ZHANG Yuejiao	People's Republic of China

WORKING GROUP
FOR THE PREPARATION OF
THE UNIDROIT PRINCIPLES (1994)

Michael Joachim BONELL — Professor of Law, University of Rome I "La Sapienza"; *Chairman of the Working Group; Rapporteur on Chapter 1 (including the Preamble), Chapter 2 and Chapter 4*

Patrick BRAZIL — Attorney, Canberra; former Secretary, Attorney-General's Department; former member of the UNIDROIT Governing Council

Paul-André CREPEAU — Director, Centre de recherche en droit privé et comparé du Québec; Professor of Law, McGill University, Montreal

Samuel K. DATE-BAH — Professor of Law, University of Accra; Special Adviser (Legal), Commonwealth Secretariat, London

Adolfo DI MAJO — Professor of Law, University of Rome I "La Sapienza"

Ulrich DROBNIG — Director, Max-Planck-Institut für ausländisches und internationales Privatrecht, Hamburg; *Rapporteur on Chapter 7, Section 2 and Co-Rapporteur on Chapter 3*

E. Allan FARNSWORTH — Professor of Law, Columbia University in the City of New York School of Law; Member of the UNIDROIT Governing Council; *Chairman of the Editorial Committee*

Marcel FONTAINE — Professor of Law, Centre de droit des Obligations, Université Catholique de Louvain, Louvain-la-Neuve; *Rapporteur on Chapter 5 and on Chapter 6, Section 1 (excluding Articles 6.1.14 to 6.1.17)*

Michael P. FURMSTON — Professor of Law, University of Bristol; *Rapporteur on Chapter 7, Section 1 (excluding Articles 7.1.4 and 7.1.6)*

Alejandro GARRO — Lecturer at the Columbia University in the City of New York School of Law; former Attorney, Buenos Aires

Arthur S. HARTKAMP — Advocate-General at the Supreme Court of the Netherlands, The Hague; Professor of Law, Utrecht University; member of the UNIDROIT Governing Council

Hisakazu HIROSE — Professor of Law, University of Tokyo, Komaba

HUANG Danhan — Professor of Law, University of International Business and Economics; former Deputy Director of the Department of Treaties and Law at the Ministry of Foreign Economic Relations and Trade of the People's Republic of China, Beijing

Alexander S. KOMAROV — President of the Court of International Commercial Arbitration at the Russian Federation Chamber of Commerce and Industry; Head of Law Department, All-Russian Academy of Foreign Trade, Moscow

Ole LANDO — Professor of Law, Institute of European Market Law, Copenhagen School of Economics and Business Administration; *Rapporteur on Chapter 7, Section 3, Co-Rapporteur on Chapter 3*

Dietrich MASKOW — Attorney, Berlin; Former Director, Institut für ausländisches Recht und Rechtsvergleichung der DDR; *Rapporteur on Articles 6.1.14 to 6.1.17 and on Chapter 6, Section 2*

Denis TALLON — Professor of Law; Former Director, Institut de droit comparé de Paris, Université de droit, d'économie et de sciences sociales (Paris 2); *Rapporteur on Article 7.1.6 and on Chapter 7, Section 4*

Secretary to the Working Group was Lena PETERS of the UNIDROIT Secretariat

Initially the Working Group also included C. Massimo Bianca (University of Rome I "La Sapienza"); Jerzy Rajski (University of Warsaw; Co-Rapporteur on the preliminary drafts of Chapters 5 and 6); Tony Wade (The Asser Institute at The Hague); Wang Zhenpu (Deputy Director of the Department of Treaties and Law at the Ministry of Foreign Economic Relations and Trade of the People's Republic of China).

OTHER PARTICIPANTS IN THE PROJECT

The following also participated in the project in one capacity or another: José M. Abascal Zamora (Panamerican University of Mexico City); Enrique Aimone Gibson (Catholic University of Valparaìso); Joseph 'Bayo Ajala (former Solicitor-General of the Federation of Nigeria and Director-General Federal Ministry of Justice); Bernard Audit (University of Paris II Panthéon-Assas); Luiz O. Baptista (President of the Bar Association of São Paolo); Jorge Barrera Graf (Universidad Nacional Autónoma de México); Henry T. Bennett (former Deputy Secretary of the Attorney-General's Department, Canberra); Eric E. Bergsten (Pace University; former Secretary to the United Nations Commission on International Trade Law); George Berlioz (Attorney in Paris); Piero Bernardini (Attorney in Rome; former Head of the Legal Office of the Ente Nazionale Idrocarburi (ENI)); Richard Buxbaum (University of California at Berkeley); Franz Bydlinski (University of Vienna); Amelia Boss (Temple University); Andrzej Calus (Warsaw School of Economics); John W. Carter (University of Sydney); James Richard Crawford (University of Cambridge); Ronald C.C. Cuming (University of Saskatchewan); Giorgio De Nova (University of Milan); Louis Del Duca (Dickinson School of Law); Arturo Diaz Bravo (Attorney in Mexico City); Aubrey L. Diamond (University of London); Alfred Duchek (Generalanwalt at the Austrian Federal Ministry of Justice); Fritz Enderlein (Attorney in Berlin; former Director of the Institut für ausländisches Recht und Rechtsvergleichung in Potsdam-Babelsberg); John Goldring (University of Wollongong); James Gordley (University of California at Berkeley); Anita Hill (University of Oklahoma); Fernando Hinestrosa (University of Bogotà); Kurt Grönfors (University of Gothenburg); Lars Hjerner (University of Stockholm); Richard Hyland (Rutgers University at Camden), *Rapporteur on Article 7.1.4*; Rafael Illescas Ortiz (University Carlos III of Madrid); Philippe Kahn (Director of the Centre de recherche sur le droit des marchés et des investissements internationaux, Dijon); Koh Kheng-Lian (University of Singapore); Lodvik Kopac (Attorney in Prague; former Deputy Director at the Federal Ministry of Foreign Trade of the CSSR); Ernest Krings (Advocate-General at the Supreme Court of Belgium); Pierre Lalive (University of Geneva); Hans Leser (University of Marburg); Berardino Libonati (University of Rome I "La Sapienza"); Giovanni Longo (Secretary-General of the Supreme Court of Italy); Kéba Mbaye (former Vice-President of the International Court of Justice); Luis Moisset de Espanés (University of Còrdova);

José C. Moreira Alves (former President of the Supreme Court of Brazil); Barry Nicholas (University of Oxford); Tinuade Oyekunle (Attorney in Lagos; former Director International and Comparative Law Division, Nigerian Federal Ministry of Justice); Grace Orleans (Acting Solicitor-General, Ghana); Alfred E. von Overbeck (University of Fribourg); Luiz G. Paes de Barros Leães (University of São Paolo); Gonzalo Parra Aranguren (University of Caracas); Michel Pelichet (Deputy Secretary-General of the Hague Conference on Private International Law); Pietro Perlingieri (University of Naples); Allan Philip (President of the Comité Maritime International); László Réczei (Professor of Law, University of Budapest; former Ambassador); Pietro Rescigno (University of Rome I "La Sapienza"); Julio C. Rivera (University of Buenos Aires); Walter Rolland (University of Halle; former Ministerialdirektor at the Federal Ministry of Justice); Eero Routamo (University of Helsinki); Arthur Rosett (University of California Los Angeles); Rodolfo Sacco (University of Turin); Claude Samson (University of Laval); Benito Sansò (University of Caracas); David Sassoon (Attorney in Tel Aviv); Peter Schlechtriem (University of Freiburg); Kurt Siehr (University of Zurich); José Luis Siqueiros (Professor of Law; Attorney in Mexico City); Sir Thomas Smith (University of Edinburgh); T. Bradbrooke Smith (former Assistant Deputy Attorney General at the Department of Justice, Ottawa); Kazuaki Sono (Hokkaido University of Sapporo; former Secretary, United Nations Commission on International Trade Law; former Legal Consultant of the World Bank); Jean-Georges Sauveplanne (University of Utrecht); Nagendra Singh (former President of the International Court of Justice); Sandro Schipani (University of Rome II "Tor Vergata"); Giuseppe Sperduti (University of Rome I "La Sapienza"); Sompong Sucharitkul (former Ambassador and former Thai member of the International Law Commission); Guido Tedeschi (Hebrew University, Jerusalem); Evelio Verdera y Tuells (University of Madrid "La Complutense"); Michael Will (University of Geneva); Hernany Veytia Palomino (Panamerican University of Mexico City); Jelena Vilus (University of Belgrade); Peter Winship (Southern Methodist University, Dallas).

4. INDEX

Definitions

Dispatch principle

Domestic law

Duty of confidentiality

Duty of co-operation

Duty to achieve specific result

Duty to use best efforts

Electronic contracting

Estoppel

Exemption clauses

Fair dealing

Force majeure

withholding performance,
6.2.3[4]
resort to court in case renegotiations fail, 6.2.3[6]
measures court may take,
6.2.3[7]
termination of contract for indefinite
period distinguished, 5.1.8
See Force majeure, Price

Illegality

contracts infringing mandatory rules,
3.3.1
effects of infringement prescribed
by mandatory rule infringed,
3.3.1[4]
according to what is reasonable in
the circumstances, 3.3.1[5]
criteria, 3.3.1[6]
restitution, 3.3.2
according to what is reasonable in
the circumstances, 3.3.2[1]
criteria, 3.3.2[2]
See Corruption, Mandatory rules,
Restitution

Impossibility

See Initial impossibility, Interference by
other party, Force majeure, Hardship,
Payment, Public permission
requirements, Remedies

Imprévision

See Hardship

Imputation

of non-monetary obligations, 6.1.13
of payments, 6.1.12

Inconsistent behaviour

prohibition of, 1.8
application of general principle of
good faith and fair dealing, 1.7,
1.8[1]
understanding caused by one party and
reasonably relied upon, 1.8[2]
means to avoid detriment caused by,
1.8[3]
See Authority of agent, Interpretation of
contract, Interpretation of statements
and other conduct, Modification in
particular from, Offer

Initial impossibility

lack of legal title to dispose, 3.1.3[2]
lack of capacity distinguished,
3.1.3[2]
performance impossible from outset,
3.1.3[1], 3.2.2[2]
objet need not be possible, 3.1.3[1]
validity of contract unaffected by,
3.1.3[1], 3.1.3[2], 7.2.2[3]
non-mandatory character of provision, 1.5[3], 3.1.4
rules on non-performance apply,
3.1.3[1], 3.1.3[2]
See Force majeure, Hardship, Public
permission requirements

Integration clause

See Merger clauses

Interest

failure to pay, 7.4.9[1]
accrues from time payment due,
7.4.9[1]
additional damages recoverable,
7.4.9[3]
rate of interest, 7.4.9[2]
on damages, 7.4.10
accrues from time of non-performance, 7.4.10
compound interest, 7.4.10
See Agreed payment for non-performance, Damages

Interference by other party

excuse for own non-performance, 7.1.1
non-performance due to act or
omission of other party, 7.1.2[1]
non-performance due to event for
which other party bears risk,
7.1.2[2]
other party may not terminate,
7.1.2[1]
performance impossible due to,
7.1.2[1], 7.4.7[3]
partial impediment, 7.1.2[1],
7.4.7[3]
See Damages

Interpretation of contract

circumstances relevant to, 4.3[1]

See Alternative dispute resolution,
Arbitration, Court, Force majeure,
Set-off

Mandatory Rules

of domestic law, 1.4
    broad notion of, 1.4[2]
    examples of, 1.2[3], 1.4[2], 3.3.1,
        3.3.2, 6.1.9[2], 6.1.14[1], 7.2.4[3],
        7.2.4[5], 7.2.4[7], 10.1[3]
    UNIDROIT Principles subject to,
        1.1[3], 1.4[1]
        when Principles govern
            contract, Preamble[3],
            Preamble[4], 1.4[4],
        when Principles incorporated
            into contract, 1.4[3]
of UNIDROIT Principles, 1.5[3]
    examples of, 1.5[3]
See Contract, Illegality

Merchants

UNIDROIT Principles do not require that
    parties be, Preamble[2]

Merger clauses

defined, 2.1.17
standard terms containing, 2.1.21
See Negotiations

Mistake

avoidance due to, 3.2.2
    conditions concerning mistaken
        party, 3.2.2[3]
    conditions concerning non-mis-
        taken party, 3.2.2[2]
    mistake must be sufficiently
        serious, 3.2.2[1]
    time period for notice of, 3.2.12
    damages, 7.4.1[3]
caused by the inconsistent behaviour of
    a party, 1.8[2]
defined, 3.2.1[1]
    mistake of law equated with
        mistake of fact, 3.2.1[1]
fraud distinguished, 3.2.5[2], 3.2.10[1]
imputable to third person, 3.2.8[1],
    3.2.8[2], 5.1.7[3]
in expression or transmission, 1.10[3],
    3.2.6[1]
loss of right to avoid, 3.2.10[3]
    damages not precluded, 3.2.10[4]

decision to perform must be made
    promptly, 3.2.10[2]
precluded after notice of avoidance
    relied on, 3.2.7[3], 3.2.10[3]
non-mandatory character of provisions
    relating to, 1.5[3], 3.1.4
non-performance distinguished,
    3.2.1[2], 3.2.4[1]
    remedy for non-performance
        preferred, 3.2.4[1], 3.2.4[2]

Modification in a particular form

clause requiring, 2.1.18
    reliance on modification not in the
        particular form notwithstanding,
        2.1.18
standard terms containing, 2.1.21
See Inconsistent behaviour

Modification of contract

by agreement of parties, 1.3[2], 3.1.2
    no need for consideration, 3.1.2[1]
    no need for *cause,* 3.1.2[2]
no requirement as to form, 1.2[1]
    exceptions under applicable law,
        1.2[3]
    unless agreed upon, 1.2[4]
See Inconsistent behaviour, Modifi-
    cation in particular form

Negotiations

breaking off of, 2.1.15[3]
conclusion of contract dependent on
    agreement on specific matters,
    2.1.13[1]
conclusion of contract dependent on
    agreement in a particular form,
    2.1.13[2]
duty of confidentiality and, 2.1.16[2]
freedom of, 2.1.15[1]
good faith and fair dealing in, 1.7[1],
    2.1.15[2], 5.1.2, 6.1.14[2]
    liability for failure to observe,
        2.1.15[2], 2.1.15[3]
interference in by third person, 3.2.8[1],
    3.2.8[2]
interpretation of contract and, 4.3[2],
    4.6
    merger clause, 2.1.17, 4.3[3]
    supplying of omitted terms, 4.8[3]
    pertaining to replacement transac-
        tion, 7.4.5[2]

court, 1.11[1]
international contracts, Preamble[1]
place of business, 1.11[2]
obligor-obligee, 1.11[3]
writing, 1.11[4]
exclusion and modification of, 1.5[1]
by implication, 1.5[2]
mandatory provisions, 1.1[3], 1.5[3],
1.7[4], 1.9[6], 3.1.4, 5.1.7[2], 7.1.6,
7.4.13
general principles underlying, 1.6[4]
absence of specific requirements as
to form, 1.2[1], 1.10[1]
freedom of contract, 1.1[1], 1.5[1]
full compensation, 7.1.1, 7.4.2[1]
good faith and fair dealing, 1.7[1]
pacta sunt servanda, 1.3[1]
reasonableness, 1.8[2],4.1[2],
4.1[4], 4.2[2], 4.3[2], 4.8[3], 5.1.2,
5.1.6[2], 5.1.7[1]
interpretation of, 1.6[1]
interpretation of contract distinguished, 1.6[1]
regard to be had to international
character, 1.6[2]
regard to be had to purposes, 1.6[3]
mandatory rules prevail over, 1.1[3],
1.3[1], 1.4[1]
when Principles govern contract,
Preamble[3], Preamble[4], 1.4[3]
when Principles incorporated into
contract, 1.4[2]
consumer transactions,
Preamble[2]
determination of applicable
mandatory rules, 1.4[4]
determination of relevant public
permission requirements,
6.1.14[1]
effects of contract on third persons,
1.3[3]
lack of capacity, 3.1.1, 3.1.3[2]
"real" contracts, 3.1.2[3]
rights of third persons in case of
restitution, 7.3.6[5]
scope of, Preamble
commercial contracts, Preamble[2]
international contracts, Preamble[1]
Principles applied to domestic
contract, Preamble[3]
supplementation of, 1.6[4]
by analogy with other provisions,
1.6[4]

by reference to general principles
underlying, 1.6[4]
by reference to particular domestic
law, 1.6[4]
usages and course of dealing prevail
over, 1.9[6]
See Arbitration, Private international
law

Usages

binding character of, 1.9[1]
agreed usages, 1.9[3]
in absence of agreement, 1.9[4]
local usages, 1.9[4]
subject to standard of reasonableness, 1.9[5]
circumstance relevant to interpretation,
4.3[2],
mistake, 3.2.2[1]
means of overcoming indefiniteness,
2.1.2[1]
modes of acceptance and, 2.1.6[3],
2.1.6[4], 2.1.7
order of performance determined by,
6.1.4, 6.1.4[1]
requiring replacement transaction,
7.2.1, 7.4.5[1]
source of implied obligation, 5.1.2
standard terms and, 2.1.19[3]
UNIDROIT Principles superseded by,
1.9[6]
See Practices

Validity of contract

grounds of invalidity not covered, 3.1.1
mandatory provisions concerning,
1.5[3]
public permission requirements affecting, 6.1.14[1], 6.1.16[2], 6.1.17[2],
7.2.2[3]
See Contract, Fraud, Gross disparity,
Initial impossibility, Mistake, Public
permission requirements, Terms of
contract, Threat, Unilateral
declarations

Venire contra factum proprium
See Inconsistent behaviour

Wegfall der Geschäft sgrundlage
See Hardship

Writing

defined, 1.11[4]
electronic communications and, 1.11[4]

Writings in confirmation

defined, 2.1.12[1]
   invoice as, 2.1.12[3]
time period for sending of, 2.1.12[2]
varying terms of contract, 2.1.12[1]
     acceptance varying terms compared,
       2.1.12[1]
     non-material alterations and,
       2.1.12[1]
See Acceptance